GREENS CONVEYANCING STATUTES

1994

GREENS CONVEYANCING STATUTES

1994

Division J of The Parliament House Book

W GREEN/Sweet & Maxwell

EDINBURGH

1994

ISBN 0 414 01099 X

A catalogue record for this
book is available from the
British Library.

PRINTED IN GREAT BRITAIN BY
Butler and Tanner Ltd.,
Frome, Somerset

The contents of this book are reproduced from the Parliament House Book which is published in looseleaf form and regularly updated by W. Green, the Scottish Law Publisher. The Parliament House Book contains all relevant statutory information on key areas in Scots Law.

Material in the Parliament House Book is set out in sections called Divisions. The first page of every Division lists its contents under the Division heading. The Division letters used in this book are those used for the equivalent Division in the Parliament House Book itself.

DIVISION J

Conveyancing, Land Tenure and Registration

Alphabetical and chronological indexes of all statutes and regulations reprinted in *Parliament House Book* can be found at the front of this binder

Statutes

		PAGE
1857:	Registration of Leases (Scotland) Act (20 & 21 Vict. c. 26)	J 3
1868:	Land Registers (Scotland) Act (31 & 32 Vict. c. 64)	J 10
	Titles to Land Consolidation (Scotland) Act (31 & 32 Vict. c. 101)	J 16
1869:	Titles to Land Consolidation (Scotland) Amendment Act (32 & 33 Vict. c. 116)	J 16
1874:	Conveyancing (Scotland) Act (37 & 38 Vict. c. 94)	J 66
1877:	Writs Execution (Scotland) Act (40 & 41 Vict. c. 40)	J 86
1887:	Conveyancing (Scotland) Acts (1874 and 1879) Amendment Act (50 & 51 Vict. c. 69)	J 88
1894:	Heritable Securities (Scotland) Act (57 & 58 Vict. c. 44)	J 90
1924:	Conveyancing (Scotland) Act (14 & 15 Geo. 5, c. 27)	J 95
1938:	Conveyancing Amendment (Scotland) Act (1 & 2 Geo. 6, c. 24)	J 132
1948:	Public Registers and Records (Scotland) Act (11 & 12 Geo. 6, c. 57)	J 134
1950:	Public Registers and Records (Scotland) Act (14 Geo. 6, c. 11)	J 136
1954:	Long Leases (Scotland) Act (2 & 3 Eliz. 2, c. 49)	J 137
1958:	Costs of Leases Act (6 & 7 Eliz. 2, c. 52)	J 153
1960:	Occupiers' Liability (Scotland) Act (8 & 9 Eliz. 2, c. 30)	J 154
1963:	Wills Act (1963 c. 44)	J 155
1970:	Conveyancing and Feudal Reform (Scotland) Act (1970 c. 35)	J 157
1971:	Redemption of Standard Securities (Scotland) Act (1971 c. 45)	J 190
1973:	Prescription and Limitation (Scotland) Act (1973 c. 52)	J 191
1974:	Land Tenure Reform (Scotland) Act (1974 c. 38)	J 207
1979:	Land Registration (Scotland) Act (1979 c. 33)	J 221
1981:	Matrimonial Homes (Family Protection) (Scotland) Act (1981 c. 59)	J 242
1982:	Administration of Justice Act (1982 c. 53)	J 256/1
1985:	Law Reform (Miscellaneous Provisions) (Scotland) Act (1985 c. 73) ss. 4–7: *See* DIVISION L. Ss. 8–10: *see* Division H.	
1987:	Register of Sasines (Scotland) Act (1987 c. 23)	J 261
	Housing (Scotland) Act (1987 c. 26), ss. 61–84A, 338, 340 (*See also* DIVISION L)	J 262
1990:	Term and Quarter Days (Scotland) Act (1990 c. 22). *See* DIVISION L.	

Statutory Instruments

1971:	Allocation of Feuduty etc. (Form of Notice) Regulations (S.I. 1971 No. 200)	J 501
	Act of Sederunt (Edictal Citations, Commissary Petitions and Petitions of Service) (S.I. 1971 No. 1165). *See* DIVISION C.	
1980:	Land Registration (Scotland) Act 1979 (Commencement No. 1) Order (S.I. 1980 No. 1412)	J 502
	Land Registration (Scotland) Rules (S.I. 1980 No. 1413)	J 502
1982:	Land Registration (Scotland) Act 1979 (Commencement No. 2) Order (S.I. 1982 No. 520)	J 541
	Matrimonial Homes (Form of Consent) (Scotland) Regulations (S.I. 1982 No. 971	J 542
1984:	Right to Purchase (Application Form) (Scotland) Order (S.I. 1984 No. 1005)	J 543
1993:	Charging Orders (Residential Accommodation) (Scotland) Order (S.I. 1993 No. 1516)	J 547

Right to Purchase (Prescribed Persons) (Scotland) Order (S.I. 1993 No. 1625) .... J 548/2
Housing (Preservation of Right to Buy) (Scotland) Regulations (S.I. 1993 No. 2164) .... J 548/3

Notes

Particular Registers of Sasines .... J 701
Register of Inhibitions and Adjudications .... J 701
"Burgh Registers" Discontinuance .... J 702
Land Register of Scotland .... J 703

Statutes

[1] Registration of Leases (Scotland) Act 1857

(20 & 21 Vict. c. 26)

An Act to provide for the registration of long leases in Scotland and assignations thereof. [10th August 1857]

NOTE

[1] Extended by the Long Leases (Scotland) Act 1954, s. 26: ss. 4, 5, 6, 13, 20 excluded by the Conveyancing and Feudal Reform (Scotland) Act 1970, s. 32 and Sched. 8. See the Heritable Securities (Scotland) Act 1894, s. 14, as to exercise of powers of sale contained in bonds and assignations in security under this Act.

Long leases, and assignations thereof, registrable in register of sasines

[1] **1.** It shall be lawful to record in the general register of sasines in Scotland, probative leases, whether executed before or after the passing of this Act, for a period exceeding twenty years of lands and heritages in Scotland, and to record respectively in the register in which any such lease as aforesaid shall have been registered the assignations, and assignations in security of such lease, and translations thereof all herein-after mentioned.

NOTE

[1] As amended by the Statute Law Revision Act 1892, the Burgh Registers (Scotland) Act 1926, s. 4 and the Land Tenure Reform (Scotland) Act 1974, Sched. 6, para. 1.

Recorded leases effectual against singular successors in the lands let

[1] **2.** Leases registrable under this Act, and valid and binding as in a question with the granters thereof, which shall have been duly recorded, as herein provided, shall, by virtue of such registration, be effectual against any singular successor in the lands and heritages thereby let, whose infeftment is posterior in date to the date of such registration: Provided always, that, except for the purposes of this Act, it shall not be necessary to record any such lease as aforesaid, but that all such leases which would, under the existing law prior to the passing of this Act, have been valid and effectual against any such singular successor as aforesaid, shall, though not recorded, be valid and effectual against such singular successor, as well as against the granters of the said leases.

NOTE

[1] As amended by the Land Tenure Reform (Scotland) Act 1974, Sched. 6, para. 2.

Assignations of recorded leases

3.—(1) When any such lease as aforesaid shall have been recorded as herein provided, it shall be lawful for the party in right of such lease, and whose right is recorded in terms of this Act, but in accordance always with the conditions and stipulations of such lease, and not otherwise, to assign the same, in whole or in part, by assignation, in the form as nearly as may be of the schedule (A) to this Act annexed; and the recording of such assignation shall fully and effectually vest the assignee with the right of the granter thereof in and to such lease to the extent assigned: Provided always that such assignation shall be without prejudice to the right of hypothec, or other rights of the landlord.

[1] (2) Notwithstanding—

(*a*) any restriction imposed by subsection (1) above on the power under that subsection to assign such a lease; or (*b*) any rule of law to the contrary,

it shall be, and shall be deemed always to have been, competent in an assignation under this section to impose conditions and make stipulations which, upon the recording of such assignation or the registration under the Land Registration (Scotland) Act 1979 of the assignee's interest, shall be as effectual against any singular successor of the assignee in the subjects assigned as if such assignee had been a grantee of the lease and it had been duly recorded or, as the case may be, the grantee's interest had been so registered.

[1] (3) Nothing in subsection (2) above makes effectual against any successor of the assignee any obligation of periodical payment other than a payment—

(*a*) of rent or of an apportionment of rent;

(*b*) in defrayal of a contribution towards some continuing cost related to the lands and heritages subject to the lease assigned; or

(*c*) under a heritable security.

[1] (4) A provision in an assignation which purports to make effectual against any successor of the assignee any obligation of periodic payment other than one specified in paragraphs (*a*) to (*c*) of subsection (3) above shall not render the deed void or unenforceable, but the assignation shall have, and shall be deemed always to have had, effect only to the extent (if any) that it would have had effect if it had not imposed such obligation.

[1] (5) Section 32 of the Conveyancing (Scotland) Act 1874 (which enables reservations, conditions, covenants etc. affecting lands to be effectually imported into one deed by reference to another) and section 17 of the Land Registration (Scotland) Act 1979 (which provides that certain obligations in deeds of conditions shall become real obligations upon the recording of the deed or registration of the obligation) shall, with the necessary modifications, respectively apply for the purposes of enabling conditions and stipulations to be effectually imported into any assignation under this section and enabling land obligations in a deed of conditions relating to the land subject to the assignation to become real obligations affecting the land.

In this subsection "land obligation" has the meaning assigned to it by section 1(2) of the Conveyancing and Feudal Reform (Scotland) Act 1970.

NOTE

[1] Inserted by the Law Reform (Miscellaneous Provisions) (Scotland) Act 1985, s. 3, with effect from 30th December 1985.

Assignations in security

4. It shall be lawful for the party in right of any such lease recorded as aforesaid, and whose right thereto is recorded in terms of this Act, but in accordance always with the conditions and stipulations of such lease, and not otherwise, to assign the same, in whole or in part, in security for the payment of borrowed money, or of annuities, or of provisions to wives or children, or in security of cash credits or other legal debt or obligation, in the form as near as may be of the schedule (B) to this Act annexed: and the recording of such assignation in security shall complete the right thereunder: and such assignation in security so recorded shall constitute a real security over such lease to the extent assigned.

Where party presenting for registration not original lessee or assignee

5. Where the party in right of any such lease or assignation in security as aforesaid is not the original lessee in such lease, or the original assignee in such assignation in security, he shall, before presenting such lease or assignation in security for registration, expede an instrument, under the hand of a notary public, in the form as nearly as may be of the schedule (C) to this Act annexed: and the keeper of the register, on such notarial instrument being produced to him, but not otherwise, shall thereupon record such lease or assignation in security, together with the said instrument.

Translation of assignations in security. Creditor's entry to possession in default of payment

6. All such assignations in security as aforesaid shall, when recorded, be transferable, in whole or in part, by translation, in the form as nearly as may be of the schedule (D) to this Act annexed: and the recording of such translation shall fully and effectually vest the party in whose favour it was granted with the right of the grantor thereof in such assignation in security to the extent assigned; and the creditor or party in right of such assignation in security, without prejudice to the exercise of any power of sale therein contained, shall be entitled, in default of payment of the capital sum for which such assignation in security has been granted, or of a term's interest thereof, or of a term's annuity, for six months after such capital sum or term's interest or annuity shall have fallen due, to apply to the sheriff for a warrant to enter on possession of the lands and heritages leased; and the sheriff, after intimation to the lessee for the time being, and to the landlord shall if he see cause grant such warrant, which shall be a sufficient title for such creditor or party to enter into possession of such lands and heritages, and to uplift the rents from any subtenants therein, and to sublet the same, as freely and to the like effect as the lessee might have done: Provided always, that no such creditor or party, unless and until he enter into possession as aforesaid, shall be personally liable to the landlord in any of the obligations and prestations of the lease.

7. [Repealed by the Succession (Scotland) Act 1964, Sched. 3.]

Executor may complete title by recording notarial instrument

[1] **8.** It shall be competent to the executor of any party who shall have died fully vested in right of any such lease or assignation in security, recorded as aforesaid, to expede a notarial instrument in the form as nearly as may be of the schedule (F) to this Act annexed; and the recording of such instrument in the register in which such lease is recorded shall complete the title of such executor to such lease or assignation in security.

NOTE

[1] As amended by the Succession (Scotland) Act 1964, Scheds. 2, 3.

[THE NEXT PAGE IS J 5]

Where assignee has died without recording assignation, mode of making up title

[1] **9.** Where any assignation, assignation in security, or translation granted in pursuance of this Act shall not have been registered as aforesaid in the lifetime of the grantee in such writ respectively, it shall be competent to the executor of such grantee to make up his title by expeding an instrument under the hand of a notary public in the form as nearly as may be of the schedule (F) to this Act annexed; and the keeper of the register, on such notarial instrument being presented to him, but not otherwise, shall thereupon record such assignation, assignation in security, or translation, together with the said instrument.

NOTE

[1] As amended by the Succession (Scotland) Act 1964, Scheds. 2, 3.

Adjudgers to complete right by recording abbreviate

[1] **10.** When an adjudication of any such lease or assignation in security recorded as aforesaid shall have been obtained against the party vested in the right thereof respectively, or against the heir of such party, the recording of the abbreviate of adjudication in the register in which the lease is recorded shall complete the right of the adjudger to such lease or assignation in security.

NOTE

[1] Amended by the Conveyancing (Scotland) Act 1924, s. 24 (7), *infra.*

Trustees on sequestrated estate may be entered on register

11. It shall be lawful for the trustee on the sequestrated estate of any party in right of any such lease or assignation in security as aforesaid to expede a notarial instrument in the form as nearly as may be of the schedule (F) to this Act annexed; and the recording of such instrument in the register in which such lease is recorded shall complete the right of such trustee to such lease or assignation in security.

Preferences regulated by date of recording transfer

12. All such leases executed after the passing of this Act and all assignations, assignations in security of any such lease recorded as aforesaid, and translations thereof, and all adjudications of such leases recorded as aforesaid, or assignations in security, shall in competition be preferable according to their dates of recording.

Renunciations and discharges to be recorded

[1] **13.** On the production to the keeper of the register of a renunciation of any such lease as aforesaid recorded therein, or of a discharge of any such assignation in security as aforesaid therein recorded, by or on behalf of the party appearing on the register as in right of such lease or assignation in security, which renunciation or discharge may be in the form of the schedules (G) and (H) respectively to this Act annexed, and may be endorsed on such lease or assignation in security, he shall forthwith duly record the same.

NOTE

[1] Amended by the Conveyancing (Scotland) Act 1924, s. 24 (5), *infra.*

Entry of decree of reduction

14. On the production to any such keeper of an extract of a decree of reduction of any such lease, assignation, assignation in security, translation, adjudication, instrument, discharge, or renunciation recorded in the register of which he is the keeper, he shall forthwith duly record the same.

Mode of registering—Extracts to make faith as writs registered

[1] **15.** Leases, assignations, assignations in security, translations, adjudications, instruments, discharges, renunciations, and other writs, duly presented for registration in pursuance of this Act, shall be forthwith shortly entered in the minute-book of the register in common form, and shall, with all due despatch, be fully registered in the register book, and thereafter redelivered to the parties, with certificates of due registration thereon, which shall be probative of such registration, such certificates specifying the date of presentation, and the book and folio in which the ingrossment has been made, and being subscribed by the keeper of the register; and the date of entry in the minute-book shall be held to be the date of registration.

NOTE

[1] As amended by the Conveyancing and Feudal Reform (Scotland) Act 1970, Sched. 11, and the Statute Law (Repeals) Act 1976.

Registration equivalent to possession

[1] **16.**—(1) The registration of all such leases, assignations, assignations in security, translations, adjudications, writs of acknowledgment, and notarial instruments as aforesaid, in manner herein provided, shall complete the right under the same respectively, to the effect of establishing a preference in virtue thereof, as effectually as if the grantee, or party in his right, had entered into the actual possession of the subjects leased under such writs respectively at the date of registration thereof.

(2) The registration of any such lease or other writ as aforesaid, in manner herein provided, on or after 1st September 1974, shall, without prejudice to the foregoing provisions of this section and to the provisions of section 2 of the Prescription and Limitation (Scotland) Act 1973, complete the right under the same to the effect of establishing in virtue thereof such a preference as aforesaid over the right of any party to any such lease or writ, or of any party in his right, granted after that date and not registered in manner herein provided at the time of the registration of the lease or writ first mentioned.

NOTE

[1] As amended by the Land Tenure Reform (Scotland) Act 1974, Sched. 6, para. 3.

Leases with obligation to renew, registerable

[1] **17.** Leases containing an obligation upon the granter to renew the same from time to time at fixed periods, or upon the termination of a life or lives, or otherwise, shall be deemed leases within the meaning of this Act, and registerable as such, provided such leases shall by the terms of such obligation be renewable from time to time so as to endure for a period exceeding twenty years.

NOTE

[1] As amended by the Land Tenure Reform (Scotland) Act 1974, Sched. 6, para. 4.

18. [Repealed by the Land Tenure Reform (Scotland) Act 1974, Sched. 7.]

Extracts registerable where leases recorded in Court of Session or sheriff-court books prior to Act

[1] **19.** Where any such lease as aforesaid registerable under this Act shall have been recorded in the books of Council and Session, or in the books of any sheriff, commissary, or burgh court, the production to the keeper of the register of an extract of such lease shall be a sufficient warrant for him to record the same, and he shall thereupon duly record it, and the recording

thereof shall be as valid and effectual as if the original lease had been presented to him.

NOTE

[1] As amended by the Registration of Leases Amendment Act 1877, s. 1, and the Land Tenure Reform (Scotland) Act 1974, Sched. 6, para. 6.

Functions of Commissary Courts now exercisable by sheriffs: see the Sheriff Courts (Scotland) Act 1876, ss. 35–39, 54; the Sheriff Courts and Legal Officers (Scotland) Act 1927, ss. 10, 11 and S.R. & O. 1933 No. 1089.

Clauses in schedules to be held to import and to have effect as declared by 10 and 11 Vict. c. 50

20. The several clauses in the schedules to this Act annexed shall be held to import such and the like meaning and to have such and the like effect as is declared by the Act of the 10th and 11th of Queen Victoria, chapter 50, sections 2 and 3, to belong to the corresponding clauses in the schedule to the said recited Act annexed, and the procedure thereby prescribed for a sale under a bond and disposition in security shall be applicable to a sale of any such lease as aforesaid under any such assignation in security as is herein-before mentioned.

Short title

21. This Act may be cited for all purposes as "The Registration of Leases (Scotland) Act 1857"

SCHEDULES

[1] SCHEDULE (A)

Form of Assignation of Lease

I, *A.B.* [*designation*], in consideration of the sum of now paid to me [*or otherwise as the case may be*], assign to *C.D.* [*designation*] a lease, dated , and recorded in the register of sasines at , of date , granted by *E.F.* [*designation*] in my favour [*or if not in assigner's favour, name and design grantee*], of [*shortly mention subjects*] in the parish of and county of , [but, (*where the lease is assigned in part only*) in so far only as regards the following portion of the subjects leased; viz. (*specify particularly the portion*)] with entry as at (*term of entry*). And [*where sub-lease*] I assign the rents from [*term*]; and I grant warrandice; and I bind myself to free and relieve the said *C.D.* of all rents and burdens due to the landlord or others at and prior to the term of entry in respect of said lease; and I consent to registration for preservation and execution.

[*Testing clause in common form.*]

NOTE

[1] As amended by the Conveyancing and Feudal Reform (Scotland) Act 1970, Sched. 11.

[1] SCHEDULE (B)

Form of Bond and Assignation in Security

I, *A.B.* [*designation*], bind myself, my heirs and executors, without the necessity of discussing them in their order, to make payment, at the terms of [*date and place of payment*], to *C.D.* [*designation*] or his heirs, executors, or assignees, of the sum of being money borrowed by me from him [*or* as a provision to the said *C.D. or* of the yearly annuity of during his life-time, *as the case may be*], with the interest of the said capital sum at the rate of per cent. per annum, payable by equal portions half-yearly at Whitsunday and Martinmas, beginning the first payment at . And, in security of the personal obligation before written, I assign to the said *C.D.* and his foresaids, heritably but redeemably, as after mentioned, yet irredeemably in the event of a sale by virtue hereof, a lease of [*shortly mention subjects leased*] in the parish of and county of , which lease was granted by *E.F.* [*designation*], of date , and recorded [*insert register, with date of recording*]; [but (*where only a portion of the subjects are assigned*) in so far only as regards the following portion of the subjects leased; viz. (*specify particularly the portion*)]. And I assign the rents; and I assign the writs; and I grant warrandice; and I reserve power of redemption; and I oblige myself and my foresaids for the expenses of assigning and discharging this security; and, on default of payment, I grant power of sale; and I consent to registration for preservation and execution.

[*Testing clause.*]

NOTE

[1] As amended by the Conveyancing and Feudal Reform (Scotland) Act 1970, Sched. 11.

[1] SCHEDULE (C)

Forms of Notarial Instrument in favour of a Party not the original Grantee

No. 1.—*Case of Lease*

Be it known, that by lease, dated , *A.B.* [*designation*] let to *C.D.* [*designation*] that piece of ground [*or as the case may be, shortly describing the property leased*] in the parish of and county of , to which lease *E.F.* [*designation*] has made up title by confirmation as executor of the said *C.D.*, dated [*insert date of confirmation*] before the [*specify the court by which confirmation has been granted*] [*or as the case may be*, as general disponee *or* assignee of the said *C.D.* in virtue of (*here mention the inter vivos deeds or decreets instructing the right, with the dates thereof, and if recorded, the register and date of recordings*)*]: Wherefore this instrument is taken by the said *E.F.* in the hands of *G.H.* [*designation of notary public*], in terms of the Registration of Leases (Scotland) Act 1857.

[*Testing clause.*]

No. 2—*Case of Assignation in Security*

Be it known, that by bond and assignation in security of date *C.D.* [*designation*] assigned to *J.K.* [*designation*], in security of a sum of [*or as the case may be*], a lease granted by *A.B.* [*designation*] of [*shortly describe the subjects leased*], in the parish of and county of , which lease is dated , and recorded [*register and date of recording*], to which assignation in security *E.F.* [*designation*] has acquired right as executor [*or as the case may be*] of the said *J.K.*, etc. [*as in Form No. 1*].

* *Note.*—If the person in whose favour the instrument is taken is not the executor or disponee of the original grantee, but of one who has acquired right to the lease or assignation in security, here specify shortly the series of titles by which the predecessor acquired the right.

NOTE

[1] As amended by the Succession (Scotland) Act 1964, Sched. 2.

[1] SCHEDULE (D)

Form of Translation of Assignation in Security

I, *A.B.* [*designation*], in consideration of the sum of now paid to me [*or as the case may be*], assign and transfer to *C.D.* [*designation*] a bond and assignation in security for the principal sum of [*or as the case may be*] granted by *E.F.* [*designation*] in my favour, [*or, if not in granter's favour, name and design the party in whose favour granted*] dated and recorded [*register and date of recording*], of and over a lease granted by *G.H.* [*designation*] of [*shortly describe subjects leased*], in the parish of , and county of , which lease is dated , and is recorded in the said register of date [but (*where the translation is partial*) only to the extent of (*insert sum*), and to the effect of giving pari passu preference to the said *C.D.* over the said lease with me, my heirs and assigns, as regards the remainder of the said principal sum and corresponding interest], with the interest from [*date*]

[*Testing clause.*]

NOTE

[1] As amended by the Conveyancing and Feudal Reform (Scotland) Act 1970, Sched. 11.

SCHEDULE (E)

[Repealed by the Succession (Scotland) Act 1964, Sched. 3]

[1] SCHEDULE (F)

Form of Notarial Instrument in favour of Executor in recorded Lease or Assignation in Security, or of Trustee on Sequestrated Estate

No. 1.—*Case of Lease*

Be it known, that by lease dated A.B. [*designation*] let to *C.D.* [*designation*] that piece of ground [*or as the case may be, shortly describing the property leased*], in the parish of and county of , which lease is recorded [*register and date of recording*], and to which *E.F.* [*designation*] has made up title by confirmation as executor of the said *C.D.*, dated the [*insert date of confirmation*], before the [*specify the court by which confirmation has been granted*], [*or as the case may be*, as executor of *L.M.* in an assignation by the said *C.D.* of date , *or* as trustee confimed on the sequestrated estate of the said *C.D.*, in virtue of (*here mention the confirmation or decreets instructing the rights, with the dates thereof*)]. Whereupon this instrument is taken by the said *E.F.*, in the hands of *G.H.* [*designation of notary public*], in terms of the " Registration of Leases (Scotland) Act 1857 ".

[*Testing clause.*]

No. 2.—*Case of Assignation in Security*

Be it known, that by bond and assignation in security of date *C.D.* [*designation*] assigned to *I.K.* [*designation*] in security of a sum of [*or as the case may be*], a lease granted by *A.B.* [*designation*] of [*shortly describe the subjects leased*] in the parish of and county of , dated , and recorded [*register and date of recording*], to which bond and assignation in security *E.F.* [*designation*] has acquired right as executor of the said *I.K.*, etc. [*as in Form No. 1*].

NOTE

[1] As amended by the Statute Law Revision Act 1892 and the Succession (Scotland) Act 1964, Sched. 2.

---

[1] SCHEDULE (G)

Renunciation of Lease

I, *A.B.* [*designation*], renounce as from the term of in favour of *C.D.* [*designation*] a lease granted by the said *C.D.* [*or as the case may be*] of [*shortly set forth subjects*] in the parish of and county of , which lease is dated and recorded [*register and date of recording*].

[*Testing clause.*]

NOTE

[1] As amended by the Conveyancing and Feudal Reform (Scotland) Act 1970, Sched. 11; see also the Conveyancing (Scotland) Act 1924, s. 24 (5).

---

[1] SCHEDULE (H)

Form of Discharge of Bond and Assignation in Security

I, *A.B.* [*designation*], in consideration of the sum of now paid to me by *C.D.* [*designation*], discharge a bond and assignation in security for the sum of , granted by the said *C.D.* in my favour [*or as the case may be**], and which is dated and recorded in the [*register and date of recording*]; and I declare to be disburdened thereof a lease granted by *E.F.* [*designation*] of [*shortly mention subjects leased*] in the parish of and county of , which lease is dated and recorded [*register and date of recording*].

[*Testing clause.*]

**Note.*—If granter not original creditor, name and design original creditor.

NOTE

[1] As amended by the Conveyancing and Feudal Reform (Scotland) Act 1970, Sched. 10.

[1] Land Registers (Scotland) Act 1868

(31 & 32 Vict. c. 64)

An Act to improve the system of registration of writs relating to heritable property in Scotland. [31st July 1868]

NOTE

[1] Functions of the Keeper of the General Register of Sasines now exercisable by the Keeper of the Registers of Scotland: see the Reorganisation of Offices (Scotland) Act 1928, s. 5, and the Public Registers and Records (Scotland) Act 1948, s. 1 (2).

Functions of the Lord Clerk Register as the Keeper of the Records, Registers and Rolls for Scotland now exercisable by the Keeper of the Registers of Scotland: see the Lord Clerk Register (Scotland) Act 1879, s. 6, the Reorganisation of Offices (Scotland) Act 1928, s. 5, and the Public Registers and Records (Scotland) Act 1948 s. 1 (2).

Short title

1. This Act may be cited for all purposes as " The Land Registers (Scotland) Act 1868 ".

Interpretation of terms

2. The term " Register of Sasines ", as used in this Act shall be held as applying to the registers directed to be kept by the Registration Act 1617, c. 16, for the registration of sasines, reversions, and other writs directed to be recorded therein by that Act or by any subsequent Act of Parliament; and the word " writ ", as used in this Act, shall apply to and include all deeds and writings which have heretofore been in the practice of being recorded in these registers, or which may under the provisions of this Act be recorded in the general register of sasines.

In general register of sasines, writs of each county to be kept separate

3. The general register of sasines for Scotland shall be so kept that the writs applicable to each county shall be entered in a separate series of presentment books, and the writs shall be minuted in a separate series of minute-books, and engrossed in a separate series of register volumes, in the order of presentment, and where any writ shall contain land in more than one county such writ shall be entered by the ingiver in the presentment book of such of these counties as may be specified in the warrant of registration hereinafter provided for, and shall be minuted in the minute-book of such of these counties or county as are specified in the said warrant, and shall be engrossed at length in the division of the register applicable to one only of the said counties; and a memorandum shall be entered in each division of the register applicable to the other counties or county in the presentment book of which it is entered as aforesaid, setting forth the volume of the register and the folio or folios of such volume in which such engrossment is made; and such memorandum shall be deemed to be equivalent to full engrossment of such writ in the division of the register wherein such memorandum shall be entered as aforesaid: For the purposes of this Act, the barony and regality of Glasgow, and also the stewartry of Kirkcudbright, shall each be treated as a county.

4. [Repealed by the Statute Law Revision Act 1875.]

Competent to record writs in other county or counties to which they refer by new warrant

5. Provided always, that where any writ containing lands or heritages in more than one county shall not have had a warrant of registration endorsed or written thereon applicable to all the counties to which it applies, the registration of such writ shall, notwithstanding, as regards the county or counties mentioned in the warrant, and in the minute-books and register volumes of which county or counties it has been recorded, or a memorandum thereof entered, be effectual; and it shall be competent afterwards to present such writ by a new warrant of registration thereon, and to minute and register such writ in the register of any other county or counties to which such writ applies in terms of such new warrant; and in the case of such subsequent registration it shall not be necessary to engross the writ at length in the division of the register applicable to such county or counties, but the same may be effected by the insertion of a memorandum in such division of the register in the manner hereinbefore provided for, and such subsequent registration shall be effectual as regards the county or counties to which such writ applies, and to which such new warrant is applicable, of and from the date of such subsequent registration.

Provision for writs transmitted by post to general register of sasines

[1] **6.** Where any writ shall be transmitted by post for registration in the general register of sasines the keeper of the said register shall, upon the receipt of such writ, cause the same to be acknowledged to the sender, and to be presented in terms of the warrant of registration thereon by a clerk in his office to be appointed by him for that purpose, and who shall be held as the ingiver of the writ: and such clerk shall in the presentment book enter the name of the sender; and such writ shall be recorded in the same manner as any other writ presented for registration; and on the writ being ready for delivery intimation to that effect shall be made by post to the sender, accompanied by a note of fees, and on receipt of the fees and postage, and a request to that effect, the keeper shall transmit the writs to the sender by post; and where two or more writs shall be received by the keeper at the same time, the entries thereof in the presentment book and minute-book shall be of the same year, month and day, and such writs shall be deemed and taken to be presented and registered contemporaneously.

NOTE

[1] As amended by the Public Registers and Records (Scotland) Act 1948, s. 3 and the Land Registration (Scotland) Act 1979, Sched. 2, para. 1 and Sched. 4.

Registration, how to be made, etc.

7. Registration of writs in the general register of sasines, shall, except in so far as altered by the provisions of this Act, continue to be made in conformity with the practice heretofore in use; and no error or omission in any presentment book of the general register of sasines to be kept as aforesaid shall invalidate, or in any way affect injuriously, the registration of any writ recorded in said register.

Particular registers of sasines abolished

[1] **8.** The whole particular registers of sasines in Scotland shall be discontinued; and all writs which, previous to the discontinuance of the said particular registers respectively, might competently have been presented for registration therein, shall after said discontinuance be registrable only in the general register of sasines; and registration in the general register of sasines as hereinbefore directed to be kept for separate counties shall have all the force and effect previously attached to registration in such particular registers of sasines respectively.

NOTE

[1] As amended by the Statute Law Revision Act 1893. For the dates at which the Particular Registers of Sasines respectively terminated, see the Notes, *infra*.

Printed abridgments, etc., and indexes, to be prepared contemporaneously with record

9. Printed abridgments and printed indexes, both of persons and of places, applicable to each county in Scotland, in the form heretofore in use in the General Register House, or in such other form as may from time to time be prescribed by the Lord Clerk Register, shall, from and after the discontinuance of all the particular registers of sasines directed to be discontinued as aforesaid, be prepared under the superintendence of the keeper of the general register of sasines, and as nearly as possible contemporaneously with the minute-books and volumes of the register; and such indexes shall be consolidated from time to time for such periods as may be deemed expedient: Provided always, that it shall be lawful at any time for the Lord Clerk Register, if he shall think fit, to direct that abridgments shall cease to be prepared separately from the minutes, and in that case, and in lieu of the preparation and printing of said abridgments, the minutes shall be printed under the superintendence of the keeper of the general register of sasines, in lieu of printing such abridgments.

10. [Repealed by the Public Registers and Records (Scotland) Act 1948, s. 7.]

11. [Repealed by the Statute Law Revision Act 1893.]

Registration in general register of sasines equivalent in certain cases to registration in the books of council and session

[1] **12.** It shall not be necessary to register in the books of council and session for the purpose of preservation, or of preservation and execution, any writ competent to be registered in the general register of sasines, and which shall have been so registered, and such writ, being registered in the said register of sasines, shall be held to be registered also in the books of council and session for preservation, or for preservation and execution, as the case may be: Provided such writ when presented for registration in the said register of sasines, shall, in the warrant of registration prescribed by this Act, have an addition, specifying that the writ is to be registered for preservation, or for preservation and execution, as well as for publication, in or as nearly as may be in the form of schedule (A) No. 3 hereto annexed; and the writ, with such warrant, being so registered in the said register of sasines, shall not be redelivered to the ingiver, but an extract only (containing as part of said extract, where the writ is registered for execution, a warrant for execution) shall be delivered, which extract may be issued without abiding the actual booking in the register of sasines, and shall be signed on each page

by the keeper of the register of sasines, or a deputy duly commissioned by him to that effect; and all writs so presented to be registered for preservation and execution shall, after having been engrossed in the general register of sasines in terms of law, be periodically transmitted by the keeper of the register of sasines to the Lord Clerk Register or his deputies, through the office of the keeper of the register of deeds and probative writs and protests in the books of council and session, or otherwise, as the Lord Clerk Register shall prescribe, and shall be indexed, either separately, or along with other writs registered in the books of council and session, as the Lord Clerk Register may direct; and such registration in the general register of sasines shall have all the legal effects of registration in the books of council and session for preservation, or for preservation and execution, as the case may be, as well as of registration in the general register of sasines: Provided always, that no writ shall be held to be registered for the purpose of execution which does not contain a procuratory for registration, or clause of consent to registration, for the purpose of execution, in the body of the writ; and extracts as aforesaid, one or more, of all writs so registered in the said register of sasines may be issued at any time by the keeper of the register of sasines, or, after transmission as aforesaid, by the deputy keeper of the records, or by any one having their authority respectively; and all such extracts, and the warrants of execution therein contained, shall have all the like force and effect as any extract from the books of council and session, or as any warrant of execution contained in or appended to such extract, or as any extract from the general register of sasines, according to the existing law and practice; and such extracts, in terms of this Act, shall be equivalent to the registered writs themselves, except where any writ so registered shall be offered to be improven; and all extracts issued in terms of this Act shall have upon them, in such form as may from time to time be prescribed by the Lord Clerk Register, a certificate or marking indicating the *cumulo* amount of stamp duty paid on the principal writ recorded and retained for preservation.

NOTE

[1] Amended by the Conveyancing (Scotland) Act 1924, s. 10 (warrants of registration).

No higher fees to be chargeable for writs registered for preservation and execution as well as publication

13. No fees shall be chargeable at the office of the keeper of the register of deeds and probative writs and protests in the books of council and session in respect of the registration of any writs in the general register of sasines for preservation, or for preservation and execution, as well as for publication, in terms of this Act; and the fees to be charged in respect thereof, and of the extract given out at the time of registration at the office of the general register of sasines, shall be the same, with the addition only of any outlay for the writing and stamps of such extract, as would have been chargeable if the writ had been registered for publication only; and the salaries of the principal keeper of the register of deeds and probative writs and protests in the books of council and session, and of the assistant keepers, shall be defrayed out of funds to be provided by Parliament for the purpose; and the fees of the department shall be accounted for in such manner as the Treasury shall direct.

Registered writs to be authenticated

[1] **14.** The certificate of registration on every writ that shall be registered in the general register of sasines, and redelivered to the ingiver shall be signed by the keeper of the said register, or a deputy duly commissioned by him to that effect; and no further signature in order to or in token of such registration shall be necessary to any writ presented for registration in the general register of sasines; but every folio of such writ shall, in token of such

registration, be impressed with an office seal or stamp to be kept in the said general register of sasines.

NOTE

[1] Repealed by the Public Registers and Records (Scotland) Act 1950, s. 1 and Sched., so far as it relates to the signing of certificates of registration. See *ibid.* s. 1, *infra.*

" 1.—(1) Save as may be otherwise prescribed by Act of Sederunt made by the Court of Session under section four of the Public Registers and Records (Scotland) Act 1948, it shall not be necessary, notwithstanding anything in any enactment, for a certificate of recording endorsed or stamped on a writ recorded in the Register of Sasines to be signed by the Keeper of the Registers of Scotland or by any other person....

(3) This section shall be deemed to have had effect as from the 30th day of July, 1948 ".

Register of interruptions of prescriptions to be discontinued

15. The register of interruptions of prescriptions shall be discontinued as a separate record, and all writs appropriate thereto may be presented and registered in the general register of sasines in the same manner as any other writs appropriate to said general register of sasines; and registration thereof in the general register of sasines shall have all the like force and effect as registration in the register of interruptions of prescriptions previous to the passing of this Act.

Particular register of inhibitions abolished

16. The particular registers of inhibitions and interdictions throughout Scotland shall be discontinued, and all diligences, executions, and other writings at present appropriate to those registers, or any of them, shall be registrable only in the general register of inhibitions, which shall be the only competent register for the registration of inhibitions and interdictions; and no publication whatever of such diligences, executions, and other writings, other than registration in said general register of inhibitions, shall in future be necessary, but such registration shall for all purposes whatsoever have all the legal effect of the publication at present in use.

17. [Repealed by the Statute Law Revision Act 1950.]

Particular registers of hornings, etc., not to be affected

18. The particular registers of hornings and expired charges shall be continued as at the date of the passing of this Act: Provided always, that where any such register has been heretofore kept as a joint register of hornings and inhibitions, it shall cease to be a competent register for the registration of inhibitions.

Provision as to official searchers

19. The Treasury shall have power, upon the application from time to time of the Lord Clerk Register, to regulate the number of official searchers of the records, and to grant to such searchers such remuneration out of funds to be provided by Parliament for that purpose as their Lordships shall deem fit: Provided that nothing herein contained shall interfere with the right of parties or their agents to employ any other persons to search the records, or shall affect any liability legally attaching to such other persons, or to agents employing them respectively.

20. [Repealed by the Public Registers and Records (Scotland) Act 1948, s. 7.]

Remuneration to sheriff-clerks

21. It shall be competent to the Treasury to pay to sheriff-clerks reasonable allowances for duties discharged by them under this Act out of funds to be voted by Parliament for that purpose.

22. [Repealed by the Statute Law Revision Act 1893.]

Responsibilities of keepers of particular registers to attach to keeper of general register

23. The keeper of the general register of sasines shall, from and after the discontinuance of the particular registers, or any of them, be subject to such and the like responsibilities and liabilities for loss and damage by reason of neglects, omissions, or errors in the registration of writs in the general register of sasines as the keepers of the particular registers of sasines have hitherto been and now are subject to with reference to the registration of writs in such particular registers.

24. [Repealed by the Public Registers and Records (Scotland) Act 1948, s. 7.]

Fees

[1] **25.** The Secretary of State, with the consent of the Treasury, may from time to time by order made by statutory instrument fix fees payable in respect of registration or recording in any register under the management and control of the Keeper of the Registers of Scotland and in respect of the provision by the Keeper of searches, reports, certificates or other documents or copies of any document or of information from any such register; and the amount of the fees so fixed shall not be greater than is reasonably sufficient for defraying the expenses of the department of the Keeper, including the expenses of the improvement of the systems of such registration and recording.

NOTE

[1] Substituted by the Land Registration (Scotland) Act 1979, s. 23.

26. [Repealed by the Lord Clerk Register (Scotland) Act 1879.]

27. [Repealed by the Burgh Registers (Scotland) Act 1926, s. 4 and Sched. 2.]

28. [Repealed by the Statute Law Revision Act 1893.]

SCHEDULES

SCHEDULE A

Nos. 1 & 2

[Repealed by the Statute Law Revision Act 1893.]

No. 3

[For substituted forms of warrant of registration and notes substituted for Sched. A No. 3, see the Conveyancing (Scotland) Act 1924, s. 10 and Sched. F, *infra.*]

SCHEDULE B

[Repealed by the Conveyancing (Scotland) Act 1924, s. 10 (7).]

[1] Titles to Land Consolidation (Scotland) Act 1868

(31 & 32 Vict. c. 101)

An Act to consolidate the statutes relating to the constitution and completion of titles to heritable property in Scotland, and to make certain changes in the law of Scotland relating to heritable rights. [31st July 1868]

NOTE

[1] The Act as printed embodies ss. 22, 24, 118, 119, 130 and 141 as substituted by the Titles to Land Consolidation (Scotland) Amendment Act 1869.

Short title

1. This Act may be cited for all purposes as " The Titles to Land Consolidation (Scotland) Act 1868 "

Commencement of Act

2. This Act shall take effect from and after the 31st day of December 1868, unless in so far as it is herein appointed to take effect at an earlier date.

Interpretation of terms

[1] **3.** The following words and expressions in this Act, and in the schedules annexed to this Act, shall have the several meanings hereby assigned to them, unless there be something in the subject or context repugnant to such construction; that is to say—

The words " superior ", " vassal ", " grantor ", " grantee ", " disponer ", " disponee ", " legatee ", " adjudger ", and " purchaser ", shall extend to and include the heirs, successors, and representatives of such superior, vassal, grantor, grantee, disponer, disponee, legatee, adjudger, or purchaser respectively; and the word " successors " shall extend to and include heirs, disponees, assignees, legal as well as voluntary, executors, and representatives:

[2] The words " Sheriff of Chancery " shall extend to and include the Sheriff of Chancery and his substitute under this Act, or under the Service of Heirs (Scotland) Act 1847; and the word " sheriff " shall extend to and include the sheriff of any county and his substitute, and the Sheriff of Chancery and his substitute:

The words " Sheriff-Clerk of Chancery " shall extend to and include the Sheriff-Clerk of Chancery acting under this Act, or who acted under the Service of Heirs (Scotland) Act 1847, and the depute of such sheriff-clerk; and the words " sheriff-clerk " shall extend to and include the Sheriff-Clerk of Chancery and the sheriff-clerk of any county and their respective deputes:

The words " Crown Writ " shall extend to and include all charters, precepts, and writs from Her Majesty, and from the Prince; and the word " Prince " shall extend to and include the Prince and Steward of Scotland and his successors:

The word " charter " and the word " writ " shall each extend to and include all Crown writs, and all charters, precepts, and writs from subject superiors:

[3] The word " deed " and the word " conveyance " shall each extend to and include all charters, writs, dispositions, whether containing a warrant or precept of sasine or not, and whether *inter vivos* or *mortis causa*, and whether absolute or in trust, feu contracts, contracts of ground annual, heritable securities, reversions, assignations, instruments, decrees of constitution relating to land to be afterwards

adjudged, decrees of adjudication for debt, and of adjudication in implement, and of constitution and adjudication combined, whether for debt or implement, decrees of declarator and adjudication, decrees of sale, and decrees of general and of special service, whether such decrees contain warrant to infeft or precept of sasine or not, and the summonses, petitions, or warrants on which any such decrees proceed, warrants to judicial factors, trustees, or beneficiaries of a lapsed trust, to make up titles to lands and the petitions on which such warrants proceed, writs of acknowledgment, contracts of excambion, deeds of entail, procuratories of resignation *ad remanentiam*, and all deeds, decrees, and writings by which lands, or rights in lands, are constituted or completed or conveyed or discharged, whether dated, granted, or obtained before or after the passing of this Act, and official extracts of all deeds and conveyances; and all codicils, deeds of nomination, and other writings annexed to or endorsed on deeds or conveyances, or bearing reference to deeds or conveyances separately granted, and decrees of declarator naming or appointing persons to exercise or enjoy the rights or powers conferred by such deeds or conveyances, shall be deemed and taken for the purposes of this Act to be part of the deeds or conveyances to which they severally relate, and shall have the same effect in all respects as to the persons so named and appointed as if they had been named and appointed in the deeds or conveyances themselves:

The words "deed of entail" shall extend to and include all deeds and conveyances of lands under the fetters of a strict entail, and all procuratories, bonds, and contracts by which lands are settled under such fetters:

[3] The word "instrument" shall extend to and include all notarial instruments authorised by this Act, or by any of the Acts hereby repealed, and also all instruments of sasine, instruments of resignation *ad remanentiam*, instruments of resignation and sasine, and instruments of cognition and sasine, and instruments of cognition:

[3] The words "heritable security" and "security" shall each extend to and include all heritable bonds, bonds and dispositions in security, bonds of annual rent, bonds of annuity, and all securities authorised to be granted by section 7 of the Debts Securities (Scotland) Act 1856, and all deeds and conveyances whatsoever, legal as well as voluntary, which are or may be used for the purpose of constituting or completing or transmitting a security over lands or over the rents and profits thereof as well as such lands themselves and the rents and profits thereof, and the sums, principal, interest, and penalties secured by such securities, but shall not include securities by way of ground annual, whether redeemable or irredeemable, or absolute dispositions qualified by back bonds or letters:

The word "creditor" shall extend to and include the party in whose favour an heritable security is granted, and his successors in right thereof:

The word "debtor" shall include the debtor and his successors:

[3] The word "lands" shall extend to and include all heritable subjects, securities, and rights:

The words "notary public" shall be held to mean a notary public duly admitted to practise in Scotland:

The word "petitioner" shall extend to and include any person who may have presented or may present a petition within the meaning of this Act, or of any Act hereby repealed:

[4] The words "judicial factor" shall extend to and include judicial factors or *curators bonis* to persons under incapacity, factors *loco absentis*, and all judicial managers:

The words "infeft" and "infeftment" shall extend to and include the due registration, in the appropriate register of sasines, of any deed or conveyance, whether before or after the commencement of this Act, by which registration a real right to lands has been or shall be constituted.

NOTES

[1] As amended by the Statute Law Revision Act 1893. Modified by the Conveyancing (Scotland) Act 1924, s.2(1).

[2] Functions of Sheriff of Chancery now exercisable by the sheriff principal of Lothian and Borders; the Administration of Justice (Scotland) Act 1933, s.31(1) as read with the Sheriff Courts (Scotland) Act 1971, s.4(1).

[3] As amended by the Conveyancing (Scotland) Act 1924, ss.2(1),5(3)(*b*).

[4] As amended by the Age of Legal Capacity (Scotland) Act 1991, s.10 and Sched. 2.

Acts specified in Schedule (A) repealed

[1] **4.** Every Act or Acts and such parts of every other Act or Acts as shall be inconsistent with this Act, shall be and the same are hereby repealed.

NOTE

[1] As amended by the Statute Law Revision Act 1893.

In conveyances of land, etc., not held burgage, certain clauses may be inserted in the short forms given in Schedule (B) No. 1

[1] **5.** It shall not be necessary to insert in any conveyance of lands in Scotland a clause of obligation to infeft, or a precept of sasine, or warrant of infeftment; and in any conveyance of such lands in which all or any of the following clauses are necessarily or usually inserted (*videlicet*), a clause declaring the term of entry, a clause expressing the manner of holding, a clause of assignation of writs and evidents, a clause of assignation of rents, a clause of obligation to free and relieve of feu-duties and casualties due to the superior, and of public burdens, a clause of warrandice, a procuratory or clause of restriction for preservation or for preservation and execution, it shall be lawful and competent to insert all or any of such clauses in the form or as nearly as may be in the form No. 1 of schedule (B) hereunto annexed; and all or any of such clauses, if so inserted in any such conveyance, or in any conveyance dated after the 30th day of September 1847, shall have the meaning and effect assigned to them in sections 6 and 8 of this Act, and shall be as valid, effectual, and operative to all intents, effects, and purposes, as if the same had been expressed in the fuller mode or form generally in use prior to the said 30th day of September 1847.

NOTE

[1] As amended by the Statute Law Revision Act 1893.

Import of clause expressing manner of holding

[1] **6.** If the lands have been or shall be conveyed to be holden *a me* only, the clause so expressing the manner of holding shall imply that the lands are to be holden from the grantor of and under his immediate lawful superiors, in the same manner as the grantor or his predecessors or authors held, hold, or might have holden the same.

NOTE

[1] As amended by the Statute Law Revision Act 1893.

In conveyances of burgage property certain clauses may be inserted in the forms given in Schedule (B) No. 2

7. It shall not be necessary to insert in any conveyance of lands in

Scotland held by burgage tenure a clause of obligation to infeft, or a procuratory of clause of resignation; and every conveyance of such lands shall imply that the lands thereby conveyed are to be holden of Her Majesty in free burgage, for service of burgh used and wont; and in any conveyance of such lands in which all or any of the following clauses are necessarily or usually inserted (*videlicet*), a clause declaring the term of entry, a clause of obligation to free and relieve of ground annual, cess, annuity, and other public burdens, a clause of assignation of rents, a clause of assignation of writs and evidents, a clause of warrandice, and a clause of registration for preservation and execution, it shall be lawful and competent to insert all or any of such clauses in the form or as nearly as may be in the Form No. 2 of schedule (B) hereto annexed; and all or any of such clauses, if so inserted in any such conveyance, or in any similar conveyance dated after the 30th day of September 1847, shall have the meaning and effect assigned to them in section 8 of this Act, and shall be as valid, effectual, and operative to all intents and purposes as if they had been expressed in the fuller mode or form generally in use prior to the said 30th day of September 1847.

Import of clauses in Schedule (B) Nos. 1 and 2

[1] **8.** The clause of assignation of writs and evidents in forms Nos. 1 and 2 of schedule (B) hereto annexed shall, unless specially qualified, be held to import an absolute and unconditional assignation to such writs and evidents, and to all open procuratories, clauses, and precepts, if any, and as the case may be, therein contained, and to all unrecorded conveyances to which the disponer has right: and the clause of assignation of rents in these forms shall, unless specially qualified, be held to import an assignation to the rents to become due for the possession following the term of entry, according to the legal and not the conventional terms, unless in the case of forehand rents, in which case it shall be held to import an assignation to the rents payable at the conventional terms subsequent to the date of entry; and the clause of warrandice in these forms shall, unless specially qualified, be held to imply absolute warrandice as regards the lands and writs and evidents, and warrandice from fact and deed as regards the rents; and the clause of obligation to free and relieve from feu-duties, casualties, and public burdens, in form No. 1 of schedule (B) hereto annexed, shall, unless specially qualified, be held to import an obligation to relieve of all feu-duties or other duties and services or casualties payable or prestable to the superior, and of all public, parochial, and local burdens due from or on account of the lands conveyed prior to the date of entry; and the clause of obligation to free and relieve from ground annuals, cess, annuity, and other public burdens, in form No. 2 of schedule (B) hereto annexed, shall, unless specially qualified, be held to import an obligation to relieve of all ground annuals, cess, annuity, and other public, parochial, and local burdens, due from or on account of the lands conveyed prior to the date of entry; and the clause of consent to registration in these two forms shall, unless specially qualified, have the meaning and import and effect assigned to them in section 138 of this Act.

NOTE

[1] As amended by the Statute Law Revision Act 1893.

Conditions of entail may, in conveyances of entailed lands, be inserted by reference merely

9. It shall not be necessary in any conveyance or deed of or relating to lands held under a deed of entail, or of or relating to lands obtained by excambion in exchange for lands held under any deed of entail, or of or relating to lands purchased or acquired for the purpose of being added to any estate held under any deed of entail, or entailed on the heirs and under the conditions specified in any deed of entail, to insert the destination of heirs, or the conditions, provisions, and prohibitory, irritant, and resolutive clauses, or clause authorising registration in the register of tailzies, contained in any such deed of entail; provided the same shall in such conveyance or deed be specially referred to as set forth at full length in such deed of entail recorded in the register of tailzies, if the same shall have been so recorded, or as set forth at full length in any conveyance or deed recorded in the appropriate register of sasines and forming part of the progress of title deeds of the said lands held under such deed of entail, such reference being made, as nearly as may be, in the terms set forth in schedule (C) hereto annexed; and the reference to such destination, or to such conditions, provisions, and prohibitory, irritant, and resolutive clauses, or clause authorising registration in the register of tailzies, if so made in any such conveyance or deed, whether dated prior or subsequent to the commencement of this Act, shall be equivalent to the full insertion thereof, and shall, to all intents and in all questions whatever, whether *inter haeredes* or with third parties, have the same legal effect as if the same had been inserted exactly as they are expressed in the recorded deed of entail, conveyance, or deed referred to, notwithstanding any law or practice to the contrary, or any injunction to the contrary contained in such deed of entail, or any enactments or provisions to the contrary contained in the Entail Act 1685, or in any other Act or Acts of the Parliament of Scotland or of Great Britain, or of the United Kingdom of Great Britain and Ireland, now in force.

Real burdens may be referred to as already in the Register of Sasines

[1] **10.** Where lands are or shall hereafter be held under any real burdens or conditions or provisions or limitations whatsoever appointed to be fully inserted in the investitures of such lands, it shall, notwithstanding such appointment, and notwithstanding any law or practice to the contrary, not be necessary in any conveyance or deed of or relating to such lands to insert such real burdens or conditions or provisions or limitations, provided the same shall, in such conveyance or deed, be specially referred to as set forth at full length in the conveyance or deed of or relating to such lands recorded in the appropriate register of sasines, wherein the same were first inserted, or in any such conveyance or deed of subsequent date recorded as aforesaid, and forming part of the progress of titles of the said lands, such reference being made in the terms or as nearly as may be in the terms set forth in schedule (D) hereto annexed; and the reference to such real burdens or conditions or provisions or limitations, if so made in any such conveyance or deed, whether dated prior or subsequent to the commencement of this Act, shall be held to be equivalent to the full insertion thereof, and shall to all intents and in all questions whatever, whether with the disponer or superior or third parties, have the same legal effect as if the same had been inserted exactly as they are expressed in the recorded conveyance or deed referred to, notwithstanding any law or practice or Act or Acts of Parliament to the contrary.

NOTE

[1] Excluded by the Land Registration (Scotland) Act 1979, s. 15 (2).

11. [Repealed by the Conveyancing (Scotland) Act 1874, s. 61.]

Clause directing part of conveyance to be recorded

[1] **12.** Immediately before the testing clause of any conveyance of lands, it shall be competent to insert a clause of direction, in or as nearly as may be in the form No. 1 of schedule (F) hereto annexed, specifying the part or parts of the conveyance which the grantor thereof desires to be recorded in the register of sasines; and when such clause is so inserted in any conveyance, whether dated before or after the commencement of this Act, and with a warrant of registration thereon, in which express reference is made to such clause of direction (such warrant being in the form as nearly as may be of No.

2 of schedule (F) hereto annexed), is presented to the keeper of the appropriate register of sasines for registration, such keeper shall record such part or parts only, together with the clause of direction and the testing clause and warrant of registration; and in the absence of such express reference in the warrant of registration as aforesaid, such conveyance shall be engrossed in the register as if it had contained no clause of direction; and the recording of such part or parts of the conveyance, together with the clause of direction and the testing clause, and the warrant of registration as before provided, shall have the same legal effect as if, at the date of such recording, a notarial instrument containing such part or parts of the conveyance had been duly expede and recorded in the appropriate register of sasines in favour of the person on whose behalf the conveyance is presented: Provided that, notwithstanding such clause of direction, it shall be competent for the person entitled to present the conveyance for registration to record the whole conveyance or to expede and record a notarial instrument thereon, as after provided, in the same manner as if the conveyance had contained no such clause of direction; and where such notarial instrument shall be expede no part or parts of the conveyance directed to be recorded shall be omitted from such instrument.

NOTE

[1] Amended (warrants of registration) by the Conveyancing (Scotland) Act 1924, s. 10.

Several lands conveyed by the same deed may be comprehended under one general name

[1] **13.** Where several lands are comprehended in one conveyance in favour of the same person or persons, it shall be competent to insert a clause in the conveyance, declaring that the whole lands conveyed and therein particularly described shall be designed and known in future by one general name to be therein specified; and on the conveyance containing such clause, whether dated before or after the commencement of this Act, or on an instrument following thereon, whether dated before or after the commencement of this Act, and containing such particular description and clause, being duly recorded in the appropriate register of sasines, it shall be competent in all subsequent conveyance and deeds and discharges, of or relating to such several lands, to use the general name specified in such clause as the name of the several lands declared by such clause to be comprehended under it; and such subsequent conveyances and deeds and discharges of or relating to such several lands under the general name so specified shall be as effectual in all respects as if the same contained a particular description of each of such several lands, exactly as the same is set forth in such recorded conveyance or instrument: Provided always that reference be made in such subsequent conveyances and deeds and discharges to a prior conveyance or instrument recorded as aforesaid, in which such particular description and clause are contained; provided also that it shall not be necessary in such clause to comprehend under one general name the whole lands contained in the conveyance in which such clause is inserted, but that it shall be competent to comprehend certain lands under one general name and certain other lands under another general name, it being clearly specified what lands are comprehended under each general name; and such reference shall be in or as nearly as may be in the terms set forth in schedule (G) hereunto annexed.

NOTE

[1] Excluded by the Land Registration (Scotland) Act 1979, s. 15 (1).

Certain clauses in entails no longer necessary

14. Where a deed of entail contains an express clause authorising registration of the deed in the register of tailzies, it shall not be necessary to insert clauses of prohibition against alienation, contracting debt, and altering the order of succession, and irritant and resolutive clauses, or any of them; and such clause of registration contained in any deed of entail of lands not held by burgage tenure dated on or after the 1st day of October 1958, or of lands held by burgage tenure dated on or after the 10th day of October 1860, shall have in every respect the same operation and effect as if such clauses of prohibition, and such irritant and resolutive clauses, had been inserted in such deed of entail, any law or practice to the contrary notwithstanding.

Instrument of sasine no longer necessary, but conveyance may be recorded instead

15. It shall not be necessary towards obtaining infeftment in land to expede and record in the case of lands not held by burgage tenure an instrument of sasine, or in the case of lands held by burgage tenure an instrument of resignation and sasine, on any conveyance or deed of or relating to such lands,[1] but it shall be competent and sufficient for the person or persons in whose favour the conveyance or deed has been or shall be granted or conceived, instead of expeding and recording such instrument of sasine or of resignation and sasine, to record the conveyance or deed itself in the appropriate register of sasines; and the conveyance or deed being presented for registration in such register, with a warrant of registration thereon, in or as nearly as may be in the form No. 1 of schedule (H) hereto annexed, and being so recorded along with such warrant, shall have the same legal force and effect in all respects as if the conveyance or deed so recorded had been followed by an instrument of sasine in the case of lands not held by burgage tenure, or in the case of lands held by burgage tenure by an instrument of resignation and sasine, expede in favour of the person on whose behalf the conveyance or deed is presented for registration, and recorded in the appropriate register of sasines, at the date of recording the said conveyance or deed; and where it is desired to give investiture *propriis manibus*, it shall be competent for the person in whose favour the conveyance or deed has been or shall be granted or conceived to record the conveyance or deed itself in the register of sasines applicable to the lands therein contained, with a warrant of registration thereon, in or as nearly as may be in the form of No. 3 of schedule (H) hereto annexed, signed by such person, and such conveyance or deed being so recorded along with such warrant, shall have the same legal force and effect in all respects as if the conveyance or deed so recorded had been followed by an instrument of sasine, or of resignation and sasine *propriis manibus* expede in favour of the wife of such person, and signed by such person, and recorded at the date of recording the said conveyance or deed according to the law and practice heretofore in force.

NOTE

[1] Distinction between feu and burgage abolished by the Conveyancing (Scotland) Act 1874, s. 25.

Not necessary to record the whole conveyance or discharge

17. Where it is not desired to record in the register of sasines the whole of a conveyance or deed, or the whole of a discharge, of or relating to lands, it shall be competent and sufficient to expede and record in the appropriate register of sasines a notarial instrument setting forth generally the nature of the conveyance or deed or discharge, and containing those portions of the same by which the lands are conveyed or discharged, and by which real burdens, conditions, provisions, or limitations are imposed or discharged; and where by any conveyance or deed or discharge separate lands or separate interests in the same lands are conveyed or discharged in favour of the same or different persons, it shall not be necessary to record the whole of such conveyance or deed or discharge, but it shall be competent and sufficient to expede and record as aforesaid a notarial instrument, setting forth generally the nature of the conveyance or deed or discharge, and containing the part or parts of the conveyance or deed or discharge by which particular lands are conveyed or discharged in favour of the person or persons in whose favour the notarial instrument is expede, and the part of the conveyance or deed or discharge which specifies the nature and extent of the right and interest of such person or persons, with the real burdens, conditions, provisions, and limitations, if any; and such notarial instrument shall be in or as nearly as may be in the form of schedule (J) hereto annexed: and upon such notarial instrument or any similar notarial instrument expede in virtue of any of the Acts of Parliament hereby repealed being so recorded, the person or persons in whose favour the same has been or shall be expede and so recorded shall be in the same position as if, at the date of such recording, the conveyance or deed or discharge on which it proceeds, along with a warrant of registration thereon, had been recorded in the appropriate register of sasines in favour of such person or persons.

Instrument of resignation ad remanentiam **unnecessary, but in place thereof conveyance in favour of superior may be recorded**

[1] **18.** [Superseded 1874.]

NOTE

[1] For consolidation of superiority and feu, see the Conveyancing (Scotland) Act 1874, s. 6.

Notarial instruments in favour of general disponees

[1] **19.** Where a person shall have granted or shall grant a general disposition of his lands, whether by conveyance *mortis causa* or *inter vivos*, or by a testamentary deed or writing within the sense and meaning of sections 20 and 21 of this Act, and whether such general disposition shall extend to the whole lands belonging to the grantor, or be limited to particular lands belonging to him, with or without full description of such lands, and whether such general disposition shall contain or shall not contain a procuratory or clause of resignation, or a precept of sasine, or an obligation to infeft, or a clause expressing the manner of holding, it shall be competent to the grantee under such general disposition to expede and record in the appropriate register of sasines a notarial instrument in or as nearly as may be in the form of schedule (L) hereto annexed; and on such notarial instrument or any similar notarial instrument expede in virtue of any Act of Parliament hereby repealed being so recorded, such grantee shall be in all respects in the same position as if a conveyance of the lands contained in such notarial instrument had been executed in his favour by the grantor of the general disposition, by such manner of holding, if any, as is expressed in the general disposition, and if no particular manner of holding is therein expressed, then to be holden in the manner and to the effect, and subject to the provisions enacted and provided in section 6 of this Act in the case of conveyances in which no manner of holding is expressed, and in the case of lands held by burgage tenure to be holden of Her Majesty in free burgage, and as if such conveyance had been followed, where such lands are not held by burgage tenure, by an instrument of sasine of the said lands in favour of such grantee, expede and recorded in the appropriate register of sasines at the date of recording such notarial instrument: Provided always that where such notarial instrument shall be expede by a person other than the original grantee under such general disposition, it shall set forth the title or series of titles by which the person in whose favour it is expede acquired right to such general disposition, and the nature of his right.

NOTE

[1] As amended by the Statute Law Revision Act 1893; repealed by the Succession (Scotland) Act 1964, s. 34 (2), Sched. 3, except in relation to general dispositions by conveyance *inter vivos*.

De praesenti words, or words of style, unnecessary in mortis causa deeds

[1] **20.** From and after the commencement of this Act it shall be competent to any owner of lands to settle the succession to the same in the event of his death, not only by conveyances *de praesenti*, according to the existing law and practice, but likewise by testamentary or *mortis causa* deeds or writings, and no testamentary or *mortis causa* deed or writing purporting to convey or bequeath lands which shall have been granted by any person alive at the commencement of this Act, or which shall be granted by any person after the commencement of this Act, shall be held to be invalid as a settlement of the lands to which such deed or writing applies, on the ground that the grantor has not used, with reference to such lands, the word " dispone ", or other word or words importing a conveyance *de praesenti*; and where such deed or writing shall not be expressed in the terms required by the existing law or practice for the conveyance of lands, but shall contain with reference to such lands any word or words which would, if used in a will or testament, with reference to moveables, be sufficient to confer upon the executor of the grantor, or upon the grantee or legatee of such moveables, a right to claim and receive the same, such deed or writing, if duly executed in the manner required or permitted in the case of any testamentary writing by the law of Scotland, shall be deemed and taken to be valid as a settlement on a grantee or legatee of the lands to which it applies; and the executor of the grantor may complete title to such lands by expeding and recording a notarial instrument as aforesaid: Provided always, that nothing herein contained shall be held to confer any right to such lands on the successors of any such grantee or legatee who shall predecease the grantor, unless the deed or writing shall be so expressed as to give them such right in the event of the predecease of such grantee or legatee.

NOTE

[1] As amended by the Succession (Scotland) Act 1964, s. 34 (1) and Sched. 2.

Trustee or executor to apply lands for purposes of trust or will

21. Where such testamentary or *mortis causa* deed or writing shall be conceived in favour of a grantee as trustee or executor of the grantor, and shall not be expressed to be wholly in favour of such trustee or executor for his own benefit, such trustee or executor shall apply such whole lands for the purposes specified in such deed or writing; and where such purposes cannot, in whole or in part, be carried into effect, or where no purposes with reference to such lands have been or shall be specified in such deed or writing, such trustee or executor shall convey such lands, or so much thereof, or shall apply so much of the proceeds thereof, if such lands shall have been sold and realised by him, as may not be required for the purposes of such deed or writing, to or for behoof of the person or the successors of the person who, but for the passing of this Act and the granting of such deed or writing, would have been entitled to succeed to such lands on the death of such grantor.

22. [Repealed by the Conveyancing and Feudal Reform (Scotland) Act 1970, Sched. 11, Pt. II.]

Notarial instruments in favour of parties acquiring rights to unrecorded conveyances

23. It shall be competent to any person having right to an unrecorded deed or conveyance originally granted in favour of another person to expede a notarial instrument, in or as nearly as may be in the form of schedule (N) hereto annexed, setting forth the deed or conveyance and the title or series of titles by which he acquired right to the same, and the nature of his right, and to record the deed or conveyance, with warrant of registration thereon, in the form or as nearly as may be in the form of No. 2 of schedule (H) hereto annexed, and also the notarial instrument, in the appropriate register of sasines; or where it is not desired to record the whole of the deed or conveyance, it shall be competent to expede a notarial instrument in or as nearly as may be in the form of schedule (J) hereto annexed, setting forth generally the nature of the deed or conveyance, and containing those portions of the deed or conveyance by which the lands in regard to which the said instrument is expeded, are conveyed, and by which real burdens, conditions, provisions, or limitations, if any, are imposed, and also setting forth the title or series of titles by which the party acquired right to the deed or conveyance and to record such notarial instrument in the appropriate register of sasines; and on the deed or conveyance, with such warrant of registration thereon, and such notarial instrument in the form of the said schedule (N), or any similar deed or conveyance with warrant of registration and notarial instrument expede in virtue of any Act of Parliament hereby repealed, being so recorded, or on such notarial instrument in the form of the said schedule (J), or any similar notarial instrument expede in virtue of any Act of Parliament hereby repealed, being so recorded, the person in whose favour the deed or conveyance and instrument, or the instrument, have or has been or shall be expede and so recorded, shall be in the same position as if the original deed or conveyance had been granted to himself, and, along with a warrant of registration thereon, had been recorded in the manner hereinbefore provided, of the date of recording the deed or conveyance and notarial instrument or the notarial instrument.

Mode of completing title by a judicial factor on a trust-estate, etc.

[1] **24.** Where, in a petition to the Court of Session for the appointment of a judicial factor, authority has been or shall be asked for the completion of a title by such factor to any lands forming the whole or part of the estate to be managed by such judicial factor, or where a judicial factor has applied or shall apply, by petition or note, to the said court for authority to complete a title to such lands, either in his own person as judicial factor, or in the person of any person under legal disability by reason of nonage, or person suffering from mental disorder within the meaning of the Mental Health (Scotland) Act 1960, to whom he may have been appointed judicial factor, and where any petition or note has specified and described or shall specify and describe the lands to which such title is to be completed, or has referred or shall refer to the description of the same in the form of schedule (G) hereto annexed, as the case may be, the warrant granted for completing such title shall also so specify and describe the lands to which such title is to be completed, or shall so refer to the description thereof; and such warrant shall be held to be a conveyance in due and common form of the lands therein specified in favour of such judicial factor granted by the person, whether in life or deceased, whose estate is under judicial management, or where the estate is that of a person under legal disability by reason of nonage, or person suffering from mental disorder within the meaning of the Mental Health (Scotland) Act 1960, in whose person a title has not been made up, such warrant shall be held to be such a conveyance in favour of the person under legal disability by reason of nonage, or person suffering from mental disorder within the meaning of the Mental Health (Scotland) Act 1960, or of the judicial factor appointed to such person under legal disability by reason of nonage, or person suffering from mental disorder within the meaning of the Mental Health (Scotland) Act 1960, as the case may be, granted by a predecessor, or author having such title, or where such judicial factor has been or shall be appointed on an estate which shall have been vested in a trustee or former judicial factor, such warrant shall be held to be such a conveyance granted by such trustee or former judicial factor, whether in life or deceased, for the purposes of such estate or trust, or factory; and such warrant may, with warrant of registration thereon, be recorded in the appropriate register of sasines as a conveyance in favour of such judicial factor or person under legal disability

by reason of nonage, or person suffering from mental disorder within the meaning of the Mental Health (Scotland) Act 1960, or of the factor on his estate, and being so recorded, shall have the same force and effect as if at the date of such recording such conveyance had been granted to the judicial factor, person under legal disability by reason of nonage, or person suffering from mental disorder within the meaning of the Mental Health (Scotland) Act 1960, or the judicial factor appointed to such person under legal disability by reason of nonage, or person suffering from mental disorder within the meaning of the Mental Health (Scotland) Act 1960, as the case may be, and recorded in the appropriate register of sasines: Provided always, that for enabling the person in whom such lands were last vested, or his representatives, or other parties interested, to bring forward competent objections against such warrant being granted, or claims upon the estate, the court shall order such intimation and service of the petition or note as to them shall seem proper: Declaring always, that the whole enactments and provisions herein contained shall extend and apply to all petitions to and warrants by the Court of Session under "The Trusts (Scotland) Act 1867", unless in so far as such provisions and enactments may be inapplicable to the form or objects of such petitions or warrants.

NOTE

[1] As substituted by the Titles to Land Consolidation (Scotland) Amendment Act 1869, s.3; as amended by the Statute Law Revision Act 1893, the Conveyancing (Scotland) Act 1924, s.5(3), the Mental Health (Scotland) Act 1960, Sched. 4 and the Age of Legal Capacity (Scotland) Act 1991, Sched. 1, para. 19. Extended by the Conveyancing (Scotland) Act 1924, s.24(6).

Mode of completing title by a trustee in sequestration, and by liquidators of joint stock companies

[1] **25.** It shall be competent to a trustee on a sequestrated estate, or to liquidators, official or voluntary, appointed for the purpose of winding up a joint stock company, to expede a notarial instrument, setting forth the Act and warrant of confirmation in favour of such trustee, or the appointment of such liquidators, official or voluntary, respectively, and specifying the lands belonging to the bankrupt or company to which a title is to be completed, and the title by which such lands are held by the bankrupt or company, in or as nearly as may be in the form of schedule (O) hereto annexed, and when the lands consist of heritable securities by a notarial instrument in or as nearly as may be in the form of schedule (LL) hereto annexed, and to record such notarial instrument in the appropriate register of sasines; and on such notarial instrument or any similar notarial instrument expede in virtue of any Act of Parliament hereby repealed, being so recorded, the trustee or liquidators in whose favour the same shall have been or shall be so recorded shall be held to be in all respects in the same position as if the bankrupt or company, or any previous trustee or liquidator, had granted a conveyance of the lands contained in the notarial instrument in favour of such trustee or such liquidators, and as if such conveyance had been recorded or followed by an instrument of sasine, or notarial instrument, in favour of such trustee or of such liquidators, duly expede and recorded in the appropriate register of sasines at the date of recording such notarial instrument.

NOTE

[1] As amended by the Statute Law Revision Act 1893.

Heritable property conveyed for religious or educational purposes to vest in disponees or their successors

26. Wherever lands have been or may hereafter be acquired by any congregation, society, or body of men associated for religious purposes, or for the promotion of education, including the General Assemblies, Synods, and Presbyteries of the Established Church of Scotland, and of all other Presbyterian Churches in Scotland, as a chapel, meeting-house or other place of worship, or as a manse or dwelling-house for the minister of such congregation or society or body of men, or offices, garden, or glebe for his use, or as a schoolhouse or schoolmaster's house, garden, or playground, or as a college, academy, or seminary, or as a hall or rooms for meeting for the transaction of business, or as part of the property belonging to such congregation, society, or body of men, and wherever the conveyance or lease of such lands has been or may be taken in favour of the moderator, minister, kirk session, vestryman, deacons, managers, or other office-bearers or office-bearer of such congregation or society or body of men, or any of them, or of trustees appointed, or to be from time to time appointed, or of any party or parties named in such conveyance or lease, in trust for behoof of the congregation or society or body of men, or of the individuals comprising the same, such conveyance, when recorded with warrant of registration thereon in terms of this Act, or when followed by notarial instrument expede, and with warrant of registration thereon recorded in terms of this Act, or such lease, shall not only vest the party or parties named therein in the lands thereby feued, conveyed, or leased, but shall also, after the death, or resignation or removal from office of such party or parties, or any of them, effectually vest their successors in office for the time being chosen and appointed in the manner provided or referred to in such conveyance or lease, or if no mode of appointment be therein set forth or prescribed, then in terms of the rules or regulations of such congregation or society or body of men, in such lands, subject to such and the like trusts and with and under the same powers and provisions as are contained or referred to in the conveyance or lease given and granted to the parties, disponees, or lessees therein, and that without any transmission or renewal of the investiture whatsoever, anything in such conveyance or lease contained to the contrary notwithstanding: And the provisions of this section shall apply also to all trusts for the maintenance, support, or endowment of ministers of religion, missionaries, or schoolmasters, or for the maintenance of the fabric of churches, chapels, meeting-houses, or other places of worship, or of manses or dwelling-houses or offices for ministers of the gospel, or of schoolhouses or schoolmasters' houses, or other like buildings.

27–50. [Repealed by the Succession (Scotland) Act 1964, s.34(2) and Sched. 3.]

Power to the Court of Session to pass Acts of Sederunt

[1] **51.** It shall be competent to the said Court of Session, and they are hereby authorised and required from time to time, to pass such Acts of Sederunt as shall be necessary or proper for regulating in all respects the proceedings under this Act before the sheriff of chancery or sheriffs of counties, and following out the purposes of this Act in regard of these proceedings, and regulating the time at which the sheriff of chancery shall hold his courts, and the fees to be paid in respect of any of the proceedings to be taken in virtue hereof; and the charges to be made by agents and solicitors, whether in the inferior court or Court of Session, for any proceedings under this Act, shall be audited and taxed in the same manner as charges for other judicial proceedings in the said courts respectively are audited and taxed: Provided always that accounts of expenses in the sheriff court of chancery shall be audited and taxed by the auditor of the Court of Session and the decree for such expenses shall be extractable by the extractor of the Court of Session in the same manner as a decree of that court, and all such decrees shall be held to be interim decrees, and the warrant shall, after extract, be re-transmitted to the sheriff-clerk of chancery.

NOTE

[1] See note 2 to s.3 on "Sheriff of Chancery," *supra*.

52. [Repealed by the Statute Law (Repeals) Act 1975.]

53. [Repealed by the Statute Law Revision Act 1893.]

54–55. [Repealed by the Statute Law (Repeals) Act 1975.]

56–57. [Repealed by the Statute Law Revision Act 1893.]

58. [Repealed by the Succession (Scotland) Act 1964, s.34(2) and Sched. 3.]

Unnecessary to libel and conclude for decree of special adjudication

59. Whereas it is inconvenient in practice to libel and conclude for general adjudication of lands as the alternative only of special adjudication, in terms of an Act of the Parliament of Scotland passed in the year 1672: It shall not be necessary to libel or conclude for special adjudication, and it shall be lawful to libel and conclude and decern for general adjudication without such alternative, anything in the said last recited Act of the Parliament of Scotland, or in any other Act or Acts of the Parliament of Scotland or of Great Britain, or of the United Kingdom of Great Britain and Ireland, to the contrary notwithstanding.

60–61. [Repealed by the Succession (Scotland) Act 1964, s.34(2) and Sched. 3.]

Effect of a decree of adjudication or sale

[1] **62.** In all cases a decree of adjudication, whether for debt or in implement, or a decree of constitution and adjudication, whether for debt or in implement, if duly obtained in the form prescribed by this Act, or obtained, if prior to the commencement of this Act, in the form then in use, or a decree of declarator and adjudication, or a decree of sale, shall, except in the case where the subjects contained in the decree of adjudication, or of constitution and adjudication, or of declarator and adjudication, are heritable securities, be held equivalent to and shall have the legal operation and effect of a conveyance in ordinary form of the lands therein contained granted in favour of the adjudger or purchaser by the ancestor of such apparent heir, or by the owner or proprietor in trust or otherwise, and whether in life or deceased, of the lands adjudged, or by the seller of the lands sold, although under legal disability by reason of nonage or of insane mind, and it shall be lawful and competent to such adjudger or purchaser to complete feudal titles to said lands, not only by infeftment on such decree as a conveyance or by using it, for the purpose of infeftment, as an assignation or as one of a series of assignations of an unrecorded conveyance, as the case may be, in the manner provided by this Act.

NOTE

[1] As substituted by the Conveyancing (Scotland) Act 1874, s.62; as amended by the Statute Law Revision (No. 2) Act 1893 and the Age of Legal Capacity (Scotland) Act 1991, Sched. 1, para. 20; repealed in so far as relating to any such decree as is therein mentioned obtained in relation to lands forming part of the estate of a deceased person, by the Succession (Scotland) Act 1964, Sched. 3.

Signature for Crown writs abolished

63. It shall not be necessary, in order to the obtaining of any Crown writ, that any signature shall be presented and passed in exchequer, or that any precept shall be framed and issued thereon as preliminary to the granting of such writ, and all Crown writs shall be obtained in the manner directed by this Act and not otherwise.

Crown writs to be obtained by lodging a draft thereof and note along with the title deeds

64. Any person seeking to obtain a Crown writ shall lodge or cause to be lodged in the office of the presenter of signatures a draft of the proposed writ, as prepared by his agent, being a writer to the signet, whose signature shall be endorsed thereon, together with a short note, in the form, or as nearly as may be in the form, of schedule (S) hereunto annexed, praying for a Crown writ in terms of the said draft; and the date of lodging such note shall be marked thereon by the presenter of signatures or his clerk; and along with such note and draft there shall be lodged the last Crown writ and retour or decree of service of the lands, and all the title deeds of the lands subsequent thereto, together with evidence of the valued rent when necessary, and an inventory and brief of the titles, according to the practice heretofore in use.

Draft Crown writ to be revised

[1] **65.** The draft Crown writ so lodged shall be forthwith revised by the presenter of signatures, who shall require the attendance of the agent of the person applying for the writ for the purpose of receiving his explanations; and the presenter of signatures shall thereafter proceed with the revision of the said draft, making such alterations and corrections as are necessary; and he shall, after his final revisal of such draft, authenticate each page thereof, and the several alterations and corrections thereon, if any, with his initials, and shall mark on such draft that the same has been revised by him, and also the date when such revisal was completed; and the fees on signatures payable prior to the 1st day of October 1847 to the presenter of signatures shall be chargeable on the draft writ to be lodged and revised as aforesaid, and all other fees payable prior to that date to the officers of exchequer on signature shall cease and determine.

NOTE

[1] The duties of the presenter of signatures are now discharged by the sheriff principal of Lothian and Borders: see the Conveyancing (Scotland) Act 1874, s. 57, and the Sheriff Courts (Scotland) Act 1971, s. 4 (1).

Rectification of mistakes in former titles

[1] **66.** If it shall appear that any mistake has occurred in the terms of the last Crown writ or retour or decree of service, to the prejudice of the Crown, the person applying for the writ shall further, on requisition made to him or his agent to that effect, by order of the presenter of signatures, lodge the prior title deeds of the said lands, and any other title deeds of and concerning the same, in so far as such title deeds may be in his possession or at his command, and in so far as the same may be necessary for the due revisal of the said draft on behalf of the Crown, and for the rectification of such mistake, which may be rectified accordingly; and, on the other hand, if the vassal shall allege any mistake to have occurred in the terms of the last Crown writ or retour or decree of service to his prejudice, the person applying for the writ shall be entitled, without such requisition, to lodge a note explaining the alleged mistake, and produce the prior titles of the said lands, and any other title deeds or other deeds of and concerning the same, in so far as these may be necessary for the due revisal of the said draft and the rectification of such mistake, which may be rectified accordingly; but no such rectification shall in either case be allowed, nor the draft be held as finally revised or authenticated as such, until the same shall have been reported by the presenter of signatures to and approved of by the Lord Ordinary in Exchequer causes appointed in terms of the Exchequer Court (Scotland) Act 1856.

NOTE

[1] See note 1 to s. 65, *supra*.

Intimation of proposed rectification to be made to solicitor for Commissioners of Woods

[1] **67.** In every case where the draft of any Crown writ shall be laid before the Lord Ordinary in Exchequer causes, as before provided for, intimation

thereof and of the relative report by the presenter of signatures, or note, as the case may be, shall be made by the agent applying for the writ to the solicitor in Scotland for the Commissioners of Woods, and the Lord Advocate shall be entitled to appear in name and on behalf of the Crown, and on behalf of the said Commissioners, or either of them, in all future proceedings relating to the said Crown writ; and the Lord Ordinary, before finally approving of any such draft writ, shall be satisfied that one calendar month's previous notice in writing of such draft having been laid before him has been given to the said solicitor, accompanied by a copy of the said draft writ, and of the report by the presenter of signatures, or note, as the case may be.

NOTE

[1] The functions of the Commissioners of Woods now exercisable by the Crown Estate Commissioners: see S.R. & O. 1924 No. 1370, the Crown Estate Acts 1956, s. 1 (1), and 1961, s. 1 (1). See note 1 to s. 65, *supra*.

Presenter of signatures, etc., may refer to copy of writ where withheld

[1] **68.** When the last Crown writ or retour or decree of service shall be withheld by the person applying as aforesaid, or cannot be so lodged from being in the possession of the proprietor of other lands therein contained, or from any other good cause, it shall be competent for the presenter of signatures, or for the person applying as aforesaid, to refer to the copy thereof engrossed in the register of the Great Seal, or in the register of retours or record of services, and to procure exhibition thereof as evidence of the terms of such last Crown writ or retour or decree of service; and the Lord Clerk Register is hereby authorised and required to make such regulation as will enable the exhibition thereof to be obtained for the purpose aforesaid, upon the joint application of the person so applying and of the presenter of signatures.

NOTE

[1] See note 1 to s. 65, *supra*.

Amount of Crown duties to be fixed

[1] **69.** The presenter of signatures shall also, with the aid of the auditor of exchequer, ascertain and fix the amount of composition or other duties due and payable to the Crown on granting such writ, and the amount of the same shall be marked on the said draft, and certified by the signatures of the said auditor of exchequer and of the presenter of signatures; and in ascertaining and fixing the amount of such composition and other duties payable to the Crown there shall be no charge added for the expense of collecting the same, any law or practice to the contrary notwithstanding.

NOTE

[1] See note 1 to s. 65, *supra*.

Clerk's fees

[1] **70.** The person applying for such Crown writ shall be bound to pay to the clerk of the presenter of signatures the fees to be fixed in manner herinafter provided, which fees shall be paid over by such clerk to the director of chancery, who shall be accountable therefor.

NOTE

[1] See note 1 to s. 65, *supra*.

Copy of revised draft to be furnished to the party

[1] **71.** Such revised draft shall, so long as it is retained in the office of the presenter of signatures, be there open to the inspection of the party applying

for the Crown writ or his agent, and a copy thereof shall be furnished on demand on payment of the fees to be fixed as hereinafter directed.

NOTE

[1] See note 1 to s. 65, *supra*.

If no objections, the revised draft to be attested, and the Crown writ prepared

[1, 2] **72.** Where no objections shall be stated to the draft as so revised, a docquet shall be put thereon certifying that the same is approved, which docquet shall be signed by the agent applying for the Crown writ and by the presenter of signatures, and the date of signing the same thereon set forth; and such draft, so docqueted, shall, without being given up to the party applying for the said writ or his agent, be officially transmitted by the presenter of signatures to the office of the director of chancery, and such draft shall form a valid and sufficient warrant for the immediate preparation of the writ in chancery in terms of such draft.

NOTES

[1] See note 1 to s. 65, *supra*.
[2] As amended by the Statute Law Revision Act 1893.

Crown writs may be applied for at any time

[1] **73.** It shall be competent to apply for any Crown writ in manner before directed, and to revise the draft of the same, and in the event of the same being docqueted as revised and approved in manner aforesaid, to prepare and deliver the writ as hereinafter directed at any period of the year, and notwithstanding that it shall not then be term time of the Court of Session acting as the Court of Exchequer in Scotland under the Exchequer Court (Scotland) Act 1856.

NOTE

[1] See note 1 to s. 65, *supra*.

Objections, if any, to draft Crown writ to be by note

[1] **74.** It shall be lawful for the person applying for the Crown writ, if dissatisfied with the draft revised as aforesaid, to state objections thereto or against the amount of duties and composition thereon marked as payable, and such objections shall be set forth in a short written note of objections, without argument, to be lodged in the office of the presenter of signatures, subscribed by the agent of such person; and the date of lodging such note of objections shall be marked thereon by the presenter of signatures or his clerk.

NOTE

[1] See note 1 to s. 65, *supra*.

Objections, how to be disposed of

[1] **75.** Where any note of objections shall be so lodged, such note shall, together with the whole other proceedings, be laid before the said Lord Ordinary in Exchequer causes, and the said Lord Ordinary shall hear the person so objecting, by himself, his counsel or his agent, being a writer to the signet, and shall also hear any report or statement by the presenter of signatures; and wherever it shall appear to the said Lord Ordinary that the said objections should to any extent receive effect, he shall cause such alterations and corrections as shall appear to him proper, either with reference to the terms of the said draft, or to the amount of duties or other payments marked thereon as payable, to be made on such draft, or to be expressed in a separate paper marked as relative thereto, and shall authenticate such draft and relative paper with his signature; and the said Lord

Ordinary shall at the same time pronounce a judgment or deliverance, to be written on the note of objections, appointing the writ, as so altered and corrected, to be prepared and executed; and the judgment or deliverance so pronounced shall form a valid and sufficient warrant for the preparation in chancery of the writ as altered and corrected.

NOTE

[1] See note 1 to s. 65, *supra*.

Procedure if objections repelled

[1] **76.** Wherever the said Lord Ordinary shall be of opinion that the said objections should not to any extent receive effect, he shall pronounce a judgment, to be written on the said note of objections, repelling the said objections; and the judgment or deliverance so pronounced shall form a valid and sufficient warrant for the preparation in chancery of the writ as revised by the presenter of signatures in manner before directed.

NOTE

[1] See note 1 to s. 65, *supra*.

Refusal to revise, how to be complained of

[1] **77.** Wherever the presenter of signatures shall be of opinion that the person applying for the Crown writ has not produced a title sufficient to show that he has right to obtain the same, the presenter of signatures shall mark on the said draft that the same is refused for want of sufficient production of titles, adding thereto his signature and the date of affixing the same; and his clerk shall intimate such refusal to the agent of the said person, and shall on demand return the draft to such agent; and in every such case it shall be competent for the person who shall have applied for the writ to bring such refusal under review of the said Lord Ordinary by a note of objections lodged in manner aforesaid; and the said Lord Ordinary shall, after considering such note, and hearing parties thereon in manner aforesaid, sustain or repel the objections, or pronounce such judgment or deliverance thereon as shall be just; and if the said Lord Ordinary shall be of opinion that a sufficient title has been shown to authorise the writ being granted, he shall in that case remit to the presenter of signatures to proceed with the revisal of the draft in manner before mentioned.

NOTE

[1] See note 1 to s. 65, *supra*.

Crown writ as revised to be engrossed and delivered

[1] **78.** As soon as the draft Crown writ shall have been docqueted as revised and approved in manner before provided, or, in case of objections being stated, as soon as the same shall have been disposed of by the said Lord Ordinary in manner before directed, the said draft shall be officially transmitted by the presenter of signatures to the office of the director of chancery; and immediately thereafter the writ shall be engrossed in the office of the director of chancery in terms of the draft as finally adjusted, signed, and officially transmitted as aforesaid, and shall be signed by the director of chancery or his depute or substitute: and it shall not be necessary to have the seal appointed by the Treaty of Union to be kept and used in Scotland in place of the Great Seal thereof formerly in use affixed to any writs from Her Majesty, or the seal of the Prince if the writs be of lands holden of the Prince, and a separate seal be then in use for such writs, affixed to any writs from the Prince, unless the receivers of such writs shall require the appropriate seal to be affixed; and when the appropriate seal is so required and affixed, the fact shall be stated at the conclusion of the writ, and the date on which the seal is

actually appended stated; and all Crown writs shall be in all respects as valid and effectual without the seal as if the same had been appended thereto; and the writ when signed, or, if required, signed and sealed, as the case may be, shall be recorded in chancery in manner hereafter provided, and shall be thereafter delivered to the person applying for the same, or his agent, in like manner in all respects, and on payment of the same fees and charges, as at present used and observed and payable, and the date of signing, or of sealing when the seal is appended shall in all cases be held and expressed to be the date of the writ: Provided always that before the writ shall be so delivered payment shall be made to the officers who are or may be entitled to receive the same of the amount of duties and compositions payable to Her Majesty or the Prince, ascertained and fixed as aforesaid; and a record of the amount of duties payable to Her Majesty or the Prince shall be kept in chancery, so as to form a charge against the officer or other person appointed to receive the same.

NOTE

[1] As amended by the Statute Law Revision Act 1893. See note 1 to s. 65, *supra*.

Crown writ to be valid

79. The engrossed Crown writ, signed, or signed and sealed, recorded and delivered as aforesaid, shall be in all respects a warrant for infeftment in the lands described or referred to in the said writ, as valid and effectual as any Crown writ of the same description hitherto in use to be granted, and notwithstanding that the same has not followed on any signature presented and passed in exchequer or precept directed thereon, any law or usage heretofore existing to the contrary notwithstanding.

80–82. [Repealed by the Statute Law Revision Act 1893.]

Crown writs and Crown charters may be in the forms given in Schedule (T)

[1] **83.** Crown charters of any denomination or nature, may be in forms as nearly approaching as may be to the examples given in schedule (T), the necessary alterations being made as the denomination or nature of the particular charter may require; and all Crown charters, when granted in or as nearly as may be in any of the forms provided by this Act, shall have the same force and legal effect in all respects as if the same had been granted in any corresponding forms heretofore in use or competent, and shall be read and construed as largely and beneficially in all respects for the holders thereof as if the same had been expressed in and had contained the whole terms and words which are now used, or were used prior to the 1st day of October, 1847, in granting such Crown writs or charters.

NOTE

[1] As amended by the Statute Law Revision Act 1893; repealed by the Succession (Scotland) Act 1964, s. 34 (2) and Sched. 3, in so far as relating to Crown precepts and Crown writs of *clare constat*.

84.–86. [Repealed by the Succession (Scotland) Act 1964, Sched. 3.]

Register of Crown writs to be kept

[1] **87.** The director of chancery,[2] or his depute or substitute, shall enter or cause to be entered in a book to be kept for the purpose, and entitled "The Register of Crown Writs", the whole Crown writ at full length: Provided always, that no Crown writ entered in the register of the Crown writs before the commencement of this Act shall be held to be invalidly entered in such register, although the whole of such writ has been so entered, anything in the "Titles to Land (Scotland) Act 1858", notwithstanding; and it is hereby

provided that extracts from the said register of Crown writs, certified by the director of chancery or his depute or substitute, shall make faith in judgment in all cases except in case of improbation.

NOTES

[1] As amended by the Statute Law Revision Act 1893.

[2] Functions of the director of chancery now exercisable by the Keeper of the Registers of Scotland: the Reorganisation of Offices (Scotland) Act 1928, s. 7, S.R. & O. 1932 No. 148 and the Public Registers and Records (Scotland) Act 1948, s. 1 (2).

Crown charters or writs of novodamus, **how to be obtained**

[1] **88.** In every case in which a Crown charter of *novodamus*, or a Crown charter containing any new or original grant, shall be sought, the person applying for the same shall, previously to lodging the note before mentioned in the office of the presenter of signatures, obtain the consent and approbation of the Commissioners of Woods, or any one of them, and of the Commissioners of the Board of Trade, under the hand of their secretary for the time being, and written evidence of such consent shall be produced along with the note to be lodged as aforesaid in the office of the presenter of signatures; and the charter shall be revised and engrossed as in the ordinary case, but the same shall be lodged with the Queen's and Lord Treasurer's Remembrancer, and be by him transmitted for the sign manual of Her Majesty, and the signatures of Her Majesty's Treasury, or in case such charter be of lands holden of the Prince, and His Royal Highness be then of full age, for the consent and approbation of the Prince, signified under his sign manual, after which the proper seal shall, if desired, be attached to such charters, and the other procedure shall be as is provided in regard to Crown writs generally.

NOTE

[1] As amended by the Statute Law Revision Act 1893.

89. [Repealed by the Statute Law Revision Act 1893.]

Crown writs to be in the English language

90. All Crown writs and instruments following thereon, or relating thereto, shall be expressed in the English language.

Court of Session to frame Regulations

91. The Court of Session performing the duty of the Court of Exchequer as aforesaid shall be and they are hereby authorised from time to time to frame and enact by rule of Court all such regulations as shall seem to them proper for giving effect to the purposes of the present Act, so far as they have reference to entries with the Crown; and the said court shall forthwith frame and enact a Rule of Court fixing and determining the fees to be paid on the various Crown writs, steps of procedure, and other matters hereby authorised with reference to such entries, but such Rule of Court shall be subject to revision by the court at any time or times thereafter.

92. [Repealed by the Statute Law Revision Act 1875.]

Power to Prince and Steward of Scotland to appoint his own presenter of signatures, etc.

[1] **93.** Notwithstanding anything in this Act contained, it shall be lawful for the Prince, being of full age, at any time or times hereafter to appoint his own presenter of signatures, and other officer or officers of exchequer and chancery, to discharge, in regard to all charters and precepts or writs of lands holden of him, the duties hereby assigned to the presenter of signatures and other officers of Her Majesty's exchequer and chancery respectively; and in case of the office of presenter of signatures, or any such other office in

exchequer or chancery as aforesaid for the Prince, being conferred on the person holding the corresponding office for the Crown, such officer shall be bound to act for the Prince without additional salary; and the fees hereby authorised to be levied in respect of all charters and writs from the Prince shall in that case be paid into the consolidated fund, but if any such appointment by the Prince shall be conferred upon a different person, the person so appointed shall draw for his own use such of the said fees as shall arise from the duties performed by him in respect of such charters and writs.

NOTE

[1] See note 1 to s. 65, *supra*.

94–95. [Repealed by the Statute Law Revision Act 1893.]

Substitute to be appointed to sheriff of chancery or presenter of signatures in event of absence or disability

[1] **96.** In the event of the temporary absence or disability of the sheriff of chancery it shall be competent to the Lord Justice General and President of the Court of Session to appoint a properly qualified person to act as substitute to the sheriff of chancery, such person receiving from the sheriff of chancery such remuneration for so acting as shall be fixed by the said Lord Justice General and President of the Court of Session.

NOTE

[1] As amended by the Statute Law Revision Act 1875.

97–99. [Repealed by the Statute Law Revision Act 1893.]

All writs and charters from subject superior may refer to tenendas and reddendo

[1] **100.** In granting all writs and charters by subject superiors it shall be competent and sufficient to refer to the *tenendas* and *reddendo* of the lands therein contained, as set forth at length either in the writ or charter produced to the superior in terms of this Act, or in any charter or other writ recorded in any public register.

NOTE

[1] As amended by the Statute Law Revision Act 1893.

101–103. [Repealed by the Succession (Scotland) Act 1964, s. 34 (2) and Sched. 3.]

Where subject superior's title incomplete, owner may in certain cases apply to Lord Ordinary on the Bills to ordain superior to complete his title and grant an entry under pain of forfeiture

104. [Virtually repealed.]

Owner may in such case apply to Lord Ordinary on Bills to authorise application for an entry by the Crown or mediate over superior as in case of the recusant superior

105. [Virtually repealed.]

Lands to be held temporarily of the Crown or mediate superior

106. [Virtually repealed.]

The party in right of the superiority may lodge a minute tendering relinquishment of his right, and if accepted by the petitioner, the Lord Ordinary may interpone his authority

107. [Virtually repealed.]

Over superior's rights not to be extended or affected

108. [Virtually repealed.]

Vassal obtaining or accepting forfeiture or relinquishment of superiority to be liable for its value, but forfeiture or relinquishment not to infer representation

109. [Virtually repealed.]

Mode of relinquishing superiorities

110. In order to facilitate still further the extinguishing of mid-superiorities not defeasible by the vassal, it shall be competent to any subject superior, whether himself entered with his superior or not, and whatever the annual value of the reddendo may be, to relinquish his right of superiority in favour of his immediate vassal, by granting a deed of relinquishment in the form or as nearly as may be in the form of No. 1 of schedule (CC) hereto annexed; and on the deed of relinquishment being accepted by the vassal, by an acceptance written on such deed in the form or as nearly as may be in the form No. 2 of schedule (CC) hereto annexed, and being followed by a writ of investiture by the over superior as hereinafter provided, also written upon the deed of relinquishment and on such deed, with the acceptance and writ of investiture written thereon, whether dated prior or subsequent to the commencement of this Act, and warrant of registration on behalf of the vassal, also written thereon, being thereafter recorded in the appropriate register of sasines, the superiority so relinquished shall be held to be extinguished, and the vassal and his successors in the lands shall hold the same as immediate vassals of the over superior by the tenure and for the reddendo by and for which such relinquished superiority was held, and the vassal and his foresaids shall be entitled to apply for an entry to such over superior accordingly as his immediate superior; and such relinquishment by a superior who shall not have completed his title to the superiority relinquished shall not infer a passive representation on his part, nor any liability for the debts of the person last infeft therein, beyond the price or consideration, if any, which he may receive for such relinquishment.

Investiture by over superior

111. On the application of the vassal in the relinquished superiority, and on production by him of the deed of relinquishment and acceptance thereof, whether dated prior or subsequent to the commencement of this Act, and on his paying or tendering such duties and casualties as may be exigible by the over superior, the over superior shall be bound to receive the vassal as his immediate vassal by writ of investiture in or as nearly as may be in the form of No. 3 of schedule (CC), to be written on the deed of relinquishment, and the tenendas and reddendo contained in the title deeds of the relinquished superiority shall be inserted therein in room of those contained in the former investiture held under the relinquished superiority; and where the lands are held of the Crown, such writ of investiture shall be obtained from chancery, in the same manner as hereinbefore directed in regard to confirmation written on the deeds confirmed; Provided always, that the party applying for such writ of investiture shall lodge or cause to be lodged in the office of the presenter of signatures a draft of the proposed writ in the same manner as when a Crown writ is applied for under the provisions of this Act; and the deed of relinquishment with the acceptance thereon shall be officially transmitted to the director of chancery, and the Crown writ of investiture engrossed thereon, and recorded in the same manner in which Crown writs are to be recorded, and shall thereafter be delivered to the vassal or his agent on payment of the same fees as are now payable for recording a writ or charter in chancery; and the investiture completed upon such relinquishment of the superiority shall be as effectual as if the grantor of the deed of relinquishment had completed his title to the superiority, and had thereafter conveyed the same to the vassal, and the latter, after having completed his titles under the over superior, had resigned *ad remanentiam* in his own hands: Provided always, that the investiture so completed shall not in any respect extend the rights or interests of such over superior, and that he shall be entitled to no more than the duties and casualties, taxed or untaxed, to which he would have been entitled if the grantor of the deed of relinquishment had remained or entered as his vassal.

Applications of price of entailed superiorities.–Price of superiorities of entailed lands may be charged on the entailed estate

112. Where the right of superiority, or the dues and casualties payable in respect thereof, forfeited or relinquished under the provisions of this Act, shall form part of an estate held under a deed of strict entail, such forfeiture or relinquishment shall not operate as a contravention of such entail, anything contained in the deed of entail or any Act of Parliament notwithstanding; and the price agreed to be paid for such superiority so forfeited or relinquished, if any, shall be consigned by the vassal in one of the chartered banks in Scotland, subject to the orders of the Court of Session, and shall be applicable and applied in such and the like manner and to such and the like purposes as purchase money or compensation coming to parties having limited interests is made applicable, under the Lands Clauses Consolidation (Scotland) Act 1845, or any Act altering or amending the same, or under the Entail Amendment Act 1848 or under the Entail Amendment Act 1853 and for that purpose it shall be competent to the heir of entail in possession to present a summary petition to the Court of Session, praying to have the price so applied, and such petition shall set forth the names, designations, and places of abode of those heirs of entail whose consents would be required to the execution of an instrument of disentail; and on such petition being served on such parties, and being intimated in the minute-book and on the walls in common form, it shall be competent for the court to direct the price to be applied to such of the said purposes as may appear to them to be most expedient: Provided always, that where the sums agreed to be paid for all the superiorities which form part of an entailed estate shall not in all exceed the sum of £200, such sum shall belong to the heir in possession, and the court shall direct such sums to be paid to him: Provided also, that the price of such superiorities may be applied by the heir in possession to such purposes and in such manner as may be authorised by any private Act of Parliament authorising the sale of the entailed estate or any portion thereof, and the application of the price thereof; and where the lands of which the superiority is so forfeited or relinquished shall be held by the vassal under a deed of strict entail, the vassal in such lands shall be entitled and he is hereby authorised to grant a bond and disposition in security over the entailed estate for the full amount of the price paid for the forfeited or relinquished superiority, together with all expenses incurred in the relative proceedings, including the estimated expense of such bond and disposition in security; and his granting such bond and disposition in security shall not operate as a contravention of such entail, anything contained in the deed of entail or any Act of Parliament notwithstanding: Provided always, that such bond and disposition in security shall be granted with the consent of those heirs of entail whose consents would be required to the execution of an instrument of disentail of the lands, or under the authority of a judicial warrant or decree of the Court of Session pronounced on a summary petition by the heir of entail in possession praying for such warrant; and the proceedings under such petition shall be the same or as nearly as may be the same as the proceedings under a petition to charge an entailed estate with provisions to younger children, as authorised by the said Entail Amendment Act 1848 and the Entail Amendment Act 1853: Provided always, that it shall not be necessary that such petition be publicly advertised in the *Gazette* or any newspaper, but that service and intimation only shall be made in common form.

Providing for payment in lieu of casualties of superiority in case of lands conveyed for religious purposes

113. [Virtually repealed.]

Writs of confirmation, etc., by subject superiors to be tested

[1] **114.** Writs of *clare constat*, and all other writs or charters granted in terms of this Act by subject superiors, shall be authenticated in the form required by the law of Scotland in the case of ordinary conveyances.

NOTE

[1] As amended by the Statute Law Revision Act 1893: repealed in so far as relating to writs of *clare constat* and writs of acknowledgment by the succession (Scotland) Act 1964, s. 34 (2) and Sched. 3.

115. [Repealed by the Statute Law Revision Act 1893.]

Stamp duty on writs of confirmation, etc.

[1] **116.** The stamp duty chargeable on writs of *clare constat*, and writs of investiture, granted or to be granted in virtue of this Act, except Crown writs, and on writs of acknowledgment under " The Registration of Leases (Scotland) Act ", shall be the same as that chargeable on precepts of *clare constat*, by subject superiors, and the said duty may be paid by means of adhesive stamps to be provided for that purpose by the Commissioners of Inland Revenue, who may from time to time make such rules as may seem fit for regulating the use of such stamps, and for insuring the proper cancellation thereof.

NOTE

[1] As amended by the Statute Law Revision Act 1893. Repealed in so far as relating to writs of *clare constat* and writs of acknowledgment by the Succession (Scotland) Act 1964, s. 34 (2) and Sched. 3.

Heritable securities to form moveable estate; except where conceived in favour of heirs, excluding executors and quoad fiscum**—Not to belong to husband,** jure mariti, **nor to wife** jure relictae**—Nor to be computed in legitim**

[1] **117.** From and after the commencement of this Act no heritable security granted or obtained either before or after that date shall, in whatever terms the same may be conceived, be heritable as regards the succession of the creditor in such security, and the same, shall be moveable as regards the succession of such creditor, provided that all heritable securities shall continue, and shall be heritable *quoad fiscum*, and that no heritable security, whether granted before or after marriage, shall to any extent pertain to the husband, *jure mariti*, where the same is or shall be conceived in favour of the wife, or to the wife, *jure relictae,* where the same is or shall be conceived in favour of the husband, unless the husband or relict has or shall have right and interest therein otherwise; declaring, nevertheless, that this provision shall in no way prejudice the rights and interests of wife or husband, or of the creditors of either, in or to the bygone interest and annual rents due under any such heritable security and *in bonis* of the husband or wife respectively prior to his or her death; and further provided, that where legitim is claimed on the death of the creditor no heritable security shall to any extent be held to be part of the creditor's moveable estate in computing the amount of the legitim.

NOTE

[1] As amended by the Succession (Scotland) Act 1964, s. 34 (1), (2), Sched. 2, para. 4 and Sched. 3.

Bonds and dispositions in security may be granted in the form No. 1 of Schedule (FF)

[1] **118.** From and after the commencement of this Act it shall be lawful and competent for any person entitled to grant an heritable security by way of bond and disposition in security to grant the same in the form or as nearly as may be in the form No. 1 of schedule (FF) hereto annexed; and the registration in the appropriate register of sasines, of such bond and disposition in security, or of any bond and disposition in security, granted according to any of the forms competent or in use prior to the commencement of this Act, shall be as effectual and operative to all intents and purposes as if such bond and disposition in security had contained an obligation to infeft, and precept of sasine, all in the words and form in use prior to the 30th day of September 1847, and as if sasine had been duly made, accepted, and given thereon in favour of the original creditor, and an instrument of sasine, as the case may be, in favour of such creditor had been duly recorded in the appropriate register of sasines of the date of the registration of the said bond and disposition in security as aforesaid.

NOTE

[1] As substituted by the Titles to Land Consolidation (Scotland) Amendment Act 1869, s.6, and amended by the Statute Law Revision Act 1893. Excluded by the Conveyancing and Feudal Reform (Scotland) Act 1970, s.32 and Sched. 8, para. 7.

Explanation of clauses in Schedule (FF) No. 1—Clauses reserving right of redemption, and of obligation to pay expense of assignation or discharge and power of sale, valid, etc.

[1] **119.** The import of the clauses of the form of No. 1 of the said schedule (FF) occurring in any bond and disposition in security, whether granted before or after the commencement of this Act, shall be as follows: *videlicet*, the cause obliging the grantor to pay the amount due under the bond, principal, interest, and penalty, to the creditor, his heirs, executors, or assignees, shall, unless where executors are excluded, be held to import an obligation to pay the same to the creditor and his representatives *in mobilibus* and his assignees, and, where there is or shall be such exclusion, to the creditor and his heirs and assignees; the clause disponing the lands to such creditor and his foresaids heritably shall, unless where executors are excluded, be held to import a disposition of such lands to such creditor and his representatives *in mobilibus* and his assignees, and, where there is or shall be such exclusion, to such creditor and his heirs and assignees in security in manner specified in the bond and disposition in security, with all the rights and powers at present competent to a creditor and his heirs under such a security; the clause of assignation of rents shall be held to import an assignation to the creditor and his representatives *in mobilibus* or his heirs as the case may be, and to his assignees, to the rents to become due or payable from and after the date from which interest on the sum in the security commences to run, in the fuller form generally in use prior to the 30th day of September 1847, including therein a power to the creditor and his foresaids to insure all buildings against loss by fire, and on default in payment to enter into possession of the lands disponed in security and uplift the rents thereof,or to uplift the rents thereof if the lands are not disponed in security, and to make all necessary repairs on the buildings, subject to accounting to the debtor for any balance of rents actually recovered beyond what is necessary for payment to such creditor and his foresaids of the sums, principal, interest, and penalty, due to him or them under such security, and of all expenses incurred by him or them in reference to such possession, including the expenses of management, insurance, and repairs; and the clause of assignation of writs shall be held to import an assignation to the creditor and his foresaids to writs and evidents to the same effect as in the fuller form generally in use in a bond and disposition in security with power of sale prior to the 30th day of September 1847; and the clause of warrandice shall be held to import absolute warrandice as regards the lands and the title deeds

thereof, and warrandice from fact and deed as regards the rents; and clause consenting to registration for preservation and execution shall have the meaning and effect assigned to such clause in section 138 of this Act; the clauses reserving right of redemption, and obliging the grantor to pay the expenses of assigning or discharging the security, and, on default in payment, granting power of sale, shall have the same import, and shall be in all respects as valid, effectual, and operative as if it had been in such bond and disposition in security specially provided and declared that the lands and others thereby disponed, should be redeemable by the grantor from the grantee, at the term and place of payment, or at any term of Whitsunday or Martinmas thereafter, upon premonition of three months, to be made by the grantor to the grantee, personally or at his dwelling-place, if within Scotland, and if furth thereof at the time, then at the office of the keeper of the record of edictal citations within the General Register House, Edinburgh, in presence of a notary public and witnesses, and that by payment to him of the whole principal sum payable under the bond and disposition in security, interest due thereon, and liquidated expenses and termly failures corresponding thereto, if incurred, and in case of his absence or refusal to receive the same, by consignation thereof in the bank specified in the security, if any bank shall be so specified, and if not, then in one or other of the banks in Scotland incorporated by Act of Parliament or royal charter, having an office or branch at the place of payment, to be made furthcoming on the peril of the consignor, the place of redemption to be within the office of such bank or branch thereof; and as if it had been thereby further provided and declared that any discharge and renunciation, disposition and assignation, or other deed, necessary to be granted by the grantee upon the rantor making payment and redeeming as aforesaid, and also the recording thereof, should always be at the expense of the grantor: and as if it had been thereby further provided and declared that if the grantor should fail to make payment of the sums that should be due by the personal obligation contained in the said bond and disposition in security, within three months after a demand of payment intimated to the grantor, although subject to any legal incapacity, personally or at his dwelling-place, if within Scotland, or if furth thereof, at the office of the keeper of the record of edictal citations above mentioned, in presence of a notary public and witnesses, and which demand for payment may be in or as nearly as may be in the form of No. 2 of schedule (FF) hereto annexed, and a copy thereof certified by such notary public in the form of No. 3 of schedule (FF) hereto annexed, or where such demand has been intimated to more persons than one, a copy so certified of the demand intimated to one of such persons with a certificate by such notary public that a similar demand has been intimated to the other persons, and stating the names and designations of such persons, and the dates and places of intimation to them, shall be sufficient evidence of such demand, then and in that case it should be lawful to and in the power of the grantee, immediately after the expiration of the said three months and without any other intimation or process of law, to sell and dispose, in whole or in lots, of the said lands and others, by public roup at Edinburgh or Glasgow, or at the head burgh of the county within which the said lands and others, or the chief part thereof, are situated, or at the burgh or town sending or contributing to send a member to Parliament, or at the burgh or town which may have previously adopted the General Police and Improvement (Scotland) Act 1862, or part thereof, which, whether within or without the county, shall be nearest to such lands, or the chief part thereof on previous advertisement, stating the time and place of sale, and published once weekly for at least six weeks subsequent to the expiry of the said three months, in any newspaper published in Edinburgh or in Glasgow, and in every case in a newspaper published in the county in which such lands are situated, or if there be no newspaper published in such county, then in any newspaper published in the next or a neighbouring county, and a certificate by the publishers of such newspapers for the time shall be *prima facie* evidence of such advertisement, the grantee being always bound, upon payment of the price, to hold count and reckoning with the grantor for the same, after deduction of the principal sum secured, interest due thereon, and liquidated penalties corresponding to both which may be incurred, and all expenses attending the sale, and for that end to enter into articles of roup, to grant dispositions containing all usual and necessary clauses, and in particular a clause binding the grantor of the said bond and disposition in security, in absolute warrandice of such dispositions, and obliging him to corroborate and confirm the same, and to grant all other deeds and securities requisite and necessary by the laws of Scotland for rendering such sale or sales effectual, in the same manner and as amply in every respect as the grantor could do himself; and as if it had been thereby further provided and declared that the said proceedings should all be valid and effectual, whether the debtor in the said bond and disposition in security for the time should be subject to any legal incapacity or not, and that such sale or sales should be equally good to the purchaser or purchasers as if the grantor himself had made them, and also that in carrying such sale or sales into execution it should be lawful to the grantee to prorogate and adjourn the day of sale from time to time as he should think proper, previous advertisement of such adjourned day of sale being given in the newspapers above mentioned, once weekly for at least three weeks; and as if the grantor had bound and obliged himself to ratify, approve of, and confirm any sale or sales that should be made in consequence thereof, and to grant absoluteand irredeemable dispositions of the lands and others so to be sold to the purchaser, and to execute and deliver all other deeds and writings necessary for rendering their rights complete.

NOTE

[1] As substituted by the Titles to Land Consolidation (Scotland) Amendment Act 1869, s. 7. Repealed by the Succession (Scotland) Act 1964, s. 34(2) and Sched. 3, in so far as relating to heritable securities from which executors are excluded. Amended by the Conveyancing (Scotland) Act 1924, s. 25. Excluded by the Conveyancing and Feudal Reform (Scotland) Act 1970, s. 32 and Sched. 8, para. 8. As amended by the Age of Legal Capacity (Scotland) Act 1991, Sched. 1, para. 21 and Sched. 2.

Securities may be registered during lifetime of grantee, or title completed after his death

120. Heritable securities, whether dated before or after the commencement of this Act, may be registered in the appropriate register of sasines at any time during the lifetime of the grantee, and shall in competition be preferred according to the date of the registration thereof: Provided always, that if an heritable security has not been so registered in the lifetime of the grantee, such heritable security shall be as full and sufficient warrant for completion of the title in favour of the party having right thereto, as if it had been a bond and disposition in security, containing precept of sasine and other clauses, in the ordinary form in use prior to the 30th day of September 1847, which title may be completed as after provided, or by service or notarial instrument as the circumstances of the case may require.

Sale carried through in terms of this Act to be valid to the purchaser

[1] **121.** Any sale duly carried through in terms of the heritable security and of this Act, or partly in terms of any Act now in force and partly in terms of this Act, if the proceedings shall have been begun before the commencement of this Act, shall be as valid and effectual to the purchaser as if made by the grantor of the security himself, and that whether the grantor shall have died before or after such sale, and without the necessity of confirmation by him or his successors, and notwithstanding that the party debtor in the security and in right of the lands at the time shall be

subject to any legal incapacity; Provided always, that nothing herein contained shall be held to affect or prejudice the obligation of the grantor and his successors to execute, or the right of the creditor or purchaser to require the grantor and his successors to execute, any deed or deeds which, independently of this enactment, would at common law be necessary for rendering the sale effectual, or otherwise completing in due form the titles of such purchaser.

NOTE

[1] As amended by the Age of Legal Capacity (Scotland) Act 1991, Sched. 2. Excluded by the Conveyancing and Feudal Reform (Scotland) Act 1970, s.32 and Sched. 8, para. 8.

Creditors selling to count and reckon for the surplus of the price and to consign the same in the bank

[1] **122.** The creditor, upon receipt of the price, shall be bound to hold count and reckoning therefor with the debtor and postponed creditors, if any such there be, or with any other party having interest, and to consign the surplus which may remain, after deducting the debt secured, with the interest due thereon and penalties incurred and expenses in reference to the possession of the estate if such creditor has been in possession, including expense of insurance, repairs, and management, and whole expenses attending such sale, and after paying all previous incumbrances and the expense of discharging the same, in one or other of the said banks, or in a branch of any such bank, in the joint names of the seller and purchaser for behoof of the party or parties having best right thereto; and the particular bank in which such consignation is to be made shall be specified in the articles of roup.

NOTE

[1] Excluded by the Conveyancing and Feudal Reform (Scotland) Act 1970, s.32 and Sched. 8, para. 8.

On sale and consignation of surplus, lands to be disencumbered of the security

[1] **123.** Upon a sale being carried through in terms of this Act, and upon consignation of the surplus of the price, if any be, as aforesaid, the disposition by the creditor to the purchaser shall have the effect of completely disencumbering the lands and others sold of all securities and diligences posterior to the security of such creditor, as well as of the security and diligence of such creditor himself.

NOTE

[1] Excluded by the Conveyancing and Feudal Reform (Scotland) Act 1970, s.32 and Sched. 8, para. 8.

Securities to be transferred in the form prescribed—When conveyance of heritable security is contained in a general deed of conveyance, the whole such deed need not be recorded

[1] **124.** Where an heritable security whether dated before or after the passing of this Act has been constituted by infeftment, whether such infeftment has been taken by recording the security or an instrument thereon in the appropriate register of sasines in terms of this Act or any of the repealed Acts, or by any mode competent or in use prior to the 30th day of September, 1847, in the appropriate register of sasines, the right of the creditor therein may be transferred, either in whole or in part, by an assignation or other conveyance in the form or as nearly as may be in the form of schedule (GG) hereto annexed; and on such assignation or conveyance being recorded in the appropriate register of sasines, the said security or part of such security, as the case may be, shall be transferred to the assignee as effectually as if such security had been disponed and assigned, and the disposition and assignation or conveyance had been followed by sasine duly recorded according to the law and practice prior to the 1st day of October

1845 at the date of recording such assignation or conveyance; and such assignee or disponee shall thereupon be held to be as fully entered as if he had obtained a renewal of the investiture in his favour according to the law and practice in use before that date: Provided always, that where the assignation or conveyance of an heritable security constituted as aforesaid is contained in any other conveyance or deed, it shall not be necessary to record the whole of such conveyance or deed, but it shall be sufficient to expede and record in the appropriate register of sasines a notarial instrument in the form or as nearly as may be in the form of schedule (HH) hereto annexed, and upon such notarial instrument being recorded the person or persons expeding the same shall be in the same position as if the assignation or conveyance of the heritable security on which it proceeds had been itself recorded as of the date of recording the said instrument.

NOTE

[1] Excluded by the Conveyancing and Feudal Reform (Scotland) Act 1970, s. 32 and Sched. 8, para. 8.

125. [Repealed by the Succession (Scotland) Act 1964, s. 34 (2) and Sched. 3.]

Completion of title of executors, etc., of creditor dying intestate

[1] **126.** Upon the death of any creditor who shall die intestate in right of an heritable security constituted by infeftment as aforesaid, it shall be competent to the executors duly confirmed to such deceased creditor to complete a title to such security by expeding and recording an instrument under the hands of a notary public in the form or as nearly as may be in the form set forth in schedule (JJ) hereto annexed; and when the executors (being more than one) duly confirmed as aforesaid shall not be entitled to the deceased's moveable estate wholly for their own interest, it shall be competent to take such notarial instrument in favour of the said executors and the survivors or survivor of them; and on such instrument being recorded in the appropriate register of sasines such executors or executor shall be held to be vested with the full right of the creditor in such security, and to be entered with the superior in the same manner and to the same effect as the original creditor himself.

NOTE

[1] As amended by the Succession (Scotland) Act 1964, s. 34 (2) and Sched. 3.

Executor-nominate or disponee mortis causa **may complete title by notarial instrument**

[1] **127.** Upon the death of any creditor in right of an heritable security constituted by infeftment as aforesaid from which executors shall not have been excluded, and who shall die leaving a testamentary or *mortis causa* deed or writing naming executors, or disponing or bequeathing his moveable estate, or disponing or bequeathing the security, it shall be competent for the executors, duly confirmed, or for the disponees, or for the legatees, as the case may be, to complete a title thereto by expending and recording in the appropriate register of sasines an instrument under the hand of a notary public in the form or as nearly as may be in the form of schedule KK hereto annexed; and when such executors or disponees, or legatees, being more than one, shall not be entitled to such security wholly for their own beneficial interest, it shall be competent to take such notarial instrument in favour of such executors or disponees or legatees, and the survivors and survivor of them, unless such a destination be expressly excluded by the terms of the deed or writing; and where any creditor has died or shall die before the commencement of this act, in right of such an heritable security, and leaving a *mortis causa* conveyance thereof, or of his heritable estate generally, or where any creditor shall die thereafter in right of such an heritable security from which executors shall have been excluded and leaving such a *mortis*

causa conveyance, or a testamentary deed or writing within the meaning of section 20 of this act, it shall be competent to the grantee or legatee under such *mortis causa* conveyance or testamentary deed or writing to complete a title to the security by notarial instrument as aforesaid; and on such instrument being so recorded the executors, disponees, legatees, or grantees, as the case may be, in whose favour such instrument has been expede, shall be vested with the full right of the creditor in such security, and shall be held to be entered with the superior in like manner and to the same effect as the original creditor himself.

NOTE

[1] As substituted by the Conveyancing (Scotland) Act 1874, s. 64. Repealed except in so far as providing for the completion of title by executors by the Succession (Scotland) Act 1964, s. 34 (2) and Sched. 3.

128. [Repealed by the Succession (Scotland) Act 1964, s. 34 (2) and Sched. 3.]

Adjudgers may complete their title by recording abbreviate of adjudication

[1] **129.** In all cases of adjudication, whether for debt or in implement, or of constitution and adjudication, whether for debt or in implement, in which the adjudger has obtained a decree of adjudication or of constitution and adjudication in the manner and to the effect provided by this Act, or in cases of declarator and adjudication, where the subjects contained in any such decree are heritable securities, it shall be competent for the adjudger to complete his title to such securities by recording either the abbreviate of adjudication or an extract of such decree in the appropriate register of sasines, in either of which cases he shall be in the same position as if an assignation of such heritable securities had been granted in his favour by the ancestor or person or creditor in trust or otherwise, and whether in life or deceased, whose estate is adjudged, and as if such assignation had been duly recorded in the appropriate register of sasines at the date of so recording such abbreviate or such extract decree.

NOTE

[1] As substituted by the Conveyancing (Scotland) Act 1874, s. 65. Repealed so far as relating to actions of constitution and adjudication by the Succession (Scotland) Act 1964, s. 34 (2) and Sched. 3.

Unregistered security or assignation to be available to executors, etc., of grantee

[1] **130.** In the event of an heritable security from which executors shall not have been excluded, dated before or after the commencement of this Act, not being constituted by infeftment during the lifetime of the grantee, or of any assignation, dated before or after the commencement of this Act, of a security from which executors shall not have been excluded, but which has been constituted by infeftment, not being completed by infeftment during the lifetime of the assignee, and where such grantee or assignee shall be in life at, or at any time subsequent to, the commencement of this Act, such security or assignation shall form a warrant for an instrument in the form or as nearly as may be in the form of schedule (MM) hereto annexed under the hands of a notary public, being passed upon the same in favour of the executors of the creditor duly confirmed, whether the same be executors nominate or executors dative, or in favour of the disponees or assignees of such security, or of the moveable estate of such creditor under any deed or conveyance *inter vivos* or *mortis causa*, or in favour of any legatees of such security; and where such executors or disponees or assignees, being more than one, shall not be entitled to such security wholly for their own beneficial interest, it shall be competent to take such notarial instrument in favour of such executors or disponees or assignees, and the survivors or survivor of them, unless such a destination be expressly excluded by the terms of the

conveyance, or deed, or writing; and where executors shall be excluded from such security, or the creditor has died before the commencement of this Act, the security or assignation, as the case may be, shall form a warrant for a notarial instrument as aforesaid, in favour of any disponees or assignees or legatees of such security, or of the heritable estate of such creditor under any deed or conveyance by him *inter vivos* or *mortis causa*, or under any testamentary deed or writing by him within the meaning of section 20 of this Act, or in favour of the heirs of such creditor having right to the security by decree of general or special service as heir to such creditor; and on such instrument being recorded in the appropriate register of sasines, the executors or disponees, or assignees or legatees or heirs, as the case may be, in whose favour such instrument is expede, shall be vested with the full right of the creditor in such security, and shall be held to be entered with the superior in like manner and to the same effect as the original creditor himself.

NOTE

[1] As substituted by the Titles to Land Consolidation (Scotland) Act 1869, s.8. Repealed except in so far as providing for the completion of title by executors and by disponees or assignees under a deed or conveyance *inter vivos* by the Succession (Scotland) Act 1964, s.34(2) and Sched. 3.

This Act not to affect liability of debtors on their lands

131. Nothing contained in this Act shall affect or interfere with the present law and practice in regard to the liability of the lands contained in any security, or of the debtor, or with the rights and remedies of the creditor, or of the creditors of the creditor.

How any heritable security may be renounced or discharged

[1] **132.** Any heritable security whether dated before or after the commencement of this Act, constituted by infeftment as aforesaid, may be effectually renounced and discharged, in whole or in part, and the lands therein contained effectually disburdened of the same, by a discharge in the form or as nearly as may be in the form of schedule (NN) hereto annexed, and by the registration of such discharge in the appropriate regiter of sasines, as aforesaid.

NOTE

[1] Excluded by the Conveyancing and Feudal Reform (Scotland) Act 1970, s.32 and Sched. 8, para. 13.

Heritable security, how restricted

[1] **133.** Any heritable security constituted as aforesaid may be restricted, as regards any portion of the lands therein contained, by a deed of restriction in the form or as nearly as may be in the form of schedule (OO) hereto annexed, and on such deed of restriction being recorded in the appropriate register of sasines the security shall be restricted accordingly to the lands therein contained, other than those discharged by such deed of restriction, which lands thereby discharged shall be released from the security to the same effect as if the same had never been contained in such security.

NOTE

[1] Excluded by the Conveyancing and Feudal Reform (Scotland) Act 1970, s.32 and Sched. 8, para. 13.

Act to apply to all heritable securities

134. The whole provisions, enactments, and forms of this Act relative to bonds and dispositions in security shall be taken to apply and shall apply as nearly as may be to all heritable securities unless in so far as such provisions, enactments, or forms may be inapplicable to the form or objects of such securities.

Parties may use the present forms if they see fit

135. Nothing in this Act contained shall prevent the constitution, transmission, or extinction of heritable securities in the forms in use prior to the lst day of October 1845.

136. [Repealed by the Burgh Registers (Scotland) Act 1926, s.4 and Sched. 2.]

This Act to apply to lands held by any description of tenure

137. The whole of this Act shall apply to lands by whatever tenure the same may be held, except in so far as any of the provisions of this Act shall be limited expressly or by necessary implication to lands held by one particular tenure.

Short clauses of consent to registration may be used in any deed

[1] **138.** The short clauses of consent to registration for preservation, and for preservation and execution, contained in forms Nos. 1 and 2 of schedule (B) hereto annexed, when occurring in any deed or conveyance under this Act or in any deed or writing or document of whatsoever nature, and whether relating to lands or not, shall unless specially qualified import a consent to registration and a procuratory of registration in the books of Council and Session, or other judges' books competent, therein to remain for preservation; and also, if for execution, that upon the issue of an extract containing a warrant for execution, all lawful execution shall pass thereon.

NOTE

[1] Excluded by the Conveyancing and Feudal Reform (Scotland) Act 1970, s.32 and Sched. 8, para. 13. As amended by the Debtors (Scotland) Act 1987, Sched. 6, para. 7.

139. [Repealed by the Age of Legal Capacity (Scotland) Act 1991, Sched. 2.]

Additional sheets may be added to writs

140. In all cases where writs or deeds of any description are by this or any other Act permitted or directed to be engrossed on any conveyance or deed, it shall be competent, when necessary, to engross such deeds or writs on a sheet or sheets of paper, or of whatever other material the conveyance itself consists, added to such conveyance, provided that the engrossing of the deed or writ shall be commenced on some part of the conveyance or deed itself on which it is permitted or directed to be engrossed; and the first of such additional sheets shall be chargeable with the stamp duty applicable to the writ or deed partly engrossed thereon, and subsequent sheets (if any) shall be chargeable with the appropriate progressive duty.[1]

NOTE

[1] Progressive duty not payable after lst January 1871.

All deeds, etc., recorded in Register of Sasines to have warrants of registration endorsed, except certain burgage deeds

[1] **141.** All conveyances and deeds, and all writings whatsoever which may be recorded in any register of sasines, shall, previous to being presented for registration, have a warrant of registration endorsed or written thereon in or as nearly as may be in such one or other of the forms of warrants of registration contained in the following schedules hereto annexed, viz. schedule (F) No. 2 and schedule (H) Nos. 1, 2, and 3, as may be applicable to the particular conveyance, deed, or writing, so to be presented, which warrant shall in every case specify the person or persons on whose behalf the conveyance, deed, or writing is presented for registration, and in the case of lands not held by burgage tenure the register or registers of the county or counties, and in the case of lands held by burgage tenure the register or registers of the burgh or burghs in which the lands to which such conveyance or deed or writing has reference are situated, and shall be signed by such person or persons, or by his or their agent or agents, and in the latter case the warrant may be signed either by an individual agent or by the subscription of any firm of which such agent may be a partner: Provided always, that where registration has been or shall be made in any particular register of sasines, it shall be sufficient that such register is specified in the warrant of registration, without any specification of a county or counties.

NOTE

[1] As substituted by the Titles to Land Consolidation (Scotland) Amendment Act 1869, s. 9; as amended by the Conveyancing (Scotland) Act 1874, s. 33, the Conveyancing (Scotland) Act 1924, s. 10 (1), and the Burgh Registers (Scotland) Act 1926, s. 4 and Sched. 2.

Recording of conveyances in the register of sasines authorised

[1] **142.** All conveyances and deeds, and all instruments hereby authorised to be recorded in the register of sasines, may, with warrants of registration written thereon respectively, be recorded at any time in the life of the person on whose behalf the same shall be presented for registration, in the same manner as instruments of sasine, or notarial instruments, are at present recorded, and the same when presented for registration shall be forthwith shortly registered in the minute-books of the said register in common form, and shall with all due despatch be fully registered in the register books, and thereafter re-delivered to the parties with certificates of due registration thereon, which shall specify the date of presentation, and the book and folios in which the engrossment has been made, and shall be probative of such registration, and when so registered shall in competition be preferable according to the date of registration, and the date of entry in the minute-book shall be held to be the date of registration; provided that where two or more deeds or conveyances, shall be received by the keeper of the register of sasines on the same day, the entries thereof in the presentment book and minute-book shall be of the same year, month, and day, and such deeds and conveyances shall be deemed and taken to be presented and registered contemporaneously.

NOTE

[1] As amended by the Statute Law Revision Act 1893, the Public Registers (Scotland) Act 1950, s. 1 and Sched., the Conveyancing and Feudal Reform (Scotland) Act 1970, s. 52 (3) and Sched. II, Pt. III, and the Land Registration (Scotland) Act 1979, s. 29 (4) and Sched. 4.

Conveyances and instruments may be recorded of new

[1] **143.** In case of any error or defect in any instrument or in the recording of any deed or conveyance, or of any warrant of registration, recorded or to be recorded in any register of sasines, or in any warrant of registration thereon, or in the recording of such warrant, it shall be competent of new to make and record such instrument, or of new to record the deed or con-

veyance with the original or a new warrant of registration, as the case may require.

NOTE

[1] See the Land Registration (Scotland) Act 1979, s. 8 (2).

Recorded instruments not to be challenged on the ground of erasures

144. The Erasures in Deeds (Scotland) Act 1836 shall extend and be applicable to all instruments.

Not competent to challenge existing warrants of registration on certain grounds

145. It shall not be competent to challenge the validity of any existing warrants of registration upon conveyances under the Titles to Lands (Scotland) Acts 1858 and 1860 hereby repealed, or the real rights completed in the persons of those in whose favour the said conveyances are recorded by the registration thereof in the appropriate register of sasines, on the ground that the said warrants of registration are disconform to the terms of the schedules annexed to the said Acts, provided that the said warrants contain the name of the party or parties on whose behalf the warrant is written, and contain the designation of such party or parties, or refer to the same as given in the conveyance on which such warrants are engrossed, and are signed by the party or parties themselves, or by his or their agent or agents, either individually or as a partnership; and the designation " agent " or " agents " without any further designation, shall be valid and sufficient in the case of all warrants expede in virtue of the said repealed Acts.

Obligations appointed to be inserted in instruments of sasine shall be inserted in notarial instruments

[1] **146.** Where any real burden, condition, provision, or limitation, or other matter has been or shall be appointed to be inserted or referred to in the instruments of sasine or of resignation *ad remanentiam*, or other instruments applicable to any lands, such real burden, condition, provision, or limitation, or other matter, shall be inserted or referred to in manner provided by this Act in every instrument applicable to such lands to be expede in virtue of this Act, and in every conveyance or deed of or relating to such lands the registration of which in the register of sasines is by this Act equivalent to infeftment or resignation *ad remanentiam*: Provided always that where such real burdens, conditions, provisions, limitations, or other matters have been already inserted in any conveyance or deed or instrument recorded in the appropriate register of sasines, it shall not be necessary to insert the same at length in any subsequent conveyance or deed or instrument, provided the same be therein referred to in manner provided in section 9 or 10 of this Act, as the circumstances of the case may require.

NOTE

[1] Applied by the Conveyancing (Scotland) Act 1924, s. 3 (dispositions, etc., by person uninfeft), and s. 6 (1) (Notice of Title equivalent to Notarial Instrument). Excluded by the Land Registration (Scotland) Act 1979, s. 15 (2).

Prohibition against sub-infeudation not to be affected

147. Where the investiture of any lands has imposed or shall impose a prohibition against sub-infeudation or against alternative holding, nothing contained in this Act shall operate to authorise subinfeudation or an alternative holding in respect to such lands; and nothing in this Act contained shall be construed to take away or impair any of the rights or remedies competent to a superior against his vassal lying out unentered.

148. [Repealed by the Bankruptcy (Scotland) Act 1985, Sched. 8, with effect from 1st April 1986].

Deeds and instruments may be partly written and partly printed or engraved

149. All deeds and conveyances, and all documents whatever mentioned or not mentioned in this Act, and whether relating or not relating to land, having a testing clause, may be partly written and partly engraved or lithographed: Provided always, that in the testing clause the date, if any, and the names and designations of the witnesses, and the number of the pages of the deed or conveyance or document, if the number be specified, and the name and designation of the writer of the written portions of the body of the deed or conveyance or document shall be expressed at length, and all such deeds, conveyances, and documents shall be as valid and effectual as if they had been wholly in writing: Declaring that no such deeds, conveyances, and documents executed prior to the commencement of this Act shall be challengeable on the ground that the name of the writer of the written portions of the testing clause is not mentioned.

Debts affecting lands exchanged for other lands to affect such other lands in lieu thereof

150. When any lands disponed before or after the commencement of this Act, under the authority of an Act of Parliament, in excambion for other lands, are burdened with debts, the lands so disponed shall, from and after the date of registration, whether before or after the commencement of this Act, in the appropriate register of sasines of the contract or deed of excambion of such lands, be freed and disburdened of such debts so far as previously affecting the same, and shall be burdened with the debts, if any, which previously affected the lands acquired in exchange for the same, in the order of preference in which such debts were a burden upon said last-mentioned lands: Provided always, in the case of excambions after the 31st day of December 1868, that before any such excambion is authorised (in addition to such procedure as may be prescribed by such Act) such intimation as the Court of Session may consider necessary shall be made to all creditors having interest, and such creditors shall be entitled to state any objections thereto, of which the court shall judge: Provided also, that in such contract or deed of excambion, whether executed before or after the commencement of this Act, or in a schedule subscribed as relative thereto, and declared to be part thereof, and recorded therewith, there have been or shall be set forth as to each of the said debts the following particulars: namely, the amount of the debt, the date of recording the writ by which its constitution was originally published, the register in which the same was so published, the name and designation of the original creditor, and, if the debt has been transferred, the name and designation of the creditor understood to be in right thereof for the time, and the date of recording the writ whereby his right was published, and the register in which the same was so published: Provided further, that in such contract or deed of excambion such debts have been or shall be expressly declared to burden the lands to which the same are transferred as aforesaid.

151. [Repealed by the Statute Law (Repeals) Act 1975.]

Provisions for lands in the burgh of Paisley held by booking tenure

[1] **152.** All the provisions of this Act applicable to lands held by the ordinary burgage tenure shall be applicable also to lands in the burgh of Paisley held by the peculiar tenure of booking; and all the provisions of this Act applicable to instruments of sasine, and register of booking, respectively, of lands held burgage, shall be applicable also to booking, and to

extract bookings, and to the register of booking, respectively, of lands in the said burgh of Paisley held by said tenure of booking.

NOTE

[1] As amended by the Statute Law Revision Act 1893.

153. [Repealed by the Statute Law (Repeals) Act 1975.]

Official Acts of town clerks and keepers of registers of sasines not to be affected by their personal interests in recorded writs

154. It shall be competent for the town clerk of any burgh to expede and record, and for the keeper of any burgh or other register of sasines, reversions, etc., to record, any conveyance or deed in which such town clerk or keeper may be personally interested, either individually or as trustee for another or otherwise; and no conveyance or deed expede or recorded prior to the date of the passing of this Act, or which may hereafter be expede or recorded, shall be challengeable or in any way affected by reason of personal interest in the town clerk or keeper of the register by whom the same has been expede or recorded as aforesaid: Provided that this enactment shall not prejudice or affect any action or proceeding which may have been instituted prior to the passing of this Act.

Inhibitions to take effect from date of registration of notice, etc.

[1] **155.** It shall be competent, before or after execution of any inhibition, whether by separate letters or contained in a summons before the Court of Session, to register in the general register of inhibitions a notice thereof, setting forth the names and designations of the persons by and against whom the same is raised, and the date of signeting the same, in the form or as nearly as may be in the form of schedule (PP) hereto annexed; and where any such inhibition and the execution thereof shall be duly registered in the general register of inhibitions not later than twenty-one days from the date of the registration therein of such notice thereof, such inhibitions shall take effect from the date when such notice was registered as aforesaid, but otherwise only from the date of the registration of such inhibition and the execution thereof; and no inhibition shall have any effect against any act or deed done, committed, or executed prior to the registration of such notice thereof, or of such inhibition and the execution thereof, as the case may be.

NOTE

[1] See the Conveyancing (Scotland) Act 1924, s.44(3)(*a*); s.44(6). (General Register of Inhibitions and Register of Adjudications to be combined: limitation of effect of entries therein.) See also the Drug Trafficking Offences Act 1986, s.22. Applied by the Criminal Justice (Scotland) Act 1987, s.11(2), the Criminal Justice Act 1988, s.92(2), and the Prevention of Terrorism (Temporary Provisions) Act 1989, Sched. 4, para. 16(3).

Short form of letters of inhibition

156. Letters of inhibition may be in the form as nearly as may be of the schedule (QQ) to this Act annexed; and letters of inhibition in such form shall have all the like force and effect as letters of inhibition in the form in use at the passing of this Act.

No inhibition to have effect against acquirenda, unless in case of heir under entail or other indefeasible title

157. No inhibition to be recorded from and after the 31st day of December 1868 shall have any force or effect as against any lands to be acquired by the person or persons against whom such inhibition is used after the date of recording such inhibition, or of recording the previous notice thereof prescribed by this Act, as the case may be: Provided always, that where such inhibition is used against a person or persons who shall thereafter succeed to any lands which, at the date of recording the inhibition or previous notice thereof, as the case may be, were destined to such person or persons by a deed of entail, or by a similar indefeasible title, then and in that case such inhibition shall affect the said person or persons in so far as regards the land so destined, and to which he or they shall succeed as aforesaid, but no further.

Inhibitions on depending summons to be recalled on petition to Lord Ordinary

[1] **158.** It shall be competent to the Lord Ordinary in the Court of Session, before whom any summons containing warrant for inhibition shall be enrolled as judge therein, or before whom any action on the dependence whereof letters of inhibition have been executed, has been or shall be enrolled as judge therein, and to the Lord Ordinary on the Bills in time of vacation, on the application of the defender or debtor by petition duly intimated to the creditor or pursuer, to which answers may be ordered, to recall or restrict such inhibition on caution, or without caution, and dispose of the question of expenses as shall appear just: provided that his judgment shall be subject to the review of the court by a reclaiming note duly lodged within ten days from the date thereof.

NOTE

[1] See the Drug Trafficking Offences Act 1986, s.22. See also the Criminal Justice (Scotland) Act 1987, s.11(3). Applied by the Criminal Justice Act 1988, s.92(3), and the Prevention of Terrorism (Temporary Provisions) Act 1989, Sched. 4, para. 16(4).

Litigiosity not to begin before date of registration of notice of summons

[1,2] **159.** It shall be competent to register in the general register of inhibitions a notice of any signeted summons of reduction of any conveyance or deed of or relating to lands, and in the register of adjudications a notice of any signeted summons of adjudication or of constitution and adjudication combined for debt or in security or in implement, which notice shall set forth the names and designations of the pursuer and defender of such action and the date of signeting such summons and contain a description of the lands to which the summons relates in the form or as nearly as may be in the form of schedule (RR) hereto annexed; and no summons of reduction, constitution, adjudication, or constitution and adjudication combined, shall have any effect in rendering litigious the lands to which such summons relates, except from and after the date of the registration of such notice.

NOTES

[1] See the Conveyancing (Scotland) Act 1924, s.44(3)(*a*), (6) (General Register of Inhibitions and Register of Adjudications to be combined; limitation of effect of entries therein).

[2] As amended by the Law Reform (Miscellaneous Provisions) (Scotland) Act 1985, Sched. 2, para. 4.

160. [Repealed by the Succession (Scotland) Act 1964, s.34(2) and Sched. 3.]

Judgment of Lord Ordinary on the Bills subject to review of Inner House, and judgments in certain cases to be final

161. Any judgment pronounced by the Lord Ordinary in virtue of this Act shall be subject to review by a reclaiming note in ordinary form; and the judgment of either division of the court upon such reclaiming note, or upon any advocation or appeal, shall be subject to review by appeal to the House of Lords, or in any other competent mode or form; but the judgments of the Lord Ordinary and of the court respectively, if not so brought under review, and whether the same shall have been pronounced in absence of the respondent or not, shall be final, and not subject to review in any mode or form whatever; provided always, that the judgments of the Lord Ordinary in petitions relating to the forfeiture or relinquishment of superiority under this or any of the repealed Acts, if not so brought under review, and the judgment of either division of the Court of Session upon a reclaiming note against such judgment of the Lord Ordinary, whether such judgment shall have been pronounced in absence of the respondent or not, shall be final and conclusive, and not subject to review in any mode or form whatever; and it shall be competent to the Lord Ordinary, or to either division of the court reviewing any judgment of the Lord Ordinary, if it shall appear to him or them to be just in the whole circumstances of the case, to find and decern in ordinary form for the expenses of any proceedings.

Court of Session may fix and regulate fees

[1] **162.** The Court of Session may meet for the purpose of passing and may pass all such Acts of Sederunt and rules of court as they deem proper for carrying into effect the purposes of this Act, and that either during session or vacation, and may from time to time repeal Acts of Sederunt and rules of court or alter such Acts and rules of court and tables of fees: Provided that all Acts of Sederunt and rules of court passed under the authority of this Act shall be laid before both Houses of Parliament.

NOTE

[1] As repealed in part by the Statute Law (Repeals) Act 1975, and the Statute Law (Repeals) Act 1986, Sched., Pt. XII.

Old forms of conveyances may be used

163. Nothing contained in this Act shall prevent the constitution, transmission, completion, or extinction of land rights, or of securities affecting lands, in the forms which were in use or competent for these purposes prior to the passing of the Acts hereby repealed, except in so far as such prior forms are hereby expressly abolished; and, notwithstanding the repeal of the said Acts, the same shall be held to be still in force so far as regards any reference which may be made to them or any of them in any statute not hereby repealed, and to the effect of giving full effect to such reference.

SCHEDULES

SCHEDULE (A)

No. 1

Acts and Part of Act repealed

[Repealed by the Statute Law Revision Act 1894.]

No. 2

CAP. XXXV

An Act to simplify the form and diminish the expense of obtaining infeftment in heritable property in Scotland. [21st July 1845]

How sasine to be given in future

[1] I. Whereas it is expedient to simplify the form and diminish the expense of obtaining infeftment in heritable property in Scotland: Be it therefore enacted by the Queen's Most Excellent Majesty, by and with the advice and consent of the Lords Spiritual and Temporal, and Commons, in this present Parliament assembled, and by the authority of the same, that from and after the 1st day of October in the present year 1845 it shall not be necessary to proceed to the lands in which sasine is to be given, or to perform any act of infeftment thereon, but sasine shall be effectually given therein and infeftment obtained by producing to a notary public the warrants of sasine and relative writs, as now in use to be produced at taking infeftment, and by expeding and recording in the general register of sasines, applicable to the lands contained in the warrant of infeftment, in manner herinafter directed, an instrument of sasine, setting forth that sasine had been given in the said lands, and subscribed by the said notary public and witnesses, according to the form and as nearly as may be in the terms of schedule (B) hereto annexed; and such form of infeftment shall be effectual whether the lands lie contiguous or discontiguous, or are held by the same or by different titles, or of one or more superiors, or whether the deed entitling the party to obtain infeftment be dated prior or subsequent to the present Act, or whether the precept of sasine therein be in the form heretofore in use, or in the form authorised by the present Act.

NOTE

[1] As amended by the Statute Law Revision Act 1893.

Instruments of sasine to be entered and recorded

II. And be it enacted, that from and after the said 1st day of October every such instrument of sasine shall be recorded in manner heretofore in use with regard to instruments of sasine, and the keepers of the registers of sasines are hereby required to receive and register the same accordingly; and such instrument of sasine, being so recorded, shall in all respects have the same effect as if sasine had been taken and an instrument of sasine duly recorded according to the law and practice heretofore in use.

May be recorded at any time, but the date of the presentment to be the date of the infeftment

III. And be it enacted, that from and after the said 1st day of October every such instrument of sasine may be competently and effectually recorded at any time during the life of the party in whose favour such instrument has been expede, but the date of presentment and entry set forth on any such instrument by the keeper of the record shall be taken to be the date of the instrument of sasine and infeftment.

In case of error or defect another instrument may be recorded

IV. And be it enacted that in case of any error or defect in any such instrument of sasine, or in the recording thereof, it shall be competent of new to make and record an instrument of sasine, which shall have effect from the date of the recording thereof, as if no previous instrument or instruments had been made or recorded.

Forms of the precept and instrument of sasine

V. And be it enacted, that in all deeds containing a precept of sasine such precept may be in the form and as nearly as may be in the terms of the schedule (A) hereto annexed, and the instrument of sasine on any such deed shall be in the form and as nearly as may be in the terms of the said schedule (B) hereto annexed, which precepts and instruments of sasine respectively shall be as valid and effectual as the precepts and instruments of sasine heretofore in use.

Precept from Chancery to be issued to notaries upon payment of retour duties and casualties—Fees to be paid to sheriffs and sheriff-clerks for a limited period

VI. [Repealed by this Act].

VII–IX. [Repealed by the Statute Law Revision Act 1893.]

Interpretation of Act

X. And be it enacted, That in the construction of this Act the words " Notary Public " shall be held to mean a notary public in Scotland duly admitted and practising there; the word " Deed " shall be held to include any warrant or document upon which sasine may follow; and the word " Lands ", or the words " Heritable Property ", shall be held to include houses, fishings, mills, minerals, patronages, teinds, and in general all heritable subjects or rights in which infeftment may be taken; and all words in the singular number shall be held to include a plurality of persons or things; and in general this Act shall be construed in the most liberal manner, so as to accomplish the objects thereby intended.

XI. [Repealed by the Statute Law Revision Act 1893.]

SCHEDULES

Schedule (A)

[Repealed by the Statute Law Revision Act 1894.]

Schedule (B)

Form of Instrument of Sasine

At   there was, by or on behalf of *A.B.* of Z., Esquire, presented to me, notary public subscribing, a disposition [*or other deed, or an extract of a deed (as the case may be)*] granted by *C.D.* of *Y.*, Esq., and bearing date as in the precept of sasine hereinafter inserted [*here describe also any connecting deed or writ, or extract thereof, in virtue of which the sasine is to be given to A.B.*], by which disposition the said *C.D.* sold, alienated, and disponed to the said *A.B.* [*or*, to *E.F.* *(as the case may be)*] and his heirs and assignees [*here insert the destination, if any*], heritably and irredeemably [*or* redeemably, *or* in liferent, *or otherwise (as the case may be)*]. All and Whole [*here insert the description of the subjects conveyed; and if the disposition by C.D. was not to A.B. himself, but is vested in him as assignee, heir, or adjudger, or otherwise, in whole or in part, state the successive transferences, and the way in which he has right thereto*], which disposition contains an obligation to infeft [*here state whether* a se *or* de se, *or both or either (as the case may be)*], and a precept of sasine in the following terms [*here insert the precept, which may be either according to the form at present in use, or according to the abbreviated form in schedule (A)*], in virtue of which precept I hereby give sasine [*or* liferent sasine, *or* sasine in liferent and fee respectively] to the said *A.B.* of the lands and others above described. [*If the precept of sasine contains a reference to a real burden, or to any conditions or qualifications of the right, or to a power of redemption, then add,* " but always under the burden of the real right, etc., before specified ".]

In witness whereof I have subscribed these presents, written on this and the preceding pages by *G.H.*, my clerk, before these witnesses, the said *G.H.* and *J.K.*, accountants in Edinburgh.

(Signed)   *L.M.*, Notary Public.

G.H., witness.
J.K., witness.

SCHEDULE (B)

[1] No. 1

Formal Clauses of a Disposition of Land, etc.

[*After the inductive and dispositive clauses the deed may proceed thus*:] With entry at the term of [*here specify the date of entry*]; to be holden the said lands and others [*or* subjects] a me [*or* a me vel de me, *as the case may be*]; and I assign the writs, and have delivered the same according to inventory; and I assign the rents; and I bind myself to free and relieve the said disponee and his foresaids of all feu-duties, casualties, and public-burdens; and I grant warrandice; and I consent to registration hereof for preservation [*or* for preservation and execution]. In witness whereof [*insert a testing clause in the usual form*].

NOTE.—The clauses are assumed here as occurring in a disposition, but they may be used in other deeds and conveyances; and in the event of it being necessary to omit, vary, or qualify any one or more of them, this may be done, and the other clauses may be retained.

NOTE.

[1] As amended by the Statute Law Revision Act 1893.

No. 2

Formal Clauses of a Disposition of Land, etc., held Burgage

[*After the inductive and dispositive clauses the deed may proceed thus*:] With entry at the term of [*here specify the date of entry*]; to be holden the said lands and others [*or* subjects] of Her Majesty in free burgage; and I assign the writs, and have delivered the same according to inventory; and I assign the rents; and I bind myself to free and relieve the said disponee and his foresaids of all ground annual, cess, annuity, and other public burdens; and I grant warrandice; and I consent to the registration hereof for preservation [*or* for preservation and execution]. In witness whereof [*insert a testing clause in the usual form*].

NOTE.—The clauses are assumed here as occurring in a disposition, but they may be used in other deeds and conveyances; and in the event of it being necessary to omit, vary, or qualify any one or more of them, this may be done, and the other clauses may be retained.

SCHEDULE (C)

Clause of Reference to Destinations and Conditions of Entail, etc.

[*After inserting such part of the destination as may be thought necessary, add*] and to the other heirs specified in a disposition and deed of entail [*or as the case may be*] of the said lands executed by the deceased *E.F.*, dated the   day of   in the year   , and recorded in the register of tailzies on the   day of   in the year   [*or* in the said disposition and deed of entail dated and recorded as aforesaid, *or* in a deed [*or* instrument *specify the deed or conveyance*] recorded [*specify register of sasines*] upon the   day   in the year   ].

[*And after the description of the lands insert*] but always with and under the conditions, provisions, and prohibitory irritant and resolutive clauses [*or* clause authorising registration in the register of tailzies, *as the case may be*], contained in the said disposition and deed of entail, dated and recorded as aforesaid [*or* in (*specify deed or conveyance*) recorded in (*specify register of sasines*) upon the   day of   in the year   ].

[*And in subsequent clauses in which it is usual or requisite to refer again to the conditions of the entail, etc., the reference may be made thus*:] but always with and under the conditions, provisions, and prohibitory irritant and resolutive clauses [*or* clause authorising registration in the register of tailzies, *as the case may be*] before referred to.

[1] SCHEDULE (D)

Clause of Reference to Real Burdens, Conditions, etc., in Investiture

[*After the Description of the Lands, instead of inserting the Burdens, etc., at Length, these may be referred to as follows, viz.*:] but always with and under the real Burdens, Conditions,

Provisions, and Limitations [*or such of these as may apply or have reference to the Case*] specified in a Deed [*or* Instrument *here specify a Deed or Conveyance in which the Burdens, etc., were first inserted, or any subsequent Deed or Conveyance in which they are inserted, forming Part of the Progress of the Titles to the Lands*] recorded [*specify Register of Sasines or, if the Deed or Conveyance as recorded has been previously referred to, say* in the said Deed [*or* Instrument] recorded as aforesaid] on the day of in the year

[*And in subsequent Clauses in which it is requisite or usual to refer again to the Burdens, etc., the Reference may be made thus:*] but always with and under the real Burdens, Conditions, Provisions, and Limitations [*or such of these as may apply or have reference to the Case*] before referred to.

NOTE

[1] Excluded by the Land Registration (Scotland) Act 1979, s. 15 (2).

SCHEDULE (E)

[Repealed by the Statute Law Revision Act 1893.]

SCHEDULE (F)

No. 1

Clauses of Direction, specifying part of Deed which Grantor desires to be recorded

And I direct to be recorded in the register of sasines the part of this deed from its commencement to the words [*insert words*] on the line of the page [and also the part from the words [*insert words*] on the line of the page to the words [*insert words*] on the line of the page]. [*Or*, I direct the whole of this deed to be recorded in the register of sasines, with the exception of the part [*or* parts, *as the case may be, specifying the part or parts excepted, as above*].]

[1] No. 2

Warrant of Registration to be written on Deed where it is intended to record it in terms of a Clause of Direction

---

NOTE

[1] See the Conveyancing (Scotland) Act 1924, s. 10 and substituted form of registration warrant and notes in Sched. F thereto.

---

[1] SCHEDULE (G)

Clause of Reference to Conveyance containing general Designation of Lands

[*After giving the general name or names of the lands and the name of the county, or burgh and county, as the case may be, add*] as particularly described in the disposition [*or other deed, as the case may be*] granted by *C. D.*, and bearing date [*here insert date*], and recorded in the [*specify the register of sasines*] on the day of in the year , and in which the lands hereby conveyed are declared to be designed and known by the said name of [*here insert name*], [*or* " as particularly described in the instrument (*specify instrument*) recorded, etc., and in which the lands hereby conveyed are declared ", etc.] [*If part only of lands is conveyed, then follow form for similar case given in schedule (E).*]

NOTE

[1] Excluded by the Land Registration (Scotland) Act 1979, s. 15 (1).

[1] SCHEDULE (H)

Warrants of Registration

NOTE

[1] See the Conveyancing (Scotland) Act 1924, s. 10, and substituted form of registration of warrant and notes in Sched. F thereto.

SCHEDULE (I)

[Repealed by the Statute Law Revision Act 1893.]

SCHEDULE (J)

Notarial Instrument in favour of Disponee or his Assignee, etc.

At there was by [*or* on behalf of] *A.B.* of Z., presented to me, notary public subscribing, a disposition [*or other deed, or* an extract of a deed, *as the case may be*], granted by *C.D.* of *Y.*, and dated [*insert the date*], by which disposition [*or otherwise as the case may be*], the said *C.D.* sold, alienated, and disponed to the said *A.B.* [*or* gave, granted, and disponed, *or otherwise as the case may be*, to the said *A.B.*] [*or to E.F.*] and his heirs and assignees [*insert the destination, if any, so far as may be necessary*], heritably and irredeemably [*or* redeemably, *or* in liferent, *or otherwise as the case may be*], all and whole [*insert the description of the lands conveyed, and any real burdens, conditions, provisions, and limitations, or any reference to the same, all as in the disposition of the deed, etc.*] [*If the person expeding the instrument be other than the original disponee, add*], As also there was presented to me [*here specify the title or series of titles by which such person acquired right, and the nature of his right.*] Whereupon this instrument is taken in the hands of *L.M.* [*insert name and designation of notary public*] in the terms of the " Titles to Land Consolidation (Scotland) Act 1868 ". In witness whereof [*insert testing clause as in schedule (I)*].

SCHEDULE (K)

Instrument of Resignation ad remanentiam

[See the Conveyancing (Scotland) Act 1874, s. 6.]

SCHEDULE (L)

Notarial Instrument in favour of a general Disponee, or his Assignee, etc.

At there was by [*or* on behalf of] *A.B.* of *Z.*, presented to me, notary public subscribing, a disposition [*specify the disposition or other deed or instrument or extract thereof, as the case may be*] recorded in the [*specify register of sasines and date of recording*], by which recorded disposition [*or otherwise as the case may be*] *C.D.* of *Y.* was infeft in all and whole [*describe the lands or other subjects, as the case may be, as the same are described in the said disposition or other deed or instrument*]; as also there was presented to me a general disposition [*or other deed or conveyance or testamentary deed or writing, as the case may be, or an extract of such deed*] granted by the said *C.D.*, and dated [*insert date*], by which general disposition [*or otherwise as the case may be*] the said *C.D.* disponed [*or* gave *or* granted *or* bequeathed, *or otherwise as the case may be*] to the said *A.B.* and his heirs and assignees [*or otherwise as the case may be*], heritably and irredeemably [*or* in liferent, *or otherwise as the case may be*], all and sundry the whole heritable estate [*or otherwise as the case may be*], of which he was [*or* might die] possessed [*or otherwise as the case may be*]. [*If the deed be granted under any real burden or condition or qualification, add here,* but always under the real burdens, etc.; *and if the deed be granted in trust, or for specific purposes, add,* but always in trust *or* for the uses and purposes mentioned in said general disposition, *or otherwise as the case may be. If the person expeding the instrument be other than the original disponee, or grantor or legatee under the deed, add,* as also there was presented to me (*specify the title or series of titles by which such person acquired right, and the nature of his right*).] Whereupon, *etc., as in schedule (J) to the end.*

SCHEDULE (M)

[Repealed by the Conveyancing and Feudal Reform (Scotland) Act 1970, Sched. 11.]

SCHEDULE (N)

Notarial Instrument in favour of an Assignee to an unrecorded Conveyance to be recorded along with the Conveyance

At   there was by [*or* on behalf of] *A.B.* of *Z.*, presented to me, notary public subscribing, a disposition [*or other deed or extract, as the case may be, specifying the nature of the deed*] granted by *C.D.* of *Y.*, and dated [*insert date*], by which disposition the said *C.D.* conveyed to *E.F.* all and whole the lands of *X.*, as therein described, and which disposition is to be recorded along with this instrument; as also there was presented to me [*specify the title or series of titles by which A.B. acquired right, and the nature of his right*]. Whereupon, *etc.*, *as in schedule (J) to the end.*

NOTE.—Before being presented for registration along with the disposition or other deed and warrant of registration thereon, the notarial instrument must be docqueted in or as nearly as may be in the form following, viz.:—" Docqueted with reference to warrant of registration on behalf of *A.B.*, written on the said disposition [*or other deed, as the case may be*] ". The docquet shall be signed by the person or his agent or agents signing the warrant.

SCHEDULE (O)

Notarial Instrument in favour of a Trustee in a Sequestration or of Liquidators of Joint Stock Companies

At   there was by [*or* on behalf of] *A.B.*, as trustee on the sequestrated estate of *C.D.* [*or* as liquidator for winding up the, *specify name of company, or partner thereof for whom liquidator acts*] presented to me, notary public subscribing, a disposition [*or other deed or extract, as the case may be*] [*insert date*], recorded in the [*specify register and date of recording*], by which, *etc.* [*specify the title or series of titles by which the bankrupt, or company, or partner thereof, as the case may be, held the lands*], as also there was presented to me an extract act and warrant of confirmation in favour of the said *A.B.*, dated [*insert date*] [*or here specify the appointment of the liquidator or liquidators, and the date thereof*]. Whereupon, *etc.*, *as in schedule (J) to the end.*

SCHEDULE (P)

[Repealed by the Succession (Scotland) Act 1964, s. 34 (2) and Sched. 3.]

SCHEDULE (Q)

[Repealed by the Succession (Scotland) Act 1964, s. 34 (2) and Sched. 3.]

SCHEDULE (R)

[Repealed by the Statute Law Revision Act 1893.]

SCHEDULE (S)

Note for *A.B.* [*insert name and designation*]

The said *A.B.* humbly prays that a writ [*or* charter, *or* precept, *or other deed, as the case may be*] may be granted by Her Majesty [*or* the Prince and Steward of Scotland, *as the case may be*] in terms of the draft herewith lodged and marked as relative hereto.

(Signed) *C.D.* (W.S.), Agent for the said *A.B.*

SCHEDULE (T)

No. 1

[Repealed by the Statute Law Revision Act 1893.]

No. 2

Crown Charter of Resignation

Victoria, *etc.* We do hereby give, grant, and dispone, and for ever confirm to *A.B.* and his heirs and assignees, whomsoever [*or in case there be a substitution of heirs, here insert it at full length, or refer to it as in schedule (C)*], heritably and irredeemably, all and whole [*here insert or refer as in schedule (E)* [1] *or in schedule (G), as the case may be, to the lands. In case there be any conditions of entail, or any real burdens, etc., proper to be inserted or referred to, insert them here immediately after the description of the lands, or refer to them as in schedule (C) or schedule (D), as the case may be*], which lands and others formerly belonged to *C.D.*, holden by him immediately of the Crown, in terms of [*here state briefly the investiture of the last entered vassal, whether a Crown precept and sasine, or Crown charter and sasine, or other Crown writ, as recorded in the register of sasines, or otherwise as the case may be*], and were at the date of applying for these presents resigned by him into our hands by virtue of a procuratory [*or* clause] of resignation contained in a disposition [*or other deed or conveyance, as the case may be*] of the said lands and others granted by him in favour of the said *A.B.*, dated [*here insert the date*], to be holden, the said lands and others, of us, and our royal successors, in free blench farm forever, paying therefor a penny Scots yearly of blench duty, if asked only, [*or if the lands were held formerly in ward, say here,* in free blench as in room of ward, paying therefor a penny Scots yearly, as in room of the ward duties, if asked only, *or if held in feu farm, say here,* in feu farm, *and specify the feu-duty and other duties and services, or otherwise, as the case may be*].

In witness whereof, we have ordered the seal now used for the Great Seal of Scotland, to be appended hereto of this date [*if the vassal desires the seal to be appended, say here,* and the same is accordingly at the request of the said *A.B.* appended], at Edinburgh, the day of [*state the day, month, and year*].

[*Signed by the director of chancery or his depute or substitute.*]

NOTE

[1] See the Conveyancing (Scotland) Act 1924, s. 31.

No. 3

[Repealed by the Statute Law Revision Act 1893.]

No. 4

Crown Charter of Confirmation

Victoria, *etc.* We do hereby confirm for ever, to and in favour of *A.B.*, and his heirs and assignees whomsoever [*or in case there be a substitution of heirs, here insert it at full length, or refer to it as in schedule (C)*], heritably and irredeemably, all and whole [*here insert or refer as in schedule (E) or schedule (G), as the case may be, to the lands to be confirmed. In case there be any conditions of entail, or any real burdens, etc., proper to be inserted or referred to, insert them here immediately after the description of the lands, or refer to them as in schedule (C) or schedule (D), as the case may be,*] and a [*here specify the deed or conveyance which is to be confirmed in favour of A.B., and if the same has been recorded with warrant of registration in his favour, add* with warrant of registration thereon in favour of the said *A.B.*], recorded in the [*here describe the register in which the said deed or conveyance is recorded*], on the day of , [*or of whatever other date the said deed or conveyance, or recording thereof may be*], in so far as they relate to the lands and others hereby confirmed, to be holden, the said lands and others, of us, *etc.* [*as in No. 2 of this schedule*].

In witness whereof, *etc.* [*as in No. 2 of this schedule*].

General Note to Schedule (T).—When the writs and charters Nos. 1, 2, 3, and 4 are to be granted by or on behalf of the Prince and Steward of Scotland, they will be in similar form but will run in name of the " Prince and Steward of Scotland ", without adding His Highness' other titles; and the lands, instead of being described as holding of Her Majesty and her royal successors, will, where it is necessary by the form of the writ or charter to specify the holding, and be described as holding of the " Prince and Steward of Scotland ", and the seal referred to in the testing clause will be the Prince's seal.

SCHEDULE (U)

[Repealed by the Succession (Scotland) Act 1964, s. 34 (2) and Sched. 3.]

SCHEDULE (V)

[Repealed by the Statute Law Revision Act 1893.]

SCHEDULES (W-CC)

[The proceedings indicated by these Schedules now obsolete, infeftment implying entry.—the Conveyancing (Scotland) Act 1874, s. 4; Schedule W repealed by the Succession (Scotland) Act 1964, s. 34 (2) and Sched. 3; Scheds. AA 1 and 2 repealed by the Statute Law Revision Act 1893.]

SCHEDULE (DD)

[Repealed by the Succession (Scotland) Act 1964, s. 34 (2) and Sched. 3.]

SCHEDULE (EE)

[Repealed by the Succession (Scotland) Act 1964, s. 34 (2) and Sched. 3.]

[1] SCHEDULE (FF)

NOTE

[1] As amended by the Conveyancing (Scotland) Act 1874 and the Succession (Scotland) Act 1964, s. 34 (2) and Sched. 3.

No. 1

Form of a Bond and Disposition in Security

I, *A.B.* [*here name and design the grantor*], grant me to have instantly borrowed and received from *C.D.* [*here name and design the creditor*] the sum of [*insert the sum*] sterling; which sum I bind myself, and my heirs, executors, and representatives whomsoever, without the necessity of discussing them in their order, to repay to the said *C.D.*, his executors or assignees whomsoever, at the term of [*here insert the date and place of payment*], with a fifth part more of liquidate penalty in case of failure, and the interest of said principal sum at the rate of   per centum per annum from the date hereof to the said term of payment, and half-yearly, termly, and proportionally thereafter during the not payment of the same, and that at two terms in the year, Whitsunday and Martinmas, by equal portions, beginning the first term's payment of the said interest at the term of   next, for the interest due preceding that date, and the next term's payment thereof at   following and so forth half-yearly, termly, and proportionally thereafter during the not payment of the principal sum, with a fifth part more of the interest due at each term of liquidate penalty in case of failure in the punctual payment thereof. And in security of the personal obligation before written, I dispone to and in favour of the said *C.D.* and his foresaids, heritably, but redeemably, as after mentioned, yet irredeemably in the event of a sale by virtue hereof, all and whole [*here describe or refer as in schedule (E)*[1] *or schedule (G) to the lands*] (*a*), and that in real security to the said *C.D.* and his foresaids of the whole sums of money above written, principal, interest, and penalties; [and I assign the rents, and I assign the writs, and I grant warrandice, and I reserve power of redemption, and I oblige myself for the expenses of assigning and discharging this security; and on default in payment I grant power of sale; and I consent to registration for preservation and execution. In witness whereof] *etc.* [*insert a testing clause in usual form*].

(*a*) If the lands are held under any real burdens, conditions, provisions, or limitations, insert them here or refer to them in or as nearly as the circumstances may require in the form of schedule (D). [*But see the Conveyancing (Scotland) Act 1924, s. 9.*—Ed.]

NOTE

[1] See the Conveyancing (Scotland) Act 1924, s. 31 (description of lands and deduction of title unnecessary in certain deeds relating to heritable securities).

No. 2

Form of Schedule of Intimation, Requisition, and Protest

I, *A.B.* [*design him*], procurator for *C.D.* [*design creditor in right of the security*], in whose favour the bond and disposition in security after mentioned was granted, [*or if he is not the original creditor,* now in right of the bond and disposition in security after mentioned], do hereby give notice to you *E.F.* [*design debtor under the security*] that payment is now required of the sum of £ , being the principal sum due under the bond and disposition in security dated and recorded , granted by you *E.F.* [*or by G.H.*] in favour of the said *C.D.* [*or original creditor,*] [*if C.D. is not the original credtor, add,* to which *C.D.* has now right by various transmissions, *but these transmissions need not be particularly specified,*] and of the sum of £ , being the interest due at present on the said principal sum, with such further sum of interest as shall accrue on the said principal sum till paid. And I further give you notice, that if at the expiry of the period of three months from the date hereof the sums, principal and interest, and liquidate penalty incurred and to be incurred, of which payment is now required shall not be paid in terms of the said bond and disposition in security, then the said *C.D.*, or the person or persons who may then be in right of the said bond and disposition in security, may proceed to sell the lands and others [*or* subjects] thereby conveyed in the manner provided by the " Titles to Land Consolidation (Scotland) Act 1868 ", and with all powers and privileges conferred on or competent to creditors under bonds and dispositions in security by that Act. This I do at on the day of before and in presence of *L.M.*, notary public, and *N.O.* and *P.Q.* [*design them*], witnesses to the premises, called and required, and hereto with me subscribing.

(Signed) *A.B.*

N.O., witness.
P.Q., witness.

No. 3

Certificate by Notary on Copy of foregoing Schedule

I certify that what is above written is a true copy.

(Signed) *L.M.*, Notary Public.

[1] SCHEDULE (GG)

NOTE

[1] As amended by the Succession (Scotland) Act 1964, s. 34 (2) and Sched. 3.

[*Form of Assignation of a Bond and Disposition in Security constituted by Infeftment*]

I, *A.B.* [*name and design cedent*], in consideration of the sum of [*insert sum*] now paid to me by *C.D.* [*name and design assignee*], do hereby assign and dispone to and in favour of *C.D.* and his executors and assignees whomsoever, a bond and disposition in security [*or* heritable bond, *or other security as the case may be*], dated the [*insert the date, and when recorded, add,* and recorded as after mentioned], for the sum of [*insert sum*] granted by *E.F.* [*name and design debtor*] in my favour [*or* in favour of *G.H., as the case may be*], with interest from the [*insert date*], and also all and whole [*describe or refer as in schedule (E)* [1] *or schedule (G), as the case may be, to the lands*] (*a*) all as specified and described in the said bond and disposition in security and instrument of sasine thereon, [*if the bond is recorded omit the words* " and instrument of sasine thereon ",] recorded in the [*here specify the register of sasines in which the sasine or bond is registered*] on the [*specify date of registration*] (*b*). In witness whereof, *etc.* [*insert a testing clause in usual form*].

(Signed) *A.B.*

G.H., witness.
I.K., witness.

Note.—(*a*) Where the assignation is made under any real burdens, conditions, provisions, or limitations, here insert or refer to them in or as nearly as the circumstances of the case may require in the form of schedule (D).[2]

(*b*) If the assignation is granted, not by the original creditor in the security, but by a person to whom the security has already been assigned, or in whom it has become vested by succession or diligence, the conveyance will shortly narrate here the title or series of titles by which the grantor of the conveyance has right to it.

NOTE

[1] See the Conveyancing (Scotland) Act 1924, s. 31 (description of land and deduction of title unnecessary in certain deeds relating to heritable securities).

[2] But see the Conveyancing (Scotland) Act 1924, s. 9.

SCHEDULE (HH)

Form of Instrument in favour of an Assignee to an Heritable Security following on a deed granted for further purposes or objects

At   there was by [*or* on behalf of] *A.B.* of *Z.*, presented to me, notary public subscribing, a bond and disposition in security [*or other security, or extract, as the case may be*], dated [*insert date, and where recorded in the register of sasines insert date of recording, and specify register of sasines, and where sasine has been expede thereon, add* and sasine thereon, recorded in the (*specify register of sasines*) on the (*insert date*)], granted by *C.D.* [*insert designation*] in favour of *E.F.* [*insert designation*], by which bond and disposition in security [*or as the case may be*], the said *C.D.* bound and obliged himself [*insert the personal obligation so far as necessary, and disposition of the lands in security, with the description of them, and also all real burdens, etc., if any, all as set forth at full length or by reference in the bond and disposition or other security*]. As also there was presented to me an assignation [*or other conveyance or extract*] dated [*insert date*], granted by the said *E.F.*, by which the said *E.F.* assigned the said bond and disposition in security [*or other security, as the case may be*], and sums of money and lands therein contained, to the said *A.B.*, and his heirs, executors, and representatives whomsoever [*or otherwise as the case may be, and if the deed be granted in trust, or for specific purposes, add,* but in trust always, *or* for the uses and purposes specified in said assignation, *or otherwise as the case may be. If the person in whose favour the instrument is taken is not the disponee of the original creditor, but of one who has acquired right to the security, here specify shortly the title or series of titles by which the deceased acquired such right*]. Whereupon, *etc.* [*as in schedule (J) to the end*].

SCHEDULE (II)

[Repealed by the Succession (Scotland) Act 1964, s. 34 (2) and Sched. 3.]

[1] SCHEDULE (JJ)

NOTE

[1] Repealed except in so far as relating to completion of title by executors and by disponees or assignees under a deed or conveyance *inter vivos*: the Succession (Scotland) Act 1964, s. 34 (2) and Sched. 3.

Form of instrument in favour of an executor or Heir of a Creditor who died intestate in right of an Heritable Security

At there was by [*or* on behalf of] *A.B.*, of *Z.*, *etc.* [*as in schedule (HH) down to and including the description of the lands and the reference, if any, to real burdens*]. As also there was presented to me testament dative of the said deceased *E.F.*, expede before the commissary of the county of on the [*insert date of confirmation*], whereby the said *A.B.* was ordained and confirmed executor dative of the said deceased *E.F.* (*if there are more than one executors dative appointed the necessary alterations to be made*) [*or* a decree of general (*or* special) service in favour of the said *A.B.* as (*specify character in which heir was served*) to the said *E.F.*, dated (*insert date of service*) expede before the sheriff of and recorded in chancery the day of], whereby the said *A.B.* acquired right to the said bond and disposition in security [*or as the case may be, and if the person in whose favour the instrument is taken is not the executor or heir of the original creditor, but of one who has acquired right to the security, here specify shortly the title or series of titles by which the deceased acquired such security*]. Whereupon, *etc.* [*as in schedule (J) to the end*].

[1] SCHEDULE (KK)

NOTE

[1] Repealed except in so far as relating to completion of title by executors and by disponees or assignees under a deed or conveyance *inter vivos*: the Succession (Scotland) Act 1964, s. 34 (2) and Sched. 3.

Form of instrument in favour of the Executors or Executor nominate, or of the Disponee or Legatee of a Creditor in right of an Heritable Security

At there was by [*or* on behalf of] *A.B.*, of *etc.*, [*as in schedule (HH) down to and including description of lands and the reference to real burdens*]. As also there was presented to me a testament [*or general disposition, or trust disposition and settlement, or other testamentary deed or writing, or extract, or otherwise as the case may be*], dated [*insert date*], granted by the said deceased *E.F.* [*if necessary, say,* who died after (*or* before, *as the case may be*) the commencement of the Titles to Land Consolidation Act, 1868], by which the said *E.F.* nominated the said *A.B.* to be his executor, [*or* assigned and disponed his whole heritable and moveable estate, *or otherwise as the case may be, or* gave and bequeathed his whole moveable estate, and effects to the said deceased *A.B.*; *or* gave and bequeathed the said bond and disposition in security, and sums therein contained, to the said *A.B.*; *and if the deed be granted in trust, or for specific purposes, add,* but in trust always, *or* for the uses and purposes specified in said deed, *or otherwise as the case may be*, whereby the said *A.B.* is now in right of said bond and disposition in security (*or as the case may be*). *If the person in whose favour the instrument is taken is not the executor, disponee, assignee, or legatee of the original creditor, but of one who has acquired right to the security, here specify shortly the title or series of titles by which the deceased acquired such security*]. Whereupon, *etc.* [*as in schedule (J) to the end*].

SCHEDULE (LL)

Form of Instrument in favour of a Trustee on a Sequestrated Estate, or of Liquidators of a Joint Stock Company in right of an Heritable Security

At there was by [*or* on behalf of] *A.B.* [*design him as in schedule (O)*] presented to me, *etc.* [*as in schedule (HH) down to and including description of lands and reference to real burdens, if any*]. As also there was presented to me extract act and warrant of confirmation in favour of the said *A.B.* [*or here specify the appointment of the liquidator or liquidators*], dated [*insert date*], whereby the said *A.B.*, as trustee [*or* liquidator *or as the case may be*], has right to the said bond and disposition in security [*or as the case may be*]. [*If the bankrupt or company or partner is not the original creditor, here specify shortly the title or series of titles by which the bankrupt or company or partner acquired right to the debt.*] Whereupon, *etc.* [*as in schedule (J) to the end*].

[1] SCHEDULE (MM)

NOTE

[1] Repealed except in so far as relating to completion of title by execution and disponees or assignees under a deed or conveyance *inter vivos* by the Succession (Scotland) Act 1964, s. 34 (2) and Sched. 3.

Form of Instrument on an unrecorded Bond and Disposition in Security, or unrecorded Assignation in favour of the Executor, or Disponee, or Assignee, or Legatee or Heir of the Creditor.

At there was by [*or* on behalf of] *A.B.* [*insert designation*], presented to me, notary public subscribing, a bond and disposition in security [*or other security, or* an assignation of the bond and disposition in security, after mentioned, *or* extracts, *as the case may be*] granted by *C.D.* [*insert designation*] and dated [*insert date*], by which bond and disposition in security the said *C.D.* bound and obliged himself, [*insert the personal obligation and disposition of the lands in security, with the description of them, and also all real burdens, etc., if any, all as set forth at full length or by reference in the bond and disposition in security, or other security, or, in the case of an assignation, say,* by which assignation the said *C.D.* assigned to the said *A.B.* a bond and disposition in security, *or other security*, granted by (*insert name and designation of grantor of bond*) in favour of the said *C.D.* dated (*insert date*), and recorded (*insert date of recording and specify register, or in the case of the security having been followed by sasine, say*), and sasine thereon, recorded (*insert date of recording and specify register*), for the sum of (*insert sum*), and also all and whole (*insert the description of the lands and real burdens, etc., or references thereto, all as contained in the assignation*)]: As also there was presented to me [*here specify the title or series of titles by which the party acquired right to the bond and disposition in security, or to the assignation, in or as nearly as the circumstances of the case will admit in the form of schedule (KK), or in the case of a bond and disposition in security, or other security to heirs excluding executors, etc., or the creditor in which died before the commencement of this Act, say,* as also there was presented to me extract decree of the general (*or* special) service of the said *A.B.* as heir (*specify character in which served*), of the said *E.F.* (*here specify date, and date of recording in chancery*)]: Whereupon, *etc.* [*as in schedule (J) to the end*].

SCHEDULE (NN)

Form of Discharge of Bond and Disposition in Security, etc.

I, *A.B.*, in consideration of the sum of [*specify sum*] now paid to me by *C.D.*, do hereby discharge a bond and disposition in security [*or other security*], dated [*insert date*], and recorded [*insert date of recording, if recorded, and register of sasines*], for the sum of [*insert sum*] granted by [*insert name and designation of debtor*], in favour of [*insert name and designation of grantee*], and all interest due thereon; and I declare to be redeemed and disburdened thereof, and of the infeftment following thereon; all and whole [*describe the lands*], all as specified and described in the said bond and disposition in security, dated and recorded as aforesaid, [*and if the same has been followed by sasine, here omit the words* " and recorded ", *and add*] and instrument of sasine thereon, as the same is recorded in the [*specify the register of sasines in which the sasine is recorded*], on the [*specify date of registration*].* In witness whereof, *etc.* [*here insert a testing clause in usual form*].

(Signed) *A.B.*

E.F., witness.
G.H., witness.

* If the grantor of the discharge is not the original creditor, but one who has acquired right to the security, specify shortly here the title or series of titles by which the grantor acquired such right.

SCHEDULE (OO)

Form of Deed of Restriction of an Heritable Security

I, *A. B.*, in consideration of the sum [*or if no price is paid for the restriction*, considering that *C.D.* (*the debtor*) has requested me to release the lands hereinafter described (*or* referred to) from the security hereinafter specified, but without any consideration having been paid to me therefor], do hereby declare to be redeemed and disburdened of the security constituted by a bond and disposition in security [*or other security*], dated [*insert date*], and recorded [*insert date of recording if recorded, and register of sasines*], for the sum of [*insert sum*] granted by [*insert name and designation of debtor*], in favour of [*specify name and designation of grantee*], [*and if the bond has been followed by sasine add*] and instrument of sasine thereon, dated [*insert date, if any*] and recorded [*specify the register and date of registration*], all and whole [*here describe the lands to be disburdened*], and I restrict the security thereby constituted to the lands and others contained in the said bond and disposition in security other than those hereby disburdened. [*If the grantor of the deed is not the original creditor, but one who has acquired right to the security, here specify shortly the title or series of titles by which the grantor acquired such right.*] In witness thereof, *etc.* [*here insert a testing clause in usual form*].

(Signed) *A.B.*

E.F., witness.
G.H., witness.

SCHEDULE (PP)

Notice of Inhibition

Notice of letters of inhibition [*or* of summons containing inhibition, *as the case may be*].—*A.B.* [*insert designation of the inhibitor*] against *C.D.* [*insert designation of the inhibited*].—Signeted [*insert date of signeting*].

E.F. W.S. [*or* S.S.C.], Agent.

SCHEDULE (QQ)

Form of Letters of Inhibition

Victoria, *etc.* To messengers-at-arms and others, our sheriffs, greeting: Whereas it is humbly shown to us by our lovite *A.B.* [*insert designation*], complainer, against *C.D.* [*insert designation*] that [*set forth as concisely as possible the document on which the inhibitor proceeds*]: Our will is herefore, and we charge you, that ye lawfully inhibit the said *C.D.*, personally or at his dwelling-place if within Scotland, and if furth thereof at the office of the keeper of the record of edictal citations at Edinburgh, from selling, disponing, conveying, burdening, or otherwise affecting his lands or heritages to the prejudice of the complainer; and ye cause register these our letters and execution hereof in the general register of inhibitions at Edinburgh for publication to our lieges. Given under our signet at Edinburgh this
day of in the year

[1,2] SCHEDULE (RR)

NOTES

[1] See the Conveyancing (Scotland) Act 1924, s. 44(2)(*a*).

[2] As amended by the Law Reform (Miscellaneous Provisions) (Scotland) Act 1985, Sched. 2, para. 5, with effect from 30th December 1985.

Notice of Summons of Reduction, Adjudication, etc.

Notice of summons of reduction [*or* of adjudication, *or* of constitution and adjudication, *as the case may be*].—*A.B.* [*insert designation of pursuer*] against *C.D.* [*insert designation of defender*].—Signeted [*insert date of signeting*]. The summons relates to [*insert description of lands*].

E.F., W.S. [or S.S.C.]. Agent

[1] Conveyancing (Scotland) Act 1874

(37 & 38 Vict., c. 94)

An Act to amend the law relating to land rights and conveyancing, and to facilitate the transfer of land in Scotland.

[7th August 1874]

NOTE

[1] The Act is printed as amended by the Conveyancing (Scotland) Acts (1874 and 1889) Amendment Act 1887.

Short title

1. This Act may be cited for all purposes as "The Conveyancing (Scotland) Act 1874."

Commencement of Act

2. This Act shall, except where otherwise provided come into operation on the 1st day of October 1874, which date is herein-after referred to as the commencement of this Act.

Interpretation

[1] **3.** The following words and expressions in this Act shall have the several meanings hereby assigned to them, that is to say—

"Land" or "lands" shall include all subjects of heritable property which are or may be held of a superior according to feudal tenure, or which prior to the commencement of this Act have been or might have been held by burgage tenure, or by tenure of booking:

"Estate in land" shall mean any interest in land, whether in fee, liferent, or security, and whether beneficial or in trust, or any real burden on land, and shall include an estate of superiority:

"Superior" shall include the Crown, the Prince and Steward of Scotland, and all subject superiors, and shall also include mid-superiors; "superiority" shall include mid-superiority:

"Conveyance" and "deed" and "instrument" shall each have the meaning attached thereto by the Titles to Land Consolidation (Scotland) Act 1868, and the Titles to Land Consolidation (Scotland) Amendment Act 1869, and shall also, when used in this Act, include all the deeds, instruments, decrees, petitions, and writings specified in this Act; and the words "heritable securities" and "securities" shall have the meaning attached thereto by the said recited Acts, and shall also, when used in this Act, include real burdens and securities by way of ground annual:

"Infeftment" shall include every title to an estate in land requiring and admitting of infeftment which is duly recorded in the appropriate register of sasines:

"Feu" shall include "blench," and "feu-duty" shall include "blench-duty".

"Casualties" shall include the relief duty payable on the entry or succession of an heir, the composition or other duty payable on the entry of a singular successor, whether by law or under the conditions of the feu, and all payments exigible in lieu of such duties and compositions, and all periodical fixed sums or quantities which may be stipulated for under this Act:

"Sheriff" shall include sheriff-substitute.

NOTE

[1] Amended by the Conveyancing (Scotland) Act 1924, s. 2(1).

[1] **4.** When lands have been feued, whether before or after the commencement of this Act,—

Renewal of investiture abolished

(1) It shall not, notwithstanding any provision, declaration, or condition to the contrary in any statute in force at the passing of this Act, or in any deed, instrument, or writing, whether dated before or after the passing of this Act, be necessary, in order to the completion of the title of any person having a right to the lands in whole or in part, whether such rights shall have been acquired by succession, bequest, gift, or conveyance, that he shall obtain from the superior any charter, precept, or other writ by progress; and it shall not be competent for the superior in any case to grant any such charter, precept, or other writ by progress: Provided always, that nothing in this Act contained shall prevent the granting of charters of novodamus or precepts or writs from Chancery:

Infeftment to imply entry with superior

(2) Every proprietor who is at the commencement of this Act or thereafter shall be duly infeft in the lands shall be deemed and held to be, as at the date of the registration of such infeftment in the appropriate register of sasines, duly entered with the nearest superior whose estate of superiority in such lands would according to the law existing prior to the commencement of this Act have been not defeasible at the will of the proprietor so infeft, to the same effect as if such superior had granted a writ of confirmation according to the existing law and practice, and that whether the superior's own title or that of an over superior has been completed or not, but such implied entry shall not be held to confer or confirm any rights more extensive than those contained in the original charter or feu rights of the lands or in the last charter or other writ by which the vassal was entered therein: Provided always, that nothing herein contained shall be held to validate any subfeu in cases where subinfeudation has been effectually prohibited; and provided further, that notwithstanding such implied entry, the proprietor last entered in the lands, and his heirs and representatives, shall continue personally liable to the superior for payment of the whole feu-duties affecting the said lands, and for performance of the whole obligations of the feu, until notice of the change of ownership of the feu shall have been given to the superior; but without prejudice to the superior having all his remedies against the entered proprietor under the entry implied by this Act, and without prejudice also to the right of the proprietor last entered in the lands and his foresaids to recover from the entered proprietor of the lands all feu-duties which such proprietor last entered in the lands or his foresaids may have had to pay in consequence of any failure or omission to give such notice; and for this purpose all the remedies competent to the superior for recovery of feu-duties shall by virtue of this Act be held to be assigned to the proprietor last entered in the lands and his foresaids to the effect of enabling them to recover payment of any sums so paid by them as aforesaid, but that always under reservation of, and without prejudice to the superior's rights, remedies, and securities for making effectual and recovering all other feu-duties due and to become due to him; and such notice may be in the form of schedule A hereto annexed, or as nearly in that form as the circumstances in each particular case will permit. In the event of the proprietor last entered in the lands or his foresaids desiring to preserve evidence of his or their having sent such notice, it shall be sufficient if a copy of such notice, certified by the sender thereof as having been delivered or put into the post-office by him in presence of two witnesses, who shall also subscribe the certificate, is preserved, or that the notice is acknowledged by the superior or his agent to have been received, either on a duplicate thereof or by a separate acknowledgment, and the superior or his agent on receiving such intimation in

duplicate, with a fee of 25p, shall, if required, be bound to return one of the copies with an acknowledgment of intimation thereon subscribed by him:

Implied entry not to affect rights of superiors to feu-duties, etc.

(3) Such implied entry shall not prejudice or affect the right or title of any superior to any casualties, feu-duties, or arrears of feu-duties which may be due or exigible in respect of the lands at or prior to the date of such entry; and all rights and remedies competent to a superior under the existing law and practice or under the conditions of any feu right, for recovering, securing, and making effectual such casualties, feu-duties, and arrears, or for irritating the feu *ob non solutum canonem*, and all the obligations and conditions in the feu rights prestable to or exigible by the superior, in so far as the same may not have ceased to be operative in consequence of the provisions of this Act or otherwise, shall continue to be available to such superior in time coming; but provided always, that such implied entry shall not entitle any superior to demand any casualty sooner than he could, by the law prior to this Act or by the conditions of the feu right, have required the vassal to enter or to pay such casualty irrespective of his entering:

Action in lieu of a declarator of non-entry

(4) No lands shall, after the commencement of this Act, be deemed to be in non-entry, but a superior who would but for this Act be entitled to sue an action for declarator of non-entry against the successor of the vassal in the lands, whether by succession, bequest, gift, or conveyance, may raise in the Court of Session against such successor, whether he shall be infeft or not, an action of declarator and for payment of any casualty exigible at the date of such action, and no implied entry shall be pleadable in defence against such action; and any decree for payment in such action shall have the effect of and operate as a decree of declarator of non-entry, according to the now-existing law, but shall cease to have such effect upon the payment of such casualty, and of the expenses (if any) contained in said decree; but such payment shall not prejudice the right or title of the superior to the rents due for the period while he is in possession of the lands under such decree, nor to any feu-duties or arrears thereof which may be due or exigible at or prior to the date of such payment, or the rights and remedies competent to him under the existing law and practice for recovering and securing the same; and the summons in such action may be in or as nearly as may be in the form of schedule B hereto annexed.

NOTE

[1] As amended by the Statute Law Revision (No. 2) Act 1893, the Succession (Scotland) Act 1964, s. 34 (2) and Sched. 3, and the Decimal Currency Act 1969, s. 10 (1).

Compositions payable by corporations or trustees or persons having separate interests

5. Unless where it has been or shall be otherwise stipulated, corporations shall pay at the date at which the first composition would have been payable if this Act had not been passed, and every twenty-fifth year thereafter, a sum equal to what but for the passing of this Act would have been payable on entry by a singular successor; and where a composition payable on the death of the vassal shall become exigible from any trustee or body of trustees, another composition shall be payable at the end of every twenty-five years, so long as the lands shall be vested in such trustee or trustees; and where by the terms of the feu rights of the lands a taxed composition is payable on the occasion of each sale or transfer of the property, as well as on the occasion of the death of each vassal, and a composition shall in consequence of the acquisition of the property become exigible from any corporation or from any trustee or body of trustees, another composition, unless where it has been or shall be otherwise stipulated, shall be payable at the end of every fifteen years from the date of such acquisition by such corporation or trustee or trustees, so long as the lands shall be vested in such corporation or trustee or trustees, with such interest, if any, as may be stipulated for in the feu rights during the not payment of casualties; provided always, that in the event of such corporation or of such trustee or trustees ceasing to be proprietors of the lands after having paid a composition or compositions in terms of this section the successor of such corporation or of such trustee or trustees who shall be duly infeft in the lands at the expiration of twenty-five years, where a composition is payable on the death of the vassal, or at the expiration of fifteen years where a composition is payable on the occasion of each sale or transfer as well as on the occasion of each death, from the date of the last payment of composition as aforesaid, shall then pay a composition, and the casualties for and in respect of such lands shall thereafter become due and payable at the same time and in the same manner as if such lands had never been vested in such corporation or in such trustee or trustees; and where, by the terms of the feu rights of the lands a taxed composition is payable on the occasion of each sale or transfer of the property as well as on the occasion of the death of each vassal, and where an entry is implied in terms of this Act in favour of two or more parties having separate interests as life-renter and fiar respectively or as successive life-renters, a composition, or in the case of parties interested *pro indiviso* a rateable share of a composition, shall be due by and exigible from each of the parties who shall take or derive benefit under the implied entry in the order in which they shall severally take or derive benefit under such implied entry, with such interest, if any, as may be stipulated for in the feu right during the not payment of casualties.

Consolidation of superiority with property

[1] **6.** When a superior has acquired and completed or shall acquire and complete a title by infeftment to the property or mid-superiority of lands, or where the proprietor of the property or of the mid-superiority has acquired and completed or shall acquire and complete a title by infeftment to the superiority, a minute in the form, or as nearly as may be in the form, of schedule C hereto annexed, shall, when recorded in the appropriate register of sasines, be held to consolidate the property or the mid-superiority, as the case may be, with the superiority, all to the same effect as consolidation effected by resignation *ad perpetuam remanentiam* duly completed according to the present law and practice.

NOTE

[1] Applied by the Conveyancing (Scotland) Act 1924, s. 11(1).

Consolidation not to affect or extend superior's right

7. No consolidation that may be effected under this Act or otherwise shall in any way affect or extend the rights or interests of any over superior, or entitle him to any more that the duties or casualties to which he would have been entitled had there been no consolidation.

Memorandum of allocation of feu-duty

8. Where a proprietor desires to obtain the benefit of any provision as to allocation of feu-duty, or where the superior agrees to an allocation of feu-duty contained in the original grant with or without augmentation, such proprietor may, either before or after the deed in his favour is recorded in the appropriate register of sasines, obtain a memorandum indorsed thereon in or as nearly as may be in the form of schedule D hereto annexed, and the allocation contained in such memorandum shall be binding on all having interest: Provided always, that such allocation shall not prejudice or affect the rights of heritable creditors who are not parties thereto.

9. [Repealed by the Succession (Scotland) Act 1964, s.34(2) and Sched. 3.]

Completion of title when deceased heir not served. Petition to be proceeded with as if it were a petition for special service

[1]**10.** A title of an heir to, or disponee of, a proprietor of any lands who was neither infeft nor served, but vested only with a personal right to such lands, by virtue of this Act, or of any person acquiring right from such heir or disponee, may be made up in like manner as if the person making up a title had held a disposition from the proprietor last infeft in the lands in favour of his immediate successor therein, and a disposition and assignation from each heir or disponee, if any, intervening between such immediate successor and the person so making up a title in favour of his immediate successor therein; and such title may be made up in manner following, viz: The heir or disponee or other successor making up such title shall present to the sheriff of Chancery, or to the sheriff of the county where the lands are situated, a petition which may embrace several separate lands or estates, and may be in the form of schedule E hereto annexed, or as nearly in that form as the circumstances in each particular case will permit setting forth the name of the proprietor last infeft, a description of the lands, or a valid reference thereto, and the names and, so far as known, the designations of every proprietor having only a personal right therein, whether by succession, bequest, gift, or conveyance, who has intervened between the proprietor last infeft and the petitioner, and also setting forth the petitioner's own right to the said lands; and on the decree pronounced on said petition finding the facts therein set forth proved, and that the petitioner is entitled to be infeft in the said lands, being extracted in one or several extracts, and on such extract decree or decrees, as the case may be, being recorded in the appropriate register of sasines, the petitioner shall be held to be duly infeft in the said lands contained in the extract or extracts so recorded. Such petition shall be presented, published, and carried through in all respects as if the same were a petition for special service under the now existing law; and the extract decree or decrees on such petition, as the case may be, shall be equivalent to a decree of special service, and when duly recorded as aforesaid in the appropriate register of sasines, shall have the same effect as regards the lands therein contained as an extract decree of special service duly recorded under the now existing law.

NOTE

[1] This section was repealed by the Succession (Scotland) Act 1964, s. 34(2) and Sched. 3, but is reprinted owing to its potential relevance to the transmission of the estate of persons dying before 10th September 1964.

11–13. [Repealed by the Succession (Scotland) Act 1964, s. 34(2) and Sched. 3.]

Legal remedies to prevent entry preserved

14. Nothing herein contained shall prejudice or affect the legal remedies of any person having lawful title and interest to prevent any other person from entering into possession of an estate in land as heir, or to remove him from possession, or to obtain sequestration of such estate, or the appointment of a judicial factor pending the trial of any question regarding the right of succession; and it shall be lawful for a court of competent jurisdiction to regulate possession pending such trial, as the court shall see just, notwithstanding the completion, under this Act, of the title of any person as heir.

15–17. [Repealed by the Feudal Casualties (Scotland) Act 1914, Sched. E.]

Entails not to bar redemption

[1] **18.** Casulaties subject to the fetters of an entail may be redeemed as aforesaid, notwithstanding such entail, the redemption money being consigned in one of the banks in Scotland incorporated by royal charter or Act of Parliament in name of the accountant of the Court of Session, who shall be allowed a reasonable fee for his trouble out of such money, and being applied by the heir of entail in possession under the orders of the said court for the benefit of the entailed estate, the accruing interest being payable to the heir of entail in possession during the time the same shall arise: Provided always, that when the redemption money so consigned during any period of three years shall not exceed in whole the sum of £100, the same may at the end of that period be paid over by the accountant for the time, without orders or authority from the court, to the person or persons, or the representatives of the person or persons, in possession of the entailed estate at the time or times when the consignment or consignments was or were respectively made.

NOTE

[1] As amended by the Feudal Casualties (Scotland) Act 1914, Sched. E.

Redemption of casualties by a mid-superior

19. The person in right of any estate of superiority created prior to the commencement of this Act shall be entitled to redeem the casualties, legal or conventional, which may be payable to an over superior, in the same manner and on the same terms and conditions as are herein-before enacted with respect to the redemption of casualties by a person in right of an estate of property.

Commutation of carriages and services by agreement, or by sheriff

[1] **20.** Where carriages and services, or any of them, exigible by the superior, shall, for any period of five years, have been commuted to an annual money payment by agreement between the parties, whether reduced to writing or not, and whether express or implied from the conduct or actings of parties, and have not thereafter been exacted and performed, the said annual payment shall thereafter be deemed to be the value in all time coming of such carriages and services respectively, and the superior shall be bound to accept the same in lieu of such carriages and services respectively: With respect to carriages and services which have not been so commuted, it shall be competent to either party to apply to the sheriff, within whose jurisdiction the lands lie, to determine summarily the annual value thereof, and the determination of the sheriff shall be final and not subject to review, and the

[THE NEXT PAGE IS J 71]

superior shall be bound thereafter to accept of the annual sum so determined in lieu of such carriages and services.

NOTE

[1] See the Conveyancing (Scotland) Act 1924, s. 12 (7) (carriages and services not now exigible).

[1] Commuted value to be feu-duty—Not barred by entails

21. The annual money value, where ascertained as aforesaid by agreement, may be stated in a memorandum in the form set forth in the said schedule G, hereto annexed, or in a similar form, signed by the parties or their respective agents, and on such memorandum, or the extract decree pronounced by the sheriff, as the case may be, being recorded in the appropriate register of sasines, such annual money value shall be deemed to be feu-duty with all the legal qualities thereof, and shall form an addition to any existing feu-duty, and the superior's right to the carriages and services shall be held to be discharged. Such discharge, redemption, and commutation may be validly effected, notwithstanding the fetters of any entail.

NOTE

[1] See the Conveyancing (Scotland) Act 1924, s. 12 (7) (carriages and services not now exigible).

Monopolies of superior's agents annulled

22. All conditions, whether made before or after the commencement of this Act, to the effect that the superior shall be entitled to select or appoint an agent to prepare or record sasines or warrants of registration, or conveyances or other deeds having reference to any estate in land, or restraining or restricting the proprietor of any estate in land in the selection of an agent to prepare or record such sasines, warrants, conveyances, or other deeds, or securing any privilege or monopoly to the superior's agent, or to any agent or agents selected or appointed by him, or to the effect that any proprietor of lands shall be bound to intimate to the superior of such lands any change of ownership, whether by succession or singular title, except as hereinbefore provided, or to pay any fees or expenses in connection with such change of ownership, and further all conditions made after the commencement of this Act, to the effect that it shall not be lawful to the proprietor of lands to sub-feu the same to be holden of himself as immediate lawful superior thereof, or to grant conveyances thereof to be holden *a me vel de me* or with an alternative manner of holding, shall, with all irritant clauses applicable thereto, be null and void, and not capable of being enforced, and all enactments to the contrary of, or at variance with, this enactment in any Act of Parliament shall be and the same are hereby repealed.

23. [Repealed by the Feudal Casualties (Scotland) Act 1914, Sched. E.]

Where feu rights stipulating or inferring casualties are contracted to be granted

24. In all cases where superiors have agreed or contracted prior to the passing of this Act to feu land, but have not granted the feu rights thereto prior to the commencement of this Act, and but for the provisions of this Act would have been entitled in the feu rights to stipulate for the payment of casualties as well as of feu-duties, nothing in this Act contained shall be construed or held as depriving such superiors of their right to such casualties, but such casualties may, if desired by such superiors or their vassals in such feus, be converted into annual sums equal to four per cent. on the amount of the price of the redemption of such casualties ascertained as provided in section 15 hereof, and such annual sum shall be deemed to be feu-duties, with all the legal qualities thereof, and shall form additions to the feu-duties which may have been contracted for, and in the feu rights to be granted of such feus superiors shall be entitled, in the event of the casualties being converted as aforesaid, to state as one feu-duty the feu-duty which has been contracted for or agreed upon, and that formed by the converted casualty, and shall have all competent remedies for recovery thereof. But in the event of neither the superiors nor the vassals in such feus desiring to convert casualties agreed or contracted for before the passing of this Act as aforesaid, it shall be competent in such feu rights to stipulate for payment of the casualties which the vassals may expressly or by force of law have agreed or contracted to pay, in the same manner as might have been done prior to the commencement of this Act; and it shall also be competent in such feu rights to stipulate that the same shall be recorded by the agent of the superior at the expense of the vassal if such or a similar stipulation shall have been made and agreed prior to the passing of this Act in the agreement or contract for feuing such land.

Distinction between burgage and feu abolished. Registration of writs in burgh register. Provisions for lands in Paisley held by booking tenure

[1] **25.** The proprietors of and all others having any estate in land held burgage shall have the same rights and interest in such estate as would have belonged to them under this Act or otherwise had the tenure been feu instead of burgage, and there shall not after the commencement of this Act be any distinction between estates in land held burgage and estates in land held feu, in so far as regards the conveyances relating thereto, or the completion of titles, or any of the matters or things to which the provisions of this Act relate: and the proprietors of estates in land which were held burgage shall be entitled to grant feus of the same in the same manner and to the like effect as if such estate in land had been held by feudal tenure; and the titles of all such feus granted before the commencement of this Act shall be unchallengeable on the grounds that such feus are of land held by burgage tenure, or that such titles have been recorded in the burgh register of sasines. Writs affecting land which immediately prior to the commencement of this Act was held burgage shall be recorded in the burgh register of sasines. The provisions of this section in regard to land held by ordinary burgage tenure shall be applicable also to lands in the burgh of Paisley held by the peculiar tenure of booking, except that writs affecting land in said burgh held by the tenure of booking shall be recorded in the register of booking therein.

NOTE

[1] Repealed in part by the Burgh Registers (Scotland) Act 1926, s. 4.

Form of conveyances

26. Conveyances of land hitherto held burgage or by the tenure of booking may be in the forms allowed by the Titles to Land Consolidation (Scotland) Act 1868, in regard thereto; provided always, that it shall not be necessary to insert in any such conveyances a procuratory or clause of resignation, and that such procuratory or clause if inserted shall be held *pro non scripto*, and that the forms applicable to lands held feu shall be applicable likewise, and shall have the same or a similar effect with reference to lands which were held burgage or by the tenure of booking prior to the commencement of this Act.

The word " dispone " unnecessary

27. It shall not be competent to object to the validity of any deed or writing as a conveyance of heritage coming into operation after the passing of this Act, on the ground that it does not contain the word " dispone ", provided it contains any other word or words importing conveyance or transference, or present intention to convey or transfer.

Date of entry

28. Where no term of entry is stated in a conveyance of lands, the entry shall be at the first term of Whitsunday or Martinmas after the date or last date of the conveyance, unless it shall appear from the terms of the conveyance that another term of entry was intended.

General dispositions forming links of series of titles not objectionable on certain grounds

29. No decree, instrument, or conveyance under this Act, and no other decree, instrument, or conveyance, whether dated before or after the commencement of this Act, shall be deemed to be invalid because the series of titles connecting the person obtaining such decree, or expeding such instrument, or holding such conveyance, with the person last infeft, shall contain as links of the series two or more general dispositions, or because any general disposition forming a part of the series does not contain a clause of assignation of writs.

Conveyances and discharges of real burdens. Real burdens effectual in competition from date of recording; mode of completing title to real burdens

[1] **30.** It shall be lawful to record in the appropriate register of sasines any deed, instrument, or writing whereby any real burden upon land is assigned, conveyed, or transferred, or is extinguished or restricted. No deed, instrument, or writing, executed or dated after the commencement of this Act, whereby any real burden upon land shall be hereafter assigned, conveyed, or transferred, shall be effectual in competition with third parties, unless the same is recorded in the appropriate register of sasines; and such deed, instrument, or writing shall take effect in competition with third parties only from the date of such registration, and intimation according to the existing law and pactice shall be unnecessary when such deed, instrument, or writing is recorded; and real burdens upon land may be assigned, conveyed, or transferred, and extinguished or restricted, and titles thereto may be completed as nearly as may be in the same manner as in the case of heritable securities constituted or requiring to be constituted by infeftment in favour of the creditor as defined by the Titles to Land Consolidation (Scotland) Act 1868, and the whole provisions, enactments, and forms of that Act and of this Act relative to the assignation, conveyance, or transference and extinction or restriction of bonds and dispositions in security, and other heritable securities constituted or requiring to be constituted by infeftment as aforesaid, and to the completing of titles thereto, and also the forms referred to, as well as the provisions and enactments contained in section 117 of the said Act shall be taken to apply and shall apply as nearly as may be to real burdens upon land; provided always, that where a real burden upon land shall have been assigned, conveyed, or transferred by any deed, instrument, or writing which has entered the appropriate register of sasines, it shall not be necessary to produce to the notary public expeding any notarial instrument applicable to such real burden, or to set forth in such notarial instrument, as a warrant thereof, the deed, instrument, or writing constituting the said real burden; but it shall be sufficient to produce to him, and to specify shortly in such notarial instrument, the deed, instrument, or writing, or the deeds, instruments, or writings whereby the said real burden shall have been assigned, conveyed, or transferred, and which, or one or more of which, if there are more than one, shall have entered the appropriate register of sasines.

NOTE

[1] As amended by the Succession (Scotland) Act 1964, s.34(2) and Sched. 3.

31. [Repealed by the Succession (Scotland) Act 1964, s.34(2) and Sched. 3.]

Reservations, conditions, and covenants affecting lands may be imported by reference

[1] **32.** Reservations, real burdens, conditions, provisions, limitations, obligations, and stipulations affecting land may be validly and effectually imported into any deed, instrument, or writing relating to such lands by reference to a deed, instrument, or writing applicable to such lands, or to the estate of which such lands form a part, recorded in the appropriate register of sasines, and in which such reservations, real burdens, conditions, provisions, limitations, obligations, and stipulations are set forth at full length, and a reference in the form set forth in schedule H hereto annexed, or in a similar form, shall be sufficient. And it shall be lawful for any proprietor of lands to execute a deed, instrument, or writing, setting forth the reservations, real burdens, conditions, provisions, limitations, obligations, and stipulations under which he is to feu or otherwise deal with or affect his lands, or any part thereof, and to record the same in the appropriate register of sasines; and the same being so recorded, such reservations, real burdens, conditions, provisions, limitations, obligations, and stipulations may be effectually imported in whole or in part by reference into any deed or conveyance relating to such lands subsequently granted by such proprietor, or by his heir or successor, or by any person whatsoever provided it is expressly stated in such deed or conveyance that it is granted under the reservations, real burdens, conditions, provisions, limitations, obligations, and stipulations set forth in such deed, instrument, or writing.

NOTE

[1] See the Land Registration (Scotland) Act 1979, s.17(1). Excluded (in part) by the Land Registration (Scotland) Act 1979, s.15(2). See also the Registration of Leases (Scotland) Act 1857, s.3(5).

33. [Repealed by the Statute Law Revision Act 1883.]

34. [Repealed by the Conveyancing (Scotland) Act 1924, s.16(5).]

Registration of a decree of division

35. A decree of division of commonty or of common property or runrig lands, whether pronounced by a court of law, or by arbiters or by an oversman, shall have the effect of a conveyance containing assignations of writs by all the joint proprietors in favour of the several parties participating in the division of the shares severally allotted to them, and the extract decree pronounced by the court, or the decree pronounced by the arbiters or oversman, or an extract thereof from any competent court books may be recorded in the appropriate register of sasines in ordinary form on behalf of all or any of the parties, or may be used by all or any of the parties for the purpose of infeftment in, or of acquiring a personal right to the shares severally allotted to them, or to any portion thereof, as an assignation, or one of a series of assignations, of an unrecorded conveyance or of a personal right under this Act.

Effect of decree of sale of glebe

36. A decree of sale obtained in terms of section 17 of the Glebe Lands (Scotland) Act 1866, shall have the effect of a conveyance by the minister of the parish at the sight of the heritors of the parish and of the presbytery of the bounds, to the heritor in whose favour it is pronounced, and his heirs and assignees whomsoever, of the glebe or portion of glebe therein contained; and, on an extract of such decree being recorded in the appropriate register of sasines, shall vest in such heritor the glebe or portion of the glebe described therein, with a holding of the Crown for payment of a penny Scots yearly, if asked only, as fully and completely as if he had obtained a charter from the Crown by virtue of such decree, and been infeft thereon in common form.

Distinction between heritage and conquest abolished

37. The distinction between fees of heritage and fees of conquest is hereby abolished with respect to all successions opening after the commencement of this Act, and fees of conquest shall descend to the same persons, in the same manner, and subject to the same rules as fees of heritage.

Certain rules as to probative deeds altered

38. It shall be no objection to the probative character of a deed, instrument, or writing, whether relating to land or not, that the writer or printer is not named or designed, or that the number of pages is not specified, or that the witnesses are not named or designed in the body of such deed, instrument, or writing, or in the testing clause thereof, provided that where the witnesses are not so named and designed their designations shall be appended to or follow their subscriptions; and such designations may be so appended or added at any time before the deed, instrument, or writing shall have been recorded in any register for preservation, or shall have been founded on in any court, and need not be written by the witnesses themselves.

Deed not to be invalid because improbative

[1] **39.** No deed, instrument, or writing subscribed by the grantor or maker thereof, and bearing to be attested by two witnesses subscribing, and whether relating to land or not, shall be deemed invalid or denied effect according to its legal import because of any informality of execution, but the burden of proving that such deed, instrument, or writing so attested was subscribed by the grantor or maker thereof, and by the witnesses by whom such deed, instrument, or writing bears to be attested, shall lie upon the party using or upholding the same, and such proof may be led in any action or proceeding in which such deed, instrument, or writing is founded on or objected to, or in a special application to the Court of Session, or to the sheriff within whose jurisdiction the defender in any such application resides, to have it declared that such deed, instrument, or writing was subscribed by such grantor or maker and witnesses.

NOTE

[1] Amended by the Conveyancing (Scotland) Act 1924, s. 18, and the Succession (Scotland) Act 1964, s. 21 (evidence as to holograph wills in commissary proceedings); applied by the Prescription and Limitation (Scotland) Act 1973, ss. 5 (2), 25 (2).

Holograph testamentary writings

40. Every holograph writing of a testamentary character shall, in the absence of evidence to the contrary, be deemed to have been executed or made of the date it bears.

One notary or justice of the peace and two witnesses to be sufficient where party cannot write

41. Without prejudice to the present law and practice, any deed, instrument, or writing, whether relating to land or not, may, after having been read over to the grantor, be validly executed on behalf of such grantor, who, from any cause, whether permanent or temporary, is unable to write, by one notary public or justice of the peace subscribing the same for him in his presence and by his authority, without the ceremony of touching the pen, all before two witnesses, and the docquet thereto shall set forth that the grantor of the deed authorised the execution thereof, and that the same had been read over to him in presence of the witnesses. Such docquet may be in the form set forth in schedule I hereto annexed, or in any words to the like effect.

42. [Repealed by the Conveyancing (Scotland) Act 1924, s. 44 (6).]

43. [Repealed by the Succession (Scotland) Act 1964, s. 34 (2) and Sched. 3.]

Provisions for the case of a person appointed by the court to administer a trust

[1] **44.** When a trust title has been duly completed and recorded, and any person is subsequently appointed by the court to administer the trust in whole or in part as a trustee or judicial factor the interlocutor whereby the appointment is made shall specify the trust-deed, and the other title or titles (if any) by which the trust title had been completed as aforesaid, in such manner as to identify the same, and shall refer to the register or registers of sasines where such deed or title or titles is or are recorded, and also set forth the lands by description or reference; and an extract of such interlocutor, being recorded in the appropriate register of sasines, shall operate a title by infeftment in the estate in favour of the trustee or judicial factor thereby appointed, in the same manner as if he had been a trustee named in the completed and recorded title in conformity always with the nature and terms of the appointment, and to the effect of enabling him to perform the duties of the office to which he is appointed.

NOTE

[1] Amended by the Conveyancing (Scotland) Act 1924, s. 5 (3) (deduction of title); applied by s. 24 (6) (registered leases).

How title shall be completed when the holder of an office or proprietor is ex officio a trustee and his successor in office takes the trust

45. When by the tenor of the title to any estate in land held in trust duly completed in favour of the trustee or trustees therein named, or any of them, and recorded in the appropriate register of sasines, the office of a trustee has been or shall be conferred upon the holder of any place or office, or proprietor of any estate, and his successors therein, any person subsequently becoming a trustee by appointment or succession to the place or office or estate to which the office of trustee has thus been or shall be annexed shall be deemed and taken to have a valid and complete title by infeftment in the estate, in the same manner and to the same effect as if he had been named in the completed and recorded title, without the necessity of any deed of conveyance or other procedure.

46. [Repealed by the Succession (Scotland) Act 1964, s. 34 (2) and Sched. 3.]

Securities upon land, and relative personal obligations, shall transmit against heirs and disponees

[1] **47.** An heritable security for money duly constituted upon an estate in land shall, together with any personal obligation to pay principal, interest, and penalty contained in the deed or instrument whereby the security is constituted, transmit against any person taking such estate by succession, gift, or bequest, or by conveyance, when an agreement to that effect appears *in gremio* of the conveyance, and shall be a burden upon his title in the same manner as it was upon that of his ancestor or author, without the necessity of a bond of corroboration or other deed or procedure; and the personal obligation may be enforced against such person by summary diligence or otherwise, in the same manner as against the original debtor. A warrant to charge may be applied for and validly granted in the bill-chamber or in a sheriff court in the form set forth in schedule K hereto annexed, or in a similar form, and all diligence may thereafter proceed against the party in common form. A discharge of the personal obligation of the original or any subsequent debtor, whether granted before or after the commencement of this Act, shall not where the debt still exists prejudice the security on the

estate or the obligation as hereby made transmissible against the existing proprietor.

NOTE

[1] As amended by the Succession (Scotland) Act 1964, Sched. 3. Restricted by the Conveyancing (Scotland) Act 1924, s. 15.

Provisions for disencumbering lands sold under heritable securities when no surplus emerges

[1] **48.** Where lands are sold by an heritable creditor under the powers competent to creditors in heritable securities, and it shall occur that no surplus remains after deducting the debt secured, with the interest due thereon, and penalties incurred, and expenses in reference to the possession of the estate (if the creditor had been in possession), including expense of insurance, repairs and management, and whole expense attending such sale, and after paying all previous incumbrances, and the expense of discharging the same, it shall be competent to any notary public to execute a certificate to that effect, in, or as nearly as may be in, the terms of schedule L, No. 1, hereto annexed, and the disposition by the creditor to the purchaser shall, along with such certificate, when recorded in the appropriate register of sasines, have the effect of completely disencumbering the lands and others sold of all securities and diligences prior and posterior to the security of such creditor, as well as of the security and diligence of such creditor himself, save and except when the security and diligence of such creditor shall be assigned by way of further or collateral security to the purchaser.

NOTE

[1] Excluded by the Conveyancing and Feudal Reform (Scotland) Act 1970, s. 32, Sched. 8, para. 16.

Provision for disencumbering lands of heritable security

[1] **49.** Where the debtor in any heritable security, whether granted before or after the commencement of this Act, shall have exercised the power or right of redemption contained therein, but where from the death or absence of the creditor, or any other cause, the debtor cannot obtain a discharge of the incumbrance created by the security, it shall be competent to him to consign the amount, principal and interest, due, and thereupon it shall be competent to any notary public to expede a certificate in, or as nearly as may be in, the terms of schedule L, No. 2, hereto annexed, and the recording of the said certificate in the appropriate register of sasines shall, provided the principal debt and all interest due thereon in terms of the security shall have been so consigned, have the effect of completely disencumbering the lands contained in such heritable security of the debt and of all interest and penalties corresponding thereto.

NOTE

[1] Excluded by the Conveyancing and Feudal Reform (Scotland) Act 1970, s. 32, Sched. 8, para. 17.

Form and effect of assigning right of relief or other right affecting land

[1] **50.** An assignation or conveyance of any obligation or right of relief or other right connected with lands, but the title to which does not, according to the present law, pass under the general assignation of writs in the disposition of the lands, may be granted in, or as nearly as may be in, the form of schedule M, hereto annexed, and may either be a separate deed or part of another deed, and shall have the effect of vesting in the person or persons in whose favour it is granted, and his or their successors, a valid and complete right and title to the obligation or right thereby assigned or conveyed, with all the intermediate transmissions thereof, to the same effect in all respects

as if an assignation or conveyance in the form at present in use had been granted in his or their favour.

NOTE

[1] Excluded by the Land Registration (Scotland) Act 1979, s. 15 (4).

Probate equivalent to will or extract for completing title

[1] **51.** The production to any notary public of the probate of the will or other testamentary settlement of a person deceased, issued (*a*) by any court of probate in England or in Ireland, or in any British colony or dependency, (*b*) a district court in Palestine before 15th May 1948, or of an exemplification of such probate, shall for the purpose of expeding a notarial instrument, or otherwise completing a title to any estate in land or to any heritable security, be held to be equivalent to and as effectual as the production to such notary of the will or settlement itself, or of an extract thereof from the books of council and session, and it shall not be competent to institute any challenge of any notarial instrument in respect of the probate or exemplification having been used as the warrant for expeding the same prior to the commencement of this Act.

NOTE

[1] As amended by the Statute Law (Repeals) Act 1981, s. 1 (2) and Sched. 2. See the Foreign Jurisdiction Act 1890, s. 5 and Sched. 1.

Decrees of service unchallengeable on certain grounds

[1] **52.** It shall not be competent to challenge any judgment or decree of service pronounced in terms of the Service of Heirs (Scotland) Act 1847 or of the Titles to Land Consolidation (Scotland) Act 1868, and dated before the commencement of this Act, or any extract of any such judgment or decree, or any titles following upon such judgment, decree, or extract, on account of any objection to the manner or form in which such judgment or decree was recorded or extracted by the director of Chancery or his depute, or on the ground that the manner and form of recording or extracting such judgments or decrees in use by the director of Chancery or his depute for the time had not been directed or approved of by the Lord Clerk Register in terms of the said Acts, or on the ground that evidence was led in the petition on which such decree followed, and that the decree itself was pronounced before the expiry of the *induciae,* or days of publication prescribed under section 10 of the former Act, or under section 33 of the latter Act.

NOTE

[1] The functions of the Director of Chancery now exercisable by the Keeper of the Registers of Scotland: Reorganisation of Offices (Scotland) Act 1928, s. 7, S.R. & O. 1932 No. 148 and the Public Registers and Records (Scotland) Act 1948, s. 1 (2).

Form of completing title to heritable securities under a general disposition

[1] **53.** It shall be competent to the grantee under a general disposition within the sense and meaning of section 19 of the Titles to Land Consolidation (Scotland) Act 1868, or to a person acquiring or deriving right from such grantee, to complete a title to an heritable security belonging to the grantor of such general disposition, and in which such grantor was infeft, by expeding and recording in the appropriate register of sasines a notarial instrument in, or as nearly as may be in, the form of schedule N hereto annexed, and on such notarial instrument being so expede and recorded the grantee or the person acquiring or deriving right from such grantee, as the case may be, in whose favour such instrument has been expede shall be vested with the full right of the creditor in such security, and shall be held to be entered with the superior in like manner and to the same effect as the original creditor himself; and it shall not be competent to challenge the

validity of any notarial instrument expede and recorded before or after the commencement of this Act with reference to any heritable security in terms of the said section 19 of the said Act upon the ground that such notarial instrument is not in the form of schedule L annexed to the said Act, or that the said form is not adapted to heritable securities.

NOTE

[1] Repealed except in relation to general dispositions by conveyance *inter vivos* by the Succession (Scotland) Act 1964, s. 34 (2) and Sched. 3.

Recorded deed or instrument unchallengeable on certain grounds

54. No challenge of any deed, instrument, or writing recorded in any register of sasines shall receive effect on the ground that any part of the record of such deed, instrument, or writing is written on erasure, unless such erasure be proved to have been made for the purpose of fraud, or the record is not conformable to the deed, instrument, or writing as presented for registration.

55. [Repealed by the Statute Law Revision Act 1883.]

56. [Repealed by the Companies (Consolidation) Act 1908.]

Certain offices abolished, and the duties of the sheriff of Chancery, etc. enlarged

[1] **57.** The duties of the office of presenter of signatures, so far as the same continue to be necessary, shall be discharged by the sheriff of Chancery, and the duties of the office of clerk to the presenter of signatures shall be performed by the sheriff-clerk of Chancery. After the commencement of this Act it shall not be necessary either for the sheriff of Chancery or for the sheriff of any county to hold a court for the consideration or disposal of any unopposed petition for service.

NOTE

[1] As amended by the Statute Law Revision Act 1893. Functions of sheriff of Chancery now exercisable by the sheriff principal of Lothian and Borders: see the Administration of Justice (Scotland) Act 1933, s. 31 (1) and the Sheriff Courts (Scotland) Act 1971, s. 4.

Provisions as to Chancery office

[1] **58.** The office, duties, and emoluments of the director of Chancery, and of the deputy directors and clerks of Chancery, or any of them, may be regulated at any time by the Treasury, and it shall be the duty of the director of Chancery, in addition to the duties at present discharged by him, to send to every sheriff-clerk in Scotland a copy of the printed index or abridgment of the record of services provided to be kept by him by section 38 of the Titles to Land Consolidation (Scotland) Act 1868, and it shall be the duty of every sheriff-clerk to keep the same in his office open for the inspection of the public.

NOTE

[1] The functions of the director of Chancery now exercisable by the Keeper of the Registers of Scotland: Reorganisation of Offices (Scotland) Act 1928, s. 7, S.R. & O. 1932 No. 148 and the Public Registers and Records (Scotland) Act 1948, s. 1 (2).

Act shall apply to lands held of the Crown and Prince

59. The provisions of this Act shall apply to lands held of the Crown and of the Prince, in the same way as to lands held of a subject superior, but shall not prejudice or affect the *jus coronae* as a title to lands or heritages.

Title to private estates of Her Majesty in Scotland

60. Notwithstanding the provisions of this Act, private estates in land of

Her Majesty, her heirs or successors, as defined in the Crown Private Estates Act 1862, and situate or arising in Scotland, which are or shall be held feudally directly under the Crown as superior, may lawfully be held by Her Majesty, or her heirs or successors, of and under herself or themselves as sovereign or sovereigns of the realm and feudal superiors, and the *dominium utile* thereof shall not be held to merge in the *dominium directum* or superiority, or to be consolidated therewith; and such private estates shall not thereby fall or revert to the Crown *jure coronae*, but shall remain beneficially separate estates of Her Majesty, her heirs and successors.

Section 11 of Titles to Land Consolidation Act repealed. Description of lands contained in recorded deeds may be inserted in subsequent writs by reference merely. Reference already made in unrecorded deed not challengeable if certain particulars correctly given

[1] **61.** Section 11 of the Titles to Land Consolidation (Scotland) Act 1868, is hereby repealed; and in all cases where any lands have been particularly described in any conveyance, deed, or instrument of or relating thereto, recorded in the appropriate register of sasines, it shall not be necessary in any subsequent conveyance, deed, or instrument, conveying or referring to the whole or any part of such lands, to repeat the particular description of the lands at length; but it shall be sufficient to specify the name of the county, and where the lands were held by burgage or by any similar tenure prior to the commencement of this Act, the name of the burgh and county in which the lands are situated, and to refer to the particular description of such lands as contained in such prior conveyance, deed, or instrument so recorded in or as nearly as may be in the form set forth in schedule O, hereto annexed; and the specification and reference so made in any such subsequent conveyance, deed, or instrument, whether dated prior or subsequent to the commencement of this Act, shall be held to be equivalent to the full insertion of the particular description contained in such prior conveyance, deed, or instrument, and shall have the same effect as if the particular description had been inserted in such subsequent conveyance, deed, or instrument exactly as it is contained in such prior conveyance, deed, or instrument; and it shall not be competent to object to any specification and reference to any particular description of lands contained in any conveyance, deed, or instrument recorded prior to the commencement of this Act provided such specification and reference states correctly the name of the county, and where the lands were held by burgage or by any similar tenure prior to the commencement of this Act, the name of the burgh and county in which the lands are situated, and refers correctly to the prior recorded conveyance, deed, or instrument containing the particular description of such lands; and where any conveyance, deed, or instrument recorded prior to the commencement of this Act contains a specification and reference stating these particulars correctly, the specification and reference so made shall be held to have been equivalent to the full insertion of the particular description contained in the prior conveyance, deed, or instrument referred to, as if the particular description had been inserted in such recorded conveyance, deed, or instrument exactly as it is contained in the prior conveyance, deed, or instrument referred to.

NOTE

[1] As amended by the Statute Law Revision Act 1893. Extended by the Conveyancing (Scotland) Act 1924, s. 8 (1) (2), the Land Commission Act 1967, s. 9 (5), the Countryside (Scotland) Act 1967, ss. 16 (4), 38 (4) and the Town and Country Planning (Scotland) Act 1972, s. 278, Sched. 24, para. 1 (2). Excluded by the Land Registration (Scotland) Act 1979, s. 15.

62. [Substitutes new section 62 in the Titles to Land Consolidation (Scotland) Act 1868.]

63. [Repealed by the Succession (Scotland) Act 1964, s. 34(2) and Sched. 3.]

64, 65. [Substitutes new sections 127 and 129 in the Titles to Land Consolidation (Scotland) Act 1868.]

Schedules to be part of Act

66. The schedules annexed to this Act, and the directions therein contained, and notes thereto appended, shall have the same effect as if they were contained in the body of this Act.

Repeal of Acts, etc.

67. All statutes, laws, and usages at variance with any of the provisions of this Act are hereby repealed.

68. [Repealed by the Statute Law Revision Act 1893.]

SCHEDULES

SCHEDULE A

Form of Notice to be given to a Superior of Change of Ownership

[*Place and Date.*]

Sir I hereby intimate to you that[1] has [*or have*] now right to[2] which lands [*or subjects*] formerly belonged to[3].—I am, sir, your most obedient servant,[4].

NOTES

[1] Here state name, designation, and address of the new proprietor or proprietors of the feu.

[2] Here mention the names by which the lands or subjects are generally known, so as to distinguish them to the superior, but without giving any detailed description of the lands or subjects, and if in a town or village mention the number of the street or otherwise distinguish the feu, and if a reference to the feu right will more easily and clearly distinguish the lands or subjects a reference to the feu right can be given, but the superior shall not be entitled to object either that the name or designation or address of the new proprietor or proprietors of the feu is erroneous, or that the form in which the lands or subjects are referred to is insufficient or erroneous, unless it can be shewn that the notice given as to these particulars or any of them was intended to mislead the superior as to the identity of the new proprietor or proprietors of the feu or as to the particular lands or subjects to which the notice should have referred.

[3] Insert the name of, the last entered vassal, whether by actual entry previous to the commencement of this Act or by implied entry under it.

[4] To be signed (but not attested) by the seller of the feu, or by heir or the trustees or executors, of a deceased proprietor, or by any one of the trustees or executors for himself and his co-trustees or co-executors, or by an agent of any of these parties.

To be addressed and posted or delivered to the superior or to his known agent, or to the person to whom the feu-duties of the feu have been paid, and in the event of the superior being unknown or doubtful, the notice to be addressed "to the superior", of the lands mentioned in the notice without name (in the event of the proprietor being unable to ascertain name of the superior), and to be posted or sent to the keeper of the office of edictal citations in Edinburgh, and published in the register of these citations, and also (where there is doubt as to the superior) to the person or to the agent of the person as to whom such doubt exists.

SCHEDULE B

Form of Summons of Declarator and for Payment of a Casualty

Victoria, etc.—Whereas it is humbly meant and shewn to us by our lovite A. [*design him*] immediate lawful superior of the lands [*or* subjects] after described [*or* referred to], and duly infeft therein conform to [*here mention title and date of recording same in the register of sasines*], pursuer, against *B.* [*design him*], defender, in terms of the condescendence and note of pleas in law hereunto annexed: Therefore it ought and should be found and declared by decree of the Lords of our Council and Session, that in consequence of the death of *C.[or otherwise as the case may be]*, who was the vassal last vest and seised in all and whole the lands of *X, [describe or refer to the lands, and if the casualty due is a taxed composition, or an heir's relief duty, say]* the casualty of [*or, if a singular successor's untaxed composition be due, say*] a casualty, being one year's rent of the lands, became due to the said *A.* as superior of the said lands upon the day of , being the date of the death of the said *C. [or]* the date of the infeftment of the said *B.* in the said lands of *X.* [*or otherwise as the case may be*], and that the said casualty is still unpaid, and that the full rents, maills, and duties of the said lands of *X.*, after the date of citation herrein do belong to the pursuer, the said *A.*, as superior thereof, until the said casualty and the expenses after mentioned be otherwise paid to the said *A.*: And the said *B.* ought and should be decerned and ordained by decree foresaid forthwith to make payment to the pursuer, the said *A.*, of the said sum of £ , being the casualty foresaid, [*or* of the sum of £ , or such other sum, more or less, as shall be ascertained in the course of the process to follow hereon to be one year's rent of the said lands], together with the sum of £ , or such other sum, more or less, as our said Lords shall modify as the expenses of the process to follow hereon, conform to the laws and daily practice of Scotland, used and observed in the like cases, as is alleged.—Our will is herefore, etc.

Note.—In the event of the summons being one at the instance of the Crown or Prince and Steward of Scotland, the necessary alteration will be made, and the summons will be at the instance of the Lord Advocate on behalf of the Commissioners of Woods.

SCHEDULE C

Form of Minute for effecting Consolidation of Lands

I, *A.B.*, heritable proprietor both of the immediate superiority and of the property [*or* of the mid-superiority] of all and whole [*describe or refer to the lands*], hereby consolidate the property of the said lands [*or* the mid-superiority of the said lands] with the immediate superiority thereof. In witness whereof [*testing clause*].

SCHEDULE D

Form of Memorandum of Allocation of Feu-Duty

The proportion of the original feu-duty of £ allocated upon the lands within disponed [*or as the case may be*], is hereby fixed at £ , [*and if an augmentation has been stipulated for, add*] with £ of augmentation, making a total of £

(Signed) *A.B.* (*the superior of the lands or his commissioner*).

[1] SCHEDULE E

Form of Petition for completing a Title to Lands where a Proprietor or Proprietors having only a Personal Right have intervened between the Proprietor last infeft and the Petitioner.

Unto the Honourable the Sheriff of [*specify the county, or say* "of Chancery".] the Petition of A.B. of G.

Humbly sheweth,

That the late C.D. of G. died last vest and seised in all and whole [*describe or refer to the lands as the same are described or referred to in the recorded deed or instrument in favour of the person who was last vest and seised in the lands, or refer to them as described in some other recorded deed or instrument*] conform to instrument of sasine [*or other recorded deed or instrument, as the case may be*], recorded in the [*specify the register of sasines and date of recording, and where there are any real burdens, conditions or qualifications, here specify or refer to them, or where the lands are held under entail, here specify the conditions of the entail, or refer to them as contained in the entail, as recorded in the register of tailzies, or if it is not so recorded, in the entail or other deed or instrument recorded in the register of sasines*].

Or, that *M.N.* of *Y.* was last vest and seised in all and whole [*describe or refer and specify title and date of recording, etc., as above*]. That the said *M.N.* by disposition dated [*specify date*] conveyed the said lands to *C.D.* of *G.* That the said *C.D.* died never having been infeft in the said lands.

That *E.F.*, eldest son of the said *C.D.* [*or otherwise, as the case may be*], is his heir in the said lands, but has only a personal right thereto.

That the said *E.F.*, by disposition dated [*specify date*] conveyed the said lands to the petitioner.

Or, that upon the death of the said *C.D.*, he was succeeded by *E.F.*, his eldest son [*or otherwise, as the case may be*], as his heir in the said lands. That the said *E.F.* died unserved and uninfeft, [*or* that the said E.F. expede a special service as heir of the said *C.D.*, conform to decree of the sheriff of Chancery [*or as the case may be*], in his favour as heir aforesaid, dated [*insert date*], but died without being infeft thereon], *or* that the said *E.F.* expede a general service as heir of the said *C.D.*, conform to decree [*specify the decree*], but made up no further title.

Or otherwise specify the nature of the right in the person of E.F.

That the said *E.F.* disponed the said lands or conveyed his whole estate, heritable and moveable, to *G.H.* conform to [*describe title by name and date, and where there are any real burdens, conditions, or qualifications, specify or refer to them*].

That the said *G.H.* also died, having only a personal right to the said lands, and was succeeded by his eldest son, *K.L.*, his nearest and lawful heir in the said lands [*or otherwise, as the case may be*].

That the said *K.L.* died unserved, and having only a personal right to the said lands, [*if the petitioner is his heir, say*] and was succeeded by the petitioner, the said *A.B.*, his eldest son [*or otherwise as the case may be*] and nearest and lawful heir in the said lands [*or when the petitioner is a disponee, or has otherwise acquired right from K.L., say*], That the said *K.L.*, disponed the said lands [*or* conveyed his whole estate, heritable and moveable, *or otherwise, as the case may be*] to the petitioner, the said *A.B.*, conform to disposition *or* general disposition [*or otherwise, as the case may be*], dated [*specify date*], granted in his favour by the said *K.L.* who died unserved and having only a personal right to the said lands; [*and if the deed be granted under any real burden, or condition, or qualification, add*] but always under the real burden, etc.; [*and if the deed be granted in trust or for specific purposes, add*] but always in trust *or* for the uses, ends, and purposes mentioned in the said general disposition [*or otherwise, as the case may be*].

May it therefore please your Lordship to find the facts above set forth proved, and that the petitioner is entitled to procure himself infeft in the foresaid lands, in terms of "The Conveyancing (Scotland) Act, 1874", and to decern.

According to Justice, etc.

[*Signed by the petitioner or his mandatory.*]

Note.—If any of the transmissions have been judicial, as by adjudication, act and warrant of court, or otherwise, or if by any of the transmissions a part or parts only of the lands are transferred, the necessary alterations may be made on the form of the petition.

NOTE

[1] This Schedule was repealed by the Succession (Scotland) Act 1964, s. 34(2) and Sched. 3, but is reprinted owing to its potential relevance to the transmission of estate of persons dying before 10th September 1964.

SCHEDULE F

Form of Discharge of Casualties

I, A.B. [*design him*], proprietor of the estate of superiority in the lands of [*describe or refer to a description of the lands discharged*], whereof the estate of property belongs to C.D. [*design him*], in consideration of [*state cause of granting*], hereby discharge in favour of the said C.D., and his heirs and successors, all casualties incident to my said estate of superiority exigible in respect of the said estate of property [*if only some of the casualties are redeemed specify what they are*], and I consent to the registration hereof for preservation.—In witness whereof [*testing clause*].

[1] SCHEDULE G

NOTE

[1] Applied by the Conveyancing (Scotland) Act 1924, s. 12(2) (3) (abolition and commutation of grain, etc., feu-duties).

[THE NEXT PAGE IS J 83]

Form of Memorandum constituting a Feu-Duty or additional Feu-Duty

It is agreed between *A.* [*name and designation of superior*] immediate lawful superior of the lands of [*describe or refer to a description of the lands*] on the one part, and *B.* [*name and designation of proprietor of estate of property*] the proprietor of the *dominium utile* of the said lands on the other part, that the *dominium utile* of the said lands shall, from and after the term of [*state term*], be liable in payment to the superior thereof of a feu-duty of £ [*or if there be a feu-duty already payable*, of an additional feu-duty of £ over and above the existing feu-duty of £]; and that yearly, at two terms in the year [*state the terms at which the feu-duty is to be paid, or* and that at the term of (*state term*) yearly], beginning the first term's payment [*state term, and whether with interest*]: which feu-duty [*or* additional feu-duty] is constituted in respect of [*state here whether the additional feu-duty is in respect of a commutation of casualties, or of carriages, etc., or as the case may be*].—In witness whereof [*testing clause*].

Note.—If the memorandum be executed by the agents of either or both of the parties, it will be stated in the testing clause that the memorandum is signed by them in that capacity for and on behalf of their constituent or respective constituents.

SCHEDULE H

Form of Reference to a Deed, Instrument, or Writing for Reservations, Burdens, and Conditions affecting Lands

The reservations, real burdens, conditions, provisions, limitations obligations, and stipulations [*or as the case may be*] specified in [*refer to the deed, instrument, or writing in such terms as shall be sufficient to identify it, and specify the register in which it is recorded, and the date of registration, or where the deed, instrument, or writing referred to is recorded on the same date as the deed, instrument, or writing containing the reference, here say*, recorded of even date with the recording of these presents].

SCHEDULE I

Form of Docquet where Grantor of Deed cannot write

By authority of the above named and designed *A.B.*, who declares that he cannot write, on account of sickness and bodily weakness [*or* never having been taught, *or otherwise as the case may be*] I *C.D.* [*design him*] notary public, [*or* justice of peace for the county of (*name it*), *or as regards wills or other testamentary writings executed by a parish minister as notary public in his own parish*, minister of the parish of (*name it*)], subscribe these presents for him, he having authorised me for that purpose, and the same having been previously read over to him, all in presence of the witnesses before named and designed, who subscribe this docquet in testimony of their having heard [*or* seen] authority given to me as aforesaid, and heard these presents read over to the said *A.B.*

(Signed) *A.B.*, Notary Public [*or* Justice of the Peace *or* Parish Minister].

E.F., witness.
G.H., witness.

SCHEDULE J

[Repealed by the Conveyancing (Scotland) Act 1924, s. 44 (6).]

SCHEDULE K

Form of Minute to be presented in Bill-Chamber of Court of Session, or in Sheriff Court, for Warrant to charge an Heir or Disponee under a personal Obligation by his Ancestor or Author.

Warrant is craved, in virtue of the Conveyancing (Scotland) Act 1874 at the instance of *A.B.* [*name and design applicant*], the creditor [*if he is not the original creditor or only a partial creditor, add*, in virtue of (*or* to the extent and in virtue of) the assignation (*or* general disposition and notarial instrument, *or other writ or writs forming the title in the creditor's person*) in his favour after mentioned] under a bond and disposition in security over the lands of [*specify shortly the lands*], for the principal sum of £ with corresponding interest and penalties, granted by *C.D.* [*design him*], then proprietor of the said lands, in favour of the said *A.B.* [*or* of *G.H.* (*design him*), *as the case may be*], and dated [*state date*] [*and if recorded say*, and recorded in the register of sasines (*state register and date of recording*), *or* and instrument of sasine thereon recorded, etc., *as the case may be*]; To charge *E.F.* [*design him*], the present proprietor of the said lands, and as such the present debtor in the said bond and disposition in security, to make payment to the said *A.B.* of the said principal sum of £ contained in and due by the said bond and disposition in security [*if A.B. is only a partial creditor, say,* of the principal sum of £ being the extent to which the said *A.B.* is in right of the said bond and disposition in security]: and also of the further sum of £ , being the amount of the interest now due thereon. Produced herewith the said bond and disposition in security [*or an extract thereof from the books of Council and Session or from the register of sasines; if the applicant is not the original creditor, the title in his own person to the security will also be stated and produced*].

Dated the day of

(Signed) *A.B.*, W.S., Edinburgh,
[*or as the case may be*].

The Clerk of the Bills, or Sheriff Clerk, as the case may be, will subjoin Fiat ut petitur.
[*To be dated and signed by the Clerk.*]

SCHEDULE L

No. 1

Form of Certificate where Lands are sold under Heritable Security and no Surplus emerges

I, *A.B.* [*insert designation*], notary public, with reference to the sale of all and whole the lands of [*describe or refer to the lands*], which sale took place at upon the day of at the instance of *C.D.* [*design him*], in virtue of the power of sale contained in a bond and disposition in security for the sum of £ with interest and penalties corresponding thereto, dated and recorded in the register of sasines for the day of granted by *G.H.* [*design him*] in favour of the said *C.D.* [*or* in favour of *E.F.* (*design him*), but to which the said *C.D.* has acquired right by progress (*or otherwise as the case may be*)], do hereby certify that there has been submitted to me a statement of the intromissions of the said *C.D.* with the price of the said lands, subscribed as authentic by the said *C.D.*, [*or* by *M.N.*, agent of the said *C.D.*, on his behalf], from which it appears that no surplus remains for consignation in bank, in terms of the 122d and 123d sections of the Titles to Land Consolidation (Scotland) Act 1868 and I make this certificate in terms of the Conveyancing (Scotland) Act 1874.—In witness whereof [*testing clause*].

No. 2

Form of Certificate where Lands have been redeemed of Heritable Security, but Discharge cannot be obtained

I, *A.B.* [*design him*], notary public, do hereby certify that *C.D.* [*design him*], proprietor of the lands of *X.* [*name the lands as shortly as possible*] and others in the county of *Y.*, being the lands contained in the bond and disposition in security [*or other deed of security*] for £ after mentioned, has appeared before me and represented that he did on the day of consign in the bank at the sum of £ with £ being the whole interest due under the said bond and disposition in security [*or other deed of security*] in name of *E.F.* [*design him*] the creditor in the said bond and disposition in security [*or other deed of security; if only a partial creditor say* to the extent of £]; which consignation was made in virtue of the power of redemption reserved in the said bond and disposition in security [*or other deed of security*] which was granted by the said *C.D.* [*or* by *J.K.* (*design him*), then proprietor of the said lands] in favour of the said *E.F.* [*or L.M.* (*design him*) the original creditor in the said security], and is dated [*insert date*] and recorded in the register of sasines for the day of [*if sasine was expede on the bond and disposition in security or other deed of security, instead of* and recorded, etc., *say*, on which bond and disposition in security (*or other deed of security*) the said *E.F.* (*or L.M. as the case may be*) was infeft, conform to instrument of sasine in his favour recorded in the register of sasines for the day of]; and the said consignation was rendered necessary by the refusal of the said *E.F.* to receive the said sum of £ and interest thereon [*or* by the absence of the said *E.F.*, *or otherwise as the case may be, stating the reason why discharge could not be obtained*], notwithstanding that the requisite notice of redemption was given to him; and I make this certificate in terms of the Conveyancing (Scotland) Act 1874.—In witness whereof [*testing clause*].

[1] SCHEDULE M

NOTE

[1] Excluded by the Land Registration (Scotland) Act 1979, s.15(4).

Form of Assignation of Right of Relief, etc.

I [*here insert the name and designation of the grantor, and the cause of granting, unless the assignation forms part of another deed*] hereby assign to *C.D.* [*here insert the designation of the grantee, unless already given*], and his *heirs* and assignees [*or* and his foresaids], a disposition [*or other deed, as the case may be*] granted by [*here insert the names and designations of the persons by and in whose favour the deed to be assigned was granted, with its date, and also the date of registration, and the register in which it is recorded, if it has been recorded*], whereby the said [*name of the original grantor of the disposition or obligation*] bound and obliged himself, his heirs and successors [*here insert the terms of the obligation in the terms so far as possible of the disposition or other deed, e.g.*], "to warrant the parsonage teinds of the lands of" [*here specify by description or reference, if not already done, the lands to which the obligation or right refers*] "from all future augmentations of minister's stipend or other burden imposed or to be imposed upon the said parsonage teinds except the stipend presently payable to the minister of ", [*or as the case may be. If the right to be assigned was originally granted in favour of some other person than the granitor of the assignation, here specify the series of writs by which he acquired right, and add testing clause*].

SCHEDULE N

Form of Instrument in favour of a General Disponee or his Assignee in right of an Heritable security

At there was by [*or* on behalf of] *A.B.* of *Z.*, presented to me, notary public subscribing, a bond and disposition in security [*or other security or extract as the case may be*] dated [*insert date, and where recorded in the register of sasines insert date of recording and specify register of sasines*], granted by *C.D.* [*insert designation*] in favour of *E.F.* [*insert designation*] [*if sasine has been expede thereon add,* and instrument of sasine thereon in favour of the said *E.F.*, recorded in the [*specify register of sasines and date of registration*] by which bond and disposition in security [*or as the case may be*] the said *C.D.* bound and obliged himself [*insert the personal obligation so far as necessary, and disposition of the lands in security, with the description of them, and also all real burdens, etc., if any, all as set forth at full length or by reference in the bond and disposition in security or other security*]: As also, there was presented to me a general disposition [*or other deed or writing containing a general conveyance, or an extract of such deed or writing, or otherwise, as the case may be*] granted by the said *E.F.*, and dated [*insert date*], by which general disposition [*or otherwise as the case may be*] the said *E.F.* assigned and disponed [*or otherwise as the case may be*] to the said *A.B.* and his executors and assignees [*or otherwise as the case may be*] heritably and irredeemably [*or*, in liferent, *or otherwise as the case may be*], all and sundry his whole heritable and moveable estate [*or otherwise as the case may be, and if the deed be granted in trust or for specific purposes add,* but in trust always, *or*, for the uses and purposes specified in the said general disposition (*or otherwise as the case may be*)], in which general conveyance was included the said bond and disposition in security [*or other security*] [and infeftment following thereon, *if infeftment was expede*], the said *E.F.* being then vest therein as aforesaid. [*If the grantor of the general disposition or other deed or writing was not the original creditor, but one who had acquired right to the security, instead of* as aforesaid *here say* in virtue of the following writs, viz. [*specify shortly the title or titles by which he acquired right to the security. If the person expeding the instrument be other than the original grantee under the generaql disposition or other deed or writing, add,* As also, there were presented to me the following writs whereby the said *A.B.* acquired the said general disponee's right to the said bond and disposition in security [and infeftment following thereon], [*or otherwise as the case may be*], viz. [*specify the title or series of titles by which such person acquired right, and the nature of his right*]. Whereupon this instrument is taken in the hands of *L.M.* [*insert name and designation*], notary public in terms of the Titles to Land Consolidation (Scotland) Act 1868, and the Conveyancing (Scotland) Act 1874. In witness whereof [*testing clause*].

SCHEDULE O

[Repealed by s.8(1) of the Conveyancing (Scotland) Act 1924 and Schedule D of that Act substituted (see *infra*).]

[1] Writs Execution (Scotland) Act 1877

(40 & 41 Vict., c. 40)

An Act to amend the form of warrant of execution on certain extracts of writs registered in the Books of Council and Session and sheriff court books in Scotland; and to provide for the authentication of certain extracts of writ. [10th August 1877]

NOTE

[1] By the Short Titles Act 1896 this Act may be cited as "The Writs Execution (Scotland) Act 1877"; amended by the Court of Session (Extracts) Act 1916.

Extracts of writs registered in books of Council and Session to have, in certain cases, warrant for execution.—Form of warrant of execution inserted in extracts of all protests, etc.

1. In all extracts of writs, deeds, or other documents which contain a clause of registration for preservation and execution, and which are registered in the register of deeds and probative writs and protests in the books of Council and Session in Scotland, the keeper or assistant keeper of the said register shall insert a warrant for execution in the form, or as nearly as may be in the form, of the schedule to this act annexed.

The warrants for execution inserted in the extracts of all protests of bills, promissory notes, or bankers' notes, or certificates of judgment registered for execution under the Judgments Extension Act 1868, shall be as nearly as may be in the form of the said schedule to this Act annexed.

Extracts of writs registered in sheriff court books to have warrant of execution in certain cases

2. In all extracts of writs, deeds, or other documents which contain a clause of registration for preservation and execution, and which are registered in the sheriff court books of any county in Scotland, and in all extracts of protests of bills, promissory notes, or bankers' notes registered in the sheriff court books, the sheriff clerk shall insert a warrant of execution in the form, or as nearly as may be in the form, of the schedule to this Act annexed.

Competent to arrest, charge, and poind by virtue of the extract, with warrant for execution thereon

[1] **3.** It shall be lawful, by virtue of the warrant inserted in any extract under the provisions of the two preceding sections, to arrest the readiest goods, debts, and sums of money of the debtor or obligant mentioned in such extract, in payment and satisfaction of the sum or sums of money or obligation or obligations therein specified, as also to charge the debtor or obligant therein mentioned to pay the sum or sums of money or to perform the obligation or obligations therein specified within the appropriate days of charge, under the pain of poinding and imprisonment, so far as competent, the terms of payment or implement being first come and byegone, and if he fail to obey the said charge, then, so far as competent, to apprise, poind, and distrain all his readiest goods, gear, and other effects, in payment and satisfaction of the said sum or sums or obligation or obligations, and if necessary for effecting said poinding, to open shut and lockfast places.

NOTE

[1] Extended by the Conveyancing (Scotland) Act 1924, s.10(5)(registration for execution). Substituted (*prosp.*) by the Debtors (Scotland) Act 1987, s.87(4).

4. [Repealed by the Statute Law (Repeals) Act 1969.]

Extracts of deeds registered in the books of Council and Session, and register of sasines, to be authenticated

[1] **5.** Extracts of all writs, deeds, or other documents of what nature soever, which may be registered in the books of Council and Session, shall be equivalent to the registered writs, deeds, or other documents themselves, except where any writ, deed, or other document so registered shall be offered to be improven, and such extracts shall be signed, on the last page thereof, by the keeper or assistant keeper of the register of deeds and probative writs and protests in the books of Council and Session; and extracts of all writs registered in and issued from the office of the general register of sasines shall be signed, on the last page thereof, by the keeper of the said register, or by a deputy duly commissioned by him to that effect, and no further signature on any other page of such extracts shall be necessary; but each sheet of all such extracts shall be impressed with an office seal or stamp to be kept in the respective offices of the said keepers; provided that it shall be necessary and sufficient in the case of marginal additions occurring in any extract that the same shall be authenticated by the signature of the officer certifying such extract.

NOTE

[1] The functions of the Keeper of the General Register of Sasines now exercisable by the Keeper of the Registers of Scotland: see the Reorganisation of Offices (Scotland) Act 1928 and the Public Registers and Records (Scotland) Act 1948.

Writs registered in the register of sasines for preservation only may afterwards be registered for preservation and execution

[1] **6.** Where any writ containing *in gremio* thereof a procuratory or clause of registration for preservation and execution shall have been registered in the general register of sasines upon a warrant of registration for preservation but not for execution, it shall be competent to present for registration in the said register an extract of such registered writ having a warrant of registration written thereon, bearing that such extract is to be registered for preservation and execution; and it shall be lawful to register such extract accordingly, and to issue one or more extracts thereof with warrant of execution in terms (*mutatis mutandis*) of schedule B annexed to the Land Registers (Scotland) Act 1868, and every such warrant of execution shall have all the like force and effect as any warrant of execution issued in terms of section 12 of the said last-mentioned Act; and in making such subsequent registration it shall not be necessary to engross *ad longum* in the said register the extract so presented, but the registration thereof may be effected by the insertion of a memorandum of such extract in the appropriate division or divisions of said register, setting forth the volume of the register and the folio or folios of such volume in which said original writ is engrossed, and the insertion of such memorandum shall be deemed equivalent to the full engrossment in the division or divisions of the register in which such memorandum shall be entered as aforesaid of the extract so presented for registration.

NOTE

[1] Amended by the Conveyancing (Scotland) Act 1924, s. 10 (7).

After transmission of volumes of records of books of Council and Session to the Lord Clerk Register the deputy keeper of records may issue extracts of any deeds recorded in said volumes, and authenticate the same as well as other extracts

[1] **7.** Whereas, in terms of section 12 of the Public Records (Scotland) Act 1809, the volumes of records of the books of Council and Session are,

along with the warrants thereof, periodically transmitted by the keeper of the register of deeds and probative writs and protests in the books of Council and Session, to the Lord Clerk Register [2] or his deputies; be it enacted, that the deputy keeper of the records, or any officer holding a commission to that effect from the Lord Clerk Register, may, at any time, issue extracts one or more of any writ, deed, or other document registered in said volumes of records transmitted as aforesaid, in the same or in a similar form to the extracts of such writs, deeds, or other documents which might have been issued previous to such transmission; and all such extracts, and the warrants of execution therein contained, shall have all the like force and effect as any extract from the books of Council and Session, made and issued previous to such transmission, or as any warrant of execution contained in or appended to such extract; and in all extracts issued as aforesaid, and also in all extracts issued of writs contained in any record in the custody of the Lord Clerk Register, it shall be sufficient that the last page thereof shall be signed by the said deputy keeper of the records or by any officer duly commissioned by the Lord Clerk Register to that effect, and no further signature on any other page of such extracts shall be necessary, but each sheet of all such extracts shall be impressed with an office seal or stamp to be kept in the office of the Lord Clerk Register; provided that it shall be necessary and sufficient in the case of marginal additions occurring in any such extract that the same shall be authenticated by the signature of the officer certifying such extract.

NOTES

[1] Amended by the Conveyancing (Scotland) Act 1924, s. 10 (7).

[2] The functions of the Lord Clerk Register now exercisable by the Keeper of the Registers of Scotland: see the Lord Clerk Register (Scotland) Act 1879, the Reorganisation of Offices (Scotland) Act 1928 and the Public Registers and Records (Scotland) Act 1948.

Commencement and extent of Act

8. This Act shall take effect from and after the 1st day of October 1877, and shall apply to Scotland only.

[1] SCHEDULE

NOTE

[1] Extended by the Conveyancing (Scotland) Act 1924, s. 10 (5) (registration for execution).

At   the   day of   one thousand eight hundred and   the deed herein-after engrossed was presented for registration in the books of the Lords of Council and Session [*or* sheriff court books of the county of   ], for preservation [*or* for preservation and execution], and is registered in the said books as follows:—

[*Insert full copy of the deed: and where the deed is registered for execution, insert warrant for execution, as follows*]:—

And the said Lords grant [*or* the sheriff grants, *as the case may be*] warrant for all lawful execution hereon.

Extracted, etc.

Conveyancing (Scotland) Acts (1874 and 1879) Amendment Act 1887

(50 & 51 Vict., c. 69)

An Act to amend the Conveyancing (Scotland) Act 1874, and the Conveyancing (Scotland) Act (1874) Amendment Act 1879. [16th September 1887]

Limitation of liability of trustees for casualties

1. Where by a trust-disposition and settlement, or other *mortis causa* writing, any heritable estate is conveyed to trustees for behoof of, or with directions to convey the same to, the heir of the testator, whether forthwith or after the expiration of any period of time not exceeding twenty-five years, or by virtue of which the heir of the testator has the ultimate beneficial interest in such estate, the trustees under such trust, disposition and settlement, or other *mortis causa* writing, shall not, upon their entering, or by reason of their having prior to the date of this Act entered, with the superior, by infeftment or otherwise, be liable for any other or different casualty than would have been payable by the heir if he had taken the estate by succession to the testator without the same having been conveyed to trustees; and the heir upon thereafter entering with the superior, by infeftment or otherwise, shall not be liable for any further casualty in respect of his entry, but whether the heir shall have been entered or not, another casualty shall become exigible upon his death in the same manner as if he had been duly entered with the superior.

2. [Repealed by the Bankruptcy (Scotland) Act 1913, Sched. I.]

Novodamus not challengeable because lands not resigned into superior's hands

3. It shall not be competent to object to the validity of any charter of novodamus, whether granted prior to or after the passing of this Act, on account of the lands therein contained not having previously, and in order to the granting thereof, been resigned into the hands of the superior.

Decree of irritancy not final till extract recorded

4. No decree of declarator of irritancy at the instance of a superior against his vassal *ob non salutum canonem* obtained after the passing of this Act shall be deemed to be final until an extract thereof shall have been recorded in the appropriate register of sasines.

Letters of administration of will, etc., equivalent to will for authorization of notary to expede instrument

5. The production to any notary public of letters of administration of the will or other testamentary settlement of a person deceased issued by any Court of Probate in England or in Ireland, or in any British colony or dependency, or of an exemplification of such letters of administration, shall for the purpose of expeding a notarial instrument, or otherwise completing a title to any estate in land or to any heritable security, be held to be equivalent to and as effectual as the production to such notary of the will or settlement itself, or of an extract thereof from the books of Council and Session; and it shall not be competent to institute any challenge of any notarial instrument in respect of the letters of administration or exemplification thereof having been used as the warrant for expeding the same prior to the commencement of this Act.

Short title

6. This Act may be cited for all purposes as the Conveyancing (Scotland) Acts (1874 and 1879) Amendment Act 1887.

[1] Heritable Securities (Scotland) Act 1894

(57 & 58 Vict., c. 44)

An Act to amend the law relating to heritable securities in Scotland. [25th August 1894]

NOTE

[1] Applied by the Conveyancing (Scotland) Act 1924, s. 23 (4) (ground-annuals) and s. 26 (heritable creditors' remedies for recovery of feu-duties and ground-annuals).

Ss. 6–10, 12, 15 excluded by the Conveyancing and Feudal Reform (Scotland) Act 1970, s. 32 and Sched. 8.

Short title

1. This Act may be cited for all purposes as the Heritable Securities (Scotland) Act 1894.

Extent and commencement of Act

2. This Act shall apply to Scotland only.

Tenants need not be parties to actions of maills and duties

3. The creditor in a heritable security may, without calling the tenants of the lands disponed in security as defenders, raise an action of maills and duties either in the sheriff court, in the form as nearly as may be of Schedule (A) annexed to this Act, or in the Court of Session in common form, with the necessary alterations consequent upon the provisions of this Act, and may give notice of the raising of such action to the tenants by registered letter in the form as nearly as may be of Schedule (B) annexed to this Act, and from and after the date when such notice is received by the tenants they shall be held as interpelled from making payment of the rents due by them, in the same manner and to the same effect as if they were called as defenders in an action of maills and duties according to the present law and practice, and upon intimation of the decree obtained in said action being made to the tenants by registered letter [1] in the form as nearly as may be of Schedule (C) annexed to this Act, the said tenants shall make payment of the rents due by them respectively in the same manner and under the like legal compulsitors as if the same had been decerned for and a charge for payment given in an action of maills and duties according to the existing law and practice, and payment when so made shall be a complete exoneration and discharge to such tenants respectively: Provided always, that no decree in such action shall affect the right of the tenants to refuse payment of such rents on any ground not affecting the title of such creditor or the right of any prior creditor to enter into possession, and nothing herein contained shall prevent an action of maills and duties from being raised in the form heretofore in use, or deprive a creditor of any existing right competent to him of entering into possession without having recourse to an action of maills and duties.

NOTE

[1] Now also recorded delivery service: see the Recorded Delivery Service Act 1962, s. 1.

Power to interpel security holder

4. Any person interested may take proceedings to interpel the creditor from entering into possession of the lands disponed in security or collecting the rents thereof.

Power to eject proprietor in personal occupation

5. Where a creditor desires to enter into possession of the lands disponed in security, and the proprietor thereof is in personal occupation of the same, or any part thereof, such proprietor shall be deemed to be an occupant without a title, and the creditor may take proceedings to eject him in all respects in the same way as if he were such occupant: Provided that this section shall not apply in any case unless such proprietor has made default in the punctual payment of the interest due under the security, or in due payment of the principal after formal requisition.

Power to lease security subjects for seven years or under

6. Any creditor in possession of lands disponed in security may let such lands held in security, or part thereof, on lease, for a period not exceeding seven years in duration.

Sheriff may grant power to lease security subjects for longer periods, not more than twenty-one years for heritable property in general, and thirty-one years for minerals

7. Any creditor in possession of lands disponed in security may apply to the sheriff for warrant to let the lands disponed in security or part thereof, for a period exceeding seven years, setting forth the name of the proposed tenant or tenants, the duration and conditions of the proposed lease; and the sheriff may, after service on the proprietor and on the other heritable creditors, if any, and after such intimation and inquiry as he may think proper, and if satisfied that a lease for a longer period than seven years is expedient for the beneficial occupation of the lands, approve of the proposed lease on the terms and conditions proposed, or on such other terms and conditions as may appear to him expedient: Provided always, that such lease shall in no case exceed twenty-one years for heritable property in general and thirty-one years for minerals.

Provisions for security holders becoming proprietors of security subjects

[1] **8.** Any creditor who has exposed for sale under his security the lands held in security, at a price not exceeding the amount due under the said security, and under any prior security, and any security or securities ranking *pari passu* with the exposer's security (exclusive of the expenses attending the exposure or prior exposures), and has failed to find a purchaser, may apply to the sheriff for decree, in the terms of Schedule (D) hereto annexed; and the sheriff may, after service on the proprietor and on the other creditors, if any, and after such intimation and inquiry as he may think fit, grant such application and issue decree in the said terms. On such decree being pronounced, and an extract thereof in which said lands shall be described at length or by reference recorded in the appropriate register of sasines, the right of redemption reserved to the debtor shall be extinguished, and as from the date of the said recording the creditor shall have right to the lands disponed in security in the same manner and to the same effect as if the disposition in security had been an irredeemable disposition as from that date, and upon registration of an extract of such decree in the appropriate register, the lands shall be disencumbered of all securities and diligences posterior to the security of the said creditor; or instead of granting such decree the sheriff may, upon any such application being made to him as aforesaid appoint the lands held subject to the security to be re-exposed for sale at a price to be fixed by him, and in that event the said creditor shall have right to bid for and purchase the said lands at such sale, and, in the event of the creditor purchasing, the sheriff may issue decree in the form and to the effect aforesaid, or the creditor may grant a disposition of the lands to himself in the same manner as if he had been a stranger.

NOTE

[1] As amended by the Conveyancing and Feudal Reform (Scotland) Act 1970, s.39(1).

Completion of title of security holders. Personal obligation of debtor to remain so far as not extinguished by price

9. Upon a sale being carried through under the immediately preceding section, and upon consignation of the surplus of the price, if any, over the sum due under the security, in terms of the Titles to Land Consolidation (Scotland) Act 1868, or upon the execution and recording of a certificate that there is no surplus, in terms of the Conveyancing (Scotland) Act 1874, the right and title of the creditors to the lands shall be absolute and irredeemable, and the lands shall be disencumbered of securities and diligences in the manner and to the effect provided for in the said statutes as regards sales carried through in virtue thereof. Provided always, that the personal obligation of the debtor shall be reserved in full force and effect so far as not exthinguished by the price at which the lands have been acquired.

Purchaser's title indefeasible

10. No purchaser from the creditor or other successor in title in the lands shall be under any duty to inquire into the regularity of the proceedings under which such creditor has acquired right to the lands held under his security by virtue of the provisions contained herein, or be affected by any irregularity therein, without prejudice to any competent claim of damages against such creditor.

Sheriff may grant power to pari passu **security holder to sell** pari passu **security**

[1] **11.** Any creditor holding a security ranking *pari passu* with another security who desires to sell the lands conveyed in security by his security, and who is unable to obtain the consent of the creditor holding such other *pari passu* security to a sale, may apply to the sheriff for warrant to sell the said lands, calling such other creditor as defender; and the sheriff, after hearing parties and making such inquiry as he thinks fit, may order a sale of the said lands, if in his opinion it is reasonable and expedient that such sale should take place; and in case of difference of opinion, the sheriff may fix the price, authorise both or either of the parties or some other person to carry through the sale, and upon payment or consignation of the price to grant a conveyance and disencumber the lands of the said securities in the same way and as fully as if the creditors therein were by agreement carrying through said sale, and also to fix the times and conditions of sale in conformity with the law and practice relating to premonition and advertisement. And the expenses of and connected with the sale shall be payable preferably out of the price or proceeds of the sale, and the balance of such price or proceeds after providing for such expenses shall be paid to the creditors in the securities charged upon the lands according to their just rights and preferences.

NOTE

[1] See the Conveyancing and Feudal Reform (Scotland) Act 1970, ss.29 (standard securities) and 35(3).

Provisions anent procedure

12. The following provisions shall have effect with regard to applications under sections 7, 8 and 11 of this Act:—

(1) The interlocutor of the sheriff who pronounces any order or decree shall be final, and not subject to review, except (1) as to questions of title and (2) where the principal sum due under the heritable security exceeds £1,000.

(2) The sheriff may award expenses, or may direct that the expenses be treated as part of the expenses of the sale.

Provisions of Act to have effect notwithstanding incapacity of debtor. Trustees and others to have powers conferred by Act

[1] **13.** The rights and powers conferred by this Act may be exercised by any

creditor, although the debtor or any other creditor holding a security over the same lands, or other person to whom intimation may require or be ordered to be given is subject to any legal disability by reason of nonage or otherwise, and any action or proceeding under this Act shall have the same force and effect as it would have had if such debtor, proprietor, creditor, or other person had been of full age and not subject to any legal incapacity when such action or proceeding was taken; and trustees, executors, tutors, curators, guardians, judicial factors, and other officers of court may exercise all or any of the powers conferred by this Act.

NOTE

[1] As amended by the Age of Legal Capacity (Scotland) Act 1991, Sched. 1, para. 23.

Security holders under the Registration of Leases Act to have same powers as security holders

14. From and after the passing of this Act the powers of sale contained in bonds and assignations in security granted in terms of the Registration of Leases (Scotland) Act 1857, may be exercised by adopting the procedure provided in the case of sales under the powers of sale contained in bonds and dispositions in security by the Titles to Land Consolidation (Scotland) Act 1868, and the Conveyancing (Scotland) Act 1874, and this Act, and any sales under such bonds and assignations in security carried through by adopting the said procedure shall be as valid and effectual in every aspect as if they had been carried through in accordance with the provisions of the Registration of Leases (Scotland) Act 1857.

Sheriff to have jurisdiction whatever value of lands

15. The sheriff of the county in which the lands held in security or part thereof are situate, or where lands are situate in more counties than one, the sheriff of any of such counties, shall have jurisdiction in all cases instituted under or in connection with this Act, whatever the value of the lands may be.

Provisions as to notice where debtor has died and heir cannot be ascertained

[1] **16.** Where (*a*) the debtor in an heritable security has died and no heritable title has been completed to the lands by his heir or other representative, and the name and address of such heir cannot be ascertained by the creditor, or (*b*) the creditor cannot ascertain the address of the debtor in the security, or whether such debtor is still alive, or (*c*) the creditor cannot ascertain the address of the person who, in terms of such heritable security, is the person legally entitled to receive intimation of the demand of payment hereinafter mentioned, the creditor in such security may, in any such case, apply to the sheriff of the county in which any portion of the lands disponed by such heritable security is situate, for warrant to intimate the demand of payment specified in section 119 of the Titles to Land Consolidation (Scotland) Act 1868, to the debtor, at the office of the keeper of the Record of Edictal Citations, within the General Register House, Edinburgh, in such form and addressed to such person or persons by name, or in his or their representative character, or as the sheriff may, after such inquiry (if any) as he may think fit, prescribe, and a demand for payment so made shall have the same effect as a demand for payment delivered personally to the debtor in such security.

NOTE

[1] Functions of the Keeper of the Record of Edictal Citations now exercised by such clerks and officers of the Court of Session as may be appointed: see the Reorganisation of Offices (Scotland) Act 1928, S.R. & O. 1929 No. 588 and the Public Records (Scotland) Act 1937, s.13.

Rights under existing law reserved

17. Nothing herein contained shall prejudice or restrict the powers, rights, and privileges of creditors in heritable securities according to the present law and practice.

Interpretation clause

18. In this Act the words "conveyance", "heritable security", "security", "creditor", "debtor", and "purchaser" shall have the same meanings respectively as in the Titles to Land Consolidation (Scotland) Act 1868.

The word "lands" shall extend to and include all heritable subjects.

Saving as to right of Crown

19. Nothing in this Act contained shall affect the present law and practice in regard to the preferential character of debts due to the Crown, nor shall anything done under the new procedure by this Act authorised prejudice the rights of the Crown as these exist according to the present law and practice.

SCHEDULES

SCHEDULE (A)

In the sheriff court of at

A.B., Pursuer.
against
C.D., Defender.

The above-named pursuer submits to the court the condescendence and note of plea-in-law hereto annexed, and prays the court—

To grant a decree against the above-named defender, finding and declaring that the pursuer has right to the rents, maills, and duties of the subjects and other specified in the bond and disposition in security for £ , granted by in favour of , dated the and recorded in the register or, at least so much of the said rents, maills, and duties as will satisfy and pay the pursuer the principal sum of £ with interest thereon at the rate of per centum per annum from the day of 18 , liquidate penalty and termly failures all as specified and contained in the said bond and disposition in security dated and recorded as aforesaid, and to find the said *C.D.* liable in expenses, and to decern therefor.

Add condescendence and pleas in law

SCHEDULE (B)

In the Court of Session [or]
In the sheriff court of shire, at

Notice

An action has been raised of this date [*specify place and date*] in the above court, at the instance of *A.B.* [*design him*], pursuer, against *C.D.* [*design him*], defender, in which the said pursuer asks that it be declared that as holding a bond and disposition in security over the subjects situated at [*here give such description of the subjects, e.g., their name or the number of street in which they are situated, as may identify them*], he has right to the rents due, current, and to become due, from the subjects.

Should you, after receiving this notice, pay your rent to the defender, you will do so at the risk of having to pay again to the pursuer should he obtain decree in the action.

[*To be signed by the pursuer or his law agent or messenger-at-arms or sheriff-officer.*]

SCHEDULE (C)

In the Court of Session [or]
In the sheriff court of shire, at

Notice

Decree having been obtained of this date [*specify place and date*] in the above court, at the instance of *A.B.* [*design him*], pursuer, against *C.D.* [*design him*], defender, finding and declaring that the pursuer has right to the rents, maills, and duties of the subjects and others situated at [*here give such description of the subjects, e.g., their name, or the number of street in which they are situated, as may identify them*] specified in a bond and disposition in security for £ granted by in favour of dated the and recorded in the register, you are hereby notified of the same, and desired and required to make payment to the said *A.B.* of the rents, maills, and duties due by you in respect of the occupancy of said subjects or part thereof.

[*To be signed by the pursuer or his law agent or messenger-at-arms or sheriff-officer.*]

[1] SCHEDULE (D)

NOTE

[1] Amended by the Conveyancing (Scotland) Act 1924, s. 9 (1) (conditions of title), and by the Conveyancing and Feudal Reform (Scotland) Act 1970, s. 39 (2).

The sheriff having resumed consideration of the said petition, finds and declares that *X.Y.* [the debtor in the bond] has forfeited the right of redemption reserved to him in the said bond and disposition in security, and that the said right is extinguished as from and after the date on which an extract of this decree is recorded in the appropriate register, and that *A.B.* [*design him*], the petitioner as from the said date, has right to, and is vested in, the lands described in the said bond and disposition in security, dated and recorded as aforesaid, as absolute proprietor thereof, but subject always to the burdens and conditions contained or referred to in the said bond and disposition in security, at the price of £ [*here mention the price at which the lands were last exposed, or the price at which the lands have been bought in, as the case may be*], and decerns; and grants warrant to record the decree to be extracted hereon in the register of sasines.

Note.—The extract decree is to describe the subject.

[1] Conveyancing (Scotland) Act 1924

(14 & 15 Geo. 5, c. 27)

An Act to amend the law of conveyancing in Scotland.

[1st August 1924]

NOTE

[1] Act applied with modifications by the Conveyancing and Feudal Reform (Scotland) Act 1970, s. 35 (2).

Short title, extent and commencement of Act

1.—(1) This Act may be cited as the Conveyancing (Scotland) Act 1924.

(2) [Repealed by the Statute Law Revision Act 1950.]

(3) This Act shall apply to Scotland only.

Interpretation clause

[1] **2.** The words and expressions after mentioned or referred to shall have the several meanings hereby assigned to them, unless there be something in the subject or context repugnant to such construction (that is to say):—

(1) The words and expressions used in this Act and in the schedules annexed to this Act which are interpreted in the Titles to Land Consolidation (Scotland) Act 1868 and the Conveyancing (Scotland) Act 1874, shall have the meaning assigned thereto respectively by these Acts, subject to the following qualifications:—

(*a*) " Land " or " lands " shall not include " securities ";

[2] (*b*) " Heritable securities " and " securities " shall include real burdens and securities by way of ground annual, which either appear in the appropriate Register of Sasines as a burden on the land out of which they are payable or are contained in a deed the recording of which in such Register on behalf of the original creditor would infeft him therein and in the land out of which the same are payable, or either of them, and securities over a lease, but shall not include securities constituted by ex facie absolute disposition; and

(*c*) " Conveyance " and " deed " and " instrument " shall include all deeds, notices of title, decrees, petitions and writings specified in this Act; and these words and the words " writing ", " writ " and " decree " occurring in the said Acts and in this Act shall each mean and include an extract or office copy of such " conveyance ", " deed ", " instrument ", " writing ", " writ " or " decree ":

(2) " Extract " and " office copy " shall each mean and include a duly authenticated extract of any Act, decree or warrant of the Lords of Council and Session, or any inferior court, or a duly authenticated extract or office copy from the Register of the Great Seal, or from the Books of Council and Session, or of any sheriff court, or of any other public authentic register of probative writs, or from the appropriate Register of Sasines, of any conveyance, deed, instrument, writing, writ or decree, and shall also mean and include a probate of the will or testamentary settlement of a person deceased issued by any court of probate in England or Northern Ireland, or in any part of His Majesty's Dominions, or an exemplification of such probate:

(3) " Deductions of title " shall mean the specification in a deed, decree or instrument of the writ or series of writs (without narration of the contents thereof) by which the person granting such deed or in whose favour such decree is conceived or by whom such instrument is expede, has acquired right from the person from whom such title is deduced, and such specification shall be a compliance with an instruction to " deduce " a title in terms of this Act:

(4) " Adjudication " shall include adjudication whether for debt or in implement, and constitution, and adjudication whether for debt or in implement, and declarator and adjudication:

(5) " Lease " shall mean a lease which has been registered or is registrable in the Register of Sasines in virtue of the Registration of Leases (Scotland) Act 1857, and Acts amending the same:

(6) " Law agent " shall mean and include writers to the signet, solicitors in the supreme courts, procurators in any sheriff court, and every person entitled to practise as an agent in a court of law in Scotland:

(7) " Agent " in the Schedules hereto shall mean law agent or notary public:

(8) " Register of Sasines " shall mean and include the General Register of Sasines, the Particular Registers of Sasines now discontinued, the Register of Sasines kept for any royal or other burgh and the Register of Booking in the burgh of Paisley.

NOTES

[1] Definition of " deed " and " Register of Sasines " applied by the Land Registration (Scotland) Act 1979, s. 28 (1).

[2] Applied by the Countryside (Scotland) Act 1967, s. 70 (6) and the Mines and Quarries (Tips) Act 1969, s. 35. Applied (mod.) by the Civil Aviation Act 1982, Sched. 7, para. 11 (2).

Disposition, etc., by person uninfeft

[1] **3.** If a disposition of land, or an assignation, discharge or deed of restriction of a heritable security duly recorded in the appropriate Register of Sasines, or any part of such security, is granted by a person having a right

to such land, or to such heritable security, or such part thereof, but whose title to such land or heritable security or part thereof has not been completed by being so recorded, and who in such disposition or other deed deduces his title from the person last infeft or having the last recorded title, in or as nearly as may be in the terms of Form No. 1 of Schedule A to this Act in the case of land, or in or as nearly as may be in manner prescribed in Note 2 to Schedule K to this Act in the case of a heritable security, then on such disposition or other deed being recorded in the appropriate Register of Sasines, the title of the grantee thereof shall be in all respects in the same position as if his title were completed as at the date of such recording by notarial instrument duly expede and recorded according to the present law and practice; and the provisions of section 146 of the Titles to Land Consolidation (Scotland) Act 1868, shall apply to such disposition.

NOTE

[1] See the Conveyancing Amendment (Scotland) Act 1938, s.1 and the Land Registration (Scotland) Act 1979, s.15(3).

Completion of title

[1] **4.** Any person having right either to land or to a heritable security by a title which has not been completed by being recorded in the appropriate Register of Sasines, may complete his title in manner following:—

(1) A person having such right to land may complete a title thereto by recording in the appropriate Register of Sasines a notice of title in or as nearly as may be in the terms of Form No. 1 of Schedule B to this Act, in which notice of title such person shall deduce his title from the person last infeft:

(2) When the writ forming the immediate connection with the person last infeft is an unrecorded conveyance, deed or decree, the recording of which in the appropriate Register of Sasines on behalf of the person in whose favour the same is conceived would have completed his title by infeftment, the person having such right to the land therein contained or part thereof may complete a title thereto by recording in the appropriate Register of Sasines such conveyance, deed or decree, docqueted in manner prescribed in Note 7 to Schedule B to this Act, along with a notice of title in or as nearly as may be in the terms of Form No. 2 of that Schedule, in which notice of title such person shall deduce his title, from the person in whose favour such conveyance, deed or decree is conceived:

(3) A person having such right to a heritable security, or part thereof, which appears in the appropriate Register of Sasines as a burden on land, may complete a title thereto by recording in the appropriate Register of Sasines a notice of title in or as nearly as may be in the terms of Form No. 3 of Schedule B to this Act, or in the case of a ground-annual in or as nearly as may be in the terms of Form No. 4 of that Schedule, in which notice of title such person shall deduce his title from the person last infeft in such heritable security or holding the last recorded title thereto:

(4) A person having such right to an unrecorded heritable security or part thereof contained in a deed the recording of which in the appropriate Register of Sasines on behalf of the original creditor would have infeft him therein and in the land out of which it is payable, or either of them, but which has not been so recorded, may complete a title thereto by recording in the appropriate Register of Sasines such heritable security, which shall be docqueted in manner prescribed in Note 7 to Schedule B to this Act, along with a notice of title in or as nearly as may be in the terms of Form No. 5 of that Schedule, or in the case of a ground-annual in or as nearly as may be in the terms of Form No. 6 of that Schedule, in which notice of title such person shall deduce his title from the original creditor in such heritable security.

And on such notice of title being recorded as in this section provided, the title of the person on whose behalf it is recorded shall be in all respects in the same position as if his title were completed as at the date of such recording by notarial instrument in the appropriate form duly expede and recorded according to the present law and practice.

NOTE

[1] See the Conveyancing Amendment (Scotland) Act 1938, s.1. Excluded by the Land Registration (Scotland) Act 1979, s.3(6).

Deduction of title

[1] **5.**—(1) In a deduction of title in terms of this Act it shall be competent to specify as a title or as a midcouple or link of title, any statute, conveyance, deed, instrument, decree or other writing whereby a right to land or to any estate or interest in or security over land is vested in or transmitted to any person, or in virtue of which a notarial instrument could be expede, or which could be used as a midcouple or link of title in expeding such instrument, or any minute of a meeting at which any person is appointed to any place or office, if such appointment involves a right to land or to an estate or interest in or security over land; and any copy of or excerpt from such minute of meeting certified as correct by the chairman of such meeting or other person duly authorised to sign such minute or to give extracts therefrom, or by any law agent or notary public, shall be prima facie evidence of the terms of such minute of meeting.

[2] (2)—(*a*) When the holder of a heritable security has died, whether infeft or uninfeft, or with or without a recorded title, and whether testate or intestate, any confirmation in favour of an executor of such deceased which includes such security shall of itself be a valid title to the debt thereby secured, and shall also be a warrant for such executor dealing with such debt and also with such security in terms of sections 3 and 7 of this Act, and also for completing a title to such security in terms of section 4 of this Act.

(*b*) For the purposes of this subsection, "conformation" shall include any probate or letters of administration or other grant of representation to moveable or personal estate of a deceased person issued—

(*a*) by any court in England and Wales or Northern Ireland and noting his domicile in England and Wales or in Northern Ireland, as the case may be, or

(*b*) by any court outwith the United Kingdom and sealed in Scotland under section 2 of the Colonial Probates Act 1892

and the confirmation thereby implied shall operate in favour of the person or the persons or the survivors or survivor of them to whom such probate, letters of administration or other grant of representation were granted; and "executor" shall include such person or persons; and such implied confirmation shall be deemed to include all heritable securities which belonged to the deceased.

(3)—(*a*) It shall be competent in any warrant, interlocutor or decree of court conferring a right to land or to a heritable security, or granting authority to complete a title thereto, and also in the application upon which such warrant, interlocutor or decree proceeds, to insert a deduction of title from the person last infeft or holding the last recorded title, and an extract of such warrant, interlocutor or decree shall be equivalent to a disposition of land or an assignation of a heritable security granted in terms of section 3 of this Act and on being recorded in the appropriate Register of Sasines shall have the same force and effect as such a disposition or assignation duly recorded in such register.

(*b*) Section 24 of the Titles to Land Consolidation (Scotland) Act 1868, and section 44 of the Conveyancing (Scotland) Act 1874, are hereby amended in accordance with the provisions of this subsection, and the procedure prescribed in section 44 of the said Act of 1874, as hereby amended, shall be competent irrespective of whether the trust title has or has not been duly completed and recorded, and shall be applicable to all judicial factors within the meaning of section 3 of the said Act of 1868, and both of such sections hereby amended shall apply to heritable securities, and such heritable security may be referred to in any warrant, interlocutor or decree, or in any application upon which the same proceeds, in the manner prescribed in the forms relative thereto, referred to in section 4 of this Act.

NOTES

[1] As amended by the Succession (Scotland) Act 1964, Sched. 3, and the Administration of Estates Act 1971, Sched. 1. Excluded by the Land Registration (Scotland) Act 1979, s. 15(3). See the Electricity Act 1989, Sched. 10, para. 6(1).

[2] See the Succession (Scotland) Act 1964, s. 15(1).

Notice of title equivalent to notarial instrument

6.—(1) A notice of title expede in terms of this Act shall be equivalent to a notarial instrument expede according to the present law and practice, and the provisions of section 146 of the Titles to Land Consolidation (Scotland) Act 1868, shall apply to such notice of title.

(2) [Repealed by the Finance Act 1985, Sched. 27, Pt. IX(2).]

7. [Repealed by the Conveyancing and Feudal Reform (Scotland) Act 1970, s. 48 and Sched. 11, Pt. II.]

Description by reference and short reference to deed bearing more than one date

[1] **8.**—(1) It shall be no objection to a description by reference to a particular description of land in accordance with section 61 of the Conveyancing (Scotland) Act 1874, that the description referred to contains a description by reference of a larger piece of land of which the land particularly described forms part, and Schedule O annexed to the said Act of 1874 is hereby repealed and Schedule D to this Act is substituted therefor: The provisions of this section shall be retrospective.

(2) From and after the commencement of this Act, where land in Scotland is held under and by virtue of a deed of entail registered in the Register of Sasines in which such land has been particularly described, it shall not be necessary in any proceedings for disentail of the whole or any part of such land, or in any instrument of disentail to be executed under the authority of the Court of Session, or in any instrument of disentail to which the authority of the Court of Session falls to be interponed in the course of such proceedings, to repeat the particular description of the land at length, but it shall be sufficient that such land shall be described by reference in the manner provided for by section 61 of the Conveyancing (Scotland) Act 1874.

(3) In specifying any writ recorded in any Register of Sasines, it shall be competent for the better identification of such writ, to state the number of the volume or book of the register in which, and of the folio on which, the same has been recorded; but it shall be no objection to the specification of any writ that such volume or book and folio or either of them are not stated or are mis-stated, provided that such specification is sufficient for the identification of such writ.

[2] (4) Where any deed, instrument, or writing bearing more than one date is for any purpose specified or referred to in any other deed, instrument, or writing, it shall be no objection to such specification or reference that only the first date is given with the addition of the words "and subsequent date" (or "dates").

[3] (5) Note 1 to Schedule D to this Act shall apply to a reference competently made to any deed for reservations, real burdens, conditions, provisions, limitations, obligations and stipulations affecting lands and to the

form of such references given in Schedule H of the Conveyancing (Scotland) Act 1874.

NOTES
[1] Excluded by the Land Registration (Scotland) Act 1979, s. 15(1).
[2] As amended by the Conveyancing Amendment (Scotland) Act 1938, s. 2(1)(*a*).
[3] Subs. (5) added by the Conveyancing Amendment (Scotland) Act 1938, s. 2(1)(*b*).

Amendment of law as to reference to conditions of title

9.—[1] (1) Notwithstanding any conditions or clauses affecting land, whether prohibitory, irritant, resolutive or otherwise, expressed in any deed, instrument, or writing relating to such land, whether dated before or after the commencement of this Act, it shall not be necessary in any deed, instrument, or writing by which any heritable security over such land is constituted, transmitted, or otherwise dealt with, to repeat or to refer to any such conditions or clauses: Provided that this subsection shall not apply to any disposition or other conveyance granted in virtue of any power of sale contained in a heritable security (including any disposition granted by a creditor to himself pursuant to section 8 of the Heritable Securities (Scotland) Act 1894, nor to any decree by which a security right is or may be converted into a right of property, and where in any heritable security, whether dated before or after the commencement of this Act, such conditions or clauses have not been repeated or referred to, any decree pronounced in connection with such security pursuant to the Heritable Securities (Scotland) Act 1894, and Schedule D to that Act, shall repeat or refer to such conditions or clauses, and the said Schedule D is hereby amended accordingly.

(2) It shall be no objection to any deed, instrument, or writing by which a heritable security was constituted, transmitted, or otherwise affected, although dated before the commencement of this Act, that the same neither contained nor referred to conditions or clauses affecting the security subjects, repetition of or reference to which was required by any deed or otherwise in accordance with the law as existing prior to the commencement of this Act.

[2] (3) When any conditions or clauses affecting land have been duly referred to in the title thereto of the proprietor for the time duly recorded in the appropriate Register of Sasines, whether before or after the commencement of this Act, it shall not be competent to object to such title on the ground that in any prior deed, instrument, or writing applicable to such land such conditions or clauses were neither repeated nor referred to.

[2] (4) In any case in which there has been or shall be an omission or failure in any deed, instrument, or writing applicable to land, and forming the title of the proprietor for the time, to repeat or refer to conditions or clauses affecting such land, it shall be competent for such proprietor to grant and to record in the appropriate Register of Sasines a deed of acknowledgment setting forth the omission or failure, and repeating or referring to the conditions or clauses, and thenceforth the deed, instrument, or writing as to which such omission or failure occurred shall be deemed to have duly contained or referred to such conditions or clauses. Such deed of acknowledgment may be in the form of Schedule E hereto, and may be founded on by all concerned, although the warrant of registration thereon shall be on behalf of the granter only.

NOTES
[1] Excluded (in part) by the Land Registration (Scotland) Act 1979, s. 15(2).
[2] Excluded by the Land Registration (Scotland) Act 1979, s. 15(2).

Warrants of registration

10.—(1) The forms of warrant of registration provided in Schedule F hereto and the notes to that Schedule shall be substituted for the forms of warrant of registration provided in Schedule F, No. 2, and Schedule H, Nos. 1 and 2, annexed to the Titles to Land Consolidation (Scotland) Act 1868, and in Schedule A, No. 3, annexed to the Land Registers (Scotland) Act 1868; and (except as after provided) it shall be sufficient to insert in the warrant of registration on any conveyance, deed, or writing, the name of the person on whose behalf it is to be recorded accompanied by the words " within named ", or such other words as will identify such person, provided that when a conveyance, deed, or writing is to be recorded on behalf of any person not mentioned therein, the designation of such person shall be inserted in such warrant.

(2) It shall not be competent to challenge the validity of any warrant of registration on any conveyance, deed, or writing recorded before the commencement of this Act, on the ground that the person in whose favour such warrant is conceived is not designed therein, or that the nature of his right is not stated therein, if such warrant, on being read as forming part of such conveyance, deed, or writing, shall identify such person as a person therein named and designed.

(3) When any conveyance, deed, or writing, whether recorded before or after the commencement of this Act, is in favour of two or more persons, or of trustees *ex officiis,* and contains a destination to the survivors of such persons, or to the successors of such trustees, all the qualities of such destination shall be presumed to be imported into a warrant of registration in their favour written or such conveyance, deed, or writing, and it shall not be necessary that such destination be inserted therein.

[1] (4) When an unrecorded disposition or unrecorded bond and disposition in security, or other unrecorded deed, decree or heritable security is to be recorded along with a notice of title, the same shall be so recorded in virtue of one warrant of registration in or as nearly as may be in, the terms indicated in Note 5 to the said Schedule F to this Act, which shall be written on such notice of title.

(5) Where any conveyance, deed, or writing, or an extract thereof, can be competently recorded in the General Register of Sasines for preservation and execution as well as for publication, and is so recorded, there shall be inserted in any extract to be issued of the same a warrant of execution in the short form provided for in the Schedule to the Writs Execution (Scotland) Act 1877 and execution may competently follow upon such extract in manner provided in section 3 of that Act.

(6) From and after the commencement of this Act it shall not be competent to give investiture ex propriis manibus.

(7) Section 141 of the Titles to Land Consolidation (Scotland) Act 1868, and section 12 of the Land Registers (Scotland) Act 1868, and sections 6 and 7 of the Writs Execution (Scotland) Act 1877, are hereby amended in accordance with the enactments of this section, and Schedule F, No. 2, and Schedule H annexed to the first-mentioned Act of 1868, and Schedule A, No. 3, and Schedule B annexed to the second-mentioned Act of 1868, are hereby repealed.

NOTE

[1] As amended by the Conveyancing and Feudal Reform (Scotland) Act 1970; Sched. 11.

Consolidation of superiority and property

11.—(1) Where a superior infeft has acquired the property or mid-superiority of land, or where the proprietor of the property or of the mid-superiority infeft therein has acquired the superiority, a minute in or as nearly as may be in the terms of Schedule G to this Act, written on the disposition whereby such property, mid-superiority, or superiority has been acquired, and recorded along with such disposition in the appropriate Register of Sasines, shall be held to consolidate the property, or the mid-superiority as the case may be, with the superiority, all to the same effect as a minute of consolidation executed in terms of section 6 of the Conveyancing (Scotland) Act 1874, and duly recorded.

(2) Where a superior infeft has acquired the property or mid-superiority of land, and the disposition in his favour contains a clause of resignation *ad perpetuam remanentiam*, the recording of such disposition in the appropriate Register of Sasines, whether before or after the commencement of this Act, shall be deemed to have had and shall have the effect of consolidating the property, or the mid-superiority as the case may be, with the superiority.

Abolition and commutation of grain, etc., feu-duties

[1] **12.**—(1) In feus granted after the commencement of this Act, the feu-duty shall be payable in sterling money, and it shall not be lawful to stipulate for a feu-duty payable in grain or other fungible, or the amount of which falls to be ascertained by reference to the price or value of grain or other fungible, or otherwise than from the expression of the amount thereof in sterling money in the feu contract or feu charter.

(2) In the case of feus granted before the commencement of this Act, in which the feu-duty, or part thereof, is payable in grain or other fungible, or the amount of which falls to be ascertained by reference to the price or value of grain or other fungible, or otherwise than from the expression of the amount thereof in sterling money in the feu contract or feu charter, it shall be competent for the superior and the proprietor of the land burdened by such feu-duty to agree as to the amount in sterling money representing the amount of such feu-duty, and to enter into an agreement, in or as nearly as may be in the terms of Schedule G annexed to the Conveyancing (Scotland) Act 1874, as the circumstances will admit, commuting such feu-duty into a specified annual amount of sterling money, and such agreement being duly recorded in the appropriate Register of Sasines shall be binding on the parties thereto, and their respective successors in title, and on heritable creditors and all other persons interested in the superiority and in the feu in all time thereafter.

(3) In the case of feus, such as are described in the immediately preceding subsection, the feu-duty payable from which shall not, before the 31st day of December, 1932 have been commuted into an annual feu-duty expressed in sterling money, the annual feu-duty thenceforth payable therefrom shall be a sum in sterling money representing the average annual value of the feu-duty actually paid, or payable, or delivered or deliverable, for the ten years from the 1st day of January 1923 to the 31st day of December 1932 inclusive. It shall thereafter be incumbent, on either the superior or the proprietor, on the demand of the other, to enter into an agreement in or as nearly as may be in the terms of the said Schedule G, specifying the commutation into sterling money of the feu-duty and to concur in recording the same in the appropriate Register of Sasines. Each party shall pay his own expenses of such agreement, and the amount of stamp duty and recording dues shall be paid equally. If either party shall fail when duly required to enter into such agreement, it shall be competent for either party to apply to the sheriff for a decree declaring the commuted value in sterling money of the feu-duty, and such decree, if and when pronounced, shall be recorded by the party obtaining such decree in the appropriate Register of Sasines. The expenses of such application and procedure thereon shall be in the discretion of the sheriff. Such agreement, or such decree, being duly recorded in the appropriate Register of Sasines, shall be binding on the parties thereto, and their respective successors in title, and on all persons interested in the superiority and in the feu in all time thereafter.

(4) In cases in which a feu-duty has been allocated by the superior or by an allocation binding on the superior, each part of the feu shall, for the

purposes of this section, be regarded as a separate feu. In all other cases in which a feu has been divided, then, after the 31st day of December 1932, the proprietor of any part thereof may exercise, as regards the whole feu, the whole powers conferred by this section, and the proceedings shall be as binding and effectual as if exercised by the whole proprietors, and the costs thereby incurred, as far as payable by the proprietors of the feu, shall be borne by such proprietors in proportions corresponding to their ultimate liability for feu-duty.

(5) The provisions of this section, and any procedure following thereon, shall not affect any liability for feu-duty, or any obligation of relief as regards feu-duty, and such liability and such obligations shall remain in force and be applicable to the feu-duty as commuted.

(6) The provisions of this section applicable to the commutation of feu-duty payable in grain or other fungible, or the amount of which is ascertainable by reference to the price or value of grain or other fungible, shall be applicable to dry multures as hereinafter defined, in like manner as if the person whose lands are subject to the payment of such dry multures were the feudal vassal in these lands holding of and immediately under the person entitled to exact such dry multures. For the purposes of this subsection, dry multures shall mean and include (*a*) compensation payable in respect of commutation pursuant to the Thirlage Act 1799 and (*b*) all multures and other dues and payments of a similar nature which are exigible irrespective of services rendered, provided that in either case such compensation or multures or dues or payments are payable in grain or other fungible, or that the amount thereof is ascertainable by reference to the price or value of grain or other fungible. Provided also, that in all future proceedings under the last-mentioned Act the compensation shall be fixed in sterling money.

(7) On the expiry of ten years from the commencement of this Act carriages and services such as are referred to in sections 20 and 21 of the Conveyancing (Scotland) Act 1874, and which shall not have been commuted in terms of those sections, shall cease to be exigible.

(8) All heirs of entail, liferenters, corporations, trustees, judicial factors, tutors, curators and other guardians, heritable creditors in possession, and other persons who are in actual receipt of the income of any estate of property or of superiority are, notwithstanding any limitations in their titles, hereby authorised, without any further sanction, to exercise all the powers conferred by this section.

NOTE

[1] Extended by the Local Government (Scotland) Act 1973, s. 228 (2).

Allocation of feu-duty

13. The allocation contained in a memorandum of allocation of feu-duty by a superior separate from the deed in favour of the proprietor, which is dated either before or after the commencement of this Act, shall on the memorandum being recorded in the appropriate Register of Sasines, be binding on heritable creditors and all others having interest. Provided always that such allocation shall not prejudice or affect the rights of existing heritable creditors who are not parties thereto. Any such memorandum dated after the commencement of this Act may be in or as nearly as may be in the form of Schedule H hereto.

Abolition of real warrandice

14.—(1) From and after the commencement of this Act, it shall not be competent to dispone lands in real warrandice of a conveyance of other lands, and such real warrandice shall not arise *ex lege* from any contract or agreement entered into after the commencement of this Act.

(2) [Repealed by the Conveyancing Amendment (Scotland) Act 1938, s. 3.]

Transmission of personal obligation

15.—(1) The personal obligation contained in any deed or writing whereby any heritable security is constituted shall not transmit in terms of section 47 of the Conveyancing (Scotland) Act 1874, against any person taking the estate by conveyance in the sense of that section dated after the commencement of this Act, unless such conveyance be signed by such person.

(2) After the commencement of this Act, summary diligence, in terms of the said section, shall not be competent against any obligant whose obligation is created by succession, gift or bequest, unless in cases in which there shall be an agreement to the transmission of such obligation executed by such obligant.

(3) An agreement for transmission of a personal obligation pursuant to the said section may be in terms of Form No. 2 of Schedule A to this Act, or in any other form sufficiently expressing such agreement.

16.–17. [Repealed by the Prescription and Limitation (Scotland) Act 1973, Sched. 5, Pt. I.]

Notarial execution

[1] **18.**—(1) Any deed, instrument or writing, granted after the commencement of this Act, whether relating to land or not, may, after having been read over to the granter, be validly executed on behalf of such granter if he, from any cause, permanent or temporary, is blind or unable to write, by a law agent or notary public, or a justice of the peace, or, as regards wills or other testamentary writings, by a parish minister acting in his own parish, or his assistant and successor so acting, subscribing the same in the presence of the granter and by his authority, all before two witnesses who have heard such deed, instrument or writing read over to the granter, and heard or seen such authority given, and a holograph docquet in the form of Schedule I hereto, or in any words to the like effect, shall precede the signature of such law agent or notary public or justice of the peace, or parish minister, or his assistant and successor.

(2) For the purposes of section 39 of the Conveyancing (Scotland) Act 1874, a deed executed on behalf of the granter or maker thereof in accordance with subsection (1) hereof shall be deemed to be a deed subscribed by such granter or maker.

NOTE

[1] Extended by the Church of Scotland (Property and Endowments) Amendment Act 1933, s. 13. Excluded from the provision in the Stock Transfer Act 1963, s. 1 (2), that a stock transfer need not be attested.

Applicability of forms prescribed by Act

19. The forms prescribed by this Act for the completion of the titles to and the conveyance, assignation, discharge or restriction of rights of property or fee in land or heritable securities shall respectively be applicable to all other rights in or over land or in or over a heritable security the title to which may according to the present law and practice be competently completed by the recording of such title in the appropriate Register of Sasines.

Ratification by married woman

20. It shall be no objection to any deed or writing, whether relating to land or not, granted or concurred in by a married woman before or after the commencement of this Act, that the same has not been judicially ratified by her.

21. [Repealed by the Succession (Scotland) Act 1964, s. 34 (2) and Sched. 3.]

Assimilation of law as regards legitim and jus relictae, **etc.**

22.—(1) In the case of any person dying after the commencement of this Act, the rules of law which determine what estate belonging to a deceased is subject to claims for legitim shall be applicable in determining what estate belonging to the deceased is subject to the claim for *jus relictae* or *jus relicti*: And the estates of all such persons shall be distributed on the footing that there shall no longer be any distinction between the description of estate subject to claims for legitim and the description of estate subject to claims for *jus relictae* and *jus relicti*.

(2) All debts which if due to any person dying after the commencement of this Act would, according to the present law and practice or in terms of this section, be subject to legitim and *jus relictae* or *jus relicti* shall, if due by the deceased or out of his or her estate, form, so far as the estate on which such debts are secured may be insufficient to meet the same, deductions from the deceased's moveable estate before ascertaining legitim and *jus relictae* or *jus relicti*.

Ground-annuals

0 **23.**—(1) Any ground-annual which appears in the appropriate Register of Sasines as a burden on the land out of which it is payable may be transferred in whole or in part by the creditor therein by an assignation in, or as nearly as may be in, the terms of Form No. 2 of Schedule K to this Act; and upon such assignation being recorded in the appropriate Register of Sasines it shall have the same force and effect as a duly recorded assignation or disposition and assignation in the form generally in use at the passing of this Act. Such assignation shall, unless otherwise expressed, imply:—

(*a*) That the same is granted in favour of the assignee, heritably and irredeemably, with a destination to his heirs and assignees whomsoever:

(*b*) That the ground-annual and duplications or other casual payments, if any, or (if such duplications or casual payments have been commuted into an additional ground-annual) thwe additional ground-annual thereby assigned, are to be uplifted and taken by the assignee furth of and from the land specified in such assignation as being the land out of which the same are payable, or furth of any part or portion of such land, and readiest rents, maills and duties of the same, in terms of the contract of ground-annual or other deed or memorandum of agreement constituting such ground-annual and such duplications and other casual payments, or additional ground-annual, if any, and at such terms or dates or periods and with such interest and penalties in case of non-payment at the due dates as are provided for in such contract of ground-annual or other deed, or in such memorandum of agreement:

(*c*) That there are also assigned the deed constituting such ground-annual and the memorandum of agreement, if any, by which the commutation of grassums, duplications or other casual payments has been effected, and the whole clauses and obligations therein contained so far as the cedent in such ass-ignation has right thereto and all diligence and execution competent to him thereon:

(*d*) That where the cedent can competently do so he dispones to the assignee the land out of which the ground-annual and the casual payments or additional ground-annuals, if any, are payable, with the parts and pertinents thereof, and his whole right, title and interest therein, but with and under any burdens and conditions affecting the same ranking prior to his right, and that in real security to the assignee of such ground-annual and others, and of the whole other payments or prestations, conditions, obligations and others incumbent on the obligant for such ground-annual and others:

(*e*) That where the cedent can competently do so he assigns to the assignee the rents, maills and duties of the land out of which the ground-annual is payable, and also the writs thereof, and the writs constituting the title to such ground-annual, all to the full extent of his own right therein.

(2) Such ground-annual may be effectually renounced and discharged, and the land out of which the same is payable disburdened of the same, in whole or in part, by a discharge in, or as nearly as may be in the terms of Form No. 4 of Schedule K to this Act duly recorded in the appropriate Register of Sasines.

(3) Such ground-annual may be restricted as regards any portion of the land out of which the same is payable by a deed of restriction in, or as nearly as may be in, the terms of Form No. 7 of Schedule K to this Act, and on such deed of restriction being recorded in the appropriate Register of Sasines, such ground-annual shall be restricted accordingly to the land out of which the same is payable, other than the land disburdened by such deed of restriction, which land thereby disburdened shall be released from the burden of such ground-annual.

(4) The Heritable Securities (Scotland) Act 1894, as modified by the Sheriff Courts (Scotland) Act 1907, and Acts amending the same shall apply to actions of maills and duties for the recovery of a ground-annual in cases in which according to the present law and practice an action of maills and duties is competent.

[1] (5) In the event of any ground-annual falling into arrear for two years together, the creditor holding a duly recorded title thereto shall be entitled to raise an action of adjudication against the proprietor of the land out of which the same is payable, and any other persons interested therein whose rights are postponed to that of the creditor in such ground-annnual, and in such action the creditor may set forth that the ground-annual is in arrear for two years, and may crave the court to adjudge and declare that such proprietor and other persons, if any, have by their failure to pay such arrears forfeited their srights in and to such land, and that such land, together with the rents, maills, and duties thereof current and unpaid at the date of such action, do from that date belong to the pursuer absolutely and the court may, after service on the proprietor and on the other persons interested, if any, and after such intimation and procedure as the court may think fit, grant such application and issue decree in the terms craved; and on such decree, which may be in or as nearly as may be in the terms of Form No. 8 of Schedule K to this Act, being pronounced, and an extract thereof in which the land shall be described at length or by reference, being recorded in the appropriate Register of Sasines, such land shall belong and pertain to the creditor in such ground-annual freed and disencumbered of all rights and burdens postponed to the ground-annual, and the right in and to such land of such proprietor and any other persons called as defenders to such action shall be extinguished.

[2] (6) Any action raised in virtue of the immediately preceding subsection of this section may be raised in the sheriff court, or where the ground-annual is not less in amount than £2·50 per annum, in the Court of Session.

NOTES

[0] See the Debtors (Scotland) Act 1987, s.15(1)(*b*) (*prosp.*).

[1] Applied by the War Damage to Land (Scotland) Act 1939, s.4(2).

[2] As read with the Decimal Currency Act 1969, s.10(1) and as amended by the Civil Jurisdiction and Judgments Act 1982, Sched. 14.

Registered leases. Assimilation of forms

[1] **24.** All enabling powers and rights which, by this Act, are conferred upon or implied in favour of a person in right of land or of a security over

land, including power of sale and other rights under a bond and disposition in security, shall, so far as applicable, be held as conferred upon a person who has right to a lease, or to a security over a lease respectively; and the forms prescribed by this Act may be used in connection with the constitution, transmission, restriction and discharge of securities over leases, and the completion of titles to leases and to securities over the same, and to sales thereof under such securities, and such forms shall have the same force and effect as the corresponding forms prescribed by the Registration of Leases (Scotland) Act 1857, and the clauses held as implied in any of the forms prescribed by this Act shall, so far as applicable, be held as implied when such forms are used in connection with leases and securities over the same: Provided that in applying this Act and relative schedules to leases and securities over the same the following modifications and such other verbal modifications as may be necessary shall be given effect to:—

(1) For " lands ", " lands and others ", or " subjects " there shall be substituted " lease ", for " conveyance " or " disposition " there shall be substituted " assignation ", for " bond and disposition in security " there shall be substituted " bond and assignation in security ", for " assignation of a bond and disposition in security " there shall be substituted " translation of a bond and assignation in security ", for " dispone " or " convey " there shall be substituted " assign ", for " proprietor " there shall be substituted " lessee ", for " disponee " there shall be substituted " assignee ", for " in-feft " there shall be substituted " having a recorded title ", for " superior " there shall be substituted " landlord ", and for " feu-duty " there shall be substituted " rent due to the landlord ":

[2] (2) In an assignation of a lease, or in a bond and assignation in security of a lease, or in a notice of title relating to a lease, there may be substituted for a description of the land a reference to such lease in or as nearly as may be in the terms of Schedule J to this Act:

(3) In the event of the lease, to which a title is being completed by notice of title under this Act, not having been recorded in the appropriate Register of Sasines, it shall be recorded therein along with such notice of title in which the lease shall be referred to in manner prescribed in Note 5 to Schedule J to this Act, and such lease, before being so recorded, shall be docqueted in manner prescribed in Note 7 to Schedule B to this Act, and, on the same being so recorded, it shall have the same force and effect as a recorded title under the Registration of Leases (Scotland) Act 1857, and Acts amending the same:

(4) [Repealed by the Succession (Scotland) Act 1964, Sched. 3.]

(5) A renunciation of a lease in terms of Schedule G to the Registration of Leases (Scotland) Act 1857, may competently be granted by a person not holding a recorded title to such lease, provided that he shall therein deduce his title from the person holding the last recorded title in manner prescribed in Note 4 to Schedule J to this Act, and on such renunciation being recorded in the appropriate Register of Sasines such lease shall be as effectually renounced as if the title of the granter of such renunciation had been completed as at the date of such recording by notarial instrument in the appropriate form duly expede and recorded according to the present law and practice, and section 13 of the said Act of 1857, and Schedule G annexed to that Act, are hereby amended accordingly:

(6) Section 24 of the Titles to Land Consolidation (Scotland) Act 1868, and section 44 of the Conveyancing (Scotland) Act 1874, as amended by section 5 of this Act, shall apply to a lease and to a security over a lease, and in the warrant, interlocutor or decree of court conferring a right to such lease or security over the same or granting authority to complete title thereto, and also in the application upon which such warrant, interlocutor or decree proceeds, such lease may be referred to in or as nearly as may be in the terms of Schedule J hereto:

(7) An adjudger or purchaser of a lease, or an adjudger or assignee of a security over a lease, may complete his title thereto by recording in the appropriate Register of Sasines an extract of the decree of adjudication or of sale (as the case may be) or may use such extract decree as an assignation or one of a series of assignations of an unrecorded lease or of an unrecorded security over a lease, and section 10 of the Registration of Leases (Scotland) Act 1857, is hereby amended accordingly.

NOTES

[1] As amended by the Conveyancing and Feudal Reform (Scotland) Act 1970, s. 48 and Sched. 11, Pt. II, and the Conveyancing (Amendment) (Scotland) Act 1938, s. 1; excluded by the Conveyancing and Feudal Reform (Scotland) Act 1970, s. 32 and Sched. 8, para. 25.

[2] Excluded by the Land Registration (Scotland) Act 1979, s. 15 (1).

Form of bond and disposition in security

[1] **25.**—(1) The import of the after-mentioned clauses of the Form No. 1 of Schedule FF annexed to the Titles to Land Consolidation (Scotland) Act 1868, occurring in any bond and disposition in security (whether granted before or after the commencement of this Act) shall from and after the commencement of this Act be as follows, *videlicet:*—

(*a*) The clause of assignation of rents shall be held to import an assignation to the creditor of the rents and other duties (including feu-duties and casualties in the case of a superiority, and ground-annuals and grassums in the case of a ground-annual) payable after the date from which interest on the principal sum in the security commences to run, irrespective of whether the terms of payment of such rents and others are the legal or the conventional terms, and including therein a power to the creditor to insure all buildings against loss by fire, but only for such sum as may be necessary to cover the creditor's interest therein, and to recover from the debtor the premiums paid for that purpose, and also on default in payment of principal or interest, or on the notour bankruptcy of the proprietor of the land conveyed in security or on his granting a trust deed for behoof of his creditors, to enter into possession of such land and to uplift the rents and other duties thereof, and to insure against loss by breakage of glass and against claims by tenants and third parties, and all such other incidental risks as a prudent proprietor would reasonably insure against, and to make all necessary renewals and repairs on the security subjects, including the roads, fences, ditches and drains, subject to accounting to the debtor for any balance of rents or other sums actually received beyond what is necessary for payment to such creditor of the principal and interest and penalty due to him, and of all expenses incurred by him in reference to such possession, including the expenses of factorage, management, insurance, renewals and repairs:

(*b*) The clause of assignation of writs shall be held to import an assignation to the creditor of writs and evidents, including searches, and all unrecorded and unfeudalised conveyances, with power to the creditor in the event of a sale under the powers of the bond, but subject to the rights of any person holding prior rights to possession of such writs and evidents, to deliver the same, so far as in the creditor's possession, to the purchaser, and to assign to the purchaser any right he may possess to have the writs and evidents made forthcoming:

(*c*) The clause reserving right of redemption shall be held to import a right to redeem the security, which may be exercised by the persons and in manner prescribed in this Act:

(*d*) The clause granting power of sale shall be held to import a right to the creditor in default of payment to exercise power of sale in the manner prescribed in this Act, and also power to the creditor, after there has been failure to comply with a demand for payment, and to the same extent as would have been competent to the debtor, to obtain an allocation of any feu-duty or ground-annual affecting the security subjects in such proportions and on such terms as to augmentation or otherwise as may be agreed upon between the superior or the holder of the ground-annual and the creditor, and the memorandum of such allocation of feu-duty may be endorsed on the deed or instrument or notice of title forming the infeftment of the debtor, or may be a separate memorandum in or as nearly as may be in the terms of Schedule H to this Act, but such allocation of feu-duty or ground-annual shall be without prejudice to the rights of other persons liable therefor.

(2) Such bond and disposition in security shall also import that the debtor shall be personally liable to the creditor in the whole expenses of the preparation and execution thereof, and of recording the same, and all reasonable expenses incurred by the creditor in calling up the same and realising or attempting to realise the subjects of security, and exercising the other powers conferred upon him.

(3) Section 119 of the said Act of 1868 is hereby amended in accordance with this section.

NOTE

[1] Excluded by the Conveyancing and Feudal Reform (Scotland) Act 1970, s. 32 and Sched. 8, para. 26.

Heritable creditors' remedies for recovery of feu-duties and ground-annuals

26. Where the security subjects in a bond and disposition in security, whether granted before or after the commencement of this Act, consist of or include one or more superiorities or one or more ground-annuals, the creditor, provided his title to the debt and security be complete and the debtor be in default in payment of principal or interest, may raise an action against the superior or person in right of the ground-annual, concluding for declarator that he has right to the feu-duties and casualties or ground-annuals and grassums payable to such superior or person, and may give notice by registered letter [1] signed by the creditor or his law agent of the raising of such action to the vassals or the proprietors of the land from which such ground-annuals are payable, and from and after the date when such notice is received by them they shall be interpelled from making payment of the feu-duties, including duplicands or other multiples thereof, and casualties or ground-annuals and grassums, or additional feu-duties or ground annuals constituted in lieu of such duplicands or other multiples, casualties and grassums, to the superior or person in right of the ground-annuals, and any payment thereafter made by them to such superior or person shall be of no effect in a question with the creditor in the event of his obtaining decree; and upon intimation of the decree obtained in such action to the vassals or proprietors of the land by registered letter [1] signed by the creditor or his law agent, they shall make payment to the creditor of the feu-duties including duplicands or other multiples thereof and casualties or ground-annuals and grassums, and failing their doing so the creditor shall be entitled to recover the same in the same manner and subject to the same defences on the part of the vassals or proprietors of the land as if he were the superior or person in right of the ground-annuals duly infeft, and subject to accounting therefor to the superior or person in right of the ground-annuals, and payment to the creditor shall be a complete exoneration and discharge to such vassals or proprietors; and the action and the notice thereof and the intimation of the decree may be in or as nearly as may be in the forms, with the necessary modifications, authorised by section 3 of the Heritable Securities (Scotland) Act 1894, and contained in Schedules A, B and C to that Act as modified by the Sheriff Courts (Scotland) Act 1907, and Acts amending the same: Provided that such action may be combined with an action for recovery of maills and duties and that nothing in this section contained shall deprive the creditor of any existing remedy competent to him for recovering such feu-duties, duplicands, multiples and casualties or ground-annuals and grassums.

NOTE

[1] Now also recorded delivery service: see the Recorded Delivery Service Act 1962, s. 1 and Sched.

Restriction of agent's lien

27. From and after the commencement of this Act it shall be incompetent for any law agent or notary public acting for the proprietor or creditors or others, whose rights in or over land conveyed in security are postponed to those of the creditor in such heritable security, to acquire over the writs and evidents as against such creditor any right of hypothec, lien or retention after the date of recording such heritable security.

Assignation of bond and disposition in security

[1] **28.** Any bond and disposition in security, whether dated before or after the commencement of this Act, duly recorded in the appropriate Register of Sasines, may be transferred, in whole or in part, by the creditor in right thereof by an assignation in or as nearly as may be in the terms of Form No. 1 of Schedule K to this Act, and upon such assignation being recorded in the appropriate Register of Sasines, it shall have the same force and effect as a duly recorded assignation granted in the form prescribed in section 124 of the Titles to Land Consolidation (Scotland) Act 1868. Such assignation shall, except so far as otherwise therein stated, be deemed to convey to the grantee all rights competent to the granter to the writs, and to the effect inter alia of vesting the assignee in the full benefit of all corroborative or substitutional obligations for the debt or any part thereof, whether contained in bonds or clause of corroboration or agreements *in gremio* of conveyances, or by operation of law or otherwise, and right to recover payment from the debtor of all expenses properly incurred by the creditor in connection with such security, and shall have the effect of entitling the grantee, or those deriving right from or through him, to the benefit of any notices which have been served calling up the security, and all procedure which may have followed thereon, to the effect that the grantee or those deriving right from or through him may proceed as if he or they had originally served or instituted the same.

NOTE

[1] Excluded by the Conveyancing and Feudal Reform (Scotland) Act 1970, s. 32 and Sched. 8, para. 27.

Discharge of bond and disposition in security

[1] **29.** Any bond and disposition in security, whether dated before or after the commencement of this Act, duly recorded in the appropriate Register of Sasines, may be effectually renounced and discharged and the land therein effectually disburdened of the same, in whole or in part, by a discharge in or as nearly as may be in the terms of Form No. 3 of Schedule K to this Act, duly recorded in the appropriate Register of Sasines.

NOTE

[1] Excluded by the Conveyancing and Feudal Reform (Scotland) Act 1970, s. 32 and Sched. 8, para. 27.

Restriction of bond and disposition in security

[1] **30.** The security constituted by any bond and disposition in security,

whether dated before or after the commencement of this Act, duly recorded in the appropriate Register of Sasines, may be restricted as regards any portion of the land thereby conveyed by a deed of restriction in or as nearly as may be in the terms of Form No. 5 of Schedule K to this Act, and, upon such deed of restriction being recorded in the appropriate Register of Sasines, the security shall be restricted to the land therein contained other than the land disburdened by such deed, and the land thereby disburdened shall be released from such security wholly, or to the extent specified in such deed of restriction. A partial discharge and deed of restriction of a bond and disposition in security may be combined in one deed, which may be in or as nearly as may be in the terms of Form No. 6 of the said Schedule K.

NOTE

[1] Excluded by the Conveyancing and Feudal Reform (Scotland) Act 1970, s. 32 and Sched. 8, para. 27.

Description of lands and deduction of title unnecessary in certain deeds relating to heritable securities

[1,2] **31.** In assignations and discharges, whether total or partial, granted in accordance with the provisions of sections 28 and 29 of this Act, a description of the land shall not be necessary, provided that the bond and disposition in security to which it relates is therein referred to in manner prescribed in Schedule K to this Act; and in such assignations and discharges, and in deeds of restriction granted in accordance with section 30 of this Act, it shall not be necessary to deduce the title of the granter if such granter holds or such deceasing creditor held a recorded title and the date is given of the recording of the same in the appropriate Register of Sasines in manner prescribed in Note 2 to Schedule K to this Act.

NOTES

[1] Excluded by the Conveyancing and Feudal Reform (Scotland) Act 1970, s. 32 and Sched. 8, para. 27.

[2] Repealed by the Succession (Scotland) Act 1964, s. 34 (2) and Sched. 3 so far as relating to writs of acknowledgment and to s. 125 of and Sched. (II) to the Titles to Land Consolidation (Scotland) Act 1868.

Redemption of bond and disposition in security. Notice and procedure and evidence of service

[1] **32.**—(1) A debtor in a bond and disposition in security, whether dated before or after the commencement of this Act, or the proprietor of the land disponed in security or part thereof shall be entitled to redeem the security at the place and at the date of payment or at any term of Whitsunday or Martinmas thereafter, on giving three months' premonition to the creditor, which premonition may be in or as nearly as may be in the terms of Form No. 1 of Schedule L to this Act, and may be delivered to the creditor or sent by registered post [2] to him at his last known address, and an acknowledgment signed by the creditor in or as nearly as may be in the terms of Form No. 2 of the said schedule, or a certificate in or as nearly as may be in the terms of Form No. 3 of the said schedule, accompanied (if the premonition has been posted) by the postal receipt, shall be sufficient evidence of such premonition, which, if posted, shall be held to have been given on the day next after the day of posting; and, if the address of the creditor is not known, or if the registered packet containing such premonition is returned to the debtor or proprietor, or his law agent, with intimation that the same could not be delivered, such premonition shall be sent to the Keeper of the Record of Edictal Citations, General Register House, Edinburgh, and shall be equivalent to premonition to the creditor, and an acknowledgment of receipt by the Keeper of the Record of Edictal Citations on a copy of such premonition shall be sufficient evidence thereof; and, at the term of payment mentioned in such premonition, and on payment of the principal sum secured, interest due thereon, and all expenses incurred by the creditor, as provided in section

25 of this Act, the creditor shall be bound to grant in favour of the debtor or proprietor, a valid discharge of such security; and where, on account of the death or absence of the creditor or from any other cause, the debtor or proprietor cannot obtain a discharge, it shall be competent to him to consign the amount due, including interest and expenses, if any, in the bank specified in the bond, if any bank shall be so specified, and, if not, in one or other of the banks in Scotland, incorporated by or under Act of Parliament or Royal Charter, to be made forthcoming to the creditor or his representatives, and thereupon a certificate may be expede by any agent, in, or as nearly as may be in, the terms of Form No. 4 of Schedule L to this Act, and the recording thereof in the appropriate Register of Sasines shall have the effect of completely disencumbering the land of such security as at the date of such consignation to the extent of the amount so consigned. For the purposes of this section the creditor shall be the person appearing on the record as holding the last recorded title to the bond and disposition in security to be redeemed, or if such person be dead, the executor or reputed substitute or person entitled to succeed thereto in terms of the bond or any recorded transmission thereof, notwithstanding any alteration of the succession not appearing on the Register of Sasines.

(2) The stamp duty chargeable on any such certificate granted by a law agent shall be the same as if it were granted by a notary public.

NOTES

[1] As amended by the Succession (Scotland) Act 1964, s. 34 (2) and Scheds. 2 and 3; excluded by the Conveyancing and Feudal Reform (Scotland) Act 1970, s. 32 and Sched. 8, para. 29. Functions of Keeper of Record of Edictal Citations now exercisable by officers of the Court of Session: see the Reorganisation of Offices (Scotland) Act 1928, s. 8 and the Public Records (Scotland) Act 1937, s. 13.

[2] Now also recorded delivery service: see the Recorded Delivery Service Act 1962, s. 1 and Sched.

Notice calling up bond and disposition in security

[1] **33.** Without prejudice to his rights and remedies under the personal obligation the creditor in a bond and disposition in security, or any part thereof, whether dated before or after the commencement of this Act, may serve a notice calling up the same in or as nearly as may be in the terms of Form No. 1 of Schedule M to this Act. Such notice shall be given to the person infeft in the land disponed in security and appearing on the record as the proprietor, or if the person last infeft in the land or any part thereof be dead, then to the executor or reputed substitute or person entitled to succeed to the same in terms of the last recorded title thereto, notwithstanding any alteration of the succession not appearing on the Register of Sasines. If the last proprietor was an incorporated company which has been removed from the Register of Joint Stock Companies or a person deceased who has left no heirs or whose heirs are unknown, notice shall be given to the Lord Advocate. Where the estates of the debtor have been sequestrated under the Bankruptcy (Scotland) Act 1913, or any Act thereby repealed, notice shall be given to the trustee in the sequestration (unless such trustee has been discharged) as well as to the bankrupt. If the proprietor be a body of trustees, it shall be sufficient if the notice is given to a majority of the trustees infeft in the land. There shall be no obligation on the creditor to give notice to any other person unless for the purpose of preserving recourse against such other person. Notice under this section shall cease to be effective for the purposes of a sale under the powers of a bond and disposition in security after a period of five years from the date of such notice if no exposure to sale of the land or any part thereof has followed thereon, or otherwise after five

years from the date of the last exposure to sale of the land or part thereof following on such notice.

NOTE

[1] As amended by the Succession (Scotland) Act 1964, s. 34 (1) and Sched. 2: excluded by the Conveyancing and Feudal Reform (Scotland) Act 1970, s. 32 and Sched. 8, para. 30; see also s. 33 (1).

Service of notice

[1] **34.** Notice under the immediately preceding section may be delivered to the person to whom it is desired to be given or sent by registered post[2] to him at his last known address, or in the case of the Lord Advocate at the Crown Office, Edinburgh, and an acknowledgment signed by such person in or as nearly as may be in the terms of Form No. 2 of Schedule M to this Act, or a certificate in or as nearly as may be in the terms of Form No. 3 of that schedule, accompanied (if the notice has been posted) by the postal receipt, shall be sufficient evidence of the service of such notice, and if the address of the person to whom such notice is desired to be given is not known, or if it is not known whether such a person is still alive, or if the registered packet, containing such notice, is returned to the creditor or his law agent, with an intimation that the same could not be delivered, such notice shall be sent to the Keeper of the Record of Edictal Citations, General Register House, Edinburgh, and shall be equivalent to notice to such person, and an acknowledgment of receipt by the Keeper of the Record of Edictal Citations, on a copy of such notice, shall be sufficient evidence thereof. Such notice shall be deemed to be formal requisition for all purposes, including the purposes of the Heritable Securities (Scotland) Act 1894; and if posted shall be held to be given on the next day after the day of posting.

NOTES

[1] As amended by the Conveyancing and Feudal Reform (Scotland) Act 1970, s. 34: excluded by s. 32 and Sched. 8, para. 30 of that Act. See note 1 to s. 32 *supra*, as to Keeper of the Record of Edictal Citations.

[2] Now also recorded delivery service: see the Recorded Delivery Service Act 1962, s. 1 and Sched.

Power to dispense with or shorten inducaie

35. It shall be competent to the person to whom such notice has been given, with the consent of the creditors, if any, holding securities ranking pari passu with or postponed to the security held by the creditor giving notice, to dispense with the whole or part of the period of notice by a minute written upon the said notice or upon a copy thereof, in or as nearly as may be in the terms of Form No. 2 of Schedule M to this Act.

Advertisement

36. After the expiry of three months from the date of giving such notice, or the expiry of such shorter period as may have been agreed to under the immediately preceding section, the creditor, failing payment of the whole sums to which he is entitled, may advertise the land or any part thereof for sale by public roup.

Contents of advertisement

37. Such advertisement shall specify shortly the land to be sold, and the day, hour, and place of sale, and the upset price or prices, and it shall not be necessary to state that the sale is proceeding under the powers contained in a bond and disposition in security.

Periods during which, and newspapers in which, advertisement required

[1] **38.**—(1) An advertisement for the purposes of an exposure to sale shall

be inserted at least once weekly during a period of not less than three consecutive weeks in accordance with the provisions of this section, and the exposure to sale so advertised shall take place within a period of 14 days beginning with the day following the day of the publication of the third advertisement required under this subsection.

(2) An advertisement for the purposes of an offer for sale by private bargain shall be inserted in like manner during a period of not less than two consecutive weeks, and it shall be a requirement of a competent sale that an enforceable contract to sell shall be concluded within a period of 28 days beginning with the day following the day of the publication of the second advertisement required under this subsection.

(3) Insertion of an advertisement for the purposes of the two foregoing subsections shall be as follows, that is to say–

(*a*) in the case of land situated in the county of Midlothian, in at least one daily newspaper published in Edinburgh;

(*b*) in the case of land situated in the county of Lanark, in at least one daily newspaper published in Glasgow;

(*c*) in the case of land situated elsewhere in Scotland, in at least one daily newspaper published in Scotland circulating in the district where the land or the main part thereof is situated and in at least one newspaper (if any) circulating as aforesaid and published either in the county in which the land, or any part thereof, is situated or in a county (being a county in Scotland) adjacent to that county.

(4) A copy of an advertisement required by this section shall, when supported by a certificate of publication by the publisher, printer, or editor of the newspaper in which that advertisement is inserted, be sufficient evidence of the insertion and publication thereof.

(5) For the purposes of this section–

(*a*) a week means the period between midnight on Saturday night and midnight on the succeeding Saturday night, and

(*b*) " exposure to sale " and " offer for sale " respectively include re-exposure to sale and re-offer for sale.

NOTE

[1] As substituted by the Conveyancing and Feudal Reform (Scotland) Act 1970, s. 36. Excluded by that Act, s. 32 and Sched. 8, para. 30.

Where exposure to sale to take place

[1] **39.** Any exposure to sale may take place in Edinburgh or Glasgow, or at any burgh within the meaning of the Town Councils (Scotland) Acts 1900 to 1923, which is situated within the county in which the land, or the chief part thereof, lies, or which is nearest to such land, or the chief part thereof, whether within the same county or not.

NOTE

[1] Excluded by the Conveyancing and Feudal Reform (Scotland) Act 1970, s. 32 and Sched. 8, para. 30.

Exposure in lots and apportionment of feu-duty

40.—[1] (1) The land, or any part thereof, may be exposed to, or offered for, sale either in whole or in lots, and in the former case at such upset price or prices as the creditor may think proper, and in the latter case at the best price that can be reasonably obtained, subject to such proportion of any existing feu-duty, ground-annual, stipend, valued rent or land tax, as the creditor may think proper, and, without prejudice to the rights of any third party, the creditor may, in selling the land in lots, provide that the proprietor for the time being of any lot shall be obliged to relieve the proprietor or proprietors of another lot or lots of the whole or such part of an existing feu-duty and casualties, ground-annual, stipend or land tax, as the creditor may think proper, and for that purpose the creditor may create such obligation a real burden on such lot.

[2] (2) Where there is a sale as aforesaid in lots, the creditor shall have power to create such rights and impose such duties and conditions as he considers may be reasonably required for the proper management, maintenance and use of any part of the land to be held in common by the owners for the time being of the lots.

[2] (3) For the purpose of exercising the power conferred by the last foregoing subsection, a creditor shall have the like right as has a proprietor by virtue of section 32 of the Conveyancing (Scotland) Act 1874 to execute and record to the like effect a deed of declaration of conditions in the manner prescribed by that section.

NOTES

[1] As amended by the Conveyancing and Feudal Reform (Scotland) Act 1970, s. 37.

[2] Added by the Conveyancing and Feudal Reform (Scotland) Act 1970, s. 37.

Purchasers protected

41.—[0] (1) All proceedings under sections 32 to 40, inclusive, of this Act shall be valid and effectual notwithstanding that any person to whom premonition or notice requires to be given in terms of this Act may be subject to any legal disability by reason of nonage or otherwise, and any sale and disposition in implement thereof shall be as valid to the purchaser as if made by the proprietor of the land not being under disability, and any such disposition shall import an assignation to the purchaser of the warrandice contained or implied in the bond and disposition in security under which the land is sold, and also an obligation by the granter of the security to ratify, approve and confirm the sale and disposition.

[1] (2) Where a disposition of land is duly recorded in the appropriate Register of Sasines and that disposition bears to be granted in the exercise of a power of sale contained in a deed granting a bond and disposition in security, and the exercise of that power was *ex facie* regular, the title of a *bona fide* purchaser of the land for value shall not be challengeable on the ground that the debt had ceased to exist, unless that fact appeared in the said Register, or was known to the purchaser prior to the payment of the price, or on the ground of any irregularity relating to the sale or in any preliminary procedure thereto; but nothing in the provisions of this subsection shall affect the competency of any claim for damages in respect of the sale of land against the person exercising the said power.

NOTES

[0] As amended by the Age of Legal Capacity (Scotland) Act 1991, Sched. 1, para. 26.

[1] Substituted by the Conveyancing and Feudal Reform (Scotland) Act 1970, s. 38; but in relation to a disposition duly recorded before the commencement of this Act, the said subsection shall continue to have effect as originally enacted.

Mode of disburdening land sold under power of sale in heritable security

[1] **42.**—(1) Where land is sold by a heritable creditor under the powers competent to creditors in heritable securities, and no surplus of the price remains for consignation in terms of section 122 of the Titles to Land Consolidation (Scotland) Act 1868, or where such surplus remains and the same has been consigned in bank in terms of the said section 122, it shall be competent to any law agent or notary public to execute a certificate to the effect that no surplus remains where such is the case, or where such surplus remains and has been so consigned in bank, to the effect that such consignation has taken place, which certificate shall be in or as nearly as may be in the terms of Schedule N to this Act, and the disposition by the creditor to the purchaser shall, along with such certificate, when recorded in the appropriate Register of Sasines, have the effect of completely disencum-

bering the land sold of all securities and diligences posterior to the security of such creditor, as well as of the security and diligence of such creditor himself, save and except when the security and diligence of such creditor and any prior securities and diligences shall be assigned by way of further or collateral security to the purchaser.

(2) [Repealed by the Finance Act 1985, Sched. 27, Pt. IX(2).]

NOTE

[1] Excluded by the Conveyancing and Feudal Reform (Scotland) Act 1970, s. 32 and Sched. 8, para. 31.

Act to apply to all heritable securities

43. The forms provided by this Act relative to bonds and dispositions in security or transactions incidental thereto, shall except as in this Act otherwise expressly provided apply, as nearly as may be, to all heritable securities, whether granted before or after the commencement of this Act, and deeds transmitting, discharging and restricting the same, and all notices of title completing a title thereto, except in so far as such provisions, enactments or forms may be inapplicable to the form or objects of such securities, and nothing in this Act contained shall prejudice or restrict the powers, rights, privileges and immunities of creditors in heritable securities, or of those deriving right from them, according to the present law and practice.

General Register of Inhibitions and Register of Adjudications to be combined; limitation of effect of entries therein

44.—(1) The General Register of Inhibitions and Interdictions and the Register of Adjudications shall be combined, and the Keeper thereof shall keep only one register for inhibitions, interdictions, adjudications, reductions, and notices of litigiosity, and such register shall be called the Register of Inhibitions and Adjudications; and a reference in any public, general or local Act to the General Register of Inhibitions or the Register of Adjudications shall be deemed to mean and include such Register of Inhibitions and Adjudications.

[1] (2)(*a*) No action whether raised before or after the commencement of this Act relating to land or to a lease or to a heritable security, shall be deemed to have had or shall have the effect of making such land, lease or heritable security litigious, unless and until—

(i) a notice relative to such action in or as nearly as may be in the form of Schedule (RR) annexed to the Titles to Land Consolidation (Scotland) Act 1868, shall have been or shall be registered in the Register of Inhibitions and Adjudications in the manner provided by section 159 of that Act; or

(ii) a notice of an application under section 8 of the Law Reform (Miscellaneous Provisions) (Scotland) Act 1985 has been registered in the said register.

(*b*) No decree in any action of adjudication of land or of a lease of a heritable security, whether pronounced before or after the commencement of this Act, and no abbreviate of any such decree shall be deemed to have had or to have any effect in making such land, lease or heritable security litigious.

[1] (3)(*a*) All inhibitions and all notices of litigiosity registered in terms of section 159 of the Titles to Land Consolidation (Scotland) Act 1868, subsisting at the commencement of this Act shall prescribe and be of no effect on the lapse of five years after such commencement or at such earlier date as they would prescribe according to the present law and practice; and all inhibitions, notices of litigiosity and notices of applications under section 8 of the Law Reform (Miscellaneous Provisions) (Scotland) Act 1985 which

relate to land or to a lease or to a heritable security and which shall be first registered after the commencement of this Act, shall prescribe and be of no effect on the lapse of five years from the date on which the same shall respectively take effect: Provided that in no case shall litigiosity be pleadable or be founded on to any effect after the expiry of six months from and after final decree is pronounced in the action creating such litigiosity.

(*b*) From and after the commencement of this Act interdiction, whether judicial or voluntary, shall be incompetent, and any interdiction which is legally operative at such commencement shall remain legally operative for not longer than the period of five years thereafter.

(4)(*a*) and (*b*) [Repealed by the Bankruptcy (Scotland) Act 1985, Sched. 8, with effect from 1st April 1986.]

[1] (*c*) No deed, decree, instrument or writing granted or expede by a person whose estates have been sequestrated under the Bankruptcy (Scotland) Act 1856, or the Bankruptcy (Scotland) Act 1913 or the Bankruptcy (Scotland) Act 1985, or the heirs, executors, successors or assignees of such person relative to any land or lease or heritable security belonging to such person at the date of such sequestration or subsequently acquired by him shall be challengeable or denied effect on the ground of such sequestration if such deed, decree, instrument or writing shall have been granted or expede, or shall come into operation at a date when the effect of recording (*a*) the abbreviate provided for under section 44 of the said Act of 1913, as amended by this Act, shall have expired in terms of the said section as amended as aforesaid; or (*b*) under subsection (1)(*a*) of section 14 of the Bankruptcy (Scotland) Act 1985 the certified copy of an order shall have expired by virtue of subsection (3) of that section, unless the trustee in such sequestration shall before the recording of such deed, decree, instrument or writing in the appropriate Register of Sasines have completed his title to such land, lease or heritable security by recording the same in such register or have recorded a memorandum in such register in the form provided by Schedule O to this Act: Provided always, in the case of sequestrations awarded under the Bankruptcy (Scotland) Act 1856, that the provisions of this section shall not apply to any deed, decree, instrument or writing dated within five years after the commencement of this Act.

(5) The provisions of this section shall not affect the ranking of adjudgers inter se, or any real right obtained in virtue of a decree of adjudication, or in virtue of a decree pronounced in an action creating litigiosity, or by a trustee in bankruptcy, if such right has been completed by the recording in the appropriate Register of Sasines of any deed, decree, abbreviate, or instrument necessary to effect the completion of such right.

[2] (6) Section 159 of the Titles to Land Consolidation (Scotland) Act 1868, and sections 16 and 17 of the Land Registers (Scotland) Act 1868, are hereby amended in accordance with this section, and section 42 of the Conveyancing (Scotland) Act 1874, and Schedule J thereto annexed, are hereby repealed.

NOTES

[0] As amended by the Law Reform (Miscellaneous Provisions) (Scotland) Act 1985, Sched. 2, para. 6, with effect from 30th December 1985.

[1] As amended by the Conveyancing Amendment (Scotland) Act 1938, s. 7(1)(*a*) and by the Bankruptcy (Scotland) Act 1985, Sched. 7, para. 5, with effect from 1st April 1986.

[2] As amended by the Bankruptcy (Scotland) Act 1985, Sched. 8, with effect from 1st April 1986.

Provision for termination of perpetual trusts of moveables

45. In any case where the provisions of section 9 of the Trusts (Scotland) Act 1921, would apply to any deed, and to the right of any party thereunder if such deed had been dated after the 31st day of July 1868, the provisions of the said section shall, from and after the passing of this Act, apply to such deed and to the right of any party thereunder notwithstanding that the same be dated on or prior to the said 31st day of July 1868.

Provided that, in the application of the said provisions to the deeds to which this section refers and to the right of any party thereunder, the date of such deeds shall be deemed to be the date of the passing of this Act.

Extract decree of reduction to be recorded

[1,2] **46.**—(1) In the case of the reduction of a deed, decree or instrument recorded in the Register of Sasines or forming a midcouple or link of title in a title recorded in the said register there shall be recorded in the said register either an extract of the decree of reduction of such deed, decree or instrument, or a title in which such extract decree forms a midcouple or link of title, and such decree of reduction shall not be pleadable against a third party who shall in *bona fide* onerously acquire right to the land, lease or heritable security contained in the deed, decree, or instrument reduced by such decree of reduction prior to an extract of such decree of reduction, or a title, in which it forms a midcouple or link of title, being recorded in the Register of Sasines.

(2) This section shall apply to the rectification of a document by an order under section 8 of the Law Reform (Miscellaneous Provisions) (Scotland) Act 1985 as it applies to the reduction of a deed but with the substitution of any reference to the decree of reduction of the deed with a reference to the order rectifying the document.

NOTES

[1] See the Conveyancing and Feudal Reform (Scotland) Act 1970, s. 41(2).

[2] As amended by the Law Reform (Miscellaneous Provisions) (Scotland) Act 1985, Sched. 2, para. 7, with effect from 30th December 1985.

Re-recording of deeds, relative to leasehold subjects

47. Where in terms of the Registration of Leases (Scotland) Act 1857, or of section 24 of this Act, any deed or extract shall have been recorded in the appropriate Register of Sasines, and where in terms of that Act or of the said section any such deed or extract shall fall to be recorded again, or where any extract from a competent register of any deed the principal of which has: already been recorded in the appropriate Register of Sasines falls to be so recorded, it shall not be necessary for the keeper of the Register of Sasines in which such deed or extract falls to be recorded, or in which such extract of any recorded deed falls to be recorded, to engross such deed or extract in the register at length, but the keeper of such Register of Sasines may in place of such engrossment enter in the register a short memorandum specifying the deed or extract and the book and folio in which the same is already engrossed, and in the case of an extract of a deed the principal of which has already been recorded in the appropriate Register of Sasines the book and folio in which the principal is already engrossed, and such memorandum shall have the same effect as if the deed or extract were engrossed in the register at length in place of such memorandum.

Duplicate plans may be retained with Register

48. Where any writ which refers to a plan signed as relative thereto is presented or transmitted by post for registration in the General Register of Sasines it shall be competent to ingive to the said register along therewith a duplicate of such plan, docqueted with reference to the said writ and authenticated in the same manner as the principal plan, and such duplicate plan shall be retained in the said register. The ingiving of such duplicate plan shall be noted in the register, and acknowledgment of the receipt thereof shall be marked by the keeper of the register on the plan signed as relative to the writ.

Along with each register volume transmitted to the Keeper of the

Records for custody there shall be sent the duplicate plans, if any, relative to any of the writs engrossed in such volume.

Such duplicate plans when transmitted to the Keeper of the Records shall remain in his custody, subject to the same rights on the part of the public to have access thereto as apply to the Record Volumes.

Saving clause

49.—(1) Nothing in this Act contained shall affect any action now in dependence or that shall be instituted before the commencement of this Act, or shall prevent the constitution, transmission, completion, or extinction of land rights or securities affecting land in the forms which were in use for these purposes prior to the passing of this Act, except in so far as such prior forms are hereby expressly repealed.

(2) Nothing in this Act contained shall affect the preparation of the printed minutes and printed indexes of persons and places applicable to each county in Scotland, and the Keeper of the General Register of Sasines shall supply as full information in the printed minute books as hitherto according to the existing law and practice.

SCHEDULES

SCHEDULE A

Section 3

[1] FORM No. 1

NOTE

[1] Excluded by the Land Registration (Scotland) Act 1979, s. 15 (3).

CLAUSE OF DEDUCTION OF TITLE IN A DISPOSITION OF LAND WHERE THE GRANTER IS NOT INFEFT

[To be inserted immediately after the clause specifying the date or term of entry or after the dispositive clause where no date or term of entry is specified.]

Which lands and others (*or* subjects) were last vested [*or* are part of the lands and others (*or* subjects) last vested] in *A.B.* (*designation of person last infeft*), whose title thereto is recorded in (*specify Register of Sasines and date of recording or if the last infeftment has already been mentioned say* in the said *A.B.* as aforesaid), and from whom I acquired right by (*here specify shortly the writ or series of writs by which right was so acquired*).

Note. If any conditions, reservations, provisions, obligations, servitudes or other burdens which affect the land or any part thereof or qualify the granter's right thereto be contained in or imposed by the writ or any of the writs by which the granter acquired right and are proper to be inserted, insert the same at length in the dispositive clause, and if they affect only part of the land specify the part or parts of the land affected thereby, and in case of money burdens specify the amounts thereof and the name and designation or designative description of the creditor therein, all as in the writ containing or imposing such money burdens, and in all cases specify the writ or writs containing or imposing such conditions and others.

Section 15

FORM No. 2

CLAUSE TRANSMITTING PERSONAL OBLIGATION IN A Heritable SECURITY IN A DISPOSITION OF LAND

I, *A.B.* (*designation*), in consideration of (*specify any part of price paid in money*) and in consideration also of *C.D.* (*designation*) undertaking as by his signature hereto he undertakes the personal obligation contained in a bond and disposition in security for the sum of (*insert amount*) granted by me [*or* by *E.F.* (*original debtor*)] in favour of *G.H.* (*original creditor*), dated (*insert date*), and recorded in (*specify Register of Sasines and date of recording*) do hereby dispone, etc.

SCHEDULE B

NOTICE OF TITLE

Section 4 (1)

FORM NO. 1

ON BEHALF OF A PERSON WHO HAS RIGHT TO LAND BY A TITLE WHICH HAS NOT BEEN RECORDED IN THE APPROPRIATE REGISTER OF SASINES AND WHICH IS NOT TO BE RECORDED ALONG WITH THE NOTICE OF TITLE

Be it known that *A.B.* (*designation*) has right as proprietor (*or* life-renter *or* proprietor in trust *or otherwise, as the case may be*) to all and whole [*here describe the land or refer to description thereof as in Schedule D to this Act or as in Schedule G to the Titles to Land Consolidation (Scotland) Act*, 1868; *and if there are any conditions, reservations, provisions, obligations, servitudes, or other burdens which affect the land or any part thereof and have entered the record and are proper to be inserted or referred to, here insert the same at length or refer thereto as in Schedule H to the Conveyancing (Scotland) Act*, 1874, *and if any such conditions and others which affect the land or any part thereof or qualify A.B.'s right thereto be contained in or imposed by the writ or any of the writs by which A.B. acquired right and are proper to be inserted, here insert the same at length, and if they affect only part of the land specify the part or parts of the land affected thereby, and in case of money burdens specify the amount thereof and the name and designation or designative description of the creditor therein all as in the writ containing or imposing such money burdens, and in all cases specify the writ or writs containing or imposing such conditions and others*]; Which lands and others (*or* subjects) were last vested [*or* are part of the lands and others (*or* subjects) last vested] in *C.D.* (*design person last infeft*), whose title thereto was recorded in (*specify Register of Sasines and date of recording, or if the last infefiment has already been mentioned say* in the said *C.D.* as aforesaid), and from whom the said *A.B.* acquired right by (*here specify shortly the writ or series of writs by which he acquired right*): Which last recorded title and subsequent writ (*or* writs) have been presented to me, *Y.Z.* (*designation*), Notary Public (*or* Law Agent).

[To be attested.] *Y.Z.*

Section 4 (2)

FORM NO. 2

ON BEHALF OF A PERSON WHO HAS RIGHT TO LAND CONVEYED BY AN UNRECORDED SPECIAL CONVEYANCE WHICH IS TO BE RECORDED ALONG WITH THE NOTICE OF TITLE

Be it known that *A.B.* (*designation*) has right as proprietor (*or* life-renter *or* proprietor in trust *or otherwise, as the case may be*) to all and whole the lands and others (*or* subjects) disponed by (*or* contained in) the disposition (*or feu charter or other special conveyance*) granted by *C.D.* (*designation*) in favour of *E.F.* (*designation*) dated (*insert date*), and recorded in (*specify Register of Sasines*) of even date herewith [*if any conditions, reservations, provisions, obligations, servitudes or other burdens affecting the land or any part thereof or qualifying A.B.'s right thereto be contained in or imposed by the writ or any of the writs by which A.B. acquired right other than such special conveyance and are proper to be inserted, here insert the same at length, and if they affect only part of the land specify the part or parts of the land affected thereby, and in case of money burdens specify the amount thereof and the name and designation or designative description of the creditor therein, all as in the writ containing or imposing such money burdens, and in all cases specify the writ or writs containing or imposing such conditions and others*]; To which lands and others (*or* subjects) the said *A.B.* acquired right by the foresaid disposition (*or as the case may be*) and by (*here specify shortly the subsequent writ or series of writs by which he acquired right*); Which disposition and subsequent writ (*or* writs) have been presented to me (*as in Form No. 1 of this Schedule*).

[To be attested.]

Section 4 (3)

FORM NO. 3

ON BEHALF OF A PERSON WHO HAS RIGHT TO A RECORDED HERITABLE SECURITY BY A TITLE WHICH HAS NOT BEEN RECORDED IN THE APPROPRIATE REGISTER OF SASINES AND WHICH IS NOT TO BE RECORDED ALONG WITH THE NOTICE OF TITLE

Be it known that *A.B.* (*designation*) has right (*adding if such be the case* to the extent after-mentioned) to a bond and disposition in security (*or as the case may be*) for the sum of (*insert amount*) granted by *C.D.* (*design original debtor*) in favour of *E.F.* (*design original *creditor*), dated (*insert date*) and recorded in [*specify Register of Sasines and date of recording; adding, if necessary*, but only to the extent of (*insert sum*) of principal]: Which bond and disposition in security was last vested in the said *E.F.* as aforesaid [*or if E.F. is not the person last infeft therein, or holding the last recorded title thereto, say*, Which bond and disposition in security (*adding, if necessary*, to the extent foresaid *or as the case may be*) was last vested in *G.H.* (*design person holding the last recorded title thereto*), whose title thereto was recorded in said Register of Sasines (*or as the case may be, and give date of recording*)], and from whom the said *A.B.* acquired right (*adding, if necessary*, to the extent foresaid, *or as the case may be*), by (*here specify shortly the writ or series of writs by which he acquired right*); Which last recorded title and subsequent writ (*or* writs) have been presented to me (*as in Form No. 1 of this Schedule*).

[To be attested.]

Section 4 (3) FORM No. 4

ON BEHALF OF A PERSON WHO HAS RIGHT TO A GROUND ANNUAL WHICH HAS APPEARED IN THE APPROPRIATE REGISTER OF SASINES BY A TITLE WHICH HAS NOT BEEN RECORDED THEREIN, AND WHICH IS NOT TO BE RECORDED ALONG WITH THE NOTICE OF TITLE

Be it known that *A.B.* (*designation*) has right (*adding if such be the case* to the extent after-mentioned) to the ground annual of (*insert amount*) exigible yearly at (*state term or date of payment*) in each year [*or* in equal portions half-yearly at (*state terms or dates of payment*) in each year *or otherwise as the case may be; and if there be any duplications or other casual payments add*, with duplication every nineteenth year, *or otherwise as the case may be*, from and after (*state the term or date from which the current duplication or other casual payment is running*)] constituted by a contract of ground annual (*or other deed by which the ground annual was constituted, giving the names and designations of the parties thereto or of the granter and grantee*) recorded in [*specify Register of Sasines and date of recording; and if any duplications or other casual payments have been redeemed and commuted into an additional annual payment say* and also to the additional ground annual of (*insert sum*) exigible at the same term (*or* date) in each year (*or as the case may be*) in lieu and commutation of casual payments; *adding if necessary* but only to the extent of (*insert sum or respective sums*)] payable out of All and Whole (*here describe the land or refer to description thereof as in Schedule D to this Act or as in Schedule G to the Titles to Land Consolidation (Scotland) Act 1868*); Which ground annual was (*or* which ground annual and others were) last vested (*adding if necessary* to the extent foresaid *or as the case may be*) in *C.D.* (*design person having the only or last recorded title*), whose title thereto was recorded in (*specify Register of Sasines and date of recording; or if the only or last recorded title has already been mentioned say* in the said *C.D.* as aforesaid), and from whom the said *A.B.* acquired right (*adding if necessary* to the extent foresaid *or as the case may be*) by (*here specify shortly the writ or series of writs by which he acquired right*); Which last recorded title and subsequent writ (*or writs*) have been presented to me (*as in Form No. 1 of this Schedule*).

[To be attested.]

Section 4 (4) FORM No. 5

ON BEHALF OF A PERSON WHO HAS RIGHT TO AN UNRECORDED HERITABLE SECURITY WHICH IS TO BE RECORDED ALONG WITH THE NOTICE OF TITLE

Be it known that *A.B.* (*designation*) has right (*adding if such be the case* to the extent after-mentioned) to a bond and disposition in security (*or as the case may be*) for the sum of (*insert amount*) granted by *C.D.* (*designation*) in favour of *E.F.* (*designation*) dated (*insert date*), and recorded in (*specify Register of Sasines*) of even date herewith [*adding if necessary* but only to the extent of (*insert sum*) of principal]; To which bond and disposition in security (*adding if necessary* to the extent foresaid *or as the case may be*) the said *A.B.* acquired right by (*here specify shortly the writ or series of writs by which he acquired right*); Which bond and disposition in security (*or as the case may be*) and subsequent writ (*or writs*) have been presented to me (*as in Form No. 1 of this Schedule*).

[To be attested.]

Section 4 (4) FORM No. 6

ON BEHALF OF A PERSON WHO HAS RIGHT TO A GROUND ANNUAL CONSTITUTED BY A DEED THE RECORDING OF WHICH IN THE APPROPRIATE REGISTER OF SASINES ON BEHALF OF THE ORIGINAL CREDITOR WOULD HAVE INFEFT HIM THEREIN AND IN THE LANDS OUT OF WHICH IT IS PAYABLE, OR EITHER, BUT WHICH HAS NOT BEEN SO RECORDED, AND WHICH IS TO BE RECORDED ALONG WITH THE NOTICE OF TITLE

Be it known that *A.B.* (*designation*) has right (*adding if such be the case* to the extent after-mentioned) to a ground annual of (*insert amount, and if there be any duplications or other casual payments add* with duplication every nineteenth year, *or as the case may be*) payable under a contract of ground annual (*or other deed by which the ground annual was constituted, giving the names and designations of the parties thereto or of the granter and grantee*) dated (*insert date*), and recorded in (*specify Register of Sasines*) of even date herewith [*adding, if necessary*, but only to the extent of (*insert sum or respective sums*)]; To which ground annual (*adding, if necessary*, to the extent foresaid *or as the case may be*) the said *A.B.* acquired right by the foresaid contract of ground annual (*or as the case may be*) and by (*here specify shortly the writ or series of writs by which he acquired right*); Which contract of ground annual (*or as the case may be*) and subsequent writ (*or writs*) have been presented to me (*as in Form No. 1 of this Schedule*).

[To be attested.]

Sections 4 (2) (4), 24 (3) NOTES TO SCHEDULE B

Note 1.—Where the description in the last infeftment is a particular description, the description in Form No. 1 of this Schedule should be by reference thereto, unless there is reason to the contrary.

Note 2.—In adapting Form No. 2 of this Schedule to the case of a person who has right to only a part of the land contained in an unrecorded conveyance, deed, or decree there shall be inserted immediately before the words " all and whole " a description of such part of the land, and the form may then proceed *which lands and others* (or *subjects*) *are part of.*

Note 3.—If the original infeftment upon a bond and disposition in security or other heritable security including a ground annual has been taken otherwise than by recording the same in the appropriate Register of Sasines add immediately after the mention of the date thereof *and instrument of sasine* (or *notarial instrument*, or if such be the case *and along with notice of title*) *thereon* (adding if such instrument or notice is not in favour of the original creditor the name and designation of the person in whose favour it is conceived) *recorded in* (specify Register of Sasines and date of recording).

Note 4.—In adapting Forms Nos. 3 and 5 of this Schedule to real burdens for capital sums, there shall be substituted for the specification of the bond and disposition in security the following: *A real burden for the sum of* (insert amount) *payable to E.F.* (designation) *in terms of* (specify the disposition or other deed under which the real burden was reserved or constituted, giving the names and designations of the granter and grantee, or of the parties thereto), *dated* (insert date) *and recorded in* (specify Register of Sasines and date of recording); and in specifying the writs by which *A.B.* acquired right to such real burden there shall in Form No. 5 be mentioned as the first of such writs *the said disposition* (or other deed as above), and the same shall along with the other writ or writs be presented to the Agent expeding the notice of title.

Note 5.—[Repealed by the Conveyancing and Feudal Reform (Scotland) Act 1970, Sched. 11.]

Note. 6.—Where in place of the principal titles or writs on which any notice of title bears to proceed there are presented to the agent expeding such notice extracts or office copies thereof, the statement in the notice as to the presentation of such titles or writs may be varied accordingly; but it shall be no objection to any notice of title that it states that the principal titles or writs were so presented although there were presented only extracts or office copies of such titles or writs.

Note 7.—Where a deed, decree or heritable security is to be recorded along with a notice of title it should be docqueted as follows:—*Docqueted with reference to notice of title in favour of* A.B. *recorded of even date herewith.*

Y.Z. (*designation*),
Agent.

SCHEDULE C

[Repealed by the Conveyancing and Feudal Reform (Scotland) Act 1970, Sched. 11]

Section 8

[1] SCHEDULE D

Clause of Reference to a Description of Land contained in a prior Conveyance, Deed, or Instrument

---

NOTE

[1] Extended by the Conveyancing and Feudal Reform (Scotland) Act 1970, s. 28 (5): excluded by the Land Registration (Scotland) Act 1979, s. 15 (1).

All and Whole the lands and others (*or* subjects) in the county of (*or* in the burgh of and county of *as the case may be*) described in (*refer to the conveyance, deed, or instrument in such terms as shall be sufficient to identify it, and specify the Register of Sasines in which it is recorded and date of recording, or where the conveyance, deed or instrument referred to is recorded on the same date as the conveyance, deed, or instrument containing the reference substitute for the date of recording the words* of even date with the recording of these presents):—

Notes to Schedule D

[1] *Note 1.*—In referring to a Deed containing a particular description or to a Deed containing reservations, real burdens, conditions, provisions, limitations, obligations and stipulations affecting lands it shall be sufficient to give the names of the granter and grantee or of the parties thereto without adding their designations, and when there are several granters or grantees or several parties acting in the same category it shall be sufficient to give the name of the first mentioned person only with the addition of the words *and others*[1]; and where the granter or granters or grantee or grantees, or the parties or one of the parties thereto acts or act in a fiduciary capacity it shall be sufficient to state such capacity without giving their individual name or names, *e.g.*:

(*a*) *Feu Charter granted by A.B. in favour of C.D.*, dated (insert date) *and recorded in* (specify Register of Sasines and give date of recording).

(*b*) *Disposition granted by C.D. and others in favour of E.F. and others, dated, etc.* (as above).

(*c*) *Notarial Instrument* (or *Notice of title*) *in favour of the Trustee* (*or Trustees*) *of G.H.* (or *the Judicial Factor of J.K. or the Trustee on the Sequestrated Estates of L.M. or the Liquidator of the N.O. Company Limited, or* as the case may be) *recorded in* (specify Register of Sasines and date of recording).

Note 2.—Where it is desired to insert a short description of the land or subjects, this may be done as follows:—*All and Whole that dwelling-house, number ten, Rosebery Crescent, Edinburgh* (or *the eastmost half-flat on the second storey of the tenement entering from number fifteen Lothian Street, Edinburgh,* or otherwise as the case may be) *in the county of Edinburgh, described in,* etc. (as above).

Note 3.—If part only of the land or subjects described in a former recorded conveyance, deed, instrument, or notice of title is being conveyed or otherwise dealt with for the first time as a separate subject, such part should be described at length, adding *being part of the lands and others* (or *subjects*) *in the county of* or *in the burgh of* *and county of* *described in*, etc. (as above); or thus: *All and Whole the lands and others* (or *subjects*) *in the county of* or *in the burgh of* *and county of* *described in,* etc. (as above), *with the exception of* (describe the part excepted).

Note 4.—If several lands or subjects are described in the conveyance, deed, or instrument referred to, and it is intended to specify one or more of them, these may be distinguished from the others thus: *All and Whole the lands and others* (or *subjects*) *first* (or *second and third*) *described in*, etc. (as above, or otherwise, as the case may be).

NOTE

[1] As amended by the Conveyancing Amendment (Scotland) Act 1938, s. 2 (2).

Section 9

[1] SCHEDULE E

Deed of Acknowledgment of Omitted Conditions

NOTE

[1] Excluded by the Land Registration (Scotland) Act 1979, s. 15 (2).

I, *A.B.* (*designation*), hereby acknowledge that in my title to the lands after referred to, namely (*specify it*), there was an omission or failure to repeat or refer to the following conditions (*or* clauses: *repeat or refer to them*), and which conditions (*or* clauses) affect the lands in the county of (*or* in the burgh of and county of), described at length (*or by* reference) in the said (*specify the title or writing*); And the said conditions (or clauses) are accordingly now referred to in terms of the Conveyancing (Scotland) Act 1924.

[To be attested.]

Section 10

[1] SCHEDULE F

Warrants of Registration

NOTE

[1] Repealed in part by the Burgh Registers (Scotland) Act 1926, s. 4.

Register on behalf of the within named A.B. [*or* on behalf of A.B. (*designation*)] in the Register of the County of G. [(*or* in the Registers of the Counties of G.H. and J.);].

A.B.
or C.D., W.S., Edinburgh, agent.
or E. & F., W.S., Edinburgh, agents.
(*or as the case may be*).

Notes to Schedule F

Note 1.—In the case of a Warrant of Registration written on a deed which is to be recorded in the Register of Sasines in terms of a clause of direction, and after the first word " Register " the words *in terms of the clause of direction herein contained.*

Note 2.—In the case of a Warrant of Registration written on a deed which is to be recorded in the General Register of Sasines for preservation (or for preservation and execution) insert the words *for preservation* (or *for preservation and execution*) *as well as for publication.*

Note 3.—When the right of the person or persons on whose behalf a deed is to be recorded is a fiduciary one the name or names of the Trustee or other person or persons acting in a fiduciary capacity shall be inserted in the Warrant of Registration written on such deed, and may be followed by a short reference to the capacity in which he or they act, *e.g.*, *as Trustee* (*or Trustees* or as the case may be) *within mentioned*, or, if desired, a fuller reference to such capacity may be given.

Note 4.—[Repealed by the Conveyancing and Feudal Reform (Scotland) Act 1970, Sched. 11.]

[1] *Note* 5.—When a disposition or bond and disposition in security or other deed, decree or heritable security is to be recorded along with a notice of title, add at the end of the Warrant of Registration on such notice of title, the words *along with the disposition* [*or bond and disposition in security*, or as the case may be] *docqueted with reference hereto.*

NOTE

[1] As amended by the Conveyancing and Feudal Reform (Scotland) Act 1970, Sched. 11.

Section 11

SCHEDULE G

Minute of Consolidation

I, *A.B.*, designed in the foregoing disposition, proprietor both of the superiority and of the property (*or* of the mid-superiority) of the lands described in the foregoing disposition, hereby consolidate the property of the said lands (*or* the mid-superiority of the said lands) with the superiority thereof.

[To be attested.]

Sections 13, 25

SCHEDULE H

Memorandum of Allocation of Feu Duty not endorsed on a Deed

I, *A.B.* (*designation*), immediate lawful superior of the lands and others (*or* subjects) after-mentioned [with consent of *C.D.* (*designation*), heritable creditor under a bond and disposition in security, granted by me in his favour (*or as the case may be*) for the sum of (*insert amount*), dated (*insert date*) and recorded in (*specify Register of Sasines and date of recording*)] hereby allocate the original feu-duty of (*specify amount*) and duplicand thereof [*or* additional feu-duty of (*specify amount*)] payable under the feu charter granted by me (*or as the case may be*) in favour of *E.F.* (*designation*), dated (*insert date*), and recorded in (*specify Register of Sasines and date of recording*) upon the following portions of the lands and others (*or subjects*) thereby disponed, namely (first) a feu-duty of £ with £ of augmentation, making a total of £ and duplicand thereof (*or as the case may be*) on all and whole (*describe or refer to a particular description*) and (second) a feu-duty of (*as above*) on all and whole (*describe or refer to a particular description*).

[To be attested.]

Section 18

SCHEDULE I

Docquet where Granter of Deed is Blind or cannot Write

Read over to, and signed by me for, and by authority of the above-named *A.B.* (*without designation*) who declares that he is blind (*or* is unable to write), all in his presence, and in presence of the witnesses hereto subscribing.

C.D., law agent (*or* notary public), Edinburgh (*or as the case may be*)
or E.F., justice of the peace for the county of
or G.H., minister (*or* assistant and successor to the minister) of the parish of

M.N., witness.
P.Q., witness.

[1] *Note.*—The above docquet shall be written on the last page of the deed, instrument or writing, and signed by the law agent or notary public or other person authorised to sign the same in the manner indicated in the form, and such law agent or notary public or other person shall not require also to sign above the docquet at the end of such deed, instrument or writing, and (in the case of a will or other testamentary writing) the prior pages thereof (if any) shall be authenticated in the usual manner by such law agent or notary public or other person adhibiting his own signature thereto. The witnesses to the signatures of such law agent or notary public or other person shall subscribe as indicated in the form, and may be designed in the testing clause of such deed, instrument or writing; but if there be no testing clause thereto, the designations of the witnesses may be added after their respective signatures, and if desired a specification of the place and date of signing may be added to the docquet.

NOTE

[1] As amended by the Conveyancing and Feudal Reform (Scotland) Act 1970, Sched. 10.

Section 24

[1] SCHEDULE J

Registrable Leases

NOTE

[1] Excluded by the Land Registration (Scotland) Act 1979, s. 15 (1).

A lease (*or* tack) granted by *E.F.* (*designation*) in my favour [*or* in favour of *G.H.* (*designation*) *or as the case may be*] of the subjects therein described lying in the county of (*or* burgh of and county of), dated (*insert date*), and recorded in (*specify Register of Sasines and date of recording*).

Notes to Schedule J

Note 1.—If the recording of a lease in the appropriate Register of Sasines has been effected by a successor of the original lessee, add immediately after the mention of the date thereof *and along with notarial instrument* (or *notice of title*) *thereon in favour of* (giving the name and designation of the person in whose favour it is conceived) *recorded in* (specify Register of Sasines and date of recording).

Note 2.—Where any deed authorised by this Act relates to part only of the subjects contained in a lease add *but in so far only as regards the following portion of the subjects leased, viz.* (here describe the portion or refer to description thereof as in Schedule D hereto).

[1] *Note* 3.—Where the granter of an assignation of a recorded lease or of a bond and assignation in security of a recorded lease is not the original lessee but has a recorded title no specification of the granter's title is required.

Note 4.—In an assignation or renunciation of a recorded lease the title of the granter of which assignation or renunciation is not recorded, and in a notice of title to a recorded lease, insert *which lease* (adding if necessary *to the extent foresaid* or as the case may be) *was last vested in the said G.H. as aforesaid* [or if *G.H.* is not the person having such title say *in J.K.* (design person having such title) *whose title thereto is recorded in said Register of Sasines* (or as the case may be, and give date of recording)], *and from whom I* (in the case of an assignation or renunciation) or *the said A.B.* (in the case of a notice of title) *acquired right by* (here specify shortly the writ or series of writs by which right was so acquired by the person granting the assignation or renunciation, or expeding the notice of title).

Note 5.—Where a title to an unrecorded lease is being completed by notice of title under this Act the lease shall be referred to in manner above prescribed except that the Register of Sasines shall be specified, and for the date of recording of the lease there shall be substituted the words *of even date herewith.*

NOTE

[1] As amended by the Conveyancing and Feudal Reform (Scotland) Act 1970, Sched. 10.

SCHEDULE K

Sections 3, 28, 31

Form No. 1

Assignation of a Bond and Disposition in Security

I, *A.B.* (*design creditor*), in consideration of the sum of (*insert sum*), paid to me by *C.D.* (*designation*), hereby assign to the said *C.D.* a bond and disposition in security for the sum of (*insert sum*) granted by *E.F.* (*design original debtor*) in my favour [*or* in favour of *G.H.* (*design original creditor*)], dated (*insert date*), and recorded in [*specify Register of Sasines and date of recording; adding if necessary*, but only to the extent of (*insert sum*) of principal]; With interest from (*insert date*).

[To be attested.]

Section 23

Form No. 2

Assignation of a Ground Annual

I, *A.B.* (*design creditor*), in consideration of the sum of (*insert sum*) paid to me by *C.D.* (*designation*), hereby assign to the said *C.D.* a ground annual of (*insert amount*) exigible yearly at (*state term or date of payment*) in each year [*or* in equal portions half-yearly at (*state terms or dates of payment*) in each year, *or otherwise, as the case may be; and if there be any duplications or other casual payments add* with duplication every nineteenth year (*or otherwise as the case may be*) from and after (*state the term or date from which the current duplication or other casual payment is running*)] constituted by a contract of ground annual (*or other deed by which the ground annual was constituted, giving the names and designations of the parties thereto, or of the granter and grantee*) recorded in [*specify Register of Sasines and date of recording; and if any duplications or other casual payments have been redeemed and commuted into an additional annual payment say*, and also the additional ground annual of (*insert sum*) exigible at the same term (*or* date) in each year (*or as the case may be*) in lieu and commutation of casual payments; *adding, if necessary*, but only to the extent of (*insert sum or respective sums*)] payable out of all and whole (*here describe the land or refer to description thereof as in Schedule D to this Act or as in Schedule* (*G*) *to the Titles to Land Consolidation* (*Scotland*) *Act* 1868); With right to the said ground annual (*or* ground annual and others) from and after (*insert date*).

[To be attested.]

Sections 3, 29 FORM No. 3

DISCHARGE OF A BOND AND DISPOSITION IN SECURITY

I, *A.B.* (*design creditor*), in consideration of the sum of (*insert sum*) paid to me by *C.D.* (*designation*), hereby discharge a bond and disposition in security for the sum of (*insert sum*) granted by the said *C.D.* [*or by E.F.* (*design original debtor*)] in my favour [*or* in favour of *G.H.* (*design original creditor*)] dated (*insert date*) and recorded in [*specify Register of Sasines and date of recording; adding, if necessary,* but only to the extent of (*insert sum*) of principal].

[To be attested.]

Section 23 FORM No. 4

DISCHARGE OF A GROUND ANNUAL

I, *A.B.* (*design creditor*), in consideration of the sum of (*insert sum*) paid to me by *C.D.* (*designation*), hereby discharge the ground annual of (*insert amount, and if there be any duplications or other casual payments add* with duplications every nineteenth year or otherwise, as the case may be), constituted by a contract of ground annual (*or other deed by which the ground annual was constituted, giving the names and designations of the parties thereto, or of the granter and grantee*) recorded in [*specify Register of Sasines and date of recording; and if any duplications or other casual payments have been redeemed and commuted into an additional annual payment say* and also the additional ground annual of (*insert sum*) constituted in lieu and commutation of casual payments; *adding, if necessary*, but only to the extent of (*insert sum or respective sums*)] payable out of all and whole (*here describe the land or refer to description thereof as in Schedule D to this Act, or as in Schedule G to the Titles to Land Consolidation (Scotland) Act* 1868).

[To be attested.]

Section 30 FORM No. 5

DEED OF RESTRICTION OF A BOND AND DISPOSITION IN SECURITY

I, *A.B.* (*design creditor*), in consideration of (*specify consideration, if any*), hereby disburden of a bond and disposition in security for the sum of (*insert sum*) granted by *C.D.* [*design original debtor*) in my favour [*or* in favour of *G.H.* (*design original creditor*], dated (*insert date*) and recorded in [*specify Register of Sasines and date of recording, adding, if necessary,* but only to the extent of (*insert sum*) of principal], all and whole (*describe the land disburdened, or refer to description thereof as in Schedule D to this Act or as in Schedule C to the Titles to Land Consolidation (Scotland) Act* 1868).

[To be attested.]

Section 30 FORM No. 6

COMBINED PARTIAL DISCHARGE AND DEED OF RESTRICTION OF A BOND AND DISPOSITION IN SECURITY

I, *A.B.* (*design creditor*), in consideration of the sum of (*insert sum*) paid to me by *C.D.* (*designation*), discharge a bond and disposition in security for the sum of (*insert sum*) granted by the said *C.D.* [or by *E.F.* (*design original debtor*)] in my favour [*or* in favour of *G.H.* (*design original creditor*)] dated (*insert date*) and recorded in [*specify Register of Sasines and date of recording*) but only to the extent of (*insert sum*) of principal; And I disburden of the said bond and disposition in security [*adding if necessary* but only to the extent of (*insert sum*) *of principal*] ALL and WHOLE (*describe the land disburdened, or refer to description thereof as in Schedule D to this Act or as in Schedule G to the Titles to Land Consolidation (Scotland) Act* 1868).

[To be attested.]

Section 23 FORM No. 7

DEED OF RESTRICTION OF A GROUND ANNUAL

I, *A.B.* (*design creditor*), in consideration of (*specify consideration, if any*), hereby disburden of the ground annual of (*insert amount, and if there be any duplications or other casual payments add* with duplications every nineteenth year *or otherwise as the case may be*) constituted by a contract of ground annual (*or other deed by which the ground annual was constituted, giving the names and designations of the parties thereto, or of the granter and grantee*) recorded in [*specify Register of Sasines and date of recording; and if any duplications or other casual payments have been redeemed or commuted into an additional payment say* and also of the additional ground annual of (*insert sum*) constituted in lieu and commutation of casual payments, *adding, if necessary*, but only to the extent of (*insert sum or respective sums*)] all and whole (*here describe the land disburdened or refer to description thereof as in Schedule D to this Act, or as in Schedule G to the Titles to Land Consolidation (Scotland) Act* 1868); which lands are part of all and whole (*describe the lands out of which the ground annual is payable or refer to description thereof as above*) being the lands and others (*or* subjects) out of which the said ground annual is (*or* the said ground annual and others are) payable.

[To be attested.]

Section 23 FORM No. 8

DECREE OF ADJUDICATION FOR A GROUND ANNUAL

Having resumed consideration of the said petition (or action) finds and declares that the ground annual of (*insert amount*) payable from the lands and others (*or* subjects) hereinafter described has fallen two years into arrear, and that the defender *C.D.* by his failure to pay said arrears has forfeited his right in and to the said lands and others (*or* subjects), and adjudges and declares that the said lands and others (*or* subjects), that is to say, all and whole (*here describe the land or refer to description thereof as in Schedule D to this Act, or as in Schedule G to the Titles to Land Consolidation (Scotland) Act* 1868), now belong to the Pursuer *A.B.*, from and after the (*insert date of raising of the action or other date fixed by the Court*), together with the rents, maills, and duties of the said lands and others (*or* subjects) current and unpaid at that date (*and if there are any conditions, reservations, provisions, obligations, servitudes, or other burdens which affect the land or any part thereof and have entered the Register of Sasines prior to the constitution of the ground annual, and which are proper to be inserted or referred to, here insert the same at length or refer thereto as in Schedule H annexed to the Conveyancing (Scotland) Act* 1874); and grants warrant to record an extract of this decree in the Register of Sasines.

NOTES TO SCHEDULE K

Note 1.—If the original infeftment upon a bond and disposition in security or other heritable security has been taken otherwise than by recording the same in the appropriate Register of Sasines, add immediately after the mention of the date of such bond and disposition in security or other deed *and instrument of sasine* (or *notarial instrument*, or if such be the case *and along with notice of title*) *thereon* (adding if such instrument or notice is not in favour of the original creditor the name and designation of the person in whose favour it is conceived) *recorded in* (specify Register of Sasines and date of recording).

Sections 3, 28, 29, 30, 31

[1]*Note* 2.—Where the granter of an assignation, discharge or deed of restriction of a bond and disposition in security is not the original creditor, but has a recorded title, no specification of the granter's title is required; or if such granter has not a recorded title, insert at the end of the deed *Which bond and disposition in security* (adding, if necessary, *to the extent aforesaid* or as the case may be) *was last vested in the said* (give name of original creditor) *as aforesaid* [or if he was not the person having the last recorded title, say *was last vested* (adding, if necessary, *to the extent aforesaid*, or as the case may be) *in J.K.* (design person having last recorded title) whose title

thereto was recorded in said Register of Sasines (or as the case may be, and give date of recording)], *and from whom I acquired right* (adding, if necessary, *to the extent aforesaid* or as the case may be) *by* (here specify the writ or series of writs by which right was so acquired). In the case of an assignation, discharge or deed of restriction of a ground annual or other real burden the same course will be followed except that the words *ground annual* or *real burden* shall be substituted for the words *bond and disposition in security*.

Note 3.—If part of the security subjects has already been disburdened there may be inserted in an assignation after the specification of the bond assigned a reference to the previous partial discharge or deed of restriction.

Note 4.—In adapting Forms Nos. 1, 3 and 5 of this schedule to real burdens for capital sums there shall be substituted for the specification of the bond and disposition in security the following:—*A real burden for the sum of* (insert sum) *payable in terms of* (specify deed under which the real burden was reserved or constituted, giving the names and designations of the granter and grantee or of the parties thereto), *dated* (insert date) *and recorded in* (specify Register of Sasines and date of recording).

NOTE

[1] As amended by the Conveyancing and Feudal Reform (Scotland) Act 1970, Sched. 10. Excluded by the Land Registration (Scotland) Act 1979, s. 15 (3).

SCHEDULE L

Premonition by Debtor or Proprietor desiring to Redeem a Heritable Security

Section 32 Form No. 1

To *A.B.* (*insert name and last known address of person to whom notice is given*).

Take Notice that at the term of (*state term and year*) *C.D.* (*name debtor or proprietor*) will repay the principal sum of (*insert sum*) and all interest thereon due under a bond and disposition in security (*or other security*) granted by the said *C.D.* [*or* by *E.F.* (*original debtor*)] in your favour [*or* in favour of *G.H.* (*original creditor*)], dated (*insert date*) and recorded in (*specify Register of Sasines and date of recording*).

Dated this day of

(*To be signed by the debtor, or proprietor, or by his Agent, who will add his designation and the words* Agent of the said *C.D.*)

Section 32 [1] Form No. 2

I, *A.B.*, above named, hereby acknowledge receipt of the foregoing Premonition (*or* of the Premonition of which the foregoing is a copy).

Dated this day of

NOTE

[1] Applied by the Conveyancing Amendment (Scotland) Act 1938, s. 9 (2).

Section 32 [1] Form No. 3

Premonition, of which the foregoing is a copy, was posted (*or otherwise as the case may be*) to *A.B.* above named on the day of

(*To be signed by the debtor, or proprietor, or by his Agent, who will add his designation and the words* Agent of the said *C.D. and if posted the postal receipt to be attached.*)

NOTE

[1] Applied by the Conveyancing Amendment (Scotland) Act 1938, s. 9 (2).

Section 32 FORM No. 4

FORM OF CERTIFICATE WHERE LAND HAS BEEN REDEEMED OF A HERITABLE SECURITY BUT DISCHARGE CANNOT BE OBTAINED

I, *A.B.* (*designation*), notary public (*or* law agent), hereby certify that *C.D.* (*designation*), proprietor (*or as the case may be*) of the lands and others (*or* subjects) contained in the bond and disposition in security (*or other heritable security*) aftermentioned [*or* that *X.Y.* (*designation*), the debtor in the bond and disposition in security (*or other heritable security*) aftermentioned] represented to me that on the (*insert date*) he caused to be consigned in the (*specify bank or branch of bank in which the money was consigned*) the sum of (*insert amount consigned*) being the cumulo amount (*or* the balance) of the principal sum, interest and expenses (*or as the case may be*) due (*or* remaining due) under the said bond and disposition in security (*or other heritable security*) conform to deposit receipt dated (*insert date*) by the said bank for said amount in the name of *E.F.* (*designation*), the creditor in (*or* now in right of) the said bond and disposition in security (*or other heritable security*) [*if he is only a partial creditor say* to the extent of (*insert amount*)], which consignation was made in virtue of the power of redemption reserved in the bond and disposition in security for the sum of (*insert amount*) granted by the said *C.D.* [*or* by *G.H.* (*design original debtor*)] in favour of the said *E.F.* [*or*, in favour of *J.K.* (*design original creditor*)] dated (*insert date*) and [*adding if such be the case* instrument of sasine *or* notarial instrument (*or* along with notice of title) thereon *and if such instrument or notice is not in favour of the original creditor specifying the name and designation of the person in whose favour it is conceived*] recorded in (*specify Register of Sasines and date of recording*); [*If E.F. is not the original creditor but has a recorded title insert* Which bond and disposition in security (*adding if necessary* to the extent aforesaid *or as the case may be*) is now vested in the said *E.F.* (*or other person holding the last recorded title, giving his name and designation*) whose title thereto is recorded in the said Register of Sasines (*or as the case may be, and give date of recording*), *and if E.F. is the successor of the person having such last recorded title specify E.F.'s right as successor to him*]; And I further certify that such consignation was rendered necessary by the refusal of the said *E.F.* to receive the sum so consigned [*or* by the refusal (*or* incapacity) of the said *E.F.* to grant a valid discharge of the said bond and disposition in security (*or other heritable security*) *or* by the absence (*or death*) of the said *E.F. or as the case may be, stating the reason why a valid discharge could not be obtained*] notwithstanding that the requisite premonition was duly given, and that the said deposit receipt for the sum so consigned was presented to me.

[To be attested.] *A.B.*

SCHEDULE M

NOTICE CALLING UP BOND

Section 33 [1] FORM No. 1

To *A.B.* (*insert name and last known address of person to whom notice is given*).

Take notice that *C.D.* (*name creditor*) requires payment of the principal sum of (*insert sum*) with interest thereon at the rate of per centum per annum from the day of due under a Bond and Disposition in Security by you [*or* by *E.F.* (*original debtor*)] in favour of the said *C.D.* [*or* of *G.H.* (*original creditor*) of which the said *C.D.* is now in right], dated (*insert date*) and recorded in (*specify Register of Sasines, and date of recording*): And that failing full payment of the said principal sum, interest and expenses within three months after this demand the lands and others (*or* subjects) held in security may be sold.

Dated this day of (*date of giving notice personally or of posting same*).

(*To be signed by the creditor, or by his Agent, who will add his designation and the words* Agent of the said *C.D.*)

NOTE

[1] See the Conveyancing and Feudal Reform (Scotland) Act 1970, s. 33.

Sections 34, 35 FORM No. 2

I, *A.B.* above named, hereby acknowledge receipt of the foregoing notice (*or* of the notice of which the foregoing is a copy), and I agree to the period of notice being dispensed with (*or* shortened to). Dated this day of

Section 34 FORM No. 3

Notice of which the foregoing is a copy was posted (*or otherwise, as the case may be*) to *A.B.* above named on the day of

(*To be signed by the creditor, or by his Agent, who will add his designation and the words* Agent of the said *C.D., and if posted the postal receipt to be attached.*)

Section 42 SCHEDULE N

CERTIFICATE AS TO SURPLUS (IF ANY), OR NO SURPLUS, WHERE LAND IS SOLD UNDER A HERITABLE SECURITY

I, *A.B.* (*insert designation*), notary public (*or* law agent) with reference to the sale of the lands and others (*or* subjects) contained in the bond and disposition in security (*or other heritable security*) aftermentioned, which sale took place at (*insert place*) upon the (*insert date*) at the instance of *C.D.* (*insert designation*) in virtue of the power of sale contained in a bond and disposition in security (*or other heritable security*) for the sum of (*insert amount*) granted by *E.F.* (*design original debtor*) in favour of the said *C.D.* [*or* in favour of *G.H.* (*design original creditor*)] dated (*insert date*) and [*adding if such be the case* instrument of sasine *or* notarial instrument (*or* along with notice of title) thereon, *and if such instrument or notice is not in favour of the original creditor, specify the name and designation of the person in whose favour it is conceived*] recorded in [*specify Register of Sasines, and date of recording; adding if such be the case* To which bond and disposition in security (*or other heritable security*), *adding if necessary* to the extent of (*insert amount*), the said *C.D.* acquired right by succession (*or* transmission *or as the case may be*)], Do hereby certify that there has been submitted to me a statement of the intromissions of the said *C.D.*, with the price of said land subscribed by the said *C.D.* [*or* by *J.K.* (*insert designation*) agent of the said *C.D.* on his behalf] from which it appears that no surplus remains for consignation in terms of section 122 of the Titles to Land Consolidation (Scotland) Act 1868 [*or where such surplus remains say* from which it appears that a surplus of (*insert amount*) remains for consignation in terms of section 122 of the Titles to Land Consolidation (Scotland) Act 1868, and I further certify that such surplus has been so consigned in (*specify bank or branch of bank in which the money was consigned*) conform to deposit receipt dated (*insert date*) by said bank for said amount in the joint names of the said *C.D.* and of *L.M.* (*insert designation of the purchaser of said land*), which deposit receipt has been presented to me].

[To be attested.] *A.B.*

Section 44 [1] SCHEDULE O

FORM OF MEMORANDUM TO BE RECORDED IN THE REGISTER OF SASINES

NOTE

[1] Added by the Conveyancing Amendment (Scotland) Act 1938, s. 7 (2).

Memorandum with regard to the subjects after described (s. 44):

With reference to the subjects (*describe particularly or by reference*) T. the trustee in the sequestration of B. has obtained a vesting order under section 98 of the Bankruptcy (Scotland) Act 1913, dated (*insert date of order*).

The memorandum should be signed by the trustee or his law agent, dated, and recorded with a warrant of registration in the appropriate division or divisions of the Register of Sasines.

The form may be adapted in the case of a lease thus:—

Memorandum with regard to the lease after-mentioned:

With reference to the lease granted by C. in favour of D. of the subjects therein described lying in the County of K., dated (*insert date*), and recorded in (*specify Register of Sasines and date of recording*), T. the trustee etc.

and in the case of a heritable security thus:—

Memorandum with regard to the bond and disposition in security after mentioned:

With reference to the bond and disposition in security for the sum of (*insert sum*) granted by E. in favour of F. dated (*insert date*) and recorded in (*specify Register of Sasines and date of recording*), T. the trustee, etc.

Conveyancing Amendment (Scotland) Act 1938

(1 & 2 Geo. 6, c. 24)

An Act to amend the law of conveyancing in Scotland.

[17th May 1938]

Provision in regard to judicial factors, etc.

1. For the purposes of sections 3 and 4 of the Act of 1924, a judicial factor appointed by the court to administer a trust estate comprising any land or any heritable security or part of any heritable security or any lease or security over a lease, or a trustee appointed by the court on such a trust estate shall be deemed to be a person having a right within the meaning of the said sections to such land or heritable security or part of a heritable security or lease or security over a lease respectively, and shall with respect to any lease or security over a lease comprised in the trust estate be entitled to the benefit of all enabling powers and rights under section 24 of the Act of 1924; and an extract of the Act and warrant appointing such judicial factor or trustee shall, for the purposes of deductions of title in terms of the said Act, be a valid midcouple or link of title.

2. (1) (2) [Amendments made to the Conveyancing (Scotland) Act 1924, s. 8 and Sched. D are given effect to in print of that Act.]

(3) [Repealed by the Statute Law Revision Act 1950.]

3. [Repealed by the Statute Law Revision Act 1950.]

4. [Repealed by the Prescription and Limitation (Scotland) Act 1973, Sched. 5.]

5. [Repealed by the Succession (Scotland) Act 1964, s. 34 (2) and Sched. 3]

Provisions as to actions of declarator of irritancy

6.—[1] (1) Where an action of declarator of irritancy *ob non solutum canonem* is raised in the Court of Session by a superior against a vassal, the pursuer shall, in addition to serving the same on the last entered vassal, give such intimation thereof, as the court may direct or require to subfeuars, heritable creditors and others who at the date of the raising of the action appear to have some real right in or security over the vassal's estate or any part thereof and who from a search in the Register of Sasines made against the vassal's estate for a period of twenty years immediately prior to the date of the raising of the action or from an examination of the relevant title sheet in the Land Register of Scotland are disclosed as having such interest.

[1] (2) The expense of such search or examination shall form part of the pursuer's expenses of process.

(3) After decree has been granted in any such action, it shall not be competent to any person to question in any legal proceedings whatsoever the validity or sufficiency of the intimation given to him under and in pursuance of subsection (1) of this section.

(4) Notwithstanding the provisions of section 24 of the Court of Session Act 1868, or of Rule 25 of the First Schedule to the Sheriff Courts (Scotland) Act 1907 a decree granted in any such action shall, as in a question with third parties who have acted onerously and in *bona fide* in reliance on the Records, be final and not subject to challenge when an extract thereof shall have been recorded in the appropriate Register of Sasines.

NOTE

[1] As amended by the Land Registration (Scotland) Act 1979, Sched. 2, para. 3.

7. [Amendments made to the Conveyancing (Scotland) Act 1924, s. 44 (4) and Sched. O, are given effect to in print of that Act.]

Prohibition of subinfeudation annulled

8. From and after the commencement of this Act all conditions of whatever date to the effect that it shall not be lawful for the proprietor of lands to sub-feu the same or any part thereof shall, with all irritant clauses applicable thereto, be null and void and not capable of being enforced.

Limitation of effect of conditions as to pre-emption

[1] **9.**—(1) Any condition or provision whether made before or after the commencement of this Act to the effect that the superior of any feu shall be entitled to a right of pre-emption in the event of a sale thereof or of any part thereof by the proprietor of the feu (whether or not that right purports to be exercisable on more than one occasion) shall, with all irritant clauses applicable thereto, be in all time coming null and void, and not capable of being enforced as regards such feu or part thereof, as the case may be, unless the person in right of the superiority (whether or not his title thereto is complete) shall within twenty-one days or such shorter period as may be specified in the charter stipulating for such right of pre-emption after an offer has been made to him by the proprietor for the time being accept the offer.

(2) Any such offer may be made by delivering it to such person or to the agent or factor of such person in use to receive and discharge the feu-duty in respect of the feu, or by sending it by registered letter [2] to such person or to such agent or factor at his usual or last known address, or, if such person is unknown or cannot be found, to the Extractor of the Court of Session. An acknowledgment endorsed on such offer, or a copy thereof, by such person or by his agent or factor, or, where the offer is sent by registered letter, a certificate subscribed by the proprietor of the feu or his solicitor that such offer was duly posted and having the Post Office receipt for the registered letter attached shall be sufficient evidence that such offer was duly made on the date stated in the acknowledgment or Post Office receipt. Any such acknowledgment and certificate may be in the form of Form No. 2 and Form No. 3, respectively, of Schedule L to the Act of 1924, the word " Offer " being substituted for the word " Premonition ".

[3] (3) The provisions of this section shall apply in the case of any right of pre-emption, created in a deed or other writing executed after 1st September 1974, in favour of any person, of an interest in land in the event of a sale thereof or of any part thereof by the proprietor for the time being as they apply in the case of such a right vested in the superior of a feu: and in the application of this section in such a case,

(*a*) " superior ", " proprietor ", " feu " and " charter " shall be construed accordingly;

(*b*) in subsection (1) of this section, for the words " person in right of the superiority (whether or not his title thereto is complete) " there shall be substituted the words " person in whom the right is vested ";

(*c*) in subsection (2) of this section, the words " in use to receive and discharge the feuduty in respect of the feu " shall not apply.

NOTES

[1] As amended by the Conveyancing and Feudal Reform (Scotland) Act 1970 s. 46.

[2] Now also recorded delivery service: see the Recorded Delivery Service Act 1962, s. 1 and Sched.

[3] Added by the Land Tenure Reform (Scotland) Act 1974, s. 13.

10. [Repealed by the Succession (Scotland) Act 1964, Sched. 3.]

Certain testamentary writings to be deemed to be probative

11. Any writing of a testamentary character on which confirmation of executors nominate has prior to the commencement of this Act been issued by the Commissary Court or by any sheriff court shall be deemed to be probative.

Interpretation, short title, construction, commencement and extent

12.—(1) In this Act the expression " the Act of 1924 " means the Conveyancing (Scotland) Act, 1924 (14 & 15 Geo. V. c. 27).

(2) This Act may be cited as the Conveyancing Amendment (Scotland) Act 1938, and shall be construed as one with the Act of 1924.

(3) [Repealed by the Statute Law Revision Act 1950.]

(4) This Act shall apply to Scotland only.

[1] SCHEDULE

NOTE

[1] This Schedule added a new Schedule O to the Conveyancing (Scotland) Act 1924, given effect to in the print of that Act.

Public Registers and Records (Scotland) Act 1948

(11 & 12 Geo. 6, c. 57)

An Act to provide for the appointment of a Keeper of the Registers of Scotland and of a Keeper of the Records of Scotland, the transference to such Keepers of the powers and duties of the Keeper of the Registers and Records of Scotland and the discontinuance of that office; to amend the law and procedure regarding registration in the General Register of Sasines, and for purposes connected with the aforesaid purposes. [30th July 1948]

Substitution of a Keeper of the Registers and a Keeper of the Records for the Keeper of the Registers and Records of Scotland

1.—(1) It shall be lawful for the Secretary of State with the consent of the Lord President of the Court of Session to appoint (*a*) a Keeper of the Registers of Scotland, and (*b*) a Keeper of the Records of Scotland, and on such appointments being made the office of Keeper of the Registers and Records of Scotland shall cease to exist.

(2) There shall be transferred to and vested in the Keeper of the Registers of Scotland the whole functions of the Keeper of the Registers and Records of Scotland with regard to the framing of the General Register of Sasines, the Register of Hornings, the Register of Inhibitions and Adjudications, the Register of Entails and the Register of Deeds, together with the powers and duties transferred to the said Keeper from the Director of Chancery under section 7 of the Reorganisation of Offices (Scotland) Act 1928.

(3) There shall be transferred to and vested in the Keeper of the Records of Scotland, the whole functions of the Keeper of the Registers and Records of Scotland with regard to the preservation of the public registers, records and rolls of Scotland.

(4) The Secretary of State may, to such number as the Treasury may sanction, appoint such officers and servants as he may deem necessary to enable each of the Keepers appointed under this section to perform the functions vested in him, and the persons employed at the date when this section comes into operation in the office of the Keeper of the Registers and

Records of Scotland shall, subject to any direction of the Secretary of State, be transferred and attached—

(*a*) in the case where they were employed at the said date in connection with functions transferred under subsection (2) of this section, to the Keeper of the Registers of Scotland; and

(*b*) in any other case, to the Keeper of the Records of Scotland,

and the persons so transferred and attached shall perform such duties in relation to the functions transferred to the said Keepers as the Secretary of State may direct.

(5) There shall be paid out of moneys provided by Parliament to each of the Keepers appointed under this section, and to the officers and servants appointed or transferred under subsection (4) of this section, such remuneration as the Treasury may, on the application of the Secretary of State, from time to time determine.

(6) In the event of a vacancy in the office of either of the Keepers appointed under this section or in the absence of either of them from any cause his functions shall be performed by such member of his staff or such other person as may be authorised by the Secretary of State.

(7) Any reference in any enactment to the Keeper of the General Register of Sasines shall be construed as a reference to the Keeper of the Registers of Scotland, and any reference in any enactment to the Keeper of the Registers and Records of Scotland shall be construed as a reference to the Keeper of the Registers of Scotland or to the Keeper of the Records of Scotland according as the enactment relates to the functions specified in subsection (2) or in subsection (3) of this section.

(8) [Repealed by the Statute Law Revision Act 1950.]

Provisions as to recording in Register of Sasines

2. The following provisions shall have effect with regard to the recording of writs in the General Register of Sasines—

(*a*) the names and designations of the presenters of writs shall not be entered in the minute book;

(*b*) each page of the minute book shall be signed by the Keeper of the Registers of Scotland or by a deputy duly authorised by him in that behalf, and no further signature shall be necessary for the authentication of the minute book; and in particular it shall not be necessary that the minute book be signed by the presenter of a writ or in the case of a writ transmitted to the Register by post by a clerk in the office of the said Keeper;

(*c*) [Repealed by the Statute Law (Repeals) Act 1975.]

. . . .

Power to make Acts of Sederunt regarding the Register of Sasines

[1] **4.** The Court of Session may, by Act of Sederunt, make provision with regard to the General Register of Sasines,—

(*a*) prescribing the forms to be used for the purposes of entries in the presentment books, minute books and relative indexes, prescribing the forms of rubrics and preambles in the register volumes, of certificates of recording to be endorsed on writs, of extracts to be issued, and generally of any documents required for the purposes of the Register, and the persons by whom any such documents shall be signed;

(*b*) requiring that in such cases and subject to such conditions as may be prescribed, where reference is made in a writ presented for recording in the Register to a writ previously recorded therein, the reference shall specify, as well as the date of such previous recording, the register volume and folio in which the writ is so recorded;

(*c*) for the transmission, at such time or times as may be prescribed, to the Keeper of the Records of Scotland, of the register volumes, presentment books, abstracts, indexes or copies thereof, and any other documents (or copies) prepared or kept for the purposes of the register.

NOTE

[1] See the Act of Sederunt of 4th February 1949 (at 1949 S.L.T. (News) 80) and S.I. 1977 No. 70: see also the Public Registers and Records (Scotland) Act 1950, s. (1).

. . . .

Interpretation

6. In this Act, unless the context otherwise requires:—

the expression " functions " includes powers and duties;

the expressions " minute book ", " presentment book " and " register volume " have the like meanings as in the Land Registers (Scotland) Act 1868.

Short title and repeal

7.—(1) This Act may be cited as the Public Registers and Records (Scotland) Act 1948.

(2) [Repealed by the Statute Law Revision Act 1950.]

SCHEDULE

[Repealed by the Statute Law Revision Act 1950.]

Public Registers and Records (Scotland) Act 1950

(14 Geo. 6, c. 11)

An Act to amend the law of Scotland with regard to the signing of certificates of recording in the Register of Sasines.

[12th July 1950]

Certificate of recording in Register of Sasines need not be signed

1.—(1) Save as may be otherwise prescribed by Act of Sederunt made by the Court of Session under section 4 of the Public Registers and Records (Scotland) Act 1948, it shall not be necessary, notwithstanding anything in any enactment, for a certificate of recording endorsed or stamped on a writ recorded in the Register of Sasines to be signed by the Keeper of the Registers of Scotland or by any other person.

(2) The enactments set forth in the Schedule to this Act are hereby repealed to the extent specified in the third column of that Schedule.

(3) This section shall be deemed to have had effect as from the 30th day of July 1948.

Citation

2. This Act may be cited as the Public Registers and Records (Scotland) Act 1950, and the Public Registers and Records (Scotland) Act 1948, and this Act may be cited together as the Public Registers and Records (Scotland) Acts 1948 and 1950.

SCHEDULE

[Repeals given effect to in prints of Acts, *supra.*]

Long Leases (Scotland) Act 1954

(2 & 3 Eliz. 2, c. 49)

An Act to enable lessees and sub-lessees occupying residential property in Scotland under certain long leases to obtain a feu right of such property on certain conditions; to extend and amend the Registration of Leases (Scotland) Act 1857; and for purposes connected with the matters aforesaid.

[30th July 1954]

PART I

GRANT OF FEU RIGHT OF PROPERTY LET UNDER CERTAIN LONG LEASES

General provisions relating to grant of feu right

Lessee or sub-lessee under certain long leases may require landlord to grant feu right

1.—(1) Subject to the provisions of this Part of this Act, where any property is let under a lease granted before the 10th day of August, 1914, for a period of not less than fifty years, and such property or a part thereof is occupied as a private dwelling-house forming his usual residence by the lessee under such lease or by the sub-lessee under a sub-lease granted for a period of not less than fifty years, such lessee or sub-lessee so occupying (hereafter in this Part of this Act referred to as the " occupying lessee ") may give notice to the landlord under the lease requiring him to grant a feu right of the property or, where the occupying lessee is so occupying a part only of the property, of such part.

(2) Any notice under this section shall be given within five years after the commencement of this Act.

(3) In this Part of this Act, unless the context otherwise requires, the following expressions have the meanings hereby assigned to them respectively:—

" landlord " means any person for the time being holding the interest of landlord under a lease;

" lease " means such a lease as is mentioned in subsection (1) of this section and does not include a sub-lease;

" lessee " means any person for the time being holding the interest of lessee under a lease;

" sub-lease " means such a sub-lease as is mentioned in subsection (1) of this section of the property let under a lease or of a part of such property; and

" sub-lessee " means any person for the time being holding the interest of lessee under a sub-lease.

(4) For the purposes of this Part of this Act,—

(*a*) where a lease or a sub-lease has been assigned by *ex facie* absolute assignation, the person for the time being having the right of reversion in such lease or sub-lease shall be deemed to hold the interest of lessee thereunder;

(*b*) any garden, yard, garage, outhouse or pertinent belonging to and occupied along with any dwelling-house shall be deemed to form part of such dwelling-house;

(*c*) a dwelling-house shall be deemed to be occupied as a private dwelling-house notwithstanding that a part thereof is used as a shop or office or for business, trade or professional purposes other than the sale of exciseable liquor for consumption on the premises.

Lessee or sub-lessee deemed to be occupying lessee in certain circumstances

2. Where any property let under a lease or a sub-lease is occupied in whole or in part by any person as a private dwelling-house forming his usual residence and—

(*a*) the interest of lessee under such lease or sub-lease is held by the trustees of a trust in which the said person is beneficially interested; or

(*b*) the said interest is held by the trustees of any religious denomination and the said person occupies the property or such part thereof by virtue of his office as a minister or full-time lay missionary of that denomination; or

(*c*) the said interest is held by a person who acquired it by inheritance and the person so occupying the property or such part thereof is a member of the family of the lessee or sub-lessee from whom the said interest was so acquired and was residing with him in the property or such part thereof at the time of his death;

the trustees or the person who acquired the said interest by inheritance, as the case may be, shall, for the purposes of this Part of this Act, be deemed to occupy the property or such part thereof as a private dwelling-house forming their usual residence and to be the occupying lessee.

Occupying lessee acquiring right on or after 10th May 1951 not entitled to require grant of feu right

3. An occupying lessee under any lease or sub-lease who acquired his interest thereunder, otherwise than by inheritance, on or after the 10th day of May 1951, shall not be entitled under this Part of this Act to require the grant of a feu right of any subjects let under such lease or sub-lease.

Refusal of grant of feu right on ground of public interest

4.—(1) Where the interest of landlord under a lease belongs to or is held for the purposes of a Government department and a notice requiring the grant of a feu right of any subjects let under such lease is given under section one of this Act by an occupying lessee, then if the Minister or Board in charge of any Government department certifies that it is not in the public interest that a feu right of the said subjects should be granted under this Part of this Act and the landlord, within three months after the date of the said Notice, sends to the occupying lessee a copy of such certificate, the occupying lessee shall not be entitled to the grant of such feu right.

(2) Where the landlord under a lease is a local authority or a development corporation and a notice requiring the grant of a feu right of any subjects let under such lease is given under section one of this Act by an occupying lessee, the landlord may apply to the Secretary of State for a certificate that it is not in the public interest that a feu right of the said subjects should be granted under this Part of this Act, and, if the Secretary of State so certifies and the landlord, within three months after the date of the said notice, sends to the occupying lessee a copy of such certificate, the occupying lessee shall not be entitled to the grant of such feu right.

(3) In this section—

"development corporation" has the same meaning as in the New Towns Act 1946;

" Government department " does not include the Commissioners of Crown Lands; and

[1] " local authority " means a regional, islands or district council.

NOTE

[1] As amended by the Local Government (Scotland) Act 1973, Sched. 27, Pt. II, para. 117.

Power to certain landlords who have acquired property for occupation as residence, etc., to apply to sheriff for declarator refusing grant of feu right

5.—(1) Where the landlord under a lease acquired his interest thereunder during the period beginning with the 1st day of January 1939 and ending with the 9th day of May 1951 and a notice requiring the grant of a feu right of any subjects let under such lease is given under section one of this Act by an occupying lessee, the provisions of this section shall have effect.

(2) Such landlord may, within two months after the date of the notice referred to in the foregoing subsection, apply to the sheriff for a declarator that the occupying lessee is not entitled under this Part of this Act to the grant of a feu right of the said subjects and the sheriff shall pronounce such declarator if he is satisfied—

(*a*) that the landlord acquired his interest under the lease—

(i) for the purpose of occupying the subjects as a residence for himself; or

(ii) for the purpose of development involving demolition, alteration or reconstruction of the subjects or a substantial part thereof, being development for which permission under the enactments relating to town and country planning has been granted, or is deemed to have been granted, or is not required; and

(*b*) that, having regard to all the circumstances of the case, greater hardship would be caused to the landlord if a feu right of the subjects were granted than would be caused to the occupying lessee if it were not granted.

(3) In determining whether greater hardship would be caused if a feu right of the said subjects were granted than if it were not granted, the sheriff shall (without prejudice to the generality of paragraph (*b*) of the last foregoing subsection)—

(*a*) have regard to the considerations that, if he pronounces a declarator under this section, the occupying lessee will not be entitled under this Part of this Act to the grant of a feu right of the subjects, and that no provision is made in this Act for payment to the occupying lessee of compensation in that event; and

(*b*) disregard the fact that, if he refuses to pronounce such declarator and a feu right of the subjects is granted under this Part of this Act, such feu right will be granted on the financial terms set out in sections 7 to 9 of this Act.

Notice requiring grant of feu right

Notice requiring grant of feu right

6.—(1) Any notice under section one of this Act shall be in writing, shall be in, or as nearly as may be in, the form set out in the First Schedule to this Act, and shall be signed by the occupying lessee or his solicitor.

(2) Where an occupying lessee who is a sub-lessee gives such a notice to the landlord, he shall at the same time send a copy thereof to each intermediate landlord.

(3) In this Part of this Act, the expression " intermediate landlord " means, where an occupying lessee is a sub-lessee, any person for the time being holding the interest of landlord under a sub-lease which comprises the property of which the occupying lessee is sub-lessee.

Payments to be made where feu right granted

Sums payable to landlord by occupying lessee in respect of feu right of subjects let under lease with 100 years or less unexpired

7.—(1) Where a feu right of any subjects is to be granted under this Part of this Act by the landlord under a lease the unexpired period of which at the date of the notice given under section 1 of this Act by the occupying lessee does not exceed 100 years, there shall be payable to the landlord by the occupying lessee in respect of the feu right—

(*a*) an amount calculated in accordance with the provisions of the next following subsection and payable—

(i) wholly by way of a lump sum; or

(ii) wholly by way of an annual sum which shall be equal to one-twentieth of the said amount and shall form part of the feu-duty hereinafter mentioned; or

(iii) as to a part thereof, by way of a lump sum, and as to the remaining part thereof, by way of an annual sum which shall be equal to one-twentieth of such remaining part and shall form part of the feu-duty hereinafter mentioned;

as may be determined by agreement between the parties and, in default of such agreement, one half of the said amount shall be payable by way of a lump sum and one half by way of an annual sum;

(*b*) a feu-duty equal to the aggregate of the following sums:—

(i) a sum equal to the rent payable under the lease or the proportion of such rent attributable to the subjects to be comprised in the feu right, as the case may be; and

(ii) a sum in respect of the casualties (if any) payable under the lease equal to one-twentieth of the appropriate amount determined in accordance with the provisions of the Second Schedule to this Act; and

(iii) any annual sum payable as provided in paragraph (*a*) of this subsection.

(2) The amount referred to in paragraph (*a*) of the foregoing subsection shall be such amount as would, with compound interest at 5 per centum per annum with yearly rests for the period of the lease which is unexpired at the date of the notice referred to in the said subsection, produce at the end of the said period a sum equal to the value, as determined in accordance with the provisions of the next following subsection, of the subjects to be comprised in the feu right.

Where the unexpired period of any lease is less than thirty years at the commencement of this Act, then for the purposes of this subsection such lease shall be deemed to expire on a date thirty years after such commencement.

(3) For the purposes of the last foregoing subsection, the value of the subjects shall be determined by agreement between the parties or, in default of such agreement, by a valuer agreed by the parties or, in case of dispute, appointed by the sheriff, and—

(*a*) such value shall be estimated as if the lease had expired at the commencement of this Act and the subjects were being sold in the open market at such commencement with vacant possession and subject to a feu-duty equal to the rent payable under the lease or the proportion of such rent attributable to the subjects, as the case may be; and

(*b*) if the lease contains a stipulation for payment of compensation by the landlord on the termination thereof, then in estimating such value account shall be taken of such compensation as if the lease had expired at the commencement of this Act.

(4) Any lump sum payable under subsection (1) of this section shall

bear interest at the rate of 5 per centum per annum from the date of entry under the feu right until paid.

Feu-duty payable in respect of feu right of subjects let under lease with over 100 years unexpired

8. Where a feu right of any subjects is to be granted under this Part of this Act by the landlord under a lease the unexpired period of which at the date of the notice given under section one of this Act by the occupying lessee exceeds 100 years, there shall be payable in respect of the feu right a feu-duty equal to the aggregate of the following two sums:—

(*a*) a sum equal to the rent payable under the lease or the proportion of such rent attributable to the subjects to be comprised in the feu right, as the case may be; and

(*b*) a sum in respect of the casualties (if any) payable under the lease equal to one-twentieth of the appropriate amount determined in accordance with the provisions of the Second Schedule of this Act.

Payment to be made to intermediate landlord by occupying lessee on grant of feu right

9.—(1) Where a feu right of any subjects is to be granted under this Part of this Act on the requirement of an occupying lessee who is a sub-lessee, there shall be paid to each intermediate landlord by the occupying lessee—

(*a*) a sum equal to the capital value, at the date of the notice given under section one of this Act by the occupying lessee, of any amount by which the rent payable to the intermediate landlord or the proportion of such rent attributable to the subjects to be comprised in the feu right, as the case may be, exceeds the rent payable by him or the proportion of such rent attributable to the said subjects, as the case may be, receivable annually for the unexpired period, at the date of the said notice, of the sublease under which the intermediate landlord holds the interest of landlord, such capital value being calculated in accordance with the table set out in the Third Schedule to this Act; and

(*b*) any sum by which the appropriate amount determined in accordance with the provisions of the Second Schedule to this Act in respect of the casualties (if any) payable to the intermediate landlord exceeds the appropriate amount determined in accordance with the provisions of the said Schedule in respect of the casualties (if any) payable by him.

(2) Any sums payable under this section shall bear interest at the rate of 5 per centum per annum from the date of entry under the feu right until paid.

Payments to creditors

10.—(1) Any lump sum received under subsection (1) of section 7 of this Act by a landlord shall be paid by him to the creditors in right of any heritable securities burdening his interest in the subjects comprised in the feu right according to the rights and preferences of such creditors, and shall be applied in extinction or reduction of the debts secured by the said securities:

Provided that the landlord and the creditor in right of any such security may agree that any amount which the landlord is liable to pay to the said creditor under this subsection shall not be so paid, or that a part only of such amount shall be so paid.

(2) Any sums received under the last foregoing section by an intermediate landlord shall be paid by him to the creditors in right of any securities which immediately before the grant of the feu right burdened his interest as intermediate landlord according to the rights and preferences of such creditors, and shall be applied in extinction or reduction of the debts secured by the said securities:

Provided that the intermediate landlord and the creditor in right of any such security may agree that any amount which the intermediate landlord is liable to pay to the said creditor under this subsection shall not be so paid, or that a part only of such amount shall be so paid.

Conveyancing provisions

Feu contract to be entered into on grant of feu right

11. Where a feu right is to be granted under this Part of this Act of any subjects let under a lease, a feu contract shall be entered into which shall be in, or as nearly as may be in, the form set out in the Fourth Schedule to this Act, and in particular—

(*a*) shall dispone the subjects subject to the conditions and restrictions specified in the lease in so far as they affect the subjects, are still subsisting and applicable and have not been implemented, departed from or discharged, and to such other conditions and restrictions, being reasonable and appropriate in the circumstances, as may be determined by agreement between the parties or, in default of such agreement, by the sheriff:

Provided that where the trustees of any religious denomination are the occupying lessee, there shall not without their consent be included in the feu contract a condition restricting the use of the subjects to use as a dwelling-house by a minister or full-time lay missionary of a religious denomination;

(*b*) shall contain a renunciation by the occupying lessee of the lease or sub-lease, as the case may be, under which he holds the interest of lessee, to the extent that such lease or sublease relates to the subjects; and

(*c*) where the occupying lessee is a sub-lessee, shall contain a renunciation by each intermediate landlord of the lease or sub-lease, as the case may be, under which such intermediate landlord holds the interest of lessee, to the extent that such lease or sub-lease relates to the subjects.

Rights to minerals

12. Where a feu right is to be granted under this Part of this Act of any subjects let under a lease, then unless the parties otherwise agree—

(*a*) if the minerals in the subjects are included in the lease, the said minerals shall be included in the feu right;

(*b*) if the said minerals are in terms of the lease expressly reserved to the landlord, they shall be reserved to the superior with such right to work the same, and subject to payment to the vassal of such compensation for surface damage, as is provided in the lease;

(*c*) if the said minerals are not in terms of the lease expressly reserved to the landlord, they shall be reserved to the superior with right to work the same (but without entering on the surface of the ground) subject to payment to the vassal of such compensation for surface damage as in default of agreement may be determined by arbitration;

and the feu contract disponing the subjects shall contain an appropriate clause relating to minerals:

Provided that this section shall not have effect in relation to coal or other minerals vested in the National Coal Board by virtue of the provisions of the Coal Industry Nationalisation Act 1946.

Execution of feu contract

13.—(1) The feu contract to be entered into on the grant of a feu right under this Part of this Act shall be signed by the landlord, the occupying lessee and, where the occupying lessee is a sub-lessee, each intermediate landlord.

(2) Where the landlord or any intermediate landlord fails to sign a feu contract as provided in the foregoing subsection within two months after he has been called upon to do so, the occupying lessee may present an application to the sheriff craving him to ordain such landlord or intermediate landlord, as the case may be, to sign the feu contract within such period as to the sheriff shall seem reasonable, and, if the landlord or intermediate landlord fails to sign the feu contract as so ordained, the sheriff may make an order dispensing with the signature to the feu contract of such landlord or intermediate landlord and directing the sheriff clerk to sign the feu contract on behalf of such landlord or intermediate landlord.

(3) Where an intermediate landlord is unknown or cannot be found, the occupying lessee may apply to the sheriff for an order dispensing with the signature to the feu contract of such intermediate landlord and directing the sheriff clerk to sign the feu contract on behalf of such intermediate landlord, and on making such an order the sheriff may, if he thinks fit, require the occupying lessee to consign in court any sums payable under section nine of this Act by him to such intermediate landlord.

(4) Where in pursuance of an order made by the sheriff under this section a feu contract is signed by the sheriff clerk on behalf of a landlord or an intermediate landlord, such feu contract shall have the like force and effect as if it had been signed by such landlord or intermediate landlord, as the case may be.

Provisions where lease or sub-lease assigned by ex facie **absolute assignation**

14. Where a feu right of any subjects is to be granted under this part of this Act and the lease or sub-lease under which the occupying lessee holds the interest of lessee has been assigned by *ex facie* absolute assignation—

(*a*) the feu contract to be entered into in accordance with the provisions of section 11 of this Act shall dispone the subjects to the occupying lessee;

(*b*) the renunciation referred to in paragraph (*b*) of the said section 11 shall be granted by the occupying lessee and the person for the time being in right of the said assignation (hereinafter in this section referred to as " the assignee ") for their respective interests in the lease or sub-lease to the extent that the lease or sub-lease relates to the subjects;

(*c*) the feu contract shall be signed also by the assignee and, where the assignee fails to sign the feu contract within two months after he has been called upon to do so, the provisions of subsections (2) and (4) of the last foregoing section shall apply as if the assignee were the landlord or an intermediate landlord;

(*d*) the occupying lessee shall forthwith dispone the subjects to the assignee by an *ex facie* absolute disposition which shall be recorded in the Register of Sasines along with the feu contract.

Continuation of certain leases and sub-leases

Continuation of leases and sub-leases expiring within five years after commencement of Act

15.—(1) Subject to the provisions of the next following section, where the ish of any lease or sub-lease falls within the period of five years beginning with the commencement of this Act and immediately before the ish the interest of lessee under such lease or sub-lease is held by an occupying lessee, not being an occupying lessee who acquired the said interest (otherwise than by inheritance) on or after the 10th day of May 1951, the lease or sub-lease, as the case may be, shall, to the extent that it relates to the subjects occupied by the occupying lessee as a private dwelling-house forming his usual residence, have effect as if for the ish there were substituted the term of Whitsunday, 1960.

(2) In this and the next following section any reference to an ish shall, in relation to a lease or a sub-lease continued by virtue of the Long Leases (Temporary Provisions) (Scotland) Act 1951, as extended by the Leasehold Property Act and Long Leases (Scotland) Act Extension Act 1953, be construed as a reference to the date to which such lease or sub-lease has at the commencement of this Act been so continued.

Power to occupying lessee to exclude operation of section 15

16.—(1) Where the occupying lessee under any lease or sub-lease gives to the person holding the interest of landlord under such lease or sub-lease, not later than forty days before the ish, notice in writing that he does not desire that the lease or sub-lease, as the case may be, shall be continued under the last foregoing section, that section shall not have effect regarding the lease or sub-lease.

(2) Where any lease or sub-lease has been continued under the last foregoing section and the occupying lessee gives to the person holding the interest of landlord under such lease or sub-lease notice in writing that he desires that the said section shall no longer apply to the lease or sub-lease, as the case may be, the lease or sub-lease shall come to an end on such date, not earlier than forty days after the date of the said notice, as may be specified therein.

Restriction on exercise of option to terminate lease or sub-lease

17. Where the person holding the interest of landlord under any lease or sub-lease has an option thereunder to terminate such lease or sub-lease on a date falling within the period of five years beginning with the commencement of this Act and immediately before the said date the interest of lessee under the lease or sub-lease is held by an occupying lessee, not being an occupying lessee who acquired the said interest (otherwise than by inheritance) on or after the 10th day of May 1951 the lease or sub-lease, as the case may be, shall, to the extent that it relates to the subjects occupied by the occupying lessee as a private dwelling-house forming his usual residence, have effect as if the said option were an option to terminate the lease or sub-lease at the term of Whitsunday, 1960.

Supplementary provisions

Rules for determining duration of lease or sub-lease

18.—(1) For the purposes of this Part of this Act, the following rules shall apply in determining the duration of any lease or sub-lease:—

(*a*) where the lease or sub-lease contains an obligation upon the person holding the interest of landlord thereunder to renew the same from time to time at fixed periods or upon the termination of a life or lives, the lease or sub-lease as the case may be, shall be deemed to endure for the full period to which the obligation to renew applies;

(*b*) where the duration of the lease or sub-lease is wholly or partly dependent upon the endurance of a life or lives, then—

(i) in the case of the life of a person no longer in existence, regard shall be had to the period for which such life existed or, if such period cannot be ascertained, the endurance of such life shall be deemed to be thirty-five years;

(ii) in the case of the life of an identifiable person in existence, the expentancy of life of such person shall be determined in accordance with the table set out in the Fifth Schedule to this Act;

(iii) in the case of the life of a person not yet in existence or not identifiable, the endurance of such life shall be deemed to be thirty-five years;

(*c*) where the person holding the interest of landlord under the lease or sub-lease has an option thereunder to terminate such lease or sub-lease on a date falling after the commencement of this Act, the lease or sub-lease, as the case may be, shall be deemed to expire on such date or, where there is more than one such date, on the first such date.

(2) For the purposes of section 1 of this Act, in determining the duration of any lease or sub-lease, regard shall not be had to the application (if any) to the lease or sub-lease of the Long Leases (Temporary Provisions) (Scotland) Act 1951, as extended by the Leasehold Property Act and Long Leases (Scotland) Act Extension Act 1953, or of sections 15 or 17 of this Act.

Rules for determining rent payable under lease or sub-lease

19. For the purposes of this Part of this Act, the following rules shall apply in determining the rent payable under any lease or sub-lease:—

(*a*) where the rent or a proportion thereof is payable in grain or other fungible or falls to be ascertained by reference to the price or value of grain or other fungible or otherwise than from the expression of the amount thereof in sterling money, the amount of such rent or of such proportion, as the case may be, shall be deemed to be equal to a sum in sterling money representing the average value, during the period of ten years immediately preceding the date of the notice given under section one of this Act by the occupying lessee, of the grain or other fungible delivered or deliverable or of the sum paid or payable in respect of such grain or other fungible;

(*b*) where lawful services or other duties of an annually recurring nature are stipulated for in the lease or sub-lease, the annual value of such services or duties in sterling money as the same shall be determined by agreement between the parties or, in default of such agreement, by the sheriff, shall be deemed to be the rent payable under the lease or sub-lease, or shall be added to any rent payable otherwise under the lease or sub-lease, as the case may be:

Provided that where such services or duties have not been exacted or insisted on within the period of ten years immediately preceding the 17th day of December 1953 no account shall be taken thereof.

Apportionment of rent

20. Where for the purposes of this Part of this Act it is necessary to apportion the rent payable under any lease or sub-lease between two or more parts of the property let under such lease or sub-lease, the apportionment shall be made by agreement amongst the parties concerned or, in default of such agreement, by the sheriff.

Provisions regarding securities

21.—(1) Where a feu right of any subjects is granted under this Part of this Act, any bond and assignation in security or other security (not being a security constituted by *ex facie* absolute assignation) which immediately prior to such grant burdened the interest of the occupying lessee shall, as from the appropriate date determined in accordance with the provisions of the next following subsection, have effect in relation to the said subjects as if it had been duly completed in accordance with the appropriate form usually employed in such cases for burdening property held in feu farm of a superior and shall burden the *dominium utile* of the subjects accordingly.

(2) The appropriate date for the purposes of the foregoing subsection shall be—

(*a*) where the bond and assignation in security or other security has been recorded in the Register of Sasines before the date of the feu contract disponing the subjects, the date of the said feu contract;

(*b*) where the bond and assignation in security or other security has not been so recorded before the date of the said feu contract, the date of recording such bond and assignation in security or other security in the Register of Sasines.

(3) Any securities which by virtue of this section burden the *dominium utile* of any subjects and any *ex facie* absolute disposition of those subjects granted in accordance with the provisions of paragraph (*d*) of section 14 of this Act shall be entitled to the same preferences *inter se* as if a feu right of those subjects had not been granted, and the creditors in right of securities which by virtue of this section burden the *dominium utile* of any subjects shall, in regard to the said subjects, be entitled to all the remedies competent to creditors holding corresponding securities over property held in feu farm for recovery of the sums due to them.

(4) Where a feu right of any subjects is granted under this Part of this Act, any bond and disposition in security or other heritable security which immediately prior to such grant burdened the interest of the landlord in the said subjects shall, as from the date of the feu contract disponing the subjects, burden only the superiority and not the *dominium utile* thereof, and the creditors in right of such securities shall, in regard to the said subjects, be entitled to all the remedies competent to creditors holding corresponding securities over an estate of superiority for recovery of the sums due to them.

(5) Where a feu right of any subjects is granted under this Part of this Act, any securities which immediately prior to such grant burdened the interest of an intermediate landlord shall, on the date of the feu contract disponing the said subjects, cease to burden such interest to the extent that such interest relates to the subjects and shall not burden or affect those subjects, but save as aforesaid such securities shall continue in full force and effect.

(6) Any reference in this section to the date of a feu contract shall, in relation to a feu contract executed on more than one date, be construed as a reference to the date on which such feu contract was last executed.

Expenses to be borne by occupying lessee

22. The expenses of any valuation carried out under subsection (3) of section 7 of this Act and the expenses of the preparation and execution of a feu contract or an *ex facie* absolute disposition under this Part of this Act, including the stamp duty payable thereon and the dues of recording the same, shall be borne by the occupying lessee.

Provisions regarding notices, etc.

23.—(1) Any notice or other document required or authorised by this Part of this Act to be given or sent to any person shall be sent by post in a registered letter addressed—

(*a*) to the said person; or

(*b*) where the said person is a landlord or an intermediate landlord, either to him or to the person to whom the rent under the lease or sub-lease, as the case may be, is in use to be paid; or

(*c*) where the said person, being an intermediate landlord, is unknown or cannot be found and no rent is being paid under the sub-lease, to the Extractor of the Court of Session; or

(*d*) where the said person is a local authority, development corporation, or an incorporated company or body, to the clerk, secretary or other proper officer of such authority, corporation, company or body.

(2) For the purposes of this section, the proper address of any person to whom any such notice or document is to be given or sent shall, in the case of

the clerk, secretary or other proper officer of a local authority, development corporation, or an incorporated company or body, be that of the principal or registered office of such authority, corporation, company or body, and in any other case shall be the last known address of the person in question.

(3) A copy of any such notice or document bearing a certificate of the due posting thereof signed by the person giving the notice or sending the document or by his solicitor, together with a post office receipt for the registered letter containing the notice or document, shall be sufficient evidence that the notice was duly given or that the document was duly sent, as the case may be, to the person to whom such registered letter was addressed at the address specified therein on the date mentioned in such receipt, which date shall be deemed to be the date of the notice or of the sending of the document, as the case may be.

(4) Any such notice or document shall be effectually given or sent notwithstanding that the person to whom it is required or authorised to be given or sent is in pupilarity or minority or otherwise subject to any legal incapacity at the date of the notice or at the date of the sending of the document, as the case may be.

Provisions regarding heirs of entail, etc.

24. It shall be lawful for all heirs of entail, trustees, judicial factors, tutors and curators, notwithstanding any limitations in their titles, to exercise all powers conferred by this Part of this Act and to execute, register and carry into effect all deeds required to render such powers fully operative, and such deeds shall be binding upon all persons whomsoever interested in the property to which such deeds relate.

Interpretation of Part I

Interpretation of Part I

25. In this Part of this Act, unless the context otherwise requires, the following expressions have the meanings hereby assigned to them respectively:—

" by inheritance " means as a beneficiary under a will or intestacy or as donee under a *mortis causa* donation;

" casualty " means any grassum, duplicand or other periodical or casual payment stipulated in a lease or a sub-lease to be payable in addition to the annual rent;

" heritable securities " and " securities " have the same meaning as in the Conveyancing (Scotland) Act 1924, except that they include securities constituted by *ex facie* absolute disposition or assignation;

" intermediate landlord " has the meaning assigned to it by section 6 of this Act;

" landlord " has the meaning assigned to it by section 1 of this Act;

" lease " has the meaning assigned to it by section 1 of this Act;

" lessee " has the meaning assigned to it by section 1 of this Act;

" occupying lessee " has the meaning assigned to it by section 1 of this Act;

" rent " includes rent, tack duty, or other services or prestations to be made under a lease or a sub-lease to the person holding the interest of landlord thereunder;

" sub-lease " has the meaning assigned to it by section 1 of this Act; and

" sub-lessee " has the meaning assigned to it by section 1 of this Act.

Part II

Extension and Amendment of Registration of Leases (Scotland) Act 1857

Extension of Registration of Leases (Scotland) Act 1857

26.—(1) Where a lease registrable under the Registration of Leases (Scotland) Act 1857, has not been recorded in the Register of Sasines and cannot be found, it shall be lawful to record a copy of such lease in the Register of Sasines under the said Act as if it were the lease if there is endorsed on such copy and recorded therewith a probative declaration signed by the landlord and lessee for the time being and containing—

(*a*) a statement that the lease cannot be found and that the copy is a true copy of the lease; and

(*b*) the names and designations of the said landlord and lessee (unless such names and designations are set forth in the copy).

(2) Where the landlord fails to sign a declaration as provided in the foregoing subsection within two months after he has been called upon to do so, the lessee may present an application to the sheriff craving him to ordain the landlord to sign the declaration within such period as to the sheriff shall seem reasonable; and, if the landlord fails to sign the declaration as so ordained, the sheriff may make an order dispensing with the signature to the declaration of the landlord and directing the sheriff clerk to sign the declaration on behalf of the landlord.

(3) Where in pursuance of an order made by the sheriff under this section a declaration is signed by the sheriff clerk on behalf of a landlord, such declaration shall have the like force and effect as if it had been signed by such landlord.

(4) Where in pursuance of this section a copy of any lease has been recorded in the Register of Sasines, such lease shall be deemed to have been so recorded on the date of the recording of the said copy.

Amendment of section 18 of Registration of Leases (Scotland) Act 1857

27.—(1) [Repealed by the Land Tenure Reform (Scotland) Act 1974, Scheds. 6 (para. 7) and 7.]

[1] (2) A lease recorded in the Register of Sasines under the said Act of 1857 before the commencement of this Act shall not be held to have been invalidly recorded by reason only that the name of the lands of which the subjects let consist or form a part is not set forth in such lease or by reason only that the extent of the land let is not set forth in such lease, if there is set forth in such lease a particular description of the subjects let under the lease or a description by reference of the said subjects in accordance with the provisions of the Conveyancing (Scotland) Act 1874, and the Conveyancing (Scotland) Act 1924.

NOTE

[1] As amended by the Land Tenure Reform (Scotland) Act 1974, Scheds. 6 (para. 7) and 7.

Part III

General

Applications to sheriff

28.—(1) Any dispute arising out of the provisions of this Act shall be referred to the sheriff and determined by him.

(2) The decision of the sheriff in any application made to him under this or any other section of this Act shall be final and not subject to review.

(3) The sheriff may in any such application make such award of expenses as he thinks proper, or may make no award of expenses.

(4) Any such application shall be conducted and disposed of in a summary manner.

(5) In this Act any reference to the sheriff shall, in relation to any lease or sub-lease, be construed as a reference to the sheriff within whose jurisdiction the property let under such lease or sub-lease, or any part of such property, is situated.

Application to Crown

29. This Act shall, subject to the provisions of section four thereof, apply where there is an interest belonging to Her Majesty in right of the Crown or to a Government department or held on behalf of Her Majesty for the purposes of a Government department in like manner as where no such interest subsists.

Construction of references to enactments

30. Any reference in this Act to any previous enactment shall, except in so far as the contrary intention appears, be construed as a reference to that enactment as amended, extended or applied by any subsequent enactment, including this Act.

Citation, commencement and extent

31.—(1) This Act may be cited as the Long Leases (Scotland) Act 1954.

(2) This Act shall come into operation on the 1st day of September, 1954.

(3) This Act shall apply to Scotland only.

SCHEDULES

Sections 1, 6

FIRST SCHEDULE

FORM OF NOTICE TO BE GIVEN BY AN OCCUPYING LESSEE WHO DESIRES THE GRANT OF A FEU RIGHT UNDER PART I OF THIS ACT

(1)

Take notice that A.B. (2) as lessee (*or* sub-lessee, *as the case may be*) of (3)
under lease (*or* sub-lease) entered into between
and dated
and recorded (*if recorded*)

(4) requires you to grant a feu right of the said subjects in accordance with the provisions of the Long Leases (Scotland) Act 1954.

Dated this day of , 19

(Signed) A.B.

or

C.D., W.S., Edinburgh.

Solicitor for the said A.B.

or

E. & F., W.S., Edinburgh,

Solicitors for the said A.B.

(*or as the case may be*)

Notes

(1) To be addressed to the landlord or to the person to whom the rent under the lease is in use to be paid.

(2) Name and design the occupying lessee.

(3) Describe here the subjects of which a feu right is required by usual name or short description sufficient for identification.

(4) Where the occupying lessee is a sub-lessee, add here—" which subjects form the whole (*or* part, *as the case may be*) of the property let under a lease entered into between and dated and recorded (*if recorded*) "

Sections 7, 8, 9

SECOND SCHEDULE

Determination of the Appropriate Amount in respect of Casualties Payable under a Lease or a Sub-lease

1. The appropriate amount in respect of the casualties payable under any lease or sub-lease shall be—

(*a*) such sum as may be determined by agreement between the landlord or intermediate landlord, as the case may be, and the occupying lessee, or

(*b*) in default of such agreement,—

(i) where casualties are exigible only on the death of the person holding the interest of lessee under the lease or sub-lease, a sum equal to the highest casualty or, if a feu right is to be granted of a part only of the property let under the lease or sub-lease, the proportion of such casualty attributable to the subjects to be comprised in the feu right:

Provided that if at the date of the notice given under section one of this Act by the occupying lessee and after payment of any casualty which may then be exigible the state of the title is such that the next casualty may be that payable on the entry or succession of an heir, and the amount of the casualty payable by an heir is less than the amount which would be payable on the entry of a singular successor, the said sum shall be subject to an abatement of one-half;

(ii) where casualties are exigible on the occasion of each transfer of the lease or sub-lease as well as on the death of the person holding the interest of lessee under the lease or sub-lease, a sum equal to one and two-thirds times the highest casualty or one and two-thirds times the proportion of such casualty attributable to the subjects to be comprised in the feu right, as the case may be:

Provided that if at the date of the said notice and after payment of any casualty which may then be exigible the state of the title is such that the next casualty may be that payable on the entry or succession of an heir, and the amount of the casualty payable by an heir is less than the amount which would be payable on the entry of a singular successor, the said sum shall be subject to an abatement of two-fifths;

(iii) where casualties are payable at fixed and regularly recurring intervals, such sum as will, with the addition of simple interest at the rate of five per centum per annum, produce on the next recurrence of the fixed interval a sum representing twenty-five times the highest casualty or twenty-five times the proportion of such casualty attributable to the subjects to be comprised in the feu right, as the case may be, divided by the number of years constituting such interval.

2. The appropriate amount determined under the foregoing paragraph shall be in respect only of casualties payable under the lease or sub-lease subsequent to the date of the notice referred to in that paragraph, and the appropriate amount shall be fixed as at the said date.

3. Where for the purposes of this Schedule it is necessary to apportion any casualty payable under a lease or a sub-lease between two or more parts of the property let under such lease or sub-lease, the apportionment shall be made by agreement amongst the parties concerned or, in default of such agreement, by the sheriff.

Section 9

[1] THIRD SCHEDULE

Table referred to in Paragraph (*a*) of Subsection (1) of Section Nine of this Act

Unexpired Period of Sub-lease	Capital Value of £1 per annum	Unexpired Period of Sub-lease	Capital Value of £1 per annum
Years	£ p	Years	£ p
1	0.95	6	5.10
2	1.85	7	5.80
3	2.70	8	6.45
4	3.55	9	7.10
5	4.35	10	7.70

TABLE REFERRED TO IN PARAGRAPH (*a*) OF SUBSECTION (1) OF SECTION NINE OF THIS ACT

Unexpired Period of Sub-lease	Capital Value of £1 per annum	Unexpired Period of Sub-lease	Capital Value of £1 per annum
11	8.30	36	16.55
12	8.85	37	16.70
13	9.40	38	16.85
14	9.90	39	17.00
15	10.40	40	17.15
16	10.85	41	17.30
17	11.25	42	17.40
18	11.70	43	17.55
19	12.10	44	17.65
20	12.45	45	17.75
21	12.80	46	17.90
22	13.15	47	18.00
23	13.50	48	18.10
24	13.80	49	18.15
25	14.10	50	18.25
26	14.40	51–55	18.50
27	14.65	56–60	18.80
28	14.90	61–65	19.10
29	15.15	66–70	19.30
30	15.35	71–75	19.45
31	15.60	76–80	19.55
32	15.80	81–85	19.65
33	16.00	86–90	19.75
34	16.20	91–95	19.80
35	16.35	96 and over	19.85

NOTE

[1] As amended by the Decimal Currency Act 1969, s. 10.

Sections 11, 12, 13, 14 FOURTH SCHEDULE

FORM OF FEU CONTRACT TO BE USED IN THE GRANT OF A FEU RIGHT UNDER PART I OF THIS ACT

It is contracted and agreed between the parties following, *viz.*:—A.B. (*designation*) heritable proprietor of the subjects hereinafter feued ON THE ONE PART and C.D. (*designation*) ON THE OTHER PART in manner following, that is to say:—WHEREAS the said subjects are the subjects (*or* a part of the property, *as the case may be*,) let by lease granted by E.F. (*designation*) in favour of G.H. (*designation*) dated   and recorded (*if recorded*)   which lease (*add, if necessary*, but only to the extent that it relates to the subjects hereinafter feued) is hereby renounced by the said C.D. as from the date of entry aftermentioned; and WHEREAS a feu right of the said subjects is hereinafter granted in accordance with the provisions of the Long Leases (Scotland) Act 1954, and (*where applicable*) the sum of £   is to be paid to the said A.B. by the said C.D. by way of a lump sum under subsection (1) of section seven of the said Act; THEREFORE the said A.B., in consideration of the payment of the said sum of £   (the receipt of which is hereby acknowledged by the said A.B.) and of the feu-duty and other prestations hereinafter mentioned, hereby in feu farm dispones to the said C.D. and his heirs and assignees whomsoever heritably and irredeemably All and Whole (*here insert description of subjects feued and include a clause relating to minerals in accordance with section twelve of this Act*); But always with and under the reservations, real burdens, conditions, provisions, restrictions, obligations and others following, *viz.*:—(*here insert conditions and restrictions specified in the lease in so far as they affect the subjects, are still subsisting and applicable and have not been implemented, departed from or discharged, and such other conditions and restrictions as have been determined by agreement between the parties or, in default of such agreement, by the sheriff*); And it is declared that all the reservations, burdens, conditions and others hereinbefore contained shall constitute real burdens on the subjects hereby feued and on all buildings erected or to be erected thereon, and it is directed that the same and the irritant and resolutive clauses hereinafter written shall be contained at full length in the infeftment to follow hereon and shall be imported in terms of law in all future transmissions and other writs of or relating to the feu or buildings or any part thereof but subject to section 9 of the Conveyancing (Scotland) Act 1924; And it is further declared that in the event of any contravention of or failure to fulfil the feuing conditions or the foregoing direction all acts and deeds of contravention shall be void and the said C.D. and his foresaids shall forfeit all right to the feu and buildings which shall revert and fall to the said A.B. or his heirs or successors free from all burdens as if these presents had never been granted; With entry at (*here insert date of notice given under section one of this Act by the occupying lessee or such other date as may be agreed between the parties*); To be holden of and under the said A.B. and his heirs and successors as immediate superiors in feu farm fee and heritage for ever paying therefor the sum of £ yearly in name of feu-duty and that at two terms in the year (*or, as the case may be, stating the terms at which the feu-duty is to be paid*), beginning the first term's payment at the term of for the period preceding and the next at the term of following and so forth half-yearly thereafter in all time coming. (*here insert provisions as to penalty and interest*); (*here insert clauses of assignation of writs and rents, obligation of relief and warrandice normal to a feu contract*); FOR WHICH CAUSES AND ON THE OTHER PART the said C.D. binds himself and his heirs, executors and representatives whomsoever to pay to the said A.B. and his foresaids the said sum of feu-duty at the respective terms of payment before mentioned with penalty and interest as aforesaid and to implement, observe and perform the whole other burdens, conditions and others hereinbefore written; (*here insert certificate of value, if applicable, and clause of registration*). [*To be attested.*]

Notes

1. Where the person to whom the subjects are to be feued is a sub-lessee, the form should be suitably adapted to include *inter alia* the following additional provisions:—

(*a*) a narrative of the sub-lease;

(*b*) a renunciation, to take effect as from the date of entry, by the intermediate landlord of the lease or sub-lease under which he holds the interest of lessee, to the extent that it relates to the subjects to be feued; and

(*c*) a narrative of any sums to be paid under section nine of this Act to the intermediate landlord by the sub-lessee and an acknowledgment of receipt of such sums.

2. If the person renouncing the lease or sub-lease is not the person in whose favour the lease or sub-lease was originally granted, add immediately after the renunciation—

(*a*) where his title is recorded—" which lease (*or* sub-lease and *add, if necessary,* ' to the extent that it relates to the subjects hereinafter feued ') is now vested in the said C.D., his title thereto being recorded in the said Division of the General Register of Sasines (*or as the case may be, and give date of recording*) "; or

(*b*) where his title is not recorded but the title of a predecessor vested in the lease or sub-lease was recorded,—" which lease (*or* sub-lease *and add, if necessary,* ' to the extent that it relates to the subjects hereinafter feued ') was last vested in the said G.H. as aforesaid (*or, if G.H. is not a person having such title, say,* ' in J.K. [*design person having said title*], whose title thereto is recorded in the said Division of the General Register of Sasines [*or as the case may be, and give date of recording*]'), and from whom the said C.D. acquired right by (*here specify shortly the writ or series of writs by which right was acquired*)"; or

(*c*) where there is no recorded title,—" And Whereas the said C.D. acquired right to the said lease (*or* sub-lease *and add, if necessary,* ' to the extent that it relates to the subjects hereinafter feued ') by (*here specify shortly the writ or series of writs by which right was acquired*) ".

3. Where the subjects disponed in the feu contract are comprised in a lease or a sub-lease which has been assigned by *ex facie* absolute assignation and the provisions of section fourteen of this Act apply, the form should be suitably adapted to fit the circumstances.

Section 18

FIFTH SCHEDULE

TABLE REFERRED TO IN PARAGRAPH (*b*) OF SUBSECTION (1) OF SECTION EIGHTEEN OF THIS ACT OF THE EXPECTANCY OF LIFE OF AN IDENTIFIABLE PERSON IN EXISTENCE

Years of age of Person	Years of expectancy	
	Male life	Female life
Birth to 4	65	69
5 to 9	63	67
10 to 14	58	62
15 to 19	53	57
20 to 24	48	52
25 to 29	44	48
30 to 34	39	43
35 to 39	35	38
40 to 44	30	33
45 to 49	26	29
50 to 54	22	25
55 to 59	18	21
60 to 64	15	17
65 to 69	12	13
70 to 74	9	10
75 to 79	7	8
80 to 84	5	6
85 and over	4	4

Costs of Leases Act 1958

(6 & 7 Eliz. 2, c. 52)

An Act to make provision for the incidence of the costs of leases.
[23rd July 1958]

Costs of leases

1. Notwithstanding any custom to the contrary, a party to a lease shall, unless the parties thereto agree otherwise in writing, be under no obligation to pay the whole or any part of any other party's solicitor's costs of the lease.

Interpretation

2. In this Act—

(*a*) " lease " includes an underlease and an agreement for a lease or underlease or for a tenancy or sub-tenancy;

(*b*) " costs " includes fees, charges, disbursements (including stamp duty), expenses and remuneration.

Short Title

3. This Act may be cited as the Costs of Leases Act 1958.

Occupiers' Liability (Scotland) Act 1960

(8 & 9 Eliz. 2, c. 30)

An Act to amend the law of Scotland as to the liability of occupiers and others for injury or damage occasioned to persons or property on any land or other premises by reason of the state of the premises or of anything done or omitted to be done thereon: and for purposes connected with the matter aforesaid.

[2nd June 1960]

Variation of rules of common law as to duty of care owed by occupiers

1.—(1) The provisions of the next following section of this Act shall have effect, in place of the rules of the common law, for the purpose of determining the care which a person occupying or having control of land or other premises (in this Act referred to as an " occupier of premises ") is required, by reason of such occupation or control, to show towards persons entering on the premises in respect of dangers which are due to the state of the premises or to anything done or omitted to be done on them and for which he is in law responsible.

(2) Nothing in those provisions shall be taken to alter the rules of the common law which determine the person on whom in relation to any premises a duty to show care as aforesaid towards persons entering thereon is incumbent.

(3) Those provisions shall apply, in like manner and to the same extent as they do in relation to an occupier of premises and to persons entering thereon,—

(*a*) in relation to a person occupying or having control of any fixed or moveable structure, including any vessel, vehicle or aircraft, and to persons entering thereon; and

(*b*) in relation to an occupier of premises or a person occupying or having control of any such structure and to property thereon, including the property of persons who have not themselves entered on the premises or structure.

Extent of occupier's duty to show care

2.—(1) The care which an occupier of premises is required, by reason of his occupation or control of the premises, to show towards a person entering thereon in respect of dangers which are due to the state of the premises or to anything done or omitted to be done on them and for which the occupier is in law responsible shall, except in so far as he is entitled to and does extend, restrict, modify or exclude by agreement his obligations towards that person, be such care as in all the circumstances of the case is reasonable to see that that person will not suffer injury or damage by reason of any such danger.

(2) Nothing in the foregoing subsection shall relieve an occupier of premises of any duty to show in any particular case any higher standard of care which in that case is incumbent on him by virtue of any enactment or rule of law imposing special standards of care on particular classes of persons.

(3) Nothing in the foregoing provisions of this Act shall be held to impose on an occupier any obligation to a person entering on his premises in respect of risks which that person has willingly accepted as his; and any question whether a risk was so accepted shall be decided on the same principles as in other cases in which one person owes to another a duty to show care.

Landlord's liability by virtue of responsibility for repairs

3.—(1) Where premises are occupied or used by virtue of a tenancy under which the landlord is responsible for the maintenance or repair of the premises, it shall be the duty of the landlord to show towards any persons who or whose property may from time to time be on the premises the same care in respect of dangers arising from any failure on his part in carrying out his responsibility aforesaid as is required by virtue of the foregoing provisions of this Act to be shown by an occupier of premises towards persons entering on them.

(2) Where premises are occupied or used by virtue of a sub-tenancy, the foregoing subsection shall apply to any landlord who is responsible for the maintenance or repair of the premises comprised in the sub-tenancy.

(3) Nothing in this section shall relieve a landlord of any duty which he is under apart from this section.

(4) For the purposes of this section, any obligation imposed on a landlord by any enactment by reason of the premises being subject to a tenancy shall be treated as if it were an obligation imposed on him by the tenancy, " tenancy " includes a statutory tenancy which does not in law amount to a tenancy and includes also any contract conferring a right of occupation, and " landlord " shall be construed accordingly.

(5) This section shall apply to tenancies created before the commencement of this Act as well as to tenancies created after its commencement.

Application to Crown

4. This Act shall bind the Crown, but as regards the liability of the Crown for any wrongful or negligent act or omission giving rise to liability in reparation shall not bind the Crown any further than the Crown is made liable in respect of such acts or omissions by the Crown Proceedings Act 1947, and that Act and in particular section 2 thereof shall apply in relation to duties under section 2 or section 3 of this Act as statutory duties.

Short title, extent and commencement

5.—(1) This Act may be cited as the Occupiers' Liability (Scotland) Act 1960, and shall extend to Scotland only.

(2) This Act shall come into operation at the end of the period of three months beginning with the day on which it is passed.

Wills Act 1963

(1963 c. 44)

An Act to repeal the Wills Act 1861, and make new provision in lieu thereof; and to provide that certain testamentary instruments shall be probative for the purpose of the conveyance of heritable property in Scotland. [31st July 1963]

General rule as to formal validity

1. A will shall be treated as properly executed if its execution conformed to the internal law in force in the territory where it was executed, or in the territory where, at the time of its execution or of the testator's death, he was domiciled or had his habitual residence, or in a state of which, at either of those times, he was a national.

Additional rules

2.—(1) Without prejudice to the preceding section, the following shall be treated as properly executed—

(*a*) a will executed on board a vessel or aircraft of any description, if the execution of the will conformed to the internal law in force in the territory with which, having regard to its registration (if any) and other relevant circumstances, the vessel or aircraft may be taken to have been most closely connected;

(*b*) a will so far as it disposes of immovable property, if its execution conformed to the internal law in force in the territory where the property was situated;

(*c*) a will so far as it revokes a will which under this Act would be treated as properly executed or revokes a provision which under this Act would be treated as comprised in a properly executed will, if the execution of the later will conformed to any law by reference to which the revoked will or provision would be so treated;

(*d*) a will so far as it exercises a power of appointment, if the execution of the will conformed to the law governing the essential validity of the power.

(2) A will so far as it exercises a power of appointment shall not be treated as improperly executed by reason only that its execution was not in accordance with any formal requirements contained in the instrument creating the power.

Certain requirements to be treated as formal

3. Where (whether in pursuance of this Act or not) a law in force outside the United Kingdom falls to be applied in relation to a will, any requirement of that law whereby special formalities are to be observed by testators answering a particular description, or witnesses to the execution of a will are to possess certain qualifications, shall be treated, notwithstanding any rule of that law to the contrary, as a formal requirement only.

Construction of wills

4. The construction of a will shall not be altered by reason of any change in the testator's domicile after the execution of the will.

5. [Repealed by the Succession (Scotland) Act 1964, Sched. 3.]

Interpretation

6.—(1) In this Act—

" internal law " in relation to any territory or state means the law which would apply in a case where no question of the law in force in any other territory or state arose;

" state " means a territory or group of territories having its own law of nationality;

" will " includes any testamentary instrument or act, and " testator " shall be construed accordingly.

(2) Where under this Act the internal law in force in any territory or state is to be applied in the case of a will, but there are in force in that territory or state two or more systems of internal law relating to the formal validity of wills, the system to be applied shall be ascertained as follows—

(*a*) if there is in force throughout the territory or state a rule indicating which of those systems can properly be applied in the case in question, that rule shall be followed; or

(*b*) if there is no such rule, the system shall be that with which the testator was most closely connected at the relevant time, and for this purpose the relevant time is the time of the testator's death where the matter is to be determined by reference to circumstances prevailing at his death, and the time of execution of the will in any other case.

(3) In determining for the purposes of this Act whether or not the execution of a will conformed to a particular law, regard shall be had to the

formal requirements of that law at the time of execution, but this shall not prevent account being taken of an alteration of law affecting wills executed at that time if the alteration enables the will to be treated as properly executed.

Short title, commencement, repeal and extent

7.—(1) This Act may be cited as the Wills Act 1963.

(2) This Act shall come into operation on 1st January 1964.

(3) The Wills Act 1861, is hereby repealed.

(4) This Act shall not apply to a will of a testator who died before the time of the commencement of this Act and shall apply to a will of a testator who dies after that time whether the will was executed before or after that time, but so that the repeal of the Wills Act 1861, shall not invalidate a will executed before that time.

[1] (5) It is hereby declared that this Act extends to Northern Ireland.

NOTE

[1] As amended by the Northern Ireland Constitution Act 1973 (c. 36), Sched. 6, Pt. I.

Conveyancing and Feudal Reform (Scotland) Act 1970

(1970 c. 35)

An Act to provide as respects Scotland for the variation and discharge of certain obligations relating to land; to facilitate the allocation of feu-duties and ground annuals; to reduce the period of positive prescription of 20 years to 10 years; to provide for a new form of heritable security; to make certain amendments to the existing law relating to heritable securities; to make certain other amendments to the law relating to conveyancing; to abolish the rights of pre-emption of heritors in respect of glebes; to amend the Lands Tribunal Act 1949; and for connected purposes. [29th May 1970]

Part I

Feudal Reform

Variation and discharge of land obligations

Variation and discharge of land obligations

[1] **1.**—(1) The provisions of this section and of section 2 of this Act shall, without prejudice to any other method of variation or discharge, apply for the variation or discharge of any land obligation, however constituted, and whether subsisting at the commencement of this Act or constituted thereafter:

Provided that the provisions of the said sections shall not apply in relation to an obligation specified or referred to in Schedule 1 to this Act.

[2] (2) For the purposes of this section and of section 2 of this Act, a land obligation is an obligation relating to land which is enforceable by a proprietor of an interest in land, by virtue of his being such proprietor, and which is binding upon a proprietor of another interest in that land, or of an interest in other land, by virtue of his being such proprietor.

For the purposes mentioned in this subsection, an obligation includes a future or contingent obligation, an obligation to defray or contribute towards some cost, an obligation to refrain from doing something, and an obligation to permit or suffer something to be done or maintained.

(3) Subject to the provisions of this section and of section 2 of this Act, the Lands Tribunal, on the application of any person who, in relation to a land obligation, is a burdened proprietor, may from time to time by order vary or discharge the obligation wholly or partially in relation to the interest in land in respect of which the application is made, on being satisfied that in all the circumstances,

(*a*) by reason of changes in the character of the land affected by the obligation or of the neighbourhood thereof or other circumstances which the Tribunal may deem material, the obligation is or has become unreasonable or inappropriate; or

(*b*) the obligation is unduly burdensome compared with any benefit resulting or which would result from its performance; or

(*c*) the existence of the obligation impedes some reasonable use of the land.

(4) An order varying or discharging a land obligation under this section may direct the applicant to pay, to any person who in relation to that obligation is a benefited proprietor, such sum as the Lands Tribunal may think it just to award under one, but not both, of the following heads—

(i) a sum to compensate for any substantial loss or disadvantage suffered by the proprietor as such benefited proprietor in consequence of the variation or discharge; or

(ii) a sum to make up for any effect which the obligation produced, at the time when it was imposed, in reducing the consideration then paid or made payable for the interest in land affected by it;

but the Tribunal may refuse to vary or discharge a land obligation on the ground specified in subsection (3)(*c*) of this section if they are of the opinion that, due to exceptional circumstances related to amenity or otherwise, money would not be an adequate compensation for any loss or disadvantage which a benefited proprietor would suffer from the variation or discharge.

(5) The power conferred by this section to vary or discharge an obligation includes power to add or substitute any such provision (not being an award of money otherwise than by way of compensation under subsection (4) of this section) as appears to the Lands Tribunal to be reasonable as the result of the variation or discharge of the obligation and as may be accepted by the applicant; and the Tribunal may accordingly refuse to vary or discharge the obligation without some such provision.

(6) On the taking effect of an order under this section varying or discharging to any extent a land obligation, any irritant or resolutive clause or other condition relating to the enforcement of the obligation shall, in relation to any act or omission occurring after the date of such taking effect, be effective (if at all) only in so far as it would have been effective if the obligation had to that extent been varied or discharged by the person entitled to enforce the obligation; and any such added or substituted provision as is referred to in subsection (5) of this section shall be enforceable in the same manner as the obligation to the variation or discharge of which it relates.

NOTES

[1] Excluded by the Ancient Monuments and Archaeological Areas Act 1979 (c. 46), s. 17(7).

[2] See the Crofters (Scotland) Act 1993 (c. 44), s. 16(6) (effective 5th January 1994: s. 64(2)). Definition of "land obligations" applied: see the Land Registration (Scotland) Act 1979 (c. 33), ss. 17(2) and 18(2) (*infra*).

Provisions supplementary to section 1

[1] **2.**—(1) On an application under section 1 of this Act, the Lands Tribunal shall give such notice thereof, whether by way of advertisement or otherwise, as may be prescribed, to the persons who, in relation to the

obligation which is the subject of the application, appear to them to be either benefited or burdened proprietors, and to such other person as the Tribunal may think fit.

(2) In an application to the Lands Tribunal under section 1 of this Act, any person who, in relation to the obligation which is the subject of the application, is either a burdened or a benefited proprietor, shall be entitled, within such time as may be prescribed, to oppose or make representations in relation to the application, and the Tribunal shall allow any such person, and may allow any other person who appears to them to be affected by the obligation or by its proposed variation or discharge, to be heard in relation to the application.

(3) An order made under section 1 of this Act shall take effect in accordance with such rules as may be prescribed.

[2] (4) Where an extract of an order made under section 1 of this Act which has taken effect is duly recorded, it shall be binding on all persons having interest.

(5) Where a land obligation is first created, whether before or after the commencement of this Act, in a conveyance, deed, instrument or writing, no application shall be brought under section 1 of this Act in relation thereto until the expiry of two years after the date of its creation.

(6) For the purposes of this section and of section 1 of this Act,

" benefited proprietor ", in relation to a land obligation, means a proprietor of an interest in land who is entitled, by virtue of his being such proprietor, to enforce the obligation; and " burdened proprietor ", in relation to such an obligation, means a proprietor of an interest in land upon whom, by virtue of his being such proprietor, the obligation is binding; and—

(i) the benefited proprietor or the burdened proprietor of an interest in land held by two or more persons jointly or in common means either all those persons or any of them;

(ii) the benefited proprietor or the burdened proprietor of an interest in land which is subject to a heritable security constituted by *ex facie* absolute disposition or assignation includes the person who, if the debt were discharged, would be entitled to be vested in that interest;

" interest in land " means any estate or interest in land which is capable of being owned or held as a separate interest and to which a title may be recorded in the Register of Sasines;

" land obligation " has the meaning assigned to it in section 1 (2) of this Act.

(7) Section 189 of the Housing (Scotland) Act 1966 (power of sheriff to authorise conversion of house into separate dwellings) shall cease to have effect.

NOTES

[1] Excluded by the Ancient Monuments and Archaeological Areas Act 1979, s. 17 (7).

[2] As amended by the Land Tenure Reform (Scotland) Act 1974, s. 19.

Allocation of feuduties, etc.

Allocation of feuduties

3.—(1) The provisions of this section and of sections 4 and 5 of this Act shall, without prejudice to any other method of allocation, apply for the purpose of allocating any *cumulo* feuduty, whether constituted before or after the commencement of this Act.

(2) For the purposes of this section and of sections 4 and 5 of this Act,

" *cumulo* feuduty " means the whole of a feuduty which at any given time is exigible in respect of land consisting of two or more parts held by separate proprietors, being a feuduty which at that time has not been allocated upon those parts by the superior or under this Act;

" feu " means the whole land burdened with a *cumulo* feuduty; and

" land " has the meaning assigned to it in section 3 of the Conveyancing (Scotland) Act 1874.

(3) Any proprietor of part of a feu may serve upon his superior or upon any other person to whom the *cumulo* feuduty is paid on his behalf a notice of allocation of the portion of the *cumulo* feuduty which has been apportioned by disposition or other document or by any other method (formal or informal) on the part of the feu of which he is proprietor.

(4) A notice of allocation shall be in, or as nearly as may be in, such form as may be prescribed by regulations made by the Secretary of State by statutory instrument, and shall contain—

(*a*) the name and address of the proprietor serving the notice and a sufficient identification of the part of the feu of which he is proprietor and on which he wishes the portion of the *cumulo* feuduty to be allocated, and the name and address of the person to whom that portion is paid;

(*b*) a statement of the amount of that portion;

(*c*) a statement to the effect that that portion of the feuduty is to be allocated under the Conveyancing and Feudal Reform (Scotland) Act 1970 on the part of the feu of which the person serving the notice is the proprietor;

and shall be signed by the proprietor or his agent.

(5) Subject to the provisions of sections 4 and 5 of this Act, a notice of allocation shall be effective to allocate on the part of the feu of which the person serving the notice is the proprietor the portion of the *cumulo* feuduty stated in the notice.

Applications to Lands Tribunal regarding allocation of feuduties

4.—(1) If a superior upon whom a notice of allocation has been served under section 3 of this Act wishes to object to the amount of the portion of feuduty of which allocation is sought by the proprietor serving the notice, he may, within such time as may be prescribed, apply to the Lands Tribunal, and on such application, the Tribunal (except in so far as they consider it impracticable to do so) shall by order allocate the *cumulo* feuduty, in such manner as they consider reasonable, on the part of the feu of which the person serving the notice is the proprietor, and on every other part of the feu which is held by a separate proprietor.

(2) On any application to the Lands Tribunal under this section, the Tribunal shall give such notice thereof, whether by way of advertisement or otherwise, as may be prescribed, to the persons who appear to them to be proprietors of parts of the feu in respect of which the *cumulo* feuduty is exigible, and to such other persons as the Tribunal may think fit; and the Tribunal shall allow the superior of the feu and any such proprietor, and may allow any other person who appears to them to have an interest in the application, to be heard in relation thereto.

Provisions supplementary to sections 3 and 4

5.—(1) Where, under the provisions of this Act, a portion of a *cumulo* feuduty has been allocated on a part of a feu, that part of the feu shall, in relation to the rights and obligations of the proprietors of the remainder of the feu relating to payment of the remainder of the feuduty, be treated as if it had never been part of the feu and as if the portion of the feuduty allocated on it had never formed part of the *cumulo* feuduty.

(2) Nothing in section 4 of this Act shall empower the Lands Tribunal to make an order which would result in any alteration of the total amount of

feuduty exigible in respect of the feu which, before the making of the order, was burdened with the *cumulo* feuduty allocated by the order.

(3) An order of the Lands Tribunal under section 4 of this Act allocating the whole of the *cumulo* feuduty to which the order relates shall supersede for all purposes any existing apportionment of that feuduty.

(4) Where an application is made to the Lands Tribunal under section 4 of this Act in respect of a notice relating to a *cumulo* feuduty, any notice of allocation relating to that feuduty shall be of no effect.

(5) Subject to the provisions of this section, an allocation of feuduty effected under section 3 or 4 of this Act shall take effect as respects the amount of the feuduty so allocated which becomes exigible at any term occurring not less than three months after the service of the notice of allocation or (in the case of an allocation effected by order of the Lands Tribunal) after the date of the order, as if it were effected by a duly recorded memorandum of allocation under the law in force before the commencement of this Act.

(6) In any proceedings, the production of a document purporting to be a copy of a notice of allocation together with a registered post or recorded delivery service receipt addressed to the superior shall be sufficient evidence of the fact and date of service of the notice; and any such copy shall be taken to be a true copy unless the contrary is shown.

(7) For the purposes of this section and of sections 3 and 4 of this Act,

"notice of allocation" means a notice under section 3 of this Act;

"proprietor", in relation to a part of a feu, includes a person having right to that part but whose title thereto is not complete, and includes a person who is obliged to relieve the proprietor of liability for payment of the whole or part of the *cumulo* feuduty burdening that feu;

"superior", in relation to a feu, means the immediate superior, and includes a person having right to a superiority but whose title thereto is not complete.

Allocation of ground annuals

6. The provisions of sections 3 to 5 of this Act shall apply in relation to a ground annual as they apply in relation to a feuduty, and for the purposes of such application—

"*cumulo* feuduty" and "feu" shall be construed accordingly; and

"superior" means the creditor in the ground annual.

Provisions for contracting out of sections 1 to 6 to be void

Provisions for contracting out of sections 1 to 6 void

7. Any agreement or other provision, however constituted, shall be void in so far as it purports to exclude or limit the operation of any enactment contained in sections 1 to 6 of this Act.

Reduction of period of positive prescription

8. [Repealed by the Prescription and Limitation (Scotland) Act 1973 (c. 52), Sched. 5, Pt. I.]

[1] PART II

THE STANDARD SECURITY

NOTE

[1] See also the Redemption of Standard Securities (Scotland) Act 1971 (c. 45), s. 2. Applied (with modification) by the Health and Social Services and Social Security Adjudications Act 1983 (c. 41), s. 23 (effective 12th April 1993: S.I. 1992 No. 2974), and S.I. 1993 No. 1516 (*infra*).

The standard security

9.—(1) The provisions of this Part of this Act shall have effect for the purpose of enabling a new form of heritable security to be created to be known as a standard security.

(2) It shall be competent to grant and record in the Register of Sasines a standard security over any interest in land to be expressed in conformity with one of the forms prescribed in Schedule 2 to this Act.

(3) A grant of any right over an interest in land for the purpose of securing any debt by way of a heritable security shall only be capable of being effected at law if it is embodied in a standard security.

(4) Where for the purpose last-mentioned any deed which is not in the form of a standard security contains a disposition or assignation of an interest in land, it shall to that extent be void and unenforceable, and where that deed has been duly recorded the creditor in the purported security may be required, by any person having an interest, to grant any deed which may be appropriate to clear the Register of Sasines of that security.

(5) A standard security may be used for any other purpose for which a heritable security may be used if any of the said forms is appropriate to that purpose, and for the purpose of any enactment affecting heritable securities a standard security, if so used, or if used as is required by this Act instead of a heritable security as defined therein, shall be a heritable security for the purposes of that enactment.

(6) *Act of the Parliament of Scotland 1696, c. 5.* The Bankruptcy Act 1696, in so far as it renders a heritable security of no effect in relation to a debt contracted after the recording of that security, and any rule of law which requires that a real burden for money may only be created in respect of a sum specified in the deed of creation, shall not apply in relation to a standard security.

(7) [Repealed by the Tenants' Rights, etc. (Scotland) Act 1980, Sched. 5.]

(8) For the purposes of this Part of this Act—

[1] (*a*) "heritable security" (except in subsection (5) of this section if the context otherwise requires) means any security capable of being constituted over any interest in land by disposition or assignation of that interest in security of any debt and of being recorded in the Register of Sasines;

(*b*) "interest in land" means any estate or interest in land, other than an entailed estate or any interest therein, which is capable of being owned or held as a separate interest and to which a title may be recorded in the Register of Sasines;

(*c*) "debt" means any obligation due, or which will or may become due, to repay or pay money, including any such obligation arising from a transaction or part of a transaction in the course of any trade, business or profession, and any obligation to pay an annuity or *ad factum praestandum*, but does not include an obligation to pay any feuduty, ground annual, rent or other periodical sum payable in respect of land, and "creditor" and "debtor", in relation to a standard security, shall be construed accordingly.

NOTE

[1] Applied by the Aviation Security Act 1982 (c. 36), Sched. 1, para. 11.

Import of forms of, and certain clauses in, standard security

10.—(1) The import of the clause relating to the personal obligation contained in Form A of Schedule 2 to this Act expressed in any standard security shall, unless specially qualified, be as follows—

(*a*) where the security is for a fixed amount advanced or payable at, or prior to, the delivery of the deed, the clause undertaking to make payment to the creditor shall import an acknowledgment of receipt by the debtor of the principal sum advanced or an acknowledgment by the debtor of liability to pay that sum and a personal obligation undertaken by the debtor to repay or pay to the creditor on demand in writing at any time after the date of delivery of the standard security the said sum, with interest at the rate stated payable on the dates specified, together with all expenses for which the debtor is liable by virtue of the deed or of this Part of this Act;

(*b*) where the security is for a fluctuating amount, whether subject to a maximum amount or not and whether advanced or due partly before and partly after delivery of the deed or whether to be advanced or to become due wholly after such delivery, the clause undertaking to make payment to the creditor shall import a personal obligation by the debtor to repay or pay to the creditor on demand in writing the amount, not being greater than the maximum amount, if any, specified in the deed, advanced or due and outstanding at the time of demand, with interest on each advance from the date when it was made until repayment thereof, or on each sum payable from the date on which it became due until payment thereof, and at the rate stated payable on the dates specified, together with all expenses for which the debtor is liable by virtue of the deed or of this Part of this Act.

(2) The clause of warrandice in the forms of standard security contained in Schedule 2 to this Act expressed in any standard security shall, unless specially qualified, import absolute warrandice as regards the interest in land over which the security is granted and the title deeds thereof, and warrandice from fact and deed as regards the rents thereof.

(3) The clause relating to consent to registration for execution contained in Form A of Schedule 2 to this Act, expressed in any standard security shall, unless specially qualified, import a consent to registration in the Books of Council and Session, or, as the case may be, in the books of the appropriate sheriff court, for execution.

(4) The forms of standard security contained in Schedule 2 to this Act shall, unless specially qualified, import an assignation to the creditor of the title deeds, including searches, and all conveyances not duly recorded, affecting the security subjects or any part thereof, with power to the creditor in the event of a sale under the powers conferred by the security, but subject to the rights of any person holding prior rights to possession of those title deeds, to deliver them, so far as in the creditor's possession, to the purchaser, and to assign to the purchaser any right he may possess to have the title deeds made forthcoming.

Effect of recorded standard security, and incorporation of standard conditions

11.—(1) Where a standard security is duly recorded, it shall operate to vest the interest over which it is granted in the grantee as a security for the performance of the contract to which the security relates.

(2) Subject to the provisions of this Part of this Act, the conditions set out in Schedule 3 to this Act, either as so set out or with such variations as have been agreed by the parties in the exercise of the powers conferred by the said Part (which conditions are hereinafter in this Act referred to as " the standard conditions "), shall regulate every standard security.

[1] (3) Subject to the provisions of this Part of this Act, the creditor and debtor in a standard security may vary any of the standard conditions, other than standard condition 11 (procedure on redemption) and the provisions of Schedule 3 to this Act relating to the powers of sale and foreclosure and to the exercise of those powers, but no condition capable of being varied shall be varied in a manner inconsistent with any condition which may not be varied by virtue of this subsection.

(4) In this Part of this Act—

(*a*) any reference to a variation of the standard conditions shall include a reference to the inclusion of an additional condition and to the exclusion of a standard condition;

(*b*) any purported variation of a standard condition which contravenes the provisions of subsection (3) of this section shall be void and unenforceable.

NOTE

[1] As amended by the Redemption of Standard Securities (Scotland) Act 1971, s. 1.

Standard security may be granted by person uninfeft

[1] **12.**—(1) Notwithstanding any rule of law, a standard security may be granted over an interest in land by a person having right to that interest, but whose title thereto has not been completed by being duly recorded, if in the deed expressing that security the grantor deduces his title to that interest from the person who appears in the Register of Sasines as having the last recorded title thereto.

(2) A deduction of title in a deed for the purposes of the foregoing subsection shall be expressed in the form prescribed by Note 2 or 3 of Schedule 2 to this Act, and on such a deed being recorded as aforesaid the title of the grantee shall, for the purposes of the rights and obligations between the grantor and the grantee thereof, and those deriving right from them, but for no other purpose, in all respects be of the same effect as if the title of the grantor of the deed to the interest to which he has deduced title therein had been duly completed; and any references to a proprietor or to a person last infeft shall in this Part of this Act be construed accordingly.

(3) There may be specified for the purposes of any deduction of title in pursuance of any provision of this Part of this Act any writing which it is competent to specify as a title, midcouple, or link in title for the purposes of section 5 of the Conveyancing (Scotland) Act 1924 (deduction of title).

NOTE

[1] Excluded by the Land Registration (Scotland) Act 1979, s. 15 (3).

Ranking of standard securities

[1] **13.**—(1) Where the creditor in a standard security duly recorded has received notice of the creation of a subsequent security over the same interest in land or any part thereof, or of the subsequent assignation or conveyance of that interest in whole or in part, being a security, assignation or conveyance so recorded, the preference in ranking of the security of that creditor shall be restricted to security for his present advances and future advances which he may be required to make under the contract to which the security relates and interest present or future due thereon (including any such interest which has accrued or may accrue) and for any expenses or outlays (including interest thereon) which may be, or may have been, reasonably incurred in the exercise of any power conferred on any creditor by the deed expressing the existing security.

(2) For the purposes of the foregoing subsection—

(*a*) a creditor in an existing standard security duly recorded shall not be held to have had any notice referred to in that subsection, by reason only of the subsequent recording of the relevant deed in the Register of Sasines;

(*b*) any assignation, conveyance or vesting in favour of or in any other person of the interest of the debtor in the security subjects or in any part thereof resulting from any judicial decree, or otherwise by operation of law, shall constitute sufficient notice thereof to the creditor.

(3) Nothing in the foregoing provisions of this section shall affect—

(*a*) any preference in ranking enjoyed by the Crown; and

(*b*) any powers of the creditor and debtor in any heritable security to regulate the preference to be enjoyed by creditors in such manner as they may think fit.

NOTE

[1] See the Tenants' Rights, Etc. (Scotland) Act 1980, s. 6 (5).

Assignation of standard security

14.—(1) Any standard security duly recorded may be transferred, in whole or in part, by the creditor by an assignation in conformity with Form A or B of Schedule 4 to this Act, and upon such an assignation being duly recorded, the security, or, as the case may be, part thereof, shall be vested in the assignee as effectually as if the security or the part had been granted in his favour.

(2) An assignation of a standard security shall, except so far as otherwise therein stated, be deemed to convey to the grantee all rights competent to the grantor to the writs, and shall have the effect *inter alia* of vesting in the assignee—

(*a*) the full benefit of all corroborative or substitutional obligations for the debt, or any part thereof, whether those obligations are contained in any deed or arise by operation of law or otherwise,

(*b*) the right to recover payment from the debtor of all expenses properly incurred by the creditor in connection with the security, and

(*c*) the entitlement to the benefit of any notices served and of all procedure instituted by the creditor in respect of the security to the effect that the grantee may proceed as if he had originally served or instituted such notices or procedure.

Restriction of standard security

15.—(1) The security constituted by any standard security duly recorded may be restricted, as regards any part of the interest in land burdened by the security, by a deed of restriction in conformity with Form C of Schedule 4 to this Act, and, upon that deed being duly recorded, the security shall be restricted to the interest in land contained in the standard security other than the part of that interest disburdened by the deed; and the interest in land thereby disburdened shall be released from the security wholly or to the extent specified in the deed.

(2) A partial discharge and deed of restriction of a standard security, which has been duly recorded, may be combined in one deed, which shall be in conformity with Form D of the said Schedule 4.

Variation of standard security

16.—(1) Any alteration in the provisions (including any standard condition) of a standard security duly recorded, other than an alteration which may appropriately be effected by an assignation, discharge or restriction of that standard security, or an alteration which involves an addition to, or an extension of, the interest in land mentioned therein, may be effected by a variation endorsed on the standard security in conformity with Form E of Schedule 4 to this Act, or by a variation contained in a separate deed in a form appropriate for that purpose, duly recorded in either case.

(2) Where a standard security has been duly recorded, but the personal obligation or any other provision (including any standard condition) relating to the security has been created or specified in a deed which has not been so recorded, nothing contained in this section shall prevent any alteration in that personal obligation or provision, other than an alteration which may be

appropriately effected by an assignation, discharge or restriction of the standard security, or an alteration which involves an addition to, or an extension of, the interest in land mentioned therein, by a variation contained in any form of deed appropriate for that purpose, and such a variation shall not require to be recorded in the Register of Sasines.

(3) [Repealed by the Finance Act 1971, Sched. 14, Pt. VI.]

(4) Any variation effected in accordance with this section shall not prejudice any other security or right over the same interest in land, or any part thereof, effectively constituted before the variation is recorded, or, where the variation is effected by an unrecorded deed, before that deed is executed, as the case may be.

Discharge of standard security

17. A standard security duly recorded may be discharged, and the interest in land burdened by that security may be disburdened thereof, in whole or in part, by a discharge in conformity with Form F of Schedule 4 to this Act, duly recorded.

Redemption of standard security

[1] **18.**—(1) Subject to the provisions of subsection (1A) of this section the debtor in a standard security or, where the debtor is not the proprietor, the proprietor of the security subjects shall be entitled to redeem the security on giving two months' notice of his intention so to do and in conformity with the terms of standard condition 11 and the appropriate Forms of Schedule 5 to this Act.

[2] (1A) Without prejudice to section 11 of the Land Tenure Reform (Scotland) Act 1974, the provisions of the foregoing subsection shall be subject to any agreement to the contrary, but any right to redeem the security shall be exercisable in conformity with the terms and Forms referred to in that subsection.

[3] (2) Where owing to the death or absence of the creditor, or to any other cause, the debtor in a standard security or, as the case may be, the proprietor of the security subjects (being in either case a person entitled to redeem the security) is unable to obtain a discharge under the foregoing provisions of this section, he may—

(*a*) where the security was granted in respect of any obligation to repay or pay money, consign in any bank in Scotland, incorporated by or under Act of Parliament or by Royal Charter, the whole amount due to the creditor on redemption, other than any unascertained expenses of the creditor, for the person appearing to have the best right thereto, and

(*b*) in any other case, apply to the court for declarator that the whole obligations under the contract to which the security relates have been performed.

(3) On consignation, or on the court granting declarator as aforesaid, a certificate to that effect may be expede by a solicitor in the appropriate form prescribed by Form D of Schedule 5 to this Act, which on being duly recorded shall disburden the interest in land, to which the standard security relates, of that security.

(4) For the purposes of this section, " whole amount due " means the debt to which the security relates, so far as outstanding, and any other sums due thereunder by way of interest or otherwise.

NOTES

[1] As amended by the Redemption of Standard Securities (Scotland) Act 1971, s. 1.

[2] Added by the Redemption of Standard Securities (Scotland) Act 1971, s. 1, and as amended by the Land Tenure Reform (Scotland) Act 1974, s. 11 (6).

[3] As amended by the Redemption of Standard Securities (Scotland) Act 1971, s. 1.

Calling-up of standard security

19.—(1) Where a creditor in a standard security intends to require discharge of the debt thereby secured and, failing that discharge, to exercise any power conferred by the security to sell any subjects of the security or any other power which he may appropriately exercise on the default of the debtor within the meaning of standard condition 9 (1) (*a*), he shall serve a notice calling-up the security in conformity with Form A of Schedule 6 to this Act (hereinafter in this Act referred to as a " calling-up notice "), in accordance with the following provisions of this section.

(2) Subject to the following provisions of this section, a calling-up notice shall be served on the person last infeft in the security subjects and appearing on the record as the proprietor and, should the proprietor of those subjects, or any part thereof, be dead then on his representative or the person entitled to the subjects in terms of the last recorded title thereto, notwithstanding any alteration of the succession not appearing in the Register of Sasines.

(3) Where the person last infeft in the security subjects was an incorporated company which has been removed from the Register of Companies, or a person deceased who has left no representatives, a calling-up notice shall be served on the Lord Advocate and, where the estates of the person last infeft have been sequestrated under the Bankruptcy (Scotland) Act 1913, the notice shall be served on the trustee in the sequestration (unless such trustee has been discharged) as well as on the bankrupt.

(4) If the proprietor be a body of trustees, it shall be sufficient if the notice is served on a majority of the trustees infeft in the security subjects.

(5) It shall be an obligation on the creditor to serve a copy of the calling-up notice on any other person against whom he wishes to preserve any right of recourse in respect of the debt.

(6) For the purposes of the foregoing provisions of this section, the service of a calling-up notice may be made by delivery to the person on whom it is desired to be served or the notice may be sent by registered post or by the recorded delivery service to him at his last known address, or, in the case of the Lord Advocate, at the Crown Office, Edinburgh, and an acknowledgment, signed by the person on whom service has been made, in conformity with Form C of Schedule 6 to this Act, or, as the case may be, a certificate in conformity with Form D of that Schedule, accompanied by the postal receipt shall be sufficient evidence of the service of that notice; and if the address of the person on whom the notice is desired to be served is not known, or if it is not known whether that person is still alive, or if the packet containing a calling-up notice is returned to the creditor with an intimation that it could not be delivered, that notice shall be sent to the Extractor of the Court of Session, and shall be equivalent to the service of a calling-up notice on the person on whom it is desired to be served.

(7) For the purposes of the last foregoing subsection, an acknowledgment of receipt by the said Extractor on a copy of a calling-up notice shall be sufficient evidence of the receipt by him of that notice.

(8) A calling-up notice served by post shall be held to have been served on the next day after the day of posting.

(9) Where a creditor in a standard security has indicated in a calling-up notice that any sum and any interest thereon due under the contract may be subject to adjustment in amount, he shall, if the person on whom notice has been served so requests, furnish the debtor with a statement of the amount as finally determined within a period of one month from the date of service of the calling-up notice, and a failure by the creditor to comply with the provisions of this subsection shall cause the calling-up notice to be of no effect.

[1] (10) The period of notice mentioned in the calling-up notice may be effectively dispensed with or shortened by the person on whom it is served,

with the consent of the creditors, if any, holding securities *pari passu* with, or postponed to, the security held by the creditor serving the calling-up notice, by a minute written or endorsed upon the said notice, or a copy thereof, in conformity with Form C of Schedule 6 to this Act.

Provided that, without prejudice to the foregoing generality, if the standard security is over a matrimonial home as defined in section 22 of the Matrimonial Homes (Family Protection) (Scotland) Act 1981, the spouse on whom the calling-up notice has been served may not dispense with or shorten the said period without the consent in writing of the other spouse.

(11) A calling-up notice shall cease to have effect for the purpose of a sale in the exercise of any power conferred by the security on the expiration of a period of five years, which period shall run—

(*a*) in the case where the subjects of the security, or any part thereof, have not been offered for or exposed to sale, from the date of the notice.

(*b*) in the case where there has been such an offer or exposure, from the date of the last offer or exposure.

NOTE

[1] As amended by the Matrimonial Homes (Family Protection) (Scotland) Act 1981, s. 20.

Exercise of rights of creditor on default of debtor in complying with a calling-up notice

20.—(1) Where the debtor in a standard security is in default within the meaning of standard condition 9 (1) (*a*), the creditor may exercise such of his rights under the security as he may consider appropriate, and any such right shall be in addition to and not in derogation from any other remedy arising from the contract to which the security relates or from any right conferred by any enactment or by any rule of law on the creditor in a heritable security.

(2) Where the debtor is in default as aforesaid, the creditor shall have the right to sell the security subjects, or any part thereof, in accordance with the provisions of this Part of this Act.

(3) A creditor in a standard security who is in lawful possession of the security subjects may let the security subjects, or any part thereof, for any period not exceeding seven years, or may make application to the court for warrant to let those subjects, or any part thereof, for a period exceeding seven years, and the application shall state the proposed tenant, and the duration and conditions of the proposed lease, and shall be served on the proprietor of the subjects and on any other heritable creditor having interest as such a creditor in the subjects.

(4) The court, on such an application as aforesaid and after such inquiry and such further intimation of the application as it may think fit, may grant the application as submitted, or subject to such variation as it may consider reasonable in all the circumstances of the case, or may refuse the application.

(5) There shall be deemed to be assigned to a creditor who is in lawful possession of the security subjects all rights and obligations of the proprietor relating to—

(*a*) leases, or any permission or right of occupancy, granted in respect of those subjects or any part thereof, and

(*b*) the management and maintenance of the subjects and the effecting of any reconstruction, alteration or improvement reasonably required for the purpose of maintaining the market value of the subjects.

Notice of default

21.—(1) Where the debtor in a standard security is in default within the meaning of standard condition 9 (1) (*b*), and the default is remediable, the creditor may, without prejudice to any other powers he may have by virtue of this Act or otherwise, proceed in accordance with the provisions of this section to call on the debtor and on the proprietor, where he is not the debtor, to purge the default.

(2) For the aforesaid purpose the creditor may serve on the debtor and, as the case may be, on the proprietor a notice in conformity with Form B of Schedule 6 to this Act (hereinafter in this Act referred to as a "notice of default") which shall be served in the like manner and with the like requirements as to proof of service as a calling-up notice.

(3) For the purpose of dispensing with, or shortening, the period of notice mentioned in a notice of default, section 19(10) of this Act shall apply as it applies in relation to a calling-up notice.

(4) Notwithstanding the failure to comply with any requirement contained in the notice, a notice of default shall cease to be authority for the exercise of the rights mentioned in section 23(2) of this Act on the expiration of a period of five years from the date of the notice.

Objections to notice of default

22.—(1) Where a person on whom a notice of default has been served considers himself aggrieved by any requirement of that notice he may, within a period of fourteen days of the service of the notice, object to the notice by way of application to the court; and the applicant shall, not later than the lodging of that application, serve a copy of his application on the creditor, and on any other party on whom the notice has been served by the creditor.

(2) On any such application the court, after hearing the parties and making such inquiry as it may think fit, may order the notice appealed against to be set aside, in whole or in part, or otherwise to be varied, or to be upheld.

(3) The respondent in any such application may make a counter-application craving for any of the remedies conferred on him by this Act or by any other enactment relating to heritable securities, and the court may grant any such remedy as aforesaid as it may think proper.

(4) For the purposes of such a counter-application as aforesaid, a certificate which conforms with the requirements of Schedule 7 to this Act may be lodged in court by the creditor, and that certificate shall be *prima facie* evidence of the facts directed by the said Schedule to be contained therein.

Rights and duties of parties after service of notice of default to which objection is not taken, or where the notice is not set aside

23.—(1) Where a person does not object to a notice of default in accordance with the provisions of the last foregoing section, or where he has so objected and the notice has been upheld or varied under that section, it shall be his duty to comply with any requirement, due to be performed or fulfilled by him, contained in the notice or, as the case may be, in the notice as so varied.

(2) Subject to the provisions of section 21(4) of this Act, where a person fails to comply as aforesaid, the creditor, subject to the next following subsection, may proceed to exercise such of his rights on default under standard condition 10(2), (6) and (7) as he may consider appropriate.

[1] (3) At any time after the expiry of the period stated in a notice of default, or in a notice varied as aforesaid, but before the conclusion of any enforceable contract to sell the security subjects, or any part thereof, by virtue of the last foregoing subsection, the debtor or proprietor (being in either case a person entitled to redeem the security) may, subject to any agreement to the contrary, redeem the security without the necessity of observance of any requirement as to notice.

NOTE

[1] As amended by the Redemption of Standard Securities (Scotland) Act 1971, s. 1.

Application by creditor to court for remedies on default

24.—(1) Without prejudice to his proceeding by way of notice of default in respect of a default within the meaning of standard condition 9(1)(*b*), a creditor in a standard security, where the debtor is in default within the meaning of that standard condition or standard condition 9(1)(*c*), may apply to the court for warrant to exercise any of the remedies which he is entitled to exercise on a default within the meaning of standard condition 9(1)(*a*).

(2) For the purposes of such an application as aforesaid in respect of a default within the meaning of standard condition 9(1)(*b*), a certificate which conforms with the requirements of Schedule 7 to this Act may be lodged in court by the creditor, and that certificate shall be *prima facie* evidence of the facts directed by the said Schedule to be contained therein.

Exercise of power of sale

[1] **25.** A creditor in a standard security having right to sell the security subjects may exercise that right either by private bargain or by exposure to sale, and in either event it shall be the duty of the creditor to advertise the sale and to take all reasonable steps to ensure that the price at which all or any of the subjects are sold is the best that can be reasonably obtained.

NOTE

[1] Applied (*mod.*) by S.I. 1986 No. 843.

Disposition by creditor on sale

26.—(1) Where a creditor in a standard security has effected a sale of the security subjects, or any part thereof, and grants to the purchaser or his nominee a disposition of the subjects sold thereby, which bears to be in implement of the sale, then, on that disposition being duly recorded, those subjects shall be disburdened of the standard security and of all other heritable securities and diligences ranking *pari passu* with, or postponed to, that security.

(2) Where on a sale as aforesaid the security subjects remain subject to a prior security, the recording of a disposition under the foregoing subsection shall not affect the rights of the creditor in that security, but the creditor who has effected the sale shall have the like right as the debtor to redeem the security.

Application of proceeds of sale

[1] **27.**—(1) The money which is received by the creditor in a standard security, arising from any sale by him of the security subjects, shall be held by him in trust to be applied by him in accordance with the following order of priority—

(*a*) first, in payment of all expenses properly incurred by him in connection with the sale, or any attempted sale;

(*b*) secondly, in payment of the whole amount due under any prior security to which the sale is not made subject;

(*c*) thirdly, in payment of the whole amount due under the standard security, and in payment, in due proportion, of the whole amount due under a security, if any, ranking *pari passu* with his own security, which has been duly recorded;

(*d*) fourthly, in payment of any amounts due under any securities with a ranking postponed to that of his own security, according to their ranking,

and any residue of the money so received shall be paid to the person entitled to the security subjects at the time of sale, or to any person authorised to give receipts for the proceeds of the sale thereof.

(2) Where owing to the death or absence of any other creditor, or to any other cause, a creditor is unable to obtain a receipt or discharge for any payment he is required to make under the provisions of the foregoing sub-

section, he may, without prejudice to his liability to account therefor, consign the amount due (so far as ascertainable) in the sheriff court for the person appearing to have the best right thereto; and where consignation is so made, the creditor shall lodge in court a statement of the amount consigned.

(3) A consignation made in pursuance of the last foregoing subsection shall operate as a discharge of the payment of the amount due, and a certificate under the hand of the sheriff clerk shall be sufficient evidence thereof.

NOTE

[1] Applied (*mod.*) by S.I. 1986 No. 843.

Foreclosure

[1] **28.**—(1) Where the creditor in a standard security has exposed the security subjects to sale at a price not exceeding the amount due under the security and under any security ranking prior to, or *pari passu* with, the security, and has failed to find a purchaser, or where, having so failed, he has succeeded in selling only a part of the subjects at a price which is less than the amount due as aforesaid, he may, on the expiration of a period of two months from the date of the first exposure to sale, apply to the court for a decree of foreclosure.

(2) In any application under the last foregoing subsection the creditor shall lodge a statement setting out the whole amount due under the security but, without prejudice to the right of the debtor or of the proprietor to challenge that statement, it shall be sufficient for the purposes of the application for the creditor to establish to the satisfaction of the court that the amount so stated is not less than the price at which the security subjects have been exposed to sale or sold, where part of the subjects has been sold as aforesaid.

(3) Any application under subsection (1) of this section shall be served on the debtor in the standard security, the proprietor of the security subjects (if he is a person other than the debtor) and the creditor in any other heritable security affecting the security subjects as disclosed by a search of the Register of Sasines for a period of twenty years immediately preceding the last date to which the appropriate Minute Book of the said Register has been completed at the time when the application is made or by an examination of the title sheet of the security subjects in the Land Register of Scotland.

(4) The court may order such intimation and inquiry as it thinks fit and may in its discretion allow the debtor or the proprietor of the security subjects a period not exceeding three months in which to pay the whole amount due under the security and, subject to any such allowance, may—

(*a*) appoint the security subjects or the unsold part thereof to be re-exposed to sale at a price to be fixed by the court, in which event the creditor in the security may bid and purchase at the sale, or

(*b*) grant a decree of foreclosure in conformity with the provisions of the next following subsection.

(5) A decree of foreclosure shall contain a declaration that, on the extract of the decree being duly recorded, any right to redeem the security has been extinguished and that the creditor has right to the security subjects or the unsold part thereof, described by means of a particular description or by reference to a description thereof as in Schedule D to the Conveyancing (Scotland) Act 1924 or in Schedule G to the Titles to Land Consolidation (Scotland) Act 1868, including a reference to any conditions or clauses affecting the subjects or the unsold part thereof or in accordance with section 15 of the Land Registration (Scotland) Act 1979, at the price at which the said subjects were last exposed to sale under deduction of the price received for any part thereof sold, and shall also contain a warrant for recording the extract of the decree in the Register of Sasines.

(6) Upon an extract of the decree of foreclosure being duly recorded, the following provisions of this subsection shall have effect in relation to the security subjects to which the decree relates—

(*a*) any right to redeem the security shall be extinguished, and the creditor shall have right to, and be vested in, the subjects as if he had received an irredeemable disposition thereof duly recorded from the proprietor of the subjects at the date of the recording of the extract of the decree;

(*b*) the subjects shall be disburdened of the standard security and all securities and diligences postponed thereto;

(*c*) the creditor who has obtained the decree shall have the like right as the debtor to redeem any security prior to, or *pari passu* with, his own security.

(7) Notwithstanding the due recording of an extract of a decree of foreclosure, any personal obligation of the debtor under the standard security shall remain in full force and effect so far as not extinguished by the price at which the security subjects have been acquired and the price for which any part thereof has been sold.

(8) Where the security subjects or any part thereof have been acquired by a creditor in the security by virtue of a decree of foreclosure under the provisions of this section, the title thereto of the creditor shall not be challengeable on the ground of any irregularity in the proceedings for foreclosure or on calling-up or default which preceded it; but nothing in the provisions of this subsection shall affect the competency of any claim for damages in respect of such proceedings against the creditor.

NOTE

[1] As amended by the Redemption of Standard Securities (Scotland) Act 1971, s.1, and the Land Registration (Scotland) Act 1979, Sched. 2, para. 4. See the Building Societies Act 1986, s.11(10), (15).

Procedure

29.—(1) The court for the purposes of this Part of this Act, and for the operation of section 11 of the Heritable Securities (Scotland) Act 1894 (application by *pari passu* creditor to sell), in relation to a standard security, shall be the sheriff having jurisdiction over any part of the security subjects, and the sheriff shall be deemed to have such jurisdiction whatever the value of the subjects.

(2), (3) [Repealed by S.I. 1990 No. 661.]

Interpretation of Part II

30.—(1) In this Part of this Act, unless the context otherwise requires, the following expressions have the meanings hereby respectively assigned to them, that is to say—

"creditor" and "debtor" shall include any successor in title, assignee or representative of a creditor or debtor;

"debt" and "creditor" and "debtor", in relation to a standard security, have the meanings assigned to them by section 9(8) of this Act;

"duly recorded" means recorded in the appropriate division of the General Register of Sasines;

"exposure to sale" means exposure to sale by public roup, and exposed or re-exposed to sale shall be construed accordingly;

"heritable security" has the meaning assigned to it by the said section 9(8);

"interest in land" has the meaning assigned to it by the said section 9(8);

"Register of Sasines" means the appropriate division of the General Register of Sasines;

"the standard condition" are the conditions (whether varied or not) referred to in section 11 (2) of this Act;

"whole amount due" has the meaning assigned to it by section 18 (4) of this Act.

(2) For the purpose of construing this Part of this Act in relation to the creation of a security over a registered lease and to any subsequent transactions connected with that security, the following expressions shall have the meanings hereby respectively assigned to them, that is to say—

"conveyance" or "disposition" means assignation;

"convey" or "dispone" means assign;

"infeft" means having a recorded title;

"proprietor" means lessee;

"security subjects" means a registered lease subject to a security.

Saving

31. Nothing in the provisions of this Part of this Act shall affect the validity of any heritable security within the meaning of this Part which has been duly recorded before the commencement of this Act, and any such security may be dealt with, and shall be as capable of being enforced, as if this Part had not been passed.

Application of enactments

32. The provisions of any enactment relating to a bond and disposition or assignation in security shall apply to a standard security, except in so far as such provisions are inconsistent with the provisions of this Part of this Act, but, without prejudice to the generality of that exception, the enactments specified in Schedule 8 to this Act shall not so apply.

PART III

PROVISIONS AS TO HERITABLE SECURITIES

Form of notice calling-up heritable security

33.—(1) For the avoidance of doubt, it is hereby declared that for the purposes of section 33 of the Act of 1924 (notice of calling-up security) a creditor in possession of the land disponed in security may adapt the form of notice contained in Form No. 1 of Schedule M to the said Act by stating that the principal sum and interest thereon specified in that notice is subject to adjustment in amount as calculated in a statement of relevant intromissions.

(2) The person on whom notice as aforesaid is served may request the creditor to furnish to him a statement as aforesaid, in a case to which the foregoing subsection applies, within a period of one month from the date of service of the notice calling-up the security, and a failure by the creditor to comply with that request shall cause the notice of calling-up to be of no effect.

Amendment of section 34 of Act of 1924

34. With a view to making provision for the service of notices required to be served for the purposes of the said section 33 on persons who are not known to be alive or dead, section 34 of the Act of 1924 (service of notice of calling-up) shall have effect as if after the words "is not known," there were inserted the words "or if it is not known whether such a person is still alive".

Power of creditor in bond and disposition in security to sell to include power to sell by private bargain

35.—(1) The creditor in a bond and disposition in security may exercise his power to sell the land disponed in security by way of sale by private bargain for the best price that can be reasonably obtained.

(2) In relation to a sale by private bargain, the Act of 1924, except as respects amendments thereto made by this Act, shall have effect subject to the following modifications—

(*a*) any reference to sale by public roup shall include a reference to a sale by private bargain, and any reference to exposure to sale, however worded, shall include a reference to an offer for sale;

(*b*) any reference to the upset price of the land, or any part thereof, shall be omitted.

(*c*) section 39 shall be omitted.

(3) Nothing in the provisions of this section shall authorise a sale under warrant of the sheriff in pursuance of section 11 of the Act of 1894 (empowering by sheriff of *pari passu* security holder to sell *pari passu* security) to be by way of private bargain.

36–37. [The amendments made by these sections to the Conveyancing (Scotland) Act 1924, ss. 38 and 40, are given effect to in the print of that Act, *supra.*]

Amendment of s. 41 of Act of 1924

38. For subsection (2) of section 41 of the Act of 1924 (protection of purchasers) there shall be substituted the following subsection—

[See the print of s. 41 (2) of the Act of 1924, *supra.*]

but in relation to a disposition duly recorded before the commencement of this Act the said subsection shall continue to have effect as originally enacted.

39. [The amendments made by this section to the Heritable Securities (Scotland) Act 1894 are given effect to in the print of that Act, *supra.*]

Discharge of heritable security constituted by ex facie absolute conveyance

40.—(1) Where land is held in security by virtue of a heritable security constituted by *ex facie* absolute conveyance, whether qualified by a back letter or not, a discharge by the creditor in security in conformity with Schedule 9 to this Act, either as a separate deed or as a deed endorsed on the conveyance, shall, as from the date on which that discharge is duly recorded, discharge that heritable security, disburden the land to the extent that it is the subject of the security, and vest that land in the person entitled thereto in like manner and to the like effect as if a conveyance containing a clause of warrandice from fact and deed only and all other usual and necessary clauses had been granted by the creditor to that person and duly recorded.

(2) Nothing in the provisions of the foregoing subsection shall affect any method of granting a discharge in existence at the commencement of this Act.

Restriction on effect of reduction of certain discharges of securities

41.—(1) Where the discharge, in whole or in part, of a security over land is duly recorded, whether before or after the commencement of this Act, and that discharge bears to be granted by a person entitled so to do, the title of a person to any subsequent interest in the land, acquired *bona fide* and for value, shall not be challengeable, after the expiration of a period of five years commencing with the date of the recording of the discharge, by reason only of the recording of an extract of a decree of reduction of the discharge, whether or not the date of that decree was before or after the date on which the acquisition of the interest was duly recorded.

(2) Section 46 of the Act of 1924 (which requires extract decrees of reduction of certain deeds to be recorded) shall cease to apply in relation to a decree of reduction of a discharge of a security where that discharge has been duly recorded for a period of five years or more, but the provisions of

this subsection shall not preclude the recording of such a decree of reduction as provided for in the said section 46.

(3) Nothing in the provisions of this section shall affect any rights of a creditor in a security as against the debtor therein.

(4) The provisions of this section shall not be pleadable to any effect in any action begun, whether before or after the date of the commencement of this Act, before the expiry of a period of two years beginning with that date.

[1] (5) This section shall apply to an order under section 8 of the Law Reform (Miscellaneous Provisions) (Scotland) Act 1985 rectifying a discharge as it applies to a decree of reduction of a discharge.

NOTE

[1] Inserted by the Law Reform (Miscellaneous Provisions) (Scotland) Act 1985, Sched. 2, para. 11, with effect from 30th December 1985.

Extension of section 13 to certain existing forms of heritable securities

42. Section 13 of this Act shall apply, in relation to the effect on the preference in ranking of any heritable security, constituted by *ex facie* absolute disposition or assignation, as it applies to the preference in ranking of a standard security.

Interpretation of Part III

43.—(1) In this Part of this Act, unless the context otherwise requires, the following expressions have the meanings hereby respectively assigned to them, that is to say—

"the Act of 1894" means the Heritable Securities (Scotland) Act 1894;

"the Act of 1924" means the Conveyancing (Scotland) Act 1924;

"land" has the meaning assigned to it by section 2(1) of the Act of 1924.

(2) For the purpose of construing this Part of this Act in relation to the creation of a security over a registered lease and to any subsequent transactions connected with that security, section 30(2) shall apply as it applies to Part II of this Act, and any reference to a security over land, however expressed, shall be construed as a reference to a registered lease subject to a security, and "land" shall be construed accordingly.

PART IV

OTHER CONVEYANCING REFORMS

Alteration of rules as to probative deeds

44.—(1) Subject to the provisions of subsection (2) of this section, where—

(*a*) a conveyance, deed, instrument or writing, whether relating to land or not;

(*b*) an inventory, appendix, schedule, plan or other document annexed to such a conveyance, deed, instrument or writing,

is subscribed and (where appropriate) sealed on the last page, it shall be no objection to its probative character that it is not subscribed or, as the case may be, subscribed and sealed on every other page.

(2) Nothing in subsection (1) of this section shall affect the law relating to wills or other testamentary writings.

Status of sasine extracts

45. An extract, whether issued before or after the commencement of this Act, of a conveyance, deed, instrument or other document bearing to have been recorded in the Register of Sasines shall be accepted for all purposes as sufficient evidence of the contents of the original so recorded and of any matter relating thereto appearing on the extract.

46. [See the Conveyancing Amendment (Scotland) Act 1938, s. 9(1).]

Abolition of requirement to specify grantee's title in certain deeds

47. The provisions of Part I of Schedule 10 and Part I of Schedule 11 to this Act shall apply for the purpose of abolishing the requirement that in certain cases the granter of a deed who has a duly recorded title must specify his title in the deed.

Abolition of forms of assignation of unrecorded conveyances, etc., and of completion of title by recording of such assignations

48. The provisions of Part II of Schedule 11 to this Act shall apply for the purpose of repealing certain provisions for the assignation of unrecorded conveyances, deeds and leases and for the completion of title by assignees under such assignations by the recording of the conveyance, deed or lease together with the assignation.

PART V

MISCELLANEOUS

Abolition of heritor's right of pre-emption of glebe

49. The obligation imposed upon the General Trustees by section 37 of the Church of Scotland (Property and Endowments) Act 1925 (powers of General Trustees), before selling or feuing a glebe or any part thereof, to give to the heritor or heritors whose lands adjoin such glebe or part an opportunity to purchase or take the same in feu, is hereby abolished.

In this section, "the General Trustees" has the meaning assigned to it in section 47 of the said Act.

Amendment of Lands Tribunal Act 1949

50.—(1) (In the Lands Tribunal Act 1949 (hereafter in this section called "the principal Act"), in section 2 (members, officers and expenses of Lands Tribunal), for paragraph (*b*) and (*c*) of subsection (9) there shall be substituted the following paragraph:—

"(*b*) subsection (2), of the following subsection:—

'(2) The President shall be a person appearing to the Lord President of the Court of Session to be suitably qualified by the holding of judicial office or by experience as an advocate or solicitor, and of the other members of the Lands Tribunal such number as the Lord President of the Court of Session may determine shall be persons so qualified, and the others shall be persons who have had experience in the valuation of land appointed after consultation with the chairman of the Scottish Branch of the Royal Institution of Chartered Surveyors.' "

(2) In section 3 of the principal Act (procedure, appeals, costs and fees), for paragraphs (*a*), (*b*) and (*c*) of subsection (12) there shall be substituted the following paragraphs:—

"(*a*) subsection (4) of this section there shall be substituted the following subsection:—

'(4) Section 9 of the Tribunals and Inquiries Act 1958 (appeals from certain tribunals) shall apply, subject to the modifications specified in subsection (6) of that section, to proceedings before the Lands Tribunal as it applies to proceedings before the tribunals referred to in subsection (1) of that section.';

(*b*) paragraph (*c*) of subsection (6) of this section there shall be substituted the following paragraph:—

'(*c*) provide for requiring persons to attend to give evidence and produce documents, and for authorising the administration of oaths to witnesses, and for granting to any person such recovery of documents as might be granted by the Court of Session.';

[1](*c*) any person who without reasonable excuse fails to comply with any requirement imposed by rules under this section in accordance with

[THE NEXT PAGE IS J 177]

paragraph (*c*) of subsection (6) of this section shall be guilty of an offence and liable on summary conviction to a fine not exceeding level 3 on the standard scale or imprisonment for a term not exceeding three months or both;

(*d*) any extract of an order[2] of the Tribunal may be recorded for execution in the Books of Council and Session and shall be enforceable accordingly;

(*e*) the rule-making authority for the purposes of this Act shall be the Secretary of State.".

NOTES

[1] As amended by virtue of the Criminal Procedure (Scotland) Act 1975, ss. 289F and 289G.

[2] See the Land Tenure Reform (Scotland) Act 1974, s. 19.

PART VI

GENERAL

Application to Crown

51. This Act shall, subject to any exceptions stated therein, apply to land held of the Crown and of the Prince and Steward of Scotland, and to land in which there is any other interest belonging to Her Majesty in right of the Crown or to a Government department, or held on behalf of Her Majesty for the purposes of a Government department, in like manner as it applies to other land.

Saving, amendment and repeal

52.—(1) Any procedure, notice, advertisement, certificate or warrant instituted, given or granted, or any other thing done under any enactment amended or disapplied by this Act, shall not be invalidated by the coming into force of that amendment or disapplication, but it and any sale or other proceedings dependent thereon shall have effect as if this Act had not come into operation.

(2) The enactments specified in Schedule 10 to this Act shall have effect subject to the amendments specified in that Schedule, being minor amendments and amendments consequential on the provisions of this Act.

(3) The enactments specified in Schedule 11 to this Act are hereby repealed to the extent specified in relation thereto in that Schedule.

Interpretation

53.—(1) It shall be sufficient compliance with any provisions in this Act which require any deed, notice, certificate or procedure to be in conformity with a Form or Note, or other requirement of this Act, that that deed, notice, certificate or procedure so conforms as closely as may be, and nothing in this Act shall preclude the inclusion of any additional matter which the person granting the deed or giving or serving the notice or giving the certificate or adopting the procedure may consider relevant.

(2) In any Form prescribed by Schedules 2, 4, 5, 6 and 9 to this Act, and in any Note to those Schedules, the expression "Register for" means the Register of Sasines appropriate for.

(3) Any reference in this Act to any other enactment is a reference thereto as amended, and includes a reference thereto as extended or applied, by or under any other enactment, including this Act.

(4) In this Act, except Part II, unless the context otherwise requires—

"conveyance", "deed" and "instrument" have the meanings assigned to them in section 3 of the Titles to Land Consolidation (Scotland) Act 1868, section 3 of the Conveyancing (Scotland) Act 1874, and section 2 of the Conveyancing (Scotland) Act 1924;

"duly recorded" means recorded in the appropriate Register of Sasines;

"Lands Tribunal" means the Lands Tribunal for Scotland;

"prescribed" means prescribed by rules made under section 3 of the Lands Tribunal Act 1949;

"Register of Sasines" has the meaning assigned to it in section 2 of the Conveyancing (Scotland) Act 1924.

Short title, commencement and extent

54.—(1) This Act may be cited as the Conveyancing and Feudal Reform (Scotland) Act 1970.

(2) This Act shall come into operation—

(*a*) except as respects sections 1 to 6, section 50, sections 51 to 53 in so far as they relate to those sections, and this section, at the expiration of a period of six months beginning with the date on which it is passed,

[1] (*b*) as respects sections 1 to 6 and sections 51 to 53 in so far as they relate to those sections, on such date as the Secretary of State may by order made by statutory instrument appoint, and different days may be appointed for different provisions,

(*c*) as respects section 50, sections 51 to 53 in so far as they relate thereto, and this section, on the passing of this Act;

and any reference in any provision of this Act to the commencement of this Act shall, unless otherwise provided by any such order, be construed as a reference to the date on which that provision comes into operation.

(3) This Act shall extend to Scotland only.

NOTE

[1] 1st March 1971 (S.I. 1971 No. 199).

SCHEDULES

Section 1

SCHEDULE 1

LAND OBLIGATIONS NOT SUBJECT TO VARIATION OR DISCHARGE UNDER SECTION 1

1. An obligation to pay feuduty, ground annual, rent, skat, dry multure, teind, stipend, standard charge or other payment of a like nature, or an obligation of relief relating to any such payment.

2. An obligation, however constituted, relating to the right to work minerals or to any ancillary right in relation to minerals within the meaning of section 2 of the Mines (Working Facilities and Support) Act 1966.

3. An obligation imposed by or on behalf of the Crown for the protection of any royal park, garden or palace.

4. An obligation created or imposed—

(i) for naval, military or air force purposes;

(ii) for civil aviation purposes under the powers conferred by section 19 or 23 of the Civil Aviation Act 1949 or any enactment replaced thereby:

Provided that this paragraph—

(i) shall exclude the application of section 1 of this Act to an obligation falling within sub-paragraph (i) above, and not created or imposed in connection with the use of any land as an aerodrome, only so long as the obligation is enforceable by or on behalf of the Crown; and

(ii) shall exclude the application of section 1 of this Act to an obligation falling within sub-paragraph (ii) above, or created or imposed in connection with the use of any land as an aerodrome, only so long as the obligation is enforceable by or on behalf of the Crown or any public or international authority.

5. An obligation created or imposed in or in relation to a lease of—

[1] (*a*) an agricultural holding, within the meaning of the Agricultural Holdings (Scotland) Act 1991;

(*b*) a holding within the meaning of the Small Landholders (Scotland) Acts 1886 to 1931; or

(*c*) a croft, within the meaning of the Crofters (Scotland) Act 1955.

NOTE

[1] As amended by the Agricultural Holdings (Scotland) Act 1991, Sched. 11, para. 32.

Sections 9 and 10 SCHEDULE 2

FORMS OF STANDARD SECURITY

FORM A

[To be used where the personal obligation is included in the deed]

I, A.B. (*designation*), hereby undertake to pay to C.D. (*designation*), the sum of £ (*or* a maximum sum of £) (*or* all sums due and that may become due by me to the said C.D. in respect of (*here specify the matter for which the undertaking is granted*)) with interest from (*or* from the respective times of advance) at per centum per annum (*or otherwise as the case may be*) (annually, half-yearly, *or otherwise as the case may be*) on in each year commencing on ; For which I grant a standard security in favour of the said C.D. over ALL and WHOLE (*here describe the security subjects as indicated in Note 1 hereto*): The standard conditions specified in Schedule 3 to the Conveyancing and Feudal Reform (Scotland) Act 1970, and any lawful variation thereof operative for the time being, shall apply: And I grant warrandice: And I consent to registration for execution.

[To be attested]

FORM B

[To be used where the personal obligation is constituted in a separate instrument or instruments]

I, A.B. (*designation*) hereby in security of (*here specify the nature of the debt or obligation in respect of which the security is given and the instrument(s) by which it is constituted in such manner as will identify these instruments*) grant a standard security in favour of C.D. (*designation*) over ALL and WHOLE (*here describe the security subjects as indicated in Note 1 hereto*): The standard conditions specified in Schedule 3 to the Conveyancing and Feudal Reform (Scotland) Act 1970, and any lawful variation thereof operative for the time being, shall apply: And I grant warrandice.

[To be attested]

NOTES TO SCHEDULE 2

[1] *Note 1*.—The security subjects shall be described by means of a particular description or by reference to a description thereof as in Schedule D to the Conveyancing (Scotland) Act 1924 or as in Schedule G to the Titles to Land Consolidation (Scotland) Act 1868. Where the security subjects consist of an interest in land, other than ownership of the land, amend the description appropriately, e.g. *a ground annual of £ constituted by a contract of ground annual* (or other deed by which the ground annual was constituted) (giving the names of the parties thereto or of the grantor and grantee), *recorded in the Register for on payable out of the subjects therein described lying in the county of* (*or in the burgh of and county of*), adding if necessary, *but only to the extent of* ; or *a lease* (*or tack*) (giving the names of the parties thereto) *of the subjects therein described lying in the county of* (or *in the burgh of and county of*) *recorded in the Register for on* adding if necessary, *but only to the extent of*

NOTE

[1] Excluded by the Land Registration (Scotland) Act 1979, s. 15 (1).

[1] *Note 2*.—Where the grantor has not a recorded title to the security subjects, insert after the description thereof a clause of deduction of title as follows:— *Which subjects* (or *ground annual* or *lease* (or *tack*) or, as the case may be) *were last vested* (or *are part of the subjects last vested*) *in E.F. whose title thereto was recorded in the Register for* (or *the said Register of Sasines*) on (or, if the last infeftment has already been mentioned, say *in the said E.F. as aforesaid*), *and from whom I acquired right by* (here specify shortly the writ or writs by which that right was so acquired).

NOTE

[1] Excluded by the Land Registration (Scotland) Act 1979, s. 15 (3).

Note 3.—Where the grantor of a standard security has granted a conveyance *ex facie* absolute of the security subjects, or any part thereof, that conveyance shall be referred to in accordance with Note 5 to this Schedule. In any such case:—(a) where the grantor has been infeft in the security subjects, no clause of deduction of title is required in the standard security, [1] (b) where the grantor has not previously been infeft in the security subjects but has right thereto by virtue of an unrecorded title insert in the standard security after the description of the security subjects a clause of deduction of title as follows.—*Which subjects* (or *ground annual* or *lease* (or *tack*) or, as the case may be) *were formerly vested in* (or *are part of the subjects formerly vested in*) (give name of person last infeft in the subjects before the grantor acquired right thereto) *whose title thereto was recorded in the Register for* (or *the said Register of Sasines*) on (or if such infeftment has already been mentioned say *in the said as aforesaid*) *and from whom I acquired right by* (here specify shortly the writ or writs by which that right was so acquired).

NOTE

[1] Excluded by the Land Registration (Scotland) Act 1979, s. 15 (3).

Note 4.—Where it is desired to vary any of the standard conditions contained in Schedule 3 to this Act, such variations shall be effected either by an instrument or instruments other than the standard security, and any such instrument shall not require to be recorded in the Register of Sasines or by inserting in the standard security after the description of the security subjects (and after the clause of deduction of title, if any) *And I agree that the standard conditions shall be varied to the effect that* (here insert particulars of the variations desired).

(As regards future variations, see section 16 of, and Form E and Notes 5 and 6 in Schedule 4 to this Act.)

Note 5.—Where the security subjects are burdened by any other standard security or heritable security, or by any security by way of *ex facie* absolute conveyance which ranks prior to the standard security which is being granted, insert immediately before the clause of warrandice the following:—*But the security hereby granted is subject to* (here specify any deed by which such preferable rights were created and any deed modifying or altering such rights), and amend the clause of warrandice to read *And, subject as aforesaid, I grant warrandice.* Where the standard security is to rank prior or postponed to, or *pari passu* with, any other existing heritable security or any other standard security, a ranking clause may be inserted in appropriate terms immediately prior to the warrandice clause, and the warrandice clause shall, where necessary, be qualified accordingly.

Note 6.—Where a standard security is granted in Form A for a fluctuating or uncertain amount, provisions for ascertaining the amount due at any time may be inserted immediately prior to the clause of granting of the security, and the registration clause shall, where necessary, be amended accordingly.

Note 7.—In the case of a standard security for a non-monetary obligation, the forms in this Schedule shall be adapted as appropriate.

Section 11

SCHEDULE 3

The Standard Conditions

Maintenance and repair

1. It shall be an obligation on the debtor—

(*a*) to maintain the security subjects in good and sufficient repair to the reasonable satisfaction of the creditor;

(*b*) to permit, after seven clear days notice in writing, the creditor or his agent to enter upon the security subjects at all reasonable times to examine the condition thereof;

(*c*) to make all necessary repairs and make good all defects in pursuance of his obligation under head (*a*) of this condition within such reasonable period as the creditor may require by notice in writing.

Completion of buildings, etc., and prohibition of alterations, etc.

2. It shall be an obligation on the debtor—

(*a*) to complete, as soon as may be practicable, any unfinished buildings and works forming part of the security subjects to the reasonable satisfaction of the creditor;
(*b*) not to demolish, alter or add to any buildings or works forming part of the security subjects, except in accordance with the terms of a prior written consent of the creditor and in compliance with any consent, licence or approval required by law;
(*c*) to exhibit to the creditor at his request evidence of that consent, licence or approval.

Observance of conditions in title, payment of duties, charges, etc., and general compliance with requirements of law relating to security subjects

3. It shall be an obligation on the debtor—
(*a*) to observe any condition or perform any obligation in respect of the security subjects lawfully binding on him in relation to the security subjects;
(*b*) to make due and punctual payment of any ground burden, teind, stipend, or standard charge, and any rates, taxes and other public burdens, and any other payments exigible in respect of the security subjects;
(*c*) to comply with any requirement imposed upon him in relation to the security subjects by virtue of any enactment.

Planning notices, etc.

4. It shall be an obligation on the debtor—
(*a*) where he has received any notice or order, issued or made by virtue of the Town and Country Planning (Scotland) Acts 1947 to 1969 or any amendment thereof, or any proposal so made for the making or issuing of any such notice or order, or any other notice or document affecting or likely to affect the security subjects, to give to the creditor, within fourteen days of the receipt of that notice, order or proposal, full particulars thereof;
(*b*) to take, as soon as practicable, all reasonable or necessary steps to comply with such a notice or order or, as the case may be, duly to object thereto;
(*c*) in the event of the creditor so requiring, to object or to join with the creditor in objecting to any such notice or order or in making representations against any proposal therefor.

Insurance

5. It shall be an obligation on the debtor—
(*a*) to insure the security subjects or, at the option of the creditor, to permit the creditor to insure the security subjects in the names of the creditor and the debtor to the extent of the market value thereof against the risk of fire and such other risks as the creditor may reasonably require;
(*b*) to deposit any policy of insurance effected by the debtor for the aforesaid purpose with the creditor;
(*c*) to pay any premium due in respect of any such policy and, where the creditor so requests, to exhibit a receipt therefor not later than the fourteenth day after the renewal date of the policy;
(*d*) to intimate to the creditor, within fourteen days of the occurrence, any occurrence which may give rise to a claim under the policy and to authorise the creditor to negotiate the settlement of the claim;
(*e*) without prejudice to any obligation to the contrary enforceable against him, to comply with any reasonable requirement of the creditor as to the application of any sum received in respect of such a claim;
(*f*) to refrain from any act or omission which would invalidate the policy.

Restriction on letting

6. It shall be an obligation on the debtor not to let, or agree to let, the security subjects, or any part thereof, without the prior consent in writing of the creditor, and "to let" in this condition includes to sub-let.

General power of creditor to perform obligations, etc., on failure of debtor and power to charge debtor

7.—(1) The creditor shall be entitled to perform any obligation imposed by the standard conditions on the debtor, which the debtor has failed to perform.

(2) Where it is necessary for the performance of any obligation as aforesaid, the creditor may, after giving seven clear days notice in writing to the debtor, enter upon the security subjects at all reasonable times.

(3) All expenses and charges (including any interest thereon), reasonably incurred by the

creditor in the exercise of a right conferred by this condition, shall be recoverable from the debtor and shall be deemed to be secured by the security subjects under the standard security, and the rate of any such interest shall be the rate in force at the relevant time in respect of advances secured by the security, or, where no such rate is prescribed, shall be the bank rate in force at the relevant time.

Calling-up

8. The creditor shall be entitled, subject to the terms of the security and to any requirement of law, to call-up a standard security in the manner prescribed by section 19 of this Act.

Default

9.—(1) The debtor shall be held to be in default in any of the following circumstances, that is to say—

(*a*) where a calling-up notice in respect of the security has been served and has not been complied with;

(*b*) where there has been a failure to comply with any other requirement arising out of the security;

(*c*) where the proprietor of the security subjects has become insolvent.

[1] (2) For the purposes of this condition, the proprietor shall be taken to be insolvent if—

(*a*) he has become notour bankrupt, or he has executed a trust deed for behoof of, or has made a composition contract or arrangement with, his creditors;

[2] (*b*) he has died and a judicial factor has been appointed under section 11A of the Judicial Factors (Scotland) Act 1889 to divide his insolvent estate among his creditors, or his estate falls to be administered in accordance with an order under section 421 of the Insolvency Act 1986;

(*c*) where the proprietor is a company, a winding-up order has been made with respect to it, or a resolution for voluntary winding-up (other than a members' voluntary winding-up) has been passed with respect to it, or a receiver or manager of its undertaking has been duly appointed, or possession has been taken, by or on behalf of the holders of any debentures secured by a floating charge, of any property of the company comprised in or subject to the charge.

NOTES

[1] Applied: see the Sex Discrimination Act 1975, Sched. 3, para. 3(5)(*b*); also the Race Relations Act 1976, Sched. 1, para. 3(5)(*b*) and the National Heritage Act 1980, Sched. 1, para. 3(4)(*b*).

[2] As amended by the Bankruptcy (Scotland) Act 1985, Sched. 7, para. 8, by the Insolvency Act 1985, Sched. 8, para. 18 and by the Insolvency Act 1986, Sched. 14.

Rights of creditor on default

10.—(1) Where the debtor is in default, the creditor may, without prejudice to his exercising any other remedy arising from the contract to which the standard security relates, exercise, in accordance with the provisions of Part II of this Act and of any other enactment applying to standard securities, such of the remedies specified in the following sub-paragraphs of this standard condition as he may consider appropriate.

(2) He may proceed to sell the security subjects or any part thereof.

(3) He may enter into possession of the security subjects and may receive or recover feu-duties, ground annuals or, as the case may be, the rents of those subjects or any part thereof.

(4) Where he has entered into possession as aforesaid, he may let the security subjects or any part thereof.

(5) Where he has entered into possession as aforesaid there shall be transferred to him all the rights of the debtor in relation to the granting of leases or rights of occupancy over the security subjects and to the management and maintenance of those subjects.

(6) He may effect all such repairs and may make good such defects as are necessary to maintain the security subjects in good and sufficient repair, and may effect such reconstruction, alteration and improvement on the subjects as would be expected of a prudent proprietor to maintain the market value of the subjects, and for the aforesaid purposes may enter on the subjects at all reasonable times.

(7) He may apply to the court for a decree of foreclosure.

Exercise of right of redemption

[1] **11.**—(1) The debtor shall be entitled to exercise his right (if any) to redeem the security on

giving notice of his intention so to do, being a notice in writing (hereinafter referred to as a " notice of redemption ").

(2) Nothing in the provisions of this Act shall preclude a creditor from waiving the necessity for a notice of redemption, or from agreeing to a period of notice of less than that to which he is entitled.

(3) (*a*) A notice of redemption may be delivered to the creditor or sent by registered post or recorded delivery to him at his last known address, and an acknowledgment signed by the creditor or his agent or a certificate of postage by the person giving the notice accompanied by the postal receipt shall be sufficient evidence of such notice having been given.

(*b*) If the address of the creditor is not known, or if the packet containing the notice of redemption is returned to the sender with intimation that it could not be delivered, a notice of redemption may be sent to the Extractor of the Court of Session and an acknowledgment of receipt by him shall be sufficient evidence of such notice having been given.

(*c*) A notice of redemption sent by post shall be held to have been given on the day next after the day of posting.

(4) When a notice of redemption states that a specified amount will be repaid, and it is subsequently ascertained that the whole amount due to be repaid is more or less than the amount specified in the notice, the notice shall nevertheless be effective as a notice of repayment of the amount due as subsequently ascertained.

(5) Where the debtor has exercised a right to redeem, and has made payment of the whole amount due, or has performed the whole obligations of the debtor under the contract to which the security relates, the creditor shall grant a discharge in the terms prescribed in section 17 of this Act.

NOTE

[1] As amended by the Redemption of Standard Securities (Scotland) Act 1971, s. 1.

---

12. The debtor shall be personally liable to the creditor for the whole expenses of the preparation and execution of the standard security and any variation, restriction and discharge thereof and, where any of those deeds are recorded, the recording thereof, and all expenses reasonably incurred by the creditor in calling-up the security and realising or attempting to realise the security subjects, or any part thereof, and exercising any other powers conferred upon him by the security.

Interpretation

In this Schedule, where the debtor is not the proprietor of the security subjects, " debtor " means " proprietor ", except

(*a*) in standard conditions 9 (1), 10 (1) and 12, and

(*b*) in standard condition 11, where " debtor " includes the proprietor.

Sections 14, 15, 16 and 17 SCHEDULE 4

FORMS OF DEEDS OF ASSIGNATION, RESTRICTION, &C.

FORM A

ASSIGNATION OF STANDARD SECURITY

Separate

I, A.B. (*designation*), in consideration of £ hereby assign to C.D. (*designation*) a standard security for £ (*or* a maximum sum of £ , to the extent of £ being the amount now due thereunder; *in other cases describe as indicated in Note 2 to this Schedule*) by E.F. in my favour (*or* in favour of G.H.) recorded in the register for on (*adding if necessary*, but only to the extent of £ of principal); With interest from

[To be attested]

FORM B

[To be endorsed on the standard security]

As above save that instead of the words " *a standard security for £* " *(or otherwise, as the case may be) insert* " the foregoing standard security ". *Where the security is for a fluctuating amount whether subject to a maximum or not, add* " to the extent of £ being the amount now due thereunder.".

FORM C

RESTRICTION OF STANDARD SECURITY

I, A.B. (*designation*), in consideration of (*specify consideration, if any*) hereby disburden of a standard security for £ (*or* a maximum sum of £ ; *in other cases, describe as indicated in Note 2 to this Schedule*) by C.D. in my favour (*or* in favour of E.F.) recorded in the Register for on (*adding if necessary,* but only to the extent of £ of principal) ALL and WHOLE (*describe the subjects disburdened in the same way as directed in Note 1 to Schedule 2 to this Act in the case of a description of security subjects*).

[To be attested]

FORM D

COMBINED PARTIAL DISCHARGE AND DEED OF RESTRICTION OF STANDARD SECURITY

I, A.B. (*designation*) in consideration of £ paid by C.D. (*designation*) (*or, as the case may be*), hereby discharge a standard security for £ (*or* a maximum sum of £ ; *in other cases, describe as indicated in Note 2 to this Schedule*) by the said C.D. (*or* by E.F.) in my favour (*or* in favour of G.H.) recorded in the Register for on but only to the extent of £ of principal; And I disburden of the said standard security (*adding if necessary,* but only to the extent of £ of principal) ALL and WHOLE (*describe the subjects disburdened in the same way as directed in Note 1 to Schedule 2 to this Act in the case of a description of security subjects*).

[To be attested]

FORM E

VARIATION OF STANDARD SECURITY

[To be endorsed on the standard security]

I, A.B. (*designation*), agree that the foregoing standard security granted by me (*or* by C.D.) in favour of E.F. recorded in the Register for on (*if there have been previous variations insert* " as varied ") shall with effect from be varied so that (*here insert particulars of the variation agreed*); *And I, E.F.* (*designation*) (*or if the creditor is not the person in whose favour the standard security was granted say* G.H. (*designation*) the creditor now in right of the said standard security) consent to the variation hereby effected.

[To be attested]

FORM F

DISCHARGE OF STANDARD SECURITY

Separate

I, A.B. (*designation*), in consideration of £ (*where the security is in respect of a maximum sum or of all sums due or to become due or is in respect of a personal obligation constituted in an instrument or instruments other than the standard security add* being the whole amount secured by the standard security aftermentioned) paid by C.D. (*designation*) (*or, as the case may be*) hereby discharge a standard security for £ (or a maximum sum of £ *in other cases describe as indicated in Note 2 to this Schedule*) by the said C.D. (or by

E.F.) in my favour (*or* in favour of G.H.) recorded in the Register for on (*adding if necessary*, but only to the extent of £ of principal).

[To be attested]

[*To be endorsed on the standard security*]

As above save that instead of the words " a standard security for £ (*or* a maximum sum of £ *in other cases describe as indicated in Note 2 to this Schedule*)" *insert* " the foregoing standard security ".

NOTES TO SCHEDULE 4

General

Note 1.—Where the grantor of an assignation, discharge or deed of restriction of a standard security, or the creditor consenting to a variation of a standard security, is not the original creditor and has not a recorded title, insert at the end of the deed a clause of deduction of title as follows: *Which standard security* (adding, if necessary, *to the extent aforesaid* or, as the case may be) *was last vested in the said* (give name of original creditor) *as aforesaid* (or where the last recorded title to the standard security was in favour of a person other than the original creditor say *in J.K. whose title thereto was recorded in the said Register of Sasines on*) *and from whom I acquired right by* (here specify shortly the writ or writs by which right was so acquired).

Where the grantor of an assignation, discharge or deed of restriction of a standard security, or the creditor consenting to a variation of a standard security, although not the original creditor, has a recorded title, no specification of the title of the grantor or creditor is required.

Note 2.—In an assignation, discharge or deed of restriction, (1) a standard security in respect of an uncertain amount may be described by specifying shortly the nature of the debt or obligation (e.g., all sums due or to become due) for which the security was granted, adding in the case of an assignation, *to the extent of £ being the amount now due thereunder* and (2) a standard security in respect of a personal obligation constituted in an instrument or instruments other than the standard security itself may be described by specifying shortly the nature of the debt or obligation and referring to the other instrument or instruments by which it is constituted in such manner as will be sufficient identification thereof.

Note 3.—If the original infeftment upon a standard security has been taken otherwise than by recording the security in the Register of Sasines, insert immediately after the word " recorded " the words *along with notice of title thereon* (adding, if such notice is not in favour of the original creditor, the name of the person in whose favour it is drawn).

Note 4.—If part of the security subjects has already been disburdened, there may be inserted in an assignation, after the specification of the standard security assigned, a reference to the previous partial discharge or deed of restriction.

Note 5.—The variation docket Form E of this Schedule shall be used only when the personal obligation or other matter to which the variation relates was contained in the standard security, or in a variation thereof which has been duly recorded. Variations in a personal obligation or other matter constituted in an instrument or instruments which have not been so recorded may be altered by an instrument in appropriate terms which shall not be required to be recorded in the Register of Sasines.

Note 6.—Where the grantor of a variation docket does not have a recorded title to the security subjects, insert at the end of the variation and immediately before the consent by the creditor a clause of deduction of title as follows: *the security subjects to which the said standard security relates being last vested in* (give the name of the person in whom the security subjects were last vested) *whose title thereto was recorded in the said Register of Sasines on and from whom I acquired right by* (here specify the writ or writs by which such right was so acquired).

Section 18

SCHEDULE 5

Procedures as to Redemption

FORM A

NOTICE OF REDEMPTION OF STANDARD SECURITY

To A.B. (*address*)
TAKE NOTICE that on (*state date of repayment*) C.D. (*designation*), will repay the sum of £ (*or* the whole amount due) secured by a standard security by the said C.D. (*or* by E.F.) in your favour (*or* in favour of G.H.) recorded in the Register for on . Dated this day of

(*To be signed by the debtor, or proprietor, or by his agent, who will add his designation and the words* Agent of the said C.D.)

In the case of a standard security for a non-monetary obligation this Form shall be adapted accordingly.

FORM B

I, A.B., above named, hereby acknowledge receipt of the Notice of Redemption of which the foregoing is a copy. Dated this day of

(*To be signed by the creditor, or by his agent, who will add his designation and the words* Agent of the said A.B.)

FORM C

Notice of Redemption, of which the foregoing is a copy, was posted (*or otherwise, as the case may be*) to A.B. above named on the day of

(*To be signed by the debtor, or proprietor, or by his agent, who will add his designation and the words* Agent of the said C.D. *and if posted the postal receipt to be attached*.)

FORM D

No. 1

Certificate of Consignation on Redemption of Standard Security where Discharge cannot be obtained

I, A.B. (*designation*) (solicitor) certify that consignation of the whole amount due under the standard security aftermentioned was made as after stated and was necessitated by reason of a discharge being unobtainable after due notice of redemption had been given.
STANDARD SECURITY for £ (*or* a maximum of £ ; *in other cases describe as indicated in Note 2 to Schedule 4 to this Act*) by C.D. in favour of E.F. recorded in the Register of Sasines for on
AMOUNT CONSIGNED £ , being £ of principal, £ of interest and £ in respect of ascertained expenses.
BANK IN WHICH CONSIGNED (*specify bank or branch of bank, with address, in which above amount consigned*) conform to deposit receipt dated in name of the person appearing to have the best right thereto (*specifying his name and designation if known*) (*or if he is only a partial creditor say* to the extent of £).

[To be attested]

No. 2

Certificate of Declarator of Performance of Debtor's Obligations under Standard Security where Discharge cannot be obtained

I, A.B. (*designation*) (solicitor) certify that a decree of declarator of performance of the obligations of the debtor under the standard security aftermentioned was pronounced as after stated and was necessitated by reason of a discharge being unobtainable after due notice of redemption had been given.
STANDARD SECURITY by C.D. in favour of E.F. recorded in the Register for on
DECREE OF DECLARATOR by the Sheriff of at in the

application of the said C.D. (*or* J.K. (*designation*), who is now the debtor (*or* the proprietor of the interest in land contained) in the said standard security).

[To be attested]

Sections 19 and 21

SCHEDULE 6

PROCEDURES AS TO CALLING-UP AND DEFAULT

FORM A

NOTICE OF CALLING-UP OF STANDARD SECURITY

To A.B. (*address*)
TAKE NOTICE that C.D. (*designation*) requires payment of the principal sum of £ with interest thereon at the rate of per centum per annum from the day of (*adding if necessary*, subject to such adjustment of the principal sum and the amount of interest as may subsequently be determined) secured by a standard security by you (*or* by E.F.) in favour of the said C.D. (*or* of G.H. to which the said C.D. has now right) recorded in the Register for on ; And that failing full payment of the said sum and interest thereon (*adding if necessary*, subject to any adjustment as aforesaid), and expenses within two months after the date of service of this demand, the subjects of the security may be sold.

Dated this day of

(*To be signed by the creditor, or by his agent, who will add his designation and the words* Agent of the said C.D.)

In the case of a standard security for a non-monetary obligation this Form shall be adapted accordingly.

FORM B

NOTICE OF DEFAULT UNDER STANDARD SECURITY

To A.B. (*address*)
TAKE NOTICE that C.D. (*designation*), the creditor in a standard security by you (*or* by E.F.) in favour of the said C.D. (*or* of G.H. to which the said C.D. has now right) recorded in the Register for on requires fulfilment of the obligation(s) specified in the Schedule hereto in respect of which there is default; And that failing such fulfilment within one month after the date of service of this notice, the powers competent to the said C.D. on default may be exercised.

Dated this day of

(*To be signed by the creditor, or by his agent, who will add his designation and the words* Agent of the said C.D.)

Schedule of Obligation(s) in respect of which there is default.

To (*specify in detail the obligation(s) in respect of which there is default*).

FORM C

I, A.B., above named, hereby acknowledge receipt of the foregoing Notice of (Calling-up), (Default) of which the foregoing is a copy of the notice *adding where appropriate* " and I agree to the period of notice being dispensed with (*or* shortened to)."

Dated this day of

(*To be signed by the person on whom notice is served, or by his agent, who will add his designation and the words* Agent of the said A.B.).

FORM D

Notice of (Calling-up) (Default), of which the foregoing is a copy, was posted (*or otherwise, as the case may be*) to A.B. above named on the day of

(*To be signed by the creditor, or by his agent, who will add his designation and the words* Agent of the said C.D. *and if posted the postal receipt to be attached.*)

Sections 22 and 24

SCHEDULE 7

CONTENTS OF CERTIFICATE STATING A DEFAULT

1. A certificate which is lodged in court by the creditor for the purposes of section 22 or 24 of this Act shall contain the information required by the following provisions of this Schedule.

2. A certificate shall state—

(i) the name and address of the creditor and shall specify the standard security in respect of which the default is alleged to have occurred by reference to the original creditor and debtor therein and to the particulars of its registration;

(ii) the nature of the default with full details thereof.

3. The certificate shall be signed by the creditor or his solicitor, and a certificate which does not comply with the foregoing requirements of this Schedule shall not be received in evidence for the purposes of the said section 22 or 24.

Section 32

SCHEDULE 8

EXCLUDED ENACTMENTS

The Debts Securities (Scotland) Act 1856

1. Section 7 (Securities for cash accounts or credits).

Registration of Long Leases (Scotland) Act 1857

2. Section 4 (Assignations in security).

3. Section 6 (Instrument to be expeded where party presenting assignation in security for registration is not original lessee or assignee) so far as affecting assignation in security.

4. Section 6 (Translation of assignations in security and creditor's entry on possession in default of payment), so far as relating to such a translation.

5. Section 13 (Renunciations and discharges to be recorded) so far as affecting discharges.

6. Section 20 (Interpretation of clauses in Schedules).

The Titles to Land Consolidation (Scotland) Act 1868

7. Section 118 (Form of bond and disposition in security).

8. Section 119 (Explanation of clauses in Schedule (FF) No. 1—Form of a Bond and Disposition in Security).

9. Section 121 (Validity of sale to purchaser).

10. Section 122 (Creditors selling to count and reckon for the surplus of the price and to consign the same in the bank).

11. Section 123 (Disburdening of lands on sale and after consignation of surplus prices).

12. Section 124 (Prescription of form of transfer of securities).

13. Section 132 (Renunciation or discharge of heritable security).

14. Section 133 (Restriction of heritable security).

15. Section 138 (Use of short clauses of consent to registration).

Conveyancing (Scotland) Act 1874

16. Section 48 (Disburdening of lands sold under heritable securities when no surplus emerges).

17. Section 49 (Disburdening of lands where debtor in a heritable security cannot obtain discharge owing to the death or absence of the creditor, or any other cause).

The Heritable Securities (Scotland) Act 1894

18. Section 6 (Power of creditor to lease security subjects for seven years or under).

19. Section 7 (Granting of power by sheriff to lease security subjects for period of more than seven years).

20. Section 8 (Foreclosure).

21. Section 9 (Completion of title of security holders and preservation of personal obligation of debtor so far as not extinguished by price on sale of land).

22. Section 10 (Purchaser's title indefeasible).

23. Section 12 (Procedure).
24. Section 15 (Jurisdiction of sheriff).

The Conveyancing (Scotland) Act 1924

25. Section 24 (Assimilation of forms for registered leases).
26. Section 25 (Form of bond and disposition in security).
27. Sections 28 to 30 (Provisions dealing with the assignation, discharge and restriction of bond and disposition in security).
28. Section 31 (Description of lands and deduction of title unnecessary in certain deeds).
29. Section 32 (Redemption of bond and disposition in security).
30. Sections 33-39 (Provisions relating to calling up bond and disposition in security and advertisement and exposure to sale of the land).
31. Section 42 (Mode of disburdening land sold by creditor under power of sale).

Section 40

SCHEDULE 9

DISCHARGE OF HERITABLE SECURITY CONSTITUTED BY EX FACIE ABSOLUTE CONVEYANCE

I, A.B. (*designation*) hereby acknowledge that [the disposition (*or assignation*) granted by C.D. (*designation*)(*or* by E.F. (*designation*) with consent of C.D. (*designation*)) in my favour (*or* in favour of G.H. (*designation of original creditor*)) recorded in the Register for on] [*or, where endorsed on the disposition or assignation,* the foregoing disposition (or assignation)] [*describe security discharged by reference to the parties thereto and to the details of its recording*] although in its terms *ex facie* absolute was truly in security of an advance of £ (*or* a maximum amount of £ *in other cases describe as indicated in Note 2 to Schedule 4 to this Act*), and that all moneys intended to be secured thereby have been fully paid.

[To be attested]

NOTES TO SCHEDULE 9

Note 1.—The discharge may be separate or endorsed on the *ex facie* absolute disposition or assignation.

Note 2.—Where the grantor of the discharge is not the original creditor, the separate form of discharge shall be used.

Note 3.—Where the grantor of the discharge is not the original creditor but has a recorded title, no specification of the grantor's title is required. Where the grantor of the discharge is not the original creditor and has not a recorded title, insert at the end of the discharge a clause of deduction of title as follows:

> *The subjects conveyed by the said disposition* (or otherwise, as the case may be) *were last vested in the said G.H. as aforesaid* (or, where the last recorded title to the subjects was in favour of a person other than the original creditor, say *in J.K. whose title thereto was recorded in the said Register of Sasines on) and from whom I acquired right by* (here specify shortly the writ or writs by which right was so acquired).

[1] SCHEDULE 10

MINOR AND CONSEQUENTIAL AMENDMENTS

NOTE
[1] Amendments incorporated in the Acts to which they relate, have not been printed.

PART II

Section 52

OTHER AMENDMENTS

THE LAND COMPENSATION (SCOTLAND) ACT 1963

5. In section 10, for the words "Lord President of the Court of Session" there shall be substituted the words "Secretary of State".

SCHEDULE 11

[1] ENACTMENTS REPEALED

NOTE

[1] Repeals to which effect has been given in the Acts to which they relate, have not been printed.

Section 52

PART III

OTHER REPEALS

Chapter	Short Title	Extent of Repeal
1925 c. 33.	The Church of Scotland (Property and Endowments) Act 1925.	In section 37, the words from "Provided that" to "either party".
1949 c. 42.	The Lands Tribunal Act 1949.	In section 8 (3), the words from "and the Statutory Instruments Act 1946" to the end of the subsection.
1966 c. 49.	The Housing (Scotland) Act 1966.	Section 189.

Redemption of Standard Securities (Scotland) Act 1971

(1971 c. 45)

An Act to amend the provisions of the Conveyancing and Feudal Reform (Scotland) Act 1970 relating to the redemption of standard securities; to make provision as respects Scotland in relation to the operation of section 89 of the Companies Act 1948; and for connected purposes. [1st July 1971]

1. [See Conveyancing and Feudal Reform (Scotland) Act 1970, ss.11, 18, 23 and 28, and Sched. 3.]

Operation of s.89 of Companies Act 1948

[1] **2.** For the avoidance of doubt, it is hereby declared that the provisions of Part II (the standard security) of the principal Act[2] do not affect (and shall be deemed never to have affected) the operation of section 193 of the Companies Act 1985 (perpetual debentures).

NOTES

[1] As amended by the Companies Consolidation (Consequential Provisions) Act 1985, Sched. 2, with effect from 1st July 1985.

[2] The "principal Act" means the Conveyancing and Feudal Reform (Scotland) Act 1970.

Application of Act to existing standard securities

3. The provisions (including the standard conditions) of and relating to a standard security granted before the commencement of this Act and duly recorded may be altered by such an agreement as is mentioned in section 1(*c*) of this Act[1] duly recorded, and the provisions of the principal Act as amended by this Act shall apply in relation to any such security as so altered.

NOTE

[1] "Such an agreement as is mentioned in s.1(*c*)" means any agreement to the contrary.

Citation and construction

4. This Act may be cited as the Redemption of Standard Securities (Scotland) Act 1971, and the principal Act and this Act shall be construed together, and may be cited together as the Conveyancing and Feudal Reform (Scotland) Acts 1970 and 1971.

[THE NEXT PAGE IS J 191]

Prescription and Limitation (Scotland) Act 1973

(1973 c. 52)

An Act to replace the Prescription Acts of 1469, 1474 and 1617 and make new provision in the law of Scotland with respect to the establishment and definition by positive prescription of title to interests in land and of positive servitudes and public rights of way, and with respect to the extinction of rights and obligations by negative prescription; to repeal certain enactments relating to limitation of proof; to re-enact with modifications certain enactments relating to the time-limits for bringing legal proceedings where damages are claimed which consist of or include damages or solatium in respect of personal injuries or in respect of a person's death and the time-limit for claiming contribution between wrongdoers; and for purposes connected with the matters aforesaid. [25th July 1973]

Part I

Prescription

Positive prescription

Interests in land: general

[1] **1.**—(1) If in the case of an interest in particular land, being an interest to which this section applies,—

(*a*) the interest has been possessed by any person, or by any person and his successors, for a continuous period of ten years openly, peaceably and without any judicial interruption, and

(*b*) the possession was founded on, and followed (i) the recording of a deed which is sufficient in respect of its terms to constitute in favour of that person a title to that interest in the particular land, or in land of a description habile to include the particular land, or (ii) registration of that interest in favour of that person in the Land Register of Scotland, subject to an exclusion of indemnity under section 12 (2) of the Land Registration (Scotland) Act 1979,

then, as from the expiration of the said period, the validity of the title so far as relating to the said interest in the particular land shall be exempt from challenge.

(1A) Subsection (1) above shall not apply where—

(*a*) possession was founded on the recording of a deed which is invalid *ex facie* or was forged; or

(*b*) possession was founded on registration in respect of an interest in land in the Land Register of Scotland proceeding on a forged deed and the person appearing from the Register to be entitled to the interest was aware of the forgery at the time of registration in his favour.

(2) This section applies to any interest in land the title to which can competently be recorded or which is registrable in the Land Register of Scotland.

(3) In the computation of a prescriptive period for the purposes of this section in a case where the deed in question is a decree of adjudication for debt, any period before the expiry of the legal shall be disregarded.

(4) Where in any question involving an interest in any foreshore or in any salmon fishings this section is pled against the Crown as owner of the regalia, subsection (1) above shall have effect as if for the words " ten years " there were substituted the words " twenty years."

(5) This section is without prejudice to the operation of section 2 of this Act.

NOTE

[1] As amended by the Land Registration (Scotland) Act 1979, s. 10.

Interests in land: special cases

[1] **2.**—(1) If in the case of an interest in particular land, being an interest to which this section applies,—

(*a*) the interest has been possessed by any person, or by any person and his successors, for a continuous period of twenty years openly, peaceably and without any judicial interruption, and

(*b*) the possession was founded on, and followed the execution of, a deed (whether recorded or not) which is sufficient in respect of its terms to constitute in favour of that person a title to that interest in the particular land, or in land of a description habile to include the particular land,

then, as from the expiration of the said period, the validity of the title so far as relating to the said interest in the particular land shall be exempt from challenge except on the ground that the deed is invalid *ex facie* or was forged.

(2) This section applies—

(*a*) to the interest in land of the lessee under a lease;

(*b*) to any interest in allodial land;

(*c*) to any other interest in land the title to which is of a kind which, under the law in force immediately before the commencement of this Part of this Act, was sufficient to form a foundation for positive prescription without the deed constituting the title having been recorded.

(3) This section is without prejudice to the operation of section 1 of this Act.

NOTE

[1] See the Registration of Leases (Scotland) Act 1857, s. 16 (2), and the Land Tenure Reform (Scotland) Act 1974, s. 18 and Sched. 6, para. 3.

Positive servitudes and public rights of way

3.—(1) If in the case of a positive servitude over land—

(*a*) the servitude has been possessed for a continuous period of twenty years openly, peaceably and without any judicial interruption, and

(*b*) the possession was founded on, and followed the execution of, a deed which is sufficient in respect of its terms (whether expressly or by implication) to constitute the servitude,

then, as from the expiration of the said period, the validity of the servitude as so constituted, shall be exempt from challenge except on the ground that the deed is invalid *ex facie* or was forged.

(2) If a positive servitude over land has been possessed for a continuous period of twenty years openly, peaceably and without judicial interruption, then, as from the expiration of that period, the existence of the servitude as so possessed shall be exempt from challenge.

(3) If a public right of way over land has been possessed by the public for a continuous period of twenty years openly, peaceably and without judicial interruption, then, as from the expiration of that period, the existence of the right of way as so possessed shall be exempt from challenge.

(4) References in subsections (1) and (2) of this section to possession of a servitude are references to possession of the servitude by any person in possession of the relative dominant tenement.

(5) This section is without prejudice to the operation of section 7 of this Act.

Judicial interruption of periods of possession for purposes of sections 1, 2 and 3

4.—(1) In sections 1, 2 and 3 of this Act references to a judicial interruption, in relation to possession, are references to the making in appropriate proceedings, by any person having a proper interest to do so, of a claim which challenges the possession in question.

(2) In this section "appropriate proceedings" means—

(*a*) any proceedings in a court of competent jurisdiction in Scotland or elsewhere, except proceedings in the Court of Session initiated by a summons which is not subsequently called;

(*b*) any arbitration in Scotland;

(*c*) any arbitration in a country other than Scotland, being an arbitration an award in which would be enforceable in Scotland.

(3) The date of a judicial interruption shall be taken to be—

(*a*) where the claim has been made in an arbitration and the nature of the claim has been stated in a preliminary notice relating to that arbitration, the date when the preliminary notice was served;

(*b*) in any other case, the date when the claim was made.

(4) In the foregoing subsection "preliminary notice" in relation to an arbitration means a notice served by one party to the arbitration on the other party or parties requiring him or them to appoint an arbiter or to agree to the appointment of an arbiter, or, where the arbitration agreement or any relevant enactment provides that the reference shall be to a person therein named or designated, a notice requiring him or them to submit the dispute to the person so named or designated.

Further provisions supplementary to sections 1, 2 and 3

5.—(1) In sections 1, 2 and 3 of this Act "deed" includes a judicial decree; and for the purposes of the said sections any of the following, namely an instrument of sasine, a notarial instrument and a notice of title, which narrates or declares that a person has a title to an interest in land shall be treated as a deed sufficient to constitute that title in favour of that person.

(2) Where a deed has been at any time *ex facie* invalid by reason of an informality of execution within the meaning of section 39 of the Conveyancing (Scotland) Act 1874, but the appropriate court has subsequently declared, in pursuance of that section, that it was subscribed by the grantor or maker and the witnesses, the deed shall be deemed for the purposes of the said sections 1, 2 and 3 not to be, and not at any time to have been, *ex facie* invalid by reason of any such informality of execution.

Extinction of obligations by prescriptive periods of five years

6.—(1) If, after the appropriate date, an obligation to which this section applies has subsisted for a continuous period of five years—

(*a*) without any relevant claim having been made in relation to the obligation, and

(*b*) without the subsistence of the obligation having been relevantly acknowledged,

then as from the expiration of that period the obligation shall be extinguished:

Provided that in its application to an obligation under a bill of exchange or a promissory note this subsection shall have effect as if paragraph (*b*) thereof were omitted.

(2) Schedule 1 to this Act shall have effect for defining the obligations to which this section applies.

(3) In subsection (1) above the reference to the appropriate date, in relation to an obligation of any kind specified in Schedule 2 to this Act is a reference to the date specified in that Schedule in relation to obligations of that kind, and in relation to an obligation of any other kind is a reference to the date when the obligation became enforceable.

[1] (4) In the computation of a prescriptive period in relation to any obligation for the purposes of this section—

(*a*) any period during which by reason of—

(i) fraud on the part of the debtor or any person acting on his behalf, or

(ii) error induced by words or conduct of the debtor or any person acting on his behalf,

the creditor was induced to refrain from making a relevant claim in relation to the obligation, and

[2] (*b*) any period during which the original creditor (while he is the creditor) was under legal disability,

shall not be reckoned as, or as part of, the prescriptive period:

Provided that any period such as is mentioned in paragraph (*a*) of this subsection shall not include any time occurring after the creditor could with reasonable diligence have discovered the fraud or error, as the case may be, referred to in that paragraph.

(5) Any period such as is mentioned in paragraph (*a*) or (*b*) of subsection (4) of this section shall not be regarded as separating the time immediately before it from the time immediately after it.

NOTES

[1] Applied by the Merchant Shipping (Liner Conferences) Act 1982, s. 8(3).
[2] See the Age of Legal Capacity (Scotland) Act 1991, s. 8.

Extinction of obligations by prescriptive periods of twenty years

7.—(1) If, after the date when any obligation to which this section applies has become enforceable, the obligation has subsisted for a continuous period of twenty years—

(*a*) without any relevant claim having been made in relation to the obligation, and

(*b*) without the subsistence of the obligation having been relevantly acknowledged,

then as from the expiration of that period the obligation shall be extinguished:

Provided that in its application to an obligation under a bill of exchange or a promissory note this subsection shall have effect as if paragraph (*b*) thereof were omitted.

[1] (2) This section applies to an obligation of any kind (including an obligation to which section 6 of this Act applies), not being an obligation to which section 22A of this Act applies or an obligation specified in Schedule 3 to this Act as an imprescriptible obligation or an obligation to make reparation in respect of personal injuries within the meaning of Part II of this Act or in respect of the death of any person as a result of such injuries.

NOTE

[1] As amended by the Prescription and Limitation (Scotland) Act 1984, Sched. 1, para. 2, as regards any obligation not extinguished before 26th September 1984: *ibid.* s.5(3), and by the Consumer Protection Act 1987, Sched. 1, para. 8.

Extinction of other rights relating to property by prescriptive periods of twenty years

8.—(1) If, after the date when any right to which this section applies has become exercisable or enforceable, the right has subsisted for a continuous period of twenty years unexercised or unenforced, and without any relevant claim in relation to it having been made, then as from the expiration of that period the right shall be extinguished.

(2) This section applies to any right relating to property, whether heritable or moveable, not being a right specified in Schedule 3 to this Act as an imprescriptible right or falling within section 6 or 7 of this Act as being a right correlative to an obligation to which either of those sections applies.

Extinction of obligations to make contributions between wrongdoers

[1] **8A.**—(1) If any obligation to make a contribution by virtue of section 3(2) of the Law Reform (Miscellaneous Provisions) (Scotland) Act 1940 in respect of any damages or expenses has subsisted for a continuous period of two years after the date on which the right to recover the contribution became enforceable by the creditor in the obligation—

(*a*) without any relevant claim having been made in relation to the obligation; and

(*b*) without the subsistence of the obligation having been relevantly acknowledged;

then as from the expiration of that period the obligation shall be extinguished.

(2) Subsections (4) and (5) of section 6 of this Act shall apply for the purposes of this section as they apply for the purposes of that section.

NOTE

[1] Inserted by the Prescription and Limitation (Scotland) Act 1984, s. 1.

Definition of "relevant claim" for purposes of sections 6, 7 and 8

[1] **9.**—[2] (1) In sections 6, 7 and 8A of this Act the expression "relevant claim," in relation to an obligation, means a claim made by or on behalf of the creditor for implement or part-implement of the obligation, being a claim made—

(*a*) in appropriate proceedings; or

[3] (*b*) by the presentation of, or the concurring in, a petition for sequestration or by the submission of a claim under section 22 or 48 of the Bankruptcy (Scotland) Act 1985; or

(*c*) by a creditor to the trustee acting under a trust deed as defined in section 5(2)(*c*) of the Bankruptcy (Scotland) Act 1985;

[4] (*d*) by the presentation of, or the concurring in, a petition for the winding up of a company or by the submission of a claim in a liquidation in accordance with rules made under section 411 of the Insolvency Act 1986;

and for the purposes of the said sections 6, 7 and 8A the execution by or on behalf of the creditor in an obligation of any form of diligence directed to the enforcement of the obligation shall be deemed to be a relevant claim in relation to the obligation.

(2) In section 8 of this Act the expression "relevant claim," in relation to a right, means a claim made in appropriate proceedings by or on behalf of the creditor to establish the right or to contest any claim to a right inconsistent therewith.

(3) Where a claim which, in accordance with the foregoing provisions of this section, is a relevant claim for the purposes of section 6, 7, 8 or 8A of this Act is made in an arbitration, and the nature of the claim has been stated in a preliminary notice relating to that arbitration, the date when the notice was served shall be taken for those purposes to be the date of the making of the claim.

(4) In this section the expression "appropriate proceedings" and, in relation to an arbitration, the expression "preliminary notice" have the same meanings as in section 4 of this Act.

NOTES

[1] As amended by the Prescription and Limitation (Scotland) Act 1984, Sched. 1, para. 3.

[2] As amended by the Bankruptcy (Scotland) Act 1985, Sched. 7, para. 11, with effect from 1st April 1986.

[3] As amended by the Prescription (Scotland) Act 1987, s.1(2).

[4] Inserted by the Prescription (Scotland) Act 1987, s.1(1). By section 1(3) of the same Act:

"The said section 9 as amended by subsection (1) above shall have effect as regards any claim (whenever submitted) in a liquidation in respect of which the winding up commenced on or after 29th December 1986."

Relevant acknowledgment for purposes of sections 6, 7 and 8A

[1] **10.**—(1) The subsistence of an obligation shall be regarded for the purposes of sections 6, 7 and 8A of this Act as having been relevantly acknowledged if, and only if, either of the following conditions is satisfied, namely—

(*a*) that there has been such performance by or on behalf of the debtor towards implement of the obligation as clearly indicates that the obligation still subsists;

(*b*) that there has been made by or on behalf of the debtor to the creditor or his agent an unequivocal written admission clearly acknowledging that the obligation still subsists.

(2) Subject to subsection (3) below, where two or more persons are bound jointly by an obligation so that each is liable for the whole, and the subsistence of the obligation has been relevantly acknowledged by or on behalf of one of those persons then—

(*a*) if the acknowledgment is made in the manner specified in paragraph (*a*) of the foregoing subsection it shall have effect for the purposes of the said sections 6, 7 and 8A as respects the liability of each of those persons, and

(*b*) if it is made in the manner specified in paragraph (*b*) of that subsection it shall have effect for those purposes only as respects the liability of the person who makes it.

(3) Where the subsistence of an obligation affecting a trust estate has been relevantly acknowledged by or on behalf of one of two or more co-trustees in the manner specified in paragraph (*a*) or (*b*) of subsection (1) of this section, the acknowledgment shall have effect for the purposes of the said sections 6, 7 and 8A as respects the liability of the trust estate and any liability of each of the trustees.

(4) In this section references to performance in relation to an obligation include, where the nature of the obligation so requires, references to refraining from doing something and to permitting or suffering something to be done or maintained.

NOTE

[1] As amended by the Prescription and Limitation (Scotland) Act 1984, Sched. 1, para. 4.

Obligations to make reparation

11.—(1) Subject to subsections (2) and (3) below, any obligation (whether arising from any enactment, or from any rule of law or from, or by reason of any breach of, a contract or promise) to make reparation for loss, injury or damage caused by an act, neglect or default shall be regarded for the purposes of section 6 of this Act as having become enforceable on the date when the loss, injury or damage occurred.

(2) Where as a result of a continuing act, neglect or default loss, injury or damage has occurred before the cessation of the act, neglect or default the loss, injury or damage shall be deemed for the purposes of subsection (1) above to have occurred on the date when the act, neglect or default ceased.

(3) In relation to a case where on the date referred to in subsection (1) above (or, as the case may be, that subsection as modified by subsection (2) above) the creditor was not aware, and could not with reasonable diligence have been aware, that loss, injury or damage caused as aforesaid had occurred, the said subsection (1) shall have effect as if for the reference therein to that date there were substituted a reference to the date when the creditor first became, or could with reasonable diligence have become, so aware.

[1] (4) Subsections (1) and (2) above (with the omission of any reference therein to subsection (3) above) shall have effect for the purposes of section 7 of this Act as they have effect for the purposes of section 6 of this Act.

NOTE
[1] As amended by the Prescription and Limitation (Scotland) Act 1984, Sched. 2.

Savings

12.—(1) Where by virtue of any enactment passed or made before the passing of this Act a claim to establish a right or enforce implement of an

[THE NEXT PAGE IS J 197]

obligation may be made only within a period of limitation specified in or determined under the enactment, and, by the expiration of a prescriptive period determined under section 6, 7 or 8 of this Act the right or obligation would, apart from this subsection, be extinguished before the expiration of the period of limitation, the said section shall have effect as if the relevant prescriptive period were extended so that it expires—

(*a*) on the date when the period of limitation expires, or

(*b*) if on that date any such claim made within that period has not been finally disposed of, on the date when the claim is so disposed of.

(2) Nothing in section 6, 7 or 8 of this Act shall be construed so as to exempt any deed from challenge at any time on the ground that it is invalid *ex facie* or was forged.

Prohibition of contracting out

[1] **13.** Any provision in any agreement purporting to provide in relation to any right or obligation that section 6, 7, 8 or 8A of this Act shall not have effect shall be null.

NOTE

[1] As amended by the Prescription and Limitation (Scotland) Act 1984, Sched. 1, para. 5.

General

Computation of prescriptive periods

14.—(1) In the computation of a prescriptive period for the purposes of any provision of this Part of this Act—

(*a*) time occurring before the commencement of this Part of this Act shall be reckonable towards the prescriptive period in like manner as time occurring thereafter, but subject to the restriction that any time reckoned under this paragraph shall be less than the prescriptive period;

[1] (*b*) any time during which any person against whom the provision is pled was under legal disability shall (except so far as otherwise provided by subsection (4) of section 6 of this Act including that subsection as applied by section 8A of this Act) be reckoned as if the person were free from that disability;

(*c*) if the commencement of the prescriptive period would, apart from this paragraph, fall at a time in any day other than the beginning of the day, the period shall be deemed to have commenced at the beginning of the next following day;

(*d*) if the last day of the prescriptive period would, apart from this paragraph, be a holiday, the period shall, notwithstanding anything in the said provision, be extended to include any immediately succeeding day which is a holiday, any further immediately succeeding days which are holidays, and the next succeeding day which is not a holiday;

(*e*) save as otherwise provided in this Part of this Act regard shall be had to the like principles as immediately before the commencement of this Part of this Act were applicable to the computation of periods of prescription for the purposes of the Prescription Act 1617.

(2) In this section "holiday" means a day of any of the following descriptions, namely, a Saturday, a Sunday and a day which, in Scotland, is a bank holiday under the Banking and Financial Dealings Act 1971.

NOTE

[1] As amended by the Prescription and Limitation (Scotland) Act 1984, Sched. 1, para. 6.

Interpretation of Part I

15.—(1) In this Part of this Act, unless the context otherwise requires, the following expressions have the meanings hereby assigned to them, namely—

"bill of exchange" has the same meaning as it has for the purposes of the Bills of Exchange Act 1882;

"date of execution," in relation to a deed executed on several dates, means the last of those dates;

"enactment" includes an order, regulation, rule or other instrument having effect by virtue of an Act;

"holiday" has the meaning assigned to it by section 14 of this Act;

"interest in land" does not include a servitude;

"land" includes heritable property of any description;

"lease" includes a sub-lease;

"legal disability" means legal disability by reason of nonage or unsoundness of mind;

"possession" includes civil possession, and "possessed" shall be construed accordingly;

[1] "prescriptive period" means a period required for the operation of section 1, 2, 3, 6, 7, 8 or 8A of this Act;

"promissory note" has the same meaning as it has for the purposes of the Bills of Exchange Act 1882;

"trustee" includes any person holding property in a fiduciary capacity for another and, without prejudice to that generality, includes a trustee within the meaning of the Trusts (Scotland) Act 1921; and "trust" shall be construed accordingly;

and references to the recording of a deed are references to the recording thereof in the General Register of Sasines.

(2) In this Part of this Act, unless the context otherwise requires, any reference to an obligation or to a right includes a reference to the right or, as the case may be, to the obligation (if any), correlative thereto.

(3) In this Part of this Act any reference to an enactment shall, unless the context otherwise requires, be construed as a reference to that enactment as amended or extended, and as including a reference thereto as applied, by or under any other enactment.

NOTE

[1] As amended by the Prescription and Limitation (Scotland) Act 1984, Sched. 1, para. 7.

Amendments and repeals related to Part I

16.—(1) The enactment specified in Part I of Schedule 4 to this Act shall have effect subject to the amendment there specified, being an amendment related to this Part of this Act.

(2) Subject to the next following subsection, the enactments specified in Part I of Schedule 5 to this Act (which includes certain enactments relating to the limitation of proof) are hereby repealed to the extent specified in column 3 of that Schedule.

[1] (3) Where by virtue of any Act repealed by this section the subsistence of an obligation in force at the date of the commencement of this Part of this Act was immediately before that date, by reason of the passage of time, provable only by the writ or oath of the debtor the subsistence of the obligation shall (notwithstanding anything in sections 16(1) and 17(2)(*a*) of the Interpretation Act 1978, which relates to the effect of repeals) as from that date be provable as if the said repealed Act had not passed.

NOTE

[1] As amended by the Interpretation Act 1978, s.25(2).

[1] Part II

Limitation of Actions

NOTE

[1] Saved by the Administration of Justice Act 1982, s. 73(5).

Part II not to extend to product liability

[1] **16A.** This Part of this Act does not apply to any action to which section 22B or 22C of this Act applies.

NOTE

[1] Inserted by the Consumer Protection Act 1987, Sched. 1, para. 9.

Actions in respect of personal injuries not resulting in death

[1] **17.**—(1) This section applies to an action of damages where the damages claimed consist of or include damages in respect of personal injuries, being an action (other than an action to which section 18 of this Act applies) brought by the person who sustained the injuries or any other person.

(2) Subject to subsection (3) below and section 19A of this Act, no action to which this section applies shall be brought unless it is commenced within a period of three years after—

(*a*) the date on which the injuries were sustained or, where the act or omission to which the injuries were attributable was a continuing one, that date or the date on which the act or omission ceased, whichever is the later; or

(*b*) the date (if later than any date mentioned in paragraph (*a*) above) on which the pursuer in the action became, or on which, in the opinion of the court, it would have been reasonably practicable for him in all the circumstances to become, aware of all the following facts—

(i) that the injuries in question were sufficiently serious to justify his bringing an action of damages on the assumption that the person against whom the action was brought did not dispute liability and was able to satisfy a decree;

(ii) that the injuries were attributable in whole or in part to an act or omission; and

(iii) that the defender was a person to whose act or omission the injuries were attributable in whole or in part or the employer or principal of such a person.

[2] (3) In the computation of the period specified in subsection (2) above there shall be disregarded any time during which the person who sustained the injuries was under legal disability by reason of nonage or unsoundness of mind.

NOTES

[1] Substituted by the Prescription and Limitation (Scotland) Act 1984, s. 2, as regards rights of action accruing both before and after the commencement of that Act: *ibid.* s. 5(1).

[2] See the Age of Legal Capacity (Scotland) Act 1991, s. 8.

Actions where death has resulted from personal injuries

[1] **18.**—(1) This section applies to any action in which, following the death of any person from personal injuries, damages are claimed in respect of the injuries or the death.

(2) Subject to subsections (3) and (4) below and section 19A of this Act, no action to which this section applies shall be brought unless it is commenced within a period of three years after—

(*a*) the date of death of the deceased; or

(*b*) the date (if later than the date of death) on which the pursuer in the action became, or on which, in the opinion of the court, it would have been reasonably practicable for him in all the circumstances to become, aware of both of the following facts—

(i) that the injuries of the deceased were attributable in whole or in part to an act or omission; and

(ii) that the defender was a person to whose act or omission the injuries were attributable in whole or in part or the employer or principal of such a person.

[2] (3) Where the pursuer is a relative of the deceased, there shall be disregarded in the computation of the period specified in subsection (2) above any time during which the relative was under legal disability by reason of nonage or unsoundness of mind.

(4) Subject to section 19A of this Act, where an action of damages has not been brought by or on behalf of a person who has sustained personal injuries within the period specified in section 17(2) of this Act and that person subsequently dies in consequence of those injuries, no action to which this section applies shall be brought in respect of those injuries or the death from those injuries.

(5) In this section "relative" has the same meaning as in Schedule 1 to the Damages (Scotland) Act 1976.

NOTES

[1] Substituted by the Prescription and Limitation (Scotland) Act 1984, s. 2, as regards rights of action accruing both before and after the commencement of that Act: *ibid*. s. 5(1).

[2] See the Age of Legal Capacity (Scotland) Act 1991, s. 8.

Limitation of defamation and other actions

[1] **18A.**—(1) Subject to subsections (2) and (3) below and section 19A of this Act, no action for defamation shall be brought unless it is commenced within a period of three years after the date when the right of action accrued.

[2] (2) In the computation of the period specified in subsection (1) above there shall be disregarded any time during which the person alleged to have been defamed was under legal disability by reason of nonage or unsoundness of mind.

(3) Nothing in this section shall affect any right of action which accrued before the commencement of this section.

(4) In this section—

(*a*) "defamation" includes *convicium* and malicious falsehood, and "defamed" shall be construed accordingly; and

(*b*) references to the date when a right of action accrued shall be construed as references to the date when the publication or communication in respect of which the action for defamation is to be brought first came to the notice of the pursuer.

NOTES

[1] Inserted by the Law Reform (Miscellaneous Provisions) (Scotland) Act 1985, s. 12(2).

[2] See the Age of Legal Capacity (Scotland) Act 1991, s. 8.

19. [Repealed by the Prescription and Limitation (Scotland) Act 1984, s. 2.]

Power of court to override time-limits, etc.

[1] **19A.**—[2] (1) Where a person would be entitled, but for any of the provisions of section 17 or section 18 and 18A of this Act, to bring an action, the court may, if it seems to it equitable to do so, allow him to bring the action notwithstanding that provision.

(2) The provisions of subsection (1) above shall have effect not only as regards rights of action accruing after the commencement of this section but also as regards those, in respect of which a final judgment has not been pronounced, accruing before such commencement.

(3) In subsection (2) above, the expression "final judgment" means an interlocutor of a court of first instance which, by itself, or taken along with previous interlocutors, disposes of the subject matter of a cause notwithstanding that judgment may not have been pronounced on every question raised or that the expenses found due may not have been modified, taxed or decerned for; but the expression does not include an interlocutor dismissing a cause by reason only of a provision mentioned in subsection (1) above.

[3] (4) An action which could not be entertained but for this section shall not be tried by jury.

NOTES

[1] Inserted by the Law Reform (Miscellaneous Provisions) (Scotland) Act 1980, s. 23(*a*).

[2] As amended by the Prescription and Limitation (Scotland) Act 1984, Sched. 1, para. 8(*a*) and by the Law Reform (Miscellaneous Provisions) (Scotland) Act 1985, s. 12(3).

[3] Added by the Prescription and Limitation (Scotland) Act 1984, Sched. 1, para. 8(*b*).

20, 21. [Repealed by the Prescription and Limitation (Scotland) Act 1984, Sched. 2.]

Interpretation of Part II and supplementary provisions

[1] **22.**—(1) In this Part of this Act—

"the court" means the Court of Session or the sheriff court; and

"personal injuries" includes any disease and any impairment of a person's physical or mental condition.

[2] (2) Where the pursuer in an action to which section 17, 18 or 18A of this Act applies is pursuing the action by virtue of the assignation of a right of action, the reference in subsection (2)(*b*) of the said section 17 or of the said section 18 or, as the case may be, subsection (4)(*b*) of the said section 18A to the pursuer in the action shall be construed as a reference to the assignor of the right of action.

(3) For the purposes of the said subsection (2)(*b*) knowledge that any act or omission was or was not, as a matter of law, actionable, is irrelevant.

(4) An action which would not be entertained but for the said subsection (2)(*b*) shall not be tried by jury.

NOTES

[1] Substituted by the Prescription and Limitation (Scotland) Act 1984, s. 3.

[2] As amended by the Law Reform (Miscellaneous Provisions) (Scotland) Act 1985, s. 12(4).

[1] PART IIA

PRESCRIPTION OF OBLIGATIONS AND LIMITATION OF ACTIONS UNDER PART I OF THE CONSUMER PROTECTION ACT 1987

NOTE

[1] Inserted by the Consumer Protection Act 1987, Sched. 1, para. 10.

Prescription of Obligations

Ten years' prescription of obligations

22A.—(1) An obligation arising from liability under section 2 of the 1987 Act (to make reparation for damage caused wholly or partly by a defect in a product) shall be extinguished if a period of 10 years has expired from the relevant time, unless a relevant claim was made within that period and has not been finally disposed of, and no such obligation shall come into existence after the expiration of the said period.

(2) If, at the expiration of the period of 10 years mentioned in subsection (1) above, a relevant claim has been made but has not been finally disposed of, the obligation to which the claim relates shall be extinguished when the claim is finally disposed of.

(3) In this section a claim is finally disposed of when—

(*a*) a decision disposing of the claim has been made against which no appeal is competent;

(*b*) an appeal against such a decision is competent with leave, and the time limit for leave has expired and no application has been made or leave has been refused;

(*c*) leave to appeal against such a decision is granted or is not required, and no appeal is made within the time limit for appeal; or

(*d*) the claim is abandoned;

"relevant claim" in relation to an obligation means a claim made by or on behalf of the creditor for implement or part implement of the obligation, being a claim made—

(*a*) in appropriate proceedings within the meaning of section 4(2) of this Act; or

(*b*) by the presentation of, or the concurring in, a petition for sequestration or by the submission of a claim under section 22 or 48 of the Bankruptcy (Scotland) Act 1985; or

(*c*) by the presentation of, or the concurring in, a petition for the winding up of a company or by the submission of a claim in a liquidation in accordance with the rules made under section 411 of the Insolvency Act 1986;

"relevant time" has the meaning given in section 4(2) of the 1987 Act.

(4) Where a relevant claim is made in an arbitration, and the nature of the claim has been stated in a preliminary notice (within the meaning of section 4(4) of this Act) relating to that arbitration, the date when the notice is served shall be taken for those purposes to be the date of the making of the claim.

Limitation of actions

Three year limitation of actions

22B.—(1) This section shall apply to an action to enforce an obligation arising from liability under section 2 of the 1987 Act (to make reparation for damage caused wholly or partly by a defect in a product), except where section 22C of this Act applies.

(2) Subject to subsection (4) below, an action to which this section applies shall not be competent unless it is commenced within the period of three years after the earliest date on which the person seeking to bring (or a person who could at an earlier date have brought) the action was aware, or on which, in the opinion of the court, it was reasonably practicable for him in all the circumstances to become aware, of all the facts mentioned in subsection (3) below.

(3) The facts referred to in subsection (2) above are—

(*a*) that there was a defect in a product;

(*b*) that the damage was caused or partly caused by the defect;

(*c*) that the damage was sufficiently serious to justify the pursuer (or other person referred to in subsection (2) above) in bringing an action to which this section applies on the assumption that the defender did not dispute liability and was able to satisfy a decree;

(*d*) that the defender was a person liable for the damage under the said section 2.

(4) In the computation of the period of three years mentioned in subsection (2) above, there shall be disregarded any period during which the person seeking to bring the action was under legal disability by reason of nonage or unsoundness of mind.

(5) The facts mentioned in subsection (3) above do not include knowledge of whether particular facts and circumstances would or would not, as a matter of law, result in liability for damage under the said section 2.

(6) Where a person would be entitled, but for this section, to bring an action for reparation other than one in which the damages claimed are confined to damages for loss of or damage to property, the court may, if it seems to it equitable to do so, allow him to bring the action notwithstanding this section.

Actions under the 1987 Act where death has resulted from personal injuries

22C.—(1) This section shall apply to an action to enforce an obligation arising from liability under section 2 of the 1987 Act (to make reparation for damage caused wholly or partly by a defect in a product) where a person has died from personal injuries and the damages claimed include damages for those personal injuries or that death.

(2) Subject to subsection (4) below, an action to which this section applies shall not be competent unless it is commenced within the period of three years after the later of—

(*a*) the date of death of the injured person;

(*b*) the earliest date on which the person seeking to make (or a person who could at an earlier date have made) the claim was aware, or on which, in the opinion of the court, it was reasonably practicable for him in all the circumstances to become aware—

(i) that there was a defect in the product;

(ii) that the injuries of the deceased were caused (or partly caused) by the defect; and

(iii) that the defender was a person liable for the damage under the said section 2.

(3) Where the person seeking to make the claim is a relative of the deceased, there shall be disregarded in the computation of the period mentioned in subsection (2) above any period during which that relative was under legal disability by reason of nonage or unsoundness of mind.

(4) Where an action to which section 22B of this Act applies has not been brought within the period mentioned in subsection (2) of that section and the person subsequently dies in consequence of his injuries, an action to which this section applies shall not be competent in respect of those injuries or that death.

(5) Where a person would be entitled, but for this section, to bring an action for reparation other than one in which the damages claimed are confined to damages for loss of or damage to property, the court may, if it seems to it equitable to do so, allow him to bring the action notwithstanding this section.

(6) In this section "relative" has the same meaning as in the Damages (Scotland) Act 1976.

(7) For the purposes of subsection (2)(*b*) above there shall be disregarded knowledge of whether particular facts and circumstances would or would not, as a matter of law, result in liability for damage under the said section 2.

Supplementary

Interpretation of this Part

22D.—(1) Expressions used in this Part and in Part I of the 1987 Act shall have the same meanings in this Part as in the said Part I.

(2) For the purposes of section 1(1) of the 1987 Act, this Part shall have effect and be construed as if it were contained in Part I of that Act.

(3) In this Part, "the 1987 Act" means the Consumer Protection Act 1987.

Amendments and repeals related to Part II

23. [Repealed by the Consumer Protection Act 1987, Sched. 1, para. 11.]

[1] PART III

SUPPLEMENTAL

NOTE

[1] Saved by the Administration of Justice Act 1982, s. 73(5).

Private international law application

[1] **23A.**—(1) Where the substantive law of a country other than Scotland falls to be applied by a Scottish court as the law governing an obligation,

the court shall apply any relevant rules of law of that country relating to the extinction of the obligation or the limitation of time within which proceedings may be brought to enforce the obligation to the exclusion of any corresponding rule of Scots law.

(2) This section shall not apply where it appears to the court that the application of the relevant foreign rule of law would be incompatible with the principles of public policy applied by the court.

(3) This section shall not apply in any case where the application of the corresponding rule of Scots law has extinguished the obligation, or barred the bringing of proceedings prior to the coming into force of the Prescription and Limitation (Scotland) Act 1984.

NOTE

[1] Inserted by the Prescription and Limitation (Scotland) Act 1984, s. 4, as regards proceedings commenced on or after 26th September 1984: *ibid.* s. 5(2).

The Crown

24. This Act binds the Crown.

Short title, commencement and extent

25.—(1) This Act may be cited as the Prescription and Limitation (Scotland) Act 1973.

[1] (2) This Act shall come into operation, as follows:—

(*a*) Parts II and III of this Act, Part II of Schedule 4 to this Act and Part II of Schedule 5 to this Act shall come into operation on the date on which this Act is passed;

(*b*) except as aforesaid this Act shall come into operation on the expiration of three years from the said date.

(3) [Repealed by the Prescription and Limitation (Scotland) Act 1984, Sched. 2.]

(4) This Act extends to Scotland only.

NOTE

[1] As amended by the Prescription and Limitation (Scotland) Act 1984, Sched. 2.

SCHEDULES

SCHEDULE 1

OBLIGATIONS AFFECTED BY PRESCRIPTIVE PERIODS OF FIVE YEARS UNDER SECTION 6

1. Subject to paragraph 2 below, section 6 of this Act applies—

(*a*) to any obligation to pay a sum of money due in respect of a particular period—

(i) by way of interest;

(ii) by way of an instalment of an annuity;

(iii) by way of feuduty or other periodical payment under a feu grant;

(iv) by way of ground annual or other periodical payment under a contract of ground annual;

(v) by way of rent or other periodical payment under a lease;

(vi) by way of a periodical payment in respect of the occupancy or use of land, not being an obligation falling within any other provision of this sub-paragraph;

(vii) by way of a periodical payment under a land obligation, not being an obligation falling within any other provision of this sub-paragraph;

(*b*) to any obligation based on redress of unjustified enrichment, including without prejudice to that generality any obligation of restitution, repetition or recompense;

(*c*) to any obligation arising from *negotiorum gestio*;

(*d*) to any obligation arising from liability (whether arising from any enactment or from any rule of law) to make reparation;

(*e*) to any obligation under a bill of exchange or a promissory note;

(*f*) to any obligation of accounting, other than accounting for trust funds;

(*g*) to any obligation arising from, or by reason of any breach of, a contract or promise, not being an obligation falling within any other provision of this paragraph.

2. Notwithstanding anything in the foregoing paragraph, section 6 of this Act does not apply—

- (*a*) to any obligation to recognise or obtemper a decree of court, an arbitration award or an order of a tribunal or authority exercising jurisdiction under any enactment;
- (*b*) to any obligation arising from the issue of a bank note;
- (*c*) to any obligation constituted or evidenced by a probative writ, not being a cautionary obligation nor being an obligation falling within paragraph 1(*a*) of this Schedule;
- (*d*) to any obligation under a contract of partnership or of agency, not being an obligation remaining, or becoming, prestable on or after the termination of the relationship between the parties under the contract;
- (*e*) except as provided in paragraph 1(*a*) of this Schedule, to any obligation relating to land (including an obligation to recognise a servitude);
- (*f*) to any obligation to satisfy any claim to terce, courtesy, legitim, *jus relicti* or *jus relictae*, or to any prior right of a surviving spouse under section 8 or 9 of the Succession (Scotland) Act 1964;
- (*g*) to any obligation to make reparation in respect of personal injuries within the meaning of Part II of this Act or in respect of the death of any person as a result of such injuries;
- [1] (*gg*) to any obligation to make reparation or otherwise make good in respect of defamation within the meaning of section 18A of this Act;
- [2] (*ggg*) to any obligation arising from liability under section 2 of the Consumer Protection Act 1987 (to make reparation for damage caused wholly or partly by a defect in a product);
- (*h*) to any obligation specified in Schedule 3 to this Act as an imprescriptible obligation.

NOTES

[1] Inserted by the Law Reform (Miscellaneous Provisions) (Scotland) Act 1985, s. 12(5).

[2] Inserted by the Consumer Protection Act 1987, Sched. 1, para. 2.

3.—(1) Subject to sub-paragraph (2) below, where by virtue of a probative writ two or more persons (in this paragraph referred to as "the co-obligants") are bound jointly and severally by an obligation to pay money to another party the obligation shall, as respects the liability of each of the co-obligants, be regarded for the purposes of sub-paragraph (*c*) of the last foregoing paragraph as if it were a cautionary obligation.

(2) Nothing in the foregoing sub-paragraph shall affect any such obligation as respects the liability of any of the co-obligants with respect to whom the creditor establishes—

- (*a*) that that co-obligant is truly a principal debtor, or
- (*b*) if that co-obligant is not truly a principal debtor, that the original creditor was not aware of that fact at the time when the writ was delivered to him.

4. In this Schedule—

- (*a*) "land obligation" has the same meaning as it has for the purposes of the Conveyancing and Feudal Reform (Scotland) Act 1970;
- (*b*) "probative writ" means a writ which is authenticated by attestation or in any such other manner as, in relation to writs of the particular class in question, may be provided by or under any enactment as having an effect equivalent to attestation.

[THE NEXT PAGE IS J 203]

SCHEDULE 2

Appropriate Dates for Certain Obligations for Purposes of Section 6

1.—(1) This paragraph applies to any obligation, not being part of a banking transaction, to pay money in respect of—

(*a*) goods supplied on sale or hire, or

(*b*) services rendered,

in a series of transactions between the same parties (whether under a single contract or under several contracts) and charged on continuing account.

(2) In the foregoing sub-paragraph—

(*a*) any reference to the supply of goods on sale includes a reference to the supply of goods under a hire-purchase agreement, a credit-sale agreement or a conditional sale agreement as defined (in each case) by section 1 of the Hire-Purchase (Scotland) Act 1965; and

(*b*) any reference to services rendered does not include the work of keeping the account in question.

(3) Where there is a series of transactions between a partnership and another party, the series shall be regarded for the purposes of this paragraph as terminated (without prejudice to any other mode of termination) if the partnership or any partner therein becomes bankrupt; but, subject to that, if the partnership (in the further provisions of this sub-paragraph referred to as "the old partnership") is dissolved and is replaced by a single new partnership having among its partners any person who was a partner in the old partnership, then, for the purposes of this paragraph, the new partnership shall be regarded as if it were identical with the old partnership.

(4) The appropriate date in relation to an obligation to which this paragraph applies is the date on which payment for the goods last supplied, or, as the case may be, the services last rendered, became due.

2.—(1) This paragraph applies to any obligation to repay the whole, or any part of, a sum of money lent to, or deposited with, the debtor under a contract of loan or, as the case may be, deposit.

(2) The appropriate date in relation to an obligation to which this paragraph applies is—

(*a*) if the contract contains a stipulation which makes provision with respect to the date on or before which repayment of the sum or, as the case may be, the part thereof is to be made, the date on or before which, in terms of that stipulation, the sum or part thereof is to be repaid; and

(*b*) if the contract contains no such stipulation, but a written demand for repayment of the sum, or, as the case may be, the part thereof, is made by or on behalf of the creditor to the debtor, the date when such demand is made or first made.

3.—(1) This paragraph applies to any obligation under a contract of partnership or of agency, being an obligation remaining, or becoming, prestable on or after the termination of the relationship between the parties under the contract.

(2) The appropriate date in relation to an obligation to which this paragraph applies is—

(*a*) if the contract contains a stipulation which makes provision with respect to the date on or before which performance of the obligation is to be due, the date on or before which, in terms of that stipulation, the obligation is to be performed; and

(*b*) in any other case the date when the said relationship terminated.

4.—(1) This paragraph applies to any obligation—

(*a*) to pay an instalment of a sum of money payable by instalments, or

(*b*) to execute any instalment of work due to be executed by instalments,

not being an obligation to which any of the foregoing paragraphs applies.

(2) The appropriate date in relation to an obligation to which this paragraph applies is the date on which the last of the instalments is due to be paid or, as the case may be, to be executed.

SCHEDULE 3

Rights and Obligations which are Imprescriptible for the Purposes of Sections 7 and 8 and Schedule 1

The following are imprescriptible rights and obligations for the purposes of sections 7(2) and 8(2) of, and paragraph 2(*h*) of Schedule 1 to, this Act, namely—

(*a*) any real right of ownership in land;

(*b*) the right in land of the lessee under a recorded lease;
(*c*) any right exercisable as a *res merae facultatis*;
(*d*) any right to recover property *extra commercium*;
(*e*) any obligation of a trustee—
(i) to produce accounts of the trustee's intromissions with any property of the trust;
(ii) to make reparation or restitution in respect of any fraudulent breach of trust to which the trustee was a party or was privy;
(iii) to make furthcoming to any person entitled thereto any trust property, or the proceeds of any such property, in the possession of the trustee, or to make good the value of any such property previously received by the trustee and appropriated to his own use;
(*f*) any obligation of a third party to make furthcoming to any person entitled thereto any trust property received by the third party otherwise than in good faith and in his possession;
(*g*) any right to recover stolen property from the person by whom it was stolen or from any person privy to the stealing thereof;
(*h*) any right to be served as heir to an ancestor or to take any steps necessary for making up or completing title to any interest in land.

SCHEDULE 4

Enactments Amended

Part I

Amendment taking effect on expiration of three years from passing of this Act

The Limitation (Enemies and War Prisoners) Act 1945

In subsection (1) of section 1, as substituted for Scotland by paragraph (*a*) of section 4, in the list of enactments appended to the subsection for the entries relating to the Acts of the Parliament of Scotland 1579 cap. 21, 1669 cap. 14 and 1695 cap. 7, and to section 37 of the Bills of Exchange (Scotland) Act 1772, there shall be substituted the words "section 6 of the Prescription and Limitation (Scotland) Act 1973".

[1] Part II

Amendments Taking Effect on Passing of this Act

NOTE

[1] As amended by the Prescription and Limitation (Scotland) Act 1984, Sched. 2.

The Carriage by Air Act 1961

In section 11(*c*), for the words "section six of the Law Reform (Limitation of Actions, &c.) Act 1954" there shall be substituted the words "section 17 of the Prescription and Limitation (Scotland) Act 1973".

The Law Reform (Miscellaneous Provisions) Act 1971

In section 4(2), for the words "section 6 of the Law Reform (Limitation of Actions, &c.) Act 1954" there shall be substituted the words "section 22(1) of the Prescription and Limitation (Scotland) Act 1973".

SCHEDULE 5

REPEALS

PART I

REPEALS COMING INTO FORCE ON EXPIRATION OF THREE YEARS FROM PASSING OF THIS ACT

Chapter	Short Title	Extent of Repeal
1469 c. 4.	The Prescription Act 1469.	The whole Act.
1474 c. 9.	The Prescription Act 1474.	The whole Act.
1579 c. 19.	The Prescription (Ejections) Act 1579.	The whole Act.
1579 c. 21.	The Prescription Act 1579.	The whole Act.
1594 c. 24.	The Prescription Act 1594.	The whole Act.
1617 c. 12.	The Prescription Act 1617.	The whole Act.
1617 c. 13.	The Reduction Act 1617.	The whole Act.
1669 c. 14.	The Prescription Act 1669.	The whole Act.
1669 c. 15.	The Interruptions Act 1669.	The whole Act.
1685 c. 14.	The Prescriptions Act 1685.	The whole Act.
1695 c. 7.	The Cautioners Act 1695.	The whole Act.
1696 c. 9.	The Prescription Act 1696.	The whole Act.
1696 c. 19.	The Interruptions Act 1696.	The whole Act.
12 Geo. 3. c. 72.	The Bills of Exchange (Scotland) Act 1772.	Sections 37, 39, 40.
31 & 32 Vict. c. 64.	The Land Writs Registration (Scotland) Act 1868.	Section 15.
45 & 46 Vict. c. 61.	The Bills of Exchange Act 1882.	In section 100, the words from "this section shall not apply" to the end of the section.
14 & 15 Geo. 5. c. 27.	The Conveyancing (Scotland) Act 1924.	Sections 16, 17.
1 & 2 Geo. 6. c. 24.	The Conveyancing Amendment (Scotland) Act 1938.	Section 4.
1969 c. 39.	The Age of Majority (Scotland) Act 1969.	In Schedule 1, the entry relating to the Prescription Act 1617.
1970 c. 35.	The Conveyancing and Feudal Reform (Scotland) Act 1970.	Section 8.

[THE NEXT PAGE IS J 207]

Land Tenure Reform (Scotland) Act 1974

(1974 c. 38)

An Act to provide as respects Scotland, for the prohibition of new feuduties and other periodical payments from land; for the right to redeem feuduties and other such perpetual payments on a term day; for the redemption by law of feuduties and other such payments on transfer of land; for limitations on the residential use of property subject to long lease and other rights of occupancy; for the variation of heritable securities in the event of residential use of the security subjects; for restrictions on certain rights of reversion, redemption and pre-emption; for limitation of the right to raise an action of irritancy for non-payment of feuduty; for abolition of the right to create leasehold casualties; for the recognition of interposed leases; for amendment of the law relating to registration of leases; for abolition of the registration and recording of documents in the Office of Chancery; and for related matters. [31st July 1974]

Part I

Prohibition of Feuduties, and Redemption of Feuduties, Etc.

Prohibition of new feuduties

1.—(1) No deed executed after the commencement of this Act shall impose feuduty; but a deed executed after that date which contains a grant of land in feu shall have effect otherwise as if the grant were subject to a feuduty.

(2) A provision in a deed executed after such commencement which purports to impose feuduty shall not render the deed void or unenforceable, but the deed, if it contains a grant of land in feu, shall be subject to the provisions of subsection (1) above.

Prohibition of new ground annuals and other periodical payments from land

2.—(1) No deed executed after the commencement of this Act shall impose ground annual, skat or any other periodical payment (other than feuduty) in respect of the tenure or use of land or under a land obligation, not being a payment in respect of a lease, liferent or other right of occupancy, a payment of teind, stipend or standard charge, a payment in defrayal of or contribution towards some continuing cost related to the land, or a payment under a heritable security.

(2) A provision in a deed executed after such commencement which purports to impose any payment to which subsection (1) above applies shall not render the deed void or unenforceable, but the deed shall have effect only to the extent (if any) that it would have had effect under the law in force before such commencement if it had not imposed any such payment.

Charters of novodamus, etc.

3.—(1) The feuduty under a charter of novodamus or other deed having equivalent effect executed after the commencement of this Act may be of any amount which does not have the effect of increasing the total amount of feuduty exigible in respect of any land; and any provision in any such deed which produces that effect shall to that extent be void and unenforceable:

Provided that, where any provisions relating to two or more feuduties, contained in such a deed or in two or more such deeds executed on the same day, have the effect cumulatively of increasing the total amount of feuduty exigible in respect of any land, they shall, to the extent that they have the effect of altering the amount or incidence of that feuduty, be void and unenforceable.

(2) This section shall apply, subject to any necessary modifications, to payments to which section 2 of this Act applies, as it applies to feuduties.

Right to redeem feuduty, ground annual, etc., on a term day

4.—(1) Subject to the provisions of this section and of any agreement in relation to the redemption of feuduty made before the commencement of this Act, and without prejudice to any existing method of redemption, any proprietor of a feu may, at any term of Whitsunday or Martinmas, redeem the feuduty which, as at the date of the notice aftermentioned, is exigible in respect thereof.

(2) A proprietor who wishes to redeem a feuduty in terms of this section shall, not later than the term of redemption,

(*a*) give to the superior or his agent a notice of redemption in or as nearly as may be in the form contained in Form 1 of Schedule 1 to this Act, and

(*b*) pay to or for behoof of the superior such a sum of money as would, if invested in 2½ per cent. Consolidated Stock at the middle market price at the close of business last preceding the date occurring one month before the said term, produce an annual sum equal to the feuduty (hereinafter in this section referred to as " the redemption money "), and also any amount of feuduty unpaid in respect of the feu, liability for which has accrued up to and including that term, and any interest or other payment exigible in respect of the feuduty last mentioned.

(3) After due notice and payment in accordance with the foregoing provisions of this section, the feuduty shall, at the said term, be redeemed, and no payment shall be exigible in respect of the feuduty so redeemed for any period after such redemption; but the feu shall continue in force otherwise as if the feuduty were not redeemed.

(4) On redemption of feuduty in terms of this section, the superior or his agent shall, at the expense of the superior, grant a receipt in or as nearly as may be in the form contained in Form 2 of Schedule 1 to this Act.

(5) The redemption of feuduty in terms of this section shall be binding on all persons having interest: Provided that such redemption shall not prejudice the rights of existing heritable creditors who are not parties thereto, but the superior shall be liable to indemnify any proprietor of the feu against liability arising after such redemption from such rights.

(6) Where the interest of the superior in a feuduty which is redeemed in terms of this section is subject to any trust, liferent or entail, the redemption money shall be treated for all purposes as capital money.

(7) For the purposes of this section " feuduty " includes any *cumulo* feuduty which is unallocated and any part of a *cumulo* feuduty which has been allocated, and includes any payment (whether unallocated or allocated as aforesaid) of ground annual, skat or any other perpetual periodical payment in respect of the tenure, occupancy or use of land or under a land obligation, not being a payment of teind, stipend or standard charge, or in defrayal of or contribution towards some continuing cost related to the land, or under a heritable security; and this section, in its application to any payment to which it is extended under this subsection, shall have effect subject to any necessary modifications.

Redemption by law of feuduty, ground annual, etc., on transfer of land for valuable consideration

[1] **5.**—(1) Subject to any agreement made before the commencement of this Act in relation to the redemption of the feuduty exigible in respect of a feu and to subsection (2) below, on the date when entry is taken under an obligation to grant a conveyance of the feu for valuable consideration or under the deed containing such a conveyance (the said date being hereinafter in this section, subject to subsection (2) below, referred to as " the date of redemption "), the feuduty exigible as at the date of redemption shall be deemed to have been redeemed: Provided that this section shall not apply in any case where the date of the obligation to grant a conveyance or of the execution of the deed occurred before the commencement of this Act.

(2) Where the date (whether before or after the commencement of this Act) when entry is taken, as specified in subsection (1) above is earlier than the date of the obligation there specified or (where there was no such obligation) the execution of the deed there specified, the date of redemption shall be the date of the said obligation or execution as the case may be.

(3) No payment shall be exigible in respect of a feuduty for any period after the date of redemption thereof; but the feu shall continue in force otherwise as if the feuduty were not redeemed.

(4) On the date of redemption, there shall be payable to the superior by the person who was the proprietor of the feu immediately before the date of the obligation specified in subsection (1) above or (where there was no such obligation) the execution of the deed there specified, or by his representatives, such a sum of money (hereinafter in this section referred to as " the redemption money ") as would, if invested in 2½ per cent. Consolidated Stock at the middle market price at the close of business last preceding the date occurring one month before the date of redemption, produce an annual sum equal to the feuduty.

(5) Subject to the provisions of subsections (6) to (8) below, at and after the date of redemption, the redemption money, if it has not been paid to the superior, shall, together with interest thereon from the date of redemption until payment at such rate or rates as may be determined, be secured in favour of the superior, as a real burden on the land subject to the feu, binding on the proprietor of the feu for the time being, in the same manner and subject to the same remedies as the feuduty redeemed.

(6) At any time after the date of the obligation specified in subsection (1) above or (where there was no such obligation) after the date of execution of the deed there specified, the proprietor of the feu for the time being or his agent may give to the superior or his agent a notice of redemption in or as nearly as may be in the form contained in Schedule 2 to this Act; and, subject to subsections (7) and (8) below, at the expiry of the period of two months after the giving of such notice or after the date of redemption, whichever is later, the land subject to the feu shall cease to be burdened by the unpaid redemption money and interest referred to in subsection (5) above, and by any feuduty unpaid in respect of the feu, liability for which has accrued up to and including the date of redemption, and any interest or other payment exigible in respect of that feuduty, and thereafter (subject to the said subsections (7) and (8) no action shall lie against any person in respect of any sum specified in this subsection, other than—

(*a*) in the case of the redemption money or interest thereon, against the person who was the proprietor of the feu immediately before the date of the said obligation or of the execution of the said deed, as the case may be, or against his representatives:

(*b*) in the case of the said unpaid feuduty or interest or other payment relative thereto, against any person who was liable therefor immediately before the date of redemption, or against his representatives.

(7) If, before the end of the relevant period of two months specified in subsection (6) above, the superior has obtained warrant to cite the defender in an action against any person mentioned in paragraph (*a*) or (*b*) thereof or his representatives for the recovery of any sum for which that person remains liable in terms of those paragraphs, the court may at any time within the said period (whether or not the defender has been cited in the action) order that the land subject to the feu shall, in respect of that sum, continue to be burdened, and that the sum shall continue to be exigible, as specified in subsection (5) above, for such additional period (which the court may by further order extend from time to time if necessary) as is reasonable to enable the superior to recover the said sum; but the superior shall not be entitled to recover any such sum from or at the expense of any person whose liability therefor arose at or after the date specified in relation to such sum in the said paragraph (*a*) or (*b*), unless the court is satisfied that it is not reasonably practicable to recover such sum from any person who remains liable therefor in terms of that paragraph.

(8) No order under subsection (7) above shall have effect unless an extract thereof has been recorded in the Register of Sasines before the expiry of the relevant period of two months referred to in that subsection or before the expiry of any such existing order.

(9) On receipt of a notice of redemption in terms of subsection (6) above in duplicate, the superior or his agent shall, at the expense of the superior, if so requested return one copy with an acknowledgement thereon subscribed by him.

(10) The deemed redemption of feuduty in accordance with this section shall be binding on all persons having interest: Provided that such redemption shall not prejudice the rights of existing heritable creditors, but the superior shall be liable to indemnify any proprietor of the feu against liability arising after the date of redemption from such rights.

(11) For the avoidance of doubt, it is hereby declared that this section shall have effect whether or not the obligation to grant a conveyance as aforesaid has been implemented.

(12) Subsections (6) and (7) of section 4 of this Act shall apply in relation to this section as they apply in relation to that section, with the addition in subsection (7), after the words " ground annual ", of the words " standard charge ", and the substitution, for the words " stipend or standard charge ", of the words " or stipend "; but in this section " feu " does not include any part of a feu which is subject to a *cumulo* feuduty, no portion of which has been allocated on that part.

(13) This section shall not apply in any case specified in subsection (1) of section 6 of this Act except to the extent (and subject to the modifications) specified in that section.

NOTE

[1] See the Land Registration (Scotland) Act 1979, s. 20 (3) (*b*) (ii).

Redemption by law of feuduty, ground annual, etc., on acquisition of land by authority possessing compulsory purchase powers

6.—(1) Subject to subsection (4) below, and notwithstanding the provisions of section 107 of the Lands Clauses Consolidation (Scotland) Act 1845, this section shall have effect in relation to the case of the redemption of the feuduty exigible in respect of a feu to which entry is taken (whether or not there is an obligation to pay valuable consideration therefor) by an authority possessing compulsory purchase powers (hereinafter in this section referred to as " the acquiring authority "); and the enactments relating to the acquisition of land by such an authority shall for the purposes of this section apply accordingly as they apply in relation to acquisition by purchase.

(2) The following provisions of section 5 of this Act shall apply for the purposes of this section as they apply for the purposes of that section:

(*a*) section 5 (1) and (2) shall apply, with the omission in the said subsection (1) of the reference to valuable consideration; and for the purposes of such application the references in the said subsections to an obligation to grant a conveyance shall include references to a notice to treat or deemed notice to treat under section 17 of the said Act of 1845 or under any other enactment having similar effect;

(*b*) section 5 (3) shall apply, subject to any of the provisions of the Lands Clauses Acts or of the Railway Clauses Consolidation (Scotland) Act 1845 which apply to the case;

(*c*) notwithstanding the provisions of section 20 of the Land Compensation (Scotland) Act 1963, section 5 (4) shall apply, with the substitution, for the reference to the person who was the proprietor of the feu immediately before the date of the obligation or (as the case may be) the execution of the deed there referred to and to his representatives, of a reference to the acquiring authority;

(*d*) section 5 (10) and (11) shall apply.

(3) Sections 109 and 111 of the Lands Clauses Consolidation (Scotland) Act 1845 (which relate to the discharge of land from feuduty, etc., and the apportionment and continuance of the charge for such payments on land not taken) shall apply in relation to the redemption of feuduty under this section (whether the land subject to the feuduty is acquired compulsorily or by agreement) as they apply in relation to the discharge of charges under that Act.

(4) The foregoing provisions of this section shall not apply in relation to the acquisition of land by means of a general vesting declaration within the meaning of Schedule 24 to the Town and Country Planning (Scotland) Act 1972; but section 5 (4) of this Act shall, notwithstanding the provisions of section 20 of the Land Compensation (Scotland) Act 1963, apply in relation to such acquisition as it applies in relation to the acquisition of land to which the said section 5 applies, with the substitution, for the reference to the person who was the proprietor of the feu immediately before the date of the obligation or (as the case may be) the execution of the deed there referred to and to his representatives, of a reference to the acquiring authority; and in such a case the date of redemption means the date of vesting of the land in the acquiring authority under paragraph 7 of the said Schedule.

(5) In every case to which, by virtue of subsection (1) or (4) above, this section applies, the acquiring authority shall—

(*a*) not later than the date of redemption, give to the superior or his agent a notice of redemption in or as nearly as may be in the form contained in Schedule 3 to this Act; and

(*b*) be liable to pay to the superior interest on the redemption money from the date of redemption until payment at such rate or rates as may be determined.

(6) Where the interest of the superior in a feuduty which is redeemed in terms of this section is subject to any trust, liferent or entail, the redemption money shall be treated for all purposes as capital money.

(7) In this section,

" authority possessing compulsory purchase powers " has the same meaning as is conferred by section 275 (1) of the Town and Country Planning (Scotland) Act 1972;

" feuduty ", in any case where part only of a feu subject to a *cumulo* feuduty is acquired, means such portion of the feuduty (if any) as may be settled thereon under section 109 of the Lands Clauses Consolidation (Scotland) Act 1845 as applied by this section or, in the case specified in subsection (4) above, by paragraph 32 of the said Schedule 24; and includes any payment (or any such portion thereof, as the case may be) of ground annual, standard charge, skat or any other perpetual periodical payment in respect of the tenure, occupancy or use of land or under a land obligation, not being a payment of teind or stipend, or in defrayal of or contribution towards some continuing cost related to the land, or under a heritable security; and this section, in its application to any payment to which it is extended under this subsection, shall have effect subject to any necessary modifications.

Transitional and supplementary provisions relative to Part I

7.—(1) A deed executed after the commencement of this Act and before 8th November 1975 shall not be subject to the provisions of section 1, 2 or 3 of this Act if—

(*a*) the deed is granted in implement of an obligation entered into before 8th November 1973 by the person who, when the obligation was entered into, was the proprietor of the land subject to the deed; and

(*b*) there is included in the deed or in a memorandum endorsed thereon a statement to that effect by or on behalf of the grantor of the deed, in or as nearly as may be in the form contained in Schedule 4 to this Act.

(2) Where a deed, containing a provision which to any extent is void or unenforceable by virtue of section 1, 2 or 3 of this Act, has been recorded in the Register of Sasines, the person who granted the deed or his successor may be required, by any person having an interest, to grant any appropriate corrective deed capable of being recorded in the Register.

(3) In this Part of this Act, unless the context otherwise requires—

" feu " includes blench holding and " feuduty " includes blench duty;

" land obligation " has the meaning assigned to it in section 1 (2) of the Conveyancing and Feudal Reform (Scotland) Act 1970;

" proprietor ", in relation to land, includes a person having right to that land but whose title thereto is not complete, and, in the case of land subject to a heritable security constituted by *ex facie* absolute disposition, means the debtor in the security, except where the creditor is in possession of the land.

PART II

LIMITATIONS ON RESIDENTIAL USE OF PROPERTY LET UNDER FUTURE LONG LEASES

Property let under future long lease, etc., not to be used as private dwelling-house

8.—(1) It shall be a condition of every long lease executed after the commencement of this Act that, subject to the provisions of this Part of this Act, no part of the property which is subject to the lease shall be used as or as part of a private dwelling-house.

(2) For the purposes of this Part of this Act, any garden, yard, garage, outhouse or pertinent used along with any dwelling-house shall be deemed to form part of a dwelling-house, and use as a dwelling-house shall not include use as the site of a caravan.

(3) The use as or as part of a private dwelling-house of part of a property which is subject to a long lease shall not constitute a breach of the condition contained in subsection (1) above if such use is ancillary to the use of the remainder of the property otherwise than as or as part of a private dwelling-house and it would be detrimental to the efficient exercise of the use last-mentioned if the said ancillary use did not occur on that property.

[1] (4) For the purposes of this Part of this Act—

"lessor" and "lessee" mean any person holding for the time being the interest of lessor or lessee (as the case may be); and

"long lease" means any grant of—

(*a*) a lease, or

(*b*) a liferent or other right of occupancy granted for payment (other than payment in defrayal of or contribution towards some continuing cost related to such liferent use or such occupancy, as the case may be),

which is either—

(i) subject to a duration, whether definite or indefinite, which could (in terms of the grant and without any subsequent agreement, express or implied, between the persons holding the interests of the grantor and the grantee) extend for more than 20 years, or

(ii) subject to any provision whereby any person holding the interest of the grantor or the grantee is under a future obligation, if so requested by the other, to renew the grant so that the total duration could so extend for more than 20 years, or whereby, if he does not so renew it, he will be liable to make some payment or to perform some other obligation, but, in relation to a lease granted before 1st September 1974, does not include its renewal (whether before or after the commencement of section 1 of the Law Reform (Miscellaneous Provisions) (Scotland) Act 1985) in implementation of an obligation in or under it.

(5) This Part of this Act shall not apply in relation to the use of property for the time being forming part or deemed to form part of—

[1a] (*a*) an agricultural holding, within the meaning of the Agricultural Holdings (Scotland) Act 1991;

(*b*) a holding, within the meaning of the Small Landholders (Scotland) Acts 1886 to 1931;

(*c*) a croft, within the meaning of the Crofters (Scotland) Acts 1955 and 1961.

(6) Nothing in this Part of this Act shall affect the right of the lessor to terminate the lease and recover possession of the property subject thereto on the ground of breach of a conventional condition of the lease which has the effect of prohibiting such use of the property as constitutes a breach of the condition contained in subsection (1) above.

[2] (7) Nothing in this Part of this Act shall prevent a tenancy from being or becoming a protected or statutory tenancy within the meaning of the Rent (Scotland) Act 1984 or a secure tenancy within the meaning of the Housing (Scotland) Act 1987, but nothing in either of those Acts restricting the power of a court to make an order for possession of a dwelling-house shall prevent the granting of a decree of removing under section 9(1) of this Act.

NOTES

[1] As amended by the Law Reform (Miscellaneous Provisions) (Scotland) Act 1985, s.1.

[1a] As amended by the Agricultural Holdings (Scotland) Act 1991, Sched. 11, para. 38.

[2] As amended by the Housing (Scotland) Act 1986, Sched. 2, para. 3 and the Housing (Scotland) Act 1987, Sched. 23.

Consequences of use as dwelling-house of property subject to long lease

9.—(1) A breach of the condition of a long lease executed after the commencement of this Act, contained in section 8(1) of this Act, shall not render the lease void or unenforceable, but, subject to the provisions of this section and of section 10 of this Act, where such a breach occurs, the lessor shall be entitled to give to the lessee notice to terminate the use constituting the breach within 28 days from the date of the notice; and, if the lessee shall fail to terminate that use within that period, the lessor shall be entitled to raise an action of removing against the lessee concluding for his removal from such part of the property as is subject to the use at the expiry of 28 days after the decree of removing is extracted, and the court may decern for the termination of the lease in respect of such part and the removal of the lessee therefrom and, failing such removal, for his ejection therefrom on expiry of the 28 days last mentioned.

(2) A notice under subsection (1) above shall be in or as nearly as may be in the form contained in Schedule 5 to this Act.

(3) It shall be a defence to an action under subsection (1) above that the breach of condition constituting the ground of action has ceased.

(4) Subject to section 10(3) of this Act, in an action under subsection (1) above, if it is proved that the use of the property constituting the ground of action has at any time been approved by the person holding at that time the interest of the lessor in the lease, either expressly or by his actings, and the said use has not subsequently been discontinued, the court shall not decern in terms of that subsection, but—

(*a*) where the lease is subject to a duration expiring in a year more than 20 years after the year in which the notice under subsection (1) above relative to the breach was given, the court shall decern that the lease shall, in respect of such part of the property as is subject to the use, have effect as if for the year of expiry there were substituted the year 20 years after the year in which the said notice was given;

(*b*) where the lease is subject to a duration expiring in a year less than 20 years after that year the lease shall continue in force according to its terms;

and the said part of the property subject to the lease (and, during the remaining period of the lease as determined by reference to this subsection, any over-lease, in so far as it relates to that part) shall cease to be subject to the condition contained in section 8(1) of this Act.

(5) Where the breach of condition constituting the ground of action under subsection (1) above relates to part only of the property subject to the lease, any decree granted to the pursuer in the action under subsection (1) or (4)(*a*) above shall contain a particular description or a description by reference (in accordance with the provisions of the Conveyancing (Scotland) Act 1874 and the Conveyancing (Scotland) Act 1924) of such part; and in such a case the court shall decern for such adjustment (if any) as it thinks fit (to take effect on the termination of the lease of such part in terms of the decree) in the rent of the remaining part of the property and in the conditions of the lease, including the addition of new conditions, but not including any provision for the payment of money.

(6) Subject to the provisions of this Part of this Act and of section 37(1) of the Sheriff Courts (Scotland) Act 1971, and notwithstanding section 35(1)(*c*) of that Act, the procedure in an action of removing under this section shall be that in an ordinary cause; and on the granting of a decree to the pursuer in such an action, or at any time before the decree is extracted, the court may sist extract of the decree for such a period or periods as it thinks fit to enable any facts to be established which (if the action were still pending) would constitute a defence thereto, and if the court is satisfied that any such facts are established it may vary or rescind the decree, subject to such conditions (if any) with regard to payment of arrears of rent and otherwise as the court thinks fit.

(7) Notwithstanding the provisions of section 24 of the Court of Session Act 1868, Rule 63(*b*) of the Rules of Court 1965 or Rule 25 of Schedule 1 to the Sheriff Courts (Scotland) Act 1907, a decree granted in an action under this section shall, as in a question with third parties who have acted onerously and in good faith in reliance on the records, be final and not subject to challenge when an extract thereof shall have been recorded in the Register of Sasines.

(8) The provisions of this section and of section 10 of this Act shall apply in relation to a grant (not being a lease) mentioned in section 8(4) of this Act as they apply in relation to a lease, and any reference to a lease, over-lease or sub-lease, to the parties thereto, or to rent, shall be construed accordingly.

Modification of section 9 where lease subject to sub-lease or heritable security

10.—(1) For the avoidance of doubt, it is hereby declared that (subject to the provisions of this section) sections 8 and 9 of this Act shall apply, as

[THE NEXT PAGE IS J 215]

between the parties to any over-lease or sub-lease executed after the commencement of this Act, as they apply as between the parties to any other lease so executed.

(2) The pursuer in an action under section 9 of this Act shall give such intimation thereof as the court may direct—

(*a*) to every person appearing, from a search in the Register of Sasines for a period of 20 years immediately prior to the raising of the action, to hold for the time being the interest of creditor in a heritable security over the lease which is the subject of the action; and

(*b*) where the said lease is, in relation to any part of the property which is subject to the use constituting the ground of action, subject to any sub-lease, to every person appearing from such a search and from examination of the valuation roll or otherwise to be the lessee in any such sub-lease (of whatever duration) or the creditor in a heritable security over any such sub-lease;

and any such creditor or lessee as aforesaid shall, subject to the provisions of this section, be entitled to plead in the action any defence which could be pleaded by the defender in the action.

(3) The defence provided under section 9 (4) of this Act shall not be available to the lessee in a lease in respect of the use of property subject to a sub-lease derived from that lease.

(4) A sub-lessee, provided that he could have pleaded the defence provided by section 9 (4) of this Act in an action by the lessor in the sub-lease, may, on being sisted to an action under the said section 9 by the lessor in any over-lease, plead that defence in relation to the approval by the lessor in that over-lease or in any sub-lease under that over-lease of property which is subject to the use constituting the ground of action; and the court, on being satisfied that the defence is established to that effect, shall be entitled to decern in terms of the said section 9 (4) as if the action had been brought by the lessor in the sub-lease first mentioned.

(5) The right provided by subsection (4) above shall be available to a sub-lessee whose lease is not a long lease to the same extent as if it had been a long lease.

Part III

Miscellaneous

Right to redeem heritable security after 20 years where security subjects used as private dwelling-house

11.—(1) The provisions of this section shall apply in relation to a heritable security executed after the commencement of this Act, including a heritable security in relation to a debenture described in section 89 of the Companies Act 1948 (perpetual debentures, etc.).

(2) The debtor in a heritable security to which this section applies, or, where the debtor is not the proprietor, the proprietor of the security subjects shall, subject to the provisions of this section, be entitled, on giving two months' notice of his intention so to do, to redeem the security at any time not less than 20 years after the execution thereof, if, at the time when he gives such notice, the security subjects or any part thereof are used as or as part of a private dwelling-house.

In determining for the purposes of this section whether such use has occurred, subsection (2) of section 8 of this Act shall apply as it applies for the purposes of that section, and the ancillary use described in subsection (3) of that section shall not render the security subjects subject to the provisions of this section.

(3) The right to redeem a heritable security conferred by this section shall not apply where the use of the security subjects which is purported to constitute the ground of the right, in terms of subsection (2) above, was, at the time of the notice aforesaid, in contravention of a conventional condition of or relating to the security, unless the person in right of the creditor at any time had approved that use expressly or by his actings, and the said use had not subsequently been discontinued.

(4) Subject to the provisions of subsection (5) below, the whole amount due to the creditor in a heritable security on redemption under this section, including any sums due thereunder by way of interest or otherwise, shall not exceed the amount remaining unredeemed of—

(*a*) where the security constituted to any extent (whether expressly or otherwise) the consideration for the acquisition of the security subjects by the debtor or proprietor or his predecessor in title, any excess of the value of the security subjects at the date of the execution of the security over the amount of money paid for the subjects, and

(*b*) any money advanced under the security to the debtor or proprietor and his predecessors in title, and

(*c*) any expense or charge reasonably incurred by the creditor in the exercise of a right to perform any obligation imposed on the debtor, which the debtor has failed to perform, and which was reasonably necessary for the protection of the security,

together with interest outstanding at the date of the said notice of redemption and interest due for the period between the date of that notice and the date of redemption, at the rate applicable in terms of the security immediately before that date.

(5) In the application of paragraph (*a*) of subsection (4) above to security subjects which are burdened with two or more heritable securities to which this section applies, the maximum amount determined in accordance with that paragraph shall be apportioned among the securities according to the rights and preferences of the creditors in the securities; and the amount so apportioned in respect of each of the securities shall, on the redemption of any of the securities, be the maximum amount due in terms of that paragraph on the redemption at any time of all such securities.

(6) [See print of the Conveyancing and Feudal Reform (Scotland) Act 1970, s. 18 (1A), *supra.*]

Restriction to 20 years of period within which certain rights of redemption and reversion are exercisable

12. A right of redemption or reversion of land (other than the right of a lessor to the reversion of a lease), created in a deed executed after the commencement of this Act, which purports to be exercisable on the happening of an event, which is bound to occur, or the occurrence of which is within the control of the person for the time being entitled to exercise the right or of a third party, shall be exercisable only within 20 years of the date of its creation.

13. [See print of the Conveyancing Amendment (Scotland) Act 1938, s. 9, *supra.*]

Amendment of section 17 of Crofters (Scotland) Act 1955

14. In section 17 of the Crofters (Scotland) Act 1955 (absentee crofters) (as amended by the Crofters (Scotland) Act 1961) the following amendments shall be made—

(*a*) in subsection (4) (right of absentee crofter, after order terminating his tenancy, to conveyance in feu of dwelling-house), for the word " feuduty ", in both places where it occurs, there shall be substituted the words " the consideration ";

(*b*) in subsection (7) (rights of creditor in heritable security over house), for the words from " in addition " to " following subsection " there shall be substituted the words " as consideration under this section ";

(*c*) in subsection (8) (consideration for assistance given by landlord in respect of house), for the words " be, in addition to any feuduty thereby exigible," there shall be substituted the word " include ".

Limitation of right of irritancy for non-payment of feuduty

15. No action of declarator of irritancy for non-payment of feuduty shall be raised by a superior after the commencement of this Act unless there has been default of payment of the feuduty to the superior for the five years preceding the raising of the action; and accordingly, in the Feu-duty Act 1597, for the reference to two years there shall be substituted a reference to five years.

No casualties in future leases

16. In leases executed after the commencement of this Act, it shall not be lawful to stipulate for the payment of any casualty, but this provision shall be without prejudice to the right to stipulate for review of rent or for a permanent or periodical variation of rent in accordance with any condition of or relating to the lease.

Interposed leases

17.—(1) It shall be competent, and shall be deemed always to have been competent, for the person in right of the lessor of a lease to grant, during the subsistence of that lease, a lease of or including his interest in the whole or part of the land subject to the lease first mentioned, and whether longer or shorter than or of the same duration as that lease, and the said grant shall be effectual (or, as the case may be, shall be deemed to have been effectual) for all purposes as a lease of land; and the grantee or person in his right shall be deemed (whether before or after the commencement of this Act) to have entered into the possession of the land leased under the grant at the date of that grant: Provided that, in the case of a lease which is registrable under the Registration of Leases (Scotland) Act 1857, or which (being a lease granted before the commencement of this Act) would have been so registrable if this Act had been in force, the rights of parties shall be determined by reference to that Act, as amended by any other enactment, including this Act.

(2) Subject to any agreement to the contrary, as from the date of the grant of a lease in terms of subsection (1) above, the lessee under the lease so granted shall become (or, as the case may be, shall be deemed to have become) the lessor of the lessee in the subsisting lease, on the same terms and conditions as if the subsisting lease had, in respect of the property subject to the lease granted as aforesaid, been assigned to the grantee of the lease so granted; and, on the determination, for any reason, of the lease so granted, any remaining rights and obligations of the person in right of the said grantee, in relation to the said subsisting lease, shall vest (or as the case may be, shall be deemed to have vested) in the person in right of the grantor of the lease granted as aforesaid, on the same terms and conditions as if that lease had not been granted.

Amendment of law relating to registration of leases

18. The Registration of Leases (Scotland) Act 1857 and the Long Leases (Scotland) Act 1954 shall have effect subject to the provisions of Schedule 6 to this Act.

Recording of extract orders of Lands Tribunal

19. Section 3 (12) (*d*) of the Lands Tribunal Act 1949 (as inserted by section 50 (2) of the Conveyancing and Feudal Reform (Scotland) Act

1970) and section 2 (4) of the said Act of 1970 shall have effect, and shall be deemed always to have had effect, with the substitution, in both of those provisions, for the word " order ", of the words " extract of an order ".

Abolition of registration and recording, etc., of documents in Office of Chancery

20. It shall cease to be competent to register or record in the books kept in the Office of Chancery in Scotland any of the documents directed to be so registered or recorded by section 7 of the Crown Lands (Scotland) Act 1833, or to enter in the minute book of that Office a minute or memorandum of any such document directed to be so entered by section 7 of the Commissioners of Works Act 1852; and accordingly the said sections shall cease to have effect, and, in paragraph 2 (*b*) of Schedule 2 to the Crown Estate Act 1961 (continuation in force of sections 7 and 8 of the said Act of 1833), for the words from " sections " onwards there shall be substituted the words " section 8 (which relates to the effect in Scotland of certain documents) ".

PART IV

GENERAL

Provisions for contracting out to be void

21. Subject to the provisions of sections 8 (6) and 11 (3) of this Act, any agreement or other provision, however constituted, which is made after the commencement of this Act, shall be void in so far as it purports to exclude or limit the operation of any enactment contained in this Act.

Application to Crown

22. This Act shall apply to land held of the Crown and of the Prince and Steward of Scotland, and to land in which there is any other interest belonging to Her Majesty in right of the Crown or to a Government department, or held on behalf of Her Majesty for the purposes of a Government department, in like manner as it applies to other land.

Interpretation and repeals

23.—(1) In this Act, unless the context otherwise requires—

" deed " has the meaning assigned to it in section 3 of the Titles to Land Consolidation (Scotland) Act 1868, section 3 of the Conveyancing (Scotland) Act 1874, and section 2 of the Conveyancing (Scotland) Act 1924;

" heritable security " (except in relation to sections 4 (5), 5 (10) and 10 (2)) does not include any security for the purpose of securing the payment of a ground annual or other periodical sum payable in respect of land, and " heritable creditors " shall be construed accordingly;

" land " has the meaning assigned to it in section 2 of the said Act of 1924.

(2) Unless the context otherwise requires, any reference in this Act to any other enactment is a reference thereto as amended, and includes a reference thereto as extended or applied, by or under any other enactment, including this Act.

(3) The enactments specified in Schedule 7 to this Act are hereby repealed to the extent specified in relation thereto in that Schedule.

Short title, commencement and extent

24.—(1) This Act may be cited as the Land Tenure Reform (Scotland) Act 1974.

(2) This Act shall come into operation on 1st September 1974.

(3) This Act shall extend to Scotland only.

SCHEDULES

Section 4

SCHEDULE 1

Forms Prescribed under Section 4

Form 1

Form of Notice Prescribed under Section 4

" Notice of Redemption

under section 4 of the Land Tenure Reform (Scotland) Act 1974 (right to redeem feuduty, ground annual, &c. on a term day).

[*Address of person sending notice, and Date*]

To [*name and address of superior, &c. or his agent*]

Take notice that, in terms of section 4 of the Land Tenure Reform (Scotland) Act 1974, I wish to redeem at the term of [Whitsunday] [Martinmas] [*year*] the [feuduty] [ground annual] [*or otherwise*] of [*amount*] per annum exigible in respect of [*give sufficient identification of the land in respect of which the payment to be redeemed is exigible*].

(*Signed*) AB.
or CD,
Agent for AB."

Form 2

Form of Receipt Prescribed under Section 4

" I hereby acknowledge to have received from [*name of proprietor*] the sum of [*amount of redemption money*] in redemption (in terms of section 4 of the Land Tenure Reform (Scotland) Act 1974) of the [feuduty] [ground annual] [*or otherwise*] of [*amount*] per annum exigible as at [*give date of notice of redemption*] in respect of [*give sufficient identification of the land in respect of which the payment being redeemed is exigible*].

Dated this day of 19

(*Signed*) XY.
or YZ,
Agent for XY."

Section 5

SCHEDULE 2

Form of Notice Prescribed under Section 5

" Notice of Redemption

under section 5 of the Land Tenure Reform (Scotland) Act 1974 (redemption by law of feuduty, ground annual, etc. on transfer of land for valuable consideration).

[*Address of person sending notice, and Date*]

To [*name and address of superior, etc., or his agent*]

Take notice that, in terms of section 5 of the Land Tenure Reform (Scotland) Act 1974 the [feuduty] [ground annual] [*or otherwise*] of [*amount*] per annum exigible in respect of [*give sufficient identification of the land in respect of which the feuduty, etc., was exigible*] as at [*give date of redemption*] [will be deemed to be redeemed] [is deemed to have been redeemed] at that date by reason of entry having been taken to the said subjects [under an obligation to convey] [*or, as the case may be,* under a deed conveying] the said subjects by [*give name(s) of obligant(s) or person(s) conveying as the case may be*] dated [*give date(s) of obligation or of execution of deed as the case may be*].

(*Signed*) AB.
or CD,
Agent for AB."

Section 6

SCHEDULE 3

FORM OF NOTICE PRESCRIBED UNDER SECTION 6

" NOTICE OF REDEMPTION

under section 6 of the Land Tenure Reform (Scotland) Act 1974 (redemption by law of feuduty, ground annual, etc., on acquisition of land by authority possessing compulsory purchase powers).

[*Name and address of authority sending notice, and Date*]

To [*name and address of superior, etc., or his agent*]

Take notice that, in terms of section 6 of the Land Tenure Reform (Scotland) Act 1974, the [feuduty] [ground annual] [*or otherwise*] of [*amount*] per annum exigible in respect of [*give sufficient identification of the land in respect of which the feuduty, etc., was exigible*] as at [*give date of redemption*] will be deemed to be redeemed at that date [to such extent (if any) as may be settled under section 109 of the Lands Clauses Consolidation (Scotland) Act 1845 as applied by virtue of section 6 of the said Act of 1974].

[*To be signed on behalf of the acquiring authority*] ".

Section 7

SCHEDULE 4

STATEMENT REFERRED TO IN SECTION 7 (1) (*b*)

" I certify that this deed is granted in implement of an obligation entered into before 8th November 1973 by [me] [XY then proprietor of the land subject to this deed]."

(*If separate memorandum*) (*Signed*) AB.

or CD,
Agent for AB."

Section 9

SCHEDULE 5

FORM OF NOTICE PRESCRIBED UNDER SECTION 9

" NOTICE

under subsection (1) of section 9 of the Land Tenure Reform (Scotland) Act 1974 (consequences of use as dwelling-house of property subject to long lease, etc.)

To Terminate Use as or as part of Private Dwelling-House of Property subject to [Lease]
[Liferent]
[Right of Occupancy]

[*Address of person sending notice, and Date*]

To [*name and address of addressee*]

You are required to terminate the use as or as part of a private dwelling-house of [*give sufficient identification of the property by reference to the lease, etc., or otherwise: if the notice relates to the use of part only of the property subject to the lease, etc., the identification should be a particular description or a description by reference of that part, in terms of section 9 (5) of this Act*] within 28 days from the date of this notice, under pain of action of removing in terms of section 9 of the Land Tenure Reform (Scotland) Act 1974.

(*Signed*) AB.
or CD,
Agent for AB."

Note to be appended to Notice

" The reason for giving this notice is contravention of the condition contained in subsection (1) of section 8 of the Land Tenure Reform (Scotland) Act 1974 (property let under long lease, etc. not to be used as private dwelling-house).

Without prejudice to any other rights, obligations or defences which you may have under section 8, 9 or 10 of the said Act or otherwise, your attention is directed to the following provisions of the Act:—

Section 9 (3):

[*Here quote the subsection verbatim*]

Section 9 (4):

[*Here quote the subsection verbatim*]

Section 10 (3):

[*Here quote the subsection verbatim*]

If you are in doubt about your position in law you should obtain legal advice promptly."

Section 18

SCHEDULE 6

Amendment of Law Relating to Registration of Leases

[Amendments to Acts printed in The Parliament House Book have been given effect in the prints of those Acts]

Notes

1. The amendments made in accordance with this Schedule to sections 1, 2 and 17 of the Registration of Leases (Scotland) Act 1857 shall have effect in relation to leases executed before the commencement of this Act as they have effect in relation to those executed thereafter.
2. Section 19 of the Registration of Leases (Scotland) Act 1857 shall be deemed always to have had effect subject to the amendment thereto made in accordance with this Schedule.
3. Section 27(1) of the Long Leases (Scotland) Act 1954 (which is repealed by this Act) shall be deemed always to have had effect subject to the substitution, before the words "there is endorsed", for the word "and", of the words "or (as the case may be)".

Section 23

SCHEDULE 7

REPEALS

[Repeals affecting Acts printed or formerly printed in *The Parliament House Book* have been given effect.]

[1] Land Registration (Scotland) Act 1979

(1979 c. 33)

An Act to provide a system of registration of interests in land in Scotland in place of the recording of deeds in the Register of Sasines; and for indemnification in respect of registered interests in land; to simplify certain deeds relating to land and to provide as to the effect of certain other such deeds; to enable tenants-at-will to acquire their landlords' interests in the tenancies; to provide for the fixing of fees payable to the Keeper of the Registers of Scotland; and for connected purposes.

[4th April 1979]

NOTE

[1] See the Agriculture Act 1986, ss.18(3) and 19.

PART I

REGISTRATION OF INTERESTS IN LAND

The Land Register of Scotland

1.—(1) There shall be a public register of interests in land in Scotland to be known as the "Land Register of Scotland" (in this Act referred to as "the register").

(2) The register shall be under the management and control of the Keeper of the Registers of Scotland (in this Act referred to as "the Keeper") and shall have a seal.

(3) In this Act "registered" means registered in the register in accordance with this Act and "registrable", "registration" and other cognate expressions shall be construed accordingly.

Registration

2.—(1) Subject to subsection (2) below, an unregistered interest in land other than an overriding interest shall be registrable—

(*a*) in any of the following circumstances occurring after the commencement of this Act—

(i) on a grant of the interest in land in feu, long lease or security by way of contract of ground annual, but only to the extent that the interest has become that of the feuar, lessee or debtor in the ground annual;

(ii) on a transfer of the interest for valuable consideration;

(iii) on a transfer of the interest in consideration of marriage;

(iv) on a transfer of the interest whereby it is absorbed into a registered interest in land;

(v) on any transfer of the interest where it is held under a long lease, udal tenure or a kindly tenancy;

(*b*) in any other circumstances in which an application is made for registration of the interest by the person or persons having that interest and the Keeper considers it expedient that the interest should be registered.

(2) Subsection (1) above does not apply to an unregistered interest which is a heritable security, liferent or incorporeal heritable right; and subsection (1) (*a*) (ii) above does not apply where the interest on transference is absorbed into another unregistered interest.

(3) The creation over a registered interest in land of any of the following interests in land—

(i) a heritable security;

(ii) a liferent;

(iii) an incorporeal heritable right,

shall be registrable; and on registration of its creation such an interest shall become a registered interest in land.

(4) There shall also be registrable—

(*a*) any transfer of a registered interest in land including any transfer whereby it is absorbed into another registered interest in land;

(*b*) any absorption by a registered interest in land of another registered interest in land;

(*c*) any other transaction or event which (whether by itself or in conjunction with registration) is capable under any enactment or rule of law of affecting the title to a registered interest in land but which is not a transaction or event creating or affecting an overriding interest.

(5) The Secretary of State may, by order made by statutory instrument, provide that interests in land of a kind or kinds specified in the order, being interests in land which are unregistered at the date of the making of the order other than overriding interests, shall be registered; and the provisions of this Act shall apply for the purposes of such registration with such modifications, which may include provision as to the expenses of such registration, as may be specified in the order.

(6) In this section, " enactment " includes sections 17, 18 and 19 of this Act.

Effect of registration

3.—(1) Registration shall have the effect of—

(*a*) vesting in the person registered as entitled to the registered interest in land a real right in and to the interest and in and to any right, pertinent or servitude, express or implied, forming part of the interest, subject only to the effect of any matter entered in the title sheet of that interest under section 6 of this Act so far as adverse to the interest or that person's entitlement to it and to any overriding interest whether noted under that section or not;

(*b*) making any registered right or obligation relating to the registered interest in land a real right or obligation;

(*c*) affecting any registered real right or obligation relating to the registered interest in land,

insofar as the right or obligation is capable, under any enactment or rule of law, of being vested as a real right, of being made real or, as the case may be, of being affected as a real right.

In this subsection, " enactment " includes sections 17, 18 and 19 of this Act.

(2) Registration shall supersede the recording of a deed in the Register of Sasines but, subject to subsection (3) below, shall be without prejudice to any other means of creating or affecting real rights or obligations under any enactment or rule of law.

(3) A—

(*a*) lessee under a long lease;

(*b*) proprietor under udal tenure;

(*c*) kindly tenant,

shall obtain a real right in and to his interest as such only by registration; and registration shall be the only means of making rights or obligations relating to the registered interest in land of such a person real rights or obligations or of affecting such real rights or obligations.

(4) The date—

(*a*) at which a real right or obligation is created or as from which it is affected under this section;

(*b*) of entry of a feuar of a registrable interest in land with his superior,

shall be the date of registration.

(5) Where an interest in land has been registered, any obligation to assign title deeds and searches relating to that interest in land or to deliver them or make them forthcoming or any related obligation shall be of no effect in relation to that interest or to any other registered interest in land.

This subsection does not apply—

(*a*) to a land or charge certificate issued under section 5 of this Act;

(*b*) where the Keeper has, under section 12 (2) of this Act, excluded indemnity under Part II of this Act.

(6) It shall not be necessary for an uninfeft proprietor of an interest in land which has been registered to expede a notice of title in order to complete his title to that interest if evidence of sufficient mid-couples or links between the uninfeft proprietor and the person last infeft are produced to the Keeper on any registration in respect of that interest and, accordingly, section 4 of the Conveyancing (Scotland) Act 1924 (completion of title by person uninfeft) shall be of no effect in relation to such an interest in land.

This subsection does not apply to the completion of title under section 74 or 76 of the Lands Clauses Consolidation (Scotland) Act 1845 (procedure on compulsory purchase of lands).

(7) Nothing in this section affects any question as to the validity or effect of an overriding interest.

Applications for registration

4.—(1) Subject to subsection (2) below, an application for registration shall be accepted by the Keeper if it is accompanied by such documents and other evidence as he may require.

(2) An application for registration shall not be accepted by the Keeper if—

(*a*) it relates to land which is not sufficiently described to enable him to identify it by reference to the Ordnance Map;

(*b*) it relates to land which is a souvenir plot, that is a piece of land which, being of inconsiderable size or no practical utility, is unlikely to be wanted in isolation except for the sake of mere ownership or for sentimental reasons or commemorative purposes; or (*c*) it is frivolous or vexatious;

(*d*) a deed which—

(i) accompanies the application;

(ii) relates to a registered interest in land; and

(iii) is executed after that interest has been registered,

does not bear a reference to the number of the title sheet of that interest.

(3) On receipt of an application for registration, the Keeper shall forthwith note the date of such receipt, and that date shall be deemed for the purposes of this Act to be the date of registration either—

(*a*) where the application, after examination by the Keeper, is accepted by him, or

(*b*) where the application is not accepted by him on the grounds that it does not comply with subsection (1) or (2) (*a*) or (*d*) above but, without being rejected by the Keeper or withdrawn by the applicant, is subsequently accepted by the Keeper on his being satisfied that it does so comply, or has been made so to comply.

Completion of registration

5.—(1) The Keeper shall complete registration—

(*a*) in respect of an interest in land which is not a heritable security, liferent or incorporeal heritable right—

(i) if the interest has not previously been registered, by making up a title sheet for it in the register in accordance with section 6 of this Act, or

(ii) if the interest has previously been registered, by making such amendment as is necessary to the title sheet of the interest;

(*b*) in respect of an interest in land which is a heritable security, liferent or incorporeal heritable right or in respect of the matters registrable under section 2 (4) of this Act by making such amendment as is necessary to the title sheet of the interest in land to which the heritable security, liferent, incorporeal heritable right or matter, as the case may be, relates,

and in each case by making such consequential amendments in the register as are necessary.

(2) Where the Keeper has completed registration under subsection (1) (*a*) above, he shall issue to the applicant a copy of the title sheet, authenticated by the seal of the register; and such copy shall be known as a land certificate.

(3) Where the Keeper has completed registration in respect of a heritable security, he shall issue to the applicant a certificate authenticated by the seal of the register; and such certificate shall be known as a charge certificate.

(4) A land certificate shall be accepted for all purposes as sufficient evidence of the contents of the title sheet of which the land certificate is a copy; and a charge certificate shall be accepted for all purposes as sufficient evidence of the facts stated in it.

(5) Every land certificate and charge certificate shall contain a statement as to indemnity by the Keeper under Part II of this Act.

The title sheet

6.—(1) Subject to subsection (3) below, the Keeper shall make up and maintain a title sheet of an interest in land in the register by entering therein—

(*a*) a description of the land which shall consist of or include a description of it based on the Ordnance Map, and, where the interest is that of the proprietor of the *dominium utile* or the lessee under a long lease and the land appears to the Keeper to extend to 2 hectares or more, its area as calculated by the Keeper;

(*b*) the name and designation of the person entitled to the interest in the land and the nature of that interest;

(*c*) any subsisting entry in the Register of Inhibitions and Adjudications adverse to the interest;

(*d*) any heritable security over the interest;

(*e*) any enforceable real right pertaining to the interest or subsisting real burden or condition affecting the interest;

(*f*) any exclusion of indemnity under section 12 (2) of this Act in respect of the interest;

(*g*) such other information as the Keeper thinks fit to enter in the register.

(2) The Keeper shall enter a real right or real burden or condition in the title sheet by entering its terms or a summary of its terms therein; and such a summary shall, unless it contains a reference to a further entry in the title sheet wherein the terms of the real right, burden or condition are set out in full be presumed to be a correct statement of the terms of the right, burden or condition.

(3) The Keeper's duty under subsection (1) above shall not extend to entering in the title sheet any over-feuduty or over-rent exigible in respect of the interest in land, but he may so enter any such over-feuduty or over-rent.

[1] (4) Any overriding interest which appears to the Keeper to affect an interest in land—

(*a*) shall be noted by him in the title sheet of that interest if it has been disclosed in any document accompanying an application for registration in respect of that interest;

(*b*) may be so noted if—

(i) application is made to him to do so;

(ii) the overriding interest is disclosed in any application for registration; or

(iii) the overriding interest otherwise comes to his notice.

In this subsection " overriding interest " does not include the interest of

(i) a lessee under a lease which is not a long lease and

(ii) a non-entitled spouse within the meaning of section 6 of the Matrimonial Homes (Family Protection) (Scotland) Act 1981.

(5) The Keeper shall issue, to any person applying, a copy, authenticated as the Keeper thinks fit, of any title sheet, part thereof, or of any document referred to in a title sheet; and such copy, which shall be known as an office copy, shall be accepted for all purposes as sufficient evidence of the contents of the original.

NOTE

[1] As amended by the Matrimonial Homes (Family Protection) (Scotland) Act 1981, s. 6 (4).

Ranking

7.—(1) Without prejudice to any express provision as to ranking in any deed or any other provision as to ranking in, or having effect by virtue of, any enactment or rule of law, the following provisions of this section shall have effect to determine the ranking of titles to interests in land.

(2) Titles to registered interests in land shall rank according to the date of registration of those interests.

(3) A title to a registered interest and a title governed by a deed recorded in the Register of Sasines shall rank according to the respective dates of registration and recording.

(4) Where the date of registration or recording of the titles to two or more interests in land is the same, the titles to those interests shall rank equally.

Continuing effectiveness of recording in Register of Sasines

8.—(1) Subject to subsection (3) below, the only means of creating or affecting a real right or a real obligation relating to anything to which subsection (2) below applies shall be by recording a deed in the Register of Sasines.

(2) This subsection applies to—

(*a*) an interest in land which is to be transferred or otherwise affected by—

(i) an instrument which, having been recorded before the commencement of this Act in the Register of Sasines with an error or defect; or

(ii) a deed which, having been recorded before the commencement of this Act in the Register of Sasines with an error or defect in the recording,

has not, before such commencement, been re-presented, corrected as necessary, for the purposes of recording of new under section 143 of the Titles to Land Consolidation (Scotland) Act 1868;

In this paragraph, "instrument" has the same meaning as in section 3 of the said Act of 1868.

(*b*) a registered interest in land which has been absorbed, otherwise than by operation of prescription, into another interest in land the title to which is governed by a deed recorded in the Register of Sasines;

(*c*) anything which is not registrable under subsections (1) to (4) of section 2 of this Act and in respect of which, immediately before the commencement of this Act, a real right or obligation could be created or affected by recording a deed in the Register of Sasines.

(3) Nothing in subsection (1) above shall prejudice any other means, other than by registration, of creating or affecting real rights or obligations under any enactment or rule of law.

(4) Except as provided in this section, the Keeper shall reject any deed submitted for recording in the Register of Sasines.

Rectification of the register

9.—(1) Subject to subsection (3) below, the Keeper may, whether on being so requested or not, and shall, on being so ordered by the court or the Lands Tribunal for Scotland, rectify any inaccuracy in the register by inserting, amending or cancelling anything therein.

(2) Subject to subsection (3)(*b*) below, the powers of the court and of the Lands Tribunal for Scotland to deal with questions of heritable right or title shall include power to make orders for the purposes of subsection (1) above.

(3) If rectification under subsection (1) above would prejudice a proprietor in possession—

(*a*) the Keeper may exercise his power to rectify only where—

(i) the purpose of the rectification is to note an overriding interest or to correct any information in the register relating to an overriding interest;

(ii) all persons whose interests in land are likely to be affected by the rectification have been informed by the Keeper of his intention to rectify and have consented in writing;

(iii) the inaccuracy has been caused wholly or substantially by the fraud or carelessness of the proprietor in possession; or

(iv) the rectification relates to a matter in respect of which indemnity has been excluded under section 12(2) of this Act;

[1] (*b*) the court or the Lands Tribunal for Scotland may order the Keeper to rectify only where sub-paragraph (i), (iii) or (iv) of paragraph (*a*) above applies or the rectification is consequential on the making of an order under section 8 of the Law Reform (Miscellaneous Provisions) (Scotland) Act 1985.

[2] (3A) Where a rectification of an entry in the register is consequential on the making of an order under section 8 of the said Act of 1985, the entry shall have effect as rectified as from the date when the entry was made:

Provided that the court, for the purpose of protecting the interests of a person to whom section 9 of that Act applies, may order that the rectification shall have effect as from such later date as it may specify.

[3] (4) In this section—

(*a*) "the court" means any court having jurisdiction in questions of heritable right or title;

(*b*) "overriding interest" does not include the interest of

(i) a lessee under a lease which is not a long lease and

(ii) a non-entitled spouse within the meaning of section 6 of the Matrimonial Homes (Family Protection) (Scotland) Act 1981.

NOTES

[1] As amended by the Law Reform (Miscellaneous Provisions) (Scotland) Act 1985, Sched. 2, para. 21, with effect from 30th December 1985.

[2] Inserted by the Law Reform (Miscellaneous Provisions) (Scotland) Act 1985, Sched. 2, para. 21, with effect from 30th December 1985.

[3] As amended by the Matrimonial Homes (Family Protection) (Scotland) Act 1981, s. 6(4).

Positive prescription in respect of registered interests in land

10. [Amendments of the Prescription and Limitation (Scotland) Act 1973, s. 1, given effect to in the print of that Act, *supra*.]

Transitional provisions for Part I

11.—(1) If an application for registration relates to land no part of which is in an operational area, the Keeper may nevertheless accept that application as if it related to land wholly within an operational area, and if the Keeper has so accepted such an application, the provisions of this Act relating to registration then in force shall apply in relation to that application.

(2) An application for registration which relates to land which is partly in an operational area shall be treated as if it related to land wholly in that area, and the provisions of this Act relating to registration in force shall apply in relation to that application.

(3) In this section an "operational area" means an area in respect of which the provisions of this Act relating to registration have come into operation.

PART II

INDEMNITY IN RESPECT OF REGISTERED INTERESTS IN LAND

Indemnity in respect of loss

12.—(1) Subject to the provisions of this section, a person who suffers loss as a result of—

(*a*) a rectification of the register made under section 9 of this Act;

(*b*) the refusal or omission of the Keeper to make such a rectification;

(*c*) the loss or destruction of any document while lodged with the Keeper;

(*d*) an error or omission in any land or charge certificate or in any information given by the Keeper in writing or in such other manner as may be prescribed by rules made under section 27 of this Act,

shall be entitled to be indemnified by the Keeper in respect of that loss.

(2) Subject to section 14 of this Act, the Keeper may on registration in respect of an interest in land exclude, in whole or in part, any right to indemnity under this section in respect of anything appearing in, or omitted from, the title sheet of that interest.

(3) There shall be no entitlement to indemnity under this section in respect of loss where—

(*a*) the loss arises as a result of a title prevailing over that of the claimant in a case where—

(i) the prevailing title is one in respect of which the right to indemnity has been partially excluded under subsection (2) above, and

(ii) such exclusion has been cancelled but only on the prevailing title having been fortified by prescription;

[1] (*b*) the loss arises in respect of a title which has been reduced, whether or not under subsection (4) of section 34, or subsection (5) of section 36, of the Bankruptcy (Scotland) Act 1985 (or either of those subsections as applied by sections 615A and 615B of the Companies Act 1985, respectively), as a gratuitous alienation or fraudulent preference, or has been reduced or varied by an order under section 6(2) of the Divorce (Scotland) Act 1976 or by an order made by virtue of section 29 of the Matrimonial and Family Proceedings Act 1984 (orders relating to settlements and other dealings) or has been set aside or varied by an order under section 18(2) (orders relating to avoidance transactions) of the Family Law (Scotland) Act 1985;

(*c*) the loss arises in consequence of the making of a further order under section 5(2) of the Presumption of Death (Scotland) Act 1977 (effect on property rights of recall or variation of decree of declarator of presumed death);

(*d*) the loss arises as a result of any inaccuracy in the delineation of any boundaries shown in a title sheet, being an inaccuracy which could not have been rectified by reference to the Ordnance Map, unless the Keeper has expressly assumed responsibility for the accuracy of that delineation;

(*e*) the loss arises, in the case of land extending to 2 hectares or more the area of which falls to be entered in the title sheet of an interest in that land under section 6(1)(*a*) of this Act, as a result of the Keeper's failure to enter such area in the title sheet or, where he has so entered such area, as a result of any inaccuracy in the specification of that area in the title sheet;

(*f*) the loss arises in respect of an interest in mines and minerals and the title sheet of any interest in land which is or includes the surface land does not expressly disclose that the interest in mines and minerals is included in that interest in land;

(*g*) the loss arises from inability to enforce a real burden or condition entered in the register, unless the Keeper expressly assumes responsibility for the enforceability of that burden or condition;

(*h*) the loss arises in respect of an error or omission in the noting of an overriding interest;

(*j*) the loss is suffered by—

(i) a beneficiary under a trust in respect of any transaction entered into by its trustees or in respect of any title granted by them the validity of which is unchallengeable by virtue of section 2 of the Trusts (Scotland) Act 1961 (validity of certain transactions by trustees), or as the case may be, section 17 of the Succession (Scotland) Act 1964 (protection of persons acquiring title), or

(ii) a person in respect of any interest transferred to him by trustees in purported implement of trust purposes;

(*k*) the loss arises as a result of an error or omission in an office copy as to the effect of any subsisting adverse entry in the Register of Inhibitions and Adjudications affecting any person in respect of any registered interest in land, and that person's entitlement to that interest is neither disclosed in the register nor otherwise known to the Keeper;

(*l*) the claimant is the proprietor of the dominant tenement in a servitude, except insofar as the claim may relate to the validity of the constitution of that servitude;

(*m*) the claimant is a superior, a creditor in a ground annual or a landlord under a long lease and the claim relates to any information—

(i) contained in the feu writ, the contract of ground annual or the lease, as the case may be, and

(ii) omitted from the title sheet of the interest of the superior, creditor or landlord,

(except insofar as the claim may relate to the constitution or amount of the feuduty, ground annual or rent and adequate information has been made available to the Keeper to enable him to make an entry in the register in respect of such constitution or amount or to the description of the land in respect of which the feuduty, ground annual or rent is payable);

(*n*) the claimant has by his fraudulent or careless act or omission caused the loss;

(*o*) the claim relates to the amount due under a heritable security;

[2] (*p*) the loss arises from a rectification of the register consequential on the making of an order under section 8 of the Law Reform (Miscellaneous Provisions) (Scotland) Act 1985.

(4) A refusal or omission by the Keeper to enter into a title sheet—

(*a*) any over-feuduty or over-rent exigible in respect of a registrable interest;

(*b*) any right alleged to be a real right on the ground that by virtue of section 6 of this Act he has no duty to do so since it is unenforceable,

shall not by itself prevent a claim to indemnity under this section.

NOTES

[1] As amended by the Matrimonial and Family Proceedings Act 1984, Sched. 1, para. 28, the Bankruptcy (Scotland) Act 1985, Sched. 7, para. 15 and the Family Law (Scotland) Act 1985, Sched. 1, para. 10.

[2] Inserted by the Law Reform (Miscellaneous Provisions) (Scotland) Act 1985, Sched. 2, para. 22.

Provisions supplementary to section 12

13.—(1) Subject to any order by the Lands Tribunal for Scotland or the court for the payment of expenses in connection with any claim disposed of by the Lands Tribunal under section 25 of this Act or the court, the Keeper shall reimburse any expenditure reasonably and properly incurred by a person in pursuing a *prima facie* well-founded claim under section 12 of this Act, whether successful or not.

(2) On settlement of any claim to indemnity under the said section 12, the Keeper shall be subrogated to all rights which would have been available to the claimant to recover the loss indemnified.

(3) The Keeper may require a claimant, as a condition of payment of his claim, to grant, at the Keeper's expense, a formal assignation to the Keeper of the rights mentioned in subsection (2) above.

(4) If a claimant to indemnity has by his fraudulent or careless act or omission contributed to the loss in respect of which he claims indemnity, the amount of the indemnity to which he would have been entitled had he

not so contributed to his loss shall be reduced proportionately to the extent to which he has so contributed.

The foreshore

14.—(1) If—

(*a*) it appears to the Keeper that—

(i) an interest in land which is registered or in respect of which an application for registration has been made consists, in whole or in part, of foreshore or a right in foreshore, or might so consist, and

(ii) discounting any other deficiencies in his title in respect of that foreshore or right in foreshore, the person registered or, as the case may be, applying to be registered as entitled to the interest will not have an unchallengeable title in respect of the foreshore or the right in foreshore until prescription against the Crown has fortified his title in that respect, and

(*b*) the Keeper wholly excludes or proposes wholly to exclude rights to indemnity in respect of that person's entitlement to that foreshore or that right in foreshore, and is requested by that person not to do so,

the Keeper shall notify the Crown Estate Commissioners that he has been so requested.

[THE NEXT PAGE IS J 231]

(2) If the Crown Estate Commissioners have—

(*a*) within one month of receipt of the notification referred to in subsection (1) above, given to the Keeper written notice of their interest, and

(*b*) within three months of that receipt informed the Keeper in writing that they are taking steps to challenge that title,

the Keeper shall—

(i) during the prescriptive period, or

(ii) until such time as it appears to the Keeper that the Commissioners are no longer taking steps to challenge that title or that their challenge has been unsuccessful,

whichever is the shorter, continue wholly to exclude or, as the case may be, wholly exclude right to indemnity in respect of that person's entitlement to that foreshore or that right in foreshore.

(3) This section, or anything done under it, shall be without prejudice to any other right or remedy available to any person in respect of foreshore or any right in foreshore.

PART III

SIMPLIFICATION AND EFFECT OF DEEDS

Simplification of deeds relating to registered interests

15.—(1) Land in respect of which an interest has been registered shall be sufficiently described in any deed relating to that interest if it is described by reference to the number of the title sheet of that interest, and accordingly, section 13 of and Schedule G to the Titles to Land Consolidation (Scotland) Act 1868, section 61 of the Conveyancing (Scotland) Act 1874, sections 8 and 24(2) of and Schedules D and J to the Conveyancing (Scotland) Act 1924 and Note 1 of Schedule 2 to the Conveyancing and Feudal Reform (Scotland) Act 1970 (sufficiency of description by reference) shall not apply to such a deed.

(2) It shall not be necessary in any deed relating to a registered interest in land to insert or refer to any real burden, condition, provision or other matter affecting that interest if that real burden, condition, provision, or other matter has been entered in the title sheet of that interest under section 6(1)(*e*) of this Act, and, accordingly, in such a case—

(*a*) sections 10 and 146 of and Schedule D to the Titles to Land Consolidation (Scotland) Act 1868, in section 32 of the Conveyancing (Scotland) Act 1874, the words from the beginning to "shall be sufficient" and in section 9 of the Conveyancing (Scotland) Act 1924, the proviso to subsection (1), subsections (3) and (4) and Schedule E to the said Act of 1924 (importation of burdens etc. by reference) shall not apply to such a deed; and

(*b*) such a deed shall import for all purposes a full insertion of the real burden, condition, provision or other matter.

(3) It shall not be necessary in any deed relating to a registered interest in land, being a deed referred to in section 3 of the Conveyancing (Scotland) Act 1924 or section 12 of the Conveyancing and Feudal Reform (Scotland) Act 1970 (dispositions etc. by persons uninfeft), to deduce title, if evidence of sufficient midcouples or links between the uninfeft proprietor and the person last infeft are produced to the Keeper on registration in respect of that interest in land and, accordingly, in such a case, section 5 of and Form 1 of Schedule A and Note 2 of Schedule K to the said Act of 1924 and Notes 2 and 3(*b*) of Schedule 2 to the Conveyancing and Feudal Reform (Scotland) Act 1970 (further provisions to deduction of title) as well as the said section 3 and the said section 12, shall not apply to such a deed, which shall be as valid as if it had contained a clause of deduction of title.

(4) It shall not be necessary, in connection with any deed relating to a registered interest in land, to include an assignation of any obligation or right of relief or to narrate the series of writs by which the grantor of the deed became entitled to enforce that obligation or exercise that right if the obligation or right has been entered in the title sheet of that interest and, accordingly, in such a case—

(*a*) section 50 of and Schedule M to the Conveyancing (Scotland) Act 1874 (form and effect of assigning right of relief or other right affecting land) shall not apply to such a deed; and

(*b*) such a deed shall for all purposes import a valid and complete assignation of that obligation or right.

Omission of certain clauses in deeds

16.—[1] (1) It shall not be necessary to insert in any deed executed after the commencement of this Act which conveys an interest in land a clause of assignation of writs and any such deed shall, unless specially qualified, import an assignation to the grantee of the title deeds and searches and all deeds not duly recorded, and shall—

(*a*) impose on the grantor or any successor an obligation—

(i) to deliver to the grantee all title deeds and searches relating exclusively to the interest conveyed;

(ii) to make forthcoming to the grantee and his successors at his or their expense on all necessary occasions any title deeds and searches which remain in the possession of the grantor or any successor and which relate partly to the interest conveyed; and

(*b*) import an assignation to the grantee by the grantor of his right to require any person having custody thereof to exhibit or deliver any title deeds and searches remaining undelivered; and

(*c*) impose on the grantee or any successor an obligation to make forthcoming on all necessary occasions to any party having an interest therein any deeds and searches which have been delivered to the grantee but which relate partly to interests other than the interest conveyed to the grantee.

[1] (2) It shall not be necessary to insert in any deed executed after the commencement of this Act which grants land in feu a clause of assignation of writs, and any such deed shall, unless specially qualified, import an assignation to the grantee of the title deeds and searches to the effect of maintaining and defending the right of the grantee in the feu; and the superior shall be held to be obliged for that purpose to make the title deeds and searches forthcoming to the grantee on all necessary occasions at the latter's expense.

(3) It shall not be necessary to insert in any deed conveying an interest in land executed after the commencement of this Act a clause of assignation of rents or a clause of obligation of relief, and any such deed so executed shall, unless specially qualified, import—

(*a*) an assignation of the rents payable—

(i) in the case of backhand rents, at the legal terms following the date of entry, and

(ii) in the case of forehand rents, at the conventional terms following that date;

(*b*) an obligation on the grantor to relieve the grantee of all feuduties, ground annuals, annuities and public, parochial and local burdens exigible in respect of the interest prior to the date of entry and, in the case of a grant of land in feu, of all feuduties payable by the grantor to his superiors from and after the date of entry.

NOTE

[1] Modified by the Electricity Act 1989 (c. 29), Sched. 10, para. 5(3), and the Railways Act 1993 (c. 43), Sched. 8, para. 4(1) and (3) (effective 6th January 1994: S.I. 1993 No. 3237).

Deeds of declaration of conditions

[1] **17.**—(1) A land obligation specified in a deed executed after the commencement of this Act under section 32 of the Conveyancing (Scotland) Act 1874 (deeds of conditions etc.) shall—

(*a*) on the recording of such deed in the Register of Sasines;

(*b*) on the obligation being registered,

become a real obligation affecting the land to which it relates, unless it is expressly stated in such deed that the provisions of this section are not to apply to that obligation.

(2) In this section "land obligation" has the meaning assigned to it by section 1(2) of the Conveyancing and Feudal Reform (Scotland) Act 1970.

NOTE

[1] See the Registration of Leases (Scotland) Act 1857, s.3(5).

Variations and discharges of land obligations

18.—(1) The terms of any—

(*a*) deed recorded in the Register of Sasines, whether before or after the commencement of this Act, whereby a land obligation is varied or discharged;

(*b*) registered variation or discharge of a land obligation,

shall be binding on the singular successors of the person entitled to enforce the land obligation, and of the person on whom the land obligation was binding.

(2) In this section "land obligation" has the meaning assigned to it by section 1(2) of the Conveyancing and Feudal Reform (Scotland) Act 1970.

Agreement as to common boundary

19.—(1) This section shall apply where the titles to adjoining lands disclose a discrepancy as to the common boundary and the proprietors of those lands have agreed to, and have executed a plan of, that boundary.

(2) Where one or both of the proprietors holds his interest or their interest in the land or lands by virtue of a deed or, as the case may be, deeds recorded in the Register of Sasines, the agreement and plan may be recorded in the Register of Sasines and on being so recorded shall be binding on the singular successors of that proprietor or, as the case may be, those proprietors and on all other persons having an interest in the land or, as the case may be, the lands.

(3) Where one or both of the interests in the lands is or are registered interests, the plan with a docquet thereon executed by both proprietors referring to the agreement shall be registrable as affecting that interest or those interests, and on its being so registered its effect shall be binding on the singular successors of the proprietor of that interest or, as the case may be, the proprietors of those intere:sts and on all other persons having an interest in the land or, as the case may be, the lands.

PART IV

MISCELLANEOUS AND GENERAL

Tenants-at-will

20.—(1) A tenant-at-will shall be entitled, in accordance with this section, to acquire his landlord's interest as such in the land which is subject to the tenancy-at-will (hereinafter referred to as the "tenancy land").

(2) Subject to section 21(2) of this Act, a tenant-at-will who wishes to acquire his landlord's interest under this section shall serve notice on him in, or as nearly as may be in, the form set out in Schedule 1 to this Act.

(3) There shall be payable by the tenant-at-will to his landlord by way of compensation in respect of an acquisition of tenancy land such amount as may be agreed between them or, failing agreement, an amount equal to—

(*a*) the value of the tenancy land, not including any buildings thereon, but assuming that planning permission for residential purposes has been granted in respect of it; or

(*b*) one twenty-fifth of the value of the tenancy land, including any buildings thereon,

whichever is the lesser, together with—

(i) subject to subsection (4) below, such further amount as may be required to discharge any heritable security over the tenancy land or, where the heritable security is granted over land including the tenancy land, such further amount (being such proportion of the sum secured over the land which includes the tenancy land as may reasonably be regarded as attributable to the tenancy land) as is required to restrict the heritable security so as to disburden the tenancy land; and

(ii) such further amount as may be required to redeem any feuduty, ground annual or other periodic payment falling to be redeemed under section 5 of the Land Tenure Reform (Scotland) Act 1974.

(4) In respect of any acquisition under this section, the amount mentioned in paragraph (i) of subsection (3) above shall not exceed ninety per cent. of the amount fixed by virtue of paragraph (*a*) or (*b*) of that subsection.

(5) The tenant-at-will shall reimburse the expenses reasonably and properly incurred by the landlord in conveying his interest in the tenancy land to the tenant-at-will, including the expenses of any discharge, restriction or redemption under subsection (3) above.

(6) The landlord shall, on there being tendered to him the compensation and expenses specified in this section, convey his interest in the tenancy land to his tenant-at-will on such terms and conditions (additional to those relating to compensation and expenses under subsections (3), (4) and (5) above) as may be agreed between them or, failing agreement, as may be appropriate to the circumstances of the case and free of all heritable securities, and all such feuduties, ground annuals or other periodical payments as are mentioned in subsection (3)(ii) above.

(7) A heritable creditor whose security is over the tenancy land or land which includes the tenancy land, on there being tendered to him the amount mentioned in paragraph (i) of subsection (3) above (as read with subsection (4) above) and his reasonable expenses, shall discharge or, as the case may be, restrict the security so as to disburden the tenancy land.

[1] (8) In this section and in sections 21 and 22 of this Act, "tenant-at-will" means a person—

(*a*) who, not being—

(i) a tenant under a lease;

(ii) a kindly tenant; or

(iii) a tenant or occupier by virtue of any enactment,

is by custom and usage the occupier (actual or constructive) of land on which there is a building or buildings erected or acquired for value by him or any predecessor of his;

(*b*) who is under an obligation to pay a ground rent to the owner of the land in respect of the said land but not in respect of the building or buildings on it, or would have been under such an obligation if the ground rent had not been redeemed; and

(*c*) whose right of occupancy of the land is without ish.

(9) In subsections (5) and (6) above, references to the conveying of the landlord's interest in tenancy land shall be construed in accordance with section 21(10) of this Act.

NOTE

[1] Excluded by the Matrimonial Homes (Family Protection) (Scotland) Act 1981, s.13(7).

Provisions supplementary to section 20

21.—(1) Any question arising under section 20 of this Act as to—
(*a*) whether a person is a tenant-at-will;
(*b*) the extent or boundaries of any tenancy land;
(*c*) the value of any tenancy land or as to what proportion of any sum secured over any land may reasonably be regarded as attributable to any tenancy land included in that land;
(*d*) whether any expenses are reasonably and properly incurred;
(*e*) what are appropriate terms and conditions,
shall be determined, on the application of the tenant-at-will, a person claiming to be the tenant-at-will or the landlord, by the Lands Tribunal for Scotland.

(2) The Lands Tribunal for Scotland may, on the application of a tenant-at-will who wishes to acquire his landlord's interest in the tenancy land under section 20 of this Act, if they are satisfied that such landlord is unknown or cannot be found, make an order—
(*a*) dispensing with notice under section 20(2) above;
(*b*) fixing an amount by way of compensation in accordance with section 20(3) of this Act;
(*c*) determining appropriate terms and conditions on which the landlord's interest in the tenancy land should be conveyed,
for the purposes of the acquisition by the tenant-at-will of his landlord's said interest.

(3) If the landlord—
(*a*) fails to convey his interest in accordance with section 20(6) of this Act, or
(*b*) is unknown or cannot be found,
the tenant-at-will may apply to the sheriff for an order dispensing with the execution by the landlord of the conveyance in favour of the tenant-at-will and directing the sheriff clerk to execute the conveyance instead of the landlord, and on making such an order the sheriff may require the tenant-at-will to consign in court any sums payable by the tenant-at-will under section 20(3) and (5) of this Act or, as the case may be, any sums specified in an order under subsection (2) above.

(4) Where, in pursuance of an order made by the sheriff under this section, a conveyance is executed by the sheriff clerk on behalf of the landlord, such conveyance shall have the like force and effect as if it had been executed by such landlord.

(5) The sheriff may, on the application of any party, order the investment, payment or distribution of any sums consigned in court under subsection (3) above, and in so doing the sheriff shall have regard to the respective interests of any parties appearing to have a claim on such sums.

(6) Nothing in section 5 of the Sheriff Courts (Scotland) Act 1907 shall entitle any party to an application to the sheriff under this section to require it to be remitted to the Court of Session on the grounds that it relates to a question of heritable right or title.

(7) A landlord shall have power to execute a valid conveyance in pursuance of this section notwithstanding that he may be under any such disability as is mentioned in section 7 of the Lands Clauses Consolidation (Scotland) Act 1845.

(8) Where a person other than the landlord is infeft in the subjects to be conveyed, references in section 20 of this Act and in this section to the landlord shall be construed as references to the landlord and such other person for their respective rights.

(9) Any condition or provision to the effect that—
(*a*) the superior of any feu shall be entitled to a right of pre-emption in the event of a sale thereof or any part thereof by the proprietor of the feu, or

(*b*) any other person with an interest in land shall be entitled to a right of pre-emption in the event of a sale thereof or of any part thereof by the proprietor for the time being.

shall not be capable of being enforced where the sale is by a landlord to his tenant-at-will under section 20 of this Act.

(10) In this section and in section 20(5) and (6) of this Act, references to the conveying of the landlord's interest in the tenancy land shall be construed as references to a grant by him of a feu of that land or, where the landlord is a lessee under a lease, an assignation of the lease but only as regards the tenancy land and, in this section, "conveyance" shall be construed accordingly.

Provisions supplementary to section 20: heritable creditors

22.—(1) The provisions of this section shall have effect where a heritable security over tenancy land or over land which includes tenancy land falls to be discharged or restricted under section 20(7) of this Act.

(2) The heritable creditor shall be entitled for his interest to apply, and to be a party to an application, under section 21(1) of this Act.

(3) The Lands Tribunal for Scotland, if they are satisfied that the heritable creditor is unknown or cannot be found, may, on the application of the tenant-at-will or his landlord or both, make an order fixing the amount required to discharge or restrict the heritable security so as to disburden the tenancy land.

(4) If the heritable creditor—

(*a*) fails to disburden the tenancy land in accordance with section 20(7) of this Act, or

(*b*) is unknown or cannot be found,

the tenant-at-will or the landlord or both may apply to the sheriff for an order dispensing with the execution by the heritable creditor of the deed of discharge or restriction in favour of the landlord and directing the sheriff clerk to execute the deed instead of the heritable creditor and on making such an order the sheriff may require the landlord to consign in court any amount or expenses which the landlord requires to pay for the purposes of section 20(3)(i), (4) and (5) of this Act to the heritable creditor or, as the case may be, any amount specified in an order under subsection (3) above.

(5) Where, in pursuance of an order made by the sheriff under this section, a deed of discharge or restriction is executed by the sheriff clerk on behalf of the heritable creditor, such deed shall have the like force and effect as if it had been executed by such heritable creditor.

(6) The sheriff may, on the application of any party, order the investment, payment or distribution of any amount consigned in court under subsection (4) above, and in so doing the sheriff shall have regard to the respective interests of any parties appearing to have a claim on such amount.

(7) Nothing in section 5 of the Sheriff Courts (Scotland) Act 1907 shall entitle any party to an application to the sheriff under this section to require it to be remitted to the Court of Session on the grounds that it relates to a question of heritable right or title.

(8) A heritable creditor shall have power to execute a valid deed of discharge or restriction in pursuance of this section notwithstanding that he may be under any such disability as is mentioned in section 7 of the Lands Clauses Consolidation (Scotland) Act 1845.

Power of sheriff to grant renewals of certain long leases

[1] **22A**—(1) Where a landlord has failed to renew a long lease in implement of an obligation in or under it, the sheriff may, on summary application by the tenant, make an order directing the sheriff clerk to execute a renewal of the lease instead of the landlord.

(2) On making an order under subsection (1) above, the sheriff may require the tenant to consign in court such amount (whether by way of rent or expenses or otherwise) in respect of the lease and its renewal as appears to the sheriff to be lawfully due and payable or appears to him would have been so due and payable had the landlord duly renewed the lease.

(3) A renewal executed under this section shall have the like force and effect as if it were executed by the landlord.

(4) Without prejudice to subsection (7)(*a*) below, a landlord shall be regarded, for the purposes of subsection (1) above, as having failed to renew a lease in implement of an obligation in or under it if, having been given written notice in accordance with subsection (5) below by the tenant that he requires the landlord, in implement of the obligation, to renew the lease, the landlord has failed to do so when he was obliged to and continues so to fail.

(5) Notice is in accordance with this subsection if it is given not less than three months before the lodging of the summary application.

(6) Subsection (4) above is subject to subsection (7)(*b*) below and to any provision in or under the lease for earlier, or a longer period of, notice requiring renewal of the lease than that mentioned in subsection (5) above.

(7) If the sheriff is satisfied that a landlord is unknown or cannot be found, he may—

(*a*) in a case where the tenant is thereby prevented from bringing the landlord, in accordance with the lease, under an obligation to renew it, order that the landlord shall be regarded, for the purposes of subsection (1) above, as having failed to renew the lease in implement of an obligation under it; and

(*b*) in any other case, dispense with notice under subsection (4) above.

(8) The sheriff may, on the application of any party, order the investment, payment or distribution of any sums consigned in court under subsection (2) above, and in so doing the sheriff shall have regard to the respective interests of any parties appearing to have a claim on such sums.

(9) The sheriff's power under subsection (8) above extends to ordering that any award of expenses of the application under this section be paid out of any sums consigned in court under subsection (2) above.

NOTE

[1] Inserted by the Law Reform (Miscellaneous Provisions) (Scotland) Act 1985, s. 2, with effect from 30th December 1985.

23. [See the Land Registers (Scotland) Act 1868, s. 25.]

Financial provisions

24. There shall be defrayed out of money provided by Parliament all expenses incurred by the Keeper in consequence of the provisions of this Act.

[THE NEXT PAGE IS J 237]

Appeals

25.—(1) Subject to subsections (3) and (4) below, an appeal shall lie, on any question of fact or law arising from anything done or omitted to be done by the Keeper under this Act, to the Lands Tribunal for Scotland.

(2) Subject to subsections (3) and (4) below subsection (1) above is without prejudice to any right of recourse under any enactment other than this Act or under any rule of law.

(3) Nothing in subsection (1) above shall enable the taking of an appeal if it is, under the law relating to *res judicata*, excluded as a result of the exercise of any right of recourse by virtue of subsection (2) above; and nothing in subsection (2) above shall enable the exercise of any right of recourse if it is so excluded as a result of the taking of an appeal under subsection (1) above.

(4) No appeal shall lie under this section, nor shall there be any right of recourse by virtue of this section in respect of a decision of the Keeper under section 2(1)(*b*) or 11(1) of this Act.

Application to Crown

26. This Act shall apply to land held of the Crown and of the Prince and Steward of Scotland, and to land in which there is any other interest belonging to Her Majesty in right of the Crown or to a Government department, or held on behalf of Her Majesty for the purposes of a Government department, in like manner as it applies to other land.

Rules

27.—(1) The Secretary of State may, after consultation with the Lord President of the Court of Session, make rules—

(*a*) regulating the making up and keeping of the register;

(*b*) prescribing the form of any search, report or other document to be issued or used under or in connection with this Act and regulating the issue of any such document;

(*c*) regulating the procedure on application for any registration;

(*d*) prescribing the form of deeds relating to registered interests in land;

(*e*) concerning such other matters as seem to the Secretary of State to be necessary or proper in order to give full effect to the purposes of this Act.

(2) The power to make rules under this section shall be exerciseable by statutory instrument subject to annulment in pursuance of a resolution of either House of Parliament.

Interpretation, etc.

28.—(1) In this Act, except where the context otherwise requires—

[1] "deed" has the meaning assigned to it by section 3 of the Titles to Land Consolidation (Scotland) Act 1868, section 3 of the Conveyancing (Scotland) Act 1874 and section 2 of the Conveyancing (Scotland) Act 1924;

"feu" includes blench holding and cognate expressions shall be construed accordingly;

"heritable security" has the same meaning as in section 9(8) of the Conveyancing and Feudal Reform (Scotland) Act 1970;

"incorporeal heritable right" does not include a right to salmon fishings;

"interest in land" means any estate, interest, servitude or other heritable right in or over land, including a heritable security but excluding a lease which is not a long lease;

"the Keeper" has the meaning assigned by section 1(2) of this Act;

"land" includes buildings and other structures and land covered with water;

[2] "long lease" means a probative lease—

(*a*) exceeding 20 years; or

(*b*) which is subject to any provision whereby any person holding the interest of the grantor is under a future obligation, if so requested by the grantee, to renew the lease so that the total duration could (in terms of the lease, as renewed, and without any subsequent agreement, express or implied, between the persons holding the interests of the grantor and the grantee) extend for more than 20 years;

"overriding interest" means, subject to sections 6(4) and 9(4) of this Act, in relation to any interest in land, the right or interest over it of—

(*a*) the lessee under a lease which is not a long lease;

(*b*) the lessee under a long lease who, prior to the commencement of this Act, has acquired a real right to the subjects of the lease by virtue of possession of them;

(*c*) a crofter or cottar within the meaning of section 3 or 28(4) respectively of the Crofters (Scotland) Act 1955, or a landholder or statutory small tenant within the meaning of section 2(2) or 32(1) respectively of the Small Landholders (Scotland) Act 1911;

(*d*) the proprietor of the dominant tenement in a servitude;

(*e*) the Crown or any Government or other public department, or any public or local authority, under any enactment or rule of law, other than an enactment or ruler of law authorising or requiring the recording of a deed in the Register of Sasines or registration in order to complete the right or interest;

[2a] (*ee*) the operator having a right conferred in accordance with paragraph 2, 3 or 5 of Schedule 2 to the Telecommunications Act 1984 (agreements for execution of works, obstruction of access, etc.);

[2b] (*ef*) a licence holder within the meaning of Part I of the Electricity Act 1989 having such a wayleave as is mentioned in paragraph 6 of Schedule 4 to that Act (wayleaves for electric lines), whether granted under that paragraph or by agreement between the parties;

[2b] (*eg*) a licence holder within the meaning of Part I of the Electricity Act 1989 who is authorised by virtue of paragraph 1 of Schedule 5 to that Act to abstract, divert and use water for a generating station wholly or mainly driven by water;

(*f*) the holder of a floating charge whether or not the charge has attached to the interest;

(*g*) a member of the public in respect of any public right of way or in respect of any right held inalienably by the Crown in trust for the public;

[3] (*gg*) the non-entitled spouse within the meaning of section 6 of the Matrimonial Homes (Family Protection) (Scotland) Act 1981;

(*h*) any person, being a right which has been made real, otherwise than by the recording of a deed in the Register of Sasines or by registration; or

(*i*) any other person under any rule of law relating to common interest or joint or common property, not being a right or interest constituting a real right, burden or condition entered in the title sheet of the interest in land under section 6(1)(*e*) of this Act or having effect by virtue of a deed recorded in the Register of Sasines,

but does not include any subsisting burden or condition enforceable against the interest in land and entered in its title sheet under section 6(1) of this Act;

"the register" and "registered" have the meanings assigned to them respectively by subsections (1) and (3) of section 1 of this Act;
"Register of Sasines" has the same meaning as in section 2 of the Conveyancing (Scotland) Act 1924;
"transfer" includes transfer by operation of law.

(2) [Repealed by the Statute Law (Repeals) Act 1981.]

NOTES

[1] As amended (retrospectively) by the Civil Aviation (Amendment) Act 1982, Sched. 1, para. 48, and the Civil Aviation Act 1982, Sched. 16.

[2] Extended by the Matrimonial Homes (Family Protection) (Scotland) Act 1981, s.13(8).

[2a] Inserted by the Telecommunications Act 1984, Sched. 4, para. 71.

[2b] Inserted by the Electricity Act 1989, Sched. 16, para. 23.

[3] Inserted by the Matrimonial Homes (Family Protection) (Scotland) Act 1981, s.6(4).

[THE NEXT PAGE IS J 239]

Amendment and repeal of enactments

29.—(1) The enactments specified in Schedule 2 to this Act shall have effect subject to the amendments set out in that Schedule.

(2) Subject to subsection (3) below, any reference, however expressed, in any enactment passed before, or during the same Session as, this Act or in any instrument made before the passing of this Act under any enactment to the Register of Sasines or to the recording of a deed therein shall be construed as a reference to the register or, as the case may be, to registration.

(3) Subsection (2) above does not apply—

(*a*) to the enactments specified in Schedule 3 to this Act;

(*b*) for the purposes of the recording of a deed in the Register of Sasines under section 8 of this Act.

(4) The enactments specified in Schedule 4 to this Act are hereby repealed to the extent specified in the third column of that Schedule.

Short title, extent and commencement

[1] **30.**—(1) This Act may be cited as the Land Registration (Scotland) Act 1979 and extends to Scotland only.

(2) Sections 1, 16 to 23 of this Act, this section and so much of the remainder of this Part of this Act as relates to the aforesaid provisions of this Act shall come into operation on the passing of this Act, and the other provisions of this Act shall come into operation on the appointed day, being such day as the Secretary of State may by order made by statutory instrument appoint; and different days may be appointed under this subsection for different areas, or for different provisions of this Act.

(3) Any reference in any provision of this Act to the commencement of this Act shall be construed as a reference to the date on which that provision comes into operation.

NOTE

[1] For commencement, see S.I. 1980 No. 1412 and list of areas, p. J 703.

SCHEDULES

Section 20

SCHEDULE 1

FORM OF NOTICE TO BE GIVEN BY A TENANT-AT-WILL WHO WISHES TO ACQUIRE HIS LANDLORD'S INTEREST AS SUCH IN THE TENANCY

To (1)

Take Notice that (2), as tenant-at-will of (3), requires you to make over to him your interest as landlord of the tenancy land in accordance with the provisions of the Land Registration (Scotland) Act 1979.

Dated this of 19

Signed

Notes

(1) To be addressed to the landlord.

(2) Insert name and designation of tenant-at-will.

(3) Give the address or a short identifying description of the property to be acquired.

Section 29(1)

[1] SCHEDULE 2

AMENDMENT OF ENACTMENTS

NOTE

[1] The amendments in this Schedule which apply to material contained in the *Parliament House Book* have been given effect to.

. . . . . .

Section 29(3) SCHEDULE 3

ENACTMENTS REFERRING TO THE REGISTER OF SASINES OR TO THE RECORDING OF A DEED IN THE REGISTER OF SASINES NOT AFFECTED BY SECTION 29(2)

1. *The Real Rights Act 1693*
The whole Act.

2. *The Register of Sasines Act 1693*
The whole Act.

3. *The Register of Sasines Act 1829*
Section 1.

4. *The Infeftment Act 1845*
Sections 1 to 4 and Schedule B insofar as relating to section 1.

5. *The Registration of Leases (Scotland) Act 1857*
(*a*) In section 6, from the beginning of the section to "to the extent assigned" and Schedule D
(*b*) Section 12
(*c*) Section 15
(*d*) Section 16

6. *The Land Registers (Scotland) Act 1868*
(*a*) Sections 2 and 3
(*b*) Sections 5 to 7
(*c*) Section 9
(*d*) Sections 12 to 14
(*e*) In section 19, the proviso
(*f*) Section 23

7. *The Titles to Land Consolidation (Scotland) Act 1868*
(*a*) Sections 9 and 10 and Schedules C and D
(*b*) Sections 12 and 13 and Schedules F and G insofar as relating to sections 12 and 13 respectively
(*c*) Section 17
(*d*) Section 19 and Schedule L
(*e*) Section 120
(*f*) Section 141
(*g*) Section 142
(*h*) Section 143
(*i*) Section 146
(*j*) Schedule D
(*k*) Schedule G

8. *The Conveyancing (Scotland) Act 1874*
(*a*) Section 8
(*b*) In section 32, from the beginning to "shall be sufficient" and Schedule H
(*c*) Section 61
(*d*) Schedule M

9. *The Writs Execution (Scotland) Act 1877*
Sections 5 and 6

10. *The Registration of Certain Writs (Scotland) Act 1891*
Section 1(2)

11. *The Conveyancing (Scotland) Act 1924*
(*a*) Section 3, form 1 of Schedule A and Note 2 to Schedule K
(*b*) Section 4 and, in Schedule B, forms 1 to 6 and Note 7, but not insofar as relating to the completion of title under section 74 or 76 of the Lands Clauses Consolidation (Scotland) Act 1845
(*c*) Section 8 and Schedule D
(*d*) Section 9(3) and (4)

[THE NEXT PAGE IS J241]

(*e*) Section 10(1) to (5) and Schedule F
(*f*) In section 24(3) from "and such lease, before" to "Schedule B to this Act"
(*g*) Section 24(2) and (5) and Schedule J
(*h*) Section 47
(*i*) Sections 48 and 49(2)

12. *The Burgh Registers (Scotland) Act 1926*
(*a*) Section 1(1) (except the words from "and any writ" to "appropriate burgh register of sasines") and Schedule 1 insofar as relating to section 1(1) with that exception
(*b*) Section 1(2)
(*c*) Section 2 and Schedule 1 insofar as relating to section 2
(*d*) Section 5 and Schedule 1 insofar as relating to section 5

13. *The Conveyancing Amendment (Scotland) Act 1938*
Section 6(1) and (2)

14. *The Public Registers and Records (Scotland) Act 1948*
(*a*) Section 2
(*b*) Section 4

15. *The Public Registers and Records (Scotland) Act 1950*
Section 1 (1)

16. *The Conveyancing and Feudal Reform (Scotland) Act 1970*
(*a*) Section 12(1) and (2) and Notes 1, 2 and 3 to Schedule 2 insofar as relating to section 12(2)
(*b*) Section 28(3)

17. *The Prescription and Limitation (Scotland) Act 1973*
Section 1.

Section 29(4)

[1] SCHEDULE 4

REPEALS

NOTE
[1] The amendments in this Schedule which apply to material contained in the *Parliament House Book* have been given effect to.

Chapter	Short Title	Extent of Repeal
1693 c. 22.	The Real Rights Act 1693.	The words "and priority"
1693 c. 23.	The Register of Sasines Act 1693	The words "and houre"

Matrimonial Homes (Family Protection) (Scotland) Act 1981

(1981 c. 59)

An Act to make new provision for Scotland as to the rights of occupancy of spouses in a matrimonial home and of cohabiting couples in the house where they cohabit; to provide for the transfer of the tenancy of a matrimonial home between the spouses in certain circumstances during marriage and on granting decree of divorce or nullity of marriage, and for the transfer of the tenancy of a house occupied by a cohabiting couple between the partners in certain circumstances; to strengthen the law relating to matrimonial interdicts; and for connected purposes. [30th October 1981]

Protection of occupancy rights of one spouse against the other

Right of spouse without title to occupy matrimonial home

[1] **1.**—(1) Where, apart from the provisions of this Act, one spouse is entitled, or permitted by a third party, to occupy a matrimonial home (an "entitled spouse") and the other spouse is not so entitled or permitted (a "non-entitled spouse"), the non-entitled spouse shall, subject to the provisions of this Act, have the following rights—

(*a*) if in occupation, a right to continue to occupy the matrimonial home;

(*b*) if not in occupation, a right to enter into and occupy the matrimonial home.

(1A) The rights conferred by subsection (1) above to continue to occupy or, as the case may be, to enter and occupy the matrimonial home include, without prejudice to their generality, the right to do so together with any child of the family.

(2) In subsection (1) above, an "entitled spouse" includes a spouse who is entitled, or permitted by a third party, to occupy a matrimonial home along with an individual who is not the other spouse only if that individual

[THE NEXT PAGE IS J 242/15]

has waived his or her right of occupation in favour of the spouse so entitled or permitted.

(3) If the entitled spouse refuses to allow the non-entitled spouse to exercise the right conferred by subsection (1)(*b*) above, the non-entitled spouse may exercise that right only with the leave of the court under section 3(3) or (4) of this Act.

(4) In this Act, the rights mentioned in paragraphs (*a*) and (*b*) of subsection (1) above are referred to as occupancy rights.

(5) A non-entitled spouse may renounce in writing his or her occupancy rights only—

(*a*) in a particular matrimonial home; or

(*b*) in a particular property which it is intended by the spouses will become a matrimonial home.

(6) A renunciation under subsection (5) above shall have effect only if at the time of making the renunciation, the non-entitled spouse has sworn or affirmed before a notary public that it was made freely and without coercion of any kind. In this subsection, "notary public" includes any person duly authorised by the law of the country (other than Scotland) in which the swearing or affirmation takes place to administer oaths or receive affirmations in that other country.

NOTE

[1] As amended by the Law Reform (Miscellaneous Provisions) (Scotland) Act 1985, s. 13 subs. (2), (3) and (4), with effect from 30th December 1985.

Subsidiary and consequential rights

[1] **2.**—(1) For the purpose of securing the occupancy rights of a non-entitled spouse, that spouse shall, in relation to a matrimonial home, be entitled without the consent of the entitled spouse—

(*a*) to make any payment due by the entitled spouse in respect of rent, rates, secured loan instalments, interest or other outgoings (not being outgoings on repairs or improvements);

[THE NEXT PAGE IS J 243]

(*b*) to perform any other obligation incumbent on the entitled spouse (not being an obligation in respect of non-essential repairs or improvements);

(*c*) to enforce performance of an obligation by a third party which that third party has undertaken to the entitled spouse to the extent that the entitled spouse may enforce such performance;

(*d*) to carry out such essential repairs as the entitled spouse may carry out;

(*e*) to carry out such non-essential repairs or improvements as may be authorised by an order of the court, being such repairs or improvements as the entitled spouse may carry out and which the court considers to be appropriate for the reasonable enjoyment of the occupancy rights;

(*f*) to take such other steps, for the purpose of protecting the occupancy rights of the non-entitled spouse, as the entitled spouse may take to protect the occupancy rights of the entitled spouse.

(2) Any payment made under subsection (1) (*a*) above or any obligation performed under subsection (1) (*b*) above shall have effect in relation to the rights of a third party as if the payment were made or the obligation were performed by the entitled spouse; and the performance of an obligation which has been enforced under subsection (1) (*c*) above shall have effect as if it had been enforced by the entitled spouse.

(3) Where there is an entitled and a non-entitled spouse, the court, on the application of either of them, may, having regard in particular to the respective financial circumstances of the spouses, make an order apportioning expenditure incurred or to be incurred by either spouse—

(*a*) without the consent of the other spouse, on any of the items mentioned in paragraphs (*a*) and (*d*) of subsection (1) above;

(*b*) with the consent of the other spouse, on anything relating to a matrimonial home.

(4) Where both spouses are entitled, or permitted by a third party, to occupy a matrimonial home—

(*a*) either spouse shall be entitled, without the consent of the other spouse, to carry out such non-essential repairs or improvements as may be authorised by an order of the court, being such repairs or improvements as the court considers to be appropriate for the reasonable enjoyment of the occupancy rights;

(*b*) the court, on the application of either spouse, may, having regard in particular to the respective financial circumstances of the spouses, make an order apportioning expenditure incurred or to be incurred by either spouse, with or without the consent of the other spouse, on anything relating to the matrimonial home.

(5) Where one spouse owns or hires, or is acquiring under a hire-purchase or conditional sale agreement, furniture and plenishings in a matrimonial home—

(*a*) the other spouse may, without the consent of the first mentioned spouse—

(i) make any payment due by the first mentioned spouse which is necessary, or take any other step which the first mentioned spouse is entitled to take, to secure the possession or use of any such furniture and plenishings (and any such payment shall have effect in relation to the rights of a third party as if it were made by the first mentioned spouse); or

(ii) carry out such essential repairs to the furniture and plenishings as the first mentioned spouse is entitled to carry out;

(*b*) the court, on the application of either spouse, may, having regard in particular to the respective financial circumstances of the spouses, make an order apportioning expenditure incurred or to be incurred by either spouse—

(i) without the consent of the other spouse, in making payments under a hire, hire-purchase or conditional sale agreement, or in paying interest charges in respect of the furniture and plenishings, or in carrying out essential repairs to the furniture and plenishings; or

(ii) with the consent of the other spouse, on anything relating to the furniture and plenishings.

(6) An order under subsection (3), (4) (*b*) or (5) (*b*) above may require one spouse to make a payment to the other spouse in implementation of the apportionment.

(7) Any application under subsection (3), (4) (*b*) or 5 (*b*) above shall be made within five years of the date on which any payment in respect of such incurred expenditure was made.

(8) Where—

(*a*) the entitled spouse is a tenant of a matrimonial home; and

(*b*) possession thereof is necessary in order to continue the tenancy; and

(*c*) the entitled spouse abandons such possession,

the tenancy shall be continued by such possession by the non-entitled spouse.

(9) In this section " improvements " includes alterations and enlargement.

Regulation by court of rights of occupancy of matrimonial home

3.—(1) Where there is an entitled and a non-entitled spouse, or where both spouses are entitled, or permitted by a third party, to occupy a matrimonial home, either spouse may apply to the court for an order—

(*a*) declaring the occupancy rights of the applicant spouse;

(*b*) enforcing the occupancy rights of the applicant spouse;

(*c*) restricting the occupancy rights of the non-applicant spouse;

(*d*) regulating the exercise by either spouse of his or her occupancy rights;

(*e*) protecting the occupancy rights of the applicant spouse in relation to the other spouse.

(2) Where one spouse owns or hires, or is acquiring under a hire-purchase or conditional sale agreement, furniture and plenishings in a matrimonial home, the other spouse, if he or she has occupancy rights in that home, may apply to the court for an order granting to the applicant the possession or use in the matrimonial home of any such furniture and plenishings; but, subject to section 2 of this Act, an order under this subsection shall not prejudice the rights of any third party in relation to the non-performance of any obligation under such hire-purchase or conditional sale agreement.

(3) The court shall grant an application under subsection (1) (*a*) above if it appears to the court that the application relates to a matrimonial home; and, on an application under any of paragraphs (*b*) to (*e*) of subsection (1) or under subsection (2) above, the court may make such order relating to the application as appears to it to be just and reasonable having regard to all the circumstances of the case including—

(*a*) the conduct of the spouses in relation to each other and otherwise;

(*b*) the respective needs and financial resources of the spouses;

(*c*) the needs of any child of the family;

(*d*) the extent (if any) to which—

(i) the matrimonial home; and

(ii) in relation only to an order under subsection (2) above, any item of furniture and plenishings referred to in that subsection,

is used in connection with a trade, business or profession of either spouse; and (*e*) whether the entitled spouse offers or has offered to make available to the non-entitled spouse any suitable alternative accommodation.

(4) Pending the making of an order under subsection (3) above, the court, on the application of either spouse, may make such interim order as it may consider necessary or expedient in relation to—

(*a*) the residence of either spouse in the home to which the application relates;

(*b*) the personal effects of either spouse or of any child of the family; or

(*c*) the furniture and plenishings:

Provided that an interim order may be made only if the non-applicant spouse has been afforded an opportunity of being heard by or represented before the court.

(5) The court shall not make an order under subsection (3) or (4) above if it appears that the effect of the order would be to exclude the non-applicant spouse from the matrimonial home.

(6) If the court makes an order under subsection (3) or (4) above which requires the delivery to one spouse of anything which has been left in or removed from the matrimonial home, it may also grant a warrant authorising a messenger-at-arms or sheriff officer to enter the matrimonial home or other premises occupied by the other spouse and to search for and take possession of the thing required to be delivered, if need be by opening shut and lockfast places, and to deliver the thing in accordance with the said order:

Provided that a warrant granted under this subsection shall be executed only after expiry of the period of a charge, being such period as the court shall specify in the order for delivery.

(7) Where it appears to the court—

(*a*) on the application of a non-entitled spouse, that that spouse has suffered a loss of occupancy rights or that the quality of the non-entitled spouse's occupation of a matrimonial home has been impaired; or

(*b*) on the application of a spouse who has been given the possession or use of furniture and plenishings by virtue of an order under subsection (3) above, that the applicant has suffered a loss of such possession or use or that the quality of the applicant's possession or use of the furniture and plenishings has been impaired,

in consequence of any act or default on the part of the other spouse which was intended to result in such loss or impairment, it may order that other spouse to pay to the applicant such compensation as the court in the circumstances considers just and reasonable in respect of that loss or impairment.

(8) A spouse may renounce in writing the right to apply under subsection (2) above for the possession or use of any item of furniture and plenishings.

Exclusion orders

4.—[1] (1) Where there is an entitled and a non-entitled spouse, or where both spouses are entitled, or permitted by a third party, to occupy a matrimonial home, either spouse, whether or not that spouse is in occupation at the time of the application, may apply to the court for an order (in this Act referred to as "an exclusion order") suspending the occupancy rights of the other spouse ("the non-applicant spouse") in a matrimonial home.

(2) Subject to subsection (3) below, the court shall make an exclusion order if it appears to the court that the making of the order is necessary for the protection of the applicant or any child of the family from any conduct or threatened or reasonably apprehended conduct of the non-applicant spouse which is or would be injurious to the physical or mental health of the applicant or child.

(3) The court shall not make an exclusion order if it appears to the court that the making of the order would be unjustified or unreasonable—

(*a*) having regard to all the circumstances of the case including the matters specified in paragraphs (*a*) to (*e*) of section 3(3) of this Act; and

(*b*) where the matrimonial home—

(i) is or is part of an agricultural holding within the meaning of section 1 of the Agricultural Holdings (Scotland) Act 1949; or

(ii) is let, or is a home in respect of which possession is given, to the non-applicant spouse or to both spouses by an employer as an incident of employment,

subject to a requirement that the non-applicant spouse or, as the case may be, both spouses must reside in the matrimonial home, having regard to that requirement and the likely consequences of the exclusion of the non-applicant spouse from the matrimonial home.

(4) In making an exclusion order the court shall, on the application of the applicant spouse,—

(*a*) grant a warrant for the summary ejection of the non-applicant spouse from the matrimonial home;

(*b*) grant an interdict prohibiting the non-applicant spouse from entering the matrimonial home without the express permission of the applicant;

(*c*) grant an interdict prohibiting the removal by the non-applicant spouse, except with the written consent of the applicant or by a further order of the court, of any furniture and plenishings in the matrimonial home;

unless, in relation to paragraph (*a*) or (*c*) above, the non-applicant spouse satisfies the court that it is unnecessary for it to grant such a remedy.

(5) In making an exclusion order the court may—

(*a*) grant an interdict prohibiting the non-applicant spouse from entering or remaining in a specified area in the vicinity of the matrimonial home;

(*b*) where the warrant for the summary ejection of the non-applicant spouse has been granted in his or her absence, give directions as to the preservation of the non-applicant spouse's goods and effects which remain in the matrimonial home;

(*c*) on the application of either spouse, make the exclusion order or the warrant or interdict mentioned in paragraph (*a*), (*b*) or (*c*) of subsection (4) above or paragraph (*a*) of this subsection subject to such terms and conditions as the court may prescribe;

(*d*) on application as aforesaid, make such other order as it may consider necessary for the proper enforcement of an order made under subsection (4) above or paragraph (*a*), (*b*) or (*c*) of this subsection.

(6) Pending the making of an exclusion order, the court may, on the application of the applicant spouse, make an interim order suspending the occupancy rights of the non-applicant spouse in the matrimonial home to which the application for the exclusion order relates; and subsections (4) and (5) above shall apply to such interim order as they apply to an exclusion order:

Provided that an interim order may be made only if the non-applicant spouse has been afforded an opportunity of being heard by or represented before the court.

(7) Without prejudice to subsections (1) and (6) above, where both spouses are entitled, or permitted by a third party, to occupy a matrimonial home, it shall be incompetent for one spouse to bring an action of ejection from the matrimonial home against the other spouse.

NOTE

[1] As amended by the Law Reform (Miscellaneous Provisions) (Scotland) Act 1985, s. 13(5), with effect from 30th December 1985.

Duration of orders under sections 3 and 4

5.—(1) The court may, on the application of either spouse, vary or recall any order made by it under section 3 or 4 of this Act, but, subject to subsection (2) below, any such order shall, unless previously so varied or recalled, cease to have effect—

(*a*) on the termination of the marriage; or

(*b*) subject to section 6(1) of this Act, where there is an entitled and a non-entitled spouse, on the entitled spouse ceasing to be an entitled spouse in respect of the matrimonial home to which the order relates; or

(*c*) where both spouses are entitled, or permitted by a third party, to occupy the matrimonial home, on both spouses ceasing to be so entitled or permitted.

(2) Without prejudice to the generality of subsection (1) above, an order under section 3(3) or (4) of this Act which grants the possession or use of furniture and plenishings shall cease to have effect if the furniture and plenishings cease to be permitted by a third party to be retained in the matrimonial home.

Occupancy rights in relation to dealings with third parties

Continued exercise of occupancy rights after dealing

6.—(1) Subject to subsection (3) below—

(*a*) the continued exercise of the rights conferred on a non-entitled spouse by the provisions of this Act in respect of a matrimonial home shall not be prejudiced by reason only of any dealing of the entitled spouse relating to that home; and

(*b*) a third party shall not by reason only of such a dealing be entitled to occupy that matrimonial home or any part of it.

(2) In this section and section 7 of this Act—

"dealing" includes the grant of a heritable security and the creation of a trust but does not include a conveyance under section 80 of the Lands Clauses Consolidation (Scotland) Act 1845;

"entitled spouse" does not include a spouse who, apart from the provisions of this Act,—

(*a*) is permitted by a third party to occupy a matrimonial home; or

(*b*) is entitled to occupy a matrimonial home along with an individual who is not the other spouse, whether or not that individual has waived his or her right of occupation in favour of the spouse so entitled;

and "non-entitled spouse" shall be construed accordingly.

(3) This section shall not apply in any case where—

(*a*) the non-entitled spouse in writing either—

(i) consents or has consented to the dealing, and any consent shall be in such form as the Secretary of State may, by regulations made by statutory instrument, prescribe[1]; or

(ii) renounces or has renounced his or her occupancy rights in relation to the matrimonial home or property to which the dealing relates;

(*b*) the court has made an order under section 7 of this Act dispensing with the consent of the non-entitled spouse to the dealing;

(*c*) the dealing occurred, or implements, a binding obligation entered into by the entitled spouse before his or her marriage to the non-entitled spouse;

(*d*) the dealing occurred, or implements, a binding obligation entered into before the commencement of this Act;

[2] (*e*) the dealing comprises a sale to a third party who has acted in good faith, if there is produced to the third party by the seller—

(i) an affidavit sworn or affirmed by the seller declaring that the subjects of sale are not or were not at the time of the dealing a matrimonial home in relation to which a spouse of the seller has or had occupancy rights; or

(ii) a renunciation of occupancy rights or consent to the dealing which bears to have been properly made or given by the non-entitled spouse.

For the purposes of this paragraph, the time of the dealing, in the case of the sale of an interest in heritable property, is the date of delivery to the purchaser of the deed transferring title to that interest; or

(*f*) the entitled spouse has permanently ceased to be entitled to occupy the matrimonial home, and at any time thereafter a continuous period of 5 years has elapsed during which the non-entitled spouse has not occupied the matrimonial home.

(4) [See the print of the Land Registration (Scotland) Act 1979, ss. 6(4), 9(4) and 28 *supra*.]

NOTES

[1] See S.I. 1982 No. 971, *infra*.

[2] As amended by the Law Reform (Miscellaneous Provisions) (Scotland) Act 1985, s. 13(6), with effect from 30th November 1985 and by the Law Reform (Miscellaneous Provisions) (Scotland) Act 1990, Sched. 8, para. 31(1) and Sched. 9. By s. 13(11) of the 1985 Act:

"Any—

(*a*) affidavit lawfully sworn or affirmed before the commencement of this section in pursuance of paragraph (*e*) of subsection (3) of section 6 or subsection (2) of section 8 of that Act;

(*b*) consent lawfully given before such commencement in pursuance of the said subsection (2),

shall have effect for the purposes of the said subsection (3) as amended by this section or, as the case may be, section 8(2A) of that Act as if it had been duly sworn, affirmed or, as the case may be, given in pursuance of the said paragraph (*e*) as so amended or, as the case may be, the said section 8(2A)."

Dispensation by court with spouse's consent to dealing

7.—(1) The court may, on the application of an entitled spouse or any other person having an interest, make an order dispensing with the consent of a non-entitled spouse to a dealing which has taken place or a proposed dealing, if—

(*a*) such consent is unreasonably withheld;

(*b*) such consent cannot be given by reason of physical or mental disability;

(*c*) the non-entitled spouse cannot be found after reasonable steps have been taken to trace him or her; or

[1] (*d*) the non-entitled spouse is under legal disability by reason of nonage.

(2) For the purposes of subsection (1)(*a*) above, a non-entitled spouse shall have unreasonably withheld consent to a dealing which has taken place or a proposed dealing, where it appears to the court—

(*a*) that the non-entitled spouse has led the entitled spouse to believe that he or she would consent to the dealing and that the non-entitled spouse would not be prejudiced by any change in the circumstances of the case since such apparent consent was given; or

(*b*) that the entitled spouse has, having taken all reasonable steps to do so, been unable to obtain an answer to a request for consent.

(3) The court, in considering whether to make an order under subsection (1) above, shall have regard to all the circumstances of the case including the matters specified in paragraphs (*a*) to (*e*) of section 3(3) of this Act.

(4) Where—

(*a*) an application is made for an order under this section; and

(*b*) an action is or has been raised by a non-entitled spouse to enforce occupancy rights, the action shall be sisted until the conclusion of the proceedings on the application.

(5) [Repealed by the Family Law (Scotland) Act 1985, Sched. 2.]

NOTE

[1] As amended by the Age of Legal Capacity (Scotland) Act 1991, s. 10 and Sched. 1, para. 37.

Interests of heritable creditors

[0] **8.**—(1) The rights of a third party with an interest in the matrimonial home as a creditor under a secured loan in relation to the non-performance of any obligation under the loan shall not be prejudiced by reason only of the occupancy rights of the non-entitled spouse; but where a non-entitled spouse has or obtains occupation of a matrimonial home and—

(*a*) the entitled spouse is not in occupation; and

(*b*) there is a third party with such an interest in the matrimonial home,

the court may, on the application of the third party, make an order requiring the non-entitled spouse to make any payment due by the entitled spouse in respect of the loan.

[1] (2) This section shall not apply to secured loans in respect of which the security was granted prior to the commencement of section 13 of the Law Reform (Miscellaneous Provisions) (Scotland) Act 1985 unless the third party in granting the secured loan acted in good faith and there was produced to the third party by the entitled spouse—

(*a*) an affidavit sworn or affirmed by the entitled spouse declaring that there is no non-entitled spouse; or

(*b*) a renunciation of occupancy rights or consent to the taking of the loan which bears to have been properly made or given by the non-entitled spouse.

[2] (2A) This section shall not apply to secured loans in respect of which the security was granted after the commencement of section 13 of the Law Reform (Miscellaneous Provisions) (Scotland) Act 1985 unless the third party in granting the secured loan acted in good faith and there was produced to the third party by the grantor—

(*a*) an affidavit sworn or affirmed by the grantor declaring that the security subjects are not or were not at the time of the granting of the security a matrimonial home in relation to which a spouse of the grantor has or had occupancy rights; or

(*b*) a renunciation of occupancy rights or consent to the granting of the security which bears to have been properly made or given by the non-entitled spouse.

[2] (2B) For the purposes of subsections (2) and (2A) above, the time of granting a security, in the case of a heritable security, is the date of delivery of the deed creating the security.

NOTES

[0] As amended by the Law Reform (Miscellaneous Provisions) (Scotland) Act 1990, Sched. 8, para. 31(2) and Sched. 9.

[1] As amended by the Law Reform (Miscellaneous Provisions) (Scotland) Act 1985, s.13(7), with effect from 30th December 1985. By section 13(11) of the same Act: "Any—

(*a*) affidavit lawfully sworn or affirmed before the commencement of this section in pursuance of paragraph (*e*) of subsection (3) of section 6 or subsection (2) of section 8 of that Act;

(*b*) consent lawfully given before such commencement in pursuance of the said subsection (2),

shall have effect for the purposes of the said subsection (3) as amended by this section or, as the case may be, section 8(2A) of that Act as if it had been duly sworn, affirmed or, as the case may be, given in pursuance of the said paragraph (*e*) as so amended or, as the case may be, the said section 8(2A)."

[2] Inserted by the Law Reform (Miscellaneous Provisions) (Scotland) Act 1985, s.13(8), with effect from 30th December 1985.

Provisions where both spouses have title

9.—(1) Subject to subsection (2) below, where, apart from the provisions of this Act, both spouses are entitled to occupy a matrimonial home—

(*a*) the rights in that home of one spouse shall not be prejudiced by reason only of any dealing of the other spouse; and

(*b*) a third party shall not by reason only of such a dealing be entitled to occupy that matrimonial home or any part of it.

(2) The definition of "dealing" in section 6(2) of this Act and sections 6(3) and 7 of this Act shall apply for the purposes of subsection (1) above as they apply for the purposes of section 6(1) of this Act subject to the following modifications—

(*a*) any reference to the entitled spouse and to the non-entitled spouse shall be construed as a reference to a spouse who has entered into, or as the case may be, proposes to enter into a dealing and to the other spouse respectively; and

(*b*) in paragraph (*b*) of section 7(4) the reference to occupancy rights shall be construed as a reference to any rights in the matrimonial home.

Protection of rights of spouse against arrangements intended to defeat them

10. [Repealed by the Bankruptcy (Scotland) Act 1985, Sched. 8.]

Poinding

[1] **11.** Where a poinding has been executed of furniture and plenishings of which the debtor's spouse has the possession or use by virtue of an order under section 3(3) or (4) of this Act, the sheriff, on the application of that spouse within 40 days of the date of execution of the poinding, may—

(*a*) declare that the poinding is null; or

(*b*) make such order as he thinks appropriate to protect such possession or use by that spouse,

if he is satisfied that the purpose of the diligence was wholly or mainly to prevent such possession or use.

NOTE

[1] Applied by the Family Law (Scotland) Act 1985, s.14(5).

Adjudication

[1] **12.**—(1) Where a matrimonial home of which there is an entitled spouse and a non-entitled spouse is adjudged, the Court of Session, on the application of the non-entitled spouse within 40 days of the date of the decree of adjudication, may—

(*a*) order the reduction of the decree; or

(*b*) make such order as it thinks appropriate to protect the occupancy rights of the non-entitled spouse,

if it is satisfied that the purpose of the diligence was wholly or mainly to defeat the occupancy rights of the non-entitled spouse.

(2) In this section, "entitled spouse" and "non-entitled spouse" have the same meanings respectively as in section 6(2) of this Act.

NOTE

[1] Applied by the Family Law (Scotland) Act 1985, s.14(5).

Transfer of tenancy

Transfer of tenancy

13.—(1) The court may, on the application of a non-entitled spouse, make an order transferring the tenancy of a matrimonial home to that spouse and providing, subject to subsection (11) below, for the payment by the non-entitled spouse to the entitled spouse of such compensation as seems just and reasonable in all the circumstances of the case.

[1] (2) In an action—

(*a*) for divorce, the Court of Session or a sheriff;

(*b*) for nullity of marriage, the Court of Session,

may, on granting decree or within such period as the court may specify on granting decree, make an order granting an application under subsection (1) above.

(3) In determining whether to grant an application under subsection (1) above, the court shall have regard to all the circumstances of the case including the matters specified in paragraphs (*a*) to (*e*) of section 3(3) of this Act and the suitability of the applicant to become the tenant and the applicant's capacity to perform the obligations under the lease of the matrimonial home.

(4) The non-entitled spouse shall serve a copy of an application under subsection (1) above on the landlord and, before making an order under subsection (1) above, the court shall give the landlord an opportunity of being heard by it.

(5) On the making of an order granting an application under subsection (1) above, the tenancy shall vest in the non-entitled spouse without intimation to the landlord, subject to all the liabilities under the lease (other than any arrears of rent for the period before the making of the order, which shall remain the liability of the original entitled spouse).

(6) The clerk of court shall notify the landlord of the making of an order granting an application under subsection (1) above.

(7) It shall not be competent for a non-entitled spouse to apply for an order under subsection (1) above where the matrimonial home—

(*a*) is let to the entitled spouse by his or her employer as an incident of employment, and the lease is subject to a requirement that the entitled spouse must reside therein;

(*b*) is or is part of an agricultural holding;

(*c*) is on or pertains to a croft or the subject of a cottar or the holding of a landholder or a statutory small tenant;

(*d*) is let on a long lease;

(*e*) is part of the tenancy land of a tenant-at-will.

[1a] (8) In subsection (6) above—

"agricultural holding" has the same meaning as in section 1 of the Agricultural Holdings (Scotland) Act 1991;

"cottar" has the same meaning as in section 28(4) of the Crofters (Scotland) Act 1955;

"croft" has the same meaning as in the Crofters (Scotland) Act 1955;

"holding", in relation to a landholder and a statutory small tenant, "landholder" and "statutory small tenant" have the same meanings respectively as in sections 2(1), 2(2) and 32(1) of the Small Landholders (Scotland) Act 1911;

"long lease" has the same meaning as in section 28(1) of the Land Registration (Scotland) Act 1979;

"tenant-at-will" has the same meaning as in section 20(8) of the Land Registration (Scotland) Act 1979.

(9) Where both spouses are joint or common tenants of a matrimonial home, the court may, on the application of one of the spouses, make an order vesting the tenancy in that spouse solely and providing, subject to subsection (11) below, for the payment by the applicant to the other spouse of such compensation as seems just and reasonable in the circumstances of the case.

(10) Subsections (2) to (8) above shall apply for the purposes of an order under subsection (9) above as they apply for the purposes of an order under subsection (1) above subject to the following modifications—

(*a*) in subsection (3) for the word "tenant" there shall be substituted the words "sole tenant";

(*b*) in subsection (4) for the words "non-entitled" there should be substituted the word "applicant";

(*c*) in subsection (5) for the words "non-entitled" and "liability of the original entitled spouse" there shall be substituted respectively the words "applicant" and "joint and several liability of both spouses";

(*d*) in subsection (7)—

(i) for the words "a non-entitled" there shall be substituted the words "an applicant";

(ii) for paragraph (*a*) there shall be substituted the following paragraph—

"(*a*) is let to both spouses by their employer as an incident of employment, and the lease is subject to a requirement that both spouses must reside there;";

(iii) paragraphs (*c*) and (*e*) shall be omitted.

[2] (11) Where the matrimonial home is a secure tenancy within the meaning of Part III of the Housing (Scotland) Act 1987, no account shall be taken, in assessing the amount of any compensation to be awarded under subsection (1) or (9) above, of the loss, by virtue of the transfer of the tenancy of the home, of a right to purchase the home under Part I of that Act.

(12) [See the print of the Housing (Scotland) Act 1987, s.48(1) and Sched. 3, Pt. I, *infra*.]

NOTES

[1] As amended by the Family Law (Scotland) Act 1985, Sched. 1, para. 11.

[1a] As amended by the Agricultural Holdings (Scotland) Act 1991, Sched. 11, para. 40.

[2] As amended by the Housing (Scotland) Act 1987, Sched. 23, para. 26.

Matrimonial interdicts

Interdict competent where spouses live together

14.—(1) It shall not be incompetent for the court to entertain an application by a spouse for a matrimonial interdict by reason only that the spouses are living together as man and wife.

(2) In this section and section 15 of this Act—

"matrimonial interdict" means an interdict including an interim interdict which—

(*a*) restrains or prohibits any conduct of one spouse towards the other spouse or a child of the family, or

(*b*) prohibits a spouse from entering or remaining in a matrimonial home or in a specified area in the vicinity of the matrimonial home.

Attachment of powers of arrest to matrimonial interdicts

[1] **15.**—(1) The court shall, on the application of the applicant spouse, attach a power of arrest—

(*a*) to any matrimonial interdict which is ancillary to an exclusion order, including an interim order under section 4(6) of this Act;

(*b*) to any other matrimonial interdict where the non-applicant spouse has had the opportunity of being heard by or represented before the court, unless it appears to the court that in all the circumstances of the case such a power is unnecessary.

(2) A power of arrest attached to an interdict by virtue of subsection (1) above shall not have effect until such interdict is together with the attached power of arrest served on the non-applicant spouse, and such a power of arrest shall, unless previously recalled, cease to have effect upon the termination of the marriage.

(3) If, by virtue of subsection (1) above, a power of arrest is attached to an interdict, a constable may arrest without warrant the non-applicant spouse if he has reasonable cause for suspecting that spouse of being in breach of the interdict.

(4) If, by virtue of subsection (1) above, a power of arrest is attached to an interdict, the applicant spouse shall, as soon as possible after service of the interdict together with the attached power of arrest on the non-applicant spouse, ensure that there is delivered—

(*a*) to the chief constable of the police area in which the matrimonial home is situated; and

(*b*) if the applicant spouse resides in another police area, to the chief constable of that other police area,

a copy of the application for the interdict and of the interlocutor granting the interdict together with a certificate of service of the interdict and where the application to attach the power of arrest to the interdict was made after the interdict was granted, a copy of that application and of the interlocutor granting it and a certificate of service of the interdict together with the attached power of arrest.

(5) Where any matrimonial interdict to which, by virtue of subsection (1)

[THE NEXT PAGE IS J 253]

above there is attached a power of arrest, is varied or recalled, the spouse who applied for the variation or recall shall ensure that there is delivered—

(*a*) to the chief constable of the police area in which the matrimonial home is situated; and

(*b*) if the applicant spouse (within the meaning of subsection (6) below) resides in another police area, to the chief constable of that other police area,

a copy of the application for variation or recall and of the interlocutor granting the variation or recall.

(6) In this section and in sections 16 and 17 of this Act—

"applicant spouse" means the spouse who has applied for the interdict; and

"non-applicant spouse" shall be construed accordingly.

NOTE

[1] As amended by the Law Reform (Miscellaneous Provisions) (Scotland) Act 1990, s.64.

Police powers after arrest

16.—(1) Where a person has been arrested under section 15(3) of this Act, the officer in charge of a police station may—

(*a*) if satisfied that there is no likelihood of violence to the applicant spouse or any child of the family, liberate that person unconditionally; or

(*b*) refuse to liberate that person;

and such refusal and the detention of that person until his or her appearance in court by virtue of—

(i) section 17(2) of this Act; or

(ii) any provision of the Criminal Procedure (Scotland) Act 1975,

shall not subject the officer to any claim whatsoever.

(2) Where a person arrested under section 15(3) of this Act is liberated under subsection (1) above, the facts and circumstances which gave rise to the arrest shall be reported forthwith to the procurator fiscal who, if he decides to take no criminal proceedings in respect of those facts and circumstances, shall at the earliest opportunity take all reasonable steps to intimate his decision to the persons mentioned in paragraphs (*a*) and (*b*) of section 17(4) of this Act.

Procedure after arrest

17.—(1) The provisions of this section shall apply only where—

(*a*) the non-applicant spouse has not been liberated under section 16(1) of this Act; and

(*b*) the procurator fiscal decides that no criminal proceedings are to be taken in respect of the facts and circumstances which gave rise to the arrest.

(2) The non-applicant spouse who has been arrested under section 15(3) of this Act shall wherever practicable be brought before the sheriff sitting as a court of summary criminal jurisdiction for the district in which he or she was arrested not later than in the course of the first day after the arrest, such day not being a Saturday, a Sunday or a court holiday prescribed for that court under section 10 of the Bail etc. (Scotland) Act 1980:

Provided that nothing in this subsection shall prevent the non-applicant spouse from being brought before the sheriff on a Saturday, a Sunday or such a court holiday where the sheriff is in pursuance of the said section 10 sitting on such a day for the disposal of criminal business.

(3) Subsections (1) and (2) of section 3 of the Criminal Justice (Scotland) Act 1980 (intimation to a named person) shall apply to a non-applicant spouse who has been arrested under section 15(3) of this Act as they apply to a person who has been arrested in respect of any offence.

(4) The procurator fiscal shall at the earliest opportunity, and in any event prior to the non-applicant spouse being brought before the sheriff under subsection (2) above, take all reasonable steps to intimate—

(*a*) to the applicant spouse; and

(*b*) to the solicitor who acted for that spouse when the interdict was granted or to any other solicitor who the procurator fiscal has reason to believe acts for the time being for that spouse,

that the criminal proceedings referred to in subsection (1) above will not be taken.

(5) On the non-applicant spouse being brought before the sheriff under subsection (2) above, the following procedure shall apply—

(*a*) the procurator fiscal shall present to the court a petition containing—

(i) a statement of the particulars of the non-applicant spouse;

(ii) a statement of the facts and circumstances which gave rise to the arrest; and

(iii) a request that the non-applicant spouse be detained for a further period not exceeding 2 days;

(*b*) if it appears to the sheriff that—

(i) the statement referred to in paragraph (*a*)(ii) above discloses a *prima facie* breach of interdict by the non-applicant spouse;

(ii) proceedings for breach of interdict will be taken; and

(iii) there is a substantial risk of violence by the non-applicant spouse against the applicant spouse or any child of the family,

he may order the non-applicant spouse to be detained for a further period not exceeding 2 days;

(*c*) in any case to which paragraph (*b*) above does not apply, the non-applicant spouse shall, unless in custody in respect of any other matter, be released from custody;

and in computing the period of two days referred to in paragraphs (*a*) and (*b*) above, no account shall be taken of a Saturday or Sunday or of any holiday in the court in which the proceedings for breach of interdict will require to be raised.

Cohabiting couples

Occupancy rights of cohabiting couples

18.—[1] (1) If a man and a woman are living with each other as if they were man and wife ("a cohabiting couple") in a house which, apart from the provisions of this section—

(*a*) one of them (an "entitled partner") is entitled, or permitted by a third party, to occupy; and

(*b*) the other (a "non-entitled partner") is not so entitled or permitted to occupy,

the court may, on the application of the non-entitled partner, if it appears that the man and the woman are a cohabiting couple in that house, grant occupancy rights therein to the applicant for such period, not exceeding six months, as the court may specify:

Provided that the court may extend the said period for a further period or periods, no such period exceeding 6 months.

(2) In determining whether for the purpose of subsection (1) above a man and woman are a cohabiting couple the court shall have regard to all the circumstances of the case including—

(*a*) the time for which it appears they have been living together; and

(*b*) whether there are any children of the relationship.

(3) While an order granting an application under subsection (1) above or an extension of such an order is in force, or where both partners of a cohabiting couple are entitled, or permitted by a third party, to occupy the house where they are cohabiting, the following provisions of this Act shall subject to any necessary modifications—

(*a*) apply to the cohabiting couple as they apply to parties to a marriage; and

(*b*) have effect in relation to any child residing with the cohabiting couple as they have effect in relation to a child of the family,

section 2;
section 3, except subsection (1)(*a*);
section 4;
in section 5(1), the words from the beginning to "Act" where it first occurs;
sections 13 and 14;
section 15, except the words in subsection (2) from "and such a power of arrest" to the end;
sections 16 and 17;
and
section 22,

and any reference in these provisions to a matrimonial home shall be construed as a reference to a house.

(4) Any order under section 3 or 4 of this Act as applied to a cohabiting couple by subsection (3) above shall have effect—

(*a*) if one of them is a non-entitled partner, for such a period, not exceeding the period or periods which from time to time may be specified in any order under subsection (1) above for which occupancy rights have been granted under that subsection, as may be specified in the order;

(*b*) if they are both entitled, or permitted by a third party, to occupy the house, until a further order of the court.

(5) Nothing in this section shall prejudice the rights of any third party having an interest in the house referred to in subsection (1) above.

[1] (6) In this section—

"house" includes a caravan, houseboat or other structure in which the couple are cohabiting and any garden or other ground or building attached to, and usually occupied with, or otherwise required for the amenity or convenience of, the house, caravan, houseboat or other structure;

"occupancy rights" means the following rights of a non-entitled partner—

(*a*) if in occupation, a right to continue to occupy the house;
(*b*) if not in occupation, a right to enter into and occupy the house;

and, without prejudice to the generality of these rights, includes the right to continue to occupy or, as the case may be, to enter and occupy the house together with any child residing with the cohabiting couple;

"entitled partner" includes a partner who is entitled, or permitted by a third party, to occupy the house along with an individual who is not the other partner only if that individual has waived his or her right of occupation in favour of the partner so entitled or permitted.

NOTE

[1] As amended by the Law Reform (Miscellaneous Provisions) (Scotland) Act 1985, s. 13(9).

Miscellaneous and General

Rights of occupancy in relation to division and sale

19. Where a spouse brings an action for the division and sale of a matrimonial home which the spouses own in common, the court, after having regard to all the circumstances of the case including—

(*a*) the matters specified in paragraphs (*a*) to (*d*) of section 3(3) of this Act; and

(*b*) whether the spouse bringing the action offers or has offered to make available to the other spouse any suitable alternative accommodation,

may refuse to grant decree in that action or may postpone the granting of decree for such period as it may consider reasonable in the circumstances or may grant decree subject to such conditions as it may prescribe.

Spouse's consent in relation to calling up of standard securities over matrimonial homes

20. [See the print of the Conveyancing and Feudal Reform (Scotland) Act 1970, s. 19(10), *supra*.]

Procedural provision

21. Section 2(2) of the Law Reform (Husband and Wife) Act 1962 (dismissal by court of delictual proceedings between spouses) shall not apply to any proceedings brought before the court in pursuance of any provision of this Act.

Interpretation

[1] **22.** In this Act—

"caravan" mean a caravan which is mobile or affixed to the land;

"child of the family" includes any child or grandchild of either spouse, and any person who has been brought up or accepted by either spouse as if he or she were a child of that spouse, whatever the age of such a child, grandchild or person may be;

"the court" means the Court of Session or the sheriff;

"furniture and plenishings" means any article situated in a matrimonial home which—

(*a*) is owned or hired by either spouse or is being acquired by either spouse under a hire-purchase agreement or conditional sale agreement; and

(*b*) is reasonably necessary to enable the home to be used as a family residence,

but does not include any vehicle, caravan or houseboat, or such other structure as is mentioned in the definition of "matrimonial home";

"matrimonial home" means any house, caravan, houseboat or other structure which has been provided or has been made available by one or both of the spouses as, or has become, a family residence and includes any garden or other ground or building attached to, and usually occupied with, or otherwise required for the amenity or convenience of, the house, caravan, houseboat or other structure but does not include a residence provided or made available by one spouse for that spouse to reside in, whether with any child of the family or not, separately from the other spouse;

"occupancy rights" has, subject to section 18(6) of this Act, the meaning assigned by section 1(4) of this Act;

"the sheriff" includes the sheriff having jurisdiction in the district where the matrimonial home is situated;

"tenant" includes sub-tenant and a statutory tenant as defined in section 3 of the Rent (Scotland) Act 1984 and a statutory assured tenant as defined in section 16(1) of the Housing (Scotland) Act 1988 and "tenancy" shall be construed accordingly;

"entitled spouse" and "non-entitled spouse", subject to sections 6(2) and 12(2) of this Act, have the meanings respectively assigned to them by section 1 of this Act.

NOTE

[1] As amended by the Law Reform (Miscellaneous Provisions) (Scotland) Act 1985, s. 13(10), and (with effect from 2 January 1989) the Housing (Scotland) Act 1988, Sched. 9, para. 3.

Short title, commencement and extent

23.—(1) This Act may be cited as the Matrimonial Homes (Family Protection) (Scotland) Act 1981.

[1] (2) This Act (except this section) shall come into operation on such day as the Secretary of State may by order made by statutory instrument appoint, and different days may be so appointed for different provisions and for different purposes.

(3) This Act extends to Scotland only.

NOTE

[1] 1st September 1982 for the whole Act: S.I. 1982 No. 972.

Administration of Justice Act 1982

(1982 c. 53)

An Act to . . . amend the law relating to wills . . .

[28th October 1982]

. . . . . .

Part IV

Wills

. . . . . .

Registration of wills

Deposit and registration of wills of living persons

23.—(1) The following, namely—

(*a*) the Principal Registry of the Family Division of the High Court of Justice;

(*b*) the Keeper of the Registers of Scotland; and

(*c*) the Probate and Matrimonial Office of the Supreme Court of Northern Ireland,

shall be registering authorities for the purposes of this section.

(2) Each registering authority shall provide and maintain safe and convenient depositories for the custody of the wills of living persons.

(3) Any person may deposit his will in such a depository in accordance with regulations under section 25 below and on payment of the prescribed fee.

(4) It shall be the duty of a registering authority to register in accordance with regulations under section 25 below—

(*a*) any will deposited in a depository maintained by the authority; and

(*b*) any other will whose registration is requested under Article 6 of the Registration Convention.

(5) A will deposited in a depository provided—

(*a*) under section 172 of the Supreme Court of Judicature (Consolidation) Act 1925 or section 126 of the Supreme Court Act 1981; or

[THE NEXT PAGE IS J 257]

(*b*) under Article 27 of the Administration of Estates (Northern Ireland) Order 1979,

shall be treated for the purposes of this section as if it had been deposited under this section.

. . . .

Designation of Principal Registry as national body under Registration Convention

24.—(1) The Principal Registry of the Family Division of the High Court of Justice shall be the national body for the purposes of the Registration Convention, and shall accordingly have the functions assigned to the national body by the Registration Convention including, without prejudice to the general application of the Convention to the Principal Registry by virtue of this section, the functions—

(*a*) of arranging for the registration of wills in other Contracting States as provided for in Article 6 of the Convention;

(*b*) of receiving and answering requests for information arising from the national bodies of other Contracting States.

(2) In this Part of this Act " the Registration Convention " means the Convention on the Establishment of a Scheme of Registration of Wills concluded at Basle on 16th May 1972.

Regulations as to deposit and registration of wills etc.

25.—(1) Regulations may make provision—

(*a*) as to the conditions for the deposit of a will;

(*b*) as to the manner of and procedure for—

(i) the deposit and registration of a will; and

(ii) the withdrawal of a will which has been deposited; and

(iii) the cancellation of the registration of a will; and

(*c*) as to the manner in which the Principal Registry of the Family Division is to perform its functions as the national body under the Registration Convention.

(2) Regulations under this section may contain such incidental or supplementary provisions as the authority making the regulations considers appropriate.

(3) Any such regulations are to be made—

(*a*) for England and Wales, by the President of the Family Division of the High Court of Justice, with the concurrence of the Lord Chancellor;

(*b*) for Scotland, by the Secretary of State after consultation with the Lord President of the Court of Session; and

(*c*) for Northern ireland, by the Northern Ireland Supreme Court Rules Committee, with the concurrence of the Lord Chancellor.

. . . .

(7) The Statutory Instruments Act 1946 shall apply to a statutory instrument containing regulations made in accordance with subsection (3) (*a*) or (*c*) above as if the regulations had been made by a Minister of the Crown.

(8) Any regulations made under section 172 of the Supreme Court of Judicature (Consolidation) Act 1925 or section 126 of the Supreme Court Act 1981 shall have effect for the purposes of this Part of this Act as they have effect for the purposes of the enactment under which they were made.

. . . .

The form of an international will

27.—(1) The Annex to the Convention on International Wills shall have the force of law in the United Kingdom.

(2) The Annex is set out in Schedule 2 to this Act.

(3) In this Part of this Act—

" international will " means a will made in accordance with the requirements of the Annex, as set out in Schedule 2 to this Act; and

" the Convention on International Wills " means the Convention providing a Uniform Law on the Form of an International Will concluded at Washington on 26th October 1973.

International wills—procedure

28.—(1) The persons authorised to act in the United Kingdom in connection with international wills are—

(*a*) solicitors; and

(*b*) notaries public.

(2) A person who is authorised under section 6 (1) of the Commissioners for Oaths Act 1889 to do notarial acts in any foreign country or place is authorised to act there in connection with international wills.

(3) An international will certified by virtue of subsection (1) or (2) above may be deposited in a depository provided under section 23 above.

(4) Section 23 above shall accordingly have effect in relation to such international wills.

(5) Subject to subsection (6) below, regulations under section 25 above shall have effect in relation to such international wills as they have effect in relation to wills deposited under section 23 above.

(6) Without prejudice to the generality of section 25 above, regulations under that section may make special provision with regard to such international wills.

(7) In section 10 of the Consular Relations Act 1968 (by virtue of which diplomatic agents and consular officials may administer oaths and do notarial acts in certain cases)—

(*a*) at the end of subsection (1) (*b*) there shall be added the words " or (*c*) in connection with an international will."; and

(*b*) at the end of subsection (4) there shall be added the words " and " international will " has the meaning assigned to it by section 27 of the Administration of Justice Act 1982 ".

. . . .

Commencement

76. . . .

(5) The provisions of this Act specified in subsection (6) below shall come into operation on such day as the Lord Chancellor and the Secretary of State may by order jointly appoint.

(6) The provisions of this Act mentioned in subsection (5) above are—

(*a*) sections 23 to 25;

(*b*) sections 27 and 28.

. . . .

Citation

78. This Act may be cited as the Administration of Justice Act 1982.

. . . .

Section 27

SCHEDULE 2

THE ANNEX TO THE CONVENTION ON INTERNATIONAL WILLS

UNIFORM LAW ON THE FORM OF AN INTERNATIONAL WILL

Article 1

1. A will shall be valid as regards form, irrespective particularly of the place where it is made, of the location of the assets and of the nationality, domicile or residence of the testator, if it is made in the form of an international will complying with the provisions set out in Articles 2 to 5 hereinafter.

2. The invalidity of the will as an international will shall not affect its formal validity as a will of another kind.

Article 2

This law shall not apply to the form of testamentary dispositions made by two or more persons in one instrument.

Article 3

1. The will shall be made in writing.

2. It need not be written by the testator himself.

3. It may be written in any language, by hand or by any other means.

Article 4

1. The testator shall declare in the presence of two witnesses and of a person authorized to act in connection with international wills that the document is his will and that he knows the contents thereof.

2. The testator need not inform the witnesses, or the authorized person, of the contents of the will.

Article 5

1. In the presence of the witnesses and of the authorized person, the testator shall sign the will or, if he has previously signed it, shall acknowledge his signature.

2. When the testator is unable to sign, he shall indicate the reason therefor to the authorized person who shall make note of this on the will. Moreover, the testator may be authorized by the law under which the authorized person was designated to direct another person to sign on his behalf.

3. The witnesses and the authorized person shall there and then attest the will by signing in the presence of the testator.

Article 6

1. The signatures shall be placed at the end of the will.

2. If the will consists of several sheets, each sheet shall be signed by the testator or, if he is unable to sign, by the person signing on his behalf or, if there is no such person, by the authorized person. In addition, each sheet shall be numbered.

Article 7

1. The date of the will shall be the date of its signature by the authorized person.
2. This date shall be noted at the end of the will by the authorized person.

Article 8

In the absence of any mandatory rule pertaining to the safekeeping of the will, the authorized person shall ask the testator whether he wishes to make a declaration concerning the safekeeping of his will. If so and at the express request of the testator the place where he intends to have his will kept shall be mentioned in the certificate provided for in Article 9.

Article 9

The authorized person shall attach to the will a certificate in the form prescribed in Article 10 establishing that the obligations of this law have been complied with.

Article 10

The certificate drawn up by the authorized person shall be in the following form or in a substantially similar form:

CERTIFICATE
(Convention of October 26th, 1973)

1. I, ... (*name, address and capacity*), a person authorized to act in connection with international wills

2. Certify that on ....

(*date*) at ....

....(*place*)

3. (*testator*) ....(*name, address, date and place of birth*) in my presence and that of the witnesses

4. (*a*) ....(*name, address, date and place of birth*)

(*b*) ....(*name, address, date and place of birth*)

has declared that the attached document is his will and that he knows the contents thereof.

5. I furthermore certify that:

6. (*a*) in my presence and in that of the witnesses
(1) the testator has signed the will or has acknowledged his signature previously affixed.
*(2) following a declaration of the testator stating that he was unable to sign his will for the following reason
....
—I have mentioned this declaration on the will
*—the signature has been affixed by ....(*name, address*)

7. (*b*) the witnesses and I have signed the will:

8. *(*c*) each page of the will has been signed by ....and numbered:

9. (*d*) I have satisfied myself as to the identity of the testator and of the witnesses as designated above;

10. (*e*) the witnesses met the conditions requisite to act as such according to the law under which I am acting;

11. *(*f*) the testator has requested me to include the following statement concerning the safekeeping of his will:

....

....

12. PLACE

13. DATE

14. SIGNATURE and, if necessary, SEAL

*To be completed if appropriate.

Article 11

The authorized person shall keep a copy of the certificate and deliver another to the testator.

Article 12

In the absence of evidence to the contrary, the certificate of the authorized person shall be conclusive of the formal validity of the instrument as a will under this Law.

Article 13

The absence or irregularity of a certificate shall not affect the formal validity of a will under this Law.

Article 14

The international will shall be subject to the ordinary rules of revocation of wills.

Article 15

In interpreting and applying the provisions of this law, regard shall be had to its international origin and to the need for uniformity in its interpretation.

. . . . . .

Register of Sasines (Scotland) Act 1987

(1987 c. 23)

An Act to make provision as to the methods of keeping the Register of Sasines. [15th May 1987]

Regulations prescribing methods of operation in the Register of Sasines

1.—(1) Subject to the following provisions of this section, the Secretary of State may by regulations prescribe methods of operation in the Register of Sasines and these methods shall apply in place of methods of operation provided for in any enactment prior to the coming into force of this Act, notwithstanding the provisions of such enactments.

(2) In subsection (1) above, "methods of operation" means—

(*a*) the manner of recording a deed and of keeping the Register, including the medium in which a deed may be recorded and the Register kept;

(*b*) the making available of the Register to the public for inspection,

and different provision may be made for different cases or classes of case.

(3) Nothing in this Act, or in regulations under this Act, or done under or by virtue of such regulations shall affect—

(*a*) any rule of law relating to the information—

(i) to be recorded in the Register; or

(ii) to be made available to the public; or

(*b*) the evidential value of the Register or of an extract from the Register.

(4) Methods of keeping the Register prescribed in accordance with subsection (1) above may apply to records of deeds, notwithstanding that they were recorded before the coming into force of the regulations.

(5) Any reference, however expressed, in any enactment to—
(*a*) a particular book, volume or folio; or
(*b*) a method of recording a deed or keeping the Register
which has been superseded by virtue of regulations made under this Act shall be construed as a reference to such document or method as has so superseded it.

(6) In this Act—
"enactment" includes any Act of Parliament, whether public, general, local or private, any Act of Sederunt and any instrument made under any enactment;
any reference to the Register of Sasines shall be construed in accordance with section 2 of The Land Registers (Scotland) Act 1868.

Making of regulations

2.—(1) Before making regulations under this Act, the Secretary of State shall consult such persons or bodies as appear to him to be appropriate.

(2) Regulations under this Act shall be made by statutory instrument which shall be subject to annulment in pursuance of a resolution of either House of Parliament.

Citation commencement and extent

3.—(1) This Act, which may be cited as the Register of Sasines (Scotland) Act 1987, shall come into force on the expiry of the period of two months beginning with the day on which it is passed.

(2) This Act extends to Scotland only.

Housing (Scotland) Act 1987

(1987 c. 26)

An Act to consolidate with amendments to give effect to recommendations of the Scottish Law Commission, certain enactments relating to housing in Scotland. [15th May 1987]

. . . . . .

Part III

Rights of Public Sector Tenants

Security of Tenure

[For sections 44–60, see Division L.]

[1] *Right to buy*

NOTE

[1] See the Finance Act 1993, s. 203 (stamp duty on dispositions under rent to loan scheme).

Secure tenant's right to purchase

[1] **61.**—(1) Notwithstanding anything contained in any agreement, a tenant of a house to which this section applies (or such one or more of joint tenants as may be agreed between them) shall, subject to this Part, have the right to purchase the house at a price fixed under section 62.

(2) This section applies to every house let under a secure tenancy where—
(*a*) the landlord is either—

(i) an islands or district council, or a joint board or joint committee of an islands or district council or the common good of an islands or district council, or any trust under the control of an islands or district council; or

(ii) a regional council, or a joint board or joint committee of 2 or more regional councils, or any trust under the control of a regional council; or

(iii) a development corporation (including an urban development corporation); or

(iv) the Scottish Special Housing Association; or

(v) the Housing Corporation; or

(vi) a registered housing association; or

(vii) a housing co-operative; or

(viii) a police authority in Scotland; or

(ix) a fire authority in Scotland; and

(*b*) the landlord is the heritable proprietor of the house or in the case of a landlord who is a housing co-operative a body mentioned in paragraph (*a*)(i) is the heritable proprietor; and

(*c*) immediately prior to the date of service of an application to purchase, the tenant has been for not less than 2 years in occupation of a house (including accommodation provided as mentioned in subsection (11)(*n*)) or of a succession of houses provided by any persons mentioned in subsection (11).

(2A) For the purposes of subsection (2)(*c*), where the house was provided by a housing association which, at any time while the house was so provided, was not a registered housing association, the association shall, if it became a registered housing association at any later time, be deemed to have been a registered housing association at all times since it first provided the house.

[2] (3) This section also applies to a house let under a secure tenancy granted in pursuance of section 282(2) or (3) (grant of secure tenancy on acquisition of defective dwelling), if the tenant would not otherwise have the right to purchase under this Part; and where it so applies—

(*a*) paragraph (*c*) of subsection (2) shall not have effect;

(*b*) the words "beyond 2" in section 62(3)(*b*) shall not have effect.

[3] (4) This section does not apply—

(*a*) to a house that is one of a group which has been provided with facilities (including a call system and the services of a warden) specially designed or adapted for the needs of persons of pensionable age or disabled persons; or

(*b*) where a landlord which is a registered housing association has at no time received a grant under—

(i) any enactment mentioned in paragraph 2 of Schedule 1 to the Housing Associations Act 1985 (grants under enactments superseded by the Housing Act 1974);

(ii) section 31 of the Housing Act 1974 (management grants);

(iii) section 41 of the Housing Associations Act 1985 (housing association grants);

(iv) section 54 of that Act (revenue deficit grants);

(v) section 55 of that Act (hostel deficit grants); or

(vi) section 59(2) of that Act (grants by local authorities); or

(*c*) where such a landlord has at no time let (or had available for letting) more than 100 dwellings;

(*d*) where such a landlord is a charity—

(i) entered in the register of charities maintained under the Charities Act 1960 by the Charity Commissioners for England and Wales; or

(ii) which but for section 4(4) of, and paragraph (g) of the Second Schedule to, that Act (exempt charities) would require to be so entered; or

(e) where by virtue of section 49(2) of the said Act of 1960 (extent) such a landlord is not one to which Part II of that Act (registration of charities etc.) applies, but—

(i) the landlord has, in respect of all periods from 14th November 1985 or from the date of first being registered by the Housing Corporation or by Scottish Homes (whichever is the later) claimed and been granted (whether or not retrospectively), under section 360(1) of the Income and Corporation Taxes Act 1970 (special exemptions for charities), exemption from tax; and

(ii) where such exemption has not been claimed and granted in respect of all periods from the said date of registration, the rules of the landlord, registered under the Industrial and Provident Societies Act 1965 and in force at that date, were such as would have admitted of such exemption had it been claimed as at that date; or

(f) where, within a neighbourhood, the house is one of a number (not exceeding 14) of houses with a common landlord, being a landlord which is a registered housing association, and it is the practice of that landlord to let at least one half of those houses for occupation by any or all of the following—

(i) persons who have suffered from, or are suffering from, mental disorder (as defined in the Mental Health (Scotland) Act 1984), physical handicap or addiction to alcohol or other drugs;

(ii) persons who have been released from prison or other institutions;

(iii) young persons who have left the care of a local authority,

and a social service is, or special facilities are, provided wholly or partly for the purpose of assisting those persons.

(5) Where the spouse of a tenant or, where there is a joint tenancy, the spouse of a joint tenant, occupies the house as his only or principal home but is not himself a joint tenant, the right to purchase the house under subsection (1) shall not be exercised without the consent of such spouse.

(6) A tenant may exercise his right to purchase, if he so wishes, together with one or more members of his family acting as joint purchasers, provided—

(a) that such members are at least 18 years of age, that they have, during the period of six months ending with the date of service of the application to purchase, had their only or principal home with the tenant and that their residence in the house is not a breach of any obligation of the tenancy; or

(b) where the requirements of paragraph (a) are not satisfied, the landlord has consented.

(7) The Secretary of State may by order made by statutory instrument amend, or add to, the descriptions of persons set out in sub-paragraphs (i) to (iii) of paragraph (f) of subsection (4).

(8) The Commissioners of Inland Revenue shall, as regards any registered housing association, at the request of the Secretary of State, provide him, the Housing Corporation and Scottish Homes with such information as will enable them to determine whether that association is a landlord in respect of which this section will not, by virtue of subsection (4)(d), apply; and where a registered housing association is refused exemption on a claim under section 360(1) of the Income and Corporation Taxes Act 1970 the Commissioners shall forthwith inform the Secretary of State, the Housing Corporation and Scottish Homes of that fact.

(9) Where information has been received by the Housing Corporation or by Scottish Homes under subsection (8) and having regard to that information the Corporation or, as the case may be, Scottish Homes is satisfied that the housing association to which it relates is not a landlord in respect of which this section applies, they shall make an entry to that effect in the

register of housing associations maintained by them under section 3(1) or, as the case may be, 3(1A) of the Housing Associations Act 1985; and they shall cancel that entry where subsequent information so received in relation to that housing association is inconsistent with their being so satisfied.

[4] (10) In this section and the following section—

(*a*) references to occupation of a house include occupation—

(i) in the case of joint tenants, by any one of them;

(ii) by any person occupying the house rent-free;

(iii) as the spouse of the tenant, joint tenant or of any such person;

(iv) as the child, or the spouse of a child, of a tenant or a person occupying the house rent free who has succeeded, directly or indirectly, to the rights of that person in a house occupation of which would be reckonable for the purposes of this section; but only in relation to any period when the child, or as the case may be spouse of the child, is at least 16 years of age; or

(v) as a member of the family of a tenant or a person occupying the house rent free who, not being that person's spouse or child (or child's spouse), has succeeded, directly or indirectly, to such rights as are mentioned in paragraph (iv); but only in relation to any period when the member of the family is at least 16 years of age.

(*b*) for the purposes of determining the period of occupation—

(i), (ii) [Repealed by the Leasehold Reform, Housing and Urban Development Act 1993 (c. 28), s. 157(2) (effective 27th September 1993: S.I. 1993 No. 2163).]

[4] (iii) there shall be added to the period of occupation of a house by a joint tenant any earlier period during which he was at least 16 years of age and occupied the house as a member of the family of the tenant or of one or more of the joint tenants of the house.

(11) The persons providing houses referred to in subsection (2)(*c*) (occupation requirement for exercise of right to purchase) and in section 62(3)(*b*) (calculation of the discount from the market value) are—

(*a*) a regional, islands or district council in Scotland; any local authority in England and Wales or in Northern Ireland; and the statutory predecessors of any such council or authority, or the common good of any such council, or any trust under the control of any such council;

(*b*) the Commission for the New Towns;

(*c*) a development corporation in Scotland, an urban development corporation; and any development corporation established under corresponding legislation in England and Wales or in Northern Ireland; and the statutory predecessors of any such authority;

(*d*) Scottish Homes and the Scottish Special Housing Association;

(*e*) a registered housing association;

(*f*) the Housing Corporation;

(*g*) a housing co-operative within the meaning of section 22 or a housing co-operative within the meaning of section 27B of the Housing Act 1985;

(*h*) the Development Board for Rural Wales;

(*i*) the Northern Ireland Housing Executive or any statutory predecessor;

(*j*) a police authority or the statutory predecessors of any such authority;

(*k*) a fire authority or the statutory predecessors of any such authority;

(*l*) a water authority in Scotland; any water authority constituted under corresponding legislation in England and Wales or in Northern Ireland; and the statutory predecessors of any such authority;

(*m*) the Secretary of State, where the house was at the material time used for the purposes of the Scottish Prison Service or of a prison service for which the Home Office or the Northern Ireland Office have responsibility;

(*n*) the Crown, in relation to accommodation provided in connection with service whether by the tenant or his spouse as a member of the regular armed forces of the Crown;

(*o*) the Secretary of State, where the house was at the material time used for the purposes of a health board constituted under section 2 of the National Health Service (Scotland) Act 1978 or for the purposes of a corresponding board in England and Wales, or for the purposes of the statutory predecessors of any such board; or the Department of Health and Social Services for Northern Ireland, where the house was at the material time used for the purposes of a Health and Personal Services Board in Northern Ireland, or for the purposes of the statutory predecessors of any such board;

(*p*) the Secretary of State, or the Minister of Agriculture, Fisheries and Food, where the house was at the material time used for the purposes of the Forestry Commission;

(*q*) the Secretary of State, where the house was at the material time used for the purposes of a State Hospital provided by him under section 90 of the Mental Health (Scotland) Act 1984 or for the purposes of any hospital provided under corresponding legislation in England and Wales;

(*r*) the Commissioners of Northern Lighthouses;

(*s*) the Trinity House;

(*t*) the Secretary of State, where the house was at the material time used for the purposes of Her Majesty's Coastguard;

(*u*) the United Kingdom Atomic Energy Authority;

(*v*) the Secretary of State, where the house was at the material time used for the purposes of any function transferred to him under section 1(2) of the Defence (Transfer of Functions) Act 1964 or any function relating to defence conferred on him by or under any subsequent enactment;

[5] (*w*) such other person as the Secretary of State may by order made by statutory instrument subject to annulment in pursuance of a resolution of either House of Parliament prescribe.

NOTES

[1] As amended by the Housing (Scotland) Act 1988 (c. 43), Sched. 2, para. 9, Sched. 7, para. 2 and Sched. 8, para. 1.

[2] As amended by the Local Government and Housing Act 1989 (c. 42), Sched. 11, para. 93.

[3] Amended (*prosp.*) by the Housing Act 1988 (c. 50), Sched. 17, para. 79 and Sched. 18 (insertion of references to ss. 50 and S.I. of that Act).

[4] As amended by the Local Government and Housing Act 1989 (c. 42), s. 176(1) and Sched. 12, Pt. II.

[5] See S.I. 1993 No. 1625 (*infra*).

The price

[1] **62.**—[2] (1) Subject to subsection (6A), the price at which a tenant shall be entitled to purchase a house under this Part shall be fixed as at the date of service of the application to purchase by subtracting a discount from the market value of the house.

(2) The market value for the purposes of this section shall be determined by either—

(*a*) a qualified valuer nominated by the landlord and accepted by the tenant; or

(*b*) the district valuer;

as the landlord thinks fit as if the house were available for sale on the open market with vacant possession at the date of service of the application to purchase.

For the purposes of this subsection, no account shall be taken of any element in the market value of the house which reflects an increase in value as a result of work the cost of which would qualify for a reimbursement under section 58.

(3) Subject to subsection (5), the discount for the purposes of subsection (1) shall be—

(*a*) 32 per cent. of the market value of the house except—

(i) where the house is a flat, it shall be 44 per cent. of the market value;

(ii) where the house is one to which section 61(3) applies, it shall be 30 per cent. or if it is a flat 40 per cent. of the market value;

together with

[3] (*b*) an additional one per cent. or, where the house is a flat, two per cent. of the market value for every year beyond two of occupation by the appropriate person, preceding the date of service of the application to purchase, of a house (including accommodation provided as mentioned in section 61(11)(*n*)) or of a succession of houses provided by any persons mentioned in section 61(11),

up to a maximum discount of 60 per cent., or where the house is a flat, 70 per cent. of the market value.

[4] (3A) There shall be deducted from the discount an amount equal to any previous discount, or the aggregate of any previous discounts, received by the appropriate person on any previous purchase of a house by any of these persons from a landlord who is a person specified in subsection (11) of section 61 or prescribed in an order made under that subsection, reduced by any amount of such previous discount recovered by such a landlord.

[5] (4) For the purposes of subsection (3)—

(*a*) the "appropriate person" is whoever of—

(i) the tenant; or

(ii) the tenant's spouse if living with him at the date of service of the application to purchase; or

(iii) a deceased spouse if living with the tenant at the time of death; or

(iv) any joint tenant who is a joint purchaser of the house,

has the longer or longest such occupation; and

(*b*) where the house was provided by a housing association which, at any time while the house was so provided was not a registered housing association, the association shall, if it became a registered housing association at any later time, be deemed to have been a registered housing association at all times since it first provided the house,

and, for the purposes of subsection (3A), the "appropriate person" is any of the persons mentioned in sub-paragraphs (i) to (iv) of paragraph (*a*).

(5) The Secretary of State may by order made with the consent of the Treasury provide that, in such cases as may be specified in the order—

(*a*) the minimum percentage discount,

(*b*) the percentage increase for each complete year of the qualifying period after the first two, or

(*c*) the maximum percentage discount,

shall be such percentage, higher than that specified in subsection (3), as may be specified in the order.

(6) An order under subsection (5)—

(*a*) may make different provision with respect to different cases or descriptions of case,

(*b*) may contain such incidental, supplementary or transitional provisions as appear to the Secretary of State to be necessary or expedient, and

(*c*) shall be made by statutory instrument and shall not be made unless a draft of it has been laid before and approved by resolution of each House of Parliament.

(6A) Except where the Secretary of State so determines, the discount for the purpose of subsection (1) shall not reduce the price below the amount which, in accordance with a determination made by him, is to be taken as representing so much of the costs incurred in respect of the house as, in accordance with the determination, is to be treated as—

(*a*) incurred in the period commencing with the beginning of the financial year of the landlord which was current five years prior to the date of service of the application to purchase the house or such other period as the Secretary of State may by order provide; and

(*b*) relevant for the purposes of this subsection,

and, if the price before discount is below that amount, there shall be no discount.

(6B) An order under subsection (6A) shall be made by statutory instrument subject to annulment in pursuance of a resolution of either House of Parliament and may make different provision in relation to different cases or circumstances or different areas.

(10) Where at the date of service of an offer to sell under section 63 any of the costs referred to in subsection (6A) are not known, the landlord shall make an estimate of such unknown costs for the purposes of that subsection.

NOTES

[1] As amended by the Housing (Scotland) Act 1988 (c. 43), s. 65(1)–(4), Sched. 8, para. 10 and Sched. 10.

[2] As amended by the Local Government and Housing Act 1989 (c. 42), Sched. 11, para. 94.

[3] As amended by the Leasehold Reform, Housing and Urban Development Act 1993 (c. 28), s. 157(3) (effective 27th September 1993: S.I. 1993 No. 2163).

[4] Inserted by the Leasehold Reform, Housing and Urban Development Act 1993 (c. 28), s. 157(3) (effective 27th September 1993: S.I. 1993 No. 2163).

[5] As amended by the Leasehold Reform, Housing and Urban Development Act 1993 (c. 28), s. 157(4) (effective 27th September 1993: S.I. 1993 No. 2163).

Eligibility for rent to loan scheme

[1] **62A.**—(1) Subject to subsection (2), a tenant who has the right under section 61 to purchase a house may exercise the right by way of the rent to loan scheme.

(2) Subsection (1) does not apply—

(*a*) to the tenant of a house which is designated as defective under Part XIV; or

(*b*) to a tenant—

(i) in respect of whom a determination has been made that he is entitled to housing benefit in respect of any part of the relevant period; or

(ii) by or on behalf of whom a claim for housing benefit has been made (or is treated as having been made) and has not been determined or withdrawn.

(3) In subsection (2), "the relevant period" means the period—

(*a*) beginning 12 months before the date of the application to purchase the house; and

(*b*) ending on the day when the contract of sale of the house is constituted under section 66(2).

NOTE

[1] Inserted by the Leasehold Reform, Housing and Urban Development Act 1993 (c. 28), s. 141 (effective 27th September 1993: S.I. 1993 No. 2163).

Procedure

Application to purchase and offer to sell

63.—(1) A tenant who seeks to exercise a right to purchase a house under section 61 shall serve on the landlord a notice (referred to in this Part as an "application to purchase") which shall be in such form as the

Secretary of State shall by order made by statutory instrument prescribe, and shall contain—

(*a*) notice that the tenant seeks to exercise the right to purchase;

(*b*) a statement of any period of occupancy of a house on which the tenant intends to rely for the purposes of sections 61 and 62; and

(*c*) the name of any joint purchaser within the meaning of section 61(6); and

[1] (*d*) in the case of a tenant who is entitled to purchase the house by way of the rent to loan scheme, a statement whether he wishes to proceed so to purchase the house.

(2) Where an application to purchase is served on a landlord, and the landlord does not serve a notice of refusal under sections 68 to 70 it shall, within two months after service of the application to purchase serve on the tenant a notice (referred to in this Part as an "offer to sell") containing—

(*a*) the market value of the house determined under section 62(2);

(*b*) the discount calculated under section 62(3);

(*c*) the price fixed under section 62(1);

[1] (*cc*) where the application to purchase contains a statement under subsection (1)(*d*) that the applicant wishes to proceed by way of the rent to loan scheme and the statement has not been withdrawn, the minimum amount of the initial capital payment, a statement that the applicant, if so minded, may make an initial capital payment greater than the minimum and a description of the deferred financial commitment including—

(i) the amount of the deferred financial commitment calculated as if due to be paid as at the date of the offer to sell;

(ii) an explanation of why and how the amount of the deferred financial commitment when payable under section 73C(3)(*a*) can vary from its amount as calculated under sub-paragraph (i); and

(iii) the procedure for paying the deferred financial commitment;

(*d*) any conditions which the landlord intends to impose under section 64; and

(*e*) an offer to sell the house to the tenant and any joint purchaser named in the application to purchase at the price referred to in paragraph (*c*) and under the conditions referred to in paragraph (*d*).

[1] (3) Where, in response to an offer to sell containing the matters referred to in paragraph (*cc*) of subsection (2), an applicant has informed a landlord in writing of his intention to make an initial capital payment of an amount greater than the minimum, the landlord shall, before the end of the period specified in subsection (2) or, if later, the expiry of one month from the date when the landlord was so informed of the tenant's intention, serve an amended offer to sell in which the calculation of the deferred financial commitment is revised accordingly.

NOTE

[1] Inserted by the Leasehold Reform, Housing and Urban Development Act 1993 (c. 28), s. 143(2) (effective 27th September 1993: S.I. 1993 No. 2163).

Conditions of sale

64.—(1) Subject to section 75, an offer to sell under section 63(2) shall contain such conditions as are reasonable, provided that—

(*a*) the conditions shall have the effect of ensuring that the tenant has as full enjoyment and use of the house as owner as he has had as tenant;

(*b*) the conditions shall secure to the tenant such additional rights as are necessary for his reasonable enjoyment and use of the house as owner (including, without prejudice to the foregoing generality, common rights in any part of the building of which the house forms part) and shall impose on the tenant any necessary duties relative to rights so secured; and (*c*) the conditions shall include such terms as are necessary to entitle the tenant to receive a good and marketable title to the house.

(2) A condition which imposes a new charge or an increase of an existing charge for the provision of a service in relation to the house shall provide for the charge to be in reasonable proportion to the cost to the landlord of providing the service.

(3) No condition shall be imposed under this section which has the effect of requiring the tenant to pay any expenses of the landlord.

(4) Subject to subsection (6), no condition shall be imposed under this section which has the effect of requiring the tenant or any of his successors in title to offer to the landlord, or to any other person, an option to purchase the house in advance of its sale to a third party, except in the case of

[THE NEXT PAGE IS J 269]

a house which has facilities which are substantially different from those of an ordinary house and which has been designed or adapted for occupation by a person of pensionable age or disabled person whose special needs require accommodation of the kind provided by the house.

(5) Where an option to purchase permitted under subsection (4) is exercised, the price to be paid for the house shall be determined by the district valuer who shall have regard to the market value of the house at the time of the purchase and to any amount due to the landlord under section 72 (recovery of discount on early re-sale).

(6) Subsection (4) shall not apply to houses in an area which is designated a rural area by the islands or district council within whose area it is situated where the Secretary of State, on the application of the islands or district council concerned, makes an order, which shall be made by statutory instrument subject to annulment in pursuance of a resolution of either House of Parliament, to that effect.

[1] (7) An order under subsection (6) may be made where—

(*a*) within the said rural area more than one-third of all relevant houses have been sold whether under this Part or otherwise; and

(*b*) the Secretary of State is satisfied that an unreasonable proportion of the houses sold consists of houses which have been resold and are not—

(i) being used as the only or principal homes of the owners; or

(ii) subject to regulated tenancies within the meaning of section 8 of the Rent (Scotland) Act 1984 or assured tenancies for the purposes of Part II of the Housing (Scotland) Act 1988.

(8) For the purposes of subsection (7)(*a*), a "relevant house" is one of which—

(*a*) at 3rd October 1980, the council concerned, or

(*b*) at 7th January 1987 a registered housing association,

is landlord.

(9) A condition imposed by virtue of subsection (6) shall not have effect in relation to any house for more than 10 years from the date of its conveyance to a tenant in pursuance of his right to purchase under this Part and subsection (5) shall apply to any option to purchase exercised under such a condition.

NOTE

[1] As amended by the Housing (Scotland) Act 1988 (c. 43), Sched. 9, para. 11.

Variation of conditions

65.—(1) Where an offer to sell is served on a tenant and he wishes to exercise his right to purchase, but—

(*a*) he considers that a condition contained in the offer to sell is unreasonable; or

(*b*) he wishes to have a new condition included in it; or

(*c*) he has not previously notified the landlord of his intention to exercise that right together with a joint purchaser, but now wishes to do so; or

(*d*) he has previously notified the landlord of his intention to exercise that right together with any joint purchaser but now wishes to exercise the right without that joint purchaser,

he may request the landlord to strike out or vary the condition, or to include the new condition, or to make the offer to sell to the tenant and the joint purchaser, or to withdraw the offer to sell in respect of the joint purchaser, as the case may be, by serving on the landlord within one month after service of the offer to sell a notice in writing setting out his request; and if the landlord agrees, it shall accordingly serve an amended offer to sell on the tenant within one month of service of the notice setting out the request.

(2) A tenant who is aggrieved by the refusal of the landlord to agree to strike out or vary a condition, or to include a new condition or to make the offer to sell to the tenant and the joint purchaser, or to withdraw the offer to sell in respect of any joint purchaser under subsection (1), or by his failure timeously to serve an amended offer to sell under the said subsection, may, within one month or, with the consent of the landlord given in writing before the expiry of the said period of one month, within two months of the refusal or failure, refer the matter to the Lands Tribunal for determination.

(3) In proceedings under subsection (2), the Lands Tribunal may, as it thinks fit, uphold the condition or strike it out or vary it, or insert the new condition or order that the offer to sell be made to the tenant and the joint purchaser, or order that the offer to sell be withdrawn in respect of any joint purchaser, and where its determination results in a variation of the terms of the offer to sell, it shall order the landlord to serve on the tenant an amended offer to sell accordingly within two months thereafter.

Notice of acceptance

66.—(1) Where an offer to sell is served on a tenant and he wishes to exercise his right to purchase and—

(*a*) he does not dispute the terms of the offer to sell by timeously serving a notice setting out a request under section 65(1) or by referring the matter to the Lands Tribunal under subsection (1)(*d*) of section 71; or

(*b*) any such dispute has been resolved;

the tenant shall, subject to section 67(1), serve a notice of acceptance on the landlord within two months of whichever is the latest of—

(i) the service on him of the offer to sell;

(ii) the service on him of an amended offer to sell (or if there is more than one, of the latest amended offer to sell);

(iii) a determination by the Lands Tribunal for Scotland under section 65(3) which does not require service of an amended offer to sell;

(iv) a finding or determination of the Lands Tribunal in a matter referred to it under section 71(1)(*d*) where no order is made under section 71(2)(*b*);

(v) the service of an offer to sell on him by virtue of subsection (2)(*b*) of section 71;

(vi) where a loan application under subsection (2)(*a*)(i) of section 216 (loans) has been served on the landlord, the service of a relative offer or refusal of loan; or

(vii) where section 216(7) (loans) is invoked, the decision of the court.

(2) Where an offer to sell (or an amended offer to sell) has been served on the tenant and a relative notice of acceptance has been duly served on the landlord, a contract of sale of the house shall be constituted between the landlord and the tenant on the terms contained in the offer (or amended offer) to sell.

Abatement of purchase price on landlord's failure before contract of sale

[1] **66A.**—(1) Where a tenant who seeks to exercise a right to purchase a house under section 61 has served an application to purchase on the landlord and the landlord—

(*a*) not having served a notice of refusal, has failed to serve an offer to sell on the tenant within two months of the application or, where an amended offer to sell falls to be served on the tenant under subsection (3) of section 63, has failed to do so within the time limit specified in that subsection;

(*b*) having agreed to serve an amended offer to sell on the tenant in response to a request under section 65(1), has failed to do so within one month of the request;

(*c*) following an order by the Lands Tribunal to serve an amended offer to sell on the tenant under section 65(3), has failed to do so within two months of the date of the order;

(*d*) following a finding by the Lands Tribunal under section 68(4), has failed to serve an offer to sell within two months of the date of the finding; or

(*e*) following an order by the Lands Tribunal under section 71(2)(*b*), has failed to serve an offer or amended offer to sell within the time specified in the order,

the tenant may serve on the landlord a notice in writing requiring the landlord to serve on him, within one month of the date of the notice, the offer to sell or (as the case may be) the amended offer to sell which the landlord has failed to serve.

(2) Where the landlord fails to serve the offer to sell or the amended offer to sell within one month of the date of the notice in writing under subsection (1), the price fixed under section 62 shall be reduced by the amount of rent paid by the tenant during the period commencing with the date on which the one month period expired and ending with the date on which the offer is served.

NOTE

[1] Inserted by the Leasehold Reform, Housing and Urban Development Act 1993 (c. 28), s. 144 (effective 27th September 1993: S.I. 1993 No. 2163).

Abatement of purchase price on landlord's failure after contract of sale

[1] **66B.**—(1) Where the landlord has failed and continues to fail to deliver a good and marketable title to the tenant in accordance with the contract of sale, the tenant may at any time serve on the landlord a notice (the "initial notice of delay") setting out the landlord's failure and specifying—

(*a*) the most recent action of which the tenant is aware which has been taken by the landlord in fulfilment of his duties under this Part;

(*b*) a period (the "response period"), of not less than one month beginning on the date of service of the notice, within which the service by the landlord of a counter notice under subsection (2) will have the effect of cancelling the initial notice of delay.

(2) If there is no action under this Part which, at the beginning of the response period it was for the landlord to take in order to grant a good and marketable title to the tenant in implementation of the contract of sale, the landlord may serve on the tenant a counter notice either during or after the responsse period.

(3) At any time when—

(*a*) the response period specified in the initial notice of delay has expired; and

(*b*) the landlord has not served a counter notice under subsection (2),

the tenant may serve on the landlord a notice (the "operative notice of delay") that this subsection shall apply to the price fixed under section 62; and thereupon the price fixed under section 62 shall be reduced by the amount of rent paid by the tenant during the period commencing with the date of service of the operative notice of delay and ending with whichever is the earlier of the following dates—

(i) the date of service by the landlord of a counter notice; or

(ii) the date of delivery by the landlord of a good and marketable title in implementation of the contract of sale.

(4) Where the landlord has served a counter notice under subsection (2) the tenant (together with any joint purchaser) may, by serving on the clerk to the Lands Tribunal a copy of the initial notice of delay and of the landlord's counter notice together with a request for the matter to be so referred, refer the matter to the Tribunal for its consideration under subsection (5).

(5) Where the matter has been so referred to the Lands Tribunal it shall consider whether or not in its opinion action which would have enabled a

good and marketable title to be delivered in implementation of the contract of sale could have been taken by the landlord and shall find accordingly.

(6) Where the Lands Tribunal finds that action could have been taken by the landlord the tenant shall be entitled to serve an operative notice of delay as if the landlord had not served a counter notice and in that event the commencement date for the purposes of subsection (3) shall be the date on which an operative notice of delay could first have been served if no counter notice had been served.

NOTE

[1] Inserted by the Leasehold Reform, Housing and Urban Development Act 1993 (c. 28), s. 144 (effective 27th September 1993: S.I. 1993 No. 2163).

Provisions relating to sections 66A and 66B

[1] **66C.**—(1) Where there is more than one period in respect of which the price fixed under section 62 can be reduced under section 66A(2) or 66B(3), the periods may be aggregated and the price reduced by the total amount of the rent.

(2) If the period in respect of which the price fixed can be so reduced is, of if the periods aggregated under subsection (1) together amount to, more than 12 months, the amount by which the price fixed under section 62 would, apart from this subsection, fall to be reduced shall be increased by 50 per cent. or such other percentage as the Secretary of State may by order made by statutory instrument and subject to annulment in pursuance of a resolution of either House of Parliament provide.

NOTE

[1] Inserted by the Leasehold Reform, Housing and Urban Development Act 1993 (c. 28), s. 144 (effective 27th September 1993: S.I. 1993 No. 2163).

Fixed price option

67.—(1) Where an offer to sell (or an amended offer to sell) is served on a tenant, but he is unable by reason of the application of regulations made under section 216(3) (loans) to obtain a loan of the amount for which he has applied, he may, within two months of service on him of an offer of loan, or (as the case may be) of the date of a declarator by the sheriff under section 216(7) (loans), whichever is the later, serve on the landlord a notice to the effect that he wishes to have a fixed price option, which notice shall be accompanied by a payment to the landlord of £100, and in that event he shall be entitled to serve a notice of acceptance on the landlord at any time within two years of the service of the application to purchase:

Provided that where, as regards the house, the tenant has served a loan application in accordance with subsection (2)(*a*)(ii) of section 216 (loans), he shall be entitled (even if the said period of two years has expired) to serve a notice of acceptance on the landlord within two months of whichever is the later of—

(*a*) the service of a relative offer, or refusal, of loan; or

(*b*) where section 216(7) is invoked, the decision of the court.

(2) The payment of £100 mentioned in subsection (1) shall be recoverable—

(*a*) by the tenant, when he purchases the house in accordance with that subsection or, if he does not, at the expiry of the period of two years mentioned therein;

(*b*) by the tenant, when the landlord recovers possession of the house under subsection (3); or

(*c*) by his personal representatives, if he dies without purchasing the house in accordance with that subsection.

(3) The existence of a fixed price option under subsection (1) shall not prevent the landlord from recovering possession of the property in any manner which may be lawful, and in that event the option shall be terminated.

[1] (4) This section does not apply where the tenant is exercising his right to purchase under section 61 by way of the rent to loan scheme.

NOTE

[1] Inserted by the Leasehold Reform, Housing and Urban Development Act 1993 (c. 28), s. 143 (effective 27th September 1993: S.I. 1993 No. 2163).

Refusal of applications

68.—(1) Where a landlord on which an application to purchase has been served disputes the tenant's right to purchase a house under section 61, it shall by notice (referred to in this Part as a "notice of refusal") served within one month after service of the application to purchase—

(*a*) refuse the application; or

(*b*) offer to sell the house to the tenant under section 14 or under any other power which the landlord has to sell the house.

(2) Where a landlord on which an application to purchase has been served, after reasonable enquiry (which shall include reasonable opportunity for the tenant to amend his application), is of the opinion that information contained in the application is incorrect in a material respect it shall issue a notice of refusal within two months of the application to purchase.

(3) A notice of refusal shall specify the grounds on which the landlord disputes the tenant's right to purchase or, as the case may be, the accuracy of the information.

(4) Where a landlord serves a notice of refusal on a tenant under this section, the tenant may within one month thereafter apply to the Lands Tribunal for a finding that he has a right to purchase the house under section 61 on such terms as it may determine.

Houses provided for special purposes

Secretary of State's power to authorise refusal to sell certain houses provided for persons of pensionable age

69.—(1) This section applies to a house which has facilities which are substantially different from those of an ordinary house and which has been designed or adapted for occupation by a person of pensionable age whose special needs require accommodation of the kind provided by the house.

[1] (1A) This section applies only to houses first let on a secure tenancy before 1st January 1990.

(2) Where an application to purchase a house is served on a landlord and it appears to the landlord that—

(*a*) the house is one to which this section applies; and

(*b*) the tenant would, apart from this section, have a right under section 61 to purchase the house,

the landlord may, within one month after service of the application to purchase, instead of serving an offer to sell on the tenant, make an application to the Secretary of State under this section.

(3) An application under subsection (2) shall specify the facilities and features of design or adaptation which in the view of the landlord cause the house to be a house to which this section applies.

(4) Where the Secretary of State has received an application under this section and it appears to him that the house concerned is one to which this section applies, he shall authorise the landlord to serve on the tenant a notice of refusal under this section, which shall be served as soon as is practicable after the authority is given and in any event within one month thereafter.

(5) A notice of refusal served under subsection (4) shall specify the facilities and features specified for the purposes of subsection (3) and that the Secretary of State's authority for service of the said notice has been given.

(6) Where the Secretary of State refuses an application made under subsection (2), the landlord shall serve on the tenant an offer to sell under section 63(2)—

(*a*) within the period mentioned in that section; or

(*b*) where the unexpired portion of that period is less than one month or there is not an unexpired portion of that period within one month of the Secretary of State's refusal.

NOTE

[1] Inserted by the Local Government and Housing Act 1989 (c. 42), s. 177, with effect from 16th January 1990.

Power to refuse to sell certain houses required for educational purposes

70.—(1) Where an application to purchase a house is served on an islands council as landlord and—

(*a*) the house is—

(i) held by the council for the purposes of its functions as education authority; and

(ii) required for the accommodation of a person who is or will be employed by the council for those purposes;

(*b*) the council is not likely to be able reasonably to provide other suitable accommodation for the person mentioned in paragraph (*a*)(ii); and

(*c*) the tenant would, apart from this section, have a right under section 61 to purchase the house,

the landlord may, within one month of service of the application to purchase, serve a notice of refusal on the tenant.

(2) A refusal by the landlord under subsection (1) shall contain sufficient information to demonstrate that the conditions mentioned in paragraphs (*a*) and (*b*) of that subsection are fulfilled in relation to the house.

Lands Tribunal

Reference to Lands Tribunal

71.—(1) Where—

[1] (*a*) a landlord who has been duly served with an application to purchase fails to issue timeously either an offer or amended offer to sell (even if only such offer or amended offer to sell as is mentioned in paragraph (*d*)) or a notice of refusal; or

(*b*) the Lands Tribunal has made a determination under section 65(3) (variation of terms of offer to sell) and the landlord has failed to issue an amended offer to sell within two months thereafter; or

(*c*) the Lands Tribunal has made a finding under section 68(4) (refusal of right to purchase) or has made an order under subsection (2)(*b*) of this section and the landlord has not duly progressed the application to purchase in accordance with that finding or, as the case may be, order, within two months thereafter; or

[1] (*d*) a landlord has served an offer or amended offer to sell whose contents do not conform with the requirements of paragraphs (*a*) to (*e*) of section 63(2) (or where such contents were not obtained in accordance with the provisions specified in those paragraphs), and, in the case of an amended offer, they do not conform with the requirements of section 63(3),

the tenant (together with any joint purchaser) may refer the matter to the Lands Tribunal by serving on the clerk to that body a copy of any notice served and of any finding or determination made under this Part, together with a statement of his grievance.

(2) Where a matter has been referred to the Lands Tribunal under subsection (1), the Tribunal shall consider whether in its opinion—

(*a*) any of paragraphs (*a*) to (*c*) of that subsection apply, and if it so finds it may—

(i) give any consent, exercise any discretion, or do anything which the landlord may give, exercise or do under or for the purposes of sections 61 to 84; and

(ii) issue such notices and undertake such other steps as may be required to complete the procedure provided for in sections 63 and 65 to 67;

and any consent given, any discretion exercised or anything done under the foregoing provisions of this subsection shall have effect as if it had been duly given, exercised or done by the landlord; or

[1] (*b*) paragraph (*d*) of that subsection applies, and if it so finds it may order the landlord to serve on the tenant an offer or amended offer to sell, in proper form, under section 63(2) and, in the case of an amended offer, under section 63(3) within such time (not exceeding two months) as it may specify.

(3) Nothing in this section shall affect the operation of the provisions of any other enactment relating to the enforcement of a statutory duty whether under that enactment or otherwise.

NOTE

[1] As amended by the Leasehold Reform, Housing and Urban Development Act 1993 (c. 28), s. 143(4) (effective 27th September 1993: S.I. 1993 No. 2163).

Recoverability of discount

Recovery of discount on early re-sale

72.—(1) A person who has purchased a house in exercise of a right to purchase under section 61, or any of his successors in title, who sells or otherwise disposes of the house (except as provided for in section 73) before the expiry of three years from the date of service of a notice of acceptance by the tenant under section 66 shall be liable to repay to the landlord, in accordance with subsection (3), a proportion of the difference between the market value determined, in respect of the house, under section 62(2) and the price at which the house was so purchased.

[1] (1A) Where a tenant has served on the landlord a notice under section 66A(1), the commencement of the period of 3 years referred to in subsection (1) shall be backdated by a period equal to the time (or, where section 66C(1) applies, the aggregate of the times) during which, by virtue of section 66A(2), any payment of rent falls to be taken into account.

(2) Subsection (1) applies to the disposal of part of a house except in a case where—

(*a*) it is a disposal by one of the parties to the original sale to one of the other parties; or

(*b*) the remainder of the house continues to be the only or principal home of the person disposing of the part.

(3) The proportion of the difference which shall be paid to the landlord shall be—

(*a*) 100 per cent. where the disposal occurs within the first year after the date of service of notice,

(*b*) 66 per cent. where it occurs in the second such year, and

(*c*) 33 per cent. where it occurs in the third such year.

(4) Where as regards a house or part of a house there is, within the period mentioned in subsection (1), more than one disposal to which that subsection would (apart from the provisions of this subsection) apply, that subsection shall apply only in relation to the first such disposal of the house, or part.

(5) Where a landlord secures the liability to make a repayment under subsection (1) the security shall, notwithstanding section 13 of the Conveyancing and Feudal Reform (Scotland) Act 1970, have priority immediately after—

(*a*) any standard security granted in security of a loan either—

(i) for the purchase of the house, or

(ii) for the improvement of the house, and any interest present or future due thereon (including any such interest which has accrued or may accrue) and any expenses or outlays (including interest thereon) which may be, or may have been, reasonably incurred in the exercise of any power conferred on the lender by the deed expressing the said standard security; and

(*b*) if the landlord consents, a standard security over the house granted in security of any other loan, and in relation thereto any such interest, expenses or outlays as aforesaid.

(6) For the avoidance of doubt, paragraph (*a*) of subsection (5) applies to a standard security granted in security both for the purpose mentioned in sub-paragraph (i) and for that mentioned in sub-paragraph (ii) as it applies to a standard security so granted for only one of those purposes.

(7) The liability to make a repayment under subsection (1) shall not be imposed as a real burden in a disposition of any interest in the house.

NOTE

[1] Inserted by the Leasehold Reform, Housing and Urban Development Act 1993 (c. 28), s. 145 (effective 27th September 1993: S.I. 1993 No. 2163).

Cases where discount etc. is not recoverable

73.—(1) There shall be no liability to make a repayment under section 72(1) where the disposal is made—

(*a*) by the executor of the deceased owner acting in that capacity; or

(*b*) as a result of a compulsory purchase order; or

(*c*) in the circumstances specified in subsection (2).

(2) The circumstances mentioned in subsection (1)(*c*) are that the disposal—

(*a*) is to a member of the owner's family who has lived with him for a period of 12 months before the disposal; and

(*b*) is for no consideration:

Provided that, if the disponee disposes of the house before the expiry of the three year period mentioned in section 72(1), the provisions of that section will apply to him as if this was the first disposal and he was the original purchaser.

[1] *Rent to loan scheme*

NOTE

[1] ss. 73A–73D inserted by the Leasehold Reform, Housing and Urban Development Act 1993 (c. 28), s. 142 (effective 27th September 1993: S.I. 1993 No. 2163).

The rent to loan scheme

73A.—(1) Under the rent to loan scheme, the price fixed for a house under section 62 shall be payable in two elements, viz—

(*a*) the initial capital payment; and

(*b*) the deferred financial commitment.

(2) In the application of subsection (3) of section 62 to the price of a house being purchased by way of the rent to loan scheme, each of the percentage figures specified in that subsection shall be reduced by 15 or such other number as may, with the consent of the Treasury, be prescribed.

(3) The conditions which are, under section 64, to be contained in an offer to sell under section 63(2) shall, in the case of a house which is to be purchased by way of the rent to loan scheme, include a condition providing that the tenant will be entitled to ownership of the house in exchange for the initial capital payment.

(4) The deferred financial commitment shall be secured by a standard security over the house.

The initial capital payment

73B.—(1) The initial capital payment in respect of a house is a sum determined by the tenant, being of an amount not less than the maximum amount of loan which could be repaid at the statutory rate of interest over the loan period by weekly payments each equal to the adjusted weekly rent for the house.

(2) In this section—

(*a*) the "statutory rate of interest" is the rate of interest which would be charged under section 219(4) on the application date by the local authority for the area in which the house is situated;

(*b*) the "loan period" is the period beginning on the application date and ending on whichever of the following is the earlier—

(i) the expiry of a period of 25 years starting on that date; and

(ii) the date when the applicant will (if he survives) reach pensionable age within the meaning of the Social Security Act 1975 or, in the case of joint applicants, the date when the one who will (if they both or all survive) reach pensionable age later than the other or the others reaches that age,

but if the period arrived at under sub-paragraph (ii) is less than 10 years, then the loan period shall be a period of 10 years beginning on the application date;

(*c*) the "adjusted weekly rent" is an amount equal to 90 per cent. of the weekly rent for the house payable as at the application date; and

(*d*) the "application date" is the date of the application to purchase the house.

The deferred financial commitment

73C.—(1) The deferred financial commitment in respect of a house is the sum arrived at by—

(*a*) finding the difference between—

(i) the price which was fixed for the purchase of the house under section 62(1); and

(ii) the initial capital payment;

(*b*) expressing that difference as a percentage of the market value which was determined under section 62(2) for the purpose of fixing the price of the house;

(*c*) reducing that percentage figure by—

(i) seven or such other number as may, with the consent of the Treasury, be prescribed; and

(ii) in a case where payment has been made under subsection (4), the percentage figure which the amount so paid represents in relation to the market value mentioned in paragraph (*b*);

(*d*) finding the sum which is equal to that resultant percentage of the resale value of the house; and

(*e*) in a case to which subsection (5) of section 73D applies, adding to that sum the amount which falls to be added under subsection (6) of that section.

(2) No interest shall accrue on the deferred financial commitment.

(3) Payment of the deferred financial commitment—

(*a*) shall, subject to section 73D, be made to the original seller of the house—

(i) on the sale or other disposal of the house by the rent to loan purchaser; or

(ii) if the rent to loan purchaser does not sell or dispose of it, on his death; and

(*b*) may be so made in whole at any earlier time.

(4) Subject to section 73D(3), payment may be made at any time for the purpose of reducing the deferred financial commitment in accordance with subsection (1)(*c*)(ii).

(5) Subject to subsection (6), payment of the deferred financial commitment shall be made as soon as may be after the destruction of or damage to the house by fire, tempest, flood or any other cause against the risk of which it is normal practice to insure.

(6) Subsection (5) does not apply where, following the destruction of or damage to a house, it is rebuilt or reinstated.

(7) A standard security granted in security of the deferred financial commitment shall, notwithstanding section 13 of the Conveyancing and Feudal Reform (Scotland) Act 1970, have priority before any standard security securing the liability to make a repayment under section 72(1) but immediately after—

(*a*) any standard security granted in security of any amount advanced by a recognised lending institution—

(i) to enable payment of the initial capital payment or payment under subsection (4);

(ii) for the improvement of the house; or

(iii) for any combination of those purposes,

(together with any interest, expenses and outlays payable thereunder); and

(*b*) with the consent of the original seller, a standard security over the house granted in security of any other loan (together with any such interest, expenses and outlays).

In this subsection—

a "recognised lending institution" is one which is recognised for the purposes of section 222;

references to interest payable under a standard security are references both to present and future interest payable thereunder including interest which has accrued or may accrue; and

references to expenses and outlays include interest thereon.

(8) In this section—

(*a*) the "resale value" of a house is, subject to subsections (9) and (10)—

(i) where it is being sold by the rent to loan purchaser on the open market with vacant possession and a good and marketable title, the price at which it is being so sold;

(ii) where the rent to loan purchaser has died not having sold or disposed of it, its value for the purpose of confirmation to his estate;

(iii) in any other case, such amount as is agreed for the purposes of this sub-paragraph between the rent to loan purchaser and the original seller or, failing such agreement, such amount as is determined for those purposes by an independent valuer as the value of the house, assuming it to be available for sale in the circumstances specified in sub-paragraph (i) on a date as near as may be to the date when payment of the deferred financial commitment is to be made; and

(*b*) the "original seller" of a house is the body which, as the landlord of the house, sold it in pursuance of this Part to the rent to loan purchaser or, where another body has succeeded to the rights and duties of that body in relation to the house, that other body.

(9) In arriving at the resale value of a house no account shall be taken of—

(*a*) anything done by the rent to loan purchaser (or any predecessor of his as secure tenant of the house) which has added to the value of the house; or

(*b*) any failure by him (but not by any such predecessor) to keep the house in good repair (including decorative repair).

(10) For the purposes of agreeing or determining the amount of the resale value of a house under subsection (8)(*a*)(iii) in a case where it has been destroyed or damaged by a cause referred to in subsection (5), that value shall be taken as including the value of any sums paid or falling to be paid to the rent to loan purchaser under a policy insuring against the risk of the cause of destruction of or damage to the house except to the extent that

they have been or fall to be applied in meeting the cost of any rebuilding or reinstatement which has been carried out.

Deferred financial commitment; further provisions

73D.—(1) This subsection applies where—

(*a*) the person who has purchased a house by way of the rent to loan scheme sells or otherwise disposes of it to his spouse or any other person with whom he is living as if they were husband and wife and the house is, at the time of the sale or disposal, the spouse's or other person's only or principal home;

(*b*) the person who has so purchased the house dies and there succeeds to the house, by operation of the law of succession, a person for whom or persons for whom or for one of more of whom the house was, for the period of 12 months immediately preceding the death, his or their only or principal home; or

(*c*) in the case of a house which was so purchased jointly, one of the joint purchasers dies and, at the time of the death, the house was the only or principal home of the survivor or the survivors or one or more of them.

(2) Where subsection (1) applies—

(*a*) the deferred financial commitment shall not be payable on the sale, disposal or death referred to in paragraph (*a*) of subsection (3) of section 73C but on the sale or other disposal of the house by the person or persons acquiring it, succeeding to it or surviving in the circumstances whereby subsection (1) applies or on the death of such person or of the last of them for whom the house was, both at the time of such acquisition, succession or survival and at the time of his death, his only or principal home; and

(*b*) paragraph (*b*) of the said subsection (3) shall have effect accordingly.

(3) A payment made under section 73C(4) shall not—

(*a*) be less than £1500 or such other sum as may, with the consent of the Treasury, be prescribed;

(*b*) exceed the statutory maximum; or

(*c*) be made within the period of one year after any previous such payment in respect of the same transaction.

(4) In subsection (3)(*b*), the "statutory maximum" is the amount by which the initial capital payment would be required to be augmented so as to produce, by operation of the calculations specified in paragraphs (*a*) to (*c*) of section 73C(1), a resultant percentage of 7.5 per cent. or such other percentage as may, with the consent of the Treasury, be prescribed.

(5) This subsection applies where—

(*a*) the subtraction of discount for the purposes of section 62(1) falls to be limited or excluded by operation of subsection (6A) of that section; and

(*b*) any part of those costs which, in accordance with that subsection, are to be represented by an amount arrived at under that subsection, was incurred in the period commencing with the beginning of the financial year of the landlord which was current five years prior to the date of payment in whole of the deferred financial commitment.

(6) Where subsection (5) applies, the amount which is, under section 73C(1)(*e*), to be added is an amount equal to the difference between the aggregate of the amounts mentioned in paragraph (*a*) and the amount mentioned in paragraph (*b*)—

(*a*) the initial capital payment and the deferred financial commitment (including any payment under section 73C(4)) which would be payable apart from this subsection;

(*b*) the price which would have been payable under section 62 had the purchase of the house proceeded otherwise than by way of the rent to loan scheme.

Duties of landlords

74. It shall be the duty of every landlord of a house to which sections 61 to 84 and section 216 apply to make provision for the progression of applications under those sections in such manner as may be necessary to enable any tenant who wishes to exercise his rights under this Part to do so, and to comply with any regulations which may be made by statutory instrument by the Secretary of State in that regard.

Agreements affecting right to purchase

75.—(1) Subject to sections 61(1), 67(1) and 72(1)—

(*a*) no person exercising or seeking to exercise a right to purchase under section 61(1) shall be obliged, notwithstanding any agreement to the contrary, to make any payment to or lodge any deposit with the landlord which he would not have been obliged to make, or as the case may be lodge, had he not exercised (or sought to exercise) the right to purchase;

(*b*) a landlord mentioned in section 61(2)(*a*)(i) or (ii) is required neither to enter into, nor to induce (or seek to induce) any person to enter into, such agreement as is mentioned in paragraph (*a*), or into any agreement which purports to restrict that person's rights under this Part.

(2) Paragraph (*a*) of subsection (1) does not apply to the expenses in any court proceedings.

Duty of local authority landlord to provide information about right to buy

[1] **75A.**—(1) A landlord which is one of those mentioned in section 61(2)(*a*)(i) or (ii) shall supply each of its secure tenants at least once every year with information about his right to purchase his house under this Part.

(2) The information supplied under subsection (1) shall be in such form as the landlord considers best suited to explain in simple terms and so far as it considers appropriate the right referred to in that subsection.

NOTE

[1] Inserted by the Leasehold Reform, Housing and Urban Development Act 1993 (c. 28), s. 148 (effective 27th September 1993: S.I. 1993 No. 2163).

[THE NEXT PAGE IS J 275]

Duty of landlord to provide information to secure tenants

[1] **76.**—(1) Whenever a new secure tenancy is to be created, if—

(*a*) the landlord is neither the heritable proprietor of the house nor holds the interest of the landlord under a registered lease of the house or of land which includes it; or

(*b*) by virtue of section 61(4), the house is not one to which that section applies; or

[2] (*c*) section 62(6A) may affect any price fixed as regards the house under section 62(1),

the landlord shall so inform the prospective tenant by written notice.

(2) Where in the course of a secure tenancy the landlord ceases to be either the heritable proprietor of the house or the holder of the interest of the landlord under a registered lease of the house or of land which includes it or the house, by virtue of section 61(4), ceases to be one to which that section applies, the landlord shall forthwith so inform the tenant by written notice.

(3) Subsections (1) and (2) do not apply if—

(*a*) the landlord is a housing co-operative within the meaning of section 22, and

(*b*) the heritable proprietor is a local authority, or a local authority is the holder of the interest of the landlord under a registered lease of the house or of land which includes it.

(4) Where—

(*a*) by way of any enactment (including an enactment made under this Act), any change is to be made in the law relating to the calculation of the price at which the tenant of a house is entitled under this Act to purchase it, being a change which does not come into force upon the passing or making of that enactment but which, when it does come into force will affect the price of the house, and

(*b*) the house is one in respect of which an application to purchase has, in the period ending with the coming into force of the change, been served under section 63(1) and not withdrawn but no contract of sale of the house has been constituted under section 66(2),

the landlord shall, upon the passing or making of that enactment or, if later, upon the service of the application to purchase, forthwith give written notice to the tenant stating the nature of the change and how it will affect the price and suggesting that the tenant should seek appropriate advice.

(5) For the purposes of subsection (4), a change in the law will affect the price of a house if, on the day it falls to be calculated under the law as changed, the price will be different from what it would have been that day had there been no such change.

NOTES

[1] As amended by the Local Government and Housing Act 1989, ss.178(1), with effect from 16th January 1990, and 181.

[2] As amended by the Housing (Scotland) Act 1988, s. 65(5), with effect from 2nd January 1989. S. 65(6) of that Act provides:

"(6) The said sections 62 and 76 shall, however, continue to apply as originally enacted in relation to the price of a house in respect of which the offer to sell (within the meaning of section 63 of the Housing (Scotland) Act 1987) was served on the tenant prior to the commencement of this section; but nothing in this subsection restricts the power of the tenant to withdraw his application to purchase or prejudices the effect of such withdrawal."

Powers of Secretary of State

Secretary of State may make provision for vesting in landlord to bring into being tenant's right to purchase house

77.—(1) Subject to subsection (2), where, but for the fact that a landlord is not the heritable proprietor of land on which houses have been let (or made available for letting) by it, one or more of its tenants would have a right to purchase under section 61, the Secretary of State may by order made by statutory instrument provide that the whole of the heritable proprietor's interest in the land shall vest in the landlord.

(2) An order under this section shall only be made where—

(*a*) the heritable proprietor is a body mentioned in paragraph (*a*) of section 61(2); and

(*b*) the Secretary of State is of the opinion, after consultation with the heritable proprietor and with the landlord that the order is necessary if the right to purchase is to come into being.

(3) An order under this section shall have the same effect as a declaration under section 278 of the Town and Country Planning (Scotland) Act 1972 (general vesting declarations) except that in relation to such an order, the enactments mentioned in Schedule 6 shall have effect subject to the modifications specified in that Schedule.

(4) Compensation under the Land Compensation (Scotland) Act 1963, as applied by subsection (3) and Schedule 6 shall be assessed by reference to values current on the date the order under this section comes into force.

(5) An order under this section shall have no effect until approved by resolution of each House of Parliament.

(6) An order under this section which would, apart from the provisions of this subsection, be treated for the purposes of the Standing Orders of either House of Parliament as a hybrid instrument shall proceed in that House as if it were not such an instrument.

(7) An order under this section may include such incidental, consequential or supplementary provisions as may appear to the Secretary of State to be necessary or expedient for the purposes of this Act.

Secretary of State may give directions to modify conditions of sale

78.—(1) Where it appears to the Secretary of State that the inclusion of conditions of a particular kind in offers to sell would be unreasonable he may by direction require landlords generally, landlords of a particular description, or particular landlords not to include conditions of that kind (or not to include conditions of that kind unless modified in such manner as may be specified in the direction) in offers to sell served on or after a date so specified.

(2) Where a condition's inclusion in an offer to sell—

(*a*) is in contravention of a direction under subsection (1) above; or

(*b*) in a case where the tenant has not by the date specified in such a direction served a relative notice of acceptance on the landlord, would have been in such contravention had the offer to sell been served on or after that date,

the condition shall have no effect as regards the offer to sell.

(3) A direction under subsection (1) above may—

(*a*) make different provision in relation to different areas, cases or classes of case and may exclude certain areas, cases or classes of case; and

(*b*) be varied or withdrawn by a subsequent direction so given.

(4) Section 211 of the Local Government (Scotland) Act 1973 (provision for default of local authority) shall apply as regards a failure to comply with a requirement in a direction under subsection (1) as that section applies as regards such failure as is mentioned in subsection (1) thereof.

Secretary of State may give financial and other assistance for tenants involved in proceedings

79.—(1) Where, in relation to any proceedings, or prospective proceedings, to which this section applies, a tenant or purchaser is an actual or prospective party, the Secretary of State may on written application to him by the tenant or purchaser give financial or other assistance to the applicant, if the Secretary of State thinks fit to do so:

Provided that assistance under this section shall be given only where the Secretary of State considers—

(*a*) that the case raises a question of principle and that it is in the public interest to give the applicant such assistance; or

(*b*) that there is some other special consideration.

(2) This section applies to

(*a*) any proceedings under sections 61 to 84 and section 216; and

(*b*) any proceedings to determine any question arising under or in connection with those sections other than a question as to market value for the purposes of section 62.

(3) Assistance by the Secretary of State under this section may include—

(*a*) giving advice;

(*b*) procuring or attempting to procure the settlement of the matter in dispute;

(*c*) arranging for the giving of advice or assistance by a solicitor or counsel;

(*d*) arranging for representation by a solicitor or counsel;

(*e*) any other form of assistance which the Secretary of State may consider appropriate.

(4) In so far as expenses are incurred by the Secretary of State in providing the applicant with assistance under this section, any sums recovered by virtue of an award of expenses, or of an agreement as to expenses, in the applicant's favour with respect to the matter in connection with which the assistance is given shall, subject to any charge or obligation for payment in priority to other debts under the Legal Aid (Scotland) Act 1986 and to any provision of that Act for payment of any sum into the Scottish Legal Aid Fund, be paid to the Secretary of State in priority to any other debts.

(5) Any expenses incurred by the Secretary of State in providing assistance under this section shall be paid out of money provided by Parliament; and any sums received by the Secretary of State under subsection (4) shall be paid into the Consolidated Fund.

Secretary of State may make contributions towards the cost of transfers and exchanges

80.—(1) The Secretary of State may with the consent of the Treasury make grants or loans towards the cost of arrangements for facilitating moves to and from homes by which—

(*a*) a secure tenant of one landlord (the "first landlord") becomes, at his own request, the secure tenant of a different landlord (whether or not by means of an exchange whereby a secure tenant of the different landlord becomes the secure tenant of the first landlord); or

(*b*) each of two or more tenants of houses, one at least of which is let under a secure tenancy, becomes the tenant of the other house (or, as the case may be, of one of the other houses).

(2) The grants or loans may be made subject to such conditions as the Secretary of State may determine, and may be made so as to be repayable (or, as the case may be, repayable earlier) if there is a breach of such a condition.

(3) In subsection (1) above, the reference to a "secure tenant" is to a tenant under a secure tenancy within the meaning of this Act or of the Housing Act 1985 or of Chapter II of Part II of the Housing (Northern Ireland) Order 1983.

Information from landlords in relation to Secretary of State's powers

81.—(1) Without prejudice to section 199 of the Local Government (Scotland) Act 1973 (reports and returns by local authorities etc.), where it appears to the Secretary of State necessary or expedient, in relation to the exercise of his powers under sections 61 to 84 and section 216, he may by notice in writing to a landlord require it—

(*a*) at such time and at such place as may be specified in the notice, to produce any document; or (*b*) within such period as may be so specified or such longer period as the Secretary of State may allow, to furnish a copy of any document or supply any information.

(2) Any officer of the landlord designated in the notice for that purpose or having custody or control of the document or in a position to give that information shall, without instructions from the landlord, take all reasonable steps to ensure that the notice is complied with.

Preservation of right to buy on disposal to private sector landlord

[1] **81A.**—(1) The right to buy provisions shall continue to apply where a person ceases to be a secure tenant of a house by reason of the disposal by the landlord of an interest in the house to a private sector landlord.

(2) The right to buy provisions shall not, however, continue to apply under subsection (1) in such circumstances as may be prescribed.

(3) The continued application under subsection (1) of the right to buy provisions shall be in accordance with and subject to such provision as is prescribed which may—

(*a*) include—

(i) such additions and exceptions to, and adaptations and modifications of, the right to buy provisions in their continued application by virtue of this section; and

(ii) such incidental, supplementary and transitional provisions;

as the Secretary of State considers appropriate;

(*b*) differ as between different cases or descriptions of case and as between different areas;

(*c*) relate to a particular disposal.

(4) Without prejudice to the generality of subsection (3), provision may be made by virtue of it—

(*a*) specifying the persons entitled to the benefit of the right to buy provisions in their continued application by virtue of this section;

(*b*) preventing, except with the consent of the Secretary of State, the disposal by the private sector landlord of less than his whole interest in a house in relation to which the right to buy provisions continue to apply by virtue of this section;

(*c*) ensuring that where, under Ground 9 of Schedule 5 to the Housing (Scotland) Act 1988 (availability of suitable alternative accommodation), the sheriff makes any order for possession of a house in relation to which the right to buy provisions continue to apply by virtue of this section and the tenant would not have the right under this Part (other than this section) to buy the house which is or will be available by way of alternative accommodation, these provisions as so continued will apply in relation to the house which is or will be so available.

(5) In this section—

(*a*) "secure tenant" means a tenant under a secure tenancy;

(*b*) "private sector landlord" means a landlord other than one of those set out in sub-paragraphs (i) to (iv) and (viii) and (ix) of paragraph (*a*) of subsection (2) of section 61;

(*c*) the "right to buy provisions" means the provisions of this Act relating to the right of a tenant of a house to purchase it under this Part and to his rights in respect of a loan.

NOTE

[1] Inserted by the Housing Act 1988, s. 128 (effective 21st February 1992).

Consultation before disposal to private sector landlord

[1] **81B.** The provisions of Schedule 6A have effect with respect to the duties of—

(*a*) a local authority proposing to dispose of houses let on secure tenancies;

(*b*) the Secretary of State in considering whether to give his consent under section 12(7) to such a disposal,

to have regard to the views of tenants liable as a result of the disposal to cease to be secure tenants (that is to say, tenants under secure tenancies).

NOTE

[1] Inserted by the Housing Act 1988 (c. 50), s. 135 (effective 21st February 1992).

General

Interpretation of this Part

[1] **82.** In this Part and in sections 14, 19, 20, 214 and 216, except where provision is made to the contrary,

"application to purchase" has the meaning assigned to it by section 63;

"family" and any reference to membership thereof shall be construed in accordance with section 83;

"fire authority" means a fire authority for the purposes of the Fire Services Acts 1947 to 1959 or a joint committee constituted by virtue of section 36(4)(*b*) of the Fire Services Act 1947;

"heritable proprietor" in relation to a house includes any landlord entitled under section 3 of the Conveyancing (Scotland) Act 1924 (disposition of the dwelling-house etc. by persons uninfeft) to grant a disposition of the house;

"housing co-operative" has the meaning assigned to it by section 22;

"landlord" means a person who lets a house to a tenant for human habitation, and includes his successors in title;

"offer to sell" has the meaning assigned to it by section 63(2) and includes such offer to sell as is mentioned in section 71(1)(*d*);

"police authority" means a police authority in Scotland within the meaning of section 2(1) or 19(9)(*b*) of the Police (Scotland) Act 1967 or a joint police committee constituted by virtue of subsection (2)(*b*) of the said section 19 and any police authority constituted in England and Wales or Northern Ireland under corresponding legislation;

the "rent to loan purchaser" of a house is the person who exercised his right to purchase it under section 61 by way of the rent to loan scheme or, where section 73D(1) applies, the person whose selling or otherwise disposing of the house or whose death is, by virtue of subsection (2) of that section, the occasion for payment of the deferred financial commitment, that person;

"rent to loan scheme" means the provisions of sections 62A and 73A to 73D;

"secure tenancy" means a secure tenancy within the meaning of section 44;

"tenancy" means any agreement under which a house is made available for occupation for human habitation, and "leases", "let" and "lets" shall be construed accordingly;

"tenant" means a person who leases a house from a landlord and who derives his right therein directly from the landlord, and in the case of joint tenancies means all the tenants.

NOTE

[1] As amended by the Leasehold Reform, Housing and Urban Development Act 1993 (c. 28), s. 143 (effective 27th September 1993: S.I. 1993 No. 2163).

Members of a person's family

83.—(1) A person is a member of another's family for the purposes of this Act if—

(*a*) he is the spouse of that person or he and that person live together as husband and wife; or (*b*) he is that person's parent, grandparent, child, grandchild, brother, sister, uncle, aunt, nephew or niece.

(2) For the purposes of subsection (1)(*b*) above—

(*a*) a relationship by marriage shall be treated as a relationship by blood;

(*b*) a relationship of the half-blood shall be treated as a relationship of the whole blood;

(*c*) the stepchild of a person shall be treated as his child; and

(*d*) a child shall be treated as such whether or not his parents are married.

Service of notices

84.—(1) A notice or other document which requires to be served on a person under any provision of this Part or of section 216 may be given to him—

(*a*) by delivering it to him;

(*b*) by leaving it at his proper address; or

(*c*) by sending it by recorded delivery post to him at that address.

(2) For the purposes of this section and of section 7 of the Interpretation Act 1978 (references to service by post) in its application to this section, a person's proper address shall be his last known address.

Application of right to buy to cases where landlord is lessee

[1] **84A.**—(1) Sections 61 to 84 (but not 76 or 77) and 216 (the "right to buy" provisions) shall, with the modifications set out in this section, apply so as to provide for—

(*a*) the acquisition by the tenant of a house let on a secure tenancy of the landlord's interest in the house as lessee under a registered lease of the house or of land which includes it or as assignee of that interest; and

(*b*) the obtaining of a loan by the tenant in that connection,

as these sections apply for the purposes of the purchase of a house by the tenant from the landlord as heritable proprietor of it and the obtaining by the tenant of a loan in that connection.

(2) References in the right to buy provisions to the purchase or sale of a house shall be construed respectively as references to the acquisition or disposal of the landlord's interest in the house by way of a registered assignation of that interest and cognate expressions shall be construed accordingly.

(3) The reference in section 61(2)(*b*) to the landlord's being the heritable proprietor of the house shall be construed as a reference to the landlord's being the holder of the interest of the lessee under a registered lease of the house or of land which includes it.

(4) References in the right to buy provisions to the market value of or price to be paid for a house shall be construed respectively as references to the market value of the landlord's interest in the house and to the price to be paid for acquiring that interest.

(5) References in section 64(1) to the tenant's enjoyment and use of a house as owner shall be construed as references to his enjoyment and use of it as assignee of the landlord's interest in the house.

(6) The reference in subsection (4) of section 64 to an option being offered to the landlord or to any other person to purchase the house in advance of its sale to a third party shall be construed as a reference to an option being offered to have the interest acquired by the tenant re-assigned to the landlord or assigned to the other person in advance of its being disposed of to a third party; and the references in subsections (5) and (9) of that section to an option to purchase shall be construed accordingly.

(7) In this section and section 76—

"registered lease" means a lease—

(*a*) which is recorded in the general register of sasines; or

(*b*) in respect of which the interest of the lessee is registered in the Land Register of Scotland

under the Registration of Leases (Scotland) Act 1857; and

"registered assignation" means, in relation to such a lease, an assignation thereof which is so recorded or in respect of which the interest of the assignee has been so registered.

NOTE

[1] Inserted by the Local Government and Housing Act 1989 (c. 42), s. 178(2).

. . . .

Part XVI

General and Miscellaneous

Interpretation

338.—(1) In this Act, unless the context otherwise requires—

. . .

"Act of 1980" means the Tenants' Rights, Etc. (Scotland) Act 1980;

. . .

"Act of 1986" means the Housing (Scotland) Act 1986;

[0] "agricultural holding" means an agricultural holding within the meaning of the Agricultural Holdings (Scotland) Act 1991;

"agriculture" means the use of land for agricultural or pastoral purposes, or for the purpose of poultry farming or market gardening, or as an orchard or woodlands, or for the purpose of afforestation, and "agricultural worker" shall be construed accordingly;

. . .

"development corporation" means a development corporation established by an order made or having effect as if made under the New Towns (Scotland) Act 1968;

[THE NEXT PAGE IS J 279]

"disabled occupant" has the meaning assigned to it by section 236;
"disabled person" has the meaning assigned to it by section 236;

. . .

"family" and any reference to membership thereof shall be construed in accordance with section 83;

. . .

"flat" means a separate and self-contained set of premises, whether or not on the same floor and forming part of a building from some other part of which it is divided horizontally;

. . .

"hostel" has the meaning assigned to it by section 2(5);
"house" (except in relation to Part XIV) includes any part of a building, being a part which is occupied or intended to be occupied as a separate dwelling, and, in particular, includes a flat, and includes also any yard, garden, out-houses and pertinents belonging to the house or usually enjoyed therewith and also includes any structure made available under section 1 of the Housing (Temporary Accommodation) Act 1944;

. . .

"housing association" has the same meaning as it has in the Housing Associations Act 1985;

. . .

"land" includes any estate or interest in land;

. . .

"Lands Tribunal" means the Lands Tribunal for Scotland;

. . .

"local authority" means an islands council or a district council, and the district of a local authority means the islands area or the district, as the case may be;

. . .

"owner" includes any person who under the Lands Clauses Acts would be enabled to sell and convey land to the promoters of an undertaking, but in Part XIII and sections 99 to 104, in relation to a house, means the person who is for the time being entitled to receive the rent of the house or who, if the house were let would be so entitled and a tenant-at-will;
"prescribed" means prescribed by regulations made by the Secretary of State by statutory instrument;

. . .

"registered housing association" means a housing association registered under the Housing Associations Act 1985;
"regular armed forces of the Crown" means the Royal Navy, the regular forces as defined by section 225 of the Army Act 1955, the regular air force as defined by section 223 of the Air Force Act 1955, Queen Alexandra's Royal Naval Nursing Service and the Women's Royal Naval Service;

. . .

"sell" and "sale" includes feu;

. . .

[1] "tenancy" in Parts IV and XIII includes a sub-tenancy, a statutory tenancy within the meaning of section 115(1) of the Rent (Scotland) Act 1984 and a contract to which Part VII of that Act applies and a statutory assured tenancy within the meaning of the Housing (Scotland) Act 1988 and "tenant" shall be construed accordingly; and any reference to a tenancy of a house or to the tenant thereof shall be construed as including a reference to all the tenancies of that house or to all the tenants thereof as the case may be;

. . .

NOTES

[0] As amended by the Agricultural Holdings (Scotland) Act 1991, Sched. 11, para. 55.

[1] As amended by the Housing (Scotland) Act 1988, Sched. 9, para. 20.

Citation, commencement and extent

340.—(1) This Act may be cited as the Housing (Scotland) Act 1987.

(2) This Act shall come into force at the end of the period of three months beginning with the day on which it is passed.

(3) This Act extends to Scotland only.

SCHEDULES

. . . . . .

[1] SCHEDULE 6A

NOTE

[1] As inserted by the Housing Act 1988, Sched. 16 (effective 21st February 1992: S.I. 1992 No. 324).

CONSULTATION BEFORE DISPOSAL TO PRIVATE SECTOR LANDLORD

Disposals to which this Schedule applies

1.—(1) This Schedule applies to the disposal by a local authority of an interest in land as a result of which a secure tenant of the local authority will become the tenant of a private sector landlord.

(2) For the purposes of this Schedule the grant of an option which if exercised would result in a secure tenant of a local authority becoming the tenant of a private sector landlord shall be treated as a disposal of the interest which is the subject of the option.

(3) Where a disposal of land by a local authority is in part a disposal to which this Schedule applies, the provisions of this Schedule apply to that part as to a separate disposal.

(4) In this paragraph "private sector landlord" means a person other than one of those set out in sub-paragraphs (i) to (iv) and (viii) and (ix) of paragraph (*a*) of subsection (2) of section 61.

Application for Secretary of State's consent

2.—(1) The Secretary of State shall not entertain an application for his consent under section 12(7) to a disposal to which this Schedule applies unless the local authority certify either—

(*a*) that the requirements of paragraph 3 as to consultation have been complied with, or

(*b*) that the requirements of that paragraph as to consultation have been complied with except in relation to tenants expected to have vacated the house in question before the disposal;

and the certificate shall be accompanied by a copy of the notices given by the local authority in accordance with that paragraph.

(2) Where the certificate is in the latter form, the Secretary of State shall not determine the application until the local authority certify as regards the tenants not originally consulted—

(*a*) that they have vacated the house in question, or

(*b*) that the requirements of paragraph 3 as to consultation have been complied with; and a certificate under sub-paragraph (*b*) shall be accompanied by a copy of the notices given by the local authority in accordance with paragraph 3.

Requirements as to consultation

3.—(1) The requirements as to consultation referred to above are as follows.

(2) The local authority shall serve notice in writing on the tenant informing him of—

(*a*) such details of their proposal as the local authority consider appropriate, but including the identity of the person to whom the disposal is to be made,

(*b*) the likely consequences of the disposal for the tenant, and
(*c*) the effect of section 81A and the provision made under it (preservation of right to buy on disposal to private sector landlord) and of this Schedule,

and informing him that he may, within such reasonable period as may be specified in the notice, which must be at least 28 days after the service of the notice, make representations to the local authority.

(3) The local authority shall consider any representations made to them within that period and shall serve a further written notice on the tenant informing him—

(*a*) of any significant changes in their proposal, and
(*b*) that he may within such period as is specified (which must be at least 28 days after the service of the notice) communicate to the Secretary of State his objection to the proposal,

and informing him of the effect of paragraph 5 (consent to be withheld if majority of tenants are opposed).

Power to require further consultation

4. The Secretary of State may require the local authority to carry out such further consultation with their tenants, and to give him such information as to the results of that consultation, as he may direct.

Consent to be withheld if majority of tenants are opposed

5.—(1) The Secretary of State shall not give his consent if it appears to him that a majority of the tenants of the houses to which the application relates do not wish the disposal to proceed; but this does not affect his general discretion to refuse consent on grounds relating to whether a disposal has the support of the tenants or on any other ground.

(2) In making his decision the Secretary of State may have regard to any information available to him; and the local authority shall give him such information as to the representations made to them by tenants and others, and other relevant matters, as he may require.

Protection of purchasers

6. The Secretary of State's consent to a disposal is not invalidated by a failure on his part or that of the local authority to comply with the requirements of this Schedule.

[THE NEXT PAGE IS J 501]

Statutory Instruments

Allocation of Feuduty etc. (Form of Notice) Regulations 1971

(S.I. 1971 No. 200)

[4th February 1971]

In exercise of the powers conferred on me by section 3 (4) of the Conveyancing and Feudal Reform (Scotland) Act 1970, and of all other powers enabling me in that behalf, I hereby make the following regulations:—

1.—(1) These regulations may be cited as the Allocation of Feuduty etc. (Form of Notice) Regulations 1971 and shall come into operation on 1st March 1971.

(2) The Interpretation Act 1889 shall apply for the interpretation of these regulations as it applies for the interpretation of an Act of Parliament.

2. A notice of allocation shall be in, or as nearly as may be in, the form set out in the Schedule hereto.

SCHEDULE

CONVEYANCING AND FEUDAL REFORM (SCOTLAND) ACT 1970

Notice of Allocation

To ....

Take notice that the sum of £ ....
which is the portion of a *cumulo* feuduty/ground annual* which has been apportioned on ....
....
....
of which ....
is the proprietor, is to be allocated on the said subjects under the Conveyancing and Feudal Reform (Scotland) Act 1970

*The said portion of *cumulo* feuduty/ground annual* is paid to ....
....
or
*The *cumulo* feuduty/ground annual* of which the said portion forms part is paid by the proprietor to the superior.

Date .... Signed ....
....

* Delete whichever is not applicable.

Name and address of Superior [Creditor in Ground Annual] or his agent.

Distinguish the property (including, where appropriate, the postal address) so that it can be clearly identified.

Name and address of proprietor.

Name and address of the person to whom the portion of *cumulo* feuduty [ground annual] is paid

To be signed by the proprietor or his agent. An agent should state his designation and add the words " Agent of .... (name of proprietor)".

Notes

1. If the Superior [Creditor in Ground Annual] wishes to object to the amount of the portion of feuduty [ground annual] specified in this Notice he *must* apply to the Lands Tribunal for Scotland within 28 days.

2. Unless an application is made to the Lands Tribunal for Scotland by the Superior [Creditor in Ground Annual] the allocation of feuduty [ground annual] specified in this Notice shall take effect in respect of any feuduty [ground annual] so allocated which becomes due at any term occurring not less than three months after service of this Notice.

Land Registration (Scotland) Act 1979 (Commencement No. 1) Order 1980

(S.I. 1980 No. 1412)

[16th September 1980]

The Secretary of State, in exercise of the powers conferred on him by section 30 (2) of the Land Registration (Scotland) Act 1979 and of all other powers enabling him in that behalf, hereby makes the following order:—

Citation and interpretation

1. This order may be cited as the Land Registration (Scotland) Act 1979 (Commencement No. 1) Order 1980.

2. In this order a reference to the Act is a reference to the Land Registration (Scotland) Act 1979.

Commencement

3. Subsections (1) and (2) of section 2 and subsection (3) of section 3 shall come into operation on 6th April 1981 in the area, for the purpose of registration of writs, of the County of Renfrew.

4. The other provisions of the Act, except those provisions which, under section 30 (2) of the Act, came into operation on the passing of the Act, shall also come into operation on 6th April 1981.

Land Registration (Scotland) Rules 1980

(S.I. 1980 No. 1413)

[16th September 1980]

In exercise of the powers conferred on me by section 27 (1) of the Land Registration (Scotland) Act 1979 and of all other powers enabling me in that behalf, and after consultation with the Lord President of the Court of Session, I hereby make the following rules:

Part I

General

Citation and Commencement

1. These rules may be cited as the Land Registration (Scotland) Rules 1980 and shall come into operation on 6th April 1981.

Interpretation

2.—(1) In these rules—

" the Act " means the Land Registration (Scotland) Act 1979;

" certificate of title " includes a land certificate and a charge certificate;

" dealing " means a transaction or event capable of affecting the title to a registered interest in land; and

" debt " has the meaning assigned to it by section 9 (8) (*c*) of the Conveyancing and Feudal Reform (Scotland) Act 1970.

(2) In these rules any reference to a numbered rule or to a numbered form is a reference to, respectively, the rule bearing that number in these rules or the form bearing that number in Schedule A to these rules.

(3) In a rule, any reference to a numbered paragraph is a reference to the paragraph in that rule bearing that number.

PART II

THE TITLE SHEET

Contents and Distinguishing Number of Title Sheet

3.—(1) A title sheet shall consist of the following sections: a Property Section, a Proprietorship Section, a Charges Section and a Burdens Section.

(2) Each title sheet of a registered interest in land shall be distinguished by a title number, consisting either of numbers or of letters and numbers.

Property Section

4.—(1) The following matters shall be entered in the Property Section—

(*a*) the description of the land in accordance with section 6 (1) (*a*) of the Act;

(*b*) the nature of the interest in the land;

(*c*) particulars of any enforceable real right pertaining to the interest;

(*d*) particulars of any exclusion of indemnity under section 12 (2) of the Act which the Keeper considers is appropriate to the Property Section; and

(*e*) such other information as the Keeper thinks fit to enter in the Property Section.

(2) The Property Section shall include a plan of the land to which the interest relates.

Proprietorship Section

[1] **5.** The following matters shall be entered in the Proprietorship Section—

(*a*) the name and designation of the person entitled to the interest in land;

(*b*) the extent of that person's entitlement to the interest in land;

(*c*) the capacity in which that person is entitled to the interest in land, if he is not so entitled as an individual;

(*d*) the destination, if any, to which the interest in land is subject;

(*e*) the date, if any, stated as the date of entry of that person to the interest in land;

(*f*) the date of registration of that person's entitlement to the interest in land;

(*g*) any consideration stated for the transfer of the interest in land;

(*h*) any subsisting entry in the Register of Inhibitions and Adjudications adverse to the interest;

(*i*) particulars of any exclusion of indemnity under section 12 (2) of the Act which the Keeper considers is appropriate to the Proprietorship Section;

(*j*) a statement that there are in respect of the interest in land no subsisting occupancy rights, in terms of the Matrimonial Homes (Family Protection) (Scotland) Act 1981, of spouses of persons who were formerly entitled to the interest in land, if the Keeper is satisfied that there are no such subsisting rights; and

(*k*) such other information as the Keeper thinks fit to enter in the Proprietorship Section.

NOTE

[1] As amended by the Land Registration (Scotland) (Amendment) Rules 1982 (S.I. No. 974).

Charges Section

6.—(1) The following matters shall be entered in the Charges Section—

(*a*) particulars of any heritable security over the interest;

(*b*) particulars of any debt, including a pecuniary real burden, affecting the interest;

(*c*) particulars of any exclusion of indemnity under section 12 (2) of the Act which the Keeper considers is appropriate to the Charges Section; and

(*d*) such other information as the Keeper thinks fit to enter in the Charges Section.

(2) There shall be noted in the Charges Section particulars of a floating charge, which, as an overriding interest, may fall to be noted in terms of section 6 (4) of the Act

Burdens Section

7.—(1) The following matters shall be entered in the Burdens Section—

(*a*) particulars of any subsisting real burden, other than a real burden which falls to be entered in the Charges Section, and of any subsisting condition affecting the interest;

(*b*) particulars of any exclusion of indemnity under section 12 (2) of the Act which the Keeper considers is appropriate to the Burdens Section; and

(*c*) such other information as the Keeper thinks fit to enter in the Burdens Section.

(2) There shall be noted in the Burdens Section particulars of any overriding interest, other than a floating charge, which may fall to be noted in terms of section 6 (4) of the Act.

(3) There shall be entered in the Burdens Section—

(*a*) particulars of a probative discharge of an overriding interest, other than a floating charge or the right of the proprietor of the dominant tenement in a servitude, but only where (i) the overriding interest has been either recorded in the Register of Sasines or noted in the Burdens Section and (ii) the applicant has requested that the particulars be noted; and

(*b*) particulars of a probative discharge of the right of the proprietor of the dominant tenement in a servitude.

Combination and Division of Title Sheets

8. When it appears to the Keeper to be desirable to do so he may—

(*a*) enter the particulars of an interest in land in the title sheet of another interest in land and cancel the title sheet in which the interest was previously entered, or (*b*) enter in another title sheet or in other title sheets a part or parts of the interest in land which was previously entered as a single interest and amend appropriately the title sheet in which the whole interest was previously entered.

[THE NEXT PAGE IS J 505]

Part III

Registration of Interests in Land and Noting of Overriding Interests and Entry of Additional Information

Application for Registration of Interest in Land

9.—(1) Any application for registration shall be made by the person in whose favour a real right will be created or affected by registration and such an application shall be on the following forms—

(*a*) Form 1, where the application is for first registration;

(*b*) Form 2, where the application is for registration of a dealing (other than the transfer of part of a registered interest in land); and

(*c*) Form 3, where the application is for registration of a transfer of part of a registered interest in land.

(2) An application for registration shall be accompanied by an inventory of the writs relevant to the application on Form 4.

(3) Subject to rule 18, an application for registration on Form 2 or on Form 3 shall be accompanied by the certificate of title of the relevant interest in land.

Withdrawal by Applicant of Application for Registration

10. An application for registration may be withdrawn by the applicant before the completion of registration.

Return by Keeper of Document for Amendment

11. Subject to rule 12, where an application for registration is not accepted by the Keeper on the grounds that it does not comply with subsection (1) or (2) (*a*) or (*d*) of section 4 of the Act, but has not been rejected by the Keeper or withdrawn by the applicant, the Keeper may return any document relating to the application to the applicant for amendment in order that the application may be made so to comply.

Failure by Applicant to Respond to Keeper's Request

12. Where the applicant, having been requested by the Keeper to supply documents and evidence in accordance with section 4 (1) of the Act or to amend a document in accordance with rule 11, fails to do so, the Keeper after the expiry of such reasonable period of time as may be fixed by him and intimated to the applicant, being not less than 60 days, may either complete registration, subject to exclusion of indemnity, or reject the application.

Application for Noting of Overriding Interest or for Entry of Discharge of Overriding Interest or of Additional Information

13. An application for—

(*a*) the noting of an overriding interest in terms of section 6 (4) of the Act; or

(*b*) the entering of—

(i) the discharge of an overriding interest in terms of rule 7 (3); or

(ii) additional information entered in terms of section 6 (1) (*g*) of the Act; or

(*c*) the deletion of a note or an entry made, respectively, under paragraph (*a*) or paragraph (*b*) of this rule

shall be on Form 5.

PART IV

CERTIFICATE OF TITLE

Form of Land Certificate

14. A land certificate issued by the Keeper in terms of section 5 (2) of the Act shall be in, or as nearly as may be in, Form 6 and shall be authenticated by the seal of the register.

Form of Charge Certificate

15. A charge certificate issued by the Keeper in terms of section 5 (3) of the Act shall be in, or as nearly as may be in, Form 7 and shall be authenticated by the seal of the register.

Application for Certificate of Title to be made to Correspond with Title Sheet

16.—(1) An application may be made to the Keeper for a certificate of title to be made to correspond with the relevant title sheet.

(2) Such an application shall be Form 8.

Amendment or Cancellation of Certificate of Title by Keeper

17.—(1) The Keeper shall have power to amend or cancel a certificate of title in order to make the certificate correspond with the relevant title sheet.

(2) Subject to rule 18, a certificate of title shall be produced to the Keeper for amendment or cancellation if the Keeper requests production.

(3) The Keeper shall not request production of a certificate of title in terms of the preceding paragraph where amendment of the certificate would inform the person entitled to the interest in land of the existence of a recorded deed or a registration upon which possession adverse to him may be founded in terms of section 1 of the Prescription and Limitation (Scotland) Act 1973.

(4) On being requested to do so, the Keeper shall make payment of such expenses occasioned by compliance with paragraph (2), as the Keeper considers to be reasonable.

Circumstances where Certificate of Title need not be Produced to Keeper

18.—(1) There shall be no obligation to produce the Certificate of title to the Keeper, in terms of rule 9 (3) or rule 17 (2), where the Keeper is satisfied of the existence of good cause for the failure to produce the certificate.

(2) For the purpose of the preceding paragraph, good cause will include—

(*a*) with reference to a land certificate or a charge certificate, the fact that the certificate has been lost or destroyed or is otherwise unobtainable; and

(*b*) with reference to a land certificate, the fact that the land certificate is held by a creditor.

Issue by Keeper of Substitute Certificate of Title

19. Where the Keeper is satisfied that a certificate of title has been lost or destroyed he shall issue a substitute certificate, marked " substitute " and shall note on the title sheet that a substitute certificate has been issued.

PART V

MISCELLANEOUS

Rectification of Register

20.—(1) An application to the Keeper, under section 9 (1) of the Act, for the rectification of the register shall be on Form 9.

(2) Where it appears to the Keeper that proceedings in the court or the Lands Tribunal for Scotland may result in an order for rectification of the register under section 9 (1) of the Act, the Keeper shall note the existence of such proceedings on the title sheet of the interest in land to which the proceedings relate.

Notifications by Keeper

21.—(1) The Keeper shall notify his decision on any matter affecting registration to any person whose interest appears from the register to be affected by that decision.

(2) Notification shall not be made under the foregoing paragraph where notification would have the effect of informing the person entitled to the interest in land of the existence of a recorded deed or a registration upon which possession adverse to his interest may be founded in terms of section 1 of the Prescription and Limitation (Scotland) Act 1973.

(3) A notification under paragraph (1) shall be made in such form as the Keeper shall think fit and shall be sufficiently made if sent by post to the person's last address shown on the register.

Affidavits to Accompany Applications for Registration

22. Affidavits intended to accompany an application for registration may be made before a notary public.

Maps of Registered Interests and Index of Proprietors

23. The Keeper shall make up and maintain—

(*a*) an index map, based on the Ordnance Map, of registered interests in land; and

(*b*) an index of the names of all persons currently entered in the proprietorship section of title sheets.

Application to Keeper for Report or Office Copy

24. An application to the Keeper for any of the documents mentioned in column 1 of the following table shall be on the appropriate form in column 2 of the said table—

(1) *Document Applied For*	(2) *Form*
(1) Report prior to Registration	Form 10
(2) Continuation of Report prior to Registration	Form 11
(3) Report over Registered Subjects	Form 12
(4) Continuation of Report over Registered Subjects	Form 13
(5) Report to ascertain whether or not subjects have been registered	Form 14
(6) Office Copy (in terms of section 6 (5) of the Act)	Form 15

Description of a Registered Interest in Land

25. Land in respect of which an interest has been registered shall be sufficiently described in any deed relating to that interest if it is described by reference to the number of the title sheet of that interest, in or as nearly as may be in, the manner prescribed by Schedule B to these rules.

SCHEDULE A

List of Forms to be Used in Connection with Registration

Form	*Purpose*	*Reference to Act*
[1] 1	Application for First Registration	section 4
[1] 2	Application for Registration of a Dealing (other than the transfer of part of a registered interest in land)	section 4
[1] 3	Application for Registration of a Transfer of part of a Registered Interest in Land	section 4
[1] 4	Inventory of Writs	section 4
5	Application for Noting of Overriding Interest or for entry of Other Information in terms of section 6 (1) (*g*)	section 6 (4)
6	Land Certificate	section 5 (2)
7	Charge Certificate	section 5 (3)
8	Application for Certificate of Title to be made to correspond with Title Sheet	—
9	Application for Rectification of Register	section 9 (1)
10	Application for Report prior to Registration	—
11	Application for Continuation of Report prior to Registration	—
12	Application for Report over Registered Subjects	—
13	Application for Continuation of Report over Registered Subjects	—
14	Application for Report to ascertain whether or not Subjects have been registered	—
15	Application for Office Copy	section 6 (5)

NOTE

[1] The Notes and Directions which follow Forms 1–4, *infra*, do not form part of the Land Registration (Scotland) Rules 1980 but are issued separately by the Keeper.

Rule 9(1)(*a*) [1] FORM 1

Form of Application for First Registration

Form 1

REGISTERS OF SCOTLAND (Land Registration (Scotland) Rules 1980, Rule 9(1)(*a*))

APPLICATION FOR FIRST REGISTRATION *(See Note 1)*
Note: No covering letter is required.

PART A

NAME OF DEED IN RESPECT OF WHICH REGISTRATION IS REQUIRED

PRICE *(See Note 5)*

FOR OFFICIAL USE
Fee

DESCRIPTION OF SUBJECTS *(See Note 2)*

Registration County of

TO

Keeper of the Registers of Scotland

Meadowbank House
153 London Road
EDINBURGH EH8 7AU

Telephone: 031-659 6111

NAME AND ADDRESS OF APPLICANT *(See Note 4)*

GRANTER/PARTY LAST INFEFT *(See Note 3)*

I/WE APPLY FOR REGISTRATION IN RESPECT OF DEED(S) No. ..... in the Inventory of Writs (Form 4). I/We certify that the information supplied in this application is correct to the best of my/our knowledge and belief.

Signature of Applicant or Applicant's Solicitor(s)

Date

Name of signatory (Block Capitals)

Address

FAS Account Number

Reference Telephone:

FOR OFFICIAL USE

Application Number	Date Stamp	Title Number

Notes 1–5 referred to are contained in Notes and Directions for Completion of Application for first Registration.

PART B

Delete **YES** or **NO** as appropriate

---

1. Is there any person in possession or occupation of the subjects or any part of them adversely to the interest of the applicant? **YES/NO**
If **YES**, please give details:

---

2. If the subjects were acquired by the applicant under any statutory provision, does the statutory provision restrict the applicant's power of disposal of the subjects? **YES/NO**
If **YES**, please indicate the statute:

---

3. (a) Are there any charges affecting the subjects or any part of them, except as stated in the Schedule of Heritable Securities etc. on page 4 of this application? **YES/NO**
If **YES**, please give details:

(b) Apart from overriding interests are there any burdens affecting the subjects or any part of them, except as stated in the Schedule of Burdens on page 4 of this application? **YES/NO**
If **YES**, please give details:

(c) Are there any overriding interests affecting the subjects or any part of them which you wish noted on the Title Sheet? **YES/NO**
If **YES**, please give details:

(d) Are there any annual monetary payments (e.g. feuduty) exigible from the subjects or any part of them? **YES/NO**
If **YES**, please give details:

---

4. Where any party to the deed inducing registration is a company registered under the Companies Acts **YES/NO**

Has, a receiver or liquidator been appointed?
If **YES**, please give details:

If **NO**, has any resolution been passed or court order made for the winding up of the company or petition presented for its liquidation? **YES/NO**
IF **YES**, please give details:

---

5. Where any party to the deed inducing registration other than the applicant is a company registered under the Companies Acts

Has the applicant relied on the provisions of section 35 of the Companies Act 1985 in this transaction? **YES/NO**

If NO, is the company acting *intra vires*? **YES/NO**

---

6. Where the applicant is a company registered under the Companies Acts

Is the company acting *intra vires*? **YES/NO**
If NO, please give details:

---

7. Where any party to the deed inducing registration is a corporate body other than a company registered under the Companies Acts

(a) Is it acting *intra vires*? **YES/NO**
If **NO**, please give details:

(b) Has any arrangement been put in hand for the dissolution of any such corporate body? **YES/NO**
If **YES**, please give details:

---

8. Are *all* the necessary consents, renunciations or affidavits in terms of section 6 of the Matrimonial Homes (Family Protection) (Scotland) Act 1981 being submitted in connection with this application? **YES/NO**

If **YES**, are you satisfied that each consent, renunciation or affidavit was produced to the appropriate purchaser at or before the time of the dealing to which it relates? **YES/NO**

N.B. If sufficient evidence to satisfy the Keeper that there are no subsisting occupancy rights in the subjects of this application is not submitted with the application then the statement by the Keeper in terms of rule 5(*j*) of the Land Registration (Scotland) Rules 1980 will not be inserted in the Title Sheet or will be qualified as appropriate without further enquiry by the Keeper.

---

9. Where the deed inducing registration is in implement of the exercise of a power of sale under a heritable security

Have the statutory procedures necessary for the proper exercise of such power been complied with? **YES/NO**

---

10. Where the deed inducing registration is a general vesting declaration or a notice of title pursuant on a compulsory purchase order

Have the necessary statutory procedures been complied with? **YES/NO**

---

11. Is any party to the deed inducing registration subject to any legal incapacity or disability? **YES/NO**
If **YES**, please give details:

---

12. Are the deed and documents detailed in the inventory (Form 4) all the deeds and documents relevant to the title? **YES/NO**
If **NO**, please give details:

---

13. Are there any facts and circumstances material to the right or title of the applicant which have not already been disclosed in this application or its accompanying documents? **YES/NO**
If **YES**, please give details:

This transaction is not in consideration of a price and the value of the subjects does not exceed £

SCHEDULE OF HERITABLE SECURITIES ETC.

N.B. New charges granted by the applicant should not be included

---

SCHEDULE OF BURDENS

If a Form 10 report has been issued in connection with this application, please quote report no.

N.B. If more space is required for any section of this form, a separate sheet, or separate sheets, may be added.

NOTE
[1] Substituted by S.I. 1988 No. 1143.

---

[1] NOTES AND DIRECTIONS FOR COMPLETION OF FORM 1 (PINK)—APPLICATION FOR FIRST REGISTRATION

NOTE
[1] The Notes and Directions which follow do not form part of the Land Registration (Scotland) Rules 1980 but are issued separately by the Keeper.

The Notes 1–5 referred to on Form 1.

1. Form 1 is to be used in the case of an Application for first Registration of an interest in land.

Any Application for Voluntary First Registration made in terms of either section 2(1)(*b*) or 11(1) of the Act should be accompanied by an explanation of the circumstances in letter form signed by the applicant or his solicitor.

Part A

Description of subjects

2. A short description only is required, e.g.

(*a*) southmost house on first floor 27 High Street, Renfrew,
(*b*) Public house 14 Canal Lane, Falkirk,
(*c*) Bungalow 42 Acacia Avenue, Helensburgh,
(*d*) Factory 40–80 Railway Cuttings, Wishaw,
(*e*) Plot 27 Avaroch Estate, Ballachulish, or
(*f*) Hillside Farm, Parish of Rothiemurchus.

In cases where the subjects comprise or include superiorities or landlord's interests in registered Leases, a Schedule of Feus or Leases must accompany the Application if an up-to-date list is not included in the title, but the Keeper may dispense with the requirement on good cause being shown. Where possible, identification should be made on a plan.

Any Schedule may be in the following form:—

Writ	Feuar (or Tenant)	Date of recording	Subjects	Feuduty (or Rent)
Feu Contract	Alexander Campbell and another	4 September 1898 (G.R.S.) Renfrew	129 Edinburgh Road, Renfrew	£4
(Lease	Ian Gow	1 May 1922 (G.R.S.) Renfrew	1 Fulbar Street, Renfrew	£10)

Granter/Party Last Infeft

3. The following information is required:—
the full name of
(i) the granter of the deed inducing registration and
(ii) the party last infeft if not the granter.

Applicant

4. (*a*) Where the applicant is an individual, the information required is his full name and address, e.g. Robert Gordon Campbell, 27 Princes Avenue, Girvan;
(*b*) where the applicant discloses that he is acting in a fiduciary or other capacity, the information required is the applicant's name and the name and address of the party for whom he is acting, e.g. George Campbell, Trustee of Robert Gordon Campbell, late of 27 Princes Avenue, Girvan; this applies where the relationship results from testamentary deed, partnership, court appointment, etc. Information which is not revealed in the documents supporting the Application is not sought;
(*c*) where the applicant is a corporate body the information required is the name of the body;
(*d*) the names and (where appropriate) the addresses of *all* the applicants should be given.

Price

5. The consideration, if monetary, should be entered in figures. If otherwise, provide a short explanation, e.g. Love, Favour and Affection, etc. If the latter, please complete the Certificate on page 4.

Explanatory notes relevant to Part B

Adverse Possession. Rights of possession under a Lease granted by any person entitled to grant the same are not to be regarded as adverse to the interest of the applicant.

The Schedule of Heritable Securities. Must list all existing heritable securities which may be specified by reference to the Inventory (Form 4). Intromissions (i.e. partial Discharges and Assignations) need not be listed in the Schedule but should be included in the Inventory.

The Schedule of Burdens. May be completed by reference to the Inventory (Form 4). It must specify at length or by specific reference to the writs containing them all burdens affecting the subjects and any variation thereof.

Overriding Interests. Where an overriding interest, as defined in section 28(1) of the Act, is constituted otherwise than by writ, particulars of its mode of constitution must be given. In terms of section 6(4) of the Act, the provisions for noting an overriding interest do not apply to the interest of a lessee under a Lease which is not a Long Lease.

Deeds and Documents are:—
(i) a sufficient progress of titles including the deed inducing registration and unrecorded links in title,
(ii) all prior writs containing rights or burdens affecting the subjects,
(iii) any Redemption Receipt for Feuduty or other annual payment,
(iv) any existing heritable securities and deeds relating thereto,
(v) where appropriate, consents to Leases and Sub-Leases and Assignations of recorded or registered Leases,
(vi) Form P16, if obtained,
(vii) any other relevant documents.

An applicant should be prepared to submit common titles (i.e. title deeds or burdens writs relating to a substantial development) to the Keeper if requested to do so. Such titles should not however be submitted in the first instance, although all those relevant to the Application must be listed on form 4.

Rule 9(1)(*b*) [1] FORM 2

Form of Application for Registration of a Dealing (other than the transfer of part of a Registered Interest in Land)

REGISTERS OF SCOTLAND
(Land Registration (Scotland) Rules 1980, Rule 9(1)(*b*))

APPLICATION FOR REGISTRATION OF A DEALING *(See Note 1)*
Note: No covering letter is required.

PART A

<table>
<tr><td>NAME OF DEED IN RESPECT OF WHICH REGISTRATION IS REQUIRED</td><td>PRICE
(See Note 5)</td><td>**FOR OFFICIAL USE**
Fee</td></tr>
<tr><td>DESCRIPTION OF SUBJECTS
(See Note 3)

Registration County of</td><td colspan="2">TO
Keeper of the Registers of Scotland
Meadowbank House
153 London Road
EDINBURGH EH8 7AU
Telephone: 031-659 6111</td></tr>
<tr><td>NAME AND ADDRESS OF APPLICANT
(See Note 4)</td><td colspan="2">I/WE APPLY FOR REGISTRATION IN RESPECT OF DEED(S) No. ..... in the Inventory of Writs (Form 4). I/We certify that the information supplied in this application is correct to the best of my/our knowledge and belief.

Signature of Applicant or Applicant's Solicitor(s)

Date
Name of signatory (Block Capitals)
Address

FAS Account Number

Reference Telephone:</td></tr>
</table>

<table>
<tr><td colspan="2">**FOR OFFICIAL USE**</td><td rowspan="2">TITLE NUMBER(S) OF REGISTERED INTEREST(S) AFFECTED BY THIS APPLICATION
(See Note 2)</td></tr>
<tr><td>Application Number</td><td>Date Stamp</td></tr>
</table>

Notes 1–5 referred to are contained in Notes and Directions for Completion of Application for Registration of a Dealing with Registered Interest(s).

PART B

Delete **YES** or **NO** as appropriate

1. Where the application is for registration as proprietor

   (a) If there any person in possession or occupation of the subjects or any part of them adversely to the interest of the applicant? **YES/NO**
   If **YES**, please give details:

   (b) If the subjects were acquired by the applicant under any statutory provision, does the statutory provision restrict the applicant's power of disposal of the subjects? **YES/NO**
   If **YES**, please indicate the statute:

   (c) Apart from overriding interests are there any burdens affecting the subjects or any part of them, except as already disclosed in the Land Certificate and in the documents produced with this application? **YES/NO**
   If **YES**, please give details:

   (d) Are there any overriding interests affecting the subjects or any part of them which you wish noted on the Title Sheet? **YES/NO**
   If **YES**, please give details:

   (e) Are there any annual monetary payments (e.g. feuduty) exigible from the subjects or any part of them? **YES/NO**
   If **YES**, please give details:

---

2. Where any party to the dealing is a company registered under the Companies Acts

   Has a receiver or liquidator been appointed? **YES/NO**
   If **YES**, please give details:

   If **NO**, has any resolution been passed or court order made for the winding up of the company or petition presented for its liquidation? **YES/NO**
   IF **YES**, please give details:

---

3. Where any party to the dealing other than the applicant is a company registered under the Companies Acts

   Has the applicant relied on the provisions of section 35 of the Companies Act 1985 in this transaction? **YES/NO**

   If **NO**, is the company acting *intra vires*? **YES/NO**

---

4. Where the applicant is a company registered under the Companies Acts

   Is the company acting *intra vires*? **YES/NO**
   If **NO**, please give details:

---

5. Where any party to the dealing is a corporate body other than a company registered under the Companies Acts

   (a) Is it acting *intra vires*? **YES/NO**
   If **NO**, please give details:

(b) Has any arrangement been put in hand for the dissolution of any such corporate body? **YES/NO**
If **YES**, please give details:

---

6. Are *all* the necessary consents, renunciations or affidavits in terms of section 6 of the Matrimonial Homes (Family Protection) (Scotland) Act 1981 being submitted in connection with this application? **YES/NO**

If **YES**, are you satisfied that each consent, renunciation or affidavit was produced to the appropriate purchaser at or before the time of the dealing to which it relates? **YES/NO**

N.B. If sufficient evidence to satisfy the Keeper that there are no subsisting occupancy rights in the subjects of this application is not submitted with the application then the statement by the Keeper in terms of rule 5(*j*) of the Land Registration (Scotland) Rules 1980 will not be inserted in the Title Sheet or will be qualified as appropriate without further enquiry by the Keeper.

---

7. Where the dealing is in implement of the exercise of a power of sale under a heritable security

Have the statutory procedures necessary for the proper exercise of such power been complied with? **YES/NO**

---

8. Where the dealing is a general vesting declaration or a notice of title pursuant on a compulsory purchase order

Have the necessary statutory procedures been complied with? **YES/NO**

---

9. In all cases

(a) Is any party to the transaction subject to any legal incapacity or disability not already disclosed on the Land Certificate? **YES/NO**
If **YES**, please give details:

(b) Are the deed and documents detailed in the inventory (Form 4) all the deeds and documents relevant to the application? **YES/NO**
If **NO**, please give details:

(c) Are there any facts and circumstances material to the right or title of the applicant which have not already been disclosed in this application or its accompanying documents? **YES/NO**
If **YES**, please give details:

The transaction is not in consideration of a price and the value of the subjects does not exceed £

OR

The deed does not state the amount of the loan which does not exceed £

N.B. If more space is required for any section of this form, a separate sheet, or separate sheets, may be added.

NOTE
[1] Substituted by S.I. 1988 No. 1143.

[1] NOTES AND DIRECTIONS FOR COMPLETION OF FORM 2 (BLUE)—APPLICATION FOR REGISTRATION OF A DEALING WITH REGISTERED INTEREST(S) (EXCLUDING DISPOSITION, FEU OR LONG LEASE OF PART OF THE PROPERTY OR A FEU OR LONG LEASE OF THE WHOLE OF THE PROPERTY)

NOTE
[1] The Notes and Directions which follow do not form part of the Land Registration (Scotland) Rules 1980 but are issued separately by the Keeper.

The Notes 1–5 referred to on Form 2

1. Form 2 is to be used in the case of an Application for Registration of a transaction or event which deals with or affects a registered interest or interests in land. The following are examples of such transactions:—

(*a*) Disposition of the whole interest in one registered title;
(*b*) Standard Security over the whole of the interest(s) in one or more registered titles;
(*c*) Standard Security over part of the interest in one registered title;
(*d*) Discharge of a registered Standard Security;
(*e*) Deed of Conditions affecting all or part of the interest in a registered title;
(*f*) Renunciation of a Registered Lease.

The above list is demonstrative only. It should be noted that the only type of transaction affecting a registered interest for which Form 2 is not suitable is a Disposition of part of property forming a registered interest in land, or a Feu or Lease of the whole or part of that property.

Part A

Title Number(s) of Registered Interest(s)

2. All the appropriate Title Numbers must be listed. If more space is required, please write all Title Numbers on a separate sheet and refer to the latter on the Form.

Description of Subjects

3. A short description only is required and, where appropriate, should be taken from the front cover(s) of the Land Certificate(s). If only part of the subjects in the registered title(s) is affected, (e.g. as in 1(*c*) above) a description of the part is required, e.g.

(*a*) southmost house on first floor 27 High Street, Renfrew,
(*b*) Public house 14 Canal Lane, Falkirk,
(*c*) Bungalow 42 Acadia Avenue, Helensburgh,
(*d*) Factory 40–80 Railway Cuttings, Wishaw,
(*e*) Plot 27 Avaroch Estate, Ballachulish, or
(*f*) Hillside Farm, Parish of Rothiemurchus.

In cases where the subjects comprise or include superiorites or landlord's interests in registered Leases, a Schedule of Feus or Leases must accompany the Application if an up-to-date list is not included in the title, but the Keeper may dispense with the requirement on good cause being shown. Where possible, identification should be made on a plan.

Any Schedule may be in the following form:—

Writ	Feuar (or Tenant)	Date of recording	Subjects	Feuduty (or Rent)
Feu Contract	Alexander Campbell and another	4 September 1898 (G.R.S.) Renfrew	129 Edinburgh Road, Renfrew	£4
(Lease	Ian Gow	1 May 1922 (G.R.S.) Renfrew	1 Fulbar Street, Renfrew	£10)

Applicant

4. (*a*) Where the applicant is an individual, the information required is his full name and address, e.g. Robert Gordon Campbell, 27 Princes AVenue, Girvan;

(*b*) where the applicant discloses that he is acting in a fiduciary or other capacity, the information required is the applicant's name and the name and address of the party for whom he is acting, e.g. George Campbell, Trustee of Robert Gordon Campbell, late of 27 Princes Avenue, Girvan; this applies where the relationship results from testamentary deed, partnership, court appointment etc. Information which is not revealed in the documents supporting the Application is not sought;

(*c*) where the applicant is a corporate body the information required is the name of the body;

(*d*) the names and (where appropriate) the addresses of *all* the applicants should be given.

Price

5. The consideration, if monetary, should be entered in figures. If otherwise, provide a short explanation, e.g. Love, Favour and Affection, etc. If the latter, please complete the Certificate on page 4.

Explanatory notes relevant to Part B

Adverse Possession. Rights of possession under a Lease granted by any person entitled to grant the same are not to be regarded as adverse to the interest of the applicant.

Overriding Interests. Where an overriding interest, as defined in section 28(1) of the Act, is constituted otherwise than by writ, particulars of its mode of constitution must be given. In terms of section 6(4) of the Act, the provisions for noting an overriding interest do not apply to the interest of a lessee under a Lease which is not a Long Lease.

Deeds and Documents are:—

(i) the Land Certificate,

(ii) any relevant Charge Certificate,

(iii) all writs which affect the registration, including all writs containing burdens not already specified in the Land Certificate or varying or discharging burdens since the Certificate was last issued,

(iv) where appropriate, consents to Leases and Sub-Leases and Assignations of recorded or registered Leases,

(v) Form P17, if obtained,

(vi) all unregistered links in title.

All the above documents should be submitted along with the Application.

Rule 9(1)(*c*) [1] FORM 3

Form of Application for Registration of a Transfer of Part of a Registered Interest in Land

REGISTERS OF SCOTLAND
(Land Registration (Scotland) Rules 1980, Rule 9(1)(*c*))

APPLICATION FOR REGISTRATION OF A TRANSFER OF PART *(See Note 1)*
Note: No covering letter is required.

PART A

NAME OF DEED IN RESPECT OF WHICH REGISTRATION IS REQUIRED	PRICE *(See Note 5)*	**FOR OFFICIAL USE** Fee

TITLE NUMBER(S) OF REGISTERED INTEREST(S) AFFECTED BY THIS APPLICATION *(See Note 3)* DEPOSIT NUMBER	TO Keeper of the Registers of Scotland Meadowbank House 153 London Road EDINBURGH EH8 7AU Telephone: 031-659 6111
DESCRIPTION OF SUBJECTS *(See Note 2)* Registration County of	I/WE APPLY FOR REGISTRATION IN RESPECT OF DEED(S) No. ..... in the Inventory of Writs (Form 4). I/We certify that the information supplied in this application is correct to the best of my/our knowledge and belief. Signature of Applicant or Applicant's Solicitor(s)
NAME AND ADDRESS OF APPLICANT *(See Note 4)*	Date Name of signatory (Block Capitals) Address FAS Account Number Reference Telephone:

FOR OFFICIAL USE

Application Number	Date Stamp	Title Number

Notes 1–5 referred to are contained in Notes and Directions for Completion of Application for Registration of a Transfer of Part of Registered Subjects.

PART B

Delete **YES** or **NO** as appropriate

1. Is there any person in possession or occupation of the subjects or any part of them adversely to the interest of the applicant? **YES/NO**
If **YES**, please give details:

2. If the subjects were acquired by the applicant under any statutory provision does the statutory provision restrict the applicant's power of disposal of the subjects? **YES/NO**
If **YES**, please indicate the statute:

3. (a) Apart from overriding interests are there any burdens affecting the subjects or any part of them, except as already disclosed in the Land Certificate and in the documents produced with this application? **YES/NO**
If **YES**, please give details:

(b) Are there any overriding interests affecting the subjects or any part of them which you wish noted on the Title Sheet? **YES/NO**
If **YES**, please give details:

(c) Are there any annual monetary payments (e.g. feuduty) exigible from the subjects or any part of them? **YES/NO**
If **YES**, please give details:

4. Where any party to the dealing is a company registered under the Companies Acts **YES/NO**

Has a receiver or liquidator been appointed?
If **YES**, please give details:

If **NO**, has any resolution been passed or court order made for the winding up of the company or petition presented for its liquidation? **YES/NO**
IF **YES**, please give details:

5. Where any party to the dealing other than the applicant is a company registered under the Companies Acts

Has the applicant relied on the provisions of section 35 of the Companies Act 1985 in this transaction? **YES/NO**

If **NO**, is the company acting *intra vires*? **YES/NO**

6. Where the applicant is a company registered under the Companies Acts

Is the company acting *intra vires*? **YES/NO**
If **NO**, please give details:

---

7. Where any party to the dealing is a corporate body other than a company registered under the Companies Acts

(a) Is it acting *intra vires*? **YES/NO**
If **NO**, please give details:

(b) Has any arrangement been put in hand for the dissolution of any such corporate body? **YES/NO**
If **YES**, please give details:

---

8. Are *all* the necessary consents, renunciations or affidavits in terms of section 6 of the Matrimonial Homes (Family Protection) (Scotland) Act 1981 being submitted in connection with this application? **YES/NO**

If **YES**, are you satisfied that each consent, renunciation or affidavit was produced to the appropriate purchaser at or before the time of the dealing to which it relates? **YES/NO**

N.B. If sufficient evidence to satisfy the Keeper that there are no subsisting occupancy rights in the subjects of this application is not submitted with the application then the statement by the Keeper in terms of rule 5(*j*) of the Land Registration (Scotland) Rules 1980 will not be inserted in the Title Sheet or will be qualified as appropriate without further enquiry by the Keeper.

---

9. Where the dealing is in implement of the exercise of a power of sale under a heritable security

Have the statutory procedures necessary for the proper exercise of such power been complied with? **YES/NO**

---

10. Where the dealing is a general vesting declaration or a notice of title pursuant on a compulsory purchase order

Have the necessary statutory procedures been complied with? **YES/NO**

---

11. Is any party to the transaction subject to any legal incapacity or disability not already disclosed on the Land Certificate? **YES/NO**
If **YES**, please give details:

---

12. Are the boundaries of the subjects defined on the ground by fencing or other type of enclosure? **YES/NO**

---

13. Are the deeds and documents detailed in the inventory (Form 4) all the deeds and documents relevant to the application? **YES/NO**
If **NO**, please give details:

---

14. Are there any facts and circumstances material to the right or title of the applicant which have not already been disclosed in this application or its accompanying documents? **YES/NO**
If **YES**, please give details:

The transaction is not in consideration of a price and the value of the subjects does not exceed £

N.B. If more space is required for any section of this form, a separate sheet, or separate sheets, may be added.

NOTE

[1] Substituted by S.I. 1988 No. 1143.

---

[1] NOTES AND DIRECTIONS FOR COMPLETION OF FORM 3 (YELLOW)—APPLICATION FOR REGISTRATION OF A TRANSFER OF PART OF REGISTERED SUBJECTS

NOTE

[1] The Notes and Directions which follow do not form part of the Land Registration (Scotland) Rules 1980 but are issued separately by the Keeper.

The Notes 1–5 referred to on Form 3.

1. Form 3 is to be used in the case of an Application for Registration of a Transfer of Part of property comprised in one or more registered titles. The following are examples of such transactions:—

(*a*) Disposition of part of the property;
(*b*) Feu of part of the property;
(*c*) Long Lease of part of the property;
(*d*) Feu of the whole of the property;
(*e*) Long Lease of whole of the property.

Part A

Description of subjects

2. A short description only is required, e.g.

(*a*) southmost house on first floor 27 High Street, Renfrew,
(*b*) Public house 14 Canal Lane, Falkirk,
(*c*) Bungalow 42 Acacia Avenue, Helensburgh,
(*d*) Factory 40–80 Railway Cuttings, Wishaw,
(*e*) Plot 27 Avaroch Estate, Ballachulish, or
(*f*) Hillside Farm, Parish of Rothiemurchus.

In cases where the subjects comprise or include superiorities or landlords' interests in registered Leases, a Schedule of Feus or Leases must accompany the Application if an up-to-date list is not included in the title, but the Keeper may dispense with the requirement on good cause being shown. Where possible, identification should be made on a plan. Any Schedule may be in the following form:—

[THE NEXT PAGE IS J 521]

Writ	Feuar (or Tenant)	Date of recording	Subjects	Feuduty (or Rent)
Feu Contract	Alexander Campbell and another	4 September 1898 (G.R.S.) Renfrew	129 Edinburgh Road, Renfrew	£4
(Lease	Ian Gow	1 May 1922 (G.R.S.) Renfrew	1 Fulbar Street, Renfrew	£10)

Title Number(s) of Registered Interest(s)

3. All the appropriate Title Numbers must be listed. If more space is required, please write all Title Numbers on a separate sheet and refer to the latter on the Form. If the Land Certificate has already been deposited with the Keeper, please quote the Deposit Number if known.

Applicant

4. (*a*) Where the applicant is an individual, the information required is his full name and address, e.g. Robert Gordon Campbell, 27 Princes Avenue, Girvan;

(*b*) where the applicant discloses that he is acting in a fiduciary or other capacity, the information required is the applicant's name and the name and address of the party for whom he is acting, e.g. George Campbell, Trustee of Robert Gordon Campbell, late of 27 Princes Avenue, Girvan; this applies where the relationship results from testamentary deed, partnership, court appointment etc. Information which is not revealed in the documents supporting the Application is not sought;

(*c*) where the applicant is a corporate body the information required is the name of the body;

(*d*) the names and (where appropriate) the addresses of *all* the applicants should be given.

Price

5. The consideration, if monetary, should be entered in figures. If otherwise, provide a short explanation, e.g. Love, Favour and Affection, etc. If the latter, please complete the Certificate on page 4.

Explanatory notes relevant to Part B

Adverse possession. Rights of possession under a Lease granted by any person entitled to grant the same are not to be regarded as adverse to the interest of the applicant.

Overriding Interests.
Where an overriding interest, as defined in section 28 (1) of the Act, is constituted otherwise than by writ, particulars of its mode of constitution must be given. In terms of section 6 (4) of the Act, the provisions for noting an overriding interest do not apply to the interest of a lessee under a Lease which is not a Long Lease.

Deeds and Documents are:—

(i) the Land Certificate,

(ii) any relevant Charge Certificate,

(iii) all writs which affect the registration, including all writs containing burdens not already specified in the Land Certificate or varying or discharging burdens since the Certificate was last issued,

(iv) where appropriate, consents to Leases and Sub-Leases and Assignations of recorded or registered Leases,

(v) Form P17, if obtained,

(vi) all unregistered links in title.

All the above documents should be submitted along with the Application.

Rule 9 (2)

FORM 4

Form of Inventory of Writs

REGISTERS OF SCOTLAND
(Land Registration (Scotland) Rules 1980 Rule 9 (2))

INVENTORY OF WRITS RELEVANT TO APPLICATION FOR REGISTRATION (*See Note 1*)
(to be completed in duplicate)

Title Number(s)*

(*See Note 2*)

Subjects (*See Note 3*) ______________

____

Registration County ______________

Please complete inventory overleaf as in specimen Inventory below.

Applicant's Reference ______________

Item No.	Please mark "S" against writs submitted	Particulars of Writs (*See Note 4*)		
		Writ	Grantee	Date of Recording
		Land Certificate[1]		
		Charge Certificate[1]		
1	–	Feu Charter	Upright Builders Ltd.	2 May 1938
2	S	Feu Disposition	Smith	4 Feb 1939
3	S	Disposition	Scott	3 Jun 1973
4	S	Standard Security	Meadowbank B.S.	3 Jun 1973
5	S	Confirmation	Scott's Executors	28 Aug 1979
6	S	Discharge	of No. 4	–
7	S	Disposition	Brown	–
8	S	Standard Security	Lochend B.S.	–

The writs marked "S" on this inventory were received on the Date of Receipt stamped on this page

FOR OFFICIAL USE		
Title No.	Date of Receipt	Application No.

* To be completed for a dealing with registered interest(s) in land.
[1] Delete if inapplicable

Notes 1–4 referred to are contained in Notes and Directions for Completion of Inventory of Writs Relevant to
Application for Registration.

Item No.	Please mark " S " against writs submitted	Particulars of Writs		
		Writ	Grantee	Date of recording
		Land Certificate* Charge Certificate*		

* Delete if inapplicable

[1] NOTES AND DIRECTIONS FOR COMPLETION OF FORM 4 (WHITE)— INVENTORY OF WRITS RELEVANT TO APPLICATION FOR REGISTRATION

NOTE

[1] The Notes and Directions which follow Forms 1–4, *infra*, do not form part of the Land Registration (Scotland) Rules 1980 but are issued separately by the Keeper.

The Notes 1–4 referred to on Form 4.

1. Each Application for Registration must be accompanied by a Form 4 listing all deeds and documents relevant to the Application whether or not such are submitted with the case. In cases where effect is to be given to, for example, a Disposition and two Standard Securities affecting the same interest, the Application Forms for which are all completed by one solicitor, it is sufficient for him to submit one Form 4 listing all the deeds and documents for the three Applications. Where more than one solicitor or applicant is involved, each should complete a Form 4 for his own deeds &c. The Form 4 should be completed in duplicate. One copy will be returned by the Keeper as his acknowledgment of receipt.

2. Insert the name and address of the party or the solicitor who is submitting the writs.

3. A short description only of the subjects is required, e.g. a postal address.

4. (*a*) In the case of an Application for First Registration (Form 1), the relevant deeds and documents to be listed on Form 4 are:—

(i) a sufficient progress of titles including the deed inducing registration and unrecorded links in title,
(ii) all prior writs containing rights or burdens affecting the subjects,
(iii) any redemption Receipt for Feuduty or other annual payment,
(iv) any existing heritable securities and deeds relating thereto,
(v) where appropriate, consents to Leases and Sub-Leases and Assignations of recorded or registered Leases,
(vi) Form P16, if obtained,
(vii) any other relevant documents.

All the above documents should be submitted along with the Application, but if any are not available when the Application is lodged, they should be listed on the Inventory and marked " To follow ".

(*b*) In the case of an Application on Form 2 or Form 3, the relevant deeds and documents to be listed on Form 4 are:—

(i) the Land Certificate,
(ii) any relevant Charge Certificate,
(iii) all writs which affect the registration, including all writs containing burdens not already specified in the Land Certificate or varying or discharging burdens since the Certificate was last issued,
(iv) where appropriate, consents to Leases and Sub-Leases and Assignations of recorded or registered Leases,
(v) Form P17, if obtained,
(vi) all unregistered links in title.

All the above documents should be submitted along with the Application, but if any are not available when the Application is lodged, they should be listed on the Inventory and marked " To follow ".

Rule 13 FORM 5

Form of Application for Noting of Overriding Interest or for entry of Other Information in terms of Section 6(1)(g)

REGISTERS OF SCOTLAND
(Land Registration (Scotland) Rules 1980 Rule 13)

APPLICATION FOR NOTING OR ENTERING ON THE REGISTER

FOR OFFICIAL USE

TO

Keeper of the Registers of Scotland

Meadowbank House
153 London Road
EDINBURGH EH8 7AU

Telephone: 031-661 6111

Title No(s) ______________________

Short description of subjects __________

____

I/We apply to have the information set out below noted or entered on the Title Sheet(s) of the above Title(s), viz.

I/We apply to have the information set out below deleted from the Title Sheet(s) of the above Title(s) viz.

To support this application, I/We enclose the documents listed on the Inventory (Form 4).

Signature of Applicant or Applicant's Solicitor ______________________

Full name of Applicant ______________________

Address of Applicant ______________________

Name of Solicitor ______________________

Address of Solicitor ______________________

Reference ______________________ Telephone No. __________

Date of Application ______________________

Note: No covering letter is required.

Rule 14 [1] FORM 6

Form of Land Certificate

(Land Registration (Scotland) Rules 1980, Rule 14)

LAND REGISTER OF SCOTLAND

LAND CERTIFICATE

TITLE NUMBER

SUBJECTS

This Land Certificate, issued pursuant to section 5(2) of the Land Registration (Scotland) Act 1979, is a copy of the Title Sheet relating to the above subjects.

STATEMENT OF INDEMNITY

Subject to any specific qualifications entered in the Title Sheet of which this Land Certificate is a copy, a person who suffers loss as a result of any of the events specified in section 12(1) of the above Act shall be entitled to be indemnified in respect of that loss by the Keeper of the Registers of Scotland in terms of that Act.

ATTENTION IS DRAWN TO THE NOTICE OVERLEAF AND GENERAL INFORMATION ON THE INSIDE BACK COVER OF THIS CERTIFICATE.

NOTICE

This Land Certificate was made to agree with the Title Sheet of which it is a copy on the most recent date entered below.

This Land Certificate may be made to agree with the Title Sheet at any time without payment. Application should be made on Form 8.

Please see inside back cover for General Information.

1. OVERRIDING INTERESTS. A registered interest in land is in terms of section 3(1) of the Land Registration (Scotland) Act 1979 subject to overriding interests defined in section 28 of that Act (hereinafter referred to as "the 1979 Act") as amended by the Matrimonial Homes (Family Protection) (Scotland) Act 1981 as:

in relation to any interest in land, the right or interest over it of

(*a*) the lessee under a lease which is not a long lease;
(*b*) the lessee under a long lease who, prior to the commencement of the 1979 Act, has acquired a real right to the subjects of the lease by virtue of possession of them;
(*c*) a crofter or cottar within the meaning of section 3 or 28(4) respectively of the Crofters (Scotland) Act 1955, or a landholder or statutory small tenant within the meaning of section 2(2) or 32(1) respectively of the Small Landholders (Scotland) Act 1911;
(*d*) the proprietor of the dominant tenement in a servitude;
(*e*) the Crown or any Government or other public department, or any public or local authority, under any enactment or rule of law, other than an enactment or rule of law authorising or requiring the recording of a deed in the Register of Sasines or registration in order to complete the right or interest;
(*ee*) the operator having a right conferred in accordance with paragraph 2, 3 or 5 of Schedule 2 to the Telecommunications Act 1984 (agreements for execution of works, obstruction of access, etc.);
(*f*) the holder of a floating charge whether or not the charge has attached to the interest;
(*g*) a member of the public in respect of any public right of way or in respect of any right held inalienably by the Crown in trust for the public;
(*gg*) the non-entitled spouse within the meaning of section 6 of the Matrimonial Homes (Family Protection) (Scotland) Act 1981;
(*h*) any person, being a right which has been made real, otherwise than by the recording of a deed in the Register of Sasines or by registration; or
(*i*) any other person under any rule of law relating to common interest or joint or common property, not being a right or interest constituting a real right, burden or condition entered in the title sheet of the interest in land under section 6(1)(*e*) of the 1979 Act or having effect by virtue of a deed recorded in the Register of Sasines,

but does not include any subsisting burden or condition enforceable against the interest in land and entered in its title sheet under section 6(1) of the 1979 Act.

2. THE USE OF ARROWS ON TITLE PLANS
(*a*) Where a deed states the line of a boundary in relation to a physical object, e.g. the centre line, that line is indicated on the Title Plan, either by means of a black arrow or verbally.
(*b*) An arrow across the object indicates that the boundary is stated to be the centre line.
(*c*) An arrow pointing to the object indicates that the boundary is stated to be the face of the object to which the arrow points.
(*d*) The physical object presently shown on the Plan may not be the one referred to in the deed. Indemnity is therefore excluded in respect of information as to the line of the boundary.

3. Lineal measurements shown in figures on Title Plans are subject to the qualification "or thereby". Indemnity is excluded in respect of such measurements.

4. SUBMISSION OF LAND CERTIFICATE WITH SUBSEQUENT APPLICATIONS FOR REGISTRATION. In terms of Rule 9(3), this Land Certificate should be submitted to the Keeper of the Registers of Scotland with any application for registration.

5. CAUTION. No unauthorised alteration to this Land Certificate should be made.

NOTE
[1] Substituted by S.I. 1988 No. 1143.

Rule 15 FORM 7

Form of Charge Certificate

(Land Registration (Scotland) Rules 1980 Rule 15)

LAND REGISTER OF SCOTLAND

CHARGE CERTIFICATE

TITLE NUMBER:

SUBJECTS:

The within-mentioned Charge has been registered against the subjects in the above Title.

Statement of Idemnity

Subject to any specific qualifications entered in the Title Sheet to which the Charge Certificate relates a person who suffers loss as a result of any of the events specified in Section 12(1) of the Land Registration (Scotland) Act 1979 shall be entitled to be indemnified in respect of that loss by the Keeper of the Registers of Scotland in terms of that Act.

NOTICE

1. This Certificate must be presented to the Keeper on every transaction affecting the interest of the within-mentioned Registered Creditor.
2. The relative Title Sheet contains a specification of the reservations and burdens affecting the subjects in the above title. An Office Copy of the Title Sheet may be obtained on application to the Keeper.
3. No unauthorised alterations to this Charge Certificate should be made.

NOTICE

This Charge Certificate was made to agree with the Title Sheet to which it relates on the most recent date entered below.

This Charge Certificate may be made to agree with the Title Sheet at any time without payment. Application should be made on Form 8.

LAND REGISTER OF SCOTLAND

CHARGE CERTIFICATE

TITLE NO.:

SUBJECTS:

Registered Proprietor of subjects:

THIS TO CERTIFY that

is the Registered Creditor in the heritable security attached
registered on
to the extent of

NOTE
There are no heritable securities ranking prior to or *pari passu* with the above mentioned heritable security appearing on the Register affecting the subjects (except as stated in the Schedule annexed).

Rule 16 (2) FORM 8

Form of Application for Certificate of Title to be made to correspond with Title Sheet

REGISTERS OF SCOTLAND

(Land Registration (Scotland) Rules 1980 Rule 16 (2))

APPLICATION FOR LAND OR CHARGE CERTIFICATE TO BE MADE TO CORRESPOND WITH THE TITLE SHEET [1]

FOR OFFICIAL USE

TO

Keeper of the Registers of Scotland

Meadowbank House
153 London Road
EDINBURGH EH8 7AU

Telephone: 031-661 6111

Title Number ______________________

Short description of subjects ______________________

I/We apply for the accompanying Land Certificate/Charge Certificate [2] to be made to correspond with the Title Sheet.

The following parties have acquired an interest in the subjects since the Land Certificate was last made to correspond with the Title Sheet [3, 4]

Signature of Applicant or Applicant's Solicitor ______________________

____

Name of Applicant ______________________

Address of Applicant ______________________

Telephone No. ________ Reference ______________________

Date of Application ______________________

[1] No covering letter is required.

[2] Delete whichever is inapplicable.

[3] To assist the Keeper to disclose in the Land Certificate any relevant entries from the Register of Inhibitions and Adjudications, the full name and designation of any party who has acquired an interest in the subjects in the title since the Land Certificate was last made to correspond with the Title Sheet should be inserted.

[4] Delete if inapplicable.

Rule 20 FORM 9

Form of Application for Rectification of Register

REGISTERS OF SCOTLAND

(Land Registration (Scotland) Rules 1980 Rule 20)

APPLICATION FOR RECTIFICATION OF THE REGISTER

FOR OFFICIAL USE

TO

Keeper of the Registers of Scotland

Meadowbank House
153 London Road
EDINBURGH EH8 7AU

Telephone: 031-661 6111

Title No(s) ____________________

Short description of subjects __________

____

I/We apply for rectification of the Title Sheet(s) for the above Title No(s) as follows:

To support this application, I/We enclose the documents listed on the inventory (Form 4).

Signature of Applicant or Applicant's Solicitor ____________________

Full name of Applicant ____________________

Address of Applicant ____________________

Name of Solicitor ____________________

Address of Solicitor ____________________

Reference ____________________ **Telephone No.** __________

Date of Application ____________________

NOTE No covering letter is required.

Rule 24 (1) FORM 10

Form of Application for Report prior to Registration

REGISTERS OF SCOTLAND

(Land Registration (Scotland) Rules 1980 Rule 24 (1))

APPLICATION FOR A REPORT PRIOR TO REGISTRATION OF THE SUBJECTS DESCRIBED BELOW [1, 2, 3]

Applicant's reference:

FROM

FOR OFFICIAL USE
Search Sheet No.
Date of Receipt
Report Number

TO

Keeper of the Registers of Scotland

Meadowbank House
153 London Road
EDINBURGH EH8 7AU

Telephone: 031-661 6111

I/We apply for a report

(1) on the subjects described below, for which an application for registration in the Land Register is to be made, from

(a) the REGISTER OF SASINES (County of ____________________)

and

(b) the LAND REGISTER
stating whether or not registration of the said subjects has been effected

DESCRIPTION OF SUBJECTS [4] ______________________________

____

____

edged red on the accompanying Plan [5, 6]
being (part of) [5] the subjects described in [5, 7] ____________________

____

____

OFFICE COPY — If the subjects have been registered, the Keeper is requested to supply an Office Copy of the Title Sheet [5, 8]

[1] To be completed in duplicate.
[2] No covering letter is required and an existing Search should not be submitted.
[3] No charge is made for this Report.
[4] The description must be sufficient to allow the subjects to be identified in both Registers and, if lengthy, may be on a separate sheet.
[5] Delete if inapplicable.
[6] A plan need not be attached if a verbal description will sufficiently identify the subjects.
[7] Describe by reference to a writ recorded in the Register of Sasines.
[8] The fee payable for an Office Copy will be intimated.

and (II) from the REGISTER OF INHIBITIONS AND ADJUDICATIONS for 5 years prior to the date of Certificate

against *

PARTY/PARTIES LAST INFEFT

OTHERS

Signature of applicant ______________________________

Telephone number ______________________________

Date of application ______________________________

*** Insert the full names, occupations and addresses of the persons on whom a Report is required.**

Rule 24 (2) FORM 11

Form of Application for continuation of Report prior to Registration

REGISTERS OF SCOTLAND

(Land Registration (Scotland) Rules 1980 Rule 24 (2))

APPLICATION FOR CONTINUATION OF REPORT PRIOR TO THE REGISTRATION OF THE SUBJECTS DESCRIBED BELOW [1,2,3]

FOR OFFICIAL USE
Date of Receipt
Report No.

Applicant's Reference: ______________________

Previous Report No.[4] ______________________

FROM

TO

Keeper of the Registers of Scotland

Meadowbank House
153 London Road
EDINBURGH EH8 7AU

Telephone: 031-661 6111

Subjects ______________________

County ______________________ Search Sheet Number ______________________

I/We apply for the Report to ______________________ [5,6]
against the above subjects to be brought down to date.

The following parties (in addition to those noted on the previous Report) should be searched against in the Register of Inhibitions and Adjudications, viz.

Signature ______________________ Date ______________________

[1] To be completed in duplicate.
[2] No covering letter is required and neither an existing search nor the previous Report should be submitted.
[3] No charge is made for this Report.
[4] Number obtainable from previous Report.
[5] Date obtainable from previous Report.
[6] Any plan sent to the Keeper along with the application for the report which is to be continued, or any plan supplied by the Keeper along with that report must be submitted along with this application.

Rule 24 (3) FORM 12

Form of Application for Report over Registered Subjects

REGISTERS OF SCOTLAND

(Land Registration (Scotland) Rules 1980 Rule 24 (3))

APPLICATION FOR A REPORT OVER REGISTERED SUBJECTS [1, 2]

Applicant's reference: ______________________

FOR OFFICIAL USE
Date of Receipt
Report Number

FROM

TO

Keeper of the Registers of Scotland

Meadowbank House
153 London Road
EDINBURGH EH8 7AU

Telephone: 031-661 6111

TITLE NUMBER(S):

I/We apply for a report from

(1) the LAND REGISTER against:

SHORT DESCRIPTION OF SUBJECTS [3]:

Tick appropriate box

(a) ☐ being the whole subjects in the above Title

(b) ☐ being part of the subjects in the above Title and edged red on the attached plan [4]

(c) ☐ being part of the subjects in the above Title and comprising the plot numbered ______________________ on the estate plan approved by the Keeper

From the date to which the Land Certificate was last brought down
To the date of the Certificate.

[1] No covering letter is required.
[2] No charge is made for this Report.
[3] If (a) applies, take the description from the title page of the Land Certificate; if (b) or (c) applies, the description must be sufficient to allow the subjects to be identified.
[4] A plan need not be attached if a verbal description will sufficiently identify the subjects.

and (ii) from the REGISTER OF INHIBITIONS AND ADJUDICATIONS

for 5 years prior to the date of Certificate

against[a]

Signature of applicant ______________________

Telephone number ______________________

Date of application ______________________

[a] Insert the full names, occupations and addresses of the persons on whom a Report is required.

Rule 24 (4) FORM 13

Form of Application for continuation of Report over Registered Subjects

REGISTERS OF SCOTLAND

(Land Registration (Scotland) Rules 1980 Rule 24 (4))

APPLICATION FOR CONTINUATION OF REPORT OVER REGISTERED SUBJECTS [1,2,3]

FOR OFFICIAL USE
Date of Receipt
Report No.

Applicant's reference:

Previous Report No.[4]

FROM

TO

Keeper of the Registers of Scotland

Meadowbank House
153 London Road
EDINBURGH EH8 7AU

Telephone: 031-661 6111

Subjects ____________________

Title Number(s) ____________________

I/We apply for the Report from the Land Register to ____________ [5,6] against the above subjects to be brought down to date.

The following parties (in addition to those noted on the previous Report) should be searched against in the Register of Inhibitions and Adjudications, viz.

Signature ____________________ Date__________

[1] To be completed in duplicate.
[2] No covering letter is required.
[3] No charge is made for this Report.
[4] Number obtainable from previous Report.
[5] Date obtainable from previous Report.
[6] Any plan sent to the Keeper along with the application for the report which is to be continued, or any plan supplied by the Keeper along with that report must be submitted along with this application.

Rule 24 (5) FORM 14

Form of Application for Report to ascertain whether or not Subjects have been registered

REGISTERS OF SCOTLAND

(Land Registration (Scotland) Rules 1980 Rule 24 (5))

APPLICATION FOR A REPORT TO ASCERTAIN WHETHER OR NOT SUBJECTS HAVE BEEN REGISTERED[1]

Applicant's reference:

FOR OFFICIAL USE
Search Sheet No.
Date of Receipt
Report Number

FROM

TO

Keeper of the Registers of Scotland

Meadowbank House
153 London Road
EDINBURGH EH8 7AU

Telephone: 031-661 6111

I/We apply for a report from
(1) the LAND REGISTER (County of ______)
stating whether or not registration has been effected of subjects

DESCRIPTION OF SUBJECTS ______

______

______

edged red on the accompanying Plan[2, 4] and being (part of [2]) the subjects described in[2, 3] ______

______

______

OFFICE COPY If the subjects have been registered, the Keeper is requested to supply an Office Copy of the Title Sheet[2, 5]

[1] No covering letter is required.
[2] Delete if inapplicable.
[3] Describe by reference to a writ recorded in the Register of Sasines.
[4] A Plan need not be attached if a verbal description will sufficiently identify the subjects.
[5] If an Office Copy is supplied the fee for it will be intimated together with the fee for this Report.

and (ii) from the REGISTER OF INHIBITIONS AND ADJUDICATIONS
for 5 years prior to the date of Certificate
against[6, 7]

Signature of applicant ________________________________

Telephone number ________________________________

Date of application ________________________________

[6] Delete if an Office Copy is not required. See overleaf.
[7] Insert the full names, occupations and addresses of the persons on whom a Report is required.

Rule 24 (6) FORM 15

Form of Application for an Office Copy

REGISTERS OF SCOTLAND

(Land Registration (Scotland) Rules 1980 Rule 24 (6))

APPLICATION FOR AN OFFICE COPY

NOTE: No covering letter is required

FOR OFFICIAL USE

TO

Keeper of the Registers of Scotland

Meadowbank House
153 London Road
EDINBURGH EH8 7AU

Telephone: 031-661 6111

Title No. ____________________

Short description of subjects ____________________

I/We apply for

(1) An Office Copy of

Tick appropriate box(es)

- ☐ Title Sheet (excluding Title Plan)[1]
- ☐ Title Plan
- ☐ Property Section
- ☐ Proprietorship Section[1]
- ☐ Charges Section
- ☐ Burdens Section
- ☐ Documents referred to in the Property Section
- ☐ Documents referred to in the Charges Section
- ☐ Documents referred to in the Burdens Section
- ☐ The following documents:

[1] See Note overleaf

and (ii) A Search in the Register of Inhibitions and Adjudications for 5 years prior to the date of the Office Copy against'

Signature of Applicant or Applicant's Solicitor ____________________

____

Name of Applicant ____________________

Address of Applicant ____________________

Telephone Number ____________ Reference ____________

Date of application ____________________

An Office Copy will show the current state of the Register. When such an Office Copy is requested, a search in the Register of Inhibitions and Adjudications should be instructed against any party who has acquired an interest in the subjects since the last date on which the Land Certificate was made to correspond with the Register.

Rule 25

SCHEDULE B

Description of Registered Interests in Land

In any conveyance of, or other dealing with, or reference to, an interest in land which has been registered in the Land Register of Scotland the interest should be described as: " the subjects registered under Title Number(s) [*here insert the appropriate number(s)*] "

NOTES

(*a*) If part only of the registered interest in land is being conveyed or otherwise dealt with for the first time, such part should either be described adequately adding " being part of the subjects registered under Title Number(s) [*here insert the appropriate number(s)*] " or thus: " All and whole the subjects registered under Title Number(s) [*here insert the appropriate number(s)*] with the exception of [*describe the part excepted*]."

(*b*) If several subjects are registered under the one Title Number and it is desired to specify one or more of them, these may be distinguished thus: " All and Whole the subjects (First) registered under Title Number [*here insert the appropriate number*] " or " the subjects (Second) and (Third) registered under Title Number [*here insert the appropriate number*]."

Land Registration (Scotland) Act 1979 (Commencement No. 2) Order 1982

(S.I. 1982 No. 520)

[1st April 1982]

The Secretary of State, in exercise of the powers conferred on him by section 30(2) of the Land Registration (Scotland) Act 1979 and all other powers enabling him in that behalf, hereby makes the following order:—

Citation and interpretation

1. This order may be cited as the Land Registration (Scotland) Act 1979 (Commencement No. 2) Order 1982.

Commencement

2. Subsections (1) and (2) of section 2 and subsection (3) of section 3 of the Land Registration (Scotland) Act 1979 shall come into operation on 4th October 1982 in the area, for the purpose of registration of writs, of the County of Dunbarton.

Matrimonial Homes (Form of Consent) (Scotland) Regulations 1982

(S.I. 1982 No. 971)

[1st September 1982]

In exercise of the powers conferred upon me by section 6 (3) (*a*) (i), and by that section as applied by section 9 (2), of the Matrimonial Homes (Family Protection) (Scotland) Act 1981, and of all other powers enabling me in that behalf, I hereby make the following regulations:

1.—(1) These regulations may be cited as the Matrimonial Homes (Form of Consent) (Scotland) Regulations 1982 and shall come into operation on 1st September 1982.

(2) In these regulations—

" the Act " means the Matrimonial Homes (Family Protection) (Scotland) Act 1981,

and, in a case where section 9 (1) of the Act applies, any reference in these regulations to the entitled spouse and to the non-entitled spouse shall be construed in accordance with section 9 (2) (*a*) of the Act.

2. The consent of the non-entitled spouse to any dealing of the entitled spouse relating to a matrimonial home shall be—

(*a*) where the consent is given in a deed effecting the dealing, in or as nearly as may be in the form set out in Schedule 1 to these regulations; or

(*b*) where the consent is given in a separate document, in or as nearly as may be in the form set out in Schedule 2 to these regulations.

SCHEDULE 1

Consent to be Inserted in the Deed Effecting the Dealing

(The following words should be inserted where appropriate in the deed. The consenter should sign as a party to the deed.)

. . . with the consent of A.B. *(designation),* the spouse of the said C.D., for the purposes of the Matrimonial Homes (Family Protection) (Scotland) Act 1981. . . [To be attested]

SCHEDULE 2

Consent in a Separate Document

I, A.B. *(designation)*, spouse of C.D. *(designation)*, hereby consent, for the purposes of the Matrimonial Homes (Family Protection) (Scotland) Act 1981, to the undernoted dealing of the said C.D. relating to *(here describe the matrimonial home or the part of it to which the dealing relates: see Note 1)*.

Dealing referred to:—

(Here describe the dealing: see Note 2.)

[To be attested.]

Note 1

The expression " matrimonial home " is defined in section 22 of the Matrimonial Homes (Family Protection) (Scotland) Act 1981 as follows:—

" " matrimonial home " means any house, caravan, houseboat or other structure which has been provided or has been made available by one or both of the spouses as, or has become, a family residence and includes any garden or other ground or building attached to, and usually occupied with, or otherwise required for the amenity or convenience of, the house, caravan, houseboat or other structure."

Note 2
The expression "dealing" is defined in section 6(2) of the Matrimonial Homes (Family Protection) (Scotland) Act 1981 as follows:—

" "dealing" includes the grant of a heritable security and the creation of a trust but does not include a conveyance under section 80 of the Lands Clauses Consolidation (Scotland) Act 1845."

Right to Purchase (Application Form) (Scotland) Order 1984

(S.I. 1984 No. 1005)

[12th July 1984]

In exercise of the powers conferred upon me by section 2(1) of the Tenants' Rights, Etc. (Scotland) Act 1980 and of all other powers enabling me in that behalf, I hereby make the following order:–

1. This order shall be cited as the Right to Purchase (Application Form) (Scotland) Order 1984, and shall come into operation on 24th July 1984.

2. Any tenant under a secure tenancy, within the meaning of Part II of the Tenants' Rights, Etc. (Scotland) Act 1980, wishing to exercise his right to purchase under section 1 of that Act shall, as required by section 2 of that Act, do so by serving on the landlord a notice in the form specified in the Schedule to this order.

3. The Right to Purchase (Application Form) (Scotland) Order 1980 is hereby revoked.

Article 2

SCHEDULE

TENANTS' RIGHTS, ETC. (SCOTLAND) ACT 1980
APPLICATION TO PURCHASE

This form is divided into several sections. Section 1 applies to sole tenants and section 2 to joint tenants; the other sections apply to both sole tenants and joint tenants, although not all of them will need to be completed in every case.

Please write clearly and complete the form in ball point pen or ink. Where a YES or NO answer is required, tick the appropriate box.

SECTION 1

FOR USE BY SOLE TENANTS

Address of house:

Telephone no:

Surname:

First names:

Do you have a husband/wife who lives with you?

YES ☐ NO ☐

If you have answered YES to the above question, please ask your husband/wife to sign this declaration:

> I understand that my husband/wife, who is the sole tenant of the house named on this form, is applying to buy the house at the above address, and that my consent to the purchase is necessary. I hereby declare that I consent to the proposed purchase.

Signed:

Date:

NOW TURN TO SECTION 3

SECTION 2

For Use by Joint Tenants

Address of house:

Telephone no:

All joint tenants should insert their names below and indicate, by ticking the appropriate boxes, whether they wish to be joint purchasers, and whether they have a husband/wife who lives with them. (Details of persons who wish to be joint purchasers but who are not joint tenants should be given in section 5.)

1. Surname:

   First names:

   Are you applying to be a joint purchaser? YES ☐ NO ☐
   Do you have a husband/wife who lives with you? YES ☐ NO ☐

2. Surname:

   First names:

   Are you applying to be a joint purchaser? YES ☐ NO ☐
   Do you have a husband/wife who lives with you? YES ☐ NO ☐

3. Surname:

   First names:

   Are you applying to be a joint purchaser? YES ☐ NO ☐
   Do you have a husband/wife who lives with you? YES ☐ NO ☐

4. Surname:

   First names:

   Are you applying to be a joint purchaser? YES ☐ NO ☐
   Do you have a husband/wife who lives with you? YES ☐ NO ☐

If any joint tenant is not applying to be a joint purchaser, he/she should be asked to sign this declaration:

> I understand that my joint tenant(s) is/are applying to buy the house at the above address. I do not wish to become a joint purchaser but I understand that my consent to the purchase is necessary. I hereby declare that I consent to the proposed purchase.

Signed:	Signed:
Date:	Date:
Signed:	Signed:
Date:	Date:

If any of the joint tenants listed above, whether or not they wish to be joint purchasers, are married and their husband/wife lives in the house with them but is not also a joint tenant, their husband/wife should be asked to sign this declaration:

I understand that those joint tenants who have indicated above their wish to be joint purchasers are applying to buy the house at the above address and that my consent to the purchase is necessary. I hereby declare that I consent to the proposed purchase.

Signed:	Signed:
Date:	Date:
Signed:	Signed:
Date:	Date:

NOW TURN TO SECTION 3

SECTION 3

For Use by Sole and Joint Tenants

Please give complete details of your present tenancy and any previous periods of occupation of publicly provided housing. In the case of joint tenants, if the details are the same for all or some of those tenants, they need only be given once. Please also give details of any breaks of less than 12 months between periods of tenancy. Once you have given details of 30 years of occupation not counting breaks, there is no need to give further details. You should also stop if you reach a break of more than 12 months.

Please now fill in the following sheet(s) using a separate page for each person.

If you have stopped before you have given details of 30 years of occupation because you have reached a break of more than 12 months, turn now to section 4. Otherwise turn now to section 5.

Surname:

First names:

Date residence began (see footnote)	Date residence finished	Name of authority	Address of house	Status (tenant, husband/wife of tenant, child of tenant)

Note: Please give details of your *present* tenancy *first*, and then details of previous tenancies, *working backwards*.

SECTION 4

For Use by Sole and Joint Tenants

If you have had a break in occupation of between 12 and 24 months turn back to the page which you have filled out in section 3, draw a line across the page, give details of the break and then add details of any earlier periods of occupation and breaks of up to 12 months. If you reach another break of between 12 and 24 months before you have listed 30 years' occupation, simply draw another line across the page and follow these instructions again.

NOW TURN TO SECTION 5

SECTION 5

For Use by Sole and Joint Tenants

(*a*) Do you wish at this stage to include any joint purchaser other than a joint tenant in your application? YES ☐ NO ☐

IF YOUR ANSWER IS NO, TURN NOW TO SECTION 6

(*b*) If so, please name joint purchaser(s)

	Surname	First names
1		
2		
3		
4		

(*c*) What relation is/are the named joint purchaser(s) to you?

1	
2	
3	
4	

If any of the joint purchasers named above is the husband or wife of the tenant (or of one of the joint tenants), and that joint purchaser's past tenancy or occupation of publicly provided accommodation is longer than that of the tenant (or of any of the joint tenants) that joint purchaser should turn back to Section 3 and fill in a new page, not forgetting to look also at Section 4.

(*d*) Is/Are the joint purchaser(s) over 18 years of age?

1	YES ☐	NO ☐
2	YES ☐	NO ☐
3	YES ☐	NO ☐
4	YES ☐	NO ☐

(*e*) Has each of the named joint purchasers lived in the house you are applying to buy for the last six months?

1	YES ☐	NO ☐
2	YES ☐	NO ☐
3	YES ☐	NO ☐
4	YES ☐	NO ☐

(*f*) If your answer to either of the above questions for any of the proposed joint purchasers is NO, it may help if you provide additional information. If you wish to provide additional information, please do so below:

(*g*) Please ask any joint purchasers to sign the declaration below:

I certify that the information given in this form concerning me is to the best of my knowledge correct. I hereby give notice that I wish to be considered as a joint purchaser.

Signed:

Date:

Signed:

Date:

Signed:

Date:

Signed:

Date:

NOW TURN TO SECTION 6

SECTION 6

FOR USE BY ALL TENANTS WHO WISH TO APPLY TO PURCHASE (JOINT PURCHASERS WHO ARE NOT TENANTS SHOULD NOT COMPLETE THIS DECLARATION)

Sole tenants and joint tenants (provided that they have indicated in Section 2 that they are applying to be joint purchasers) should complete this declaration:

The information given by me on this form is, to the best of my knowledge, correct. I hereby give notice that I seek to exercise my right under section 1 of the Tenants' Rights, Etc. (Scotland) Act 1980 to buy the house of which I am tenant.

Signed:

Date:

Signed:

Date:

Signed:

Date:

Signed:

Date:

Charging Orders (Residential Accommodation) (Scotland) Order 1993

(S.I. 1993 No. 1516)

[14th June 1993]

The Secretary of State, in exercise of the powers conferred on him by section 23(5) and (6) of the Health and Social Services and Social Security Adjudications Act 1983 and of all other powers enabling him in that behalf, hereby makes the following Order:—

Citation and commencement

1. This Order may be cited as the Charging Orders (Residential Accommodation) (Scotland) Order 1993 and shall come into force on 16th July 1993.

Interpretation

2. In this Order—

"the 1970 Act" means the Conveyancing and Feudal Reform (Scotland) Act 1970;

"the 1983 Act" means the Health and Social Services and Social Security Adjudications Act 1983;

"accommodation" has the same meaning as the expression "Part III accommodation" has in section 21(8) of the 1983 Act; and

"charging order" means a charging order made under section 23 of the 1983 Act.

Forms

3.—(1) The form set out in Form 1 of the Schedule to this Order or a form as similar thereto as circumstances permit shall be the form of a charging order.

(2) The form set out in Form 2 of the Schedule to this Order or a form as similar thereto as circumstances permit shall be the form of a discharge of a charging order.

Amount due under charging order

4. The amount due by the debtor under a charging order at any time shall be the aggregate of—

(*a*) the debt due by him at that time to the local authority in respect of the provision of accommodation referred to in section 23(1) of the 1983 Act; and

(*b*) any interest thereon at that time as specified in section 24 of the 1983 Act, as certified by the director of finance of the local authority in whose favour the charging order was made and the director of finance of that local authority may substitute an amended certificate on cause shown.

Application of Part II of the 1970 Act

5.—(1) The provisions of Part II of the 1970 Act shall apply to a charging order made under section 23 of the 1983 Act after the date of coming into force of this Order as if it was a standard security in a form prescribed in Schedule 2 to the 1970 Act, subject to the exceptions specified in paragraph (2) below and to the modifications specified in paragraph (3) below.

(2) The following provisions of Part II of the 1970 Act shall not apply to a charging order, namely—

(*a*) section 9(1) to (5) (the standard security);

(*b*) section 10(1) to (3) (import of forms of, and certain clauses in, standard security);

(*c*) section 11(1) (effect of recorded standard security);

(*d*) section 12 (standard security may be granted by person uninfeft); and

(*e*) section 14 (assignation of standard security).

(3) Subject to the exceptions specified in paragraph (2) above, the provisions of Part II of the 1970 Act shall apply subject to the following modifications, namely—

(*a*) as if there was substituted a reference to "charging order" for any reference to "standard security" in those provisions, other than in section 13 or where the context otherwise requires;

(*b*) as if, in section 10(4) (implied assignation of title deeds), for the reference to "The forms of standard security contained in Schedule

2 to this Act", there was substituted a reference to "The form of charging order set out in Form 1 in the Schedule to the Charging Orders (Residential Accommodation) (Scotland) Order 1993";

(*c*) as if, in section 13(1) (ranking of standard securities), for the words from "subsequent security" to "conveyance so recorded", there was substituted the words "charging order over the same interest in land or any part thereof, being a charging order so recorded";

(*d*) as if, in section 17 (discharge of standard security), for the reference to "Form F of Schedule 4 to this Act", there was substituted a reference to "the form of discharge set out in Form 2 in the Schedule to the Charging Orders (Residential Accommodation) (Scotland) Order 1993";

(*e*) as if, in section 19(1) (calling-up of standard security), there was inserted at the end the following proviso—

"provided that the local authority shall not be entitled to call up a charging order for non payment of the amount due by the debtor under the charging order while the debtor is alive, except in the event of—

(*a*) the insolvency of the debtor; or

(*b*) the sale or transfer of the interest in land subject to the charging order; or

(*c*) the calling up of a standard security over the security subjects.";

(*f*) as if, in section 30(1) (interpretation of Part II), there was inserted before the first definition of "creditor" the following definition:–

" 'charging order' means a charging order made under section 23 of the Health and Social Services and Social Security Adjudications Act 1983;"; and

(*g*) as if, in paragraph 8 (entitlement of creditor to call up the standard security) of Schedule 3 (the standard conditions), there was inserted at the end the following proviso:—

"provided that the local authority shall not be entitled to call up a charging order for non payment of the amount due by the debtor under the charging order while the debtor is alive, except in the event of—

(*a*) the insolvency of the debtor; or

(*b*) the sale or transfer of the interest in land subject to the charging order; or

(*c*) the calling up of a standard security over the security subjects.".

Article 3

SCHEDULE

FORM 1

Form of Charging Order

THE HEALTH AND SOCIAL SERVICES AND SOCIAL SECURITY ADJUDICATIONS ACT 1983

Charging Order

We (*name of local authority*), in exercise of the powers conferred upon us by section 23 of the Health and Social Services and Social Security Adjudications Act 1983 ("the 1983 Act"), hereby make a charging order over All and Whole (*here describe the security subjects as in Note 1 hereto*) being an interest in land held by (*name and designation of debtor*) in respect of any debt due or to become due by the said (*name of debtor*) to us in respect of the provision by us of accommodation for the said (*name of debtor*), all in terms of the said section 23, together with any interest thereon as specified in section 24 of the 1983 Act as amended [see Note 3].

[to be attested by local authority]

NOTES TO FORM 1

Note 1—The security subjects shall be described by means of a particular description or by reference to a description thereof as in Schedule D to the Conveyancing (Scotland) Act 1924 or as in Schedule G to the Titles to Land Consolidation (Scotland) Act 1868, or where appropriate in accordance with the provisions of section 15(1) of the Land Registration (Scotland) Act 1979. Where the security subjects consist of an interest in land, other than ownership of the land, amend the description appropriately.

Note 2—Where a title to the subjects is recorded in the Register of Sasines but the debtor does not have a recorded title, insert at the end a clause of deduction of title as follows:— *Which subjects* (or *as the case may be*) *were last vested* (or *are part of the subjects last vested*) *in A.B.* (*designation of person last infeft*) *whose title thereto* (*was recorded in the Register for* (or *the said Register of Sasines*) on (or, if the last infeftment has already been mentioned, say *in the said A.B. as aforesaid*)), *and from whom the said* (name of debtor) *acquired right by* (there specify shortly the writ or writs by which that right was so acquired). Where the interest in the subjects is registered in the Land Register for Scotland but the debtor is not registered as entitled to the registered interest, in terms of section 15(3) of the Land Registration (Scotland) Act 1979 it is not necessary to insert a clause of deduction of title in the deed if evidence of sufficient links in title are produced to the Keeper of the Registers of Scotland on registration.

Note 3—Insert amendments to Section 24 of the 1983 Act; the current amendments are made by section 45(3) of the National Health Service and Community Care Act 1990.

FORM 2

FORM OF DISCHARGE OF CHARGING ORDER

THE HEALTH AND SOCIAL SERVICES AND SOCIAL SECURITY ADJUDICATIONS ACT 1983

Discharge of Charging Order

We (*name of local authority*), in consideration of £ being the whole amount secured by the charging order aftermentioned paid by (*name and designation of debtor or as the case may be*) hereby discharge the charging order over All and Whole (*describe the security subjects as indicated in Note 1 to Form 1 in this Schedule*), which charging order was made by us in our favour dated and (recorded in the Register of Sasines for on) (*or as appropriate* registered under Title No.).

[to be attested by local authority]

Right to Purchase (Prescribed Persons) (Scotland) Order 1993

(S.I. 1993 No. 1625)

[28th June 1993]

The Secretary of State, in exercise of the powers conferred on him by section 61(11)(*w*) of the Housing (Scotland) Act 1987, and of all other powers enabling him in that behalf, hereby makes the following Order:—

Citation, commencement and revocation

1.—(1) This Order may be cited as the Right to Purchase (Prescribed Persons) (Scotland) Order 1993 and shall come into force on 27th July 1993.

(2) The Right to Purchase (Prescribed Persons) (Scotland) Order 1986 is hereby revoked.

... any predecessor of any of those persons ...on 61(11)(*w*) of the Housing (Scotland)

...er than a Minister specified in paragraph ...*v*) of section 61(11) of the Housing (Scot- ...n to a house used for the purpose set out

...ist,
...search Council,
...ty,
...n,
...,
...
...n,
...d,
...rating Board,
...y,
...r Wales,

...rprise,
...ncil,
...,
...rity,
...Research Council,
...ouncil for England,
...ro-Electric Board,

...ng Research Council,
...,
...il,
...oup,
...ctricity Board,
the Sports Council,
the Sports Council for Wales, and
Waverley Housing Trust Limited.

Housing (Preservation of Right to Buy) (Scotland) Regulations 1993

(S.I. 1993 No. 2164)

[27th September 1993]

The Secretary of State, in exercise of the powers conferred on him by sections 81A and 338(1) of the Housing (Scotland) Act 1987 and of all other powers enabling him in that behalf, hereby makes the following Regulations:

Citation and commencement

1. These Regulations may be cited as the Housing (Preservation of Right to Buy) (Scotland) Regulations 1993 and shall come into force on 27th September 1993.

Interpretation

2. In these Regulations, unless the context otherwise requires—

"the Act" means the Housing (Scotland) Act 1987;

"co-operative housing association" has the same meaning as in section 300(1)(*b*) of the Act;

"qualifying person" means a person occupying a house as his only or principal home and who—

(*a*) was the former secure tenant or former joint secure tenant of a house and whose former secure tenancy ceased to be such on the disposal by the landlord of the house to his current private sector landlord;

(*b*) became entitled to succeed on the death of the former secure tenant to a statutory assured tenancy under section 31 of the Housing (Scotland) Act 1988; or

(*c*) as the spouse of a former secure tenant became a tenant of a house by virtue of an order of the court under section 13 of the Matrimonial Homes (Family Protection) (Scotland) Act 1981;

"qualifying house" means the house referred to in the chapeau to paragraphs (*a*), (*b*) and (*c*) of the definition of "qualifying person".

Preserved right to buy

3. Where a landlord disposes of an interest in a house to a private sector landlord the continued application under section 81A(1) of the Act of the right to buy provisions shall be subject to regulation 5 and to the additions, exceptions, adaptations and modifications specified in Schedule 1 to these Regulations.

4. The right to buy provisions as they continue to apply in accordance with regulation 3 are set out in Schedule 2 to these Regulations.

5. The right to buy provisions shall not continue to apply where—

(*a*) the disposal of a house is in exercise of the right conferred by Part III of the Housing (Scotland) Act 1988; or

(*b*) the disposal of a house is to a co-operative housing association.

6. Where the right to buy provisions continue to apply, the private sector landlord shall not dispose of less than his whole interest in a qualifying house without the consent in writing of the Secretary of State.

7. In any case where the sheriff makes an order for possession of a qualifying house under ground 9 in Schedule 5 to the Housing (Scotland) Act 1988 (suitable alternative accommodation) the right to buy provisions and these Regulations shall apply to the house which is or will be available by way of alternative accommodation as they apply to the qualifying house.

Revocation

8. The Housing (Preservation of Right to Buy) (Scotland) Regulations 1992 are hereby revoked.

Regulation 3

SCHEDULE 1

MODIFICATIONS OF THE RIGHT TO BUY PROVISIONS OF THE ACT FOR THE PURPOSE OF THEIR APPLICATION IN CASES WHERE THE RIGHT TO BUY IS PRESERVED

1. In section 61 (secure tenant's right to purchase)—

(*a*) in subsection (1) for the words from "a tenant of a house" to "applies" substitute "a qualifying person", for the words "joint tenants" substitute "qualifying persons" and for the word "house" substitute "qualifying house";

(*b*) in subsection (2)—

(i) for the words from "This section" to "tenancy" substitute "This section applies to every qualifying house";

[THE NEXT PAGE IS J 549]

(ii) omit paragraph (*a*);
(iii) in paragraph (*b*) omit the words from "house" to the end and substitute "qualifying house"; and
(iv) in paragraph (*c*) for the word "tenant" substitute "qualifying person" and at the end add "or of the qualifying house or any other house provided by the landlord which was a qualifying house";

(*c*) in subsection (2A) after the word "house" where it occurs for the first time add "or qualifying house" and for the words "the house" where they occur for the second and third times substitute "that house";

(*d*) in subsection (3) for the words from "house" to "tenant" substitute "qualifying house let to the qualifying person following acquisition by the landlord of a defective dwelling previously purchased by the qualifying person if the qualifying person";

(*e*) in subsection (4)—
(i) in paragraphs (*a*) and (*f*) for the word "house" substitute "qualifying house"; and
(ii) omit paragraphs (*d*) and (*e*);

(*f*) in subsection (5)—
(i) for the words from "tenant" to "joint tenant", where it occurs for the first time substitute "qualifying person";
(ii) for the word "house" substitute "qualifying house"; and
(iii) for the words "joint tenant" where they occur for the second time substitute "qualifying person";

(*g*) in subsection (6) for the word "tenant" substitute "qualifying person" and for the word "house" substitute "qualifying house"; and

(*h*) omit subsections (8) and (9); and

(*i*) in subsection (10)—
(i) in paragraph (*a*) for the words "joint tenants" in sub-paragraph (i) substitute "more than one qualifying person" and in sub-paragraph (iii) for the words "tenant, joint tenant" substitute "qualifying person";
(ii) in paragraph (*a*) omit sub-paragraphs (iv) and (v); and
(iii) in paragraph (*b*) for the word "house" where it occurs in sub-paragraph (iii) for the first and second time substitute "qualifying house", for the words "joint tenant" substitute "qualifying person" and after the words "the tenant" add "or of a qualifying person".

2. In section 62 (the price)—
(*a*) in subsections (1) and (2) for the word "tenant" substitute "qualifying person" and for the word "house" substitute "qualifying house";
(*b*) in subsection (3)—
(i) for the words "the house" substitute "the qualifying house";
(ii) in paragraph (*b*) after the words "a house" insert "or of a qualifying house";
(*c*) in subsection (4)—
(i) for the word "tenant" substitute "qualifying person";
(ii) for the word "tenant's" substitute "qualifying person's";
(iii) for the words "joint tenant" substitute "qualifying person"; and
(iv) after the word "house" insert "or qualifying house"; and
(*d*) in subsection (6A) for the word "house" substitute "qualifying house".

3. Omit section 62A.

4. In section 63 (application to purchase etc.)—
(*a*) in subsection (1)—
(i) for the word "tenant" substitute "qualifying person";
(ii) for the word "house" where it occurs for the first time substitute "qualifying house";
(iii) in paragraph (*b*) after the word "house" add "including the qualifying house"; and
(iv) omit paragraph (*d*); and
(*b*) in subsection (2)—
(i) for the words "section 68 to 70" substitute "section 68 or 69";
(ii) for the word "tenant" substitute "qualifying person";
(iii) for the word "house" substitute "qualifying house"; and
(iv) omit paragraph (*cc*); and
(*c*) omit subsection (3).

5. In section 64 (conditions of sale)—
(*a*) for the word "tenant", except where it occurs for the second time in subsection (1)(*a*), substitute "qualifying person";

(*b*) for the word "house", except where it occurs for the third time in subsection (4) substitute "qualifying house";
(*c*) in subsection (4) omit the words "Subject to subsection (6)"; and
(*d*) omit subsections (6) to (9).

6. In section 65 (variation of conditions) for the word "tenant" substitute "qualifying person".

7. In section 66 (notice of acceptance)—
(*a*) for the word "tenant" substitute "qualifying person" and for the word "house" substitute "qualifying house"; and
(*b*) in paragraph (vi) of subsection (1) for the words "on the landlord" substitute "in accordance with that section".

8. In section 66A—
(*a*) for the words "tenant" and "house" substitute "qualifying person" and "qualifying house" respectively; and
(*b*) in paragraph (*a*) of subsection (1) omit from "or" to the end of that paragraph.

9. In section 66B for the word "tenant" substitute "qualifying person";

10. In section 67 (fixed price option) for the word "tenant" substitute "qualifying person", for the word "house" substitute "qualifying house" and omit subsection (4).

11. In section 68 (refusal of applications)—
(*a*) for the word "tenant's" substitute "qualifying person's";
(*b*) for the word "house" substitute "qualifying house";
(*c*) in subsection (1) omit the words from "or" where it first occurs to the end; and
(*d*) for the word "tenant" substitute the words "qualifying person".

12. In section 69 (Secretary of State's power to authorise refusal to sell)—
(*a*) for the word "house" except where it occurs for the second time in subsection (1), substitute "qualifying house";
(*b*) in subsection (1A) for the word "houses" substitute "qualifying houses"; and
(*c*) for the word "tenant" substitute "qualifying person".

13. Omit section 70 (power to refuse to sell certain houses required for educational purposes).

14. In section 71 (reference to Lands Tribunal)—
(*a*) for the word "tenant" substitute "qualifying person";
(*b*) in subsection (1)—
  (i) in paragraph (*a*) omit "or amended offer" in both places where it occurs; and
  (ii) in paragraph (*b*), omit "or amended offer" and "and, in the case of an amended offer, they do not conform with the requirements of section 63(3)"; and
(*c*) in subsection (2) omit "or amended offer" and "and, in the case of an amended offer, under section 63(3)".

15. In section 72 (recovery of discount on early re-sale)—
(*a*) for the words "person" and "tenant" respectively substitute "qualifying person" and for the word "house" substitute "qualifying house"; and
(*b*) in subsection (1) after the word "shall" insert the words "on the request of the landlord".

16. In section 73 (cases where discount etc. is not recoverable) for the word "house" substitute "qualifying house".

17. Omit sections 73A to 73D.

18. In section 74 (duties of landlords) for the word "house" substitute "qualifying house" and for the word "tenant" substitute "qualifying person".

19. In section 75 (agreements affecting right to purchase)—
(*a*) for the word "person" substitute "qualifying person"; and
(*b*) in subsection (1)(*b*) omit the words "mentioned in section 61(2)(*a*)(i) or (ii)".

20. Omit sections 75A, 76 and 77.

21. In section 78 (Secretary of State may give directions to modify conditions of sale)—
(*a*) in subsection (2)(*b*) for the word "tenant" substitute "qualifying person"; and
(*b*) omit subsection (4).

22. In section 79(1) (financial or other assistance for persons involved in proceedings) for the words "tenant or purchaser" substitute "qualifying person".

23. Omit sections 81, 81A and 81B.

24. In section 82 omit "214" and the definitions of "rent to loan purchaser" and "rent to loan scheme".

25. In section 84A (application of right to buy to cases where landlord is lessee)—
(*a*) in subsection (1)—
(i) omit the words "(but not 76 or 77)";
(ii) in paragraph (*a*) for the words "tenant of a house let on a secure tenancy" substitute "qualifying person";
(*b*) for the word "tenant" substitute "qualifying person" and for the word "house" substitute "qualifying house";
(*c*) in subsection (5) for the word "tenant's" substitute "qualifying person's"; and
(*d*) in subsection (6) for the words "subsection (5) and (9)" substitute "subsection (5)".

26. In section 216 (loans)—
(*a*) for the word "tenant" substitute "qualifying person" and for the word "house" substitute "qualifying house";
(*b*) for the word "landlord" except where it occurs for the first time, substitute "former landlord"; and
(*c*) omit subsection (10).

Regulation 4 SCHEDULE 2

THE RIGHT TO BUY PROVISIONS AS THEY APPLY IN CASES WHERE THE RIGHT TO BUY IS PRESERVED RIGHT TO BUY

Qualifying person's right to purchase

61.—(1) Notwithstanding anything contained in any agreement, a qualifying person (or such one or more of qualifying persons as may be agreed between them) shall, subject to this Part, have the right to purchase the qualifying house at a price fixed under section 62.

(2) This section applies to every qualifying house where—
(*b*) the landlord is the heritable proprietor of the qualifying house; and
(*c*) immediately prior to the date of service of an application to purchase, the qualifying person has been for not less than 2 years in occupation of a house (including accommodation provided as mentioned in subsection (11)(*n*)) or of a succession of houses provided by any persons mentioned in subsection (11) or of the qualifying house or any other house provided by the landlord which was a qualifying house.

(2A) For the purposes of subsection (2)(*c*), where the house or qualifying house was provided by a housing association which, at any time while the house was so provided, was not a registered housing association, the association shall, if it became a registered housing association at any later time, be deemed to have been a registered housing association at all times since it first provided that house.

(3) This section also applies to a qualifying house let to the qualifying person following acquisition by the landlord of a defective dwelling previously purchased by the qualifying person if the qualifying person would not otherwise have the right to purchase under this Part; and where it so applies—
(*a*) paragraph (*c*) of subsection (2) shall not have effect;
(*b*) the words "beyond 2" in section 62(3)(*b*) shall not have effect.

(4) This section does not apply—
(*a*) to a qualifying house that is one of a group which has been provided with facilities (including a call system and the services of a warden) specially designed or adapted for the needs of persons of pensionable age or disabled persons; or
(*b*) where a landlord which is a registered housing association has at no time received a grant under—
(i) any enactment mentioned in paragraph 2 of Schedule 1 to the Housing Associations Act 1985 (grants under enactments superseded by the Housing Act 1974);
(ii) section 31 of the Housing Act 1974 (management grants);
(iii) section 41 of the Housing Associations Act 1985 (housing association grants);
(iv) section 54 of that Act (revenue deficit grants);
(v) section 55 of that Act (hostel deficit grants); or
(vi) section 59(2) of that Act (grants by local authorities); or
(vii) section 50 of the Housing Act 1988 (housing association grants); or
(viii) section 51 of that Act (revenue deficit grants); or

(*e*) where such a landlord has at no time let (or had available for letting) more than 100 dwellings; or

(*f*) where, within a neighbourhood, the qualifying house is one of a number (not exceeding 14) of houses with a common landlord, being a landlord which is a registered housing association, and it is the practice of that landlord to let at least one half of those houses for occupation by any or all of the following—

(i) persons who have suffered from, or are suffering from, mental disorder (as defined in the Mental Health (Scotland) Act 1984), physical handicap or addiction to alcohol or other drugs;

(ii) persons who have been released from prison or other institutions;

(iii) young persons who have left the care of a local authority,

and a social service is, or special facilities are, provided wholly or partly for the purpose of assisting those persons.

(5) Where the spouse of a qualifying person occupies the qualifying house as his only or principal home but is not himself a qualifying person, the right to purchase the qualifying house under subsection (1) shall not be exercised without the consent of such spouse.

(6) A qualifying person may exercise his right to purchase, if he so wishes, together with one or more members of his family acting as joint purchasers, provided—

(*a*) that such members are at least 18 years of age, that they have, during the period of 6 months ending with the date of service of the application to purchase, had their only or principal home with the qualifying person and that their residence in the qualifying house is not a breach of any obligation of the tenancy; or

(*b*) where the requirements of paragraph (*a*) are not satisfied, the landlord has consented.

(7) The Secretary of State may by order made by statutory instrument amend, or add to, the descriptions of persons set out in sub-paragraphs (i) to (iii) of paragraph (*f*) of subsection (4).

(10) In this section and the following section—

(*a*) references to occupation of a house include occupation—

(i) in the case of more than one qualifying person, by any one of them;

(ii) by any person occupying the house rent-free;

(iii) as the spouse of the qualifying person or of any such person;

(*b*) for the purpose of determining the period of occupation—

(iii) there shall be added to the period of occupation of a qualifying house by a qualifying person any earlier period during which he was at least 16 years of age and occupied the qualifying house as a member of the family of the tenant or of a qualifying person or of one or more of the joint tenants of the house.

(11) The persons providing houses referred to in subsection (2)(*c*) (occupation requirement for exercise of right to purchase) and in section 62(3)(*b*) (calculation of the discount from the market value) are—

(*a*) a regional, islands or district council in Scotland; any local authority in England and Wales or in Northern Ireland; and the statutory predecessors of any such council or authority, or the common good of any such council, or any trust under the control of any such council;

(*b*) the Commission for the New Towns;

(*c*) a development corporation, an urban development corporation; and any development corporation established under corresponding legislation in England and Wales or in Northern Ireland; and the statutory predecessors of any such authority;

(*d*) Scottish Homes and the Scottish Special Housing Association;

(*e*) a registered housing association;

(*f*) the Housing Corporation;

(*g*) a housing co-operative within the meaning of section 22 or a housing co-operative within the meaning of section 27B of the Housing Act 1985;

(*h*) the Development Board for Rural Wales;

(*i*) the Northern Ireland Housing Executive or any statutory predecessor;

(*j*) a police authority or the statutory predecessors of any such authority;

(*k*) a fire authority or the statutory predecessors of any such authority;

(*l*) a water authority in Scotland; any water authority constituted under corresponding legislation in England and Wales or in Northern Ireland; and the statutory predecessors of any such authority;

(*m*) the Secretary of State, where the house was at the material time used for the purposes of the Scottish Prison Service or of a prison service for which the Home Office or the Northern Ireland Office have responsibility;

(*n*) the Crown, in relation to accommodation provided in connection with service whether by the tenant or his spouse as a member of the regular armed forces of the Crown;

(*o*) the Secretary of State, where the house was at the material time used for the purposes of a health board constituted under section 2 of the National Health Service (Scotland) Act 1978 or for the purposes of a corresponding board in England and Wales, or for the purposes of the statutory predecessors of any such board; or the Department of Health and Social Services for Northern Ireland, where the house was at the material time used for the purposes of a Health and Personal Services Board in Northern Ireland, or for the purposes of the statutory predecessors of any such board;

(*p*) the Secretary of State, or the Minister of Agriculture, Fisheries and Food, where the house was at the material time used for the purposes of the Forestry Commission;

(*q*) the Secretary of State, where the house was at the material time used for the purposes of a State Hospital provided by him under section 90 of the Mental Health (Scotland) Act 1984 or for the purposes of any hospital provided under corresponding legislation in England and Wales;

(*r*) the Commissioners of Northern Lighthouses;

(*s*) the Trinity House;

(*t*) the Secretary of State, where the house was at the material time used for the purposes of Her Majesty's Coastguard;

(*u*) the United Kingdom Atomic Energy Authority;

(*v*) the Secretary of State, where the house was at the material time used for the purposes of any function transferred to him under section 1(2) of the Defence (Transfer of Functions) Act 1964 or any function relating to defence conferred on him by or under any subsequent enactment;

(*w*) such other person as the Secretary of State may by order made by statutory instrument subject to annulment in pursuance of a resolution of either House of Parliament prescribe.

The price

62.—(1) Subject to subsection (6A), the price at which a qualifying person shall be entitled to purchase a qualifying house under this Part shall be fixed as at the date of service of the application to purchase by subtracting a discount from the market value of the qualifying house.

(2) The market value for the purposes of this section shall be determined by either—

(*a*) a qualified valuer nominated by the landlord and accepted by the qualifying person; or

(*b*) the district valuer,

as the landlord thinks fit as if the qualifying house were available for sale on the open market with vacant possession at the date of service of the application to purchase.

For the purposes of this subsection, no account shall be taken of any element in the market value of the qualifying house which reflects an increase in value as a result of work the cost of which would qualify for a reimbursement under section 58.

(3) Subject to subsection (5), the discount for the purposes of subsection (1) shall be—

(*a*) 32 per cent. of the market value of the qualifying house except—

(i) where the qualifying house is a flat, it shall be 44 per cent. of the market value;

(ii) where the qualifying house is one to which section 61(3) applies, it shall be 30 per cent. or, where it is a flat, 40 per cent. of the market value;

together with

(*b*) an additional one per cent. or, where the qualifying house is a flat, two per cent., of the market value for every year beyond 2 of occupation by the appropriate person, preceding the date of service of the application to purchase, of a house or of a qualifying house (including accommodation provided as mentioned in section 61(11)(*n*)) or of a succession of houses provided by any persons mentioned in section 61(11),

up to a maximum discount of 60 per cent., or where the qualifying house is a flat, 70 per cent. of the market value.

(3A) There shall be deducted from the discount an amount equal to any previous discount, or the aggregate of any previous discounts, received by the appropriate person on any previous purchase of a house by any of these persons from a landlord who is a person specified in subsection (11) of section 61 or prescribed in an order made under that subsection, reduced by any amount of such previous discount recovered by such a landlord.

(4) For the purposes of subsection (3)—

(*a*) the "appropriate person" is whoever of—

(i) the qualifying person; or

(ii) the qualifying person's spouse if living with him at the date of service of the application to purchase; or

(iii) a deceased spouse if living with the qualifying person at the time of death; or

(iv) any qualifying person who is a joint purchaser of the house, has the longer or longest such occupation; and

(*b*) where the house or qualifying house was provided by a housing association which, at any time while the house or qualifying house was so provided was not a registered housing association, the association shall, if it became a registered housing association at any later time, be deemed to have been a registered housing association at all times since it first provided the house or qualifying house,

and, for the purposes of subsection (3A), the "appropriate person" is any of the persons mentioned in sub-paragraphs (i) to (iv) of paragraph (*a*).

(5) The Secretary of State may by order made with the consent of the Treasury provide that, in such cases as may be specified in the order—

(*a*) the minimum percentage discount,

(*b*) the percentage increase for each complete year of the qualifying period after the first two, or

(*c*) the maximum percentage discount,

shall be such percentage higher than that specified in subsection (3), as may be specified in the order.

(6) An order under subsection (5)—

(*a*) may make different provision with respect to different cases or descriptions of case,

(*b*) may contain such incidental, supplementary or transitional provisions as appear to the Secretary of State to be necessary or expedient, and

(*c*) shall be made by statutory instrument and shall not be made unless a draft of it has been laid before and approved by resolution of each House of Parliament.

(6A) Except where the Secretary of State so determines, the discount for the purpose of subsection (1) shall not reduce the price below the amount which, in accordance with a determination made by him, is to be taken as representing so much of the costs incurred in respect of the qualifying house as, in accordance with the determination, is to be treated as—

(*a*) incurred in the period commencing with the beginning of the financial year of the landlord which was current 5 years prior to the date of service of the application to purchase the qualifying house or such other period as the Secretary of State may by order provide; and

(*b*) relevant for the purposes of this subsection,

and if the price before discount is below that amount, there shall be no discount.

(6B) An order under subsection (6A) shall be made by statutory instrument subject to annulment in pursuance of a resolution of either House of Parliament and may make different provision in relation to different cases or circumstances or different areas.

(10) Where at the date of service of an offer to sell under section 63 any of the costs referred to in subsection (6A) are not known, the landlord shall make an estimate of such unknown costs for the purposes of that subsection.

PROCEDURE

Application to purchase and offer to sell

63.—(1) A qualifying person who seeks to exercise a right to purchase a qualifying house under section 61 shall serve on the landlord a notice (referred to in this Part as an "application to purchase") which shall be in such form as the Secretary of State shall by order made by statutory instrument prescribe, and shall contain—

(*a*) notice that the qualifying person seeks to exercise the right to purchase;

(*b*) a statement of any period of occupancy of a house including the qualifying house on which the qualifying person intends to rely for the purposes of sections 61 and 62; and

(*c*) the name of any joint purchaser within the meaning of section 61(6).

(2) Where an application to purchase is served on a landlord, and the landlord does not serve a notice of refusal under section 68 or 69 it shall, within 2 months after service of the application to purchase, serve on the qualifying person a notice (referred to in this Part as an "offer to sell") containing—

(*a*) the market value of the qualifying house determined under section 62(2),

(*b*) the discount calculated under section 62(3);

(*c*) the price fixed under section 62(1);

(*d*) any conditions which the landlord intends to impose under section 64; and

(*e*) an offer to sell the qualifying house to the qualifying person and any joint purchaser named in the application to purchase at the price referred to in paragraph (*c*) and under the conditions referred to in paragraph (*d*).

Conditions of sale

64.—(1) Subject to section 75, an offer to sell under section 63(2) shall contain such conditions as are reasonable, provided that—

(*a*) the conditions shall have the effect of ensuring that the qualifying person has as full enjoyment and use of the qualifying house as owner as he has had as tenant;

(*b*) the conditions shall secure to the qualifying person such additional rights as are necessary for his reasonable enjoyment and use of the qualifying house as owner (including, without prejudice to the foregoing generality, common rights in any part of the building of which the qualifying house forms part) and shall impose on the qualifying person any necessary duties relative to rights so secured; and

(*c*) the conditions shall include such terms as are necessary to entitle the qualifying person to receive a good and marketable title to the qualifying house.

(2) A condition which imposes a new charge or an increase of an existing charge for the provision of a service in relation to the qualifying house shall provide for the charge to be in reasonable proportion to the cost to the landlord of providing the service.

(3) No condition shall be imposed under this section which has the effect of requiring the qualifying person to pay any expenses of the landlord.

(4) No condition shall be imposed under this section which has the effect of requiring the qualifying person or any of his successors in title to offer to the landlord, or to any other person, an option to purchase the qualifying house in advance of its sale to a third party, except in the case of a qualifying house which has facilities which are substantially different from those of an ordinary house and which has been designed or adapted for occupation by a person of pensionable age or disabled person whose special needs require accommodation of the kind provided by the qualifying house.

(5) Where an option to purchase permitted under subsection (4) is exercised, the price to be paid for the qualifying house shall be determined by the district valuer who shall have regard to the market value of the qualifying house at the time of the purchase and to any amount due to the landlord under section 72 (recovery of discount on early re-sale).

Variation of conditions

65.—(1) Where an offer to sell is served on a qualifying person and he wishes to exercise his right to purchase, but—

(*a*) he considers that a condition contained in the offer to sell is unreasonable; or

(*b*) he wishes to have a new condition included in it; or

(*c*) he has not previously notified the landlord of his intention to exercise that right together with a joint purchaser, but now wishes to do so; or

(*d*) he has previously notified the landlord of his intention to exercise that right together with any joint purchaser but now wishes to exercise the right without that joint purchaser,

he may request the landlord to strike out or vary the condition, or to include the new condition, or to make the offer to sell to the qualifying person and the joint purchaser, or to withdraw the offer to sell in respect of the joint purchaser, as the case may be, by serving on the landlord within one month after service of the offer to sell a notice in writing setting out his request; and if the landlord agrees, it shall accordingly serve an amended offer to sell on the qualifying person within one month of service of the notice setting out the request.

(2) A qualifying person who is aggrieved by the refusal of the landlord to agree to strike out or vary a condition, or to include a new condition, or to make the offer to sell to the qualifying person and the joint purchaser, or to withdraw the offer to sell in respect of any joint purchaser under subsection (1), or by his failure timeously to serve an amended offer to sell under the said subsection, may, within one month or, with the consent of the landlord given in writing before the expiry of the said period of one month, within two months of the refusal or failure, refer the matter to the Lands Tribunal for determination.

(3) In proceedings under subsection (2), the Lands Tribunal may, as it thinks fit, uphold the condition or strike it out or vary it, or insert the new condition or order that the offer to sell be made to the qualifying person and the joint purchaser, or order that the offer to sell be withdrawn in respect of any joint purchaser, and where its determination results in a variation of the terms of the offer to sell, it shall order the landlord to serve on the qualifying person an amended offer to sell accordingly within 2 months thereafter.

Notice of acceptance

66.—(1) Where an offer to sell is served on a qualifying person and he wishes to exercise his right to purchase and—

(*a*) he does not dispute the terms of the offer to sell by timeously serving a notice setting out a request under section 65(1) or by referring the matter to the Lands Tribunal under subsection (1)(*d*) of section 71; or

(*b*) any such dispute had been resolved;

the qualifying person shall, subject to section 67(1), serve a notice of acceptance on the landlord within 2 months of whichever is the latest of—

(i) the service on him of the offer to sell;

(ii) the service on him of an amended offer to sell (or if there is more than one, of the latest amended offer to sell);

(iii) a determination by the Lands Tribunal under section 65(3) which does not require service of an amended offer to sell;

(iv) a finding or determination of the Lands Tribunal in a matter referred to it under section 71(1)(*d*) where no order is made under section 71(2)(*b*);

(v) the service of an offer to sell on him by virtue of subsection (2)(*b*) of section 71;

(vi) where a loan application under subsection (2)(*a*)(i) of section 216 (loans) has been served in accordance with that section, the service of a relative offer or refusal of loan; or

(vii) where section 216(7) (loans) is invoked, the decision of the court.

(2) Where an offer to sell (or an amended offer to sell) has been served on the qualifying person and a relative notice of acceptance has been duly served on the landlord, a contract of sale of the qualifying house shall be constituted between the landlord and the qualifying person on the terms contained in the offer (or amended offer) to sell.

Abatement of purchase price on landlord's failure before contract of sale

66A.—(1) Where a qualifying person who seeks to exercise a right to purchase a qualifying house under section 61 has served an application to purchase on the landlord and the landlord—

(*a*) not having served a notice of refusal, has failed to serve an offer to sell on the qualifying person within 2 months of the application;

(*b*) having agreed to serve an amended offer to sell on the qualifying person in response to a request under section 65(1), has failed to do so within one month of the request;

(*c*) following an order by the Lands Tribunal to serve an amended offer to sell on the qualifying person under section 65(3), has failed to do so within 2 months of the date of the order;

(*d*) following a finding by the Lands Tribunal under section 68(4), has failed to serve an offer to sell within 2 months of the date of the finding; or

(*e*) following an order by the Lands Tribunal under section 71(2)(*b*), has failed to serve an offer or amended offer to sell within the time specified in the order,

the qualifying person may serve on the landlord a notice in writing requiring the landlord to serve on him, within one month of the date of the notice, the offer to sell or (as the case may be) the amended offer to sell which the landlord has failed to serve.

(2) Where the landlord fails to serve the offer to sell or the amended offer to sell within one month of the date of the notice in writing under subsection (1), the price fixed under section 62 shall be reduced by the amount of rent paid by the qualifying person during the period commencing with the date on which the one month period expired and ending with the date on which the offer is served.

Abatement of purchase price on landlord's failure after contract of sale

66B.—(1) Where the landlord has failed and continues to fail to deliver a good and marketable title to the qualifying person in accordance with the contract of sale, the qualifying person may at any time serve on the landlord a notice (the "initial notice of delay") setting out the landlord's failure and specifying—

(*a*) the most recent action of which the qualifying person is aware which has been taken by the landlord in fulfilment of his duties under this Part;

(*b*) a period (the "the response period"), of not less than one month beginning on the date of service of the notice, within which the service by the landlord of a counter notice under subsection (2) will have the effect of cancelling the initial notice of delay.

(2) If there is no action under this Part which, at the beginning of the response period it was for the landlord to take in order to grant a good and marketable title to the qualifying person in implementation of the contract of sale, the landlord may serve on the qualifying person a counter notice either during or after the response period.

(3) At any time when—

(*a*) the response period specified in the initial notice of delay has expired; and

(*b*) the landlord has not served a counter notice under subsection (2),

the qualifying person may serve on the landlord a notice (the "operative notice of delay") that this subsection shall apply to the price fixed under section 62; and thereupon the price fixed under section 62 shall be reduced by the amount of rent paid by the qualifying person during the period commencing with the date of service of the operative notice of delay and ending with whichever is the earlier of the following dates—

(i) the date of service by the landlord of a counter notice; or

(ii) the date of delivery by the landlord of a good and marketable title in implementation of the contract of sale.

(4) Where the landlord has served a counter notice under subsection (2) the qualifying person (together with any joint purchaser) may, by serving on the clerk to the Lands Tribunal a copy of the initial notice of delay and of the landlord's counter notice together with a request for the matter to be so referred, refer the matter to the Tribunal for its consideration under subsection (5).

(5) Where the matter has been so referred to the Lands Tribunal it shall consider whether or not in its opinion action which would have enabled a good and marketable title to be delivered in implementation of the contract of sale could have been taken by the landlord and shall find accordingly.

(6) Where the Lands Tribunal finds that action could have been taken by the landlord the qualifying person shall be entitled to serve an operative notice of delay as if the landlord had not served a counter notice and in that event the oommencement date for the purposes of subsection (3) shall be the date on which an operative notice of delay could first have been served if no counter notice had been served.

Provisions relating to sections 66A and 66B

66C.—(1) Where there is more than one period in respect of which the price fixed under section 62 can be reduced under section 66A(2) or 66B(3), the periods may be aggregated and the price reduced by the total amount of the rent.

(2) If the period in respect of which the price fixed can be so reduced is, or if the periods aggregated under subsection (1) together amount to, more than twelve months, the amount by which the price fixed under section 62 would, apart from this subsection, fall to be reduced shall be increased by 50 per cent. or such other percentage as the Secretary of State may by order made by statutory instrument and subject to annulment in pursuance of a resolution of either House of Parliament provide.

Fixed price option

67.—(1) Where an offer to sell (or an amended offer to sell) is served on a qualifying person, but he is unable by reason of the application of regulations made under section 216(3) (loans) to obtain a loan of the amount for which he has applied, he may, within 2 months of service on him of an offer of loan, or (as the case may be) of the date of a declarator by the sheriff under section 216(7) (loans), whichever is the later, serve on the landlord a notice to the effect that he wishes to have a fixed price option, which notice shall be accompanied by a payment to the landlord of £100, and in that event he shall be entitled to serve a notice of acceptance on the landlord at any time within 2 years of the service of the application to purchase:

Provided that where, as regards the qualifying house, the qualifying person has served a loan application in accordance with subsection (2)(*a*)(ii) of section 216 (loans), he shall be entitled (even if the said period of 2 years has expired) to serve a notice of acceptance on the landlord within 2 months of whichever is the later of—

(*a*) the service of a relative offer, or refusal, of loan; or

(*b*) where section 216(7) is invoked, the decision of the court.

(2) The payment of £100 mentioned in subsection (1) shall be recoverable—

(*a*) by the qualifying person, when he purchases the qualifying house in accordance with that subsection or, if he does not, at the expiry of the period of 2 years mentioned therein;

(*b*) by the qualifying person, when the landlord recovers possession of the qualifying house under subsection (3); or

(*c*) by his personal representatives, if he dies without purchasing the qualifying house in accordance with that subsection.

(3) The existence of a fixed price option under subsection (1) shall not prevent the landlord from recovering possession of the property in any manner which may be lawful, and in that event the option shall be terminated.

Refusal of applications

68.—(1) Where a landlord on which an application to purchase has been served disputes the qualifying person's right to purchase a qualifying house under section 61, it shall by notice (referred to in this Part as a "notice of refusal") served within one month after service of the application to purchase—

(*a*) refuse the application.

(2) Where a landlord on which an application to purchase has been served, after reasonable enquiry (which shall include reasonable opportunity for the qualifying person to amend his application), is of the opinion that information contained in the application is incorrect in a material respect it shall issue a notice of refusal within 2 months of the application to purchase.

(3) A notice of refusal shall specify the grounds on which the landlord disputes the qualifying person's right to purchase or, as the case may be, the accuracy of the information.

(4) Where a landlord serves a notice of refusal on a qualifying person under this section, the qualifying person may within one month thereafter apply to the Lands Tribunal for a finding that he has a right to purchase the qualifying house under section 61 on such terms as it may determine.

Houses Provided for Special Purposes

Secretary of State's power to authorise refusal to sell certain qualifying houses provided for persons of pensionable age

69.—(1) This section applies to a qualifying house which has facilities which are substantially different from those of an ordinary house and which has been designed or adapted for occupation by a person of pensionable age whose special needs require accommodation of the kind provided by the qualifying house.

(1A) This section applies only to qualifying houses first let on a secure tenancy before 1st January 1990.

(2) Where an application to purchase a qualifying house is served on a landlord and it appears to the landlord that—

(*a*) the qualifying house is one to which this section applies; and

(*b*) the qualifying person would, apart from this section, have a right under section 61 to purchase the qualifying house,

the landlord may, within one month after service of the application to purchase, instead of serving an offer to sell on the qualifying person, make an application to the Secretary of State under this section.

(3) An application under subsection (2) shall specify the facilities and features of design or adaptation which in the view of the landlord cause the qualifying house to be a qualifying house to which this section applies.

(4) Where the Secretary of State has received an application under this section and it appears to him that the qualifying house concerned is one to which this section applies, he shall authorise the landlord to serve on the qualifying person a notice of refusal under this section, which shall be served as soon as is practicable after the authority is given and in any event within one month thereafter.

(5) A notice of refusal served under subsection (4) shall specify the facilities and features specified for the purposes of subsection (3) and that the Secretary of State's authority for service of the said notice has been given.

(6) Where the Secretary of State refuses an application made under subsection (2), the landlord shall serve on the qualifying person an offer to sell under section 63(2)—

(*a*) within the period mentioned in that section; or

(*b*) where the unexpired portion of that period is less than one month or there is not an expired portion of that period, within one month of the Secretary of State's refusal.

Lands Tribunal

Reference to Lands Tribunal

71.—(1) Where—

(*a*) a landlord who has been duly served with an application to purchase fails to issue timeously either an offer to sell (even if only such offer to sell as is mentioned in paragraph (*d*)) or a notice of refusal; or

(*b*) the Lands Tribunal has made a determination under section 65(3) (variation of terms of offer to sell) and the landlord has failed to issue an amended offer to sell within 2 months thereafter; or

(*c*) the Lands Tribunal has made a finding under section 68(4) (refusal of right to purchase) or has made an order under subsection (2)(*b*) of this section and the landlord has not duly progressed the application to purchase in accordance with that finding or, as the case may be, order, within 2 months thereafter; or

(*d*) a landlord has served an offer to sell whose contents do not conform with the requirements of paragraphs (*a*) to (*e*) of section 63(2) (or where such contents were not obtained in accordance with the provisions specified in those paragraphs), the qualifying person (together with any joint purchaser) may refer the matter to the Lands Tribunal by serving on the clerk to that body a copy of any notice served and of any findings or determination made under this Part, together with a statement of his grievance.

(2) Where a matter has been referred to the Lands Tribunal under subsection (1), the Tribunal shall consider whether in its opinion—

(*a*) any of paragraphs (*a*) to (*c*) of that subsection apply, and if it so finds it may—

(i) give any consent, exercise any discretion, or do anything which the landlord may give, exercise or do under or for the purposes of sections 61 to 84; and

(ii) issue such notices and undertake such other steps as may be required to complete the procedure provided for in sections 63 and 65 to 67;

and any consent given, any discretion exercised, or anything done, under the foregoing provisions of this subsection shall have effect as if it had been duly given, exercised or done by the landlord; or

(*b*) paragraph (*d*) of that subsection applies, and if it so finds it may order the landlord to serve on the qualifying person an offer to sell, in proper form, under section 63(2) within such time (not exceeding 2 months) as it may specify.

(3) Nothing in this section shall affect the operation of the provisions of any other enactment relating to the enforcement of a statutory duty whether under that enactment or otherwise.

Recoverability of Discount

Recovery of discount on early re-sale

72.—(1) A qualifying person who has purchased a qualifying house in exercise of a right to purchase under section 61, or any of his successors in title, who sells or otherwise disposes of the qualifying house (except as provided for in section 73) before the expiry of 3 years from the date of service of a notice of acceptance by the qualifying person under section 66, shall on the request of the landlord be liable to repay to the landlord, in accordance with subsection (3), a proportion of the difference between the market value determined, in respect of the qualifying house, under section 62(2) and the price at which the qualifying house was so purchased.

(1A) Where a qualifying person has served on the landlord a notice under section 66A(1), the commencement of the period of 3 years referred to in subsection (1) shall be backdated by a period equal to the time (or, where section 66C(1) applies, the aggregate of the times) during which, by virtue of section 66A(2), any payment of rent falls to be taken into account.

(2) Subsection (1) applies to the disposal of part of a qualifying house except in a case where—

(*a*) it is a disposal by one of the parties to the original sale to one of the other parties; or

(*b*) the remainder of the qualifying house continues to be the only or principal home of the person disposing of the part.

(3) The proportion of the difference which shall be paid to the landlord shall be—

(*a*) 100 per cent. where the disposal occurs within the first year after the date of service of notice,

(*b*) 66 per cent. where it occurs in the second such year, and

(*c*) 33 per cent. where it occurs in the third such year.

(4) Where as regards a qualifying house or part of a qualifying house there is, within the period mentioned in subsection (1), more than one disposal to which that subsection would (apart from the provisions of this subsection) apply, that subsection shall apply only in relation to the first such disposal of the qualifying house, or part of the qualifying house.

(5) Where a landlord secures the liability to make a repayment under subsection (1) the security shall, notwithstanding section 13 of the Conveyancing and Feudal Reform (Scotland) Act 1970, have priority immediately after—

(*a*) any standard security granted in security of a loan either—

(i) for the purchase of the qualifying house, or

(ii) for the improvement of the qualifying house,

and any interest present or future due thereon (including any such interest which has accrued or may accrue) and any expenses or outlays (including interest thereon) which may be, or may have been, reasonably incurred in the exercise of any power conferred on the lender by the deed expressing the said standard security; and

(*b*) if the landlord consents, a standard security over the qualifying house granted in security of any other loan, and in relation thereto any such interest, expenses or outlays as aforesaid.

(6) For the avoidance of doubt, paragraph (*a*) of subsection (5) applies to a standard security granted in security both for the purpose mentioned in sub-paragraph (i) and for that mentioned in sub-paragraph (ii) as it applies to a standard security so granted for only one of those purposes.

(7) The liability to make a repayment under subsection (1) shall not be imposed as a real burden in a disposition of any interest in the qualifying house.

Cases where discount etc. is not recoverable

73.—(1) There shall be no liability to make a repayment under section 72(1) where the disposal is made—

(*a*) by the executor of the deceased owner acting in that capacity; or
(*b*) as a result of a compulsory purchase order; or
(*c*) in the circumstances specified in subsection (2).

(2) The circumstances mentioned in subsection (1)(*c*) are that the disposal—

(*a*) is to a member of the owner's family who has lived with him for a period of 12 months before the disposal; and
(*b*) is for no consideration:

Provided that, if the disponee disposes of the qualifying house before the expiry of the 3 year period mentioned in section 72(1), the provisions of that section will apply to him as if this was the first disposal and he was the original purchaser.

Duties of Landlords

Duties of landlords

74. It shall be the duty of every landlord of a qualifying house to which sections 61 to 84 and section 216 apply to make provision for the progression of applications under those sections in such manner as may be necessary to enable any qualifying person who wishes to exercise his rights under this Part to do so, and to comply with any regulations which may be made by statutory instrument by the Secretary of State in that regard.

Agreements affecting right to purchase

75.—(1) Subject to sections 61(1), 67(1) and 72(1)—

(*a*) no qualifying person exercising or seeking to exercise a right to purchase under section 61(1) shall be obliged, notwithstanding any agreement to the contrary, to make any payment to or to lodge any deposit with the landlord which he would not have been obliged to make, or as the case may be lodge, had he not exercised (or sought to exercise) the right to purchase;
(*b*) a landlord is required neither to enter into, nor to induce (or seek to induce) any qualifying person to enter into, such agreement as is mentioned in paragraph (*a*), or into any agreement which purports to restrict that qualifying person's right under this Part.

(2) Paragraph (*a*) of subsection (1) does not apply to the expenses in any court proceedings.

Powers of Secretary of State

Secretary of State may give directions to modify conditions of sale

78.—(1) Where it appears to the Secretary of State that the inclusion of conditions of a particular kind in offers to sell would be unreasonable he may by direction require landlords generally, landlords of a particular description, or particular landlords not to include conditions of that kind (or not to include conditions of that kind unless modified in such manner as may be specified in the direction) in offers to sell served on or after a date so specified.

(2) Where a condition's inclusion in an offer to sell—

(*a*) is in contravention of a direction under subsection (1) or
(*b*) in a case where the qualifying person has not by the date specified in such a direction served a relative notice of acceptance on the landlord, would have been in such contravention had the offer to sell been served on or after that date,

the condition shall have no effect as regards the offer to sell.

(3) A direction under subsection (1) may—

(*a*) make different provision in relation to different areas, cases or classes of case and may exclude certain areas, cases or classes of case; and
(*b*) be varied or withdrawn by a subsequent direction so given.

Secretary of State may give financial and other assistance for qualifying persons involved in proceedings

79.—(1) Where, in relation to any proceedings, or prospective proceedings, to which this section applies, a qualifying person is an actual or prospective party, the Secretary of State may on written application to him by the qualifying person give financial or other assistance to the applicant, if the Secretary of State thinks fit to do so:

Provided that assistance under this section shall be given only where the Secretary of State considers—

(*a*) that the case raises a question of principle and that it is in the public interest to give the applicant such assistance; or

(*b*) that there is some other special consideration.

(2) This section applies to—

(*a*) any proceedings under sections 61 to 84 and section 216; and

(*b*) any proceedings to determine any question arising under or in connection with those sections other than a question as to market value for the purposes of section 62.

(3) Assistance by the Secretary of State under this section may include—

(*a*) giving advice;

(*b*) procuring or attempting to procure the settlement of the matter in dispute;

(*c*) arranging for the giving of advice or assistance by a solicitor or counsel;

(*d*) arranging for representation by a solicitor or counsel;

(*e*) any other form of assistance which the Secretary of State may consider appropriate.

(4) In so far as expenses are incurred by the Secretary of State in providing the applicant with assistance under this section, any sums recovered by virtue of an award of expenses, or of an agreement as to expenses, in the applicant's favour with respect to the matter in connection with which the assistance is given shall, subject to any charge or obligation for payment in priority to other debts under the Legal Aid (Scotland) Act 1986 and to any provision of that Act for payment of any sum into the Scottish Legal Aid Fund, be paid to the Secretary of State in priority to any other debts.

(5) Any expenses incurred by the Secretary of State in providing assistance under this section shall be paid out of money provided by Parliament; and any sums received by the Secretary of State under subsection (4) shall be paid into the Consolidated Fund.

General

Interpretation of this Part

82. In this Part and in sections 14, 19, 20 and 216, except where provision is made to the contrary,

"application to purchase" has the meaning assigned to it by section 63;

"family" and any reference to membership thereof shall be construed in accordance with section 83;

"fire authority" means a fire authority for the purposes of the Fire Services Acts 1947 to 1959 or a joint committee constituted by virtue of section 36(4)(*b*) of the Fire Services Act 1947;

"heritable proprietor" in relation to a house, includes any landlord entitled under section 3 of the Conveyancing (Scotland) Act 1924 (disposition of the dwelling-house etc. by persons uninfeft) to grant a disposition of the house;

"housing co-operative" has the meaning assigned to it by section 22;

"landlord" means a person who lets a house to a tenant for human habitation, and includes his successors in title;

"offer to sell" has the meaning assigned to it by section 63(2) and includes such offer to sell as is mentioned in section 71(1)(*d*);

"police authority" means a police authority in Scotland within the meaning of section 2(1) or 19(9)(*b*) of the Police (Scotland) Act 1967 or a joint police committee constituted by virtue of subsection (2)(*b*) of the said section 19 and any police authority constituted in England and Wales or Northern Ireland under corresponding legislation;

"secure tenancy" means a secure tenancy within the meaning of section 44;

"tenancy" means any agreement under which a house is made available for occupation for human habitation, and "leases", "let" and "lets" shall be construed accordingly;

"tenant" means a person who leases a house from a landlord and who derives his right therein directly from the landlord, and in the case of joint tenancies means all the tenants.

Members of a person's family

83.—(1) A person is a member of another's family for the purposes of this Act if—

(*a*) he is the spouse of that person or he and that person live together as husband and wife; or

(*b*) he is that person's parent, grandparent, child, grandchild, brother, sister, uncle, aunt, nephew or niece.

(2) For the purposes of subsection (1)(*b*)—
(*a*) a relationship by marriage shall be treated as a relationship by blood;
(*b*) a relationship of the half-blood shall be treated as a relationship of the whole blood;
(*c*) the stepchild of a person shall be treated as his child; and
(*d*) a child shall be treated as such whether or not his parents are married.

Service of notices

84.—(1) A notice or other document which requires to be served on a person under any provision of this Part or of section 216 may be given to him—
(*a*) by delivering it to him;
(*b*) by leaving it at his proper address; or
(*c*) by sending it by recorded delivery post to him at that address.

(2) For the purposes of this section and of section 7 of the Interpretation Act 1978 (references to service by post) in its application to this section, a person's proper address shall be his last known address.

Application of right to buy to cases where landlord is lessee

84A—(1) Sections 61 to 84 and 216 (the "right to buy" provisions) shall, with the modifications set out in this section, apply so as to provide for—
(*a*) the acquisition by the qualifying person of the landlord's interest in the qualifying house as lessee under a registered lease of the qualifying house or of land which includes it or as assignee of that interest; and
(*b*) the obtaining of a loan by the qualifying person in that connection,
as these sections apply for the purposes of the purchase of a qualifying house by the qualifying person from the landlord as heritable proprietor of it and the obtaining by the qualifying person of a loan in that connection.

(2) References in the right to buy provisions to the purchase or sale of a qualifying house shall be construed respectively as references to the acquisition or disposal of the landlord's interest in the qualifying house by way of a registered assignation of that interest and cognate expressions shall be construed accordingly.

(3) The reference in section 61(2)(*b*) to the landlord's being the heritable proprietor of the qualifying house shall be construed as a reference to the landlord's being the holder of the interest of the lessee under a registered lease of the qualifying house or of land which includes it.

(4) References in the right to buy provisions to the market value of or price to be paid for a qualifying house shall be construed respectively as references to the market value of the landlord's interest in the qualifying house and to the price to be paid for acquiring that interest.

(5) References in section 64(1) to the qualifying person's enjoyment and use of a qualifying house as owner shall be construed as references to his enjoyment and use of it as assigneee of the landlord's interest in the qualifying house.

(6) The reference in subsection (4) of section 64 to an option being offered to the landlord or to any other person to purchase the qualifying house in advance of its sale to a third party shall be construed as a reference to an option being offered to have the interest acquired by the qualifying person reassigned to the landlord or assigned to the other person in advance of its being disposed of to a third party; and the references in subsection (5) of that section to an option to purchase shall be construed accordingly.

(7) In this section and section 76—

"registered lease" means a lease—
(*a*) which is recorded in the general register of sasines; or
(*b*) in respect of which the interest of the lessee is registered in the Land Register of Scotland, under the Registration of Leases (Scotland) Act 1857; and

"registered assignation" means, in relation to such a lease, an assignation thereof which is so recorded or in respect of which the interest of the assignee has been so registered.

Qualifying House Loans: Special Cases

Qualifying house loans to qualifying persons exercising right to purchase

216.—(1) A qualifying person who seeks to exercise his right to purchase a qualifying house under Part III and who has received an offer to sell (or, as the case may be, an amended offer to sell) from the landlord shall be entitled, together with any joint purchaser under section 61(6) (and the said qualifying person and any joint purchaser are referred to in this section as "the applicant") to apply—
(*a*) in the case where the former landlord is a development corporation (including an urban development corporation) or Scottish Homes, to that body; or

(*b*) in a case where the former landlord is the Housing Corporation or a housing association registered in the register maintained by the Housing Corporation, to the Housing Corporation;

(*bi*) in a case where the former landlord is a housing association registered in the register maintained by Scottish Homes, to Scottish Homes;

(*c*) in any other case, to the local authority for the area in which the qualifying house is situated,

for a loan of an amount not exceeding the price fixed under section 62 to assist him to purchase the qualifying house.

(2) A loan application under subsection (1)—

(*a*) must be served on the former landlord or other body—

(i) within one month after service on the qualifying person of the offer to sell (or, where there has been service of one or more amended offers to sell or there has been a determination by the Lands Tribunal under section 65(3) which does not require the issue of an amended offer to sell, of the latest of these); or

(ii) within one year and 10 months after service of the application to purchase if the qualifying person has, in terms of section 67, a fixed price option as regards the qualifying house;

(*b*) shall be in such form as the Secretary of State shall by order made by statutory instrument prescribe, and shall contain—

(i) the amount of the loan which the applicant seeks;

(ii) the applicant's annual gross income and his net income after payment of income tax and national insurance contributions;

(iii) any liabilities in respect of credit sales or other fixed outgoings of the applicant; and

(iv) a statement that the applicant has applied for and been unable to obtain a sufficient building society loan; and

(*c*) shall be accompanied by evidence of the matters referred to in sub-paragraphs (ii) to (iv) of paragraph (*b*).

(3) subject to such requirements as the Secretary of State may by order made by statutory instrument impose, a former landlord or other body which receives an application under subsection (1) shall, where it is satisfied on reasonable inquiry (which shall include reasonable opportunity for the applicant to amend his application) that the information contained in the loan application is correct, serve on the applicant an offer of loan, which shall specify a maximum amount of loan calculated in accordance with regulations made by statutory instrument by the Secretary of State.

(4) A former landlord or other body to which the application has been made under subsection (1) shall complete its inquiries and either—

(*a*) issue the offer of loan under subsection (3); or

(*b*) refuse the application on the ground that information contained in the loan application is incorrect in a material respect,

within 2 months of the date of service of the loan application.

(5) An applicant who wishes to accept an offer of loan shall do so along with his notice of acceptance under sections 66(1) or 67(1).

(6) An offer of loan under subsection (3) together with an acceptance under subsection (5) shall constitute an agreement by the former landlord or other body, subject to such requirements as the Secretary of State may by order made by statutory instrument impose, to lend to the applicant for the purpose of purchasing the qualifying house—

(*a*) the maximum amount of loan mentioned in subsection (3); or

(*b*) the amount of loan sought by the applicant,

whichever is the lesser, on the execution by the applicant of a standard security over the qualifying house.

(7) An applicant who is aggrieved by a refusal under subsection (4)(*b*), or by a failure to comply with the said subsection, or by the calculation of maximum amount of loan mentioned in subsection (3) may, within 2 months of the date of the refusal or failure or of the offer of loan, as the case may be, raise proceedings by way of summary application in the sheriff court for the district in which the qualifying house is situated for declarator that he is entitled to a loan in accordance with subsection (3).

(8) Where in proceedings under subsection (7) the sheriff grants declarator that the applicant is entitled to a loan, such declarator shall have effect as if it were an offer of loan of the amount specified in the declaration duly issued under this section by the former landlord or other body.

(9) A statutory instrument made under subsection (3) or (6) shall be subject to annulment in pursuance of a resolution of either House of Parliament.

[THE NEXT PAGE IS J 701]

Notes

Particular Registers of Sasines

Districts and Shires for which Particular Registers were kept prior to the passing of the Land Registers (Scotland) Act 1868, with the respective dates of termination

	Date of Termination
Aberdeenshire and Kincardineshire	Feb. 6, 1869
Argyllshire, Dumbartonshire, Buteshire, Arran, and Tarbert	Jan. 12, 1871
Ayrshire, and Bailiaries of Kyle, Carrick, and Cunninghame	Sept. 30, 1869
Banffshire	Feb. 28, 1869
Berwickshire and Bailiary of Lauderdale	Mar. 17, 1869
Caithness-shire	Feb. 28, 1869
Dumfriesshire and Stewartries of Kirkcudbright and Annandale	Sept. 30, 1869
Edinburghshire, and Constabularies of Haddington, Linlithgow and Bathgate	Feb. 6, 1869
Elginshire, Forres, and Nairnshire	Feb. 28, 1869
Fifeshire	Jan. 12, 1871
Forfarshire	Feb. 28, 1869
Inverness-shire, Ross-shire, Sutherlandshire, and Cromartyshire	Feb. 6, 1869
Kinross-shire	Dec. 31, 1871
Lanarkshire (excepting the Regality of Glasgow)	Mar. 17, 1869
Orkney	Feb. 6, 1869
Perthshire (excepting the Stewartry of Menteith)	Jan. 12, 1871
Renfrewshire, and the Regality of Glasgow	Mar. 30, 1871
Roxburghshire, Selkirkshire, and Peeblesshire	Sept. 30, 1869
Shetland	Feb. 6, 1869
Stirlingshire, Clackmannanshire, and Stewartry of Menteith	Jan. 12, 1871
Wigtownshire	Sept. 30, 1869

Register of Inhibitions and Adjudications

The Land Registers Act 1868 abolished the Particular Registers of Inhibitions and Interdictions. The Conveyancing Act 1924 combined the General Register of Inhibitions and Interdictions and the Register of Adjudications into one Register called the Register of Inhibitions and Adjudications.

Registers of Sasines

[1]Kept in Royal Burghs and now discontinued, the Deeds whereof are now Registrable in the respective undernoted Counties of the General Register of Sasines

NOTE

[1] See Burgh Registers (Scotland) Act 1926.

Burgh Register	Date of Discontinuance	County in which Relative Deeds are now applicable for Registration (Gen. Reg. of Sasines)
Glasgow	1st June 1927	Barony and Regality of Glasgow.
Kinghorn	1st June 1927	Fife.
Kirkcaldy	1st June 1927	Fife.
Paisley (Bookings, etc.)	1st July 1927	Renfrew.
Lochmaben	30th June 1927	Dumfries.
Edinburgh	31st August 1927	Edinburgh.
Inverbervie	31st December 1927	Kincardine.
Wigtown	31st March 1928	Wigtown.
Dundee	31st December 1928	Angus.
Renfrew	30th April 1929	Renfrew.
Dysart	31st December 1930	Fife.
Aberdeen	30th September 1931	Aberdeen.
Queensferry	31st July 1932	West Lothian.
Linlithgow	31st January 1934	West Lothian.
Forres	28th February 1934	Moray.
Forfar	30th April 1935	Angus.
New Galloway	31st May 1935	Kirkcudbright.
Nairn	31st July 1935	Nairn.
Auchtermuchty	30th September 1935	Fife.
Inverness	30th September 1935	Inverness.
Cullen	30th June 1936	Banff.
Kirkcudbright	31st March 1938	Stewartry of Kirkcudbright.
Culross	31st May 1938	Fife.
Falkland	31st August 1938	Fife.
Dumfries	31st October 1938	Dumfries.
Rutherglen	31st October 1938	(1) Barony and Regality of Glasgow; or (2) Lanark.
Tain	31st January 1939	Ross and Cromarty.
Stirling	30th September 1939	Stirling.
Inverkeithing	30th September 1939	Fife.
Jedburgh	31st May 1941	Roxburgh.
Lanark	31st July 1941	Lanark
Dumbarton	31st July 1941	Dunbarton.
Arbroath	31st August 1941	Angus.
Elgin	31st October 1941	Moray.
Burntisland	28th February 1942	Fife.
Kintore	31st March 1942	Aberdeen.
Banff	31st August 1942	Banff.
Fortrose	30th November 1942	Ross and Cromarty.
North Berwick	31st March 1943	East Lothian.
Cupar	30th April 1943	Fife.
Stranraer	31st August 1943	Wigtown.
Perth	31st March 1944	Perth.
Whithorn	31st March 1944	Wigtown.
Montrose	31st July 1944	Angus.
Irvine	31st August 1944	Ayr.
Annan	31st October 1944	Dumfries.
Kirkwall	31st October 1945	Orkney and Zetland.
Selkirk	31st December 1945	Selkirk.

Burgh register	Date of Discontinuance	County in which Relative Deeds are now applicable for registration (Gen. Reg. of Sasines)
Newburgh	28th February 1946	Fife.
Inverurie	31st May 1946	Aberdeen.
Ayr	30th June 1946	Ayr.
Dunfermline	31st July 1946	Fife.
Brechin	30th November 1946	Angus.
Dunbar	31st December 1946	East Lothian.
Rothesay	31st October 1947	Bute.
St. Andrews	31st August 1948	Fife.
Lauder	31st August 1948	Berwick.
Peebles	31st October 1948	Peebles.
Haddington	31st May 1951	East Lothian.
Anstruther (Wester)	31st March 1953	Fife.
Crail	31st March 1953	Fife.
Sanquhar	30th September 1959	Dumfries.
Pittenweem	29th February 1960	Fife.
Earlsferry	1st November 1960	Fife.
Dingwall	30th June 1963	Ross and Cromarty.

Land Register of Scotland

Areas, for the purpose of registration of writs, for which the Land Registration (Scotland) Act 1979, ss. 2(1) and (2) and 3, has been brought into force.

Area	Date of commencement	Order
County of Renfrew	6th April 1981	S.I. 1980 No. 1412
County of Dunbarton	4th October 1982	S.I. 1982 No. 520
County of Lanark	3rd January 1984	S.I. 1983 No. 745
County of the Barony and Regality of Glasgow	30th September 1985	S.I. 1985 No. 501
County of Clackmannan	1st October 1992	S.I. 1992 No. 815
County of Stirling	1st April 1993	S.I. 1992 No. 2060
County of West Lothian	1st October 1993	S.I. 1993 No. 922
Proposed future dates		
County of Fife	1st April 1995	
County of Aberdeen	1st April 1996	
County of Kincardine		
County of Ayr	1st April 1997	
County of Dumfries		
County of Angus	1st April 1998	
County of Perth		
County of Kinross		
County of Midlothian	1st April 2000	
County of Argyll	1st April 2002	
County of Berwick		
County of Bute		
County of East Lothian		
County of Kirkcudbright		
County of Peebles		
County of Roxburgh		
County of Selkirk		
County of Wigtown		
County of Banff	1st April 2003	
County of Caithness		
County of Inverness		
County of Moray		
County of Nairn		
Counties of Orkney and Zetland		
County of Ross and Cromarty		
County of Sutherland		